# Lecture Notes in Computer Science 2481

Edited by G. Goos, J. Hartmanis, and J. van Leeuwen

T0216402

Bill Pugh   Chau-Wen Tseng (Eds.)

# Languages and Compilers for Parallel Computing

15th Workshop, LCPC 2002
College Park, MD, USA, July 25-27, 2002
Revised Papers

 Springer

Series Editors

Gerhard Goos, Karlsruhe University, Germany
Juris Hartmanis, Cornell University, NY, USA
Jan van Leeuwen, Utrecht University, The Netherlands

Volume Editors

Bill Pugh
Chau-Wen Tseng
University of Maryland, Department of Computer Science
College Park, MD 20814, USA
E-mail: {pugh, tseng}@cs.umd.edu

Library of Congress Control Number: 2005937164

CR Subject Classification (1998): D.3, D.1.3, F.1.2, B.2.1, C.2.4, C.2, E.1

ISSN        0302-9743
ISBN-10     3-540-30781-8 Springer Berlin Heidelberg New York
ISBN-13     978-3-540-30781-5 Springer Berlin Heidelberg New York

Springer is a part of Springer Science+Business Media

springer.com

© Springer-Verlag Berlin Heidelberg 2005
Printed in Germany

Typesetting: Camera-ready by author, data conversion by Scientific Publishing Services, Chennai, India
Printed on acid-free paper     SPIN: 11596110     06/3142     5 4 3 2 1 0

# Preface

The 15th Workshop on Languages and Compilers for Parallel Computing was held in July 2002 at the University of Maryland, College Park. It was jointly sponsored by the Department of Computer Science at the University of Maryland and the University of Maryland Institute for Advanced Computer Studies (UMIACS). LCPC 2002 brought together over 60 researchers from academia and research institutions from many countries.

The program of 26 papers was selected from 32 submissions. Each paper was reviewed by at least three Program Committee members and sometimes by additional reviewers. Prior to the workshop, revised versions of accepted papers were informally published on the workshop's website and in a paper proceedings that was distributed at the meeting. This year, the workshop was organized into sessions of papers on related topics, and each session consisted of two to three 30-minute presentations. Based on feedback from the workshop, the papers were revised and submitted for inclusion in the formal proceedings published in this volume. Two papers were presented at the workshop but later withdrawn from the final proceedings by their authors.

We were very lucky to have Bill Carlson from the Department of Defense give the LCPC 2002 keynote speech on "UPC: A C Language for Shared Memory Parallel Programming." Bill gave an excellent overview of the features and programming model of the UPC parallel programming language.

LCPC workshop presentations were held on campus in a spacious 140-person auditorium in the newly constructed Computer Science Instructional Center (CSIC). Workshop participants also enjoyed an afternoon excursion downtown to the Smithsonian's National Museum of Natural History, followed by a banquet held in the wine room of the D.C. Coast restaurant.

The success of LCPC 2002 was due to many people. We would like to thank the Program Committee members for their timely and thorough reviews, and the LCPC Steering Committee (especially David Padua) for providing invaluable advice and continuity for LCPC. We wish to thank Lawrence Rauchwerger and Silvius Rus for providing scripts and templates for formatting the proceedings. We appreciate the hard work performed by Cecilia Khullman, Christina Beal, and Johanna Weinstein (from UMIACS) handling local arrangements and workshop registration. Finally, we would like to thank all the LCPC 2002 authors for their patience in waiting for the long overdue publication of the formal workshop proceedings.

July 2005

Bill Pugh
Chau-Wen Tseng

# Organization

The 15th Workshop on Languages and Compilers for Parallel Computing was hosted by the Department of Computer Science at the University of Maryland and the University of Maryland Institute for Advanced Computer Studies (UMIACS).

## Steering Committee

Utpal Banerjee          Intel Corporation
David Gelernter          Yale University
Alex Nicolau            University of California at Irvine
David Padua             University of Illinois at Urbana-Champaign

## General and Program Co-chairs

Bill Pugh               University of Maryland
Chau-Wen Tseng          University of Maryland

## Program Committee

Hank Dietz              University of Kentucky
Manish Gupta            IBM T.J. Watson Research Center
Sam Midkiff             Purdue University
Jose Moreira            IBM T.J. Watson Research Center
Dave Padua              University of Illinois at Urbana-Champaign
Bill Pugh               University of Maryland
Lawrence Rauchwerger    Texas A&M University
Chau-Wen Tseng          University of Maryland

# Table of Contents

# Memory-Constrained Communication Minimization for a Class of Array Computations

Daniel Cociorva[1], Gerald Baumgartner[1], Chi-Chung Lam[1],
P. Sadayappan[1], and J. Ramanujam[2]

[1] Department of Computer and Information Science,
The Ohio State University, Columbus, OH 43210, USA
{cociorva, gb, clam, saday}@cis.ohio-state.edu
[2] Department of Electrical and Computer Engineering,
Louisiana State University, Baton Rouge, LA 70803, USA
jxr@ece.lsu.edu

**Abstract.** The accurate modeling of the electronic structure of atoms and molecules involves computationally intensive tensor contractions involving large multidimensional arrays. The efficient computation of complex tensor contractions usually requires the generation of temporary intermediate arrays. These intermediates could be extremely large, but they can often be generated and used in batches through appropriate loop fusion transformations. To optimize the performance of such computations on parallel computers, the total amount of interprocessor communication must be minimized, subject to the available memory on each processor. In this paper, we address the memory-constrained communication minimization problem in the context of this class of computations. Based on a framework that models the relationship between loop fusion and memory usage, we develop an approach to identify the best combination of loop fusion and data partitioning that minimizes inter-processor communication cost without exceeding the per-processor memory limit. The effectiveness of the developed optimization approach is demonstrated on a computation representative of a component used in quantum chemistry suites.

## 1 Introduction

The development of high-performance parallel programs for scientific applications is usually very time consuming. The time to develop an efficient parallel program for a computational model can be a primary limiting factor in the rate of progress of the science. Our overall goal is to develop a program synthesis system to facilitate the rapid development of high-performance parallel programs for a class of scientific computations encountered in quantum chemistry. The domain of our focus is electronic structure calculations, as exemplified by coupled cluster methods [4], in which many computationally intensive components are expressible as a set of tensor contractions. We are developing a synthesis system that will transform an input specification expressed in a high-level notation into efficient parallel code tailored to the characteristics of the target architecture.

A number of compile-time optimizations are being incorporated into the program synthesis system. These include algebraic transformations to minimize the number

B. Pugh and C.-W. Tseng (Eds.): LCPC 2002, LNCS 2481, pp. 1–15, 2005.

of arithmetic operations [8,13], loop fusion and array contraction for memory space minimization [13,12], tiling and data locality optimization [1,2], space-time trade-off optimization [3], and data partitioning for communication minimization [9,10]. Since the problem of determining the set of algebraic transformations to minimize operation count was found to be NP-complete, we developed a pruning search procedure [8] that is very efficient in practice. The operation-minimization procedure results in the creation of intermediate temporary arrays. Often, these intermediate arrays that help in reducing the computational cost create a problem with the memory required. Loop fusion was found to be effective in significantly reducing the total memory requirement. However, since some fusions could prevent other fusions, the choice of the optimal set of fusion transformations is important. So we addressed the problem of finding the choice of fusions for a given operator tree that minimizes the space required for all intermediate arrays after fusion [12,11].

We have also previously addressed the problem of communication optimization in the context of the operator trees [9,10]. An efficient polynomial-time dynamic programming algorithm was developed for the determination of optimal distributions of the various arrays through the evaluation of the operator tree so as to minimize interprocessor communication overhead. However, that model did not consider the effects of loop fusion for memory minimization. As we elaborate later with examples, it is not feasible to simply apply the previously developed loop fusion algorithm and the previous communication minimization algorithm (in either order) to optimize for the parallel context when memory size constraints are severe. For many computations of interest to quantum chemists, the unoptimized form of the computation could require in excess of hundreds of terabytes of memory. Therefore, the following optimization problem is of great interest: given a set of computations expressed as a sequence of tensor contractions (explained later on), an empirically derived measure of the communication cost for a given target computer, and a specified limit on the amount of available memory on each processor, re-structure the computation so as to minimize the total execution time while staying within the available memory. In this paper, we present a framework that we have developed to address this problem. The memory-constrained communication minimization algorithm we develop here will be incorporated into the synthesis system being developed.

The computational structures that we target arise in scientific application domains that are extremely compute-intensive and consume significant computer resources at national supercomputer centers. They are present in various computational chemistry codes such as ACES II, GAMESS, Gaussian, NWChem, PSI, and MOLPRO. In particular, they comprise the bulk of the computation with the coupled cluster approach to the accurate description of the electronic structure of atoms and molecules [14,15]. Computational approaches to modeling the structure and interactions of molecules, the electronic and optical properties of molecules, the heats and rates of chemical reactions, etc., are very important to the understanding of chemical processes in real-world systems.

There has been some recent work on using loop fusion for memory reduction for sequential execution. Fraboulet et al. [5] use loop alignment to reduce memory requirement between adjacent loops by formulating the one-dimensional version of the problem as a network flow problem; they did look at the effect of their solution on cache behavior or communication. Song et al. [17,18] present a different network flow formulation of the memory reduction problem and they include a simple model of cache misses as well. They do not consider trading off memory for recomputation or the impact of data distribution on communication costs while meeting per-processor memory constraints in a distributed memory machine. There has been much less work investigating the use of loop fusion as a means of reducing memory requirements [6,16]. To the best of our knowledge, loop fusion transformation for memory reduction, in combination with data partitioning for communication minimization in the parallel context, has not been previously considered.

The paper is organized as follows. In the next section, we elaborate on the computational context of interest and the pertinent optimization issues. Section 3 presents our multi-dimensional processor model, discusses the interaction between distribution of arrays and loop fusion, and describes our algorithm for the memory-constrained communication minimization problem. Section 4 presents results from the application of the new algorithm to an example abstracted from NWChem [7]. Conclusions are provided in Section 5.

## 2   Elaboration of Problem

In the class of computations considered, the final result to be computed can be expressed as multi-dimensional summations of the product of several input arrays. Due to commutativity, associativity, and distributivity, there are many different ways to obtain the same final result and they could differ widely in the number of floating point operations required. Consider the following example:

$$S(t) = \sum_{i,j,k} A(i,j,t) \times B(j,k,t).$$

If implemented directly as expressed above, the computation would require $2N_iN_jN_kN_t$ arithmetic operations to compute. However, assuming associative reordering of the operations and use of distributive law of multiplication over addition is acceptable for the floating-point computations, the above computation can be rewritten in various ways. One equivalent form that only requires $N_iN_jN_t + N_jN_kN_t + 2N_jN_t$ operations is as shown in Fig. 1(a).

Generalizing from the above example, we can express multi-dimensional integrals of products of several input arrays as a sequence of formulae. Each formula produces some intermediate array and the last formula gives the final result. A formula is either:

- a multiplication formula of the form: $Tr(\ldots) = X(\ldots) \times Y(\ldots)$, or
- a summation formula of the form: $Tr(\ldots) = \sum_i X(\ldots)$,

where the terms on the right hand side represent input arrays or intermediate arrays produced by a previously defined formula. Let $IX$, $IY$ and $ITr$ be the sets of indices in $X(\ldots)$, $Y(\ldots)$ and $Tr(\ldots)$, respectively. For a formula to be well-formed, every index in $X(\ldots)$ and $Y(\ldots)$, except the summation index in the second form, must appear in $Tr(\ldots)$. Thus $IX \cup IY \subseteq ITr$ for any multiplication formula, and $IX - \{i\} \subseteq ITr$ for any

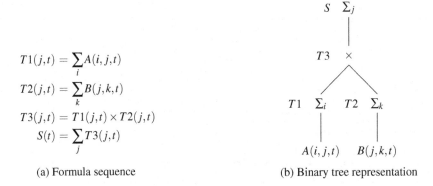

$$T1(j,t) = \sum_i A(i,j,t)$$

$$T2(j,t) = \sum_k B(j,k,t)$$

$$T3(j,t) = T1(j,t) \times T2(j,t)$$

$$S(t) = \sum_j T3(j,t)$$

(a) Formula sequence                    (b) Binary tree representation

**Fig. 1.** A formula sequence and its binary tree representation

summation formula. Such a sequence of formulae fully specifies the multiplications and additions to be performed in computing the final result.

A sequence of formulae can be represented graphically as a binary tree to show the hierarchical structure of the computation more clearly. In the binary tree, the leaves are the input arrays and each internal node corresponds to a formula, with the last formula at the root. An internal node may either be a multiplication node or a summation node. A multiplication node corresponds to a multiplication formula and has two children which are the terms being multiplied together. A summation node corresponds to a summation formula and has only one child, representing the term on which summation is performed. As an example, the binary tree in Fig. 1(b) represents the formula sequence shown in Fig. 1(a).

The operation-minimization procedure discussed above usually results in the creation of intermediate temporary arrays. Sometimes these intermediate arrays that help in reducing the computational cost create a problem with the memory capacity required. For example, consider the following expression:

$$S_{abij} = \sum_{cdefkl} A_{acik} \times B_{befl} \times C_{dfjk} \times D_{cdel}$$

If this expression is directly translated to code (with ten nested loops, for indices $a - l$), the total number of arithmetic operations required will be $4N^{10}$ if the range of each index $a - l$ is $N$. Instead, the same expression can be rewritten by use of associative and distributive laws as the following:

$$S_{abij} = \sum_{ck} \left( \sum_{df} \left( \sum_{el} B_{befl} \times D_{cdel} \right) \times C_{dfjk} \right) \times A_{acik}$$

This corresponds to the formula sequence shown in Fig. 2(a) and can be directly translated into code as shown in Fig. 2(b). This form only requires $6N^6$ operations. However, additional space is required to store temporary arrays $T1$ and $T2$. Often, the space requirements for the temporary arrays poses a serious problem. For this example,

$$T1_{bcdf} = \sum_{el} B_{befl} \times D_{cdel}$$

$$T2_{bcjk} = \sum_{df} T1_{bcdf} \times C_{dfjk}$$

$$S_{abij} = \sum_{ck} T2_{bcjk} \times A_{acik}$$

(a) Formula sequence

```
T1=0; T2=0; S=0
for b, c, d, e, f, l
 ⌈T1bcdf += Bbefl Dcdel
 for b, c, d, f, j, k
 ⌈T2bcjk += T1bcdf Cdfjk
 for a, b, c, i, j, k
 ⌈Sabij += T2bcjk Aacik
```

(b) Direct implementation
(unfused code)

```
S = 0
for b, c
⌈T1f = 0; T2f = 0
 for d, f
 ⌈ for e, l
 │ ⌈T1f += Bbefl Dcdel
 │ for j, k
 │ ⌈T2fjk += T1f Cdfjk
 for a, i, j, k
 ⌊Sabij += T2fjk Aacik
```

(c) Memory-reduced
implementation (fused)

**Fig. 2.** Example illustrating use of loop fusion for memory reduction

abstracted from a quantum chemistry model, the array extents along indices $a - d$ are the largest, while the extents along indices $i - l$ are the smallest. Therefore, the size of temporary array $T1$ would dominate the total memory requirement.

We have previously shown that the problem of determining the operator tree with minimal operation count is NP-complete, and have developed a pruning search procedure [8,9] that is very efficient in practice. For the above example, although the latter form is far more economical in terms of the number of arithmetic operations, its implementation will require the use of temporary intermediate arrays to hold the partial results of the parenthesized array subexpressions. Sometimes, the sizes of intermediate arrays needed for the "operation-minimal" form are too large to even fit on disk.

A systematic way to explore ways of reducing the memory requirement for the computation is to view it in terms of potential loop fusions. Loop fusion merges loop nests with common outer loops into larger imperfectly nested loops. When one loop nest produces an intermediate array which is consumed by another loop nest, fusing the two loop nests allows the dimension corresponding to the fused loop to be eliminated in the array. This results in a smaller intermediate array and thus reduces the memory requirements. For the example considered, the application of fusion is illustrated in Fig. 2(c). By use of loop fusion, for this example it can be seen that $T1$ can actually be reduced to a scalar and $T2$ to a 2-dimensional array, without changing the number of arithmetic operations.

For a computation comprised of a number of nested loops, there will generally be a number of fusion choices, that are not all mutually compatible. This is because different fusion choices could require different loops to be made the outermost. In prior work, we have addressed the problem of finding the choice of fusions for a given operator tree that minimizes the total space required for all arrays after fusion [13,12,11].

A data-parallel implementation of the unfused code for computing $S_{abij}$ would involve a sequence of three steps, each corresponding to one of the loops in Fig. 2(b). The communication cost incurred will depend on the way the arrays $A, B, C, D$, $T1, T2$, and $S$ are distributed. We have previously considered the problem of minimization of communication with such computations [13,9]. However, the issue of memory space requirements was not addressed. In practice, many of the computations of interest in quantum chemistry require impractically large intermediate arrays in the unfused operation-minimal form. Although the collective memory of parallel machines is very large, it is nevertheless insufficient to hold the full intermediate arrays for many computations of interest. Thus, array contraction through loop fusion is essential in the parallel context too. However, it is not satisfactory to first find a communication-minimizing data/computation distribution for the unfused form, and then apply fusion transformations to minimize memory for that parallel form. This is because 1) fusion changes the communication cost, and 2) it may be impossible to find a fused form that fits within available memory, due to constraints imposed by the chosen data distribution on possible fusions. In this paper we address this problem of finding suitable fusion transformations and data/computation partitioning that minimize communication costs, subject to limits on available per-processor memory.

## 3   Memory-Constrained Communication Minimization

Given a sequence of formulae, we now address the problem of finding the optimal partitioning of arrays and operations among the processors and the loop fusions on each processor in order to minimize inter-processor communication and computational costs while staying within the available memory in implementing the computation on a message-passing parallel computer. Section 3.1 introduces a multi-dimensional processor model used to represent the computational space. Section 3.2 discusses the combined effects of loop fusions and array/operation partitioning on communication cost, computational cost, and memory usage. An integrated algorithm for solving this problem is presented in Section 3.3.

### 3.1   Preliminaries: A Multi-dimensional Processor Model

A logical view of the processors as a multi-dimensional grid is used, where each array can be distributed or replicated along one or more of the processor dimensions. As will be clear later on, the logical view of the processor grid does not impose any restriction on the actual physical interconnection topology of the processor system since empirical characterization of the cost of redistribution between different distributions is performed on the target system.

Let $p_d$ be the number of processors on the $d$-th dimension of an $n$-dimensional processor array, so that the number of processors is $p_1 \times p_2 \times \ldots \times p_n$. We use an $n$-tuple to denote the partitioning or *distribution* of the elements of a data array on an $n$-dimensional processor array. The $d$-th position in an $n$-tuple $\alpha$, denoted $\alpha[d]$, corresponds to the $d$-th processor dimension. Each position may be one of the following: an index variable distributed along that processor dimension, a '*' denoting replication of data along that processor dimension, or a '1' denoting that only the first processor along that processor dimension is assigned any data. If an index variable appears as an array subscript but not in the $n$-tuple, then the corresponding dimension of the array is not distributed. Conversely, if an index variable appears in the $n$-tuple but not in the array, then the data are replicated along the corresponding processor dimension, which is the same as replacing that index variable with a '*'.

As an example, suppose 128 processors form a 4-dimensional $2 \times 2 \times 4 \times 8$ array. For the array $B(b,e,f,l)$ in Fig. 2(a), the 4-tuple $\langle b,e,*,1 \rangle$ specifies that the first and the second dimensions of $B$ are distributed along the first and second processor dimensions respectively (the third and fourth dimensions of $B$ are not distributed), and that data are replicated along the third processor dimension and are assigned only to processors whose fourth processor dimension equals 1. Thus, a processor whose id is $P_{z_1,z_2,z_3,z_4}$ will be assigned a portion of $B$ specified by $B(myrange(z_1, N_b, p_1), myrange(z_2, N_e, p_2), 1 : N_f, 1 : N_l)$ if $z_4 = 1$ and no part of $B$ otherwise, where $myrange(z, N, p)$ is the range $(z-1) \times N/p + 1$ to $z \times N/p$.

   We assume the data-parallel programming model and do not consider distributing the computation of different formulae on different subsets of processors. A child array (or a part of it) is redistributed before the evaluation of its parent if their distributions do not match. For instance, suppose the arrays $B(b, e, f, l)$ and $D(c, d, e, l)$ have distributions $\langle b, e, *, 1 \rangle$ and $\langle c, d, *, 1 \rangle$ respectively. If we want $T1$ to have the distribution $\langle c, d, f, 1 \rangle$ when evaluating $T1(b, c, d, f) = \sum_{e,l} B(b, e, f, l) \times D(c, d, e, l)$, $B$ would have to be redistributed from $\langle b, e, *, 1 \rangle$ to $\langle *, *, f, 1 \rangle$ because the two distributions do not match. But since for $D(c, d, e, l)$, the distribution $\langle c, d, *, 1 \rangle$ is the same as $\langle c, d, f, 1 \rangle$, $D$ is not redistributed.

## 3.2   Interaction Between Array Partitioning and Loop Fusion

The partitioning of data arrays among the processors and the fusions of loops on each processor are inter-related. Although in our context there are no constraints to loop fusion due to data dependences (there are never any fusion preventing dependences), there are constraints and interactions with array distribution: (*i*) both affect memory usage, by fully collapsing array dimensions (fusion) or by reducing them (distribution), (*ii*) loop fusion does not change the communication volume, but increases the number of messages, and therefore the start-up communication cost, and (*iii*) fusion and communications patterns may conflict, resulting in mutual constraints. We discuss these issues next.

(*i*) **Memory Usage and Array Distribution.** The memory requirements of the computation depend on both loop fusion and array distribution. Fusing a loop with index $t$ between a node $v$ and its parent eliminates the $t$-dimension of array $v$. If the $t$-loop is not fused but the $t$-dimension of array $v$ is distributed along the $d$-th processor dimension, then the range of the $t$-dimension of array $v$ on each processor is reduced to $N_t/p_d$. Let $DistSize(v, \alpha, f)$ be the size on each processor of array $v$, which has fusion $f$ with its parent and distribution $\alpha$. We have

$$DistSize(v, \alpha, f) = \prod_{i \in v.dimens} DistRange(i, v, \alpha, Set(f))$$

where $v.dimens = v.indices - \{v.sumindex\}$ is the array dimension indices of $v$ before loop fusions, $v.indices$ is the set of loop indices for $v$ including the summation index $v.sumindex$ if $v$ is a summation node, $Set(f)$ is the set of fused indices for fusion $f$, and

$$DistRange(i, v, \alpha, x) = \begin{cases} 1 & \text{if } i \in x \\ N_i/p_d & \text{if } i \notin x \text{ and } i = \alpha[d] \\ N_i & \text{if } i \notin x \text{ and } i \notin \alpha \end{cases}$$

In our example, assume that $N_a = N_b = N_c = N_d = 1000$, $N_e = N_f = 70$, and $N_j = N_k = N_l = 30$. These are index ranges typical of the quantum chemistry calculations

$$C(i,k) = \sum_j A(i,j) \times B(j,k)$$
$$E(i,l) = \sum_k C(i,k) \times D(k,l)$$

(a) Formula sequence

```
for i = 1, Ni                          for i = 1, Ni
⎡ for k = (z-1) * Nk/4 + 1, z * Nk/4   ⎡ Initialize C(k) to zero
⎢ ⎡ for j = 1, Nj                      ⎢ for k = (z-1) * Nk/4 + 1, z * Nk/4
⎢ ⎣ ⎣C(i,k) += A(i,j) * B(j,k)         ⎢ ⎡ for j = 1, Nj
Redistribute C(i,k) from <k> to <l>=<*> ⎢ ⎣ ⎣C(k) += A(i,j) * B(j,k)
for i = 1, Ni                          Redistribute C(k) from <k> to <l>=<*>
⎡ for l = (z-1) * Nl/4 + 1, z * Nl/4   for l = (z-1) * Nl/4 + 1, z * Nl/4
⎢ ⎡ for k = 1, Nk                      ⎡ for  k = 1, Nk
⎢ ⎣ ⎣E(i,l) += C(i,k) * D(k,l)         ⎣ ⎣E(i,l)  += C(k) * D(k,l)
```

(b) Before loop fusion                 (c) After loop fusion

**Fig. 3.** An example of the increase in communication cost due to loop fusion

of interest, and are used elsewhere in the paper in relation to this example. If the array $B(b,e,f,l)$ has distribution $\langle b,e,*,1\rangle$ and fusion $\langle bf\rangle$ with $T_2$, then the size of $B$ on each processor whose fourth dimension equals one would be $N_e/2 \times N_l = 1050$ words, since the $e$ and $l$ dimensions are the only unfused dimensions, and the $e$ dimension is distributed onto 2 processors. Note that if array $v$ undergoes redistribution from $\alpha$ to $\beta$, the array size on each processor after redistribution is $DistSize(v,\beta,f)$, which could be different from $DistSize(v,\alpha,f)$, the size before redistribution.

(*ii*) **Loop Fusion Increases Communication Cost.** The initial and final distributions of an array $v$ determines the communication pattern and whether $v$ needs redistribution, while loop fusions change the number of times array $v$ is redistributed and the size of each message. Let $v$ be an array that needs to be redistributed. If node $v$ is not fused with its parent, array $v$ is redistributed only once. Fusing a loop with index $t$ between node $v$ and its parent puts the collective communication code for redistribution inside the loop. Thus, the number of redistributions is increased by a factor of $N_t/p_d$ if the $t$-dimension of $v$ is distributed along the $d$-th processor dimension and by a factor of $N_t$ if the $t$-dimension of $v$ is not distributed. In other words, loop fusions cannot reduce communication cost. Instead, the number of messages increases with loop fusion, while the total volume of communication stays the same. Therefore, the communication cost increases, due to higher start-up costs. Consider the computation sequence presented in Fig. 3(a), where the array $C(i,k)$ is first "produced" from $A(i,j)$ and $B(j,k)$, and then "consumed" to produce $E(i,l)$. For this simple example, we assume that the computation is executed in parallel on 4 processors, with a one-dimensional logical processor view. Figure 3(b) shows the pseudo-code in the absence of fusion: the array $C(i,k)$ is re-distributed from $\langle k\rangle$ to $\langle l\rangle$ only once. In the presence of fusion, where the $i$-loop is the outermost loop, the dimensionality of the array $C$ is reduced to $C(k)$, but the re-distribution is performed $N_i$ times. The pseudo-code in Fig. 3(c) illustrates this effect.

(*iii*) **Potential Conflict Between Array Distribution and Loop Fusion. Solution of the Conflict by Virtual Partitioning.** For the fusion of a loop between nodes $u$ and $v$ to be possible, the loop must either be undistributed at both $u$ and $v$, or be distributed onto

```
for i = 1, Ni                          for i = (z-1) * Ni/4 + 1, z * Ni/4
⎡for k = (z-1) * Nk/4 + 1, z * Nk/4   ⎡for ii = 1, 4
⎢ ⎡for j = 1, Nj                      ⎢ ⎡for k = (z-1) * Nk/4 + 1, z * Nk/4
⎣ ⎣[C(i,k) += A(i,j) * B(j,k)         ⎢ ⎢ ⎡for j = 1, Nj
Redistribute C(i,k) from <k> to <i>   ⎣ ⎣ ⎣[C(ii,k) += A(i + (ii-1) * Ni/4,j) * B(j,k)
for i = (z-1) * Ni/4 + 1, z * Ni/4    Redistribute C(ii,k) from <k> to <i>=<ii>
⎡for l = 1, Nl                        for l = 1, Nl
⎢ ⎡for k = 1, Nk                      ⎡for k = 1, Nk
⎣ ⎣[E(i,l) += C(i,k) * D(k,l)         ⎣ ⎣[E(i,l) += C(1,k) * D(k,l)
```

    (a) Before virtualization            (b) After virtualization

**Fig. 4.** An example of the increase in loop fusion due to a virtual process view

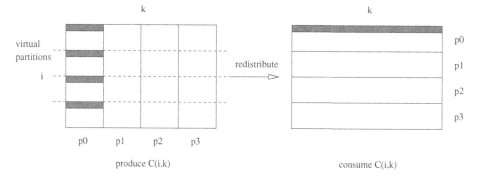

**Fig. 5.** Virtual partitioning of an array

the same number of processors at $u$ and at $v$. Otherwise, the range of the loop at node $u$ would be different from that at node $v$, preventing fusion of the loops. Let us consider again the computation given in Figure 3(a), with a different distribution of the array $C(i,k)$ at the two nodes: assume that we have a $\langle k \rangle$ distribution at the first node, and a $\langle i \rangle$ distribution at the second node. The pseudo-code for this computation on 4 processors is presented in Fig. 4(a). Fusion of the $i$-loop is no longer possible, due to the different loop ranges at the two nodes. However, we can overcome this problem by taking a virtualized view of the computation on a larger set of virtual processors, mapped onto the actual physical processors. Consider a virtual partitioning of the computation and split the $i$-loop into two loops, $i$ and $ii$. (see the pseudo-code in Fig. 4(b)). With this modification, the outermost $i$-loop can be fused, and the size of the array $C$ is reduced from $N_i \times N_k$ to $4N_k$.

This transformation of the $i$-loop is presented graphically in Fig. 5. At the first node (where it is produced), the array $C$ is distributed among the 4 processors along the $k$ dimension ($\langle k \rangle$ distribution, or vertical partitioning in the Figure). In addition, each physical processor can be further viewed as 4 "virtual processors", as showed by the horizontal virtual partitioning lines in Fig. 5. The purpose of the virtual partitioning along the $i$ dimension at the first (produce) node is to match the actual $i$ partitioning at the second (consume) node and allow for fusion of the $i$-loop. Fusion of the $i$-loop no longer produces a one-dimensional $C(k)$ array in this case. Each processor stores the equivalent of 4 such arrays, corresponding to the 4 virtual processors. In Fig. 5, the elements stored on processor $P_0$, before and after re-distribution, are represented by shaded areas.

In general, the virtual partitioning of the computation depends on the distribution at the nodes involved. Let $u$ and $v$ be two nodes in the operator tree $T$ that have a common loop index $t$. The $t$-loop is distributed onto $p_u$ processors at node $u$ and onto $p_v$ processors at node $v$. Let $p_{\text{virtual}}$ be lowest common multiple of $p_u$ and $p_v$. With these notations, the $t$-loop can be virtually partitioned by a factor of $p_{\text{virtual}}/p_u$ at the $u$ node, and by a factor of $p_{\text{virtual}}/p_v$ at the $v$ node. The resulting virtual partitions along the $t$ dimension at the $u$ and $v$ nodes become identical, allowing for loop fusion.

Virtual partitioning is essential for the success of our combined loop fusion — data distribution approach. Since both fusion and distribution impose constraints on the array dimensions, the potential for conflict is enormous. In practice, unless we allow virtual partitioning, we often find that optimal array distribution for minimizing inter-processor communication precludes effective memory reduction by fusion. The number of compatible loop fusion and array distribution configurations is very limited. Virtual partitioning relaxes the mutual constraints imposed by the loop fusion and data distribution, allowing for the optimal solution(s) to be found.

### 3.3  Memory-Constrained Communication Minimization Algorithm

In this section, we present an algorithm addressing the communication minimization problem with memory constraint. Previously, we have solved the communication minimization problem but without considering loop fusion or memory usage [9]. In practice, the arrays involved are often too large to fit into the available memory even after partitioning among the processors. We assume the input arrays can be distributed initially among the processors in any way at zero cost, as long as they are not replicated. We do not require the final results to be distributed in any particular way. Our approach works regardless of whether any initial or final data distribution is given.

The main idea of this method is to search among all combinations of loop fusions and array distributions to find one that has minimal total communication and computational cost and uses no more than the available memory. A dynamic programming algorithm for this purpose is given in this section.

Let $Mcost(localsize, \alpha, \beta)$ be the communication cost in moving the elements of an array, with $localsize$ elements distributed on each processor, from an initial distribution $\alpha$ to a final distribution $\beta$. We empirically measure $Mcost$ for each possible non-matching pair of $\alpha$ and $\beta$ and for several different $localsizes$ on the target parallel computer. Let $MoveCost(v, \alpha, \beta, f)$ denote the communication cost in redistributing the elements of array $v$, which has fusion $f$ with its parent, from an initial distribution $\alpha$ to a final distribution $\beta$. It can be expressed as:

$$MoveCost(v, \alpha, \beta, f) = MsgFactor(v, \alpha, Set(f)) \times Mcost(DistSize(v, \alpha, Set(f)), \alpha, \beta) \qquad \text{where}$$

$$MsgFactor(v, \alpha, x) = \prod_{i \in v.dimens} LoopRange(i, v, \alpha, x) \qquad \text{and}$$

$$LoopRange(i, v, \alpha, x) = \begin{cases} 1 & \text{if } i \notin x \\ N_i/p_d & \text{if } i \in x \text{ and } i = \alpha[d] \\ N_i & \text{if } i \in x \text{ and } i \notin \alpha \end{cases}$$

Let $CalcCost(v,\gamma)$ be the computational cost in calculating an array $v$ with $\gamma$ as the distribution of $v$. Note that the computational cost is unaffected by loop fusions. For multiplication and for summation where the summation index is not distributed, the computational cost for $v$ can be quantified as the total number of operations for $v$ divided by the number of processors working on distinct parts of $v$. In our example in Fig. 2(a), if the array $T1(b,c,d,f)$ has distribution $\langle c,d,f,1 \rangle$, its computational cost would be $N_b \times N_c \times N_d \times N_e \times N_f \times N_l/p_1/p_2/p_3 = 9.1875 \times 10^{12}$ multiply-add operations on each participating processor. Formally,

$$CalcCost(v,\gamma) = \frac{\Pi_{i \in v.indices}\, N_i}{\Pi_{\gamma[d]\, \in\, v.dimens}\, P_d}$$

For the case of summation where the summation index $i = v.sumindex$ is distributed, partial sums of $v$ are first formed on each processor and then either consolidated on one processor along the $i$-dimension or replicated on all processors along the same processor dimension. We denote by $CalcCost1$ and $MoveCost1$ the computational and communication costs for forming the sum without replication, and by $CalcCost2$ and $MoveCost2$ those with replication.

Finally, we define $Cost(v,\alpha)$ to be the total cost for the subtree rooted at $v$ with distribution $\alpha$. After transforming the given sequence of formulae into an expression tree $T$ (see Section 2), we initialize $Cost(v,\alpha)$ for each leaf node $v$ in $T$ and each distribution $\alpha$ as follows (where $NoRep(\alpha)$ is a predicate meaning $\alpha$ involves no replication.):

$$Cost(v,\alpha) = \begin{cases} 0 & \text{if } NoRep(\alpha) \\ \min_{NoRep(\beta)}\{MoveCost(v,\beta,\alpha,0)\} & \text{otherwise} \end{cases}$$

For each internal node $u$ and each distribution $\alpha$, we can calculate $Cost(u,\alpha)$ according to the following procedure:

**Case (a):** $u$ is a multiplication node with two children $v$ and $v'$. We need both $v$ and $v'$ to have the same distribution, say $\gamma$, before $u$ can be formed. After the multiplication, the product could be redistributed if necessary. Thus,

$$Cost(u,\alpha) = \min_{\gamma}\{Cost(v,\gamma) + Cost(v',\gamma) + CalcCost(u,\gamma) + MoveCost(u,\gamma,\alpha,0)\}$$

**Case (b):** $u$ is a summation node over index $i$ and with a child $v$, which may have any distribution $\gamma$. If $i \in \gamma$, each processor first forms partial sums of $u$ and then we either combine the partial sums on one processor along the $i$ dimension or replicate them on all processors along that processor dimension. Afterwards, the sum could be redistributed if necessary. Let $Calc\_Move\_Cost1(u,\gamma,\alpha,0)$ be $CalcCost1(u,\gamma) + MoveCost1(u,\gamma,\alpha,0)$, and $Calc\_Move\_Cost2(u,\gamma,\alpha,0)$ be $CalcCost2(u,\gamma) + MoveCost2(u,\gamma,\alpha,0)$. Thus,

$$Cost(u,\alpha) = \min_{\gamma}\{Cost(v,\gamma) + \min(Calc\_Move\_Cost1(u,\gamma,\alpha,0), Calc\_Move\_Cost2(u,\gamma,\alpha,0))\}$$

With these definitions, the bottom-up dynamic programming algorithm proceeds as follows: At each node $v$ in the expression tree $T$, we consider all combinations of array distributions for $v$ and loop fusions between $v$ and its parent. If loop fusion of the same index $t$ between $v$ and its parent is not possible because of different distribution ranges, then a virtual processor view is considered in order to allow the fusion. The array size, communication cost, and computational cost are determined according to the equations in Sections 3.1 and 3.3. If the size of an array before and after redistribution is different, the higher of the two should be used in determining memory usage. At each node $v$, a set of solutions is formed. Each solution contains the final distribution of $v$, the loop nesting at $v$, the loop fusion between $v$ and its parent, the total communication and computational cost, and the memory usage for the subtree rooted at $v$. A solution $s$ is said to be inferior to another solution $s'$ if they have the same final distribution, $s$ has less potential fusions with $v$'s parent than $s'$, $s.totalcost \geq s'.totalcost$, and the memory usage of $s$ is higher than that of $s'$. An inferior solution and any solution that uses more memory than available can be pruned. At the root node of $T$, the only two remaining criteria are the total cost and the memory usage of the solutions. The set of solutions is ordered in increasing memory usage and decreasing cost. The solution with the lowest total cost and whose memory usage is below the available memory limit is the optimal solution for the entire tree.

# 4   An Application Example

In this section, we present an application example of the memory-constrained communication minimization algorithm. Consider again the sequence of computations in Fig. (2(a)), representative of the multi-dimensional tensor contractions often present in quantum chemistry codes. The sizes of the array dimensions are chosen to be compatible with the dimensions found in typical chemistry problems, where they represent occupied or virtual orbital spaces: $N_i = N_j = N_k = N_l = 40, N_a = N_b = N_c = N_d = 1000$, and $N_e = N_f = 70$.

As an example, we investigate the parallel execution of this calculation on 32 processors of a Cray T3E, assuming 512MB of memory available at each node, and on 16 processors of an Intel Itanium cluster, assuming 2GB of memory available at each node. The best partitioning of the algorithm depends on the number of processors and the amount of memory available. It also depends on the empirical characterization data that we use to describe the communication costs of a given machine. We generated this data by measuring the communication times for each possible non-matching pair of array distributions and different array sizes for both the Cray T3E and the Itanium cluster. Although generating the characterization is somewhat laborious, once a characterization file is completed, it can be used to predict, by interpolation or extrapolation, the communication times for arbitrary array distributions and sizes.

Tables 1 and 2 present the solutions of the memory-constrained communication minimization algorithm on the Cray T3E and Itanium cluster, respectively. For the system of 32 processors of the Cray T3E, the optimal logical view of the processor space is found to be a two-dimensional $4 \times 8$ distribution. Table 1 shows the full four-dimensional arrays involved in the computation, their reduced (fused) representations, their initial and final distributions, their memory requirements, and the communication costs involved in their re-distribution. The final distribution is defined in the same way for both input and intermediate arrays: it is the distribution at the multiplication node at which the array is used or consumed. The initial distribution is defined differently for input and intermediate arrays: it is the distribution at the leaf node for an input array, and the distribution at the multiplication node where the array is generated, or produced,

**Table 1.** Loop fusions, memory requirements and communication costs on 32 processors of a Cray T3E for the arrays presented in Fig. 2(a)

| Full array | Reduced array | Initial dist. | Final dist. | Memory/processor | Comm. cost |
|---|---|---|---|---|---|
| $D(c,d,e,l)$ | $D(c,e,l)$ | $\langle c,e \rangle$ | $\langle *,* \rangle$ | 22.4MB | 552.8 sec. |
| $B(b,e,f,l)$ | $B(b,e,f,l)$ | $\langle b,f \rangle$ | $\langle b,f \rangle$ | 49.0MB | 0 |
| $C(d,f,j,k)$ | $C(f,j,k)$ | $\langle j,f \rangle$ | $\langle *,* \rangle$ | 0.9MB | 362.3 sec. |
| $A(a,c,i,k)$ | $A(c,i,k)$ | $\langle i,c \rangle$ | $\langle *,* \rangle$ | 12.8MB | 460.9 sec. |
| $T1(b,c,d,f)$ | $T1(b,c,f)$ | $\langle b,f \rangle$ | $\langle b,c \rangle$ | 17.5MB | 791.8 sec. |
| $T2(b,c,j,k)$ | $T2(b,c,j,k)$ | $\langle b,c \rangle$ | $\langle b,j \rangle$ | 400.0MB | 20.5 sec. |
| $S(a,b,i,j)$ | $S(b,i,j)$ | $\langle b,j \rangle$ | $\langle b,j \rangle$ | 0.4MB | 0 |

for an intermediate array. The total memory requirement of an array is defined as the largest memory usage of the two distributions (initial and final).

The optimal solution has the $a$ and $d$ loops fused, each across its own range: the fusion of the $d$-loop reduces $C$, $D$, and $T1$ to three-dimensional arrays, while the fusion of the $a$-loop reduces $A$ and $S$ to 3-dimensional arrays as well. Notice that $B$ and $T2$ are the only four-dimensional arrays left, and, consequently, they have the largest storage requirements of all arrays: 49MB per processor and 400MB per processor, respectively. The total memory requirements for the solution of the example are 503MB per processor, within the imposed limit of 512MB. Notice that further memory reduction is possible, for example, by partially fusing the $c$-loop and collapsing $D$ and $T1$ to two-dimensional arrays. However, this is unnecessary, as the communication cost of the computation would increase, and nothing can be gained by further memory reduction.

Based on the empirical characterization data of the Cray T3E, the total communication cost for this example is 2188 seconds, or 0.61 hours. Most of this load can be attributed to the re-distribution of the arrays $A$, $C$, $D$, and $T1$. Since they are collapsed onto three dimensions for better memory management, they have to be partially re-distributed at each iteration of the fused loop, resulting in large message-passing start-up costs.

Table 2 presents the solution of the algorithm for a system of 16 processors on the Itanium cluster. The optimal logical view of the processor space is found to be a two-dimensional $4 \times 4$ distribution. The total memory requirement of the optimal solution is 1.77GB per processor, which is within the 2GB memory limit. The total communication cost is 3076 seconds, or 0.85 hours. The optimal distributions of the arrays are different for the two cases presented here (see Tables 1 and 2).

It is important to note that a decoupled approach of first performing loop fusion followed by array distribution fails to provide a feasible solution in this example. In particular, minimizing the communication cost without taking memory usage into account produces a final distribution $\langle a,b \rangle = \langle *,* \rangle$ for the array $T2(b,c,j,k)$. The array $T2$ would be replicated on all processors, resulting in a memory usage of 12.8GB per processor. Reduction from this amount is possible by fusion, but the constraints imposed by the communication-optimal solution do not permit effective memory reduction. In this example, starting from the unfused communication-optimal solution, no

**Table 2.** Loop fusions, memory requirements and communication costs on 16 processors of an Intel Itanium cluster for the arrays presented in Fig. 2(a)

| Full array | Reduced array | Initial dist. | Final dist. | Memory /processor | Comm. cost |
|---|---|---|---|---|---|
| $D(c,d,e,l)$ | $D(c,e,l)$ | $\langle e,l \rangle$ | $\langle *,* \rangle$ | 22.4MB | 704.8 sec. |
| $B(b,e,f,l)$ | $B(b,e,f,l)$ | $\langle f,b \rangle$ | $\langle f,b \rangle$ | 98.0MB | 0 |
| $C(d,f,j,k)$ | $C(f,j,k)$ | $\langle j,f \rangle$ | $\langle *,* \rangle$ | 0.9MB | 389.7 sec. |
| $A(a,c,i,k)$ | $A(c,i,k)$ | $\langle c,k \rangle$ | $\langle *,* \rangle$ | 12.8MB | 546.0 sec. |
| $T1(b,c,d,f)$ | $T1(b,c,f)$ | $\langle f,b \rangle$ | $\langle c,b \rangle$ | 35.0MB | 1391.7 sec. |
| $T2(b,c,j,k)$ | $T2(b,c,j,k)$ | $\langle c,b \rangle$ | $\langle j,b \rangle$ | 800.0MB | 43.9 sec. |
| $S(a,b,i,j)$ | $S(a,b,i,j)$ | $\langle j,b \rangle$ | $\langle j,b \rangle$ | 800.0MB | 0 |

loop fusion structure exists that can bring the memory usage under the limit. Only an integrated approach to memory reduction and communication minimization is able to provide a solution.

## 5   Conclusion

In this paper we have addressed a compile-time optimization problem arising in the context of a program synthesis system. The goal of the synthesis system is the facilitation of rapid development of high-performance parallel programs for a class of computations encountered in computational chemistry. These computations are expressible as a set of tensor contractions and arise in electronic structure calculations.

We have described the interactions between distributing arrays on a parallel machine and minimizing memory through loop fusion. We have presented an optimization approach that can serve as the basis for a key component of the system, for minimizing the communication cost on a parallel computer under memory constraints. The effectiveness of the algorithm was demonstrated by applying it to a computation that is representative of those used in quantum chemistry codes such as NWChem.

*Acknowledgments.* We thanks the support of the National Science Foundation through the Information Technology Research program (CHE-0121676 and CHE-0121706), and NSF grants CCR-0073800 and EIA-9986052.

## References

1. D. Cociorva, J. Wilkins, C. Lam, G. Baumgartner, P. Sadayappan, J. Ramanujam. Loop Optimizations for a Class of Memory-Constrained Computations. In *Proc. 15th ACM Intl. Conf. on Supercomputing*, pp. 103–113, Sorrento, Italy, June 2001.
2. D. Cociorva, J. Wilkins, G. Baumgartner, P. Sadayappan, J. Ramanujam, M. Nooijen, D. Bernholdt, and R. Harrison. Towards Automatic Synthesis of High-Performance Codes for Electronic Structure Calculations: Data Locality Optimization. *Proc. of the Intl. Conf. on High Performance Computing*, Lecture Notes in Computer Science, Vol. 2228, pp. 237–248, Springer-Verlag, 2001.

3.  D. Cociorva, G. Baumgartner, C. Lam, P. Sadayappan, J. Ramanujam, M. Nooijen, D. Bernholdt, and R. Harrison. Space-Time Trade-Off Optimization for a Class of Electronic Structure Calculations. *Proceedings of ACM SIGPLAN 2002 Conference on Programming Language Design and Implementation (PLDI)*, June 2002.
4.  T. D. Crawford and H. F. Schaefer III. An Introduction to Coupled Cluster Theory for Computational Chemists. In *Reviews in Computational Chemistry*, vol. 14, pp. 33–136, Wiley-VCH, 2000.
5.  A. Fraboulet, G. Huard and A. Mignotte. Loop alignment for memory access optimization. In *Proc. 12th International Symposium on System Synthesis,* pages 71–77, San Jose, California, November 1999.
6.  G. Gao, R. Olsen, V. Sarkar, and R. Thekkath. Collective loop fusion for array contraction. In *Languages and Compilers for Parallel Processing,* New Haven, CT, August 1992.
7.  High Performance Computational Chemistry Group. NWChem, A computational chemistry package for parallel computers, Version 3.3, 1999. Pacific Northwest National Laboratory, Richland, WA 99352.
8.  C. Lam, P. Sadayappan, and R. Wenger. On optimizing a class of multi-dimensional loops with reductions for parallel execution. *Parallel Processing Letters,* Vol. 7 No. 2, pp. 157–168, 1997.
9.  C. Lam, P. Sadayappan, and R. Wenger. Optimization of a class of multi-dimensional integrals on parallel machines. In *Proc. Eighth SIAM Conference on Parallel Processing for Scientific Computing,* Minneapolis, MN, March 1997.
10. C. Lam, P. Sadayappan, D. Cociorva, M. Alouani, and J. Wilkins. Performance optimization of a class of loops involving sums of products of sparse arrays. In *Proc. Ninth SIAM Conference on Parallel Processing for Scientific Computing,* San Antonio, TX, March 1999.
11. C. Lam, D. Cociorva, G. Baumgartner, and P. Sadayappan. Memory-optimal evaluation of expression trees involving large objects. In *Proc. International Conference on High Performance Computing*, Calcutta, India, December 1999.
12. C. Lam, D. Cociorva, G. Baumgartner, and P. Sadayappan. Optimization of memory usage requirement for a class of loops implementing multi-dimensional integrals. In *Languages and Compilers for Parallel Computing*, San Diego, August 1999.
13. C. Lam. *Performance optimization of a class of loops implementing multi-dimensional integrals.* Ph.D. Dissertation, Ohio State University, Columbus, August 1999. Also available as Technical Report No. OSU-CISRC-8/99-TR22, Dept. of Computer and Information Science, The Ohio State University.
14. T. Lee and G. Scuseria. Achieving chemical accuracy with coupled cluster theory. In S. R. Langhoff (Ed.), *Quantum Mechanical Electronic Structure Calculations with Chemical Accuracy,* pages 47–109, Kluwer Academic, 1997.
15. J. Martin. In *Encyclopedia of Computational Chemistry.* P. Schleyer, P. Schreiner, N. Allinger, T. Clark, J. Gasteiger, P. Kollman, H. Schaefer III (Eds.), Wiley & Sons, Berne (Switzerland). Vol. 1, pp. 115–128, 1998.
16. V. Sarkar and G. Gao. Optimization of array accesses by collective loop transformations. In *Proc. ACM International Conference on Supercomputing,* pages 194–205, Cologne, Germany, June 1991.
17. Y. Song, R. Xu, C. Wang and Z. Li. Data locality enhancement by memory reduction. In *Proc. of ACM 15th International Conference on Supercomputing,* pages 50–64, June 2001.
18. Y. Song, C. Wang and Z. Li. Locality enhancement by array contraction. In *Proc. 14th International Workshop on Languages and Compilers for Parallel Computing,* August 2001.

# Forward Communication Only Placements and Their Use for Parallel Program Construction

Martin Griebl[1], Paul Feautrier[2], and Armin Größlinger[1]

[1] FMI, University of Passau, Germany
{griebl, groessli}@fmi.uni-passau.de
[2] INRIA, Unité de Recherche de Rocquencourt, France
Paul.Feautrier@inria.fr

**Abstract.** The context of this paper is automatic parallelization by the space-time mapping method. One key issue in that approach is to adjust the granularity of the derived parallelism. For that purpose, we use tiling in the space and time dimensions. While space tiling is always legal, there are constraints on the possibility of time tiling, unless the placement is such that communications always go in the same direction (*forward communications only*). We derive an algorithm that automatically constructs an FCO placement – if it exists. We show that the method is applicable to many familiar kernels and that it gives satisfactory speedups.

## 1 Introduction

In the field of automatic parallelization the question of selecting the right granularity is still not completely solved. Especially for imperfectly nested loops or non-uniform dependences (not to talk about irregular programs) many questions remain open.

In this paper, we present a method that allows to freely choose the granularity of the parallelism – if possible. Note that it is not the focus of this paper to *find* the optimal granularity for a given program and actual machine parameters, but to offer a technique that yields a parallel program in which the desired granularity can be set freely.

Our parallelization framework is space-time mapping, based on the polytope model [7, 9, 16]. It is designed for automatic parallelization of imperfect loop nests, and has been extended so as to be widely applicable, e.g., to non-uniform dependences, or, sometimes, with a slight loss in efficiency, even to irregular programs. The main idea is that every instance of every statement is mapped to a virtual point in time (*schedule*) and to a virtual processor (*placement*). In other words, the space-time mapping distributes all computations of the source program to as many processors as required. In order to map the parallel program on a machine with a fixed number of physical processors, we must apply standard tiling techniques.

Note that the initial idea and the technical basis of tiling in our setting is the same as in traditional tiling, namely coalescing iterations, but its application is different: we do not discover parallelism by tiling (this is the task of the preceding

B. Pugh and C.-W. Tseng (Eds.): LCPC 2002, LNCS 2481, pp. 16–30, 2005.

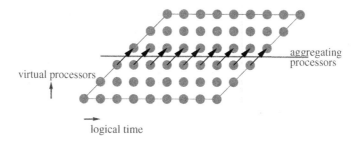

**Fig. 1.** Target space before tiling the time dimension

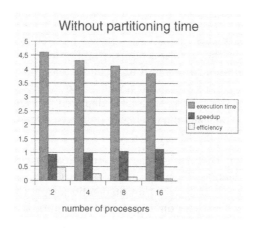

**Fig. 2.** Execution times, speedup and efficiency after tiling space dimensions only

scheduling phase), but we limit parallelism to the physically possible amount by applying tiling techniques.

When running the resulting parallel programs on distributed memory systems, we usually find that (even for few physical processors) the granularity is still too fine for being efficient. The reason is that typically there are communications after every single virtual time step.

*Example 1.* Consider the program fragment

```
for k=0 to m
    for i=1 to n-1
        A[k,i] = ( A[k,i-1] + 2 * A[k-1,i] ) /3
    end
end
```

After space-time mapping and tiling (partitioning) the one-dimensional processor space, we obtain a space-time mapped iteration domain as in Figure 1. The black arrows represent communications.

The execution times, speedups and efficiency for $(n, m) = (393216, 128)$ are given in Figure 2. The speedups for 2, 4, 8, and 16 processors are 0.94, 1.0, 1.05, and 1.13, which gives poor efficiency values of 0.47, 0.25, 0.13, and 0.07, respectively.

Our solution is to add another tiling phase, which adapts the granularity of the parallelism by coalescing virtual time steps. The idea behind this partitioning of time is (in the setting of distributed memory machines) to postpone and collect all send operations within a time partition and to execute the communications only at the end of the partition. Obviously, this reduces the number of communications. On the other hand, the larger the time partition, the longer the receiver has to wait for its data, i.e., the longer the receiver is delayed. The optimal size for the time partitions depends on the program and on the machine parameters.

*Example 2.* If we apply this idea to the space-time mapped iteration domain of Figure 1, we obtain the iteration domain in Figure 3, which shows the reduced number of communications and also the increased latency for the upper processor. The efficiency for the same problem size as above and for different values of the width of the time partitions is depicted in Figure 4. The presence of a maximum in the efficiency curve clearly points to a trade-off between fewer communications and less latency.

The problem is that time tiling may generate deadlocks: suppose that some operation in tile $t_1$ generates data for a later operation in $t_2$ while an operation in $t_2$ generates data for $t_1$. It is clear that no deadlock can occur if the time is not tiled (since we need at least two operations with different schedules in each tile) or if all communications roughly go into the same direction (e.g. from $t_1$ to $t_2$ but not the reverse). A formal definition and proof are given in Section 2. We call this property *forward communications only (FCO)*. A placement satisfying this constraint allows any size for the time partitions [10]. (Note that this constraint is not necessary but sufficient.)

Using FCO placements is not a novel idea. It has been suggested many times as a sure way of avoiding deadlocks. Our aim here is not to advocate the use of FCO placements, but to give an automatic method for building them.

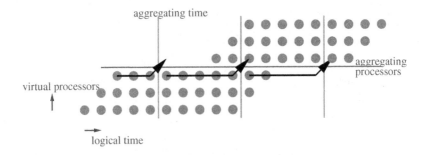

**Fig. 3.** Target space after partitioning time

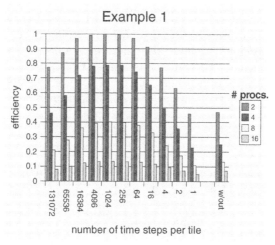

**Fig. 4.** Execution times after partitioning time

The rest of this paper is organized as follows. Section 2 sets the formal background and derives the FCO placement algorithm. Sections 3 and 4 discuss variants of this algorithm: Section 3 uses a different placement approach, and Section 4 points out some future extensions. Section 5 discusses related work. Section 6 shows some preliminary experimental results and Section 7 concludes.

## 2  Forward Communication Only Placement

In the presence of loops, every statement $S$ in the body has several instances at run-time. We call them *operations* and denote them by $\langle i, S \rangle$ where the *iteration vector* $i$ is the vector of all loop indices surrounding $S$. The set of all instances of a given statement $S$ is called the *index set* of $S$.

In order to use efficient mathematical tools, we require the loop bounds to be affine functions in surrounding loop indices and *structure parameters*, i.e., symbolic constants [7, 16]. (A method avoiding this restriction is given elsewhere [9].)

In our mathematical notation, we often use the *homogeneous representation* of index vectors: we join the $l$-vector $i$ of surrounding loops indices and the $m$-vector $n$ of structure parameters in order to obtain the $d$-dimensional homogeneous index vector. Note that the $m$-vector of structure parameters shall always contain one entry for the constant 1.

In the affine setting, the $c$ bounds of the loops surrounding a statement $S$ can be expressed as a system of linear inequalities and represented as a $c \times d$ matrix $D_S$ with

$$D_S . \binom{i}{n} \geq 0 \tag{1}$$

where $i$ is the iteration vector of $S$, and $n$ is the vector of all structure parameters. For consistency, we take care that the trivial inequality $1 \geq 0$ is always included in $D_S$.

A *computation placement* $\pi$ is a function which maps every operation to an integer vector that represents a virtual processor. Again, we require placements to be affine in the loop indices and the structure parameters. Hence, the placement of every statement $S$, $\pi_S$, can be represented by a $p \times d$ matrix $\Pi_S$ where $p$ is the number of processor dimensions, and $d = l + m$, i.e. $d$ is the dimensionality of the index set of $S$ plus the number of symbolic parameters:

$$\pi_S(i, n) = \Pi_S \cdot \binom{i}{n} \tag{2}$$

Similarly, a *data placement* maps array elements to virtual processors. For each array $A$, we express this placement as:

$$\pi_A(a, n) = \Pi_A \cdot \binom{a}{n} \tag{3}$$

where $a$ is the vector of $A$ subscripts and $n$ is as above.

Lastly, we need a *schedule* function $\theta$, which maps operations to (virtual) time. Schedules are assumed to be affine in the loop indices and the structure parameters, as this is necessary for subsequent target code generation.

In general, each operation $\langle i, S \rangle$ both reads and writes memory. Our basic assumption is that these accesses are to array cells. Let $A$ be one of the arrays accessed by $S$. We assume that we have been able to extract from the program text a subscript function $f_{AS}$ such that the cell of $A$ accessed by $S$ is $A[f_{AS}(i, n)]$. Here again we suppose $f_{AS}$ to be affine: there exists a matrix $F_{AS}$ such that:

$$f_{AS}(i, n) = F_{AS} \cdot \binom{i}{n}. \tag{4}$$

In Example 1, the $F$ matrix for the rightmost reference to $A$ is $\begin{pmatrix} 1 & 0 & 0 & 0 & -1 \\ 0 & 1 & 0 & 0 & 0 \end{pmatrix}$.

Let $A[f_{AS}(i, n)]$ be a read reference to $A$ in $S$. If this array cell is not on the same processor as operation $\langle i, S \rangle$, a communication is necessary. This communication will be forward if:

$$\pi_A(f_{AS}(i, n), n) \leq \pi_S(i, n). \tag{5}$$

On the other hand, if the distinguished reference is a write, it will be forward if:

$$\pi_S(i, n) \leq \pi_A(f_{AS}(i, n), n). \tag{6}$$

These inequalities are to be understood component-wise. They are to be verified everywhere in the index set $D_S$ of $S$. The conjunction of these properties for all references in the program defines a forward communication only (FCO) placement. (Note that the definition of the direction is arbitrary: we can always reorder processors independently in each dimension).

A *tile* is a set of operations which are executed atomically by one processor. Operations of a tile are executed sequentially. In this paper, we use a very simple tiling scheme. Let $T$ be the tile size in time and $B$ be the tile size in space[1]. Operation $\langle i, S \rangle$ is executed by physical processor $\pi_S(i, n) \div B$ in its $\theta_S(i, n) \div T$-th time step.

Arrays are tiled according to the same scheme: cell $A[x]$ is in the memory of physical processor $\pi_A(x, n) \div B$. The communication graph has the tiles as vertices; there is an edge from tile $a$ to $b$ if $a$ sends data to $b$.

**Theorem 1.** *Any space/time tiling according to an FCO placement is valid.*

*Proof.* For easier understanding, the proof will be written as if the schedule and placement were one-dimensional. Extension to several dimensions is trivial.

A tiling is valid if there are no cycles in the communication graph. Let us suppose a contrario that such a cycle exists. For $k = 0, \ldots, \ell - 1$, tile $(t_k, p_k)$ sends data to tile $(t_{k+1}, p_{k+1})$ and tile $(t_\ell, p_\ell)$ sends data to tile $(t_0, p_0)$. For each communication, there is an emitter $x$ (a memory cell or an operation) and a receiver $y$ (an operation or a memory cell), each one having a placement function $\pi_e$ (resp. $\pi_r$). The FCO condition implies:

$$\pi_e(x) \leq \pi_r(y),$$

from which follows:

$$p_e = \pi_e(x) \div B \leq \pi_r(y) \div B = p_r,$$

where $p_e$ (resp. $p_r$) is the name of the (real) processor executing (or holding) $x$ (resp. $y$). Furthermore, the inequality is strict, since there actually is a communication.

We have just proved that $p_k < p_{k+1}$ for $k = 0, \ldots, \ell - 1$ and $p_\ell < p_0$ which is impossible since $<$ is an order.

Let us now consider one of the FCO conditions, (5) for instance. It can be rewritten as:

$$\forall \begin{pmatrix} i \\ n \end{pmatrix} : D_S . \begin{pmatrix} i \\ n \end{pmatrix} \geq 0 \Rightarrow \Pi_S . \begin{pmatrix} i \\ n \end{pmatrix} - \Pi_A . F_{AS} \begin{pmatrix} i \\ n \end{pmatrix} \geq 0. \tag{7}$$

Farkas' lemma [20] shows how such an affine inequation system can be transformed into an equivalent equation system by adding non negative variables. Thus, (7) is equivalent to:

$$\Pi_S - \Pi_A . F_{AS} = \lambda_{AS} D_S. \tag{8}$$

where the Farkas multipliers $\lambda_{AS}$ are non negative. In this equation, the $\Pi_S, \Pi_A$ and $\lambda_{AS}$ are unknowns, while $F_{AS}$ and $D_S$ can be deduced from the source program. Similar considerations apply to (6).

Let $\Pi$ be the vector obtained by concatenating the $\Pi_A$ and $\Pi_S$ in some order, and $\lambda$ be the vector obtained by concatenating the $\lambda_{AS}$. (The fact that

---

[1] When the schedule and/or placement are multidimensional, $T$ and $B$ become vectors, the integer division operator $\div$ being extended componentwise.

the entries of $\Pi$ and $\lambda$ are $p$-vectors themselves is irrelevant for the following reasoning.) It is clear that there exist matrices $C$ and $D$ such that the FCO condition is equivalent to:

$$C.\Pi = D.\lambda, \tag{9}$$

$$\lambda \geq 0. \tag{10}$$

The set of solutions of this system (i.e. the set of valid FCO placements) is a cone $\mathcal{C}$ (it is closed both by addition and by multiplication by a non-negative constant). Let $\langle \Pi, \lambda \rangle$ be such a solution; let us consider a specific reference to $A$ in $S$. There is a part of $\lambda$ which corresponds to $\lambda_{AS}$ in (8). If this part is null, then the distinguished reference entails no communication. Let $\langle \Pi_1, \lambda_1 \rangle$ and $\langle \Pi_2, \lambda_2 \rangle$ be two solutions. It is clear that $\langle \Pi_1 + \Pi_2, \lambda_1 + \lambda_2 \rangle$ is another solution whose residual communications are the union of the residual communications of the two initial solutions. This leads us to consider only extremal solutions, which cannot be obtained as a weighted sum of other solutions.

Any cone can be characterized [20] by its extremal rays $r_1, \ldots, r_s$ and its lines $l_1, \ldots, l_t$ in such a way that:

$$\mathcal{C} = \{\sum x_k r_k + \sum y_k l_k \mid x_k \geq 0\}. \tag{11}$$

There are well known algorithms for finding the rays and lines of a cone, and at least one efficient implementation, the Polylib [21].

Let us now consider a line $l_k = \langle \Pi_k, \lambda_k \rangle$. Since $l_k$ is a line, $\langle -\Pi_k, -\lambda_k \rangle$ is also in $\mathcal{C}$. By (10) we obtain $\lambda_k \geq 0$ and $-\lambda_k \geq 0$ which implies $\lambda_k = 0$.

Conversely, if $\langle \Pi_k, \lambda_k \rangle$ is a ray with $\lambda_k = 0$, then $\langle -\Pi_k, -\lambda_k \rangle$ is also a solution and the ray is a line. It follows that lines correspond to communication-free placements, and that rays correspond to FCO placements with residual communications. Furthermore, an analysis of the null components of the $\lambda$ part of a ray allows one to identify residual communications. If we assign a weight to each reference (e.g. an estimate of the number of transmitted values), we can associate a weight to each ray and select the one with minimum weight (remember that in this context, lines will show up as zero weight solutions).

However, we still have to consider parallelism. Let $\Pi_S$ be the part of a solution which corresponds to statement $S$. While up to now we have considered $\Pi_S$ as a vector, it is in fact a matrix with $p$ rows, where $p$ is the dimension of the processor grid. The set of active processors is the image of the index set of $S$ by $\Pi_S$. In order to preserve efficiency, we want this set to have the same dimension as the processor grid (however, this dimension cannot be higher than the dimension of $S$ index set). Finding the dimension of the set of active processors is a simple rank computation.

We can thus propose the following algorithm:

- Build the matrices $C$ and $D$ from the source program.
- Build the rays and lines of the cone $\mathcal{C}$ associated to $C$ and $D$.
- Filter out rays and lines which do not satisfy the rank condition above.

– Compute the weight of each remaining ray or line.
– Select the ray or line with the smallest weight.

If a line has survived the filtering process, it has zero weight and will be selected, giving a communication free placement. If the selectee is a ray, it will give an FCO placement with minimum communication volume. Lastly, if there are no survivors, then the problem has no FCO placement of the required dimension.

We cannot claim that the placement we find in this way is the best one, in the sense of giving the best speedup. However, if the weights we assign to communications are estimates of the communication volumes, then our algorithm is a greedy solution to the problem of finding a minimum communication FCO placement.

Let us note that the severity of the filtering increases with the dimension of the processor grid. Hence, we can always try again with a grid of a smaller dimension. In general, the higher the dimension, the higher the volume of residual communications, but also the higher the bandwidth of the communication network. Since the relative importance of these two opposite factors depends on details of the architecture, the best choice can only be found experimentally.

## 3    Another Approach: Dependence Driven Placements

The presented placement algorithm computes one computation placement per statement and one data placement per array. However, there also exists other approaches for the computation of placements. We show how our basic FCO placement algorithm can be adapted accordingly.

One possibility is to drop the notion of ownership and assume that every processor holds the data it computes, and that it sends the data directly to every consumer. We call such a placement method *dependence driven*, in contrast to the original method which we call *ownership driven*.

Note that we have a very strong notion of dependences in this context: we use *direct* dependences for this approach. On the one hand, this requires a precise dataflow analysis, e.g. [2, 4]. On the other hand, the result is as precise as if we had converted the program to single assignment form: we can tell, for every operation, where the accessed data is located – because we know the source of the direct dependence, i.e., the producer in the case of flow dependences.

Note that if some array element $A[x]$ is re-assigned, the new producer holds the new value and, as written above, sends it to those processors that need this new value. Thus, we cannot say that $A[x]$ is owned by some processor, because the "ownership" for $A[x]$ changes. In this aspect, the dependence driven approach is more flexible than the ownership driven approach.

On the other hand, the implicit owner of every element (provided that it exists, e.g., because the program is single assignment) is its producer. There is no possibility that the producer stores the value at some different processor if this would be beneficial. So, in this aspect the ownership driven approach is more flexible [8] .

```
      DO i=0,n-1
S:      C[i] = 42;
        DO j=0, n-1
T:        A[i,j] = A[i,j-1] + C[i]
        END DO
      END DO
      DO l=1,n-1
        DO k=0, n-1
U:        B[l,k] = A[l,k] + C[l-1]
        END DO
      END DO
```

**Fig. 5.** A source program that needs redistribution

The construction of a dependence driven FCO placement can be achieved along the same lines as above. There is one placement constraint per dependence in the program.

A dependence $d$ is given as a relation from the source index set to the destination index set:

$$\{\langle i, n, S \rangle \rightarrow \langle j, n, T \rangle \mid R_d \cdot \begin{pmatrix} i \\ j \\ n \end{pmatrix} \geq 0\},$$

in which we have assumed that the dependence is representable as one polyhedron. For every such dependence, we require the FCO property:

$$\pi_S(i, n) \leq \pi_T(j, n). \tag{12}$$

This can be rewritten as

$$\forall i, j, n : R_d \cdot \begin{pmatrix} i \\ j \\ n \end{pmatrix} \geq 0 \Rightarrow \Pi_T \cdot \begin{pmatrix} j \\ n \end{pmatrix} - \Pi_S \cdot \begin{pmatrix} i \\ n \end{pmatrix} \geq 0. \tag{13}$$

From then on, the algorithm follows the same lines as above. We eliminate quantifiers with the help of Farkas lemma, then find the rays and lines of the solution cone, and select the best one.

## 4   On the Use of Redistribution

The ownership driven approach has the drawback that an array has only one placement for all the execution of a program. This is unsatisfactory: many programs can be divided in successive phases with differing access patterns to arrays. Hence, we need the ability to freely determine a data placement, but also to change this data placement during program execution. Let us discuss this on an example.

*Example 3.* Consider the source program in Figure 5. There, we can avoid any communication due to the two-dimensional (hence, most important) accesses to arrays $A$ and $B$ by the following mapping: $A[x, y] \mapsto x$ and $\langle i, j, T \rangle \mapsto i$ (this eliminates the dependences cycle inside $T$), and $B[l, k] \mapsto l$ and $\langle l, k, U \rangle \mapsto l$ (this eliminates the dependence from $T$ to $U$ due to $A$ and enables a local store of $B$).

Furthermore, we map $\langle i, S \rangle \mapsto i$ and $C[z] \mapsto z$ in order to eliminate communications due to accesses of $C$ in $S$ and $T$. This solution is optimal if we allow one mapping per array and per statement – even if every of the $n^2$ accesses to $C[l-1]$ in $U$ causes a communication.

A much better solution would be if we could re-map array $C$ between its uses in $T$ and $U$. If we re-map $C[l-1]$ to $l$ before executing $U$, then there are no communications caused by $U$. The cost for the redistribution is one read/re-store per element of $C$, i.e., the redistribution causes only linearly many communications.

How can we modify our placement algorithm in order to find this solution? The first step is to split the first loop. We then add redistribution points in the source program, i.e., technically, we add artificial statements that read all elements of the array to be redistributed and copy them to a new array (and update the subsequent accesses to the new array). This scheme has the added advantage of limiting the complexity of each elementary placement problem, thus improving the scalability of our approach.

After inserting redistribution points for array $C$ between the loops on $S$ and $T$, and also between the loops on $T$ and $U$, and applying our placement algorithm, we obtain:

- between $S$ and $T$: $C'[z] \mapsto z$
- between $T$ and $U$: $C''[z] \mapsto z+1$

This means that we should not redistribute $C$ between $S$ and $T$, but between $T$ and $U$ – the expected result.

The central question for this approach is where to insert redistribution points, and for which arrays. One heuristics is to try redistribution along the edges of the acyclic condensation of the statement dependence graph. On the one hand this allows redistribution between different phases of an algorithm (where redistribution might be most important); on the other hand it guarantees that the expensive re-mapping is not executed too often, esp. not executed repeatedly back and forth, since it forbids redistribution inside dependence cycles. Of course, other strategies can be imagined as well.

In addition, there are other possibilities to make placement algorithms more flexible (e.g., to allow replication of arrays or even redundant computations, or to deal with piecewise affine placements, e.g., via index set splitting [12]). We leave this for our ongoing work.

## 5 Related Work

Tiling has many applications in program optimization. We will not consider here its use for locality improvement in sequential programs as in the work of

Wolfe [23] or Xue et. al. [26]. Tiling may be used as a parallelization method. This approach was first proposed by Triolet [15]. The shape of the tile is first chosen in such a way that deadlocks are avoided. The parallel program is then constructed by a simple application of the hyperplane method. Lastly, the size of the tiles is adjusted for minimum run time [1, 13, 14, 18, 19, 24, 25].

Another approach consists of applying tiling after parallelization in order to adjust the grain of parallelism [22]. This has lead to the definition of fully permutable loop nests. The present paper belongs to this category. It differs from previous proposals in that we do not apply tiling either to arrays or to index sets, but to time and space. In a previous work [11], the first author explained in more detail why the parallelization procedure described in Section 1 can be superior to the traditional tiling approach. The most important reasons are a wider applicability and, at the same time, a possibly better quality of the result.

There also exist multiple papers about placement functions, some of them using the same framework as this paper [3, 6, 17]. However, to the best of our knowledge, this is the first time that automatic construction of FCO placements is considered. In Lim and Lam terminology [17], our methods apply when constant parallelism is not sufficient for taking benefit of all processors.

The use of Farkas lemma for quantifier elimination in formulas like (7) has been first proposed by the second author [5], however in a different application area.

## 6   Experiments

Our placement algorithm has been implemented as an extension to the LooPo parallelizer and tested on about ten kernels, some real and some artificial. These kernels are available on demand from the authors. We found FCO placements for all examples, and even some communication free placements. The largest examples where "burg" (a signal processing kernel with 22 lines of code) and "LCZOS" (a Lanczos iteration with 60 lines). The algorithm has removed 31 communications out of 44 in the first case and 62 out of 64 in the second case.

We then tested the performances of our target code on an SCI-connected network of 32 nodes, every node (board) with two Pentium 3 processors at 1 GHz and 512 MB of main memory. In order to avoid effects due to the shared memory on the boards, we only used one processor per node. We took gcc-2.96 -O2 for the compilation and SCAMPI as communication library.

Our first experiments show that tiling time is necessary for some cases. As a rule of thumb, these cases arise for loop nests where one dimension goes to space and all other dimensions are covered by the schedule. In this situation, we must reduce the number of communication phases which, before tiling time, take place at every iteration of the sequential loops.

We use the programs in Figure 6. The SOR algorithm has uniform, the LUBKSB (LU Backward Substitution) non-uniform but affine dependences; the complex array indices in LUBKSB result from loop normalization (in the initial program, the loops are counting backward). The schedules for SOR and the three

```
                                        DO k=0, n-1
        DO J=1,M                           sum[n-k] = b[n-k]
           DO I=2,N-1                       DO l=0, k-1
              A(I)=(A(I-1)+                    sum[n-k]=sum[n-k]-
                    A(I+1))/2.0                            a[n-k][n-l]*b[n-l]
           END DO                          END DO
        END DO                             b[n-k]=sum[n-k]/a[n-k][n-k]
                                        END DO
```

SOR 1-dimensional                    LUBKSB

**Fig. 6.** Example programs that need partitioning of time

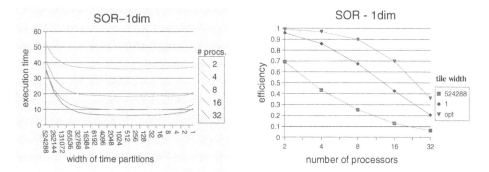

**Fig. 7.** Execution time and efficiency for SOR

statements of LUBKSB are $2*J+I-4$ and $0$, $2*l+2$, $2*k+1$, and the FCO placements generated by our algorithm are $J$ and $k$, $k$, $k$, respectively. We give the execution time and speedup for different numbers of processors and different widths of the time partitions in Figures 7 and 8.

For the SOR experiment, we set $M$ to 6144 and $N$ to 1048576; the resulting original sequential execution time was 180.5 seconds. Due to cache effects, the optimized parallel program on one processor needed only 71.4 seconds. This is an important collateral benefit: the aim of placement algorithms is to improve locality. This results not only in less communications, but also in less cache misses. Figure 7, right, shows the efficiency (with respect to this improved sequential time). We can see that the efficiency for the optimal time partitioning is about 15 to 30 % higher than without partitioning time, i.e., with time partition width of 1. On the other end of the spectrum, long time partitions (width = 524288) give up nearly all parallelism and so do not scale at all. Note that for the chosen value for parameter $M$, the 32 processors are not fully used; this becomes better for larger $M$ (but at the same time the importance of partitioning time decreases for the smaller number of processors).

In the LUBKSB experiment we use $N = 10240$ and obtain a sequential execution time of 19.81 seconds. The parallel version executes in 20.69 seconds on a single processor. We do not observe a speedup due to cache effects here since

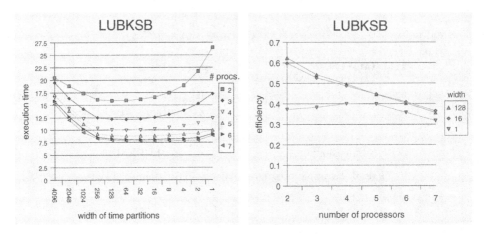

**Fig. 8.** Execution time and efficiency for LUBKSB

both programs access the array $a$ in a cache friendly way. Figure 8 shows that we achieve the highest speedup with tile sizes between 16 (on 7 processors) and 128 (on 2 processors). This example does not scale as well as the SOR example, because the iteration space is triangular, hence the work is distributed unevenly among the processors. A possible solution is to build tiles with variable size, but we have not worked out all the details of this technique.

## 7   Conclusions

As we have seen in Section 6, partitioning in the time direction is important in order to obtain good speedups for some kinds of algorithms. However, partitioning time is not always legal. A sufficient condition for legality is that all communications of the parallel program go forward in every dimension (FCO). This condition is also necessary in one dimension.

The main theme of this paper has been the development of an algorithm for the automatic construction of FCO placements. This algorithm has been implemented as an extension to the LooPo parallelizer and used for all the examples in this paper. Experiments show that the transformed programs have satisfactory performances on a cluster of PC, although better load balancing is needed in some cases.

Although we have not emphasized the point, the method can be generalized to handle programs beyond the strict polytope model: modulo and integer division in the subscripts, min and max operators in the loop bounds, tests on the loop indices, union of polytopes in the dependence descriptions, and even infinite iteration domains as in signal processing.

We intend to pursue this work in several directions:

- Analyze the FCO placement algorithm. Can its complexity be reduced? Find examples in which no FCO placement can be found.

- Build a rough cost model for the tiled program, in order to help the selection of a good tile size. Can this model help in the construction of programs with tiles of varying size?
- Compare the ownership driven and the dependence driven approaches as to applicability, complexity and efficiency.
- Explore the redistribution approach, with a view of improving the scalability of the compiler.

## Acknowledgments

The first author would like to thank Michael Classen for his support with the experiments, and Max Geigl for his fruitful comments on a draft version of this paper.

All authors acknowledge the help of the French-German exchange program PROCOPE (grant 02969TB on the French side).

## References

1. Pierre Boulet, Alain Darte, Tanguy Risset, and Yves Robert. (Pen)-ultimate tiling? *INTEGRATION*, 17:33–51, 1994.
2. Jean-François Collard and Martin Griebl. A precise fixpoint reaching definition analysis for arrays. In Larry Carter and Jeanne Ferrante, editors, *Languages and Compilers for Parallel Computing, 12th International Workshop, LCPC'99*, LNCS 1863, pages 286–302. Springer-Verlag, 1999.
3. Michèle Dion and Yves Robert. Mapping affine loop nests: New results. In Bob Hertzberger and Giuseppe Serazzi, editors, *High-Performance Computing & Networking (HPCN'95)*, LNCS 919, pages 184–189. Springer-Verlag, 1995.
4. Paul Feautrier. Dataflow analysis of array and scalar references. *Int. J. Parallel Programming*, 20(1):23–53, February 1991.
5. Paul Feautrier. Some efficient solutions to the affine scheduling problem. Part I. One-dimensional time. *Int. J. Parallel Programming*, 21(5):313–348, 1992.
6. Paul Feautrier. Toward automatic distribution. *Parallel Processing Letters*, 4(3):233–244, 1994.
7. Paul Feautrier. Automatic parallelization in the polytope model. In Guy-René Perrin and Alain Darte, editors, *The Data Parallel Programming Model*, LNCS 1132, pages 79–103. Springer-Verlag, 1996.
8. Paul Feautrier. Automatic distribution of data and computation. Technical Report 2000/3, Laboratoire PRiSM, Université de Versailles, URL: http://www.prism.uvsq.fr/rapports/2000/abstract_2000_3.html, March 2000. English translation of TSI vol. 15 pp 529–557, 1996.
9. Martin Griebl. *The Mechanical Parallelization of Loop Nests Containing while Loops*. PhD thesis, Fakultät für Mathematik und Informatik, Universität Passau, January 1997. Technical Report MIP-9701.
10. Martin Griebl. On the mechanical tiling of space-time mapped loop nests. Technical Report MIP-0009, Fakultät für Mathematik und Informatik, Universität Passau, August 2000.

11. Martin Griebl. On tiling space-time mapped loop nests. In *Thirteenth annual ACM symposium on parallel algorithms and architectures (SPAA 2001)*, pages 322–323, July 2001.

12. Martin Griebl, Paul A. Feautrier, and Christian Lengauer. Index set splitting. *Int. J. Parallel Programming*, 28(6):607–631, 2000.

13. Edin Hodžić and Weijia Shang. On time optimal supernode shape. In *Eighth Int. Workshop on Compilers for Parallel Computers (CPC 2000)*, pages 367–379, Boca Raton,FL, 2000. CRC Press.

14. Karin Högstedt, Larry Carter, and Jeanne Ferrante. Selecting tile shape for minimal execution time. In *11th Annual ACM Symposium on Parallel Algorithms and Architectures (SPAA'99)*, pages 201–211. ACM Press, June 1999. Also available with proofs as UCSD Tech Report CS99-616.

15. François Irigoin and Remi Triolet. Supernode partitioning. In *Proc. 15th Ann. ACM Symp. on Principles of Programming Languages (POPL'88)*, pages 319–329, San Diego, CA, USA, January 1988. ACM Press.

16. Christian Lengauer. Loop parallelization in the polytope model. In Eike Best, editor, *CONCUR'93*, LNCS 715, pages 398–416. Springer-Verlag, 1993.

17. Amy W. Lim and Monica S. Lam. Maximizing parallelism and minimizing synchronization with affine partitions. *Parallel Computing*, 24(3–4):445–475, May 1998.

18. Daniel A. Reed, Loyce M. Adams, and Merrell L. Patrick. Stencils and problem partitionings: Their influence on the performance of multiple processor systems. *IEEE Trans. on Computers*, C-36(7):845–858, July 1987.

19. Robert Schreiber and Jack J. Dongarra. Automatic blocking of nested loops. Technical Report CS-90-108, University of Tennessee, Computer Science, May 1990.

20. A. Schrijver. *Theory of Linear and Integer Programming*. Series in Discrete Mathematics. John Wiley & Sons, 1986.

21. Doran K. Wilde. A library for doing polyhedral operations. Technical Report 785, IRISA, December 1993.

22. Michael Wolf and Monica Lam. A loop transformation theory and an algorithm to maximize parallelism. *IEEE Trans. on Parallel and Distributed Systems*, 2(4):452–471, October 1991.

23. Michel Wolfe. Iteration space tiling for memory hierarchies. In Gary Rodrigue, editor, *Proc. of the 3rd conference on Parallel Processing for Scientific Computing*, pages 357–361. SIAM, 1989.

24. Jingling Xue. Communication-minimal tiling of uniform dependence loops. *J. Parallel and Distributed Computing*, 42(1):42–59, April 1997.

25. Jingling Xue. On tiling as a loop transformation. *Parallel Processing Letters*, 7(4):409–424, 1997.

26. Jingling Xue and Chua-Huang Huang. Reuse-driven tiling for improving data locality. *Int. J. Parallel Programming*, 26(6):671–696, December 1998.

# Hierarchical Parallelism Control for Multigrain Parallel Processing

Motoki Obata[1,2], Jun Shirako[1], Hiroki Kaminaga[1],
Kazuhisa Ishizaka[1,2], and Hironori Kasahara[1,2]

[1] Dept. of Electrical, Electronics and Computer Engineering, Waseda University
{obata, shirako, kaminaga, ishizaka, kasahara}@oscar.elec.waseda.ac.jp
[2] Advanced Parallelizing Compiler Reserch Group
http://www.apc.waseda.ac.jp

**Abstract.** To improve effective performance and usability of shared memory multiprocessor systems, a multi-grain compilation scheme, which hierarchically exploits coarse grain parallelism among loops, subroutines and basic blocks, conventional loop parallelism and near fine grain parallelism among statements inside a basic block, is important. In order to efficiently use hierarchical parallelism of each nest level, or layer, in multigrain parallel processing, it is required to determine how many processors or groups of processors should be assigned to each layer, according to the parallelism of the layer. This paper proposes an automatic hierarchical parallelism control scheme to assign suitable number of processors to each layer so that the parallelism of each hierarchy can be used efficiently. Performance of the proposed scheme is evaluated on IBM RS6000 SMP server with 8 processors using 8 programs of SPEC95FP.

## 1 Introduction

As a parallel processing scheme on multiprocessor systems, loop level parallelism has been widely used by automatic parallelizing compilers[1,2]. As examples of loop parallelizing research compilers, Polaris compiler[3,4,5] exploits loop parallelism by using inline expansion of subroutine, symbolic propagation, array privatization[4,6] and run-time data dependence analysis[5] and SUIF compiler[7,8,9] parallelizes loops with inter-procedure analysis, unimodular transformation and data locality optimization [10,11]. Effective optimization of data locality is more and more important because of the increasing gap between memory and processor speeds. Currently, many researches for data locality optimization using program restructuring techniques such as blocking, tiling, padding and data localization, has been proceeded for high performance computing and single chip multiprocessor systems [10,12,13,14].

However, by those research efforts, the loop parallelization techniques are reaching maturity. In light of this fact, new generation parallelization techniques like multigrain parallelization are desired to overcome the limitation of the loop parallelization.

B. Pugh and C.-W. Tseng (Eds.): LCPC 2002, LNCS 2481, pp. 31–44, 2005.

OSCAR FORTRAN compiler realizes multigrain parallelization [15,16,17] which uses coarse grain task parallelism [15,16,17,18,19,20,21] among loops, subroutines and basic blocks and near fine grain parallelism[22,23] among statements inside a basic block in addition to conventional loop parallelism among loop iterations. Also, NANOS compiler[24,25] based on Parafrase2 has been trying to exploit multi-level parallelism including the coarse grain parallelism by using extended OpenMP API. PROMIS compiler[26,27] hierarchically combines Parafrase2 compiler[28] using HTG[29] and symbolic analysis techniques[30] and EVE compiler for fine grain parallel processing.

Based on OSCAR compiler, Advanced Parallelizing Compiler (APC) project [31] was started in Fiscal Year of 2000 to improve the effective performance, ease of use and cost performance of shared memory multiprocessor systems as a part of Japanese Government Millennium Project IT21 with industries and universities.

In the coarse grain parallelization in OSCAR multigrain compiler, a sequential program is decomposed into three kinds of Macro-Tasks, namely Block of Pseudo Assignment statements (basic block), Repetition Block (loop) and Subroutine Block. Earliest Executable Condition analysis is applied to the generated macro-tasks and generates a macro-task graph. A macro-task graph expresses coarse grain parallelism among macro-tasks. A sequential Repetition Block with a large loop body part or Subroutine Block is decomposed into coarse grain tasks hierarchically as shown in Fig.2. By these hierarchical definition of coarse grain tasks, OSCAR compiler can exploit more parallelism in a program in addition to the loop parallelism.

However, compiler must decide which layer should be parallelized and how many processors should be used for the layer. This decision is very difficult for the ordinary users since analysis of hierarchical parallelism and examination of the combination of hierarchical parallelism are very hard. This paper proposes an automatic determination scheme of the number of processors to be assigned to each program layer.

## 2   Coarse Grain Task Parallel Processing

This section describes a coarse grain task parallel processing scheme to decompose a sequential code to coarse grain tasks hierarchically and to generate hierarchical macro-task graph.

The macro-tasks on a macro-task graph are assigned to processor clusters (PC) or processor elements(PE) by a static or dynamic task scheduling method.

### 2.1   Generation of Coarse Grain Tasks

In the coarse grain task parallelization, a Fortran source program is decomposed into three kinds of macro-tasks, namely, Block of Pseudo Assignment statements (BPA), or Basic Block(BB), repetition Block(RB), or an outermost natural loop in the treated hierarchy, and Subroutine Block(SB). RBs composed of sequential

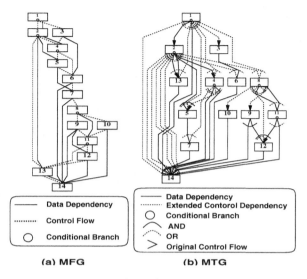

**Fig. 1.** A macro flow graph (MFG) and a macro-task graph (MTG)

loops having large processing cost and SBs to which inline expansion can not be applied effectively, are hierarchically decomposed into macro-tasks as shown in Fig.2.

## 2.2 Exploitation of Coarse Grain Parallelism

After the generation of macro-tasks in each layer, or each nest level, control and data flow among macro-tasks are analyzed. A macro flow graph in each layer is generated as shown in Fig.1(a). In the figure, nodes represent macro-tasks, solid edges represent data dependencies among macro-tasks and dotted edges represent control flow. A small circle inside a node represents a conditional branch inside the macro-task. Though arrows of edges are omitted in the macro-flow graph, it is assumed that the directions are downward.

Then, compiler analyzes Earliest Executable Condition[15,18,19] of all macro-task to exploit coarse grain parallelism among macro-tasks. This condition shows parallelism among macro-tasks considering both data dependency and control dependency. Earliest executable condition of each macro-task is shown as macro-task graph in Fig.1(b). In the macro-task graph, nodes represent macro-tasks. A small circle inside nodes represents conditional branches. Solid edges represent data dependencies. Dotted edges represent extended control dependencies. Extended control dependency means ordinary normal control dependency and the condition on which a data dependent predecessor of a macro-task is not executed.

## 2.3 Processor Clusters and Processor Elements

In the coarse grain parallelization, macro-tasks on hierarchical macro-task graphs are assigned to processor clusters, or groups of processors. OSCAR compiler

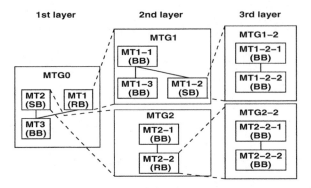

**Fig. 2.** Hierarchical macro-task graph

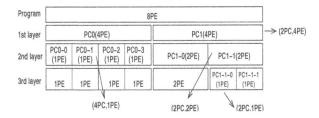

**Fig. 3.** Hierarchical definition of processor clusters and processor elements

groups processor elements(PE) into processor clusters(PC) logically, and assigns macro-tasks in a macro-task graph to PCs. If a hierarchical macro-task graph is defined inside a macro-task as shown in Fig.2, processors are also grouped by software logically into PCs hierarchically as shown in Fig.3. Fig.3 shows 8 processors are grouped into 2 processor clusters PC0 and PC1 having 4 processor elements respectively in the first layer. In the second layer, 4 processors in PC0 are grouped into 4 processor clusters PC0-0~PC0-3. On the other hand, PC1 is decomposed hierarchically to 2 processor clusters PC1-0 and PC1-1 having 2 processor elements respectively in the second layer. Again, PC1-1 having 2 processor elements is grouped hierarchically into 2 processor clusters PC1-1-0 and PC1-1-1 each of which has one PE in the third layer.

Compiler must decide how many PCs should be assigned to each layer of macro-task graphs to exploit full hierarchical parallelism efficiently. Next section handles this problem.

## 3   Automatic Determination of Parallel Processing Layer

This section describes how to decide the number of PCs to be assigned to each layer of macro-task graph (MTG). The parallel processing in the upper layer reduces overheads for synchronization and scheduling because the upper layer tasks usually have larger processing cost compared with overheads. The proposed scheme allows us to use coarse grain task parallelism and loop level parallelism.

## 3.1   Estimation of Macro-task Execution Cost

First, the compiler estimates processing cost of each macro-task. Sequential cost of each macro-task graph is the sum of sequential cost of macro-tasks considering control flow. If a macro-task is a DO-loop with undefined number of loop iterations and arrays with loop index are accessed in the loop, the compiler estimates the loop processing cost using the dimension size of arrays as the number of loop iterations. However, when the array appeared in the loop doesn't have any relationship with loop index or the number of iterations, the compiler assigns the all PE to the outermost parallelism. If conditional branches are included in a macro-task graph, execution cost is calculated by using branch probability. In this paper, since it is assumed that the compiler doesn't use execution profiles, the cost of macro-tasks is estimated using equal branch probability of 50% for the both conditional branch directions. However, if execution profile can be used, the cost of macro-tasks can be estimated more precisely. The compiler estimates sequential execution cost of each macro-task graph by using the hierarchical sum of inner macro-tasks.

## 3.2   Calculation of Parallelism of Each Layer of MTG

Coarse grain task parallelism of each macro-task graph(MTG) is calculated by sequential execution cost and critical path length of each MTG. Coarse grain task parallelism $Para_i$ of MTG$_i$ is defined as

$$Para_i = Seq_i/CP_i \tag{1}$$

where $CP_i$ is critical path length and $Seq_i$ is a sequential execution cost in MTG$_i$. Therefore, $\lceil Para_i \rceil$ shows the minimum number of processor clusters(PC) to execute MTG$_i$ in $CP_i$.

Next, $Para\_ALD_i$ (Para After Loop Division) is defined as total parallelism of coarse grain and loop iteration level parallelism. In the proposed determination scheme of parallel processing layer, $T_{min}$ is defined as a minimum task cost for loop parallelization considering overheads of parallel thread fork/join and task scheduling on each target multiprocessor system. This scheme assumes that parallelizable RB in MTG$_i$ is divided into sub RBs having larger cost than $T_{min}$. However, if the cost of iteration of RB is larger than $T_{min}$, the maximum number of decomposed tasks is the number of loop iterations of the RB. This task decomposition is considered for only calculation of $Para\_ALD$ and real task decomposition isn't performed at this phase. Critical path length after the temporary task decomposition is represented as $CP\_ALD_i$. Therefore, $Para\_ALD$ is defined by using $Seq_i$ and $CP\_ALD_i$.

$$Para\_ALD_i = Seq_i/CP\_ALD_i \tag{2}$$

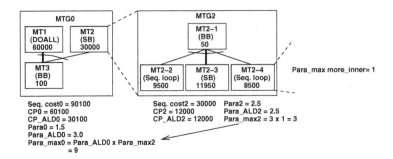

**Fig. 4.** Calculation of $Para, Para\_ALD Para\_max$

If $MT_i$ including $MTG_i$ as a loop body is parallelizable loop, it is necessary to reflect loop parallelism of $MT_i$ itself in $Para\_ALD_i$ hierarchically. In this case, $Para\_ALD_i$ is the product of the inner $Para\_ALD$ of $MTG_i$ and the number of task decomposition of $MT_i$, where the generated macro-tasks by the decomposition of $MT_i$ have larger cost than $T_{min}$. $\lceil Para\_ALD_i \rceil$ is the total number of processors which is necessary to execute $MTG_i$ in $CP\_ALD_i$ and shows the suitable number of processor clusters to balance execution cost among processor clusters. If more processors than $\lceil Para\_ALD_i \rceil$ were assigned to the MTG, possibility of processors being idle is high.

Also, as the enough number of processors for using all parallelism in lower layers of $MTG_i$, $Para\_max_i$ is defined as the following equation:

$$Para\_max_i = \lceil Para\_ALD_i \rceil \times \lceil Para\_max_{inner} \rceil \qquad (3)$$

where $Para\_max_{inner}$ is the maximum $Para\_max$ among macro-tasks in $MTG_i$. However, if RB is a parallelizable loop, the proposed scheme assumes that the loop is divided by $\lceil Para\_ALD_i \rceil$ and $Para\_max$ of the parallelizable loop in $MTG_i$ is calculated by considering the loop decomposition of parallelizable loop. Practically, after the number of processor clusters is determined, the actual number of decomposed tasks of a parallelizable loop is determined in the later stage of compilation by considering the number of processor clusters or cache size. In this phase calculating maximum parallelism, it is assumed that the parallelizable loop in $MTG_i$ is divided by $\lceil Para\_ALD_i \rceil$ which is the number of necessary processors in $MTG_i$.

As an example, $Para, Para\_ALD$ and $Para\_max$ in Fig.4 is shown. In Fig.4, "DOALL" shows parallelizable loop, "Seq. loop" shows un-parallelizable loop, namely sequential loop. Thick edges show critical path and numbers within nodes are sequential execution costs. Here, $T_{min}$, which is the minimum cost to realize efficient loop parallel processing, is defined as 10000. To explain simply, it is assumed that there are no parallelism in the body of MT1(DOALL) in $MTG_0$, MT2-2, MT2-3 and MT2-4 in $MTG_2$ which is inner macro-task graph of MT2(SB). Though hierarchical macro-task graphs can be generated inside these macro-tasks practically, the inner macro-task graphs of MT1, MT2-2, MT2-3 and

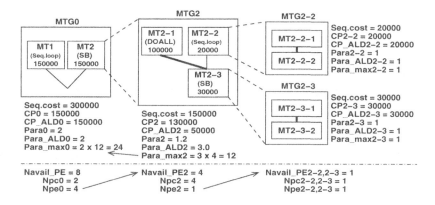

**Fig. 5.** Determination of $N_{PC}$ and $N_{PE}$

MT2-4 are omitted in this example. First, $Para$, $CP$, $Para\_ALD$, $CP\_ALD$ and $Para\_max$ are calculated from the deepest layer of a program. Since macro-task graphs within MT2-2, MT2-3 and MT2-4 don't have any parallelism as mentioned above, $Para = Para\_ALD = Para\_max = 1$ for these loops.

Sequential cost of $\mathrm{MTG}_2$ is 30000 and $CP_2$, $CP\_ALD_2$ are 12000. Therefore, $Para_2$ and $Para\_ALD_2$ of $\mathrm{MTG}_1$ are $Para_2 = 30000/12000 = 2.5$, $Para\_ALD_2 = 30000/12000 = 2.5$ Also, since $Para\_max = 1$ in MT2-2, MT2-3 and MT2-4 of $\mathrm{MTG}_2$ and $Para\_max_2 = \lceil Para\_ALD_2 \rceil \times Para\_max_{more\_inner} = 3 \times 1 = 3$, the suitable number of processors which is assigned to $\mathrm{MTG}_2$ is 3.

Also, parallelizable loop MT1 (DOALL) can be divided into 6 (60000/10000) sub macro-tasks. Therefore, $Para_1 = 1$, $Para\_ALD_1 = 6$ for MT1(DOALL). Then, each parameter in $\mathrm{MTG}_0$ is calculated. In Fig.4, $Seq_0 = 90100$ and $CP_0 = 60100$. $CP\_ALD_0 = 30100$ is the sum of sequential cost of MT2(SB) and MT3(BB) if MT1(DOALL) is divided into 6 tasks (60000/10000). Therefore, $Para_0 = 90100/60100 = 1.5$, $Para\_ALD_0 = 90100/30100 = 3.0$. For $Para\_max_0$, macro-tasks within $\mathrm{MTG}_0$ are MT1 through MT3 and it is assumed that MT1 is divided by $Para\_ALD_0 = 3$. $Para\_max_2 = 3$ of MT2(SB) which has $\mathrm{MTG}_2$ as mentioned above. Though original $Para\_max$ of MT1(DOALL) before task division is $Para\_max = 6$, $Para\_max = 6/3 = 2$ in one of divided MT1(DOALL) since MT1(DOALL) is divided by $Para\_ALD_0 = 3$. Therefore, MT having maximum $Para\_max$ in $\mathrm{MTG}_0$ is MT2 and $Para\_max_0 = \lceil Para\_ALD_0 \rceil \times Para\_max_2 = 9$.

### 3.3 Determination Scheme of PC and PE Assignment to Each Layer

This section describes an automatic determination scheme of PC and PE assignment to each layer is described by using parameters obtained in section 3.2.

**Step 1** Since execution costs of tasks in an upper layer are larger than tasks in a lower layer in a program in general, relative overheads of task scheduling and synchronization are relatively small. Thus, the proposed scheme tries to use more parallelism in an upper layer. Let's assume the number of processors which can be used in $MTG_i$ is $N_{Avail\_PEi}$. The number of processor clusters and processor elements are denoted as $N_{PCi}$ and $N_{PEi}$. Relationship between $Para_i$ and $N_{PCi}$ should be $Para_i \leq N_{PCi}$ to fully use coarse grain task parallelism. Furthermore, if the number of processor clusters is larger than $Para\_ALD_i$, the some processor clusters may become idle. Therefore, the combination of $[N_{PCi}, N_{PEi}]$ is defined as follows:

$$Para_i \leq N_{PCi} \leq Para\_ALD_i \qquad (4)$$

$$N_{PCi} \times N_{PEi} = N_{Avail\_PEi} \qquad (5)$$

If $Para_i = Para\_ALD_i$, the number of processor clusters $N_{PCi}$ for $MTG_i$ is selected as the minimum number which satisfies $Para_i \leq N_{PCi}$ and $N_{PCi} \times N_{PEi} = N_{Avail\_PEi}$ to use coarse grain task parallelism in $MTG_i$ as much as possible. If $Para_i \geq N_{Avail\_PEi}$, the combination of processor clusters and processor elements will be $N_{PCi} = N_{Avail\_PEi}$ and $N_{PEi} = 1$.

**Step 2** $MaxN_{PEi}$ is defined as the maximum $Para\_max$ among macro-tasks which are not parallelizable loop in $MTG_i$. $MaxN_{PEi}$ means an upper limit of the number of processors which can be assigned to lower layer of $MTG_i$, namely the upper limit of $N_{PEi}$. If $N_{PEi} > MaxN_{PEi}$ is used, possibility of unnecessary synchronization and number of overheads of task scheduling are high since excessive processor elements are assigned to a lower layer. To avoid such case, $N_{PEi} = MaxN_{PEi}$ is chosen in this step.

**Step 3.a** If all of the macro-tasks in $MTG_i$ is not parallelizable loops, current $N_{PCi}$ is chosen as the number of processor clusters assigned to the $MTG_i$.

**Step 3.b** If $MaxN_{PEi}$ is smaller than current $N_{PEi}$, $N_{PEi}$ is set to $MaxN_{PEi}$ in Step 2. However, when $MTG_i$ has parallelizable loops and $N_{PCi} \times N_{PEi} < N_{Avail\_PEi}$ is satisfied, possibility of lack of available processors to parallelize these loops effectively is high. In this case, $N_{PCi} \times MaxN_{PEi}$ is set to be over the upper limit of the number of processors in $MTG_i$ $MaxN_{PCPEi} = Para\_max_i$. $MaxN_{PCPEi}$ means an upper limit of total number of processors which are assigned to $MTG_i$ and its lower layer. Therefore, the proposed scheme chooses the minimum $N_{PCi}$ which satisfies $N_{PCi} \times MaxN_{PEi} \geq MaxN_{PCPEi}$. However, if $N_{PCi} \times MaxN_{PEi} > N_{Avail\_PEi}$, the proposed scheme chooses the maximum $N_{PCi}$ which is $N_{PCi} \times MaxN_{PEi} \leq N_{Avail\_PEi}$.

These steps are started from highest layer in a program to lower layers until $N_{Avail\_PEi} = 1$.

Fig.5 explains the processor assignment scheme. Fig.5 consists of 4 hierarchical macro-task graphs, namely the highest, or the first, level MTG0, the second level MTG2 and the third level MTG2-2 and MTG2-3. Sequential cost, CP, Para and so on are shown in Fig.5. It is assumed that MTG2-2 and MTG2-3 have no parallelism and no lower layers. Therefore, $Para = Para\_ALD = Para\_max = 1$. The number of available processors is eight, namely $N_{Avail\_PE0} = 8$. For

$MTG_0$, since $N_{PC0} = 2$ from $Para_0 = 2 \leq N_{PC0} \leq Para\_ALD = 2$ in Fig.5 , the combination of $[N_{PC0}, N_{PE0}]$ is [2PC, 4PE] from Step 1. Also, $MaxN_{PE0} = Para\_max_2 = 12$ since MT1 and MT2 in $MTG_0$ aren't parallelizable loops. Therefore, the proposed scheme understands that the lower layer of $MTG_0$, or $MTG_2$, needs 4 processors, and determines $N_{PE0} = 4$ from Step 2. The combination $[N_{PC2}, N_{PE2}]$ is determined. Since $N_{PE0} = 4$, $N_{Avail\_PE2} = 4$ in $MTG_2$. Here, the possible combinations of $[N_{PC2}, N_{PE2}]$ are [1, 4], [2, 2] and [4, 1]. $N_{PC2} = 2$ is satisfied $Para_2 = 1.2 \leq N_{PC2} \leq Para\_ALD_2 = 3.0$ in Fig.5 and available combinations of $[N_{PC2}, N_{PE2}]$ from Step 1. Though $N_{PE2} = 2$, $MaxN_{PE2} = Para\_max_{2-2,2-3} = 1$. Thus $N_{PE2} = 1$ from Step 2. By Step 3b, since $MaxN_{PCPE2} = 12$ in Fig.5, $N_{PC2}$ which satisfies $N_{PC2} \times MaxN_{PE2} \leq MaxN_{PCPE2} = 12$ is $N_{PC2} = 4$, thus $[N_{PC2}, N_{PE2}] = $ [4PC, 1PE]. Here, the process of assignment of PC and PE is ended since $N_{Avail\_PE2-2,2-3} = 1$.

Therefore, the proposed scheme determines $[N_{PC0}, N_{PE0}] = $ [2PC, 4PE], $[N_{PC2}, N_{PE2}] = $ [4PC, 1PE] and $[N_{PC2-2,2-3}, N_{PE2-2,2-3}] = $ [1PC, 1PE].

## 4   Performance Evaluation

This section evaluates the performance of the proposed parallelism control scheme for multigrain parallel processing on IBM RS6000 SP 604e High Node 8 processors SMP server. This scheme was implemented in OSCAR multigrain parallelizing compiler.

### 4.1   Evaluation Environment

In this evaluation, OSCAR compiler with the proposed scheme is used as a parallelizing pre-processor and generates a coarse grain task parallel program with OpenMP API. This OpenMP program uses the "one time single level thread generation" scheme which can minimize thread generation overhead by forking and joining parallel threads at the beginning and the end of the program only once and realize hierarchical coarse grain task parallel processing [32,33].

The generated OpenMP program is compiled by IBM XL Fortran for AIX Version 7.1 and executed on IBM RS6000 SP 604e High Node. This machine is a SMP server having 8 Power PC 604e processors (200MHz). Each processor has 32 Kbytes instruction / data L1 cache respectively and 1 MB unified L2 cache. A size of shared main memory is 1 GB.

In this evaluation, the best compile options, by which XL Fortran compiler gave us minimum processing time for sequential and parallel execution respectively, are used. However, the other parameter tuning for OS and runtime library isn't performed to only evaluate the pure performance of compilers.

### 4.2   Evaluation Result of SPEC95FP

In this evaluation, 8 programs from SPEC95fp, such as SWIM, TOMCATV, MGRID, HYDRO2D, SU2COR, TURB3D, APPLU and FPPPP, are used and

**Table 1.** Execution time(seconds) of SPEC95FP on 8 processors IBM RS6000 SP 604e High Node

| Benchmark | SWIM | TOMCATV | HYDRO2D | MGRID |
|---|---|---|---|---|
| Sequential | 549.1 | 636.8 | 987.7 | 592.0 |
| XLF for 8PEs | 130.6 | 1180.5 | 620.7 | 344.8 |
| XLF minimum (PE) | 112.6(6) | 373.0(3) | 426.2(4) | 193.0(4) |
| OFC for 8PEs | 64.4 | 107.2 | 116.7 | 93.6 |
| Benchmark | SU2COR | TURB3D | APPLU | FPPPP |
| Sequential | 517.2 | 649.0 | 707.4 | 505.9 |
| XLF for 8PEs | 941.9 | 2071.9 | 489.9 | 506.3 |
| XLF minimum (PE) | 197.9(4) | 649.0(1) | 489.9(8) | 505.9(1) |
| OFC for 8PEs | 120.1 | 197.9 | 423.7 | 506.0 |

*OFC: OSCAR FORTRAN COMPILER, XLF: XL Fortran
( ): the number of PEs giving the minimum time

the performance of OSCAR compiler and XL Fortran compiler is compared. Compilation options for native XL Fortran compiler are "-O3 -qsmp=noauto -qhot -qarch=ppc -qtune=auto -qcache=auto -qstrict" for OpenMP programs generated by OSCAR compiler, "-O5 -qsmp=auto -qhot -qarch=ppc -qtune=auto -qcache=auto" for automatic parallelization by XL Fortran compiler and "-O5 -qhot -qarch=ppc -qtune=auto -qcache=auto" for sequential execution. For two programs, such as SU2COR and TURB3D, manual restructuring, such as inline expansion, array renaming, loop distribution were made to avoid OSCAR compiler's bugs and the same restructured programs are used for sequential execution, automatic loop parallelization and coarse grain parallelization.

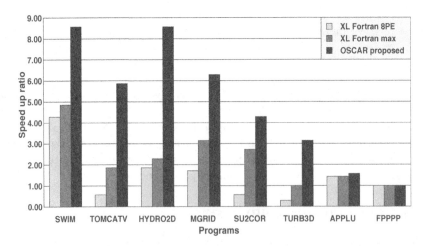

**Fig. 6.** Speedup ratio of SPEC95FP using 8 processors

Execution time of SPEC95FP is shown in Table 1. Also, Fig.6 shows speedup ratio of each SPEC95FP program by 8 processors against sequential execution time. In Table 1, the sequential processing time by XL Fortran, the automatic loop parallel processing time by XL Fortran using 8 processors, the shortest execution time by XL Fortran using up to 8 processors and the coarse grain task parallel processing time by OSCAR compiler using 8 processors are shown for each SPEC95FP programs.

In SWIM on Table 1, the sequential execution time was 549.1 seconds and the shortest parallel processing time by automatic loop parallelization by XL Fortran was 112.6 seconds. OSCAR compiler using the proposed scheme was 64.4 seconds and gave us 8.53 times speedup against the sequential time as shown in Fig.6. OSCAR compiler's "one time single level thread generation" with the parallelism control could boost up 1.75 times the maximum performance of XL Fortran though XL Fortran suffered from large thread management overhead.

In TOMCATV and HYDRO2D, sequential execution times for TOMCATV and HYDRO2D were 636.8 and 987.7 seconds. OSCAR compiler's execution times were 107.2 seconds for TOMCATV and 116.7 seconds for HYDRO2D as shown in Table 1. The shortest execution time by automatic loop parallelization of XL Fortran was 373.0 seconds for TOMCATV using 3 processors and 426.2 seconds for HYDRO2D using 4 processors. OSCAR compiler gave us 5.94 times speedup for TOMCATV and 8.46 times speedup for HYDRO2D compared with the sequential execution as shown in Fig.6 and boosted up 3.48 times for TOMCATV and 3.65 times for HYDRO2D the maximum performance of XL Fortran. Though TOMCATV and HYDRO2D consists of parallelizable loops, the proposed parallelism control scheme could find parallelizable loops which should not be processed in parallel.

In MGRID of Table 1, sequential execution time was 592.0 seconds and the shortest automatic loop parallel processing time by XL Fortran was 193.0 seconds. OSCAR compiler gave us 93.6 seconds, or 6.32 times speedup against the sequential execution as shown in Fig.6. The proposed scheme assigns all processors to the outermost parallelism in MGRID as section 3.1 because this program uses adjustable array and change array dimension in subroutines and function calls.

In SU2COR of Table 1, sequential execution time was 517.2 seconds. Though the execution time of loop parallelization by XL Fortran was 197.9 seconds, OSCAR compiler obtained 120.1 seconds, or 4.31 times speedup against the sequential execution as shown in Fig.6. Therefore OSCAR compiler boosted up 1.65 times the performance of XL Fortran. XL Fortran compiler used loop level parallelism in the deepest nest level with relatively small cost. On the contrary, the proposed scheme could find coarse grain task parallelism in the upper layer which is the inside of loop block "DO 400" in subroutine LOOPS. Since this layer has $Para = 1.90$, $Para\_ALD = 3.00$, the proposed scheme determines the combination of PC and PE [2PC, 4PE] and can use coarse grain parallelism effectively.

In TURB3D of Table 1, execution time by XL Fortran was 649.0 seconds for sequential execution time and the shortest time by loop parallel processing using up to 8 processors. The OpenMP code generated by OSCAR compiler gave us 197.9 seconds, and boosted up 3.28 times the performance of XL Fortran as shown in Fig.6. In TURB3D, coarse grain parallelism was extracted and $Para = 5.98$ was calculated by OSCAR compiler in RB of subroutine TURB3D. Therefore, the proposed scheme chooses the combination of [8PC, 1PE] since $Para \leq N_{PC}$, and gave us better performance.

In APPLU of Table 1, sequential execution time was 707.4 seconds. Though automatic loop parallel processing time by XL Fortran was 489.9 seconds, coarse grain parallel processing time by OSCAR compiler was 423.7 seconds, or 1.67 times speedup against sequential execution time as shown in Fig.6. APPLU has five subroutine including parallelizable blocks having large execution cost, namely JACLD, JACU, RHS, BUTS and BLTS. Current OSCAR compiler uses parallelism in subroutines JACLD, JACU and RHS and can not parallelize subroutine BUTS and BLTS. As the results, the proposed parallelism control scheme parallelizes the inside of subroutine JACLD, JACU and RHS automatically.

Finally, in FPPPP, execution time by XL Fortran and OSCAR compiler was the same 506 seconds as shown in Table 1. XL Fortran compiler and OSCAR compiler found no parallelism in FPPPP. However, there is statement level near fine grain parallelism in subroutine FPPPP and the parallelism can be exploited by OSCAR multigrain compiler on OSCAR chip multiprocessor[23].

## 5   Conclusions

This paper has proposed the automatic determination scheme of parallel processing layer and the number of processors to be assigned to each layer of macro-task graph for multigrain parallel processing. The performance evaluation of OSCAR compiler with the proposed scheme using SPEC95FP on IBM RS6000 SP 604e High Node 8 processors SMP server showed OSCAR compiler gave us 8.53 times speedup for SWIM, 5.94 times speedup for TOMCATV, 8.46 times speedup for HYDRO2D, 6.32 times speedup for MGRID, 4.31 times speedup for SU2COR, 3.28 times speedup for TURB3D, 1.67 time speedup for APPLU and 1.00 times speedup for FPPPP compared with the sequential execution by XL Fortran for AIX Version 7.1. Also, OpenMP coarse grain task parallel code generated by OSCAR compiler boosted up the performance of XL Fortran 1.75 times for SWIM, 3.48 times for TOMCATV, 3.65 times for HYDRO2D, 2.06 times for MGRID, 1.65 times for in SU2COR, 3.28 times for TURB3D and 1.16 times for in APPLU. From these results, it was confirmed the proposed scheme could find suitable or un-suitable layer for parallel processing and assign the suitable number of processors to each layer of macro-task graph without performance degradation with the increase processors.

Currently, the authors are researching on a chip multiprocessor[23] which supports the multigrain parallel processing and performance evaluation of the OSCAR compiler on larger scale multiprocessor systems.

# Acknowledgment

A part of this research has been supported by Japan Government Millennium Project METI/NEDO Advanced Parallelizing Compiler Project (http://www.apc.waseda.ac.jp) and Waseda University Grant for Special Research Projects No.2000A-154.

# References

1. Wolfe, M.: High Performance Compilers for Parallel Computing. Addison-Wesley (1996)
2. Banerjee, U.: Loop parallelization. Kluwer Academic Pub. (1994)
3. Polaris: (http://polaris.cs.uiuc.edu/polaris/)
4. Eigenmann, R., Hoeflinger, J., Padua, D.: On the automatic parallelization of the perfect benchmarks. IEEE Trans. on parallel and distributed systems **9** (1998)
5. Rauchwerger, L., Amato, N.M., Padua, D.A.: Run-time methods for parallelizing partially parallel loops. Proceedings of the 9th ACM International Conference on Supercomputing, Barcelona, Spain (1995) 137–146
6. Tu, P., Padua, D.: Automatic array privatization. Proc. 6th Annual Workshop on Languages and Compilers for Parallel Computing (1993)
7. Hall, M.W., Murphy, B.R., Amarasinghe, S.P., Liao, S., , Lam, M.S.: Interprocedural parallelization analysis: A case study. Proceedings of the 8th International Workshop on Languages and Compilers for Parallel Computing (LCPC95) (1995)
8. Hall, M.W., Anderson, J.M., Amarasinghe, S.P., Murphy, B.R., Liao, S.W., Bugnion, E., Lam, M.S.: Maximizing multiprocessor performance with the suif compiler. IEEE Computer (1996)
9. Amarasinghe, S., Anderson, J., Lam, M., Tseng, C.: The suif compiler for scalable parallel machines. Proc. of the 7th SIAM conference on parallel processing for scientific computing (1995)
10. Lam, M.S.: Locallity optimizations for parallel machines. Third Joint International Conference on Vector and Parallel Processing (1994)
11. Lim, A.W., Lam, M.S.: Cache optimizations with affine partitioning. Proceedings of the Tenth SIAM Conference on Parallel Processing for Scientific Computing (2001)
12. Yoshida, A., Koshizuka, K., Okamoto, M., Kasahara, H.: A data-localization scheme among loops for each layer in hierarchical coarse grain parallel processing. Trans. of IPSJ (japanese) **40** (1999)
13. Rivera, G., Tseng, C.W.: Locality optimizations for multi-level caches. Super Computing '99 (1999)
14. Han, H., Rivera, G., Tseng, C.W.: Software support for improving locality in scientific codes. 8th Workshop on Compilers for Parallel Computers (CPC'2000) (2000)
15. Kasahara, H., Honda, H., Mogi, A., Ogura, A., Fujiwara, K., Narita, S.: A multigrain parallelizing compilation scheme on oscar. Proc. 4th Workshop on Languages and Compilers for Parallel Computing (1991)
16. Okamoto, M., Aida, K., Miyazawa, M., Honda, H., Kasahara, H.: A hierarchical macro-dataflow computation scheme of oscar multi-grain compiler. Trans. of IPSJ (japanese) **35** (1994) 513–521

17. Kasahara, H., Okamoto, M., Yoshida, A., Ogata, W., Kimura, K., Matsui, G., Matsuzaki, H., H.Honda: Oscar multi-grain architecture and its evaluation. Proc. International Workshop on Innovative Architecture for Future Generation High-Performance Processors and Systems (1997)
18. Kasahara, H., Honda, H., Iwata, M., Hirota, M.: A macro-dataflow compilation scheme for hierarchical multiprocessor systems. Proc. Int'l. Conf. on Parallel Processing (1990)
19. Honda, H., Iwata, M., Kasahara, H.: Coarse grain parallelism detection scheme of fortran programs. Trans. IEICE (in Japanese) **J73-D-I** (1990)
20. Kasahara, H.: Parallel Processing Technology. Corona Publishing, Tokyo (in Japanese) (1991)
21. Kasahara, H., Obata, M., Ishizaka, K.: Automatic coarse grain task parallel processing on smp using openmp. Proceedings of the 13th International Workshop on Languages and Compilers for Parallel Computing (LCPC2000) (2000)
22. Kasahara, H., Honda, H., Narita, S.: Parallel processing of near fine grain tasks using static scheduling on oscar. Proc. IEEE ACM Supercomputing'90 (1990)
23. Kimura, K., Kato, T., Kasahara, H.: Evaluation of processor core architecture for single chip multiprocessor with near fine grain parallel processing. Trans. of IPSJ (japanese) **42** (2001)
24. Martorell, X., Ayguade, E., Navarro, N., Corbalan, J., Gozalez, M., Labarta, J.: Thread fork/join techniques for multi-level parllelism exploitation in numa multiprocessors. ICS'99 Rhodes Greece (1999)
25. Ayguade, E., Martorell, X., Labarta, J., Gonzalez, M., Navarro, N.: Exploiting multiple levels of parallelism in openmp: A case study. ICPP'99 (1999)
26. PROMIS: (http://www.csrd.uiuc.edu/promis/)
27. Brownhill, C.J., Nicolau, A., Novack, S., Polychronopoulos, C.D.: Achieving multilevel parallelization. Proc. of ISHPC'97 (1997)
28. Parafrase2: (http://www.csrd.uiuc.edu/parafrase2/)
29. Girkar, M., Polychronopoulos, C.: Optimization of data/control conditions in task graphs. Proc. 4th Workshop on Languages and Compilers for Parallel Computing (1991)
30. Haghighat, M.R., Polychronopoulos, C.D.: Symbolic Analysis for Parallelizing Compliers. Kluwer Academic Publishers (1995)
31. : (http://www.apc.waseda.ac.jp/)
32. Kasahara, H., Obata, M., Ishizaka, K.: Coarse grain task parallel processing on a shared memory multiprocessor system. Trans. of IPSJ (japanese) **42** (2001)
33. Obata, M., Ishizaka, K., Kasahara, H.: Automatic coarse grain task parallel processing using oscar multigrain parallelizing compiler. Ninth International Workshop on Compilers for Parallel Computers(CPC 2001) (2001)

# Compiler Analysis and Supports for Leakage Power Reduction on Microprocessors*

Yi-Ping You, Chingren Lee, and Jenq Kuen Lee

Department of Computer Science,
National Tsing Hua University,
Hsinchu 300, Taiwan
{ypyou, crlee}@pllab.cs.nthu.edu.tw, jklee@cs.nthu.edu.tw

**Abstract.** Power leakage constitutes an increasing fraction of the total power consumption in modern semiconductor technologies. Recent research efforts also indicate architecture, compiler, and software participations can help reduce the switching activities (also known as dynamic power) on microprocessors. This raises interests on the issues to employ architecture and compiler efforts to reduce leakage power (also known as static power) on microprocessors. In this paper, we investigate the compiler analysis techniques related to reducing leakage power. The architecture model in our design is a system with an instruction set to support the control of power gating in the component levels. Our compiler gives an analysis framework to utilize the instruction to reduce the leakage power. We present a data flow analysis framework to estimate the component activities at fixed points of programs with the consideration of pipelines of architectures. We also give the equation for the compiler to decide if the employment of the power gating instructions on given program blocks will benefit the total energy reductions. As the duration of power gating on components on given program routines is related to program branches, we propose a set of scheduling policy include *Basic_Blk_Sched*, *MIN_Path_Sched*, and *AVG_Path_Sched* mechanisms and evaluate the effectiveness of those schemes. Our experiment is done by incorporating our compiler analysis and scheduling policy into SUIF compiler tools [32] and by simulating the energy consumptions on Wattch toolkits [6]. Experimental results show our mechanisms are effective in reducing leakage powers on microprocessors.

# 1 Introduction

The demands of power-constrained mobile and embedded computing applications increase rapidly. Reducing power consumption hence becomes a crucial challenge for today's software and hardware developers. While maximization of

---

* The work was supported in part by NSC-90-2218-E-007-042, NSC-90-2213-E-007-074, NSC-90-2213-E-007-075, MOE research excellent project under grant no. 89-E-FA04-1-4, and MOEA research project under grant no. 91-EC-17-A-03-S1-0002 of Taiwan.

B. Pugh and C.-W. Tseng (Eds.): LCPC 2002, LNCS 2481, pp. 45–60, 2005.

battery life is an obvious goal, the reduction of heat dissipations is important as well. The reduction of power consumptions is also with the similar objective as the reduction of heat dissipations. Minimization of power dissipation can be considered at algorithmic, architectural, logic and circuit levels [11]. Studies on low power design are abundant in the literature [3,4,15,19,27,29,37] in which various techniques were proposed to synthesize designs with low transitional activities.

Recently, new research directions in reducing power consumptions have begun to address the issues on the aspect of architecture designs and on software arrangements at instruction-level to help reduce power consumptions [5,12,20,24,25,33,34,35]. The architecture and software efforts to reduce energy consumptions in the recent attempt have been primarily on the dynamic component of power dissipation (also known as dynamic power). The energy, $E$, consumed by a program, is given by $E = P \times T$, where $T$ is the number of execution cycles of the program [25] and $P$ the average power. The average power $P$ is given by $P = \frac{1}{2} \cdot C \cdot Vdd^2 \cdot f \cdot E$, where $C$ is the load capacitance, $Vdd$ the supply voltage, $f$ the clock frequency, and $E$ the transition count. In order to reduce the dynamic power, several research works have been proposed to reduce the dissipations. For example, software re-arrangements to utilize the value locality of registers [12], the swapping of operands for booth multiplier [25], the scheduling of VLIW instructions to reduce the power consumption on the instruction bus [24], gating clock to reduce workloads [20,34,35], cache sub-banking mechanism [33], the utilization of instruction cache [5], etc.

As transistors become smaller and faster, another mode of power dissipation has become important. This is static power dissipation or the leakage current in the absence of any switching activities. For example, consider two Intel's Pentium III processors manufactured on $0.18\mu$m process, the Pentium III 1.0 GHz and the Pentium III 1.13 GHz [21]. The datasheet lists the 1.0 GHz processor has a total power dissipation of 33.0 Watts and a deep sleep (i.e., static) power of 3.74 Watts while the maximum power dissipation at 41.4 Watts and the static power at 5.40 Watts for the 1.13 GHz one. The static power is up by 44% and comprises 13% of the total power dissipation while the total power is increased by only 25%. Figure 1 and Figure 2 show the growing ratio of static power among the total power [14,36]. Figure 1 gives the growing trend of static power. It's growing in a fast paste. Figure 2 again shows the the growing trend of static power in terms of temperatures in the hardware devices. This raises the importance of reducing static power dissipations. Recently, academic results have tried to characterize the engineering equation and cost model for analyzing static powers [14,36]. This is important, as the architecture designers and system developers can then deploy the architecture and software designs to reduce the static power according to the cost model. Previously, the availability of the cost equation for dynamic powers have prompted fruitful research results in the efforts to reduce dynamic power. The recent result in characterizing static power has the following equation. $P_{static} = V_{CC} \cdot N \cdot k_{design} \cdot \hat{I}_{leak}$, where $V_{CC}$ is the supply voltage, $N$ is the number of transistors in design, $k_{design}$ is the characteristic of

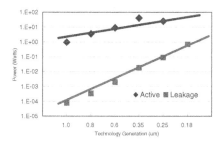 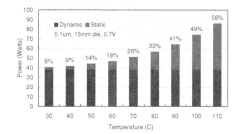

**Fig. 1.** Trends in Active and Leakage Power **Fig. 2.** Leakage Power Trend in Tempera-
Dissipation (From Thomopson et. al.)     ture (From De et. al.)

an average device, $\hat{I}_{leak}$ is the technology parameter describing the per device
subthreshold leakage [8].

In this paper, we investigate the compiler analysis techniques to reduce the
number of devices, $N$, in the static power equation above to try to ease the
problem of leakage powers. The architecture model in our design is a system
with an instruction set to support the control of power gating in the component levels. From the viewpoints of engineering equation for static power, we
attempt to reduce the number of devices by turning them off when they are
unused. Our work provides compiler solutions in giving analysis and scheduling
for the power gating control at component levels. Our compiler gives an analysis
framework to utilize the instruction to reduce the leakage power. A data-flow
analysis framework is given to estimate the component activities at fixed points
of programs with the consideration of pipelines of architectures. We also give
the equation for the compiler to decide if the employment of the power gating
instructions on given program blocks will benefit the total energy reductions.
As the duration of power gating on components on given program routines is
related to program branches, we propose a set of scheduling policy including *Ba-
sic_Blk_sched, MIN_Path_Sched, AVG_Path_Sched* mechanisms and evaluate the
effectiveness of those schemes. *Basic_Blk_Sched* mechanism schedules the power
gating instructions according to the component activities in a given basic block.
*MIN_Path_Sched* mechanism schedules the power gating instructions by assuming the minimum length among plausible program paths. *AVG_Path_Sched* schedules the power gating instructions by assuming the average length among plausible program paths. *MIN_Path_Sched* and *AVG_Path_Sched* mechanisms proposed
in our work are based-on a depth-first traversal scheme to look up the interval
in inserting power gating intsructions for components to reduce static power.
Our experiment is done by incorporating our compiler analysis and scheduling
policy into SUIF compiler tools [31,32] and by simulating the energy consumptions on Wattch [6] toolkits. Experimental results show our mechanisms are
very effective in reducing leakage powers on microprocessors. This work is also
a part of our efforts in DTC (design technology center) of our university to develop compiler toolkits[24,17,39,18,38,10,9] for high-performance and low-power
micro-processors and SoC designs.

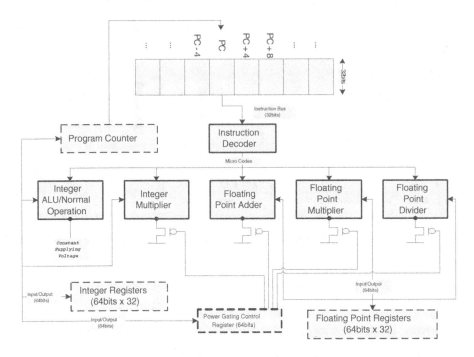

**Fig. 3.** Machine Architecture Model with Power Gating Control

## 2   Machine Architecture

The architecture model in our design is a system with an instruction set to support the control of power gating in the component levels. Figure 3 shows an example of our target machine architecture on which our optimization is based. We focus on the reduction of the power consumption of the certain function units by invoking the "Power Gating" technology. Power gating is analogous to clock gating; power gating turns off devices by switching off their supply voltage rather than the clock. It can be done by forcing transistors to be off or using multithreshold voltage CMOS technology (MTCMOS) to increase threshold voltage [8,22,30].

We build the experimental architecture within the Wattch simulation environment [6]. In the simulation environment, we can measure every CPU components's power consumption of the whole experimental program. Basically, this architecture is compatible with the DEC Alpha 21264 processor [13]. The length of an instruction in our experimental architecture is 32 bits. Memory addressing is byte address. As Alpha is a 64-bit processor and uses 64-bit data bus, our experimental architecture has 32 integer registers (R0 through R31), and each is 64 bits wide. The major difference of these two architectures is the additional "power gating" design in our experimental architecture.

Those power-gated function units in our experimental architecture are **Integer Multiplier**, **Floating Point Adder**, **Floating Point Multiplier**, and

**Floating Point Divider**. The power gating of each function unit can be controlled by the "Power Gating Control Register" ("PGCR" for short). The PGCR is a 64-bit integer register. In this case, the only lowest 4 bits of this register can affect the power gating status. The 0th bit of the lowest 4 bits of the PGCR controls the power gating of the Integer Multiplier. Setting of the bit will cause the Integer Multiplier to be turned on. Clearing of the bit will turn off the corresponding function unit in the immediately following clock. The 1st bit of the 4 bits is for Floating Point Adder, the 2nd bit is for Floating Point Multiplier, and the 3rd bit of the 4 bits is for the Floating Point Divider. Worth to mention, the Integer ALU unit within architecture also takes response to execute general operation. And, it performs the data movement to the PGCR, too. As a result of the Integer ALU is always required, this function unit is always turned on. In addition, we invoke a new instruction in the simulation environment to specify the access direction of PGCR. This instruction can operate those 4 power gated function units at once by move a proper value from a general purpose register to the PGCR.

Figure 3 is also the architecture model on which we carry out our experiments later in Section 5.

## 3   Component-Activity Data-Flow Analysis

In this section, we investigate the compiler analysis techniques to ease the problem of leakage powers. We present a data-flow analysis framework [2] for a compiler to analyze the inactive states of components on a microprocessor. The process collects the information of the utilization of components at various points in a program. We first construct basic blocks and control flow graphs of given programs. We then try to develop a data flow equation for the summary of component usages at given program points. To gather the data-flow information, we define $comp\_gen[B]$, $comp\_kill[B]$, $comp\_in[B]$, and $comp\_out[B]$ for each block $B$.

We say a component-activity $c$ is generated at a block $B$ if a component is required for this execution, symbolized as $comp\_gen[B]$, and it is killed if the component is released by the last request, symbolized as $comp\_kill[B]$. We then create two groups of equations shown below. The first group of equations follows from the observation that $comp\_in[B]$ is the union of activities arriving from all predecessors of $B$. The second group is the activities at the end of a block that are either generated within the block, or those entering at the beginning but not killed as control flows through the block. We have the data flow equation for these two groups below,

$$comp\_in[B] = \bigcup_{\substack{P \ a \ pred-\\essor \ of \ B}} comp\_out[P]$$

$$comp\_out[B] = comp\_gen[B] \cup (comp\_in[B] - comp\_kill[B]).$$

We use an iterative approach to compute the desired results of $comp\_in$ and $comp\_out$ after $comp\_gen$ have been computed for each block. The algorithm is

**Input**   A control flow graph in which each block $B$ contains only one instruction;
            a resource utilization table.
**Output**  $comp\_in[B]$ and $comp\_out[B]$ for each block $B$.

**Begin**
    **for** each block $B$ **do begin**
        **for** each component $C$ that will be used by $B$ **do begin**   /* computation of $comp\_gen$ */
            $RemainingCycle[B][C] := N$,
                where $N$ is the number of cycles needed for $C$ by $B$;
            $comp\_gen[B] := comp\_gen[B] \cup C$;
        **end**
        $comp\_in[B] := comp\_kill[B] := \emptyset$;
        $comp\_out[B] := comp\_gen[B]$;
    **end**
    **while** changes to any $comp\_out$ occur **do begin**                  /* iterative analysis */
        **for** each block $B$ **do begin**
            **for** each component $C$ **do begin**                          /* computation of $comp\_kill$ */
                $RemainingCycle[B][C] := \mathbf{MAX}(RemainingCycle[P][C]) - 1$,
                    where $P$ is a predecessor of $B$;
                    **if** $RemainingCycle[B][C] = 0$ **then** $comp\_kill[B] := comp\_kill[B] \cup C$;
            **end**
            /* computation of $comp\_in$ */
            $comp\_in[B] := \bigcup comp\_out[P]$, where $P$ is a predecessor of $B$;
            /* computation of $comp\_out$ */
            $comp\_out[B] := comp\_gen[B] \cup (comp\_in[B] - comp\_kill[B])$;
        **end**
    **end**
**End**

**Fig. 4.** Data-Flow Analysis Algorithm for Component Activities

sketched in Figure 4. This is an iterative algorithm for data flow equations [2] with the additions of resource management strcutures. A two-dimension array, called $RemainingCycle$, is used to maintain the number of required cycles to achieve requests for each component and block. In addtion, a resource utilization table is adopted to give the resource requirement for each instruction of given processors. The resource utilization table can be used to give the initial values of $RemainingCycle$. The remaining cycles of a component will be decreased by one for each propagation. Initially, both $comp\_in$ and $com\_kill$ are set to be empty. The iteration goes until the $comp\_in$ (and hence the $comp\_out$) converges. As $comp\_out[B]$ never decreases in size for any $B$, the algorithm will eventually halt while all $comp\_out$ are steady. Intuitively, the algorithm propagates activities of components as far as they will go by simulating all possible executing paths of the program. This algorithm gives the state of utilization of components for each point of programs.

## 4   Leakage Power Reduction

In this section, we present a cost model for decisions if power gating control should be applied and a set of scheduling policies to place power-gating instruction sets for given programs.

### 4.1   Cost Model

With the utilization of components obtained from last section, we can insert power gating instructions into programs at proper points, the head/tail of an inactive block, to turn off/on useless components. This can reduce the leakage power. However, both shutdown and wakeup procedures take additional penalty, especially for wakeup process due to peak voltage. The following gives our cost model for deciding if the insertions of energy instructions will profit in energy consumptions.

$$E_{turn\_off}(C) + E_{turn\_on}(C) \leq \mathbf{BreakEven_C} * P_{leak\_saving}(C),$$

where $E_{turn\_off}(C)$ is the penalty of energy for shutting down component $C$, $E_{turn\_on}$ is the penalty of energy for waking up component $C$, $\mathbf{BreakEven_C}$ is the break-even cycle for component $C$, and $P_{leak\_saving}(C)$ is the leakage power saving of component $C$ per cycle by employing power gating controls. The left-hand side of the equation shows the energy consumed by shutdown and wakeup procedures, and the right-hand side shows the leakage energy consumed for a certain cycles. It will save power for power gating control only if the amount of power of shutdown and wakeup is less than the one at RHS.

While employing power gating, there is another thing we should note. It's the latency to turn a component on. Due to the high capacitance on the circuits, several clock cycles will be needed to bring the component back to the normal operating state. Butts et al. also illustrated that it takes about 7.5 cycles at 1 GHz to charge 5 nF to 1.5 V with 1A [8]. With this consideration, we enforce power gating on a component only when the size of its inactive block, i.e. the idle region, is larger than its break-even cycle and its latency to recover. Our cost model after incorporating latency issue is now as follows.

$$\mathbf{Threshold_C} = \mathbf{MAX}(\mathbf{BreakEven_C}, \mathbf{Latency_C}),$$

where $\mathbf{Latency_C}$ is the power gating latency of component $C$. In addition, we will try to insert the on operations of the power-gating control to be ahead of the time for the use of the corresponding components to avoid the delay in the programs due to wakeup latency.

## 4.2   Scheduling Policies for Power Gating

With the component activity information gathered and the cost model for deciding if the power-gating instructions should be employed, we now give the scheduling mechanisms to place the power gating instructions for given programs. As the duration of power gating on components is related to conditional branches in programs, we propose a set of scheduling policy including *Basic_Blk_Sched*, *MIN_Path_Sched*, and *AVG_Path_Sched* to schedule power gating instructions. The details are given below.

A naive mechanism to control the power-gating instruction set will set the on and off instructions at each basic block according to the component activities gathered by the data flow equation in the previous section. We call this scheme as *Basic_Blk_Sched*.

Next, an inactive block of a component may cross over more than two adjacent basic blocks. We use a *depth-first-traveling* algorithm to traverse all possible executing paths. In general, an inactive block will be turned off while the criteria reached. In the case of conditional branches occurred in the inactive block, there should be an another consideration to take action of power gating. This is because the size of the two inactive blocks, which are targets that the branch instruction points to, may be different. There may be a situation that one of the branchings benefits for power gating while the other doesn't. It will be against power reductions if we take control of power gating considering only one branch but the other branch is taken. Hence, we propose a *MIN_Path_Sched* policy to ensure that power gating control would be activated only if the inactive lengths of both branching paths exceed the power gating threshold, that is, the minimum length of those paths reaches the criteria for power gating.

Figure 5 presents the details for *MIN_Path_Sched* algorithm. Given a control flow graph annotated with component utilizations, we define a integer variable, *Count*, to maintain the inactive length so far. It is passed around from parent blocks to successors and increased for each passing. The algorithm is recursive to guarantee the accuracy of *Count* and to ensure all paths being traversed. The algorithm is divided into four parts to handle conditions when encountering/non-encountering a conditional branch while the analyzing component is active/inactive.

1) A conditional branch reaches and the component is inactive: under this condition, current traveling will halt until both two branches having done their travelings. And then, it makes a judgement on power gating when no branch encountered before and return the minimum inactive length of two branchings.

2) A conditional branch reaches and the component is active: under this condition, it takes control of power gating if necessary, starts two new travelings for both branchings, and finally returns the current inactive length.

3) Any statement except conditional branches reaches and the component is inactive: under this condition, it only continues the current traveling, that is, it only increases *Count* for passing and returns.

4) Any statement except conditional branches reaches and the component is active: like condition 2, it takes control of power gating if necessary and starts a new traveling for its successor. And finally, it returns *Count*.

Note that cares have to be taken for recursive boundaries to reach the backward edges for a loop. As a depth-first search algorithm can find out the loop, the cycle situation can be known in our algorithm. In a cycle situation, if the the whole instructions used in the cycle of a program fragment does not use the component in the search, we will assume the loop cycle is executed for once with the minimum path scheduling policy. If some instructions in the backward edge of a program fragment does use the component in the search, the the backward edge extend to that instruction will be counted for the program path. In addition, since our proposed algorithm is based on the depth-first-traveling, the complexity of our approach is $O(N)$ where $N$ is the size of nodes in a control flow graph.

**Input**   A control flow graph annotated with component utilizations.
**Output** A scheduling for power gating instructions.

**MIN_Path_Sched**($C, B, Branched, Edge, Count$)
**Begin**
    **if** block $B$ is the end of $CFG$ or $Count > $ **MAX_COUNT** **then return** $Count$;
    **if** block $B$ has two children **then do**

        /* condition 1; conditional branch, inactive */
        **if** $C \notin comp\_out[B]$ **then do**
            $Count := Count + 1$;
            **if** left edge is a forward edge **then**
                $l\_Count := MIN\_Path\_Sched(C$, left child of $B$, **TRUE**, **FWD**, $Count$);
            **else**
                $l\_Count := MIN\_Path\_Sched(C$, left child of $B$, **TRUE**, **BWD**, $Count$);
            **if** right edge is a forward edge **then**
                $r\_Count := MIN\_Path\_Sched(C$, right child of $B$, **TRUE**, **FWD**, $Count$);
            **else**
                $r\_Count := MIN\_Path\_Sched(C$, right child of $B$, **TRUE**, **BWD**, $Count$);
            **if** **MIN**($l\_Count, r\_Count$) > **Threshold**$_C$ and !$Branched$ **then**
                schedule power gating instructions at the head and tail of inactive blocks;
            **return** **MIN**($l\_Count, r\_Count$);

        /* condition 2; conditional branch, active */
        **else**
            **if** $Count > $ **Threshold**$_C$ and !$Branched$ **then**
                schedule power gating instructions at the head and tail of inactive blocks;
            **if** $Edge = $ **FWD** **then**
                **if** right edge is a forward edge **then**
                    $MIN\_Path\_Sched(C$, left child of $B$, **FALSE**, **FWD**, $Count$);
                **else**
                    $MIN\_Path\_Sched(C$, left child of $B$, **FALSE**, **BWD**, $Count$);
                **if** left edge is a forward edge **then**
                    $MIN\_Path\_Sched(C$, right child of $B$, **FALSE**, **FWD**, $Count$);
                **else**
                    $MIN\_Path\_Sched(C$, right child of $B$, **FALSE**, **BWD**, $Count$);
            **end**
            **return** $Count$;
        **end**;
    **else**

        /* condition 3; statements except conditional branches, inactive */
        **if** $C \notin comp\_out[B]$ **then do**
            $Count := Count + 1$;
            **if** edge is a forward edge **then**
                **return** $MIN\_Path\_Sched(C$, child of $B$, $Branched$, **FWD**, $Count$);
            **else**
                **return** $MIN\_Path\_Sched(C$, child of $B$, $Branched$, **BWD**, $Count$);

        /* condition 4; statements except conditional branches, active */
        **else**
            **if** $Count > $ **Threshold**$_C$ and !$Branched$ **then**
                schedule power gating instructions at the head and tail of inactive blocks;
            **if** $Edge = $ **FWD** **then**
                **if** the edge pointing to child of $B$ is a forward edge **then**
                    $MIN\_Path\_Sched(C$, child of $B$, **FALSE**, **FWD**, $Count$);
                **else**
                    $MIN\_Path\_Sched(C$, child of $B$, **FALSE**, **BWD**, $Count$);
            **end**
            **return** $Count$;
        **end**
    **end**
**End**

**Fig. 5.** *MIN_Path_Sched* Algorithm Based on Depth-First-Traveling for Power Gating

Next, as the behavior of program branches depends on the structure and the input data of programs, some branches may be taken rarely or even not taken. To accomodate this issue, we propose an eclectic policy, called *AVG_Path_Sched*, to schedule power gating instructions. The only difference between *AVG_Path_Sched* and *MIN_Path_Sched* is the judgements made in condition 1 above. *AVG_Path_Sched* returns the average length of two branchings instead of the minimums. With this scheme, it will take advantage of power reduction if a unusual-taken branch returns a small value of *Count* which causes power gating mechanism inactivated. *AVG_Path_Sched* mechanism can be approximately done by assuming the probabilities of all branches are 50%, by assinging branch probabilities at compiler time by programmers or compilers or by incorporating path profiling schemes to examine the probabilities of all branches.

## 5   Experimental Results

### 5.1   Platform

We use an Alpha-compatible architecture with power gating control and instruction sets described in Figure 3 of Section 2 as the target architecture for our experiments. The proposed data-flow analysis and scheduling policies are incorporated into the compiler tool with SUIF [32] and MachSUIF Library [31] and evaluated by Wattch simulator [6]. Figure 6 shows the structure of the framework including compilation and simulation parts. In the compilation part, we use the SUIF library to perform compiler optimization for performances and the MachSUIF Library to perform machine-dependent optimizations for Alpha processors. After those optimizations having been done, we then analyze component activities with our proposed data-flow equation and schedule power gating instructions to reduce leakage dissipation. Finally, the compiler generates the Alpha assembly code with power gating instructions. To be recognized by Alpha assembler and linker, power gating instructions are replaced by an instruction sequence within the Alpha instruction set with annotation information to simulators. We then use the Wattch power estimator, which is based on the SimpleScalar [7] architectural simulator, to simulate power dissipation and to evaluate our approach. The SimpleScalar is a simulator that provides execution-driven and cycle-accurate simulations for various instruction set architectures (include our target architecture, Alpha ISA). Both SimpleScalar and Wattch are now widely used for simulations to evaluate performance and power dissipation [6]. We also do refinements on the Wattch estimator to catch the instruction sequences for power gating control.

### 5.2   Results

The test suits in our experiment are the common benchmarks listed in FAQ of comp.benchmarks [1]. Figure 7 and Figure 8 illustrate the power results for the simulations of power gating control over Floating Point Adder and Floating Point

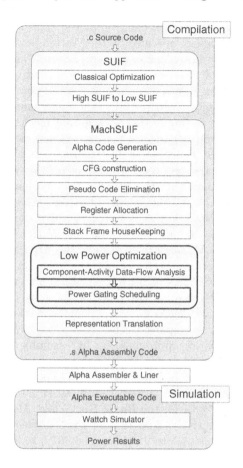

**Fig. 6.** Our Experimental Framework

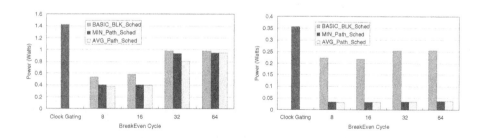

**Fig. 7.** Results of Floating Point Adder for **Fig. 8.** Results of Floating Multiplier for *nsieve* *nsieve*

Multiplier for *nsieve* application, respectively. In these figures, the X-axis represents the break-even cycle for our scheduling criteria and the Y-axis represents the power consumption. The leftest bar shows the power dissipated by function units while no power gating control being employed. This is the results of traditional clock gating mechanism provided by the Wattch power estimator. This is the version we use as the base version for comparison. The clock gating mechanism gates the clocks of those unused resources in multi-ported hardware to reduce the dynamic power. However, there is still static power leaked. Wattch assumes that clock-gated units dissipate 10% of their maximum power, rather than drawing zero power. For example, the clock gating mechanism reduces about 30% of total power consumption against the one without clock gating for several SPECint95 and SPECfp95 benchmarks [6]. The rest bars of the figures give the power gating results for the proposed scheduling policies with different break-even cycle. The results show that the power gating mechanism reduces a large amount of leakage power even if the penalty of power gating control is high (i.e., large break-even cycle). Note that we have incorporated the penalty of inserting power gating instructions into our power simulator, Wattch. In our experimental data, it also indicates the $MIN\_Path\_Sched$ and the $AVG\_Path\_Sched$ scheduling algorithms always perform better results than the $Basic\_Blk\_Sched$. This is because the $Basic\_Blk\_Sched$ algorithm schedules power gating instructions within basic blocks while the other two schedule those beyond branches. It will extend the possible inactive lengths for components while the $MIN\_Path\_Sched$ or the $AVG\_Path\_Sched$ is employed. The $AVG\_Path\_Sched$ mechanism used in our implementation is an approximation by assuming the probabilies of all branches are 50%. We think a more accurate model by incorporating path profiling schemes can further improve the results. The reduction of the power consumed by the Floating Point Adder is from 30.11% to 70.50%, 30.36% to 77.01% and 31.36% to 77.68% for the $Basic\_Blk\_Sched$, $MIN\_Path\_Sched$ and $AVG\_Path\_Sched$, respectively. And that of the Floating Point Multiplier is from 28.28% to 39.58%, 89.67% to 91.41% and 89.67% to 91.25%, respectively.

Figure 9 and Figure 10 give the power consumption of the Floating Point Adder and the Floating Point Multiplier for various benchmarks while employing the power gating mechanism with break-even cycle 32. Once again, it is observed that the $AVG\_Path\_Sched$ benefited the most power reduction while

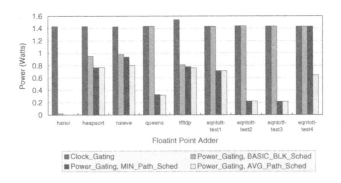

**Fig. 9.** Power Gating on Floating Point Adder for miscellaneous benchmarks ($BreakEven = 32$)

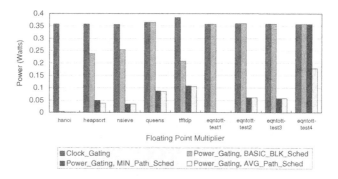

**Fig. 10.** Power Gating on Floating Point Multiplier for miscellaneous benchmarks ($BreakEven = 32$)

the $MIN\_Path\_Sched$ came second and the $Basic\_Blk\_Sched$ finished third. However, they always have better results than the one without power gating (and hence only clock gating employed). Figure 9 shows that the $Basic\_Blk\_Sched$ policy has an average 23.05% reduction for all benchmarks while the $MIN\_Path\_Sched$ and the $AVG\_Path\_Sched$ have 76.93% and 82.84%, respectively. In the case of *hanoi* benchmark, which is an integer program, it even reduces 99.03% of power for the $Basic\_Blk_Sched$ and 99.69% for the $MIN\_Path\_Sched$ and $AVG\_Path\_Sched$. Similar results can also be summarized in Figure 10.

## 6   Related Work

Several research groups have proposed and developed hardware techniques to reduce dynamic and static power dissipation in recent. Recent work by Powell et al. architectural and circuit-level techniques to reduce the power consumption in instruction caches [26]. The cache miss rate is used to determine the working set size of the application relative to that of the cache. Leakage power is then removed from the unused SRAM cells using gated-$V_{dd}$ transistors. Kaxiras et al. also attacks leakage power in cache memories. Policies and implementations for reducing cache leakage by invalidating and turning off cache lines when they enter a dead period are4 discussed [23]. This leads to power savings in the cache. Recently, we found the research work done by Zhang et al. giving a compiler approach which exploits schedule slacks in VLIW architectures to optimize leakage and dynamic energy consumption [40]. Gupta et. al gave experimental results in using software for power gating [28]. Those two work are concurrent work to our research work in compiler solutions for leakage power reduction. Note that a key part of our solution in analyzing the component activities filed a patent in Taiwan by us dated back to the year of 2000. Comparing with those two concurrent work, we have speciality in providing data flow analysis for component activities of programs. Our analysis crosses the boundary of basic blocks. In addition, we provide a family of scheduling policies in inserting energy instructions.

# 7   Conclusions

In this paper, we investigated the compiler analysis techniques related to reducing leakage power. The architecture model in our design is a system with an instruction set to support the control of power gating in the component levels. We presented a data flow analysis framework to estimate the component activities at fixed points of programs with the consideration of pipelines of architectures. A set of scheduling policy including *Basic_Blk_Sched*, *MIN_Path_Sched*, and *AVG_Path_Sched* mechanisms were proposed and evaluated. Experimental results show our mechanisms are effective in reducing leakage powers on microprocessors.

# References

1. Al Aburto, *collections of common benchmarks of FAQ of comp.benchmarks USENET newsgroup*, ftp site: ftp.nosc.mail/pub/aburto.
2. A. Aho, R. Sethi, J. Ullman, *Compilers Principles, Techniques, and Tools*, Addison-Wesley, 1985.
3. M. Alidina, J. Monteiro, S. Devadas, A. Ghosh and M. Papaefthymiou, "Precomputation-Based Sequential Logic Optimization for Low Power," *Proc. of ICCAD-94*, pp. 74-81, 1994.
4. Luca Benini and G. De Micheli, "State Assignment for Low Power Dissipation," *IEEE Journal of Solid State Circuits*, Vol. 30, No. 3, pp. 258-268, March 1995.
5. Nikolaos Bellas, Ibrahim N. Hajj, and Constantine D. Polychronopoulos, "Architectural and Compiler Techniques for Energy Reduction in High-Performance Microprocessors," *IEEE Transactions on Very Large Scale Integration (VLSI) Systems*, pp. 317-326, June 2000.
6. D. Brooks, V. Tiwari, and M. Martonosi, "Wattch: a Framework for Architectural-Level Power Analysis and Optimizations," *Proc. 27th. International Symposium on Computer Architecture*, pp. 83-94, June 2000.
7. D. Burger and T. M. Austin, "The SimpleScalar Tool Set, Version 2.0," *Computer Architecture News,* pp. 13-25, June 1997.
8. J. Adam Butts and Gurindar S. Sohi, "A Static Power Model for Architects," *Proceedings of the 33rd Annual IEEE/ACM International Symposium on Microarchitecture*, pp. 191-201, December 2000.
9. R. G. Chang, T. R. Chuang, Jenq-Kuen Lee. "Efficient Support of Parallel Sparse Computation for Array Intrinsic Functions of Fortran 90," ACM International Conference on Supercomputing, Melbourne, Australia, July 13-17, 1998.
10. Rong-Guey Chang, Jia-Shing Li, Tyng-Ruey Chuang, Jenq Kuen Lee. "Probabilistic inference schemes for sparsity structures of Fortran 90 array intrinsics," International Conference on Parallel Processing, Spain, Sep. 2001.
11. A.P. Chandrakasan, S. Sheng, and R.W. Brodersen, "Low-Power CMOS Digital Design," *IEEE Journal of Solid-State Circuits*, Vol. 27, No.4, pp. 473-484, April 1992.
12. Jui-Ming Chang, Massoud Pedram, "Register Allocation and Binding for Low Power," *Proceedings of Design Automaton Conference*, San Francisco, USA, June 1995.
13. Compaq Computer Corporation, *Alpha 21264 Microprocessor Hardware Reference Manual*, EC-RJRZA-TE, (July 1999).

14. V. De and S. Borkar, "Technology and design challenges for low power and high performance," *Proc. of Int. Symp. Low Power Electronics and Design*, pp. 163-168, 1999.

15. G. Hachtel, M. Hermida, A. Pardo, M. Poncino and F. Somenzi, "Re-Encoding Sequential Circuits to Reduce Power Dissipation," *Proc. of ICCAD' 94*, pp. 70-73, 1994.

16. G. Hadjiyiannis, S. Hanono and S. Devadas. "ISDL: An Instruction Set Description Language for Retargetability," *Design Automation Conference*, June 1997

17. Yuan-Shin Hwang, Peng-Sheng Chen, Jenq-Kuen Lee, Roy Ju. "Probabilistic Points-to Analysis," *LCPC '2001*, Aug. 2001, USA.

18. Gwan-Hwan Hwang, Jenq Kuen Lee, Roy Dz-Ching Ju. "A Function-Composition Approach to Synthesize Fortran 90 Array Operations," *Journal of Parallel and Distributed Computing*, 54, 1-47, 1998.

19. Inki Hong, Darko Dirovski, et.al., "Power Optimization of Variable Voltage Core-Based Systems," *Proc. of 35th DAC*, pp. 176-181, 1998.

20. M. Horowitz, T. Indermaur, and R. Gonzalez, "Low-Power Digital Design," *Proceedings of the 1994 IEEE Symposium on Low Power Electronics*, pp. 8-11.

21. Intel corporation, "Pentium III Processor for the SC242 at 450 MHz to 1.13 GHz Datasheet," pp. 26-30.

22. J. T. Kao and A. P. Chandrakasan, "Dual-threshold voltage techniques for low-power digital circuits," *IEEEJournal of Solid-state circuits*, 35(7):1009-1018, July 2000.

23. S. Kaxiras, Z.Hu and M.Martonosi, "Cache Decay: Exploiting Generational Behavior to Reduce Cache Leakage Power," *Proc. of the Int'l Symposium on Computer Architecture*, pp.240-251, 2001.

24. Chingren Lee, Jenq Kuen Lee, TingTing Hwang, and Shi-Chun Tsai, "Compiler Optimization on Instruction Scheduling for Low Power," *Proceedings of the 13th International Symposium on Systems Synthesis*, pp. 55 - 60, September 2000.

25. Mike Tien-Chien Lee, Vivek Tiwari, Sharad Malik, Masahiro Fujita, "Power Analysis and Minimization Techniques for Embedded DSP Software," *IEEE Transactions on VLSI Systems*, Vol. 5, no. 1, pp. 123-133, March 1997.

26. M.D. Powell, S-H. Yang, B. Falsa, K. Roy, and T.N. Vijaykumar, "Gated-Vdd: a Circuit Technique to Reduce Leakage in Deep-Submicron Cache Memories," *ACM/IEEE International Symposium on Low Power Electronics and Design (ISLPED)*, 2000.

27. S. C. Prasad and K. Roy, "Circuit Activity Driven Multilevel Logic Optimization for Low Power Reliable Operation," *Proceedings of the EDAC'93 EURO-ASIC*, pp. 368-372, Feb., 1993.

28. S. Rele, S. Pande, S. Onder, and R. Gupta, "Optimizing Static Power Dissipation by Functional Units in Superscalar Processors," *International Conference on Compiler Construction (CC)*, Grenoble, France, April 2002.

29. K. Roy and S. C. Prasad, "SYCLOP: Synthesis of CMOS Logic for Low Power Applications," *Proceedings of the ICCD*, pp. 464-467, 1992.

30. K. Roy, "Leakage Power reduction in Low-Voltage CMOS Designs," *IEEE International Conference on Circuits and Systems*, Vol. 2, pp. 167-173, 1998.

31. Michael D. Smith, "The SUIF Machine Library", *Division of of Engineering and Applied Science, Harvard University*, March 1998.

32. Stanford Compiler Group, "The SUIF Library", *Stanford Compiler Group*, Stanford, March 1995.

33. Ching-Long Su and Alvin M. Despain, "Cache Designs for Energy Efficiency," *Proceedings of the 28th Annual Hawaii International Conference on System Sciences*, pp. 306 -315, 1995.

34. V. Tiwari, R. Donnelly, S. Malik, and R. Gonzalez, "Dynamic Power Management for Microprocessors: A Case Study," *Proceedings of the 10th International Conference on VLSI Design*, pp. 185-192, 1997.

35. V. Tiwari, D.Singh, S. Rajgopal, G. Mehta, R. Patel, and F. Baez, "Reducing Power in High-Performance Microprocessors," *Proceedings of the Design Automaton Conference*, pp. 732-737, 1998.

36. Scott Thompson, Paul Packan, and Mark Bohr, "MOS Scaling: Transistor Challenges for the 21st Century," Portland Technology Development, Intel Corp. *Intel Technology Journal*, Q3 1998.

37. C.Y. Tsui, M. Pedram, and A.M. Despain, "Technology Decomposition and Mapping Targeting Low Power Dissipation," *Proc. of 30th Design Automaton Conf.*, pp.68-73, June 1993.

38. J. Z. Wu, Jenq-Kuen Lee. "A bytecode optimizer to engineer bytecodes for performances," *LCPC 00*, Aug. 2000, USA (Also in LNCS 2017).

39. Yi-Ping You, Ching-Ren Lee, Jenq-Kuen Lee, Wei-Kuan Shih. "Rea-Time Task Scheduling for Dynamically Variable Voltage Processors," *IEEE workshop on Power Management for Real-Time and Embedded Systems*, May 2001.

40. W. Zhang, N. Vijaykrishnan, M. Kandemir, M. J. Irwin, D. Duarte, and Y. Tsai. "Exploiting VLIW Schedule Slacks for Dynamic and Leakage Energy Reduction," *Proceedings of the Thirty-Fourth Annual International Symposium on Microarchitecture (MICRO-34)*. pp. 102-113. Austin, TX. December 2001.

# Automatic Detection of Saturation and Clipping Idioms

Aart J.C. Bik, Milind Girkar, Paul M. Grey, and Xinmin Tian

Intel Corporation, 2200 Mission College Blvd. SC12-301,
Santa Clara, CA 95052, USA
aart.bik@intel.com

**Abstract.** The MMX™ technology and SSE/SSE2 (streaming-SIMD-extensions) introduced a variety of SIMD instructions that can exploit data parallelism in numerical and multimedia applications. In particular, new saturation and clipping instructions can boost the performance of applications that make extensive use of such operations. Unfortunately, due to the lack of support for saturation and clipping operators in e.g. C/C++ or Fortran, these operations must be explicitly coded with conditional constructs that test the value of operands before actual wrap-around arithmetic is performed. As a result, inline-assembly or language extensions are most commonly used to exploit the new instructions. In this paper, we explore an alternative approach, where the compiler automatically maps high-level saturation and clipping idioms onto efficient low-level instructions. The effectiveness of this approach is demonstrated with some experiments.

## 1 Introduction

The MMX™ technology and SSE/SSE2 (streaming-SIMD-extensions) feature instructions that operate simultaneously on packed data elements, i.e. relatively short vectors that reside in memory or registers. The MMX™ technology [8,11,12,18,22], for example, supports instructions on eight packed bytes, four packed words or two packed dwords. The Pentium® III and Pentium® 4 Processors introduced SSE [12,26,28] and SSE2 [10,12], respectively, supporting instruction on four packed single-precision and two packed double-precision floating-point numbers, and 128-bit wide packed integers. Since a single instruction processes multiple data elements in parallel, these SIMD extensions can be used to utilize data parallelism in numerical and multimedia applications. Hand-optimizing an application to exploit data parallelism, however, can be a tedious task and means to do this exploitation automatically has been well studied in the past [2,3,14,15,19,21,24,29,30]. Some of this research dates back to the early days of supercomputing when, with a traditional focus on Fortran code, converting serial loops into vector instructions was essential to fully exploit the pipelined functional units of a vector processor. In previous work [7], we have shown how similar techniques are used by the high-performance Intel® C++/Fortran compiler to automatically convert serial code into a form that exploits the SIMD instructions of the MMX™ technology and SSE/SSE2. We refer to this process as **intra-register vectorization** to contrast it from vectorizing for traditional vector processors.

In this paper, we focus on a particular challenge arising in intra-register vectorization, namely, the effective use of saturation and clipping instructions. Saturation and

B. Pugh and C.-W. Tseng (Eds.): LCPC 2002, LNCS 2481, pp. 61–74, 2005.
© Springer-Verlag Berlin Heidelberg 2005

clipping operations are typically used in multimedia applications to avoid certain anomalies that may arise with standard wrap-around arithmetic, such as making bright pixels dark instead of brighter. Due to the lack of saturation and clipping operators in popular programming languages like C/C++ or Fortran, such operations have to be explicitly coded in a relatively obscure way, where conditional constructs test the value of operands before actual wrap-round arithmetic is performed (C++'s operator overloading [27] can hide these implementation details from the programmer, but ultimately such details are visible to the compiler). As a result, low-level saturation and clipping instructions are most commonly exploited by means of inline-assembly or language extensions (like the "saturation" attribute in SWARC [9]). Although these approaches can be quite effective, in this paper we explore an alternative approach taken by the Intel® compiler, where saturation and clipping idioms are detected automatically prior to intra-register vectorization. We present a step-wise methodology to bridge the semantic gap between high-level saturation and clipping constructs on one hand, and the low-level instructions for these idioms on the other hand. For clarity, we mainly focus on C, although other languages are handled quite similarly. Furthermore, although we focus on saturation and clipping instructions provided by the MMX™ technology and SSE/SSE2, the methodology can be easily adapted for other multimedia instruction sets. We demonstrate the effectiveness of this approach with a number of experiments.

## 2  Preliminaries

This section provides some preliminaries that are used throughout this paper.

### 2.1  Types, Operators and Expressions

This paper is concerned with the following integral types T={u8,s8,u16,s16,u32,s32}.

```
typedef unsigned char u8;      /* V_{u8}  =   {0, …,          255} */
typedef signed char   s8;      /* V_{s8}  = {-128, …,         127} */
typedef unsigned short u16;    /* V_{u16} =   {0, …,        65535} */
typedef signed   short s16;    /* V_{s16} = {-32768, …,      32767} */
typedef unsigned int   u32;    /* V_{u32} =   {0, …,   4294967295} */
typedef signed int s32;        /* V_{s32} = {-2147483648, …, 2147483647} */
```

As suggested by the names, we assume that char, short and int data types are 8, 16, and 32 bits wide, respectively. The qualifier signed or unsigned defines whether bit patterns are interpreted as numbers in $\mathbb{Z}$ (using two's complement encoding) or $\mathbb{N}$ (using ordinary binary encoding). The finite precision implies that an expression with type $t \in T$ can only have values in one of the sets $V_t$ given above. For operands with types in T, the C standard [13] states that if either operand of a binary arithmetic operator has type u32, then the other is converted into u32 as well, or else both operands are converted into s32 (this implies that shorter unsigned types alone do no propagate the unsigned property to the result). The conversion of an expression with type $t \in T$

into u32 or s32 is implemented with zero extension for t∈{u8,u16}, sign extension for t∈{s8,s16}, and no operation for t∈{u32,s32}.

The implementation of the 32-bit **relational operators** must distinguish between unsigned and signed operands to obtain correct results (the Intel® architecture uses conditional codes like "GE" or "AE" to make this distinction). We make this distinction between unsigned and signed relational operators explicit with a subscript "u" or "s" (e.g. "$<_u$" and "$<_s$"). A similar distinction is made for the 32-bit **additive operators** (e.g. "$+_u$" and "$+_s$"). The implementation of these operators (ADD/SUB in the Intel® architecture), however, does *not* distinguish between signed or unsigned operands. Instead, the outcome is merely defined by the interpretation of bit patterns after **wrap-around arithmetic**, where higher order bits of results that would require more than 32 bits are simply truncated. For example, the first addition shown below gives rise to an unsigned wrap-around interpretation 4294967295+1=0 or signed interpretation -1+1=0. The second addition has an unsigned interpretation 2147483647+1=2147483648 or a signed wrap-around interpretation 2147483647+1=-2147483648.

```
0xFFFFFFFF              0x7FFFFFFF
0x00000001              0x00000001
---------- +            ---------- +
0x00000000              0x80000000
```

We will use the notation φ(x,V) to denote the condition that the compiler can prove that an expression "x" can only have values in the set V. In the context of this paper, the following rules are useful as a basic implementation of the φ-condition.

1. φ(**c**,V) holds for a constant **c**∈V.
2. φ((t')y, V) holds for a type cast of expression "y" with type t∈T into type t'∈T where $V_t$⊆V, if either (a) t'=u32 and t∈{u8,u16}, or (b) t'=s32 and t∈{u8,u16,s8,s16}.

For example, φ((int)c, {0,255}) holds for a variable "c" of type u8, independent of the program context in which this expression appears. Clearly, this basic implementation can be enhanced by adding more rules or even using the program context of an expression to derive stricter conditions on the possible values of this expression (this would require a third parameter to the φ-condition to define this context). In this paper, we only explore the former kind of enhancement.

## 2.2 Saturation and Clipping Instructions

In this paper, we focus on the instructions of the MMX™ technology and SSE/SSE2 that are given in Table 1. The additive instructions in Table 1 differ from the common ADD/SUB instructions in three ways: (a) the instructions operate in SIMD fashion on packed data elements rather than on scalars, (b) the instructions operate in a lower 8-bit (byte) or 16-bit (word) precision rather than in 32-bit (dword) precision, and (c) the instructions perform **saturation arithmetic** rather than the wrap-around arithmetic explained earlier. In this kind of arithmetic, values that would wrap-around are saturated to the maximum or minimum value for the particular precision. For unsigned additions PADDUSB/PADDUSW, this means that each individual result that would exceed the range of an unsigned byte or word is saturated to the value 0xFF or 0xFFFF, respectively. For unsigned subtractions PSUBUSB/PSUBUWS, this implies that each individual result that would become negative is saturated to the value 0x00 or 0x0000. All signed instructions PADDSB/PSUBSB/PADDSW/PSUBWS saturate individual results to the minimum value 0x80 or 0x8000 or maximum value 0x7F or 0x7FFF.

**Table 1.** Instructions for saturation arithmetic

| Instruction | Description |
|---|---|
| PADDSB/PSUBSB | Add/Subtract signed packed bytes from source to destination and saturate |
| PADDSW/PSUBSW | Add/Subtract signed packed words from source to destination and saturate |
| PADDUSB/PSUBUSB | Add/Subtract unsigned packed bytes from source to destination and saturate |
| PADDUSW/PSUBUSW | Add/Subtract unsigned packed words from source to destination and saturate |
| PMINUB/PMAXUB | Compute minimum/maximum of unsigned packed bytes in source and destination |
| PMINSW/PMAXSW | Compute minimum/maximum of signed packed words in source and destination |

Below, for example, we illustrate the execution of "paddusb xmm0, xmm1". The individual unsigned bytes are saturated to 0xFF on overflow. As for all arithmetic SIMD instructions, there is no interaction (like a carry or borrow) between individual data elements.

```
xmm0: | 0xFF, 0xFE, 0xFD, 0xFC, 0xFB, 0xFA, 0xF9, 0xF8 |
xmm1: | 0x01, 0x01, 0x01, 0x01, 0x05, 0x05, 0x05, 0x05 |
      ------------------------------------------------- +
xmm1: | 0xFF, 0xFF, 0xFE, 0xFD, 0xFF, 0xFF, 0xFE, 0xFD |
```

The MIN/MAX instructions given in Table 1 provide a convenient way to compute the minimum or maximum of a number of unsigned packed bytes or signed packed words in parallel. We generically refer to such operations as **clipping**. Unfortunately, the instruction set is not fully orthogonal (signed bytes and unsigned words are not supported).

## 3  Automatic Detection of Saturation and Clipping Idioms

The methodology used by Intel® compiler to map saturation and clipping idioms onto efficient SIMD instructions is organized into four steps: (A) MIN/MAX operators are recognized in the intermediate representation of the original source program, (B) additive operators are moved into MIN/MAX operators, (C) saturation and clipping idioms are detected and marked, and finally (D) this information is used during intra-register vectorization. All steps are combined with traditional compiler optimizations like constant/copy propagation, forward substitution, constant folding, and expression simplification [1,5,20].

## 3.1  Detection of MIN/MAX Operators

The intermediate representation used by the Intel® compiler supports integral MIN/MAX operators in 32-bit precision. Just like the relational operators, a distinction between unsigned and signed operators must be made (e.g. "$MAX_u$," and "$MAX_s$,"). Because the operators are not directly supported in the source language, the first step focuses on detecting conditional constructs that implement MIN/MAX operations and converting the intermediate representation of these constructs accordingly. This conversion into MIN/MAX operators, making a program more amenable for analysis and enabling the code generator to select an efficient implementation for the operators, is driven by a number of rewriting rules. An example of a rule for unsigned operands is shown below. Here, $x_t$ denotes an arbitrary expression[1] with type $t \in T$ and identical symbols must be bound to equivalent expressions.

```
if (x_u32 >_u y_u32) then
    y_u32 = x_u32          ->    y_u32 = MAX_u(x_u32, y_u32)
endif
```

A rule for signed operands on a conditional construct with two branches is shown below.

```
if (x_s32 <=_s y_s32) then
    t_s32 = x_s32
else                       ->    t_s32 = MIN_s(x_s32, y_s32)
    t_s32 = y_s32
endif
```

Other rewriting rules account for the fact that relational operators on 8-bit or 16-bit operands are done in 32-bit precision, which gives rise to type conversions in the conditionals. An example of such a rule is shown below.

```
if ((s32)x_s16 <_u (s32)y_s16) then
    y_s16 = x_s16                    ->    y_s16 = (s16) MIN_s((s32)x_s16,
(s32)y_s16)
endif
```

Some other rewriting rules specifically test properties of constants to allow the detection of MIN/MAX operators that would otherwise remain unrecognized. An example of such a rule that helps to find nested MIN/MAX operators is shown below, where the comparison between **c** and **d** must be done unsigned.

```
if (d <_u x_u32) then
    t_u32 = d
else                       -> if c <_u d ->    t_u32 = MIN_u(MAX_u(x_u32,
c), d)
    t_u32 = MAX_u(x_u32, c)
endif
```

An example to detect an unsigned MIN operator in an arithmetic expression is given below.

---

[1] All rewriting rules given in this paper assume that expressions are free of side-effects.

```
if (c >u xu32) then
    tu32 = d +u xu32
else                    → if e == d +u c →        tu32 = d +u MINu(xu32,
c)
    tu32 = e                                                           c)
endif
```

Although similar rewriting rules like the five rules shown above are required to deal with all combinations of types, type conversions, alternative operators, conditional constructs, and with the commutativity of operators, these rules can be expressed quite compactly by separating a few general patterns from a number of conditions under which they become applicable. Furthermore, the Intel® compiler represents conditional expressions (viz. "(x) ? y : z") as **if-then-else** constructs, which reduces the number of required rewriting rules. A pass is made over the intermediate representation during which matches for the general patterns are found. If the associated conditions hold, the matching expression is replaced with the appropriate MIN/MAX operator. This process is repeated until no further replacements occur. As stated earlier, traditional compiler optimizations (including some specific MIN/MAX optimizations) are used to simplify the resulting expressions.

As an example, repetitive application of the rewriting rules discussed in this section recognizes a nested MIN/MAX operation in the following conditional expressions for variables "a", "b", and "c" of type s32.

```
a = (10 < ((b*c > 20) ? 20 : b*c))
        ? ((b*c > 20) ? 20 : b*c) : 10;     → … →      a = MAXs(
MINs(b*c, 20),  10);
```

## 3.2 Additive Operator Movement

The second step focuses on moving additive operators into MIN/MAX operators if it is *useful* (potentially exposing a saturation operation) and *valid* (preserving the semantics of the original code). The following rewriting rules for signed operands may be useful if the new constant $d \pm c$ is equal to 127, 255, 32767 or 65535 for a resulting MIN operator, or –32768, -128 or 0 for a resulting MAX operator. A conservative (but practical) validity test is to combine the usefulness test with the tests $-65535 \leq d \leq 65535$ and $\varphi(x_{s32}, V_{u16} \cup V_{s16})$.

```
d +s MINs(xs32, c)   →   MINs(d +s xs32, d +s c)
d +s MAXs(xs32, c)   →   MAXs(d +s xs32, d +s c)
d -s MINs(xs32, c)   →   MAXs(d -s xs32, d -s c)
d -s MAXs(xs32, c)   →   MINs(d -s xs32, d -s c)
```

These conditions, with the φ-condition as defined in Section 0, avoid a change in semantics that would occur if wrap-around could occur (for example, "1+MIN$_s$(x,0x7FFFFFFF)" always yields "1+x" whereas "MIN$_s$(x+1,0x80000000)" simply evaluates to the second argument). Allowing constant $d$ to go all the way down to –65535 may expose *unsigned saturation subtractions* in *signed* arithmetic operations, as we will see in the next section.

An unsigned addition is moved into an unsigned MIN operator, as shown below, if the new constant $d+c$ is either 255 or 65535 and, additionally, $d \in V_{u16}$ and $\varphi(x_{u32}, V_{u16})$.

```
d +u MINu(xu32, c)   →   MINu(d +u xu32, d +u c)
```

The other rewriting rules are slightly more elaborate, because negative results would wrap-around before they are involved in the unsigned comparison. Therefore, such operations are rewritten into *signed* operators as shown below. These rewriting rules are applied if the new constant is equal to 255 or 65535 for a resulting MIN operator, or 0 for a resulting MAX operator and, additionally, $d \in V_{u16}$ and $\varphi(x_{u32}, V_{u16})$ to ensure the validity of the rewriting rule.

$$
\begin{aligned}
\text{MAX}_u(x_{u32},\ c)\ -_u\ d &\rightarrow \quad (u32)\ \text{MAX}_s((s32)x_{u32}\ -_s\ d,\ c\ -_s\ d) \\
d\ -_u\ \text{MIN}_u(x_{u32},\ c) &\rightarrow \quad (u32)\ \text{MAX}_s(d\ -_s\ (s32)x_{u32},\ d\ -_s\ c) \\
d\ -_u\ \text{MAX}_u(x_{u32},\ c) &\rightarrow \quad (u32)\ \text{MIN}_s(d\ -_s\ (s32)x_{u32},\ d\ -_s\ c)
\end{aligned}
$$

After these rewriting rules (and similar rules that deal with commutativity) have been applied, the first step may be repeated to see if more rules become applicable.

### 3.3  Detection of Saturation and Clipping Idioms

In the next step, the compiler examines the intermediate representation of a program to detect saturation and clipping idioms. To separate the concerns of this idiom recognition from the details of the actual code generation that is done during intra-register vectorization, in this step the compiler merely *marks* operators in the intermediate representation as candidates that could potentially be implemented using the instructions shown in Table . Below, we discuss the conditions under which MIN/MAX operators are marked as candidates for (1) unsigned saturation, (2) signed saturation and (3) signed and unsigned clipping, respectively.

**(1) Unsigned Saturation.** Unsigned saturation addition and subtraction idioms typically arise in *single* clippings, as shown below for type u8 (with similar rules for commutativity). Note that both *signed* and *unsigned* MIN operators can be mapped onto unsigned saturation additions. Making the sign of a negative constant explicit (viz. x+c where $-255 \leq c < 0$ can be expressed as x-|c|) increases the likelihood of finding unsigned saturation subtractions in signed MAX operators.

$$
\begin{aligned}
&\text{Mark MIN}_u(x_{u32} +_u y_{u32},\ 255u) \text{ as } \textbf{sat-addu8}(x_{u32},\ y_{u32}) \text{ if } \varphi(x_{u32},\ V_{u8})\ \wedge \\
&\varphi(y_{u32},\ V_{u8}) \\
&\text{Mark MIN}_s(x_{s32} +_s y_{s32},\ 255\ ) \text{ as } \textbf{sat-addu8}(x_{s32},\ y_{s32}) \text{ if } \varphi(x_{s32},\ V_{u8})\ \wedge \\
&\varphi(y_{s32},\ V_{u8}) \\
&\text{Mark MAX}_s(x_{s32} -_s y_{s32},\ \ \ 0\ ) \text{ as } \textbf{sat-subu8}(x_{s32},\ y_{s32}) \text{ if } \varphi(x_{s32},\ V_{u8})\ \wedge \\
&\varphi(y_{s32},\ V_{u8})
\end{aligned}
$$

The $\varphi$–conditions ensure that the 32-bit operations that are implied by the language definition may actually be implemented with lower precision saturation instructions without changing the original semantics. Similar rules can be given to mark **sat-addu16** or **sat-subu16** candidates using the constants 65535u, 65535 and 0 and similar $\varphi$-conditions.

**(2) Signed Saturation.** Signed saturation addition and subtraction idioms typically arise in *double* clippings, as shown below for type s8 (with similar rules for commutativity).

$$
\begin{aligned}
&\text{Mark MAX}_s(\text{MIN}_s(x_{s32} +_s y_{s32},\ 127),\ -128) \text{ as } \textbf{sat-adds8}(x_{s32},\ y_{s32}) \text{ if } \varphi(x_{s32}, \\
&V_{s8})\ \wedge\ \varphi(y_{s32},\ V_{s8}) \\
&\text{Mark MAX}_s(\text{MIN}_s(x_{s32} -_s y_{s32},\ 127),\ -128) \text{ as } \textbf{sat-subs8}(x_{s32},\ y_{s32}) \text{ if } \varphi(x_{s32}, \\
&V_{s8})\ \wedge\ \varphi(y_{s32},\ V_{s8})
\end{aligned}
$$

The φ-conditions ensure that implementing the 32-bit operations with lower precision saturation instructions preserves the original semantics. Under certain conditions, illustrated in Fig. 1, the idioms also arise in *single* clippings, as shown below (with similar rules for commutativity).

```
Mark MINₛ(c +ₛ xₛ₃₂,   127) as sat-adds8(c, xₛ₃₂) if φ(xₛ₃₂, Vₛ₈) ∧    0 <
c ≤ 127
Mark MAXₛ(c +ₛ xₛ₃₂, -128) as sat-adds8(c, xₛ₃₂) if φ(xₛ₃₂, Vₛ₈) ∧ -128 ≤
c < 0
Mark MINₛ(c -ₛ xₛ₃₂,   127) as sat-subs8(c, xₛ₃₂) if φ(xₛ₃₂, Vₛ₈) ∧    0 <
c ≤ 127
Mark MAXₛ(c -ₛ xₛ₃₂, -128) as sat-subs8(c, xₛ₃₂) if φ(xₛ₃₂, Vₛ₈) ∧ -128 ≤
c < 0
```

Similar rules for double and single clip operations can be given to mark **sat-adds16** or **sat-subs16** candidates using the constants −32768 and 32767 and similar φ-conditions.

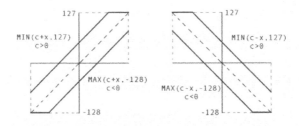

**Fig. 1.** Singed saturation in single clipping

**(3) Signed and Unsigned Clipping.** The detection of clipping idioms is straightforward. Below the rules to mark clipping idioms for type s16 are shown.

```
Mark MINₛ(xₛ₃₂, yₛ₃₂) as mins16(xₛ₃₂, yₛ₃₂) if φ(xₛ₃₂, Vₛ₁₆) ∧ φ(yₛ₃₂, Vₛ₁₆)
Mark MAXₛ(xₛ₃₂, yₛ₃₂) as maxs16(xₛ₃₂, yₛ₃₂) if φ(xₛ₃₂, Vₛ₁₆) ∧ φ(yₛ₃₂, Vₛ₁₆)
```

Similar rules can be given to mark *signed* and *unsigned* MIN/MAX operators in the intermediate representation as a candidate for **minu8** or **maxu8**. For example, both operators "MIN$_u$((u32)$z_{u8}$, 100u)" and "MIN$_s$((s32)$z_{u8}$, 100)" can be marked as **minu8** candidate (for bindings $x_{u32}=$(u32)$z_{u8}$ and $y_{u32}=$100u, and $x_{s32}=$(s32)$z_{u8}$ and $y_{s32}=$100, respectively), even though the operators perform unsigned and signed arithmetic, respectively.

Once an expression has been marked as saturation or clipping candidate for a certain type, the compiler uses this information during evaluation of other φ-conditions. This enhancement (alluded to in Section 2) enables the detection of nested idioms, as shown in the next section.

### 3.4   Intra-register Vectorization

In the fourth and final step, the information computed in the previous step affects instruction selection during the automatic conversion of serial loops into SIMD instructions. For a detailed discussion of intra-register vectorization, we must refer to previous work [7]. In essence, if the compiler can prove that a countable loop can be implemented in SIMD fashion without violating data dependences [6,29,30] or affecting the final required precision, then the loop is converted into instructions that are provided by either the MMX™ technology or SSE/SSE2. If during this conversion, an operator is encountered that has been marked as saturation or clipping candidate with a compatible data type, then the instruction selection is affected accordingly.

Consider the following fragment.

```
u8 a[256], b[256];
...
for (i = 0; i < 256; i++) {
  int x = (a[i] < 200) ? a[i]+55 : 255;
  if (x > b[i]) b[i] = x;
}
```

During the first step (A), the MIN and MAX operator performed in this fragment are recognized as shown below (where all type conversions have been made explicit).

```
for (i = 0; i < 256; i++) {
  int x = 55 + MINₛ((s32)a[i], 200);
  b[i] = (u8) MAXₛ(x, (s32)b[i]);
}
```

During the second step (B), the constant 55 is moved into the MIN operator. Combined with traditional forward substitution this eventually yields the following rewritten fragment.

```
for (i = 0; i < 256; i++) {
  b[i] = (u8) MAXₛ( MINₛ((s32)a[i]+55, 255) , (s32)b[i] );
}
```

The third step (C) marks the MIN operator as **sat-addu8** candidate. Since the φ-condition for data type u8 holds for such an idiom, subsequently the MAX operator is marked as **maxu8** candidate. Eventually, the Intel® compiler uses this information during intra-register vectorization in step (D) to generate the following assembly in which the nested idiom has been fully exploited.

```
Back:                                   ; xmm1 is preloaded with
|55,...,55|
        movdqa   xmm0, a[eax]           ; load  16 bytes from a
        paddusb  xmm0, xmm1             ; add   16 bytes and saturate
        pmaxub   xmm0, b[eax]           ; max   16 bytes from b
        movdqa   b[eax], xmm0           ; store 16 bytes into b
        add      eax, 16                ;
        cmp      eax, 256               ;
        jl       Back                   ; looping logic
```

## 4 Experiments

In this section, we demonstrate the effectiveness of the presented methodology with experimental results for some small kernels and a larger application. All experiments have been conducted with version 7.0 of the Intel® compiler on a 2GHz. Pentium® 4 Processor system with 256MB.

### 4.1 Saturation and Clipping Kernels

Consider the following saturation kernel taken from [23], which represents a typical time consuming part of an embedded application. The Intel® compiler recognizes the saturation arithmetic in this fragment, which eventually results in the selection of the instruction "paddsw" during intra-register vectorization.

```
s16 tab1[N], tab2[N], dest[N];
...
for (i = 0; i < N; i++) {
   int temp = tab1[i] + tab2[i];
   dest[i] = (temp > 32767) ? 32767 : (temp < -32768) ? -32768 :
temp;
}
```

In Fig. 2, we show the execution time for varying values of N for a serial (SEQ) and vector (VEC) version of this fragment together with the corresponding speedup (S). Implementing the conditional flow-of-control without any branch instructions yields a clear performance gain for the deeply pipelined Intel® NetBurst™ micro-architecture of the Pentium® 4 Processor. Most programmers implement saturation arithmetic in a form that strongly resembles the example given above.

For example, the application GSM in the MediaBench suite [17] defines saturation arithmetic with the following macros.

```
#define MAX_WORD (32767)
#define MIN_WORD ((-32767)-1)
#define GSM_ADD(a, b)((ltmp = (int)(a) + (int)(b)) >= MAX_WORD \
          ? MAX_WORD : ltmp <= MIN_WORD ? MIN_WORD : ltmp)
#define GSM_SUB(a, b)((ltmp = (int)(a) - (int)(b)) >= MAX_WORD \
          ? MAX_WORD : ltmp <= MIN_WORD ? MIN_WORD : ltmp)
```

A typical use like the one shown below, where all arrays have type s16, is easily recognized by the step-wise methodology as a loop that can be implemented with the instruction "paddsw" (or "psubsw").

```
for (i = 0; i <= 39; i++)
     dp[ i ] = GSM_ADD( e[5 + i], dpp[i] );
```

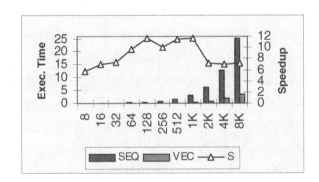

**Fig. 2.** Execution time for 16-bit saturation kernel ((in microseconds)

Likewise, take the following clipping kernel that operates on an array with type s16.

```
for (i = 0; i < N; i++) {
    if (dest[i] > 100) dest[i] = 100;
}
```

The Intel® compiler implements this loop with the "minsw" instruction. In Fig. 3, we show the serial execution time (SEQ), vector execution time (VEC) and corresponding speedup (S). For comparison, we also studied the performance obtained by a more general method for vectorizing conditional constructs, namely **IF-conversion** [3,4,29,30]. This method removes branches from a program by replacing the statements in this program with an equivalent set of guarded statements. This effectively converts all control dependences into data dependences and allows for a straightforward translation of guarded statements into vector code for vector processors that provide hardware support for conditional vector instructions. Although SSE/SSE2 does not *directly* support conditional execution, in [7] we have shown that IF-conversion can be easily implemented by means of **bit-masking**. For the example above, bit-masking results in SIMD instructions that compute the bit-wise OR of (a) the value 100 masked by the outcome of the comparison and (b) the elements of the array masked with the negation of this outcome. The execution time (MSK) and corresponding speedup (S-MSK) for this version are also shown in Fig. 3. Although vectorization by means of IF-conversion improves performance compared to serial execution, the highest performance is clearly obtained with the clipping instructions.

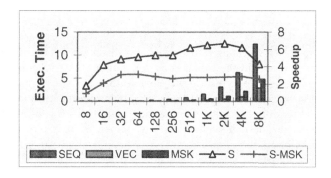

**Fig. 3.** Execution time for 16-bit clipping kernel (in microseconds)

## 4.2  Data (de)Compression Application

To demonstrate the impact of idiom recognition on a real-world application, we report some performance results for **164.gzip**, a data (de)compression program in the industry-standardized CPU-intensive benchmark suite SPEC CPU2000 (see http://www.spec.org/). Enabling intra-register vectorization for this benchmark results in the conversion of two loops of the form shown below into an SIMD form that exploits the "psubusw" instruction.

```
u16 head[N];
...
for (i = 0; i < N; i++) {
    u32 m = head[i];
    head[i] = (m >= 32768 ? m-32768 : 0);
}
```

In Table 2, we show the speedups compared to a default-optimized version (O2) for an aggressively Pentium® 4 Processor specific optimized version without intra-register vectorization (OPT) and a similarly optimized version with intra-register vectorization enabled (OPT+VEC). This data shows that the Intel® compiler obtains an improvement of 30% over a default-optimized version of this application, roughly 8% of which is due to intra-register vectorization (viz. 1.30/1.21).

**Table 2.** Speedups for164.gzip

|          | **O2** | **OPT** | **OPT+VEC** |
|----------|--------|---------|-------------|
| **164.gzip** | 1.00   | 1.21    | 1.30        |

## 5  Conclusions

In this paper, we have presented a step-wise methodology to bridge the semantic gap between high-level saturation and clipping constructs on one hand, and low-level instructions for these idioms on the other hand. The rewriting rules that drive the steps are simple, so that the validity of each individual rule can be easily verified. The rules allow for a compact representation and provide a clean separation of concerns between idiom recognition and the actual code generation. The fine granularity of the rewriting rules makes this approach more flexible than an ad-hoc pattern matching approach to idiom recognition because traditional compiler optimizations can be applied at all times (possibly exposing opportunities for further rewriting) and new rules can be easily added to the methodology as a whole (for example, to rewrite certain difficult constructs into a form that is handled by the already existing rules). The use of rewriting rules, although currently hard-coded in a separate module of the high-performance Intel® C++/Fortran compiler, makes the methodology very suited for parameterized systems that easily adapt to new multimedia instruction sets, such as the system proposed [23]. Although there are other compilers that target the instruction sets of multimedia extensions [9,16,23,25], to our knowledge this paper provides the first in-depth presentation of a methodology to bridge the semantic gap between high-level saturation and clipping idioms and low-level instructions. The results of a number of experiments on small kernels and a real-world application have been included to validate the effectiveness of this approach.

More information on intra-register vectorization in the high-performance compilers for the Intel® Architecture can be found in the upcoming book: *The Software Vectorization Handbook. Applying Multimedia Extensions for Maximum Performance.* Intel Press, June, 2004 (see http://www.intel.com/intelpress/sum_vmmx.htm).

# References

1. Alfred V. Aho, Ravi Sethi, and Jeffrey D. Ullman. *Compilers Principles, Techniques and Tools*. Addison-Wesley, 1986.
2. Randy Allen and Ken Kennedy. *Automatic Translation of Fortran Programs to Vector Form*. ACM Transactions on Programming Languages and Systems, 9:491—542, 1987.
3. Randy Allen and Ken Kennedy. *Optimizing Compilers for Modern Architectures*. Morgan Kaufmann, San Francisco, 2002.
4. Randy Allen, Ken Kennedy, Carrie Porterfield and Joe Warren. *Conversion of Control Dependence to Data Dependence*. ACM Symposium on Principles of Programming Languages. 177—189, 1983.
5. Andrew Appel. *Modern Compiler Implementation in C*. Cambridge University Press, 1998.
6. Utpal Banerjee. *Dependence Analysis*. Kluwer, Boston, 1997. A Book Series on Loop Transformations for Restructuring Compilers.
7. Aart J.C. Bik, Milind Girkar, Paul M. Grey, and Xinmin Tian. *Automatic intra-register vectorization for the Intel® Architecture*. International Journal on Parallel Processing, 2001.
8. David Bistry et.al. *The Complete Guide to MMX™ technology*. McGraw-Hill, Inc. New York, 1997.
9. R.J. Fisher and H.G. Dietz. *Compiling for SIMD within a Register*. 1998 Workshop on Languages and Compilers for Parallel Computing, University of North Carolina at Chapel Hill, North Carolina, August 7-9, 1998.
10. Glenn Hinton, Dave Sager, Mike Upton, Darrell Boggs, Doug Carmean, Alan Kyker, and Patrice Roussel. *The Microarchitecture of the Pentium® 4 Processor*. Intel Technology Journal, 2001, http://intel.com/technology/itj/.
11. Intel Corporation. *Intel Architecture MMX™ technology – Programmer's Reference Manual*. Intel Corporation, Order No. 243007-003, available at http://developer.intel.com/, 1997.
12. Intel Corporation. *Intel Architecture Software Developer's Manual, Volume 1: Basic Architecture*. Intel Corporation, available at http://developer.intel.com/, 2001.
13. Brian W. Kernighan and Dennis M. Ritchie. *The C Programming Language*. Prentice Hall, Englewood Cliffs, New Jersey, 1988.
14. David J. Kuck. *The Structure of Computers and Computations*. John Wiley and Sons, New York, 1978, Volume 1.
15. Leslie Lamport. *The Parallel Execution of DO Loops*. Communications of the ACM, 83—93, 1974.
16. Samuel Larsen and Saman Amarasinghe. *Exploiting Superword Level Parallelism with Multimedia Instruction Sets*. In Proceeding of the SIGPLAN Conference on Programming Language Design and Implementation, Vancouver, B.C., June, 2000.
17. Chunho Lee, Miodrag Potkonjak and William H. Mangione-Smith. *MediaBench: A Tool for Evaluating and Synthesizing Multimedia and Communications Systems*.
18. Oded Lempel, Alex Peleg and Uri Weiser. *Intel's MMX™ Technology – A New Instruction Set Extension*. Proceedings of COMPCON, 255—259, 1997.
19. John M. Levesque and Joel W. Williamson. *A Guidebook to Fortran on Supercomputers*. Academic Press, San Diego, 1991.
20. Steven S. Muchnick. *Advanced Compiler Design and Implementation* Morgan Kaufmann, 1997.

21. David A. Padua and Michael J. Wolfe. *Advanced Compiler Optimizations for Supercomputers*. Communications of the ACM, 29:1184—1201, 1986.
22. Alex Peleg and Uri Weiser. *MMX Technology Extension to the Intel Architecture*. IEEE Micro, 42-50, 1996.
23. Gilles Pokam, Julien Simonnet and François Bodin. A Retargetable Preprocessor for Multimedia Instructions. In Proceedings of the 9th Workshop on Compilers for Parallel Computers, 291—301, June, 2001.
24. Constantine D. Polychronopoulos. *Parallel Programming and Compilers*. Kluwer, Boston, 1988.
25. N. Sreraman and R. Govindarajan. *A vectorizing compiler for multimedia extensions*. International Journal on Parallel Processing, 2000.
26. Srinivas K. Raman, Vladimir Pentkovski, and Jagannath Keshava. *Implementing Streaming SIMD Extensions on the Pentium III Processor*. IEEE Micro, 20(4):47—57, 2000.
27. Bjarne Stroustrup. *The C++ Programming Language*. Addison-Wesley, 1991.
28. Shreekant Thakkar and Tom Huff. *Internet Streaming SIMD Extensions*. IEEE Computer, 32:26--34, 1999.
29. Michael J. Wolfe. *High Performance Compilers for Parallel Computing*. Addison-Wesley, 1996.
30. Hans Zima. Supercompilers for Parallel and Vector Computers. ACM Press, New York, 1990.

# Compiler Optimizations with DSP-Specific Semantic Descriptions

Yung-Chia Lin[1], Yuan-Shin Hwang[2], and Jenq Kuen Lee[1]

[1] Department of Computer Science, National Tsing Hua University,
Hsinchu 300, Taiwan
[2] Department of Computer Science, National Taiwan Ocean University,
Keelung 202, Taiwan

**Abstract.** Due to the specialized architecture and stream-based instruction set, traditional DSP compilers usually yield poor-quality object codes. Lack of an insight into the DSP architecture and the specific semantics of DSP applications, a compiler would have trouble selecting appropriate special instructions to exploit advanced hardware features. In order to extract optimal performance from DSPs, we propose a set of user-specified directives called *Digital Signal Processing Interface (DSPI)*, which can facilitate code generation by relaying DSP specific semantics to compilers. We have implemented a prototype compiler based on the SPAM and SUIF compiler toolkits and integrated the DSPI into the prototype compiler. The compiler is currently targeted to TI's TMS320C6X DSP and will be extended to a retargetable compiler toolkit for embedded systems and System-on-a-Chip (**SoC**) platforms. Preliminary experimental results show that by incorporating DSPI directives significant performance improvements can be achieved in several DSP applications.

## 1   Introduction

Since high-throughput data stream processing is required to deliver voice, multimedia, and data access in real-time, many embedded systems employ programmable *Digital Signal Processor*s (DSPs) as their core components. As DSP applications rapidly grow more complex, high-level development tools are vital to speedy software implementation [18]. However, this approach tends to fail to extract the optimal performance from DSPs owing to the fact that conventional code generation by DSP compilers produces very inefficient results in either speed or code size [20,8]. Those compilers cannot automatically discover the best ways to utilize the specific architecture features and to unleash proper optimized code

---

[1] The work was supported in part by NSC-90-2218-E-007-042, NSC-90-2213-E-007-074, NSC-90-2213-E-007-075, MOE research excellent project under grant no. 89-E-FA04-1-4, and MOEA research project under grant no. 91-EC-17-A-03-S1-0002 of Taiwan.

B. Pugh and C.-W. Tseng (Eds.): LCPC 2002, LNCS 2481, pp. 75–89, 2005.

composed of custom-built instructions for DSP operations without intervening from the programmers.

This paper proposes a DSP programming model with a set of user-specified directives called the *Digital Signal Processing Interface (DSPI)*. The key idea is to transform common high-level DSP operations into code of well-regulated vendor-specific instructions. Moreover, we have constructed a prototype compiler targeted to TI's TMS320C6X [16] based on the SUIF [10] and SPAM [9] compiler toolkits, and we are integrating the compiler support for processing the DSPI directives into the compiler. Furthermore, partial support for our objected-oriented architectural description framework (**ORISAL**) is being incorporated into the prototype compiler as well. Preliminary experimental results show that by incorporating DSPI directives significant performance improvement can be attained in several DSP applications. This work is also a series of our research work to attempt to develop high-performance and low-power compiler toolkit for DSP and SoC environments [15,14,22,23,6,5].

The rest of this paper is organized in the following. Section 2 discusses the background of the problems of DSP compilation and several related issues. Section 3 details the concepts of DSPI specification and optimization schemes that are furnished to the compiler. Section 4 briefly mentions our DSP compiler constructions and our ADL-based retargetable system toolkit. Experimental results are presented and analyzed in section 5. Section 6 compares the related work and Section 7 concludes this paper.

## 2   Portability and Optimization Issues for DSP Programming

The market for embedded and SOC systems with DSPs as the central processors has been expanding substantially over the past few years. Whereas there always is a need for greater product differentiation and innovation, there is also an increasing pressure to shrink design cycles by means of streamlining the complicated development process. With an eye to the unceasing upgrades and options of hardware technologies, software development tools should highlight source code portability jointly with the emphasis on target code quality.

Most software development toolkits are designed upon high-level programming languages to insulate programmers from the complexities of DSP architecture. None the less, high-level development tools seldom produce efficient software that can extract the best performance from the advanced hardware. Consequently, most decisive DSP applications are hand-coded in the low-level assembly languages.

Programming DSP applications in assembly languages is fine only when small kernels are required to be executed on a DSP. Today complicated DSP software is required to handle modern applications. Therefore, a procurable DSP software design can be achieved only by means of high-level development tools that can translate high-level languages into efficient object code. In addition, only the restricted features of traditional DSP architecture could make it easy for programmers to hand-optimize code to achieve the desired speed, size, or low-power. As more specialized architectures have been incorporated into current DSP processors, manually performing optimizations is getting exceedingly arduous. For above reasons, there is a great demand for more effective technologies for compiler optimizations of high-level languages. In this paper, we address the direction to develop high-level languages for efficiency. Our approach is to employ DSP-specific semantic descriptions to be annotated on top of high-level languages by DSP programmers. This information can also be picked up by compilers to perform optimizations.

## 3    Optimizations by DSP Specific Semantics

In order to facilitate the compilers to generate efficient object code which can take advantage of the DSP advanced hardware features, we propose a set of directives to allow programmers specifying information-rich descriptions. Our DSPI specification covers more general intrinsic operations than existing DSP directives. In the DSPI specification, each directive is specified by the following syntax:

---

#**pragma dspi** *directive-name [clause[ [,]clause]...] new-line*

---

Every directive starts with #**pragma dspi**, avoiding conflicting with other pragma directives. The remainder of the directive conforms to the conventions of the C and C++ standards for language directives. DSPI directives are classified into four categories:

- *Environment Depiction*
- *Operation Intention*
- *Data Storage Characterization*
- *Parallelism Commentary*

### 3.1    Environment Depiction

For each code segment based on the semantic of source code, programmers should specify directives to guide compiler optimizations or to specify user-controlled options. For example, any program following the first directive in Fig. 1 will be translated into a fixed-point code, while statements and variables preceded by the second directive in Fig. 1 will be converted to floating-point instructions and data formats.

In addition to specifying the data precision, the same code running on different DSP processors may actually be compiled with integers of different lengths. Therefore, we need some annotations to assist the compiler in generating code in a bit-accurate way from the portable source. Fig. 2 shows an example. The second directive in Fig. 2 will direct the compiler to load a separate file which contains a sequence of DSPI directives.

```
#pragma dspi algorithm_type fxp
/* indicating the algorithm is designed for fixed point arithmetics */

#pragma dspi algorithm_type fop
/* indicating the algorithm is designed for
   floating point arithmetics              */
```

**Fig. 1.** Environment Depiction Example 1

```
#pragma dspi int_type 32bit
/* assume that length of type int in the code is designed for 32bit */

#pragma dspi include filename.def
/* include a prepared file of DSPI directives
   at this position in the source code       */
```

**Fig. 2.** Environment Depiction Example 2

## 3.2   Operation Intention

Directives of operation intention provide several levels of comprehensive descriptions to specify DSP-specific computations, essentially ensuring that a compiler will have sufficient knowledge to generate efficient code. By providing those denotational equations or descriptions, different levels of optimizations could be applied, including low-level smart intrinsic instructions substituting, middle-level smart intrinsic function synthesizing, and high-level architectural prefab function embedding as well as possible library-level optimizations.

The general format of the operation intention directives is defined as:

**#pragma dspi op** *[label:] [enum] [&] operation-clause [[;] clause]... new-line*

Two additional directives **op_b** and **op_e** are defined to let programmers specify the starting and end points of operations respectively, if they cannot be easily determined by the compiler:

**#pragma dspi op_b** *label*
**#pragma dspi op_e** *label*

**op_b** and **op_e** DSPI descriptions should be added to demarcate effective boundaries where the semantics of the operation can apply to. Otherwise, the DSPI description **op** will automatically match the following neighboring block structure such as a function or loop if neither **op_b** nor **op_e** is annotated with *label*. The optional *enum* is an enumeration that can be used for supplying more than one alternative solution on the same specified source code. Multiple operator clauses in the same line are separated by semicolons and are operated in sequence by default if they have operand dependencies. Putting a character & before clauses means that the current line is parallelizable.

```
#pragma dspi fxp a:=<16:16>
#pragma dspi fxp b:=<16:16>
#pragma dspi fxp sadd:=<16:16>,saturated
#pragma dspi op sadd:=a.ADD<b>
int sadd(int a, int b)
{
    #pragma dspi fxp result:=<16:16>,saturated
    int result;
    #pragma dspi op saddop: result:=a.ADD<b>
    #pragma dspi op_b saddop
    result = a + b;
    if (((a ^ b) & 0x8000) == 0) {
        if ((result ^ a) & 0x8000) {
            result = (a < 0) ? 0x8000 : 0x7fff;
        }
    }
    #pragma dspi op_e saddop
    return (result);
}
```

**Fig. 3.** Operation Intention Example

The most common operations we have seen from studying many kernel routines and DSP-operation emphatic applications such as standard vocoders, which follow the European Telecommunications Standards Institute (ETSI), can be grouped into two levels of semantic operations. The low-level math operators comprise ordinary arithmetic operators such as **.ADD**, **.SUB**, **.NEG**, **.MUL**, and bit-wise manipulation like **.SHL**, **.SHR**. Operator symbol := is used for assigning values, as **.SET** is for setting values between right clause's operands or initializing operands with some values. Rotation operators **.ROR** and **.ROL** are indigenously supported in contrast to original C or C++ because most processors could carry out such operations by built-in hardware implementation. For describing the iterative operations concisely in the inner loops, we introduce the delay operator **.DLY**<*interval*> which could be applied to give the previous value of the operand before an interval.

Fig. 3 shows an example of a math operation known as the saturated addition, which can not be easily expressed in C without DSPI directives. In addition, this example shows that multiple descriptions with different boundaries could exist on some overlapped regions as well. Such a style of redundant semantics could be endowed with selectable optimizations if a compiler is able to utilize it.

Other DSP related basic operators are listed in Table 1.

It is straightforward to express critical DSP processing by these lower-level basic operators. All ETSI specific math functions can be described through one

**Table 1.** Low-level Math Operators

| | |
|---|---|
| .ABS | absolute value |
| .RND | round |
| .NRM | normalize bit number |
| .XHL<*source operand*> | extract lower half to upper half |
| .XLH<*source operand*> | extract upper half to lower half |
| .MUH<*multiplier*> | multiply upper half |
| .MAC<*multiplier, addend*> | multiply & accumulate |
| .MSU<*multiplier, subtrahend*> | multiply & subtract |
| .EXT<*pattern*> | partition and extract section (depend on pattern) |
| .PAK<*pattern, operand, ...*> | pack multiple operands into one (depend on pattern) |

**Table 2.** High-level Vector Operators

| .CONV<$vector$> | convolve two vectors |
|---|---|
| .CCRR<$vector$> | cross correlate two vectors |
| .ACRR | autocorrelate a vector |
| .RVRS | reverse a vector |
| .SCAL <$scaling\ value$> | scale a vector to range |
| .SUMM | sum a vector |
| .SQUR | square a vector |
| .CLRF <$vector$> | generic linear filtering with coefficients |
| .FIRF <$vector$> | regular FIR filtering operation |
| .IIRF <$vector,\ vector$> | regular IIR filtering operation |

**Table 3.** High-level Matrix Operators

| .KRONT <$matrix$> | Kronecker tensor product |
|---|---|
| .INVRT | inverting a square matrix |
| .LUFAC | compute LU factorization of a matrix |
| .TRACE | compute the trace of a matrix |
| .DETRM | compute the determination of a matrix |
| .EIGEN | compute the eigenvalue of a matrix |

or two directives. Furthermore, when directives operate on vectors, they properly manifest simple procurable results despite complex looped source code.

The high-level operation intentions model the familiar DSP actions that could not be directly mapped into hardware instructions but each of them has an unitary thought on vector or matrix operands. One practical example is convolution, which is the same operation as multiplying the polynomials whose coefficients are the elements of two vectors. Several of these high-level DSP operators working on vectors and matrixes are listed in Table 2 and Table 3, respectively.

### 3.3 Data Storage Characterization

Some DSP-customary fixed-length data types such as 24-bit and 40-bit integers are not defined in the ANSI/ISO C/C++ standard, and hence extra care must be taken in order to process these data types efficiently. Therefore, the compiler needs more information of data storage in the source code to process the computation and output the accurate data if using the optimized target machine instructions.

Other data storage characterizations which could let the compiler generate codes that benefit from the specific architectural ability are called accessing features. The accessing features for scalar numbers include saturated, several rounding types, etc. Vector or matrix data storage could be additionally appended with accessing conventions like interleaved, divided, circular, and so on. There is also a special accessing feature called temp, which is used to specify a temporary storage location. Suchlike temporary value is just applied to above operation intention directives. The format of data storage characterization is

```
#pragma dspi type id:=[feature[[,]feature]...] new-line
```

```
#pragma dspi fxp a:=<24:16>
int a;
/* declare that int a is actually a fixed-point number
            of bit-width 24 with integer word-length 16 */

#pragma dspi fop b:=<16>,saturated
float b;
/* declare that float b is a 16bit length
        saturated floating-point number */

#pragma dspi cfxp c:=<24:16>,real=cr,image=ci
int cr, ci;
/* declare a temporal complex number c, which consists
 of a real part cr and an imaginary part ci, could be used
        with DSPI operators in representing the semantics */

#pragma dspi fxp d:=<24:16>,circular
int d[160];
/* declare that vector d will be accessed in a circular manner */
```

**Fig. 4.** Data Storage Characterization Examples

Bit-width feature is described as ⟨width:width⟩ for fixed-point numbers and ⟨width⟩ for floating-point numbers. Interleaved or divided feature must append a ⟨number⟩ to characterize the accessing distance. Fig. 4 presents some examples.

Moreover, data storage characteristics can also be specified to the return values of functions in C or C++ language, as shown in Fig. 3.

### 3.4   Parallelism Commentary

DSP applications are practically massive data computations. Accordingly, most DSP processors are built as data flow engines, accompanied by a RISC or CISC processor, and consequently they are multiprocessors by default. From these perspectives, the directives defined in this group will allow users to create and enhance DSP programs with possible compiler optimizations when the programs running on an ILP-aware DSP processor or an SIMD-aware DSP processor. In addition, a system with multiple DSP processors may also be improved with those directives if the compiler is designed with suitable optimizations. The directives extend the C and C++ sequential programming model with data parallelism constructs and simultaneous operation semantics [13].

The directive **parallel_region** is designed to specify a parallel region, which is a part of the program that could be executed in parallel if the hardware architecture permits. This directive explicitly directs the compiler to generate parallel code, as shown in Fig. 5. Variables listed in the *shared* clause are accessed

```
#pragma dspi parallel_region [shared:=var1, [var2[,...]]]
{
   /* block of codes */
}
```

**Fig. 5.** Parallelism Commentary 1

```
#pragma dspi parallel_for [schedule:=chunksize]
for(...;...;...)
{
  /* loop body */
}
```

**Fig. 6.** Parallelism Commentary 2

```
static void Fast_Autocorrelation P2((s, L_ACF),
    word * s,        /* [0..159] IN/OUT */
    longword * L_ACF)  /* [0..8]   OUT    */
{
    ...

    #pragma dspi op s_f:=s
    #pragma dspi parallel_for
    for (i = 0; i < 160; ++i)
        sf[i] = s[i];
    #pragma dspi op f_L_ACF:=sf.ACRR.EXT<0:8>
    for (k = 0; k <= 8; k++) {
        register float L_temp2 = 0;
        register float *sfl = sf - k;
        #pragma dspi parallel_for
        for (i = k; i < 160; ++i)
            L_temp2 += sf[i] * sfl[i];
        f_L_ACF[k] = L_temp2;
    }
    scale = MAX_LONGWORD / f_L_ACF[0];
    #pragma dspi op L_ACF:=f_L_ACF.SCAL<scale>
    #pragma dspi parallel_for
    for (k = 0; k <= 8; k++) {
        L_ACF[k] = f_L_ACF[k] * scale;
    }
}
```

**Fig. 7.** Code Fragment from LPC Analysis in GSM

in the same area in parallel, so that the compiler should take a consideration about the data-path conflicting in the specific hardware.

Another fundamental parallelism is shown in Fig. 6. It specifies that the iterations of the loop could be executed in parallel if possible.

The optional clause of *schedule:=chunksize* will be used to guide the compiler to generate codes that iterations are divided into chunks of the specified size. Fig. 7 shows a code fragment of LPC analysis with parallelism commentary and other DSPI directives.

## 4   Compiler Framework

This section describes the current status of our compiler environment. It will also give a glance at the involved retargetability technology of architectural description language that we are developing for the embedded system and SoC systems. At present, our prototype compiler is based on the SPAM compiler developed by Princeton University [9]. The front-end of the SPAM compiler is actually using the SUIF1 [10]. SPAM focuses on back-end optimizations and has only a limited set of back-end support for target architectures. In our work, we

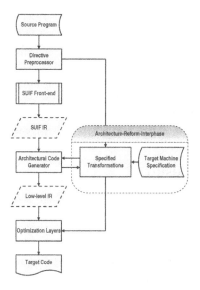

**Fig. 8.** Compiler Infrastructures

expand the SPAM to support TI TMS320C6 DSP processors. We exert the *olive* code generator-generator included in the SPAM back-end to perform instruction selections. In addition, we are in the process of incorporating compiler optimizations to fully support the DSPI directives to optimize DSP programs. The code generating procedures and our compiler infrastructures are illustrated in Fig. 8.

In addition to the attempt of supporting compiler optimizations with DSP-specific semantic descriptions specified from DSP programmers, our system is also incorporating a framework of architectural description languages in expectation to provide fast prototype and retargeting of toolkits for DSP processors. Our architecture description language is called (**ORISAL**) denoting *Object-oriented Reconfigurable Instruction Set Architecture Language*. ORISAL is represented by a Java-like syntax. From the internal design of the core library in the ORISAL framework, there are several layers of abstraction that concern the issues of compiler construction and retargeting. One of the components is a uniform semantic behavior interface that is used by both physical components and software components, providing the coherence of operation selection which the compiler or other development tools could use to match maximal architectural features. Among the predefined sets of behaviors of operations, there is one called canonical-semantics that is treated as the fundamental and the least operational interface acknowledged by instructions and hardware components. All operations except canonical-semantics must be applied with at least one self-evident identical operation semantics composed of canonical ones, thus these identical operations could provide multiple cost evaluation of different approaches or decomposed sub-operations that could be scheduled to utilize maximum hardware capability. The rules of completing one operation are configurable from several default built-in operations or user-defined methods. In order to determine the multiple selections of instructions or operation semantics, there are also several ways to reference the related cost functions. The cost of one operation can be chosen from accompanying hardware factors, instruction factors or user-defined compositions. While comparing with other existing ADLs [11] [24] [12], our ORISAL framework has several specialties which could improve the off-the-shelf design process of hardware and associated software development toolkits. ORISAL emphasizes on supporting cycle-accurate simulation, multiple IP descriptions, energy information, and the instruction set architecture for compiler toolkit optimizations.

## 5    Experimental Results

To evaluate the effects of DSPI descriptions for optimization in retargetable compiler construction, we embed *DSPI* in the DSPstone kernel benchmarks [25] and evaluate the performance. The DSP benchmark suite used in this experiments is described in Table 4.

Experiments will be performed on two sets of object programs. The first set of object programs will be generated by compiling the benchmark programs by the compiler in the TI TMS320C6201 development toolkits with option "-O3". In other words, this set is comprised of the optimized object code of the benchmark programs generated without DSPI directives. The performance of this set of object programs will be used as the baseline measurement. The other set of object programs is generated from the benchmark programs with embedded DSPI directives. The prototype compiler tries to select the TMS320C6 intrinsic instructions whenever possible based on the semantics of DSPI directives. As we are still in the early stage of compiler implementations, our software infrastructures are fragile and we manually perform code generation of statements specified by certain DSPI directives for compiler work when our system fails to do that in this early stage. However, we expect the performance will be at least the same when we have the automatic system done, as many of the optimizations with directives are quite syntactic transformations. Both sets of object programs are converted to VLIW code through the TI TMS320C6 assembly optimizer, and then executed on the TI TMS320C6201 software simulator and hardware evaluation module under different settings of data sizes and quality.

**Table 4.** DSP Benchmark suite used in this work

| Benchmark name | Description |
| --- | --- |
| convolution | This function behaves as the convolution operation. This is a modified n lags version. |
| matrix1x3 | This program multiplies a 3 by 3 matrix with 1 by 3 vector to generate and store a 3 by 1 vector |
| lms(least mean square) | This adaptive filter performs a finite impulse response filtering where the tap coefficients are adapted iteratively |
| fir | One of common kernel operations inside the central applications using DSPs. The FIR benchmark multiplies an array of state variables by an array of coefficients and accumulates the result in the output variable |
| iir_biquad_N_sections | Another intensively used digital filters in DSP applications. It inputs values through a biquad infinite impulse response filter. The IIR benchmark consists of N serial, second order subsystems named biquads, so that the output of each biquad corresponds tt the input of next biquad |
| n_complex_updates | This benchmark multiplies n complex numbers with n complex numbers, then adds other n complex numbers, and accumulates the results with n complex numbers updates |

**Table 5.** DSP Benchmark Testsuite 1 (32bit)

| Name of benchmark | convolution | matrix1x3 | lms | fir | iir_biquad_N_sections |
|---|---|---|---|---|---|
| Original code cycles | 417447 | 21984 | 110110 | 55184 | 36296 |
| DSPI code cycles | 352808 | 18284 | 106094 | 48706 | 34917 |

**Table 6.** DSP Benchmark Testsuite 2 (16bit)

| Name of benchmark | matrix1x3 | iir_biquad_N_sections | n_complex_updates |
|---|---|---|---|
| Original code cycles | 19376 | 24776 | 94284 |
| DSPI code cycles | 15273 | 23722 | 54162 |

**Table 7.** DSP Benchmark Testsuite 3 (4x Quantity)

| Name of benchmark | lms | fir | iir_biquad_N_sections | n_complex_updates |
|---|---|---|---|---|
| Original code cycles | 413400 | 194745 | 82305 | 371604 |
| DSPI code cycles | 374056 | 150441 | 60778 | 194466 |

The performance of both sets is measured by the the TMS320C6201 profiler. Table 5 and Table 6 list the numbers of cycles are executed for both sets of object programs with the data sizes of 32 bits and 16 bits, respectively. Table 7 presents the execution times when a quadruple of the data is manipulated for the benchmarks, the first two of which use the 32-bit data size and the last two use 16 bits.

The DSPI directives applied on these benchmark programs are concisely described below. Except that using basic operation intentions to construct the fundamental semantics, we use the DSPI data characteristics to indicate the

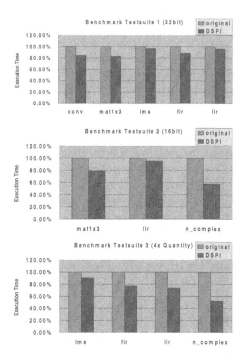

**Fig. 9.** DSP Benchmark Testsuite Performance Comparison

**Table 8.** Large Application Benchmark (G.723.1 Codec)

| Name of benchmark | Coder 6.3K | Coder 5.3K | Decoder 6.3K | Decoder 5.3K |
|---|---|---|---|---|
| Original code cycles | 8323070 | 11751868 | 850180 | 812517 |
| DSPI code cycles | 1298805 | 1565469 | 93190 | 89884 |

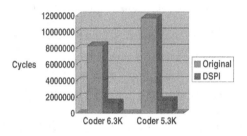

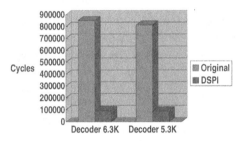

**Fig. 10.** Full G.723.1 Codec Benchmark Performance Comparison

applied vector and matrix operations. Besides, in **convolution**, **matrix1x3**, and **n_complex_updates**, we use parallelism commentary directives to annotate the loops; in **n_complex_updates**, we insert complex number feature to precisely define the data type; in the **iir_biquad_N_sections**, we make use of special storage addressing by circular buffer. These tables show that we can get some notable improvement by embedding the DSPI directives. Fig. 9 depicts the performance improvement over normalized baseline execution times.

In addition to DSP kernel program benchmarks, we also take a large application program to test the DSPI optimizations. The application is the full G.723.1 codec from ITU-T, and is compiled with both portions of rate 6.3kbit/s and rate 5.3kbit/s into single object program to simulate the condition that complex and large code could not entirely reside in the DSP core memory. The performance of coder and decoder in each rate is listed in Table 8. The comparison figures are illustrated in Fig. 10 and they reveal significant improvements gained by DSPI descriptions.

## 6   Related Works

Several methods are currently used for DSP optimizations. First, it uses the support of libraries for those frequent computation-intensive kernel procedures include FIR filters, IIR filters, FFTs, DCTs, and so on. Another way for DSP optimizations is to use intrinsics for describing specific instructions available in an architecture [2,3,7]. Rudimentary intrinsics is like the assembly statement but have the appearance of macro-usage in C/C++ source code. These words are transformed to natively supported instructions during compilation and are rewarded for some tier of optimizations. The third method is modifying the language itself to force programmers explicitly writing DSP architectural data types and expressions of DSP functionalities. Language extensions for this purpose are designed with enhanced constructs like fixed-point types, saturation types, particular memory addressing types, simultaneous execution model, etc [17,19,21]. These additions often denote special compilers that accept these none-standard dialects of C/C++ language. This decreases the portability of the programs. Our compiler directive approach is similar to HPF [4] and OpenMP [1] for the methodology, but specialized in DSP optimizations.

## 7  Conclusion

In this paper, we offered the possible solution with DSPI, a set of DSP specific semantics directives, which could make the compiler produce more optimized codes but persist source-level compatibility. We also have briefed the on-going research works of our proposed retargetable toolkit framework of SoC, ORISAL, in which the DSPI could be entailed to perform a retargetable optimization layer of the compiler and may benefit with both portability and optimizations. Preliminary experiments reveal the promising prospects of continuation in this research work.

## References

1. Eduard Ayguade, Xavier Martorell, Jesus Labarta, Marc Gonzalez, and Nacho Navarro. Exploiting multiple levels of parallelism in openmp: A case study. In *International Conference on Parallel Processing*, pages 172–180, 1999.
2. D. Batten, S. Jinturkar, J. Glossner, M. Schulte, and P. D'Arcy. A new approach to dsp intrinsic functions. In *Proceedings of the Hawaii International Conference on System Sciences*, pages 908–918, January 2000.
3. D. Batten, S. Jinturkar, J. Glossner, M. Schulte, R. Peri, and P. D'Arcy. Interaction between optimizations and a new type of dsp intrinsic function. In *Proceedings of the International Conference on Signal Processing Applications and Technology (ICSPAT'99)*, November 1999.
4. Z. Bozkus, A. Choudhary, G. Fox, T. Haupt, and S.Ranka. Fortran 90d/hpf compiler for distributed memory mimd computers: design, implementation and performance results. In *Proceedings of Supercomputing '93*, pages 351–360, November 1993.
5. R. G. Chang, T. R. Chuang, and Jenq-Kuen Lee. Efficient support of parallel sparse computation for array intrinsic functions of fortran 90. In *Proceedings of ACM International Conference on Supercomputing*, July 1998.

6. Rong-Guey Chang, Jia-Shing Li, Tyng-Ruey Chuang, and Jenq Kuen Lee. Probabilistic inference schemes for sparsity structures of fortran 90 array intrinsics. In *Proceedings of the 2001 International Conference on Parallel Processing*, September 2001.

7. D. Chen, W. Zhao, and H. Ru. Design and implementation issues of intrinsic functions for embedded dsp processors. In *Proceedings of the ACM SIGPLAN International Conference on Signal Processing Applications and Technology (ICSPAT'97)*, pages 505–509, September 1997.

8. Naji Ghazal, Richard Newton, and Jan Rabaey. Predicting performance potential of modern dsps. In *Proceedings of IEEE/ACM Design Automation Conference (DAC)*, June 2000.

9. SPAM Research Group. *SPAM Compiler User's Manual*, September 1997. *http://www.ee.princeton.edu/spam/*.

10. Stanford Compiler Group. *The SUIF Library*, 1994. *http://suif.stanford.edu/suif/suif1/docs/suif_toc.html*.

11. G. Hadjiyiannis, S. Hanono, and S. Devadas. Isdl: An instruction set description language for retargetability. In *Proceedings of ACM/IEEE Design Automation Conference*, October 1997.

12. Ashok Halambi, Peter Grun, Vijay Ganesh, Asheesh Khare, Nikil Dutt, and Alex Nicolau. Expression: A language for architecture exploration through compiler/simulator retargetability. In *Proceedings of Design, Automation, and Test in Europe conference (DATE)*, 1999.

13. Gwan-Hwan Hwang, Jenq Kuen Lee, and Dz-Ching Ju. Integrating automatic data alignment and array operation synthesis to optimize data parallel programs. In *Proceedings of the 10th International Workshop on Languages and Compilers for Parallel Computing (LCPC'97)*, Augest 1997.

14. Gwan-Hwan Hwang, Jenq Kuen Lee, and Roy Dz-Ching Ju. A function-composition approach to synthesize fortran 90 array operations. *Journal of Parallel and Distributed Computing*, 54:1–47, 1998.

15. Yuan-Shin Hwang, Peng-Sheng Chen, Jenq-Kuen Lee, and Roy Ju. Probabilistic points-to analysis. In *Proceedings of the 15th International Workshop on Languages and Compilers for Parallel Computing (LCPC'01)*, August 2001.

16. Texas Instruments Incorporated. *TMS320C62x/C67x CPU and Instruction Set*. Texas Instuments Incorporated, 1998. *http://www.ti.com/sc/psheets/spru189d/spru189d.pdf*.

17. M. Jersak and M. Willems. Fixed-point extended c compiler allows more efficient high-level programming of fixed-point dsps. In *Proceedings of the International Conference on Signal Processing Applications and Technology (ICSPAT'98)*, October 1998.

18. J.Glossner, D. Routenberg, E. Hokenek, M. Moudgill, M. Schulte, P. Balzola, and S. Vassiliadis. Towards a very high bandwidth wireless handheld device. Technical report, Sandbridge Technologies, Inc., 2001. White Paper.

19. B. Krepp. Dsp-oriented extension to ansi c. In *Proceedings of the International Conference on Signal Processing Applications and Technology (ICSPAT'97)*, pages 658–664, 1997.

20. Ashutosh K. Kulkarni and Aditya Dube. Benchmarking code generation methodologies for programmable digital signal processors. April 1997.

21. K. Leary and W. Waddington. Dsp/c: a standard high level language for dsp aad numeric processing. In *Proceedings of the International Conference on Acoustic, Speech, and Signal Processing*, pages 1065–1068, 1990.

22. Chingren Lee, Jenq Kuen Lee, TingTing Hwang, and Shi-Chun Tsai. Compiler optimization on instruction scheduling for low power. In *Proceedings of the 13th International Symposium on System Synthesis*, pages 55–60, September 2000.

23. Yi-Ping You, Ching-Ren Lee, Jenq-Kuen Lee, and Wei-Kuan Shih. Real-time task scheduling for dynamically variable voltage processors. In *Proceedings of IEEE Workshop on Power Management for Real-Time and Embedded Systems*, May 2001.

24. V. Zivojnovic, S. Pees, and H. Meyr. Lisa – machine description language and generic machine model for hw/sw co-design. In *Proceedings of IEEE Workshop on VLSI Signal Processing*, October 1996.

25. V. Zivojnovic, J.M. Velarde, C. Schlager, and H. Meyr. Dspstone, a dsp-oriented benchmarking methodology - final report. Technical report, Aachen University, Germany, August 1994. Technical Report.

# Combining Performance Aspects of Irregular Gauss-Seidel Via Sparse Tiling

Michelle Mills Strout, Larry Carter, Jeanne Ferrante, Jonathan Freeman, and Barbara Kreaseck

University of California, San Diego,
9500 Gilman Dr. La Jolla, CA 92093-0114
mstrout@cs.ucsd.edu

**Abstract.** Finite Element problems are often solved using multigrid techniques. The most time consuming part of multigrid is the iterative smoother, such as Gauss-Seidel. To improve performance, iterative smoothers can exploit parallelism, intra-iteration data reuse, and inter-iteration data reuse. Current methods for parallelizing Gauss-Seidel on irregular grids, such as multi-coloring and owner-computes based techniques, exploit parallelism and possibly intra-iteration data reuse but not inter-iteration data reuse. Sparse tiling techniques were developed to improve intra-iteration and inter-iteration data locality in iterative smoothers. This paper describes how sparse tiling can additionally provide parallelism. Our results show the effectiveness of Gauss-Seidel parallelized with sparse tiling techniques on shared memory machines, specifically compared to owner-computes based Gauss-Seidel methods. The latter employ only parallelism and intra-iteration locality. Our results support the premise that better performance occurs when all three performance aspects (parallelism, intra-iteration, and inter-iteration data locality) are combined.

## 1 Introduction

Multigrid methods are frequently used in Finite Element applications to solve simultaneous systems of linear equations. The iterative smoothers used at each of the various levels of multigrid dominate the computation time [3]. In order for iterative smoothers to improve performance, the computation can be scheduled at runtime to exploit three different performance aspects: parallelism, intra-iteration data reuse, and inter-iteration data reuse.

Figure 2 shows the iteration space graph for two commonly-used smoothers, Gauss-Seidel and Jacobi. The iteration space graph in figure 2(a) visually represents the computation and data dependences for the Gauss-Seidel pseudocode in figure 1. The $x$ and $y$ axes suggest that the unknowns of the simultaneous equations might lie in a 2-dimensional domain; however, the unknowns are indexed by a single variable $i$. The $iter$ axis shows three *convergence iterations* (applications of the smoother). Each iteration point $< iter, i >$ in the iteration space represents all the computation for the unknown $u_i$ at convergence iteration $iter$. The dark arrows show the data dependences between iteration points for one unknown $u_i$ in the three convergence iterations. At each convergence iteration $iter$ the relationships between the unknowns are shown by

B. Pugh and C.-W. Tseng (Eds.): LCPC 2002, LNCS 2481, pp. 90–110, 2005.

the lightly shaded *matrix graph*. Specifically, for each non-zero in the sparse matrix $A$, $a_{ij} \neq 0$, there is an edge $<i, j>$ in the matrix graph.

GaussSeidel($A$,$\boldsymbol{u}$,$\boldsymbol{f}$ )
    for $iter = 1, 2, ..., T$
        for $i = 1, 2, ..., R$
            $u_i = f_i$
            for all $j$ in order where $(a_{ij} \neq 0$ and $j \neq i)$
                $u_i = u_i - a_{ij}u_j$
            $u_i = u_i/a_{ii}$

**Fig. 1.** Gauss-Seidel pseudocode

In Gauss-Seidel, each iteration point $< iter, i >$ depends on the iteration points of its neighbors in the matrix graph from either the current or the previous convergence iteration, depending on whether the neighbor's index $j$ is ordered before or after $i$. In Jacobi (figure 2(b)), each iteration point $< iter, i >$ depends only on the iteration points of its neighbors in the matrix graph from the previous convergence iteration.

Tiling [35, 20, 14, 34, 8, 24] is a compile-time transformation which subdivides the iteration space for a *regular* computation so that a new tile-based schedule, where each tile is executed atomically, exhibits better data locality. However, sparse matrix computations used for irregular grids have data dependences that are not known until run-time. This prohibits the use of compile-time tiling. Instead, sparse tiling techniques use iteration space slicing [27] combined with inspector-executor [30] ideas to dynamically subdivide iteration spaces induced by the non-zero structure of a sparse matrix (like those shown in figure 2). In the case of Gauss-Seidel, it is necessary to reorder the unknowns to apply sparse tiling. The fact that we can apply an *a priori* reordering requires domain-specific knowledge about Gauss-Seidel.

There are two known sparse tiling techniques. Our previous work [33] developed a sparse tiling technique which in this paper we call *full sparse tiling*. Douglas et. al. [12] described another sparse tiling technique which they refer to as cache blocking of unstructured grids. In this paper, we will refer to their technique as *cache block sparse tiling*. Figures 3(a) and 3(b) illustrate how the full sparse tiling and the cache block sparse tiling techniques divide the Gauss-Seidel iteration space into *tiles*. Executing each tile atomically improves intra- and inter-iteration locality. *Intra-iteration locality* refers to cache locality upon data reuse within a convergence iteration, and *inter-iteration locality* refers to cache locality upon data reuse between convergence iterations.

This paper describes how sparse tiling techniques can also be used to parallelize iterative irregular computations. To parallelize cache block sparse tiled Gauss-Seidel, the "pyramid"-shaped tiles are inset by one layer of iteration points at the first convergence iteration. Then all of the pyramid-shaped tiles can execute in parallel. This however still leaves a large final tile which must be executed serially and which, because of its size, may exhibit poor inter-iteration locality. To parallelize full sparse tiled Gauss-Seidel it is necessary to create a tile dependence graph which indicates the dependences between tiles. Independent tiles can be executed in parallel. We have implemented both

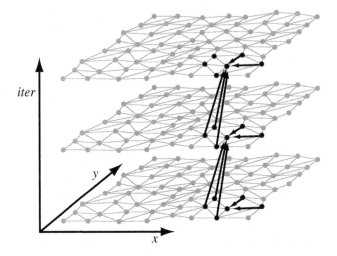

(a) Gauss-Seidel Iteration Space with 3 convergence iterations

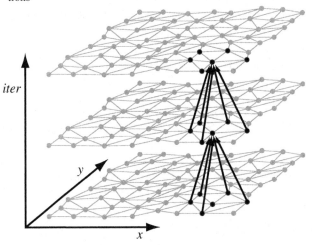

(b) Jacobi Iteration Space with 3 convergence iterations

**Fig. 2.** The arrows show the data dependences for one unknown $u_i$. The relationships between the iteration points are shown with a matrix graphs.

sparse tiling techniques within the same framework, therefore, we can compare their effectiveness.

Other methods take advantage of the ability to *a priori* reorder the unknowns in order to parallelize Gauss-Seidel. Multi-coloring is the standard way to parallelize irregular Gauss-Seidel [5]. It works by coloring the matrix graph so that adjacent nodes have different colors. Having done so, all nodes of a given color within one convergence iteration can be executed in parallel. The number of colors is the minimum number of serial

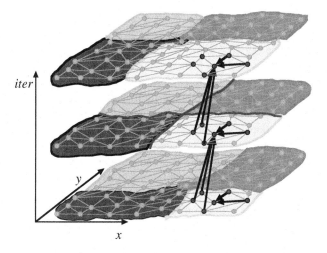

(a) Sparse tiled Gauss-Seidel iteration space using the full sparse tiling technique. Notice that the seed partition is at the middle convergence iteration.

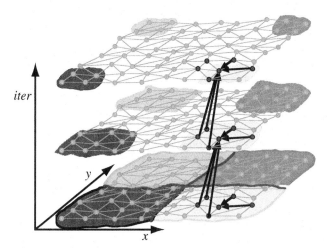

(b) Sparse tiled Gauss-Seidel iteration space using the cache block sparse tiling technique. The iteration points which are not shaded belong to a tile which will be executed last. The seed partition is at the first convergence iteration.

**Fig. 3.** A visual comparison of the two sparse tiling techniques

steps in the computation. Owner-computes methods use coloring at a coarser granularity. The nodes in the matrix graph are partitioned and assigned to processors. Adjoining partitions have data dependences. Therefore, a coloring of the partition graph can determine which cells in the partitioning can legally be executed in parallel. Adams [2] developed an owner-computes method called nodal Gauss-Seidel, which renumbers the unknowns so that good parallel efficiency is achieved. Both of these techniques require synchronization between convergence iterations.

The main difference between these techniques for parallelizing Gauss-Seidel and sparse tiling techniques is that the former do not directly result in intra-iteration and inter-iteration locality. It is relatively easy to adjust the nodal Gauss-Seidel [2] technique for intra-iteration locality, but neither multi-coloring nor owner-computes based techniques like nodal Gauss-Seidel take advantage of inter-iteration data reuse.

Sparse tiling techniques explicitly manage all three aspects of performance: parallelism, intra-iteration locality, and inter-iteration locality. Although current compilers are not able to analyze a Gauss-Seidel solver and automatically incorporate sparse tiling due to the need for domain specific knowledge, we believe that it will eventually be possible with the help of user-specified directives.

Section 2 describes sparse tiling from a traditional tiling perspective. In section 3, we describe how to create a parallel schedule for full sparse tiling and show experimental results for parallel executions of full sparse tiled and cache block sparse tiled Gauss-Seidel. In section 4, we qualitatively evaluate methods of parallelizing Gauss-Seidel, including multi-coloring, owner-computes methods, and parallel full sparse tiling, in terms of their intra- and inter-iteration data locality and parallel efficiency. Owner-computes methods are only unable to provide inter-iteration data locality, so we quantitatively compare owner-computes methods with full sparse tiling to investigate the importance of inter-iteration locality. Section 5 discusses future plans for automating sparse tiling techniques, further improving the parallelism exposed by full sparse tiling, and implementing parallel full sparse tiling on a distributed memory machine. Finally, we discuss related work and conclude.

## 2   A Simple Illustration

Although the focus of this paper is on irregular problems, we would like to introduce our techniques in a simplified setting, using a regular one-dimensional problem as an example.

Suppose we have a vector $u$ of $N$ unknowns and want to solve a set of simultaneous equations, $Au = f$. If the unknowns $u$ correspond to some property of points in a suitable one-dimensional physics problem, the matrix $A$ will be tri-diagonal, i.e. the only non-zeros will be in the major diagonal and the two adjacent diagonal. In this case, the following code corresponds to applying three iterations of a Jacobi smoother (assuming we have initialized u[0]=u[N+1]=0):

```
for iter = 1 to 3
  for i = 1 to N
    newu[i] = (f[i]-A[i,i-1]*u[i-1]
                    -A[i,i+1]*u[i+1]) / A[i,i]
  for i = 1 to N
    u[i] = newu[i]
```

Under certain assumptions about the matrix $A$, after each iteration of the $iter$ loop, $u$ will be a closer approximation to the solution of the simultaneous equations (hence the term, "convergence iterations".)

Our goal is to parallelize this computation and to improve the use of the computer's memory hierarchy through intra- and inter-iteration locality. The simplest method of parallelizing it for a shared-memory computer is to partition the *u* and *newu* vectors among the processors. Then for each convergence iteration, each processor can compute its portion of *newu* in parallel. Next, the processors perform a global synchronization, copy their portion of *newu* to *u*, resynchronize, and proceed to the next convergence iteration. On a distributed memory machine, the two synchronizations are replaced by a single communication step.

In this example, the resulting code will have decent intra-iteration locality. Specifically, the elements of *u*, *newu*, and *A* are accessed sequentially (i.e., with spatial locality). Further, in the $i$ loop, each element u[i] is used when calculating u[i-1] and u[i+1], which results in temporal locality.

However, there is no inter-iteration locality. During each convergence iteration, each processor makes a sweep over its entire portion of *A*, *u* and *newu*, and then a second sweep over *u* and *newu*. Since these data structures are typically much larger than caches, there is no temporal locality between convergence iterations. Such locality is important because even with prefetching, most processors cannot fetch data from memory as fast as they can perform arithmetic.

*Tiling* provides a method of achieving inter-iteration locality. The rectangle in figure 4 represents the $3 \times N$ iteration space for the example code - each point in the rectangle represents a computation of newu[i]. To simplify the exposition, we ignore the storage-related dependences and the copy of *newu* to *u*, but note in passing that this is a sophisticated application of tiling involving two loops, that neither tile boundary is parallel to the iteration space boundary, and that the tiling could benefit from the storage-savings techniques of [33].

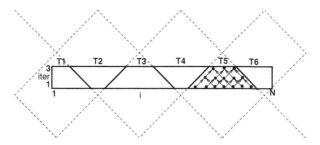

**Fig. 4.** Tiling the two-dimensional iteration space corresponding to a simple one-dimensional regular stencil computation. The dashed lines illustrate how the trapezoidal tiles arise from a regular parallelogram tiling of a conceptually infinite space. The arrows in tile T5 show the dependences between iterations.

In figure 4, there are six tiles labeled T1 to T6. For any of the odd-numbered tiles, all of the computations in the tile can be executed without needing the results from any other tiles. After all the odd-numbered tiles are completed, then the even-numbered tiles can be executed in parallel. Furthermore, assuming the tiles are made sufficiently small, each tile's portions of the three arrays will remain in cache during the execution of the tile. Thus, tiling can achieve parallelism as well as intra- and inter-iteration locality for a simple regular computation. Unfortunately, tiling requires that the dependences be regular. If we replace the tridiagonal matrix $A$ by an arbitrary sparse matrix then the implementation will use indirect memory references and non-affine loop bounds and tiling will no longer be applicable.

We now illustrate how sparse tiling achieves parallelism, as well as intra- and iter-iteration locality. Sparse tiling is a run-time technique that partitions the $newu$ vector into cells that can conveniently fit into cache, then chooses an order on the cells, and then "grows" each cell into the largest region of the iteration space that can be computed consistent with the dependences and the ordering on the cells. The tiles are grown so that each tile can be executed atomically. Since all of this is done at runtime, sparse tiling is only profitable if the overhead of forming the tiles can be amortized over multiple applications of the smoother on the same underlying matrix. Fortunately, this is often the case.

Figure 5 shows how sparse tiling would work on our simple example. The horizontal axis (representing the indices of the $u$ and $newu$ vectors) is partitioned into six cells. In the top diagram, these are numbered sequentially from left to right; in the bottom, they are given a different numbering. Then, each tile in turn is "grown" upwards assuming adjacent tiles will be executed in numerical order. If the neighboring iteration points have already been computed by an earlier tile, then the upward growth can expand outwards; otherwise, the tile contracts as it grows upwards through the iteration space.

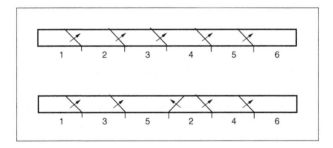

**Fig. 5.** Two applications of sparse tiling to the iteration space of figure 4. In both cases, the data was partitioned into six cells. In the top diagram, they were ordered from left to right. The resulting tiling achieves inter-iteration locality. The small arrows indicate dependences between tiles.

Both diagrams result in a tiling that achieves inter-iteration locality. However, there will be dependences between the tiles, as shown by the arrows in the diagrams. The six tiles in the top diagram must be executed sequentially — tile $i + 1$ cannot be executed until tile $i$ is completed, under the usual assumption that tiles are executed atomically. However, in the bottom diagram, the tiles numbered 1 and 2 can be executed concurrently. When 1 is complete, 3 can be started; when 2 is done, 4 can be started, and so on. Thus, sparse tiling can achieve parallelism, intra-iteration locality, and inter-iteration locality on irregular problems. However, it requires either luck or a thoughtful choice for the initial numbering of the cells given by the partitioner.

In the remainder of this paper, we will move away from the simplifying assumptions of this section. In particular, we will consider higher dimensional, unstructured problems. Thus, there will be more non-zeros in the $A$ matrix, they will occur in an irregular pattern, and a space-efficient sparse data structure will be used. Furthermore, we will concentrate on using a Gauss-Seidel smoother rather than a Jacobi one. This eliminates the temporary vector $newu$. Instead, each $i$ iteration reads and updates the $u$ vector which introduces dependences within a convergence iteration as well as between convergence iterations. As mentioned earlier, it is common with Gauss-Seidel that a reordering of the unknowns is permitted, provided that once an order is chosen, the same order is used throughout the execution of the iteration space. This allows us to choose any numbering on the cells of the partitioning as well.

## 3   Executing Sparse Tiled Gauss-Seidel in Parallel

Sparse tiling techniques perform runtime rescheduling and data reordering by partitioning the matrix graph, growing tiles from the cells of the seed partitioning, constructing the new data order, and creating the new schedule based on the sparse tiling. In order to execute tiles in parallel we construct a tile dependence graph. The tile dependence graph is used by a master-worker implementation. The master puts tiles whose data dependences are satisfied on a ready queue. The workers execute tiles from the ready queue and notify the master upon completion.

The following is an outline of the sparse tiling process for parallelism.

- **Partition** the matrix graph to create the seed partitioning. Each piece of the partition is called a *cell*. Currently we use the Metis [22] partitioning package for this step.
- **Choose a numbering** on the cells of the seed partition.
- **Grow tiles** from each cell of the seed partitioning in turn to create the tiling function $\theta$ which assigns each iteration point to a tile. The tile growth algorithm will also generate constraints on the data reordering function.
- **Reorder** the data using the reordering function.
- **Reschedule** by creating a schedule function based on the tiling function $\theta$. The schedule function provides a list of iteration points to execute for each tile at each convergence iteration.
- **Generate tile dependence graph** identifying which tiles may be executed in parallel.

Either full tile growth (called serial sparse tiling in [33]) or cache blocking tile growth [12] can be used to grow tiles based on an initial matrix graph partitioning. We show results for both methods.

Our experiments were conducted using the IBM Blue Horizon and SUN Ultra at the San Diego Supercomputer center. Details on both machines are given in table 1. We generated three matrices by solving a linear elasticity problem on a 2D bar, a 3D bar, and a 3D pipe using the FEtk [18] software package. The Sphere and Wing examples are provided by Mark Adams [1]. These are also linear elasticity problems. Table 2 shows statistics on the matrices.

In all our experiments, the sparse matrix is stored in a compressed sparse row (CSR) format. Our previous work [33] compared sparse tiled Gauss-Seidel (with a serial schedule) using CSR with a version of Gauss-Seidel which used a blocked sparse matrix format with a different format for the diagonal blocks, upper triangle blocks, and lower triangle blocks. The blocked sparse matrix format exploits the symmetric nature of the sparse matrices generated by the Finite Element package FEtk [18]. Further experimentation has shown that the CSR matrix format results in a more efficient implementation of the typical Gauss-Seidel schedule.

**Table 1.** Descriptions of architectures used in experiments

| Name | Description | L2 cache |
|------|-------------|----------|
| Ultra | SUN HPC10000, up to 32 400 MHz UltraSPARCII processors | 4MB |
| Blue Horizon Node | One node of an IBM SP, Eight 375 MHz Power3 processors | 8MB |

**Table 2.** Descriptions of input matrices

| Matrix | numrows | num non-zeros | avg non-zeros per row |
|--------|---------|---------------|-----------------------|
| 2D Bar | 74,926 | 1,037,676 | 13.85 |
| 3D Bar | 122,061 | 4,828,779 | 39.56 |
| Sphere150K | 154,938 | 11,508,390 | 74.28 |
| Pipe | 381,120 | 15,300,288 | 40.15 |
| Wing903K | 924,672 | 38,360,266 | 41.49 |

Our experiments examine the raw speedup of sparse tiled versions of Gauss-Seidel over a typical schedule for Gauss-Seidel (as shown in figure 1), the overhead of computing the sparse tiling, and the average parallelism within the tile dependence graph.

### 3.1  Raw Speedup

Figure 6 shows the raw speedups of cache blocked and full sparse tiled Gauss-Seidel for 1, 2, 4, and 8 processors on a node of the IBM Blue Horizon. Figure 7 shows the raw speedups on the SUN Ultra using up to 32 processors. In [12], cache block sparse tiling uses seed partitions which fit into half of L2 cache, and we do the same. In our experience, full sparse tiling gets better performance when we select the seed partition size to fit into one-eighth of L2 cache. More work is needed to improve on this heuristic.

While both sparse tiling techniques achieve speedups over the unoptimized Gauss-Seidel, full sparse tiling frequently achieves the best speedups. With cache block sparse tiling all of the tiles are executed in parallel except for the last tile. This last tile cannot be started until all the other tiles have completed, so parallelism is inhibited. Further, the last tile may be large and therefore have poor inter-iteration locality and intra-iteration locality.

Sparse tiling performs well in all cases but the Wing matrix on the Ultra. Further investigation is needed for the largest problem set.

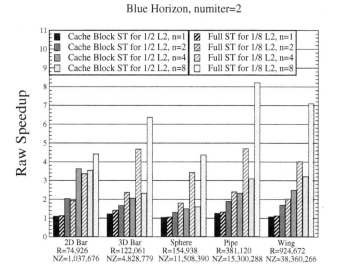

**Fig. 6.** Raw speedup of sparse tiled Gauss-Seidel with 2 convergence iterations over a typical Gauss-Seidel schedule. These experiments were run on a node of the IBM Blue Horizon at SDSC. Each node has 8 Power3 processors.

## 3.2  Overhead

Sparse tiling techniques are performed at runtime, therefore the overhead of performing sparse tiling must be considered. We present the overhead separately because Gauss-Seidel is typically called many times within applications like multigrid. We can amortize the overhead over these multiple calls which use the same sparse matrix. Our results show that Gauss-Seidel with two convergence iterations must be called anywhere from 56 to 194 times on the sample problems to amortize the overhead. Specific break even points are given in table 3. On average, 75% of the overhead is due to the graph partitioner Metis. A break down of the overhead per input matrix is given in table 4. Owner-computes parallelization methods for sparse matrices also require a partitioner and data reordering is necessary for parallelizing Gauss-Seidel.

It is possible to reduce the overhead by using faster matrix graph partitioners and by reducing the size of the matrix graph. The results in this paper use the Metis_ PartGraphRecursive function for the matrix graph partitioning. Preliminary experiments

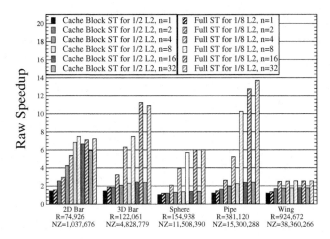

**Fig. 7.** Raw speedup of sparse tiled Gauss-Seidel with 2 convergence iterations over a typical Gauss-Seidel schedule. These experiments were run on a SUN HPC10000 which has 36 Ultra-SPARCII processors with uniform memory access.

**Table 3.** Number of Gauss-Seidel (2 convergence iterations) executions required to amortize sparse tiling overhead

| Blue Horizon, Gauss-Seidel with numiter=2, Rescheduling for parallelism | | |
|---|---|---|
| Input Matrix | Partition Time | Data Reordering |
| Matrix9 | 78.92% | 14.06% |
| Matrix12 | 71.89% | 13.42% |
| Sphere150K | 67.64% | 16.53% |
| PipeOT15mill | 81.42% | 9.73% |
| Wing903K | 83.58% | 9.95% |

**Table 4.** Break down of the overhead time. Around 80% to 90% of the overhead is due to partitioning the matrix graph plus reordering the unknown vector, right-hand side, and sparse matrix.

| Blue Horizon, Gauss-Seidel with numiter=2, Rescheduling for parallelism | | |
|---|---|---|
| Input Matrix | Partition Time | Data Reordering |
| Matrix9 | 78.92% | 14.06% |
| Matrix12 | 71.89% | 13.42% |
| Sphere150K | 67.64% | 16.53% |
| PipeOT15mill | 81.42% | 9.73% |
| Wing903K | 83.58% | 9.95% |

show that the Metis_PartGraphKway function is much faster, and the resulting raw speedups decrease only slightly. We are also experimenting with the GPART partitioner [16].

Previous sparse tiling work [33, 12] performed full sparse tiling and cache block sparse tiling on the input mesh, instead of the resulting matrix graph. Since there are often multiple unknowns per mesh node in a finite element problem, the resulting matrix graph will have multiple rows with the same non-zero structure. In such cases, the mesh will be $d^2$ times smaller than the resulting sparse matrix, where $d$ is the number of unknowns per mesh node. Future work will consider compressing general matrix graphs by discovering rows with the same non-zero structure.

### 3.3    Increasing Parallelism with Graph Coloring

The degree of parallelism within sparse tiled Gauss-Seidel is a function of the tile dependence graph. Specifically, the height of the tile dependence graph indicates the critical path of the computation. A more useful metric in determining the amount of parallelism available is the total number of tiles divided by the height of the tile dependence graph, which we refer to as the average parallelism.

For example, figure 5 gives two sparse tilings of the same iteration space graph. The tile dependence graphs for those sparse tilings are shown in figure 8. The first tile dependence graph, which exhibits no parallelism, has height equal to 6 and average parallelism equal to 1. The second tile dependence graph has height 3 and average parallelism 2. Therefore, the second sparse tiling has enough parallelism to keep two processors busy, assuming that each tile requires roughly the same amount of computation time.

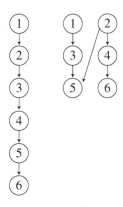

**Fig. 8.** Tile dependence graphs for the sparse tilings shown in figure 5. Each circle represents a tile, and arrows represent data flow dependences. For example, in the first tile dependence graph, tile 1 must execute before tile 2.

Potentially we can execute the second sparse tiling twice as fast. The two sparse tilings differ in their original numbering of the cells of the seed partition. The tile growth algorithms use that numbering to indicate the execution order for adjacent tiles, thus the partition numbering affects the data dependence direction between tiles.

We compared the partition numbering provided by Metis, a random numbering, and a numbering based on a coloring of the partition graph. The partition graph is an undirected graph with a node for each cell of the matrix graph partitioning. When cells $A$ and $B$ share an edge or multiple edges in the matrix graph, there is an edge $(A, B)$ in the partition graph. We color the nodes of the partition graph, and then assign consecutive numbers to the cells of the partitioning which correspond to nodes of a given color. This way, the tiles grown from the cells of a given color will probably not be data dependent. After tile growth, the data dependences between tiles must be calculated to insure correctness, since even though two partition cells are not adjacent, the tiles grown from the cells may be dependent. In our experiments, we use the greedy heuristic provided in the Graph Coloring Programs [10] to color the partition graph.

The graph in figure 9 shows the average parallelism for four different matrices with full sparse tiling using cells that fit into one eighth of an 8 MB L2 cache. Using graph coloring on the partition graph uniformly improves the degree of parallelism.

The importance of the average parallelism in the tile dependence graph can be seen when we examine the raw speedup of full sparse tiled Gauss-Seidel using the three different partition numberings. In figure 10, notice that the top two lines with speedups for the Pipe matrix show nearly linear speedup, corresponding to the fact that average parallelism for the Pipe matrix is over 16 for a random partition numbering and a graph coloring based partition numbering. However, the speedup is much less than linear when the number of processors is larger than the average parallelism in the tile dependence graph, as illustrated by the other four lines of figure 10.

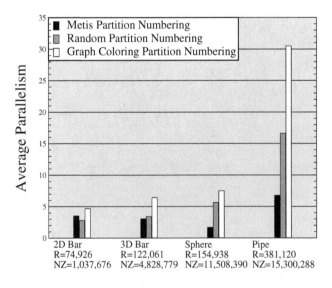

**Fig. 9.** The average parallelism in the tile dependence graph for full sparse tiled Gauss-Seidel with 2 convergence iterations

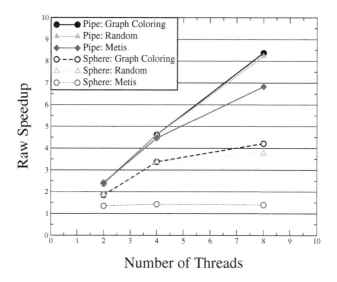

**Fig. 10.** The effect that average parallelism has on speedup for full sparse tiled Gauss-Seidel with 2 convergence iterations

## 4  Comparison with Other Gauss-Seidel Parallelization Techniques

Sparse tiling techniques differ from other Gauss-Seidel parallelization techniques, specifically multicoloring and owner-computes methods, in their focus on improving intra- and inter-iteration locality. Since in all these parallelization methods each processor is given an approximately equal amount of work, less than linear speedup may be due to parallel inefficiencies and/or poor data locality. In this section we compare the parallel efficiency, intra-iteration locality, and inter-iteration locality of multi-coloring, owner-computes methods, and sparse tiling techniques.

**Table 5.** Summary of how the various Gauss-Seidel parallelization techniques compare in how they handle the three performance aspects

|  | Parallel Efficiency | Intra-iteration locality | Inter-iteration locality |
|---|---|---|---|
| Multi-coloring | yes | no | no |
| Owner-computes | yes | yes | no |
| Sparse tiling | yes | yes | yes |

### 4.1  Parallel Efficiency

In shared memory parallel processing, the synchronization time is the amount of time that processors are waiting for data dependent results that are generated by other processors. Parallel efficiency occurs when the synchronization time is minimized. For owner-computes parallelized Gauss-Seidel there is intra-iteration synchronization because adjacent cells of the matrix graph partitioning will depend on each other. Nodal Gauss-Seidel reorders the unknowns so that intra-iteration synchronization is hidden and therefore parallel efficiency is maintained.

For multi-coloring and owner-computes methods, as long as each processor is given approximately the same number of unknowns and associated matrix rows, the synchronization barrier between convergence iterations will not cause much parallel inefficiency.

Because they group multiple convergence iterations together, sparse tiling techniques only have synchronization issues between tiles, instead of intra-iteration and inter-iteration synchronization. As long as the tile dependence graph has enough parallelism to feed the available processors, full sparse tiled Gauss-Seidel should have good parallel efficiency.

### 4.2  Intra-iteration locality

Multi-coloring techniques have poor intra-iteration locality because in order for iteration point $< iter, v >$ to be executed in parallel with other iteration points, $< iter, v >$ must not be a neighbor of the other iteration points. However, neighboring iteration points reuse the same data. When executing many iteration points that are not neighbors, data reuse is not local.

Owner-computes methods like nodal Gauss-Seidel can easily improve their intra-iteration locality by further partitioning the sub-matrix on each processor, and reordering the unknowns based on that partitioning [16].

The partitions used to grow sparse tiles are selected to be small enough to fit into (some level of) cache. Therefore the data reordering will result in intra-iteration locality.

### 4.3  Inter-iteration locality

Both multicolored and owner-computes Gauss-Seidel execute all the iteration points within one convergence iteration before continuing to the next convergence iteration. If the subset of unknowns (and their associated sparse matrix rows) assigned to a processor do not fit into a level of cache then no inter-iteration locality occurs.

Sparse tiling techniques subdivide the iteration space so that multiple convergence iterations over a subset of the unknowns occur atomically, thus improving the inter-iteration locality.

### 4.4  Experimental Comparison

Since owner-computes methods differ from sparse tiling methods only by their lack of inter-iteration locality, we compare the two by simulating an owner-computes method. We refer to the experiment as a simulation because the Gauss-Seidel dependences are violated in order to give the owner-computes method perfect intra-iteration parallel efficiency. This simulates the performance of a complete Nodal Gauss-Seidel implementation which has good intra-iteration parallel efficiency. Inter-iteration parallel efficiency within the owner-computes simulation is achieved by giving each processor the same number of unknowns. Finally, intra-iteration locality is provided by partitioning the sub-matrix graph on each processor and then reordering the unknowns accordingly.

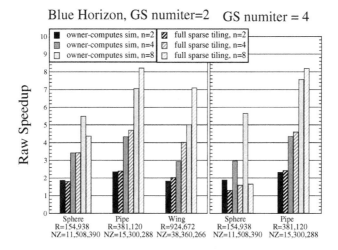

**Fig. 11.** Full sparse tiled Gauss-Seidel with 2 and 4 convergence iterations compared with the owner-computes simulation. These experiments were run on one node of the IBM Blue Horizon at SDSC.

The Sphere, Pipe, and Wing problems are the only data sets that do not fit into L2 cache once the data is partitioned for parallelism. The Sphere matrix has an average number of non-zeros per row of 74.28 (as shown in table 2). This causes sparse tiles to grow rapidly and therefore results in poor parallelism in the tile dependence graph. Recall in figure 9 that the maximum average parallelism was 7.5 for 2 convergence iterations when tiled for the Blue Horizon's L2 caches. This average parallelism worsens to 3.2 for 4 convergence iterations. The lack of parallelism causes poor performance in the full sparse tiled Gauss-Seidel on the Blue Horizon for the Sphere dataset (figure 11). However, with the Pipe and Wing matrices the average number of non-zeros per row is much lower at 40.15 and 41.49. Correspondingly, the average parallelism when tiling for one-eighth of the Blue Horizon L2 cache is 30.5 and 56.6 for 2 convergence iterations. Therefore for 2, 4, or 8 processors there is plenty of parallelism for the Pipe and Wing problems on the Blue Horizon.

On the Ultra (results shown in figure 12), the L2 cache is smaller so more tiles were used to fit into one-eighth of the L2 cache. This increased the average parallelism for the Sphere problem to 9.3 for Gauss-Seidel with 2 convergence iterations. The speedup on the Ultra for the Sphere problem is maximized around 6 even though there is more parallelism available. When sparse tiling Sphere Gauss-Seidel for 3 convergence iterations the average parallelism for Sphere reduces to 4.66, and the full sparse tiled speedup never hits 3. The owner-computes simulation outperforms full sparse tiling in this instance, because in this one case full sparse tiling doesn't generate enough parallelism.

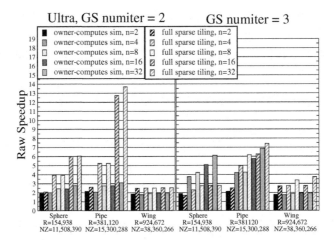

**Fig. 12.** Full sparse tiled Gauss-Seidel with 2 and 3 convergence iterations compared with the owner-computes simulation. These experiments were run on the SUN HPC10000 at SDSC.

The Wing results on the Ultra are curious. The tile dependence graph for 2 convergence iterations has 90.5 average parallelism and for 3 convergence iterations has 82.3 average parallelism. However, even though the Wing problem has been rescheduled for parallelism, inter-iteration locality, and intra-iteration locality, the speedup never breaks 4. We conjecture that this is due to the size of the problem and possible limits on the Ultra.

Our experiments show that as long as the tile dependence graph generated by full sparse tiling has enough parallelism, full sparse tiled Gauss-Seidel out performs owner-computes methods on shared memory architectures. Our owner-computes simulation made idealized assumptions about the intra-iteration parallel efficiency and added intra-iteration locality. These results show that inter-iteration locality is an important performance aspect that owner-computes methods are missing.

## 5  Future Work

Automating the use of sparse tiling techniques is an important next step to increase the usefulness of such techniques. Sparse tiling techniques use domain-specific information in order to reschedule Gauss-Seidel for parallelism, intra-iteration locality, and inter-iteration locality. Currently a number of research projects are exploring ways of optimizing the use of domain-specific libraries. Sparse tiling is most applicable to libraries which contain a large amount of sparse matrix iterative computations.

ROSE [28] is a system which generates domain-specific preprocessors. Their framework supports translating the general abstract syntax tree (AST) to a higher-level domain-specific AST, on which transformations for performance optimizations can then be performed. Interface compilation [13] and telescoping languages [9] also look at ways of optimizing uses of library interfaces. Others have looked at the specific example of compiler transformations for Matlab which is a domain-specific language [4].

Being able to attach domain-specific semantics to the library interface would allow us to construct a preprocessor which recognizes that the unknown vector being passed to a Gauss-Seidel function may be *a priori* reordered.

The Broadway compiler [7] allows the library expert to specify annotations for domain-specific, higher-level dataflow analysis. We can apply these ideas to determine what other data structures will be affected by doing an *a priori* reordering of the unknown vector in a Gauss-Seidel invocation.

Another important step for sparse tiling techniques will be the ability to run on distributed memory machines. This will require calculating the data footprint of all the tiles and creating an allocation of tiles to processors which results in parallel efficiency.

Finally, sparse matrices with a large ratio of non-zeros to rows result in tiles with many more dependences than the original cells of the seed partitioning. It might be possible to add edges to the partition graph before coloring it, so that the final tile dependence graph will have fewer dependences.

## 6    Related Work

Both iteration space slicing [27] and data shackling [23] are techniques which divide up the iteration space based on an initial data partition. This is exactly what sparse tiling does, but sparse tiling handles irregular iteration space graphs, whereas iteration space slicing and data shackling are applicable in loops with affine loop bounds and array references.

Since the smoother dominates the computation time in multigrid methods, much work revolves around parallelizing the smoother. This paper focuses on parallelizing an existing iterative algorithm with good convergence properties, Gauss-Seidel. Another approach is to use smoothers which are easily parallelizable like domain decomposition [31], blocked Jacobi, or blocked Gauss-Seidel [17]. Relative to Gauss-Seidel these approaches have less favorable convergence properties. For example, the convergence rate depends on the number of processors and degrades as this number increases [15].

There has also been work on run-time techniques for improving the intra-iteration locality for irregular grids which applies a data reordering and computation rescheduling within a single convergence iteration [25, 26, 11, 19, 16]. Some of these techniques do not apply to Gauss-Seidel because it has data dependences within the convergence iteration. We use graph partitioning of the sub-matrices to give our owner-computes simulation better intra-iteration locality.

Work which looks at inter-iteration locality on regular grids includes [6], [32], [29], [21], and [36]. The only other technique to our knowledge which handles inter-iteration locality for irregular meshes is unstructured cache-blocking by Douglas et al.[12]. We have implemented this technique in our experimental framework and refer to it as cache block sparse tiling in this paper.

## 7    Conclusion

Sparse tiling explicitly creates intra-iteration locality, inter-iteration locality, and parallelism for irregular Gauss-Seidel. The combination of these three performance aspects results in high performance. This paper describes how full sparse tiling can be used to parallelize Gauss-Seidel by creating a tile dependence graph. Full sparse-tiled Gauss-Seidel is compared with an owner-computes based parallelization, and when all aspects of performance are available, sparse tiled Gauss-Seidel has better speedups, due to the lack of inter-iteration locality in owner-computes based methods.

## Acknowledgments

This work was supported by an AT&T Labs Graduate Research Fellowship, a Lawrence Livermore National Labs LLNL grant, and in part by NSF Grant CCR-9808946. Equipment used in this research was supported in part by the UCSD Active Web Project, NSF Research Infrastructure Grant Number 9802219 and also by the National Partnership for Computational Infrastructure (NPACI). We used Rational PurifyPlus as part of the SEED program.

We would like to thank Professor Mike Holst for his assistance with the FEtk software package and general information about Finite Element Analysis. We would also like to thank the reviewers for comments which helped improve the paper.

## References

1. Mark F. Adams. Finite element market. http://www.cs.berkeley.edu/~madams/femarket/index.html.
2. Mark F. Adams. A distributed memory unstructured Gauss-Seidel algorithm for multigrid smoothers. In ACM, editor, *SC2001: High Performance Networking and Computing. Denver, CO*, 2001.
3. Mark F. Adams. Evaluation of three unstructured multigrid methods on 3D finite element problems in solid mechanics. *International Journal for Numerical Methods in Engineering*, To Appear.
4. George Almsi and David Padua. Majic: Compiling matlab for speed and responsiveness. In *PLDI 2002*, 2002.
5. R. Barrett, M. Berry, T. F. Chan, J. Demmel, J. Donato, J. Dongarra, V. Eijkhout, R. Pozo, C. Romine, and H. Van der Vorst. *Templates for the Solution of Linear Systems: Building Blocks for Iterative Methods, 2nd Edition*. SIAM, Philadelphia, PA, 1994.
6. Frederico Bassetti, Kei Davis, and Dan Quinlan. Optimizing transformations of stencil operations for parallel object-oriented scientific frameworks on cache-based architectures. *Lecture Notes in Computer Science*, 1505, 1998.
7. Emergy Berger, Calvin Lin, and Samuel Z. Guyer. Customizing software libraries for performance portability. In *10th SIAM Conference on Parallel Processing for Scientific Computing*, March 2001.
8. Steve Carr and Ken Kennedy. Compiler blockability of numerical algorithms. *The Journal of Supercomputing*, pages 114–124, November 1992.
9. Arun Chauhan and Ken Kennedy. Optimizing strategies for telescoping languages: Procedure strength reduction and procedure vectorization. In *Proceedings of the 15th ACM International Conference on Supercomputing*, pages 92–102, New York, 2001.
10. Joseph Culberson. Graph coloring programs. http://www.cs.ualberta.ca/~joe/Coloring/Colorsrc/index.html.

11. Chen Ding and Ken Kennedy. Improving cache performance in dynamic applications through data and computation reorganization at run time. In *Proceedings of the ACM SIGPLAN '99 Conference on Programming Language Design and Implementation*, pages 229–241, Atlanta, Georgia, May 1–4, 1999.

12. Craig C. Douglas, Jonathan Hu, Markus Kowarschik, Ulrich Rüde, and Christian Weiß. Cache Optimization for Structured and Unstructured Grid Multigrid. *Electronic Transaction on Numerical Analysis*, pages 21–40, February 2000.

13. Dawson R. Engler. Interface compilation: Steps toward compiling program interfaces as languages. *IEEE Transactions on Software Engineering*, 25(3):387–400, May/June 1999.

14. Dennis Gannon, William Jalby, and Kyle Gallivan. Strategies for cache and local memory management by global program transformation. *Journal of Parallel and Distributed Computing*, 5(5):587–616, October 1988.

15. M.J. Hagger. Automatic domain decomposition on unstructured grids (doug). *Advances in Computational Mathematics*, (9):281–310, 1998.

16. Hwansoo Han and Chau-Wen Tseng. A comparison of locality transformations for irregular codes. In *5th International Workshop on Languages, Compilers, and Run-time Systems for Scalable Computers (LCR'2000)*. Springer, 2000.

17. Van Emden Henson and Ulrike Meier Yang. BoomerAMG: A parallel algebraic multigrid solver and preconditioner. *Applied Numerical Mathematics: Transactions of IMACS*, 41(1):155–177, 2002.

18. Michael Holst. Fetk - the finite element tool kit. http://www.fetk.org.

19. Eun-Jin Im. *Optimizing the Performance of Sparse Matrix-Vector Multiply*. Ph.d. thesis, University of California, Berkeley, May 2000.

20. F. Irigoin and R. Triolet. Supernode partitioning. In *Proceedings of the 15th Annual ACM SIGPLAN Symposium on Priniciples of Programming Languages*, pages 319–329, 1988.

21. Guohua Jin, John Mellor-Crummey, and Robert Fowler. Increasing temporal locality with skewing and recursive blocking. In *SC2001: High Performance Networking and Computing*, Denver, Colorodo, November 2001. ACM Press and IEEE Computer Society Press.

22. George Karypis and Vipin Kumar. Multilevel $k$-way partitioning scheme for irregular graphs. *Journal of Parallel and Distributed Computing*, 48(1):96–129, 10 January 1998.

23. Induprakas Kodukula, Nawaaz Ahmed, and Keshav Pingali. Data-centric multi-level blocking. In *Proceedings of the ACM SIGPLAN Conference on Programming Language Design and Implementation (PLDI-97)*, volume 32, 5 of *ACM SIGPLAN Notices*, pages 346–357, New York, June 15–18 1997. ACM Press.

24. Kathryn S. McKinley, Steve Carr, and Chau-Wen Tseng. Improving data locality with loop transformations. *ACM Transactions on Programming Languages and Systems*, 18(4):424–453, July 1996.

25. John Mellor-Crummey, David Whalley, and Ken Kennedy. Improving memory hierarchy performance for irregular applications. In *Proceedings of the 1999 Conference on Supercomputing*, ACM SIGARCH, pages 425–433, June 1999.

26. Nicholas Mitchell, Larry Carter, and Jeanne Ferrante. Localizing non-affine array references. In *Proceedings of the 1999 International Conference on Parallel Architectures and Compilation Techniques (PACT '99)*, pages 192–202, Newport Beach, California, October 12–16, 1999. IEEE Computer Society Press.

27. William Pugh and Evan Rosser. Iteration space slicing for locality. In *LCPC Workshop*, La Jolla, California, August 1999. LCPC99 website.

28. Dan Quinlan. Rose: Compiler support for object-oriented frameworks. In *Proceedings of Conference on Parallel Compilers (CPC2000)*, Aussois, France, January 2000. Also published in a special issue of Parallel Processing Letters, Vol.10.

29. Sriram Sellappa and Siddhartha Chatterjee.   Cache-efficient multigrid algorithms.   In V.N.Alexandrov, J.J. Dongarra, and C.J.K.Tan, editors, *Proceedings of the 2001 International Conference on Computational Science*, Lecture Notes in Computer Science, San Francisco, CA, USA, May 28-30, 2001. Springer.

30. Shamik D. Sharma, Ravi Ponnusamy, Bongki Moon, Yuan-Shin Hwang, Raja Das, and Joel Saltz. Run-time and compile-time support for adaptive irregular problems. In *Supercomputing '94*. IEEE Computer Society, 1994.

31. Barry F. Smith, Petter E. Bjørstad, and William Gropp. *Domain Decomposition: Parallel Multilevel Methods for Elliptic Partial Differential Equations*. Cambridge University Press, 1996.

32. Yonghong Song and Zhiyuan Li. New tiling techniques to improve cache temporal locality. *ACM SIGPLAN Notices*, 34(5):215–228, May 1999.

33. Michelle Mills Strout, Larry Carter, and Jeanne Ferrante. Rescheduling for locality in sparse matrix computations. In V.N.Alexandrov, J.J. Dongarra, and C.J.K.Tan, editors, *Proceedings of the 2001 International Conference on Computational Science*, Lecture Notes in Computer Science, New Haven, Connecticut, May 28-30, 2001. Springer.

34. Michael E. Wolf and Monica S. Lam. A data locality optimizing algorithm. In *Programming Language Design and Implementation*, 1991.

35. Michael J. Wolfe. Iteration space tiling for memory hierarchies. In *Third SIAM Conference on Parallel Processing for Scientific Computing*, pages 357–361, 1987.

36. David Wonnacott. Achieving scalable locality with time skewing. *International Journal of Parallel Programming*, 30(3):181–221, 2002.

# A Hybrid Strategy Based on Data Distribution and Migration for Optimizing Memory Locality

I. Kadayif[1], M. Kandemir[1], and A. Choudhary[2]

[1] Department of Computer Science and Engineering,
The Pennsylvania State University, University Park, PA 16802, USA
{kadayif, kandemir}@cse.psu.edu
[2] Department of Electrical and Computer Engineering,
Northwestern University, Evanston, IL 60208, USA
choudhar@ece.nwu.edu

**Abstract.** The performance of a NUMA architecture depends on the efficient use of local memory. Therefore, software-level techniques that improve memory locality (in addition to parallelism) are extremely important to extract the best performance from these architectures. The proposed solutions so far include OS-based automatic data migrations and compiler-based static/dynamic data distributions.

This paper proposes and evaluates a hybrid strategy for optimizing memory locality in NUMA architectures. In this strategy, we employ both compiler-directed data distribution and OS-directed dynamic page migration. More specifically, a given program code is first divided into segments, and then each segment is optimized either using compiler-based data distributions (at compile-time) or using dynamic migration (at runtime). In selecting the optimization strategy to use for a program segment, we use a criterion based on the number of compile-time analyzable references in loops.

To test the effectiveness of our strategy in optimizing memory locality of applications, we implemented it and compared its performance with that of several other techniques such as compiler-directed data distribution and OS-directed dynamic page migration. Our experimental results obtained through simulation indicate that our hybrid strategy outperforms other strategies and achieves the best performance for a set of codes with regular, irregular, and mixed (regular + irregular) access patterns.

## 1 Memory Locality and Current Solutions

When a processor in a NUMA (non-uniform memory access) architecture issues a request for a data item, this item can be satisfied from local memory or remote (nonlocal) memory. Since there might be an order of magnitude between local and remote memory access times, it is extremely important to satisfy as many data requests as possible from local memory. If a processor satisfies most of its data references from its local memory, we say that it exhibits memory locality. It should be stressed that the concept of memory locality is different from that of cache locality. For example, it might be the case that a processor satisfies most of its references from its local memory but still exhibits poor cache locality. There are at least four different ways that memory accesses for data can be optimized in a NUMA architecture:

B. Pugh and C.-W. Tseng (Eds.): LCPC 2002, LNCS 2481, pp. 111–125, 2005.

- *OS-directed static data distribution:*  Under normal circumstances, an operating system tries to allocate the memory that a process uses from the node on which it runs. But once memory has been allocated, its location is fixed. Consequently, if the initial placement proves non-optimal, performance may suffer. Many NUMA OSs provide several directives for static data distribution. For example, Origin 2000 uses first-touch and round-robin policies. In the first-touch policy, a memory page is allocated from the local memory of the processor that first touches a data item from that page. In the round-robin policy, on the other hand, the data pages are distributed across local memories of processors in a round-robin fashion.

- *OS-directed page migration:*  In situations where the initial data distribution does not perform well from the memory locality viewpoint, page migration might be of help. Enabling page migration tells the operating system to (dynamically) move pages of memory to the nodes that access them most frequently, so a poor static initial page placement can be corrected at runtime. Note that page placement is not an issue for single-processor applications, so migration is only a consideration for multiprocessor programs. It might also be important to tune the aggressiveness of data migration. The best (most appropriate) level of aggressiveness for a particular program depends largely on how much time is available to move the data to their optimal location. A less aggressive migration strategy (that is, a strategy that migrates pages slowly) might do just fine for a long-running program with a poor initial data placement. But if a program can only afford a small amount of time for the data to get redistributed, a more aggressive migration strategy will perform better. It should be emphasized, however, that migrating data pages dynamically incurs a runtime cost, which is proportional to the number of times migration is invoked. Consequently, programs whose access patterns change frequently take very little advantage of automatic data migration (if any). In fact, it might even be beneficial to freeze a data page in some local memory if it is found to migrate very frequently.

- *Compiler-directed static data distribution:*  In cases where the compiler provides directives for data distribution, the programmer can distribute datasets across local memories of processors considering program-wide (global) access pattern. The MIPSpro compiler in Origin 2000, for example, provides several directives to distribute arrays across processors' memories. For instance, a compiler directive allows dividing rows of a given multi dimensional array into multiple groups (where each group contains several consecutive rows) and assigning each group to a separate local memory. These directives are very similar to those used in message-passing compilers. Note that static data distribution works only for programs where there is a program-wide (global) dominant data distribution that can lead to memory locality and it is possible to derive this data distribution (either using the programmer's help or using an optimizing compiler) at compile time.

- *Compiler-directed dynamic data distribution:* In cases where different portions of the program demand different types of data distributions (e.g., row-major versus column-major) and it is possible to identify these program portions and the corresponding data distributions at compile time, we can use dynamic data distributions. In this alternative, data distributions in different parts of the program are decided at compile time, but data distributions themselves take place at runtime (i.e., during the course of execution). However, one needs to be careful in applying dynamic data distribution as its runtime overhead can easily outweigh its memory locality benefits. It should be noted that neither static nor dynamic compiler-directed schemes are superior to dynamic page migration as these compiler-directed strategies are not effective when suitable data distributions cannot be derived at compile time (e.g., due to complex, non-analyzable array subscript expressions).

In this paper, we propose and evaluate a hybrid strategy for optimizing memory locality in NUMA architectures. In our strategy, we employ both compiler-directed data distribution and OS-directed dynamic page migration. In the rest of this paper, for brevity, we refer to these two techniques as compiler-directed strategy and OS-directed strategy (although both the strategies are initiated by the compiler). Our compiler takes an input program and optimizes each part of it using either compiler-directed strategy or OS-directed strategy. More specifically, it first divides the input program into multiple segments. Then, each segment is analyzed to see whether the data access pattern exhibited by it is compile-time optimizable. If it is, then the segment is optimized using compiler-directed (dynamic) data distribution. If not, the compiler enables data migration and lets the operating system to manage data flow between processor memories at runtime. This hybrid strategy is expected to perform best for the programs where some parts of the code have compile-time optimizable access patterns, whereas the other parts do not. We believe that most of real-life, large-scale applications fit in this description. In the rest of this paper, we give the details of our approach and present simulation data showing its effectiveness. We focus on loop-based applications where the code is structured as multiple nests and the bulk of the execution time is spent in executing loop nests.

To test the effectiveness of our strategy in optimizing memory locality of applications, we implemented it and compared its performance with that of several other techniques such as compiler-directed data distribution and OS-directed dynamic page migration. Our experimental results obtained through a custom simulation environment indicate that the hybrid strategy outperforms other strategies and achieves the best performance for a set of codes with regular, irregular, and mixed (regular + irregular) access patterns.

The remainder of this paper is organized as follows. In Section 2, we present details of our hybrid optimization strategy. In Section 3, we introduce our benchmarks, experimental setup, and the different code versions used. In Section 4, we give experimental data demonstrating the effectiveness of our optimization strategy. Finally, in Section 5, we conclude the paper by summarizing our major contributions.

## 2   Hybrid Strategy

Our hybrid strategy operates in two steps. First, it divides the input program into segments. Each segment corresponds to a portion of the program code that will be optimized uniformly. What we mean by *uniformly* is that the segment will be optimized using either compiler-directed data distribution or OS-directed page migration. In order to decide which strategy to use for each segment, our approach checks whether the segment can be optimized by the compiler using data distribution and accompanying loop parallelization. If so, then the segment is optimized at compile time using loop and data transformations. If not, the compiler inserts explicit migration activation instruction at the beginning of the segment.This instruction is a call to the operating system to activate migration when the mentioned segment is about to start executing. When the execution of the segment has completed, the migration is turned off. In the following discussion, we first explain our compiler algorithm to divide a given program into segments (Section 2.1) and then discuss how each segment is optimized (Section 2.2).

```
for(i=0;i<n;i++)
  {
    for(k=0;k<n;k++)
      {
        for(r=0;r<n;r++)
          {
            ...
          }
      }
    for(l=0;l<n;l++)
      {
        ...
      }
  }
for(j=0;j<n;j++)
  {
    ...
    ...

    ...
    for(s=0;s<n;s++)
      {
        ...
      }
  }
```

**Fig. 1.** Example program fragment

### 2.1  Dividing Program into Segments

While there might be many ways of dividing a given program code into multiple, uniformly-optimizable segments, there are at least three desirable characteristics for any code segmentation:

- The segments should be small enough to enable uniform optimization. This is because if the segment is very large, it might be the case that different portions of it require different optimization strategies (e.g., compiler-directed versus OS-directed) for the best results. In order to ensure that each segment can be decently optimized using either compiler-directed scheme or OS-directed scheme, the segment sizes should be kept sufficiently small.
- The segments should be large enough to minimize runtime overhead. Working with very small segments can increase the number of transitions between OS-directed and compiler-directed schemes and/or incur frequent dynamic data distributions. Therefore, unless large performance gains are expected, a given segment should not be divided into subsegments.
- The segment boundaries should be easy to handle. More specifically, they should preferably be expressible in terms of high-level constructs of the programming language used. Examples of these constructs are loop nests and procedures.

Considering these principles, we adopt a loop nest based program segmentation strategy. In this strategy, the loops in the code form the boundaries between different segments. Two neighboring segments differ from each other either because they prefer different optimization strategies (e.g., compiler-directed versus OS-directed) or because both prefer the compiler-directed strategy but demand different distributions for the same array.

To demonstrate the working of our program segmentation strategy, we focus on the abstract program fragment shown in Figure 1. Starting from the innermost loop positions, our approach determines whether each loop should be optimized using the compiler-directed strategy or the OS-directed strategy. Once the optimization strategy for a given inner loop has been determined, it is propagated to the (immediate) outer loop if the former is the only loop enclosed by the latter. Otherwise, i.e., if there are other (inner) loops at the same nesting level, the optimization strategy of the inner loop in question is not propagated to the outer loop. In Figure 1, we have two outermost loops: i and j. Let us start with i. This loop encloses two loops: k and l, the first of which encloses loop r. Since the loop r is the innermost, we start our analysis (of loop bodies) with that loop. Suppose that after analyzing the body of this loop (this analysis will be explained shortly), we determined that this loop can be best optimized using the OS-directed strategy. We record this at the header of this loop, and move to its (immediate) enclosing loop (k loop). Since the loop r is the only loop inside k, our optimization strategy decides that the latter should also be optimized using the OS-directed strategy. That is, the k loop inherits the optimization strategy of the r loop. Note that this is a reasonable approach because even if there are statements that are outside the r loop but inside the k loop, assigning a different optimization strategy to the k loop would lead to frequent data redistributions. We next move to i loop, which is the immediate encloser of k. Since i loop contains other loops than k, its optimization strategy is not decided at this point. Instead, our approach moves to l loop, the other loop enclosed by i. If our analysis (as explained below) indicates that this loop should be optimized using the OS-directed strategy, then we decide that the i loop should be optimized using the OS-bases strategy as well (this is because both the loops it contains prefer the OS-directed strategy). If, on the other hand, the l loop prefers a compiler-directed strategy, then we transition from one strategy to another within the i loop. More specifically, in executing the k loop, we let the operating system use page migration for ensuring memory locality, whereas for optimizing the l loop, we use the compiler-directed explicit data distribution, and disable migration during its execution.

After processing the i loop, we move to the j loop. The statements enclosed by this loop but not by loop s are dropped from consideration (as they are not enclosed by any loop other than j and it may not be wise to consider their contribution in deciding the optimization strategy for loop j). Our approach first focuses on the inner s loop and then propagates the optimization strategy selected (loop-based or OS-directed) to the j loop.

We select an optimization strategy (OS-directed or compiler-directed) for a given loop by considering the references it contains. We first divide the references in the loop into two disjoint groups. The first group (called Group I) contains compile time analyzable references (also called regular references). What we mean by this is that the data item accessed (through this reference) by each iteration of the enclosing loops can be determined (without much difficulty) at compile time. The remaining references are considered non-analyzable (also called irregular) and belong to Group II.

To clarify this grouping strategy, let us assume that i, j, and k are loop indices for a given (possibly imperfectly-nested) loop. Group I references are the ones that fall into one of the following categories:

- Scalar references, e.g., A
- Affine array references, e.g., B[i], C[i+j][k-1], D[2][5]

Examples of Group II references, on the other hand, are as follows:

- Non-affine array references, e.g., E[$i^2$][j], F[i/j], G[i*j]
- Indexed (subscripted) array references, e.g., H[IP[j]+2]

- References that contain function calls, e.g., `I[foo(i)]`
- Pointer references, e.g., `*J[i],*K`
- Struct constructs, e.g., `L.field, M->field`

After labeling each reference as a member of Group I or Group II, we calculate the following ratio:

$$R = \frac{\text{Number of References in Group I}}{\text{Number of References in Group I + Group II}}.$$

If this ratio is larger than a pre-determined *threshold* value, we decide that the loop in question should be optimized by the compiler-directed strategy. Otherwise, we decide that the loop should be optimized using the OS-directed page migration strategy. The rationale behind this approach is that if the said threshold value is kept large enough, for the loops with ratios ($R$) larger than (or equal to) the threshold, we can expect in general large performance gains by performing compiler-directed data distribution. This is because the compiler can analyze most of the data references at compile time, and based on this analysis, it can come up with suitable data distributions for the arrays involved.

An important issue in this heuristic strategy is to select a suitable threshold value. Note that while a very small threshold value would use the compiler-directed strategy aggressively and (possibly) would not be able to optimize some loops, a very large threshold value would not be able to take full advantage of the compiler-directed data distribution and (most probably) would occur unnecessary runtime overhead due to frequent activation of dynamic data migration. In our search for an appropriate threshold value, we performed experiments with different values and selected the one that generated the best result for the majority of our benchmarks. We found that a threshold value value of 60% covers most of the benefits of full optimization. Consequently, in this study, we chose a threshold value of 60%.

### 2.2   Optimizing Segments

Once we have decided the optimization strategy that will be used for each program segment, we implement these strategies. As discussed earlier, we use two types of optimization strategies: compiler-directed automatic data distribution and OS-directed dynamic page migration. In the following discussion, we give the details of each strategy.

**Compiler-Directed Data Distribution.**   In code segments where compiler can analyze access patterns, it can use data distribution to maximize memory locality. The data distribution algorithm adopted in this work is a locality-driven technique; that is, it first tries to maximize data locality by exploiting data reuse in innermost loop positions, and then, tries to parallelize outermost loops that do not carry data reuse. To achieve this, it proceeds as follows:

- *Optimizing data locality:* In the first step, for each nest, we employ loop and data transformations for maximizing data reuse in inner loop positions. It should be noted that, provided that the loop bounds are large enough, only the data reuses in the innermost loop positions can be converted into locality (i.e., can be exploited at runtime) [11]. Therefore, modifying the code structure and data layouts to move reuses into innermost loop positions is extremely important for many memory-intensive applications. Our locality optimization strategy is as follows. First, we determine the maximum exploitable temporal reuse in the code. We achieve this using the data reuse model proposed by Wolf and Lam [11]. Second, we apply loop transformations to put this reuse into innermost position as much as possible. Third, for the arrays that do not exhibit temporal reuse in the innermost loop (after applying the loop transformations), we apply data layout transformations to transform their memory layouts into suitable forms. This last step tries to improve spatial locality for the arrays in question. These three steps are executed for each nest in the code; their details are beyond the scope of this paper and can be found in [5].

- *Explicit layout conversion:* Since the first step can choose different memory layouts (for the same array) in two different nests (when optimizing their spatial locality), in the second step, we insert explicit layout conversions codes (also called copy loops) in the application code. The objective of a copy loop is to transform memory layout of a given array from one form to another. For example, if a loop nest requires row-major layout for a given array and the next nest requires column-major layout, then a copy loop transforms the layout of the array from row-major to column-major between these two nests. To do this explicit layout conversion for a two-dimensional $N \times N$ array U, we can use the following copy loop. After the execution of this copy loop, the array identifier U' is used whenever array U is used (in the original code).

```
for(i=0;i<N;i++)
  for(j=0;j<N;j++)
    U'[i][j] = U[j][i];
```

Note that the copy loops used to implement explicit layout transformations are pure overhead, so they should be optimized away as much as possible. Optimizing them means selecting the most appropriate points to transform arrays and transforming the layouts of multiple arrays simultaneously as much as possible. That is, whenever possible, our strategy transforms multiple arrays simultaneously (i.e., using the same copy loop). Note also that since copy loops do not carry any data dependence they can safely be optimized using classical locality-enhancing transformations such as loop tiling.

- *Data distribution across memories:* In the last step, we decompose the shared arrays between processors' memories. In order to do this, we first determine the parallel loops in the nest and then parallelize the outermost loop that can be parallelized. Then, we analyze the access pattern of this loop and determine the how the arrays in the nest should be decomposed across processors' memories for minimizing non-local data access under this access pattern. The distribution styles used by our current implementation are block distributions (i.e., row-block and column-block). Consequently, if a parallel loop implies any other data distribution style, we set it to row-block or column-block (depending on which one best approximates the preferred data distribution style). While it is also possible to use cyclic distributions, our experience with the codes in our experimental suite indicates that in very rare cases cyclic distributions can perform better than block distributions. In contrast, most of the nests in regular applications can take advantage of block distributions. Nevertheless, our approach can be extended to include cyclic distributions as well. In this work, however, we consider only block distributions. Once a distribution is selected, data are decomposed using a directive that allows user/compiler specify a different mapping for each dimension of the array. A distribution for an $m$-dimensional array is specified using [D1][D2]...[Dm], where each Di can be either an asterisk, meaning that the corresponding dimension is not distributed or BLOCK, meaning one block of adjacent elements is assigned to each memory. As an example, let us assume that after locality optimizations, we obtain the following code for a given nest:

```
for(i=0;i<N;i++)
 for(j=0;j<N;j++)
  for(k=1;k<N;k++)
   V[i][k][j] = V[i][k-1][j] + U[k][i][j];
```

In this nest, only i and j loops can be parallelized (as the k loop carries a data dependence). Since we favor outermost loop parallelism, we opt to parallelize only the i loop. Note that this parallelization indicates that the first dimension of array V should be distributed across processors. Similarly, the second dimension of array U needs to be distributed across processors. In other words, the data distributions for V and U are [BLOCK][*][*] and [*][BLOCK][*], respectively. In cases, where there are multiple references to the same array, and each reference demands a different distribution, our current implementation employs a simple tie-breaking strategy. Specifically, for each type of distribution, we count the number of references that require that distribution, and select the distribution with the largest number of references.

It should be noted that using a compiler-determined data distribution such as [*][BLOCK] with a row-major memory layout requires that a given page is shared by multiple processors. This leads to false sharing of data during execution. To prevent this, we also implement a page re-mapping strategy similar to the one employed by the SGI compilers. That is, a (re-mapped) page can consist of multiple consecutive columns. To allow such modifications, we assume that the program being optimized does not make any assumption about the layout of data in memory. For example, it does not assume that array elements with consecutive indexes are located in consecutive virtual addresses. With this assurance, our compiler can do several optimizations such as padding the array portion of a given processor into a full page, or modifying the page layout. Modifying page layouts can prevent false sharing by making the elements belonging to the array portion of a given processor consecutive in memory.

- *Explicit data re-distribution:* If the data distributions (for a given array) demanded by two successively executed nests are different, we explicitly re-distribute data across nest boundaries. For example, if, for a given array, a nest demands the distribution specified by [BLOCK][*][*] and the next nest demands the distribution specified by [*][*][BLOCK], our strategy performs a redistribution from [BLOCK][*][*] to [*][*][BLOCK]. In our current implementation, this step is executed together with the second step above (explicit layout conversion); that is, we transform the layout and distribution of the array simultaneously. To summarize, we first execute the first step for all nests in the code, then the third step for all nests, and finally the second and fourth steps perform memory layout conversions and array redistributions.

It should be stressed that this locality-oriented data distribution strategy has an important property. In many cases, when data reuse is placed into innermost positions, data dependences in the loop are also carried by inner loops [5]. Consequently, the outer loops in the nest become doall loops [13] and can be parallelized without too much overhead. That is, optimizing data reuse in inner loop positions allows better exploitation of outer loop (i.e., coarse-grain) parallelism.

**OS-Directed Page Migration.** In this strategy, OS keeps an array of counters (called migration counters) for each data page. Each entry in this array corresponds to a processor and gives the number of accesses made by that processor (during a given time frame) to the data page in question. Ideally, these counters are updated in each memory access made by the processors in the system. From time to time, the counters are checked and each data page is migrated to the memory of the processor that uses it most frequently. Therefore, this approach operates with two periods (that can be taken as parameters): an update period (which is the time duration between the two successive samples of memory accesses) and a migration period (which is the time duration between two successive migration counter checks and the required migrations (if any)). As an illustrative example, a given implementation can have an update period of 10000 cycles, meaning that the memory accesses are sampled once in every 10000 cycles. The same implementation can also have a migration period of 500000 cycles, which says that in every 500000 cycles the migration counters are checked and the necessary page migrations are carried out. Note that by modifying these parameters the aggressiveness of page migration can be controlled.

In addition to migration counters, we have another set of counters called freeze counters. There is a freeze counter for each data page and it keeps the count of migrations that the page has done for a given period of time. From time to time these freeze counters are checked, and if it is found that a data page has migrated very frequently, it is frozen in a specific memory (called home memory). The home memory can be the memory that would be selected by the OS for this page had round-robin or first-touch page allocation policies been used; or, it can be an arbitrarily selected memory. Note that at regular intervals the freeze counters can be reset to enable the frozen pages to migrate again.

An important advantage of this OS-directed strategy is that it is both programmer and compiler transparent. That is, neither the programmer nor the compiler needs to do anything for optimizing memory locality, other than inserting calls to activate migration. However, dynamic data migration has two major disadvantages. First, there is a runtime overhead introduced by migration. The degree of this overhead is proportional to the aggressiveness of the migration policy used. Second, in some cases, there might be short-lived localities (frequent references, in a short period of time, to the same group of pages by a given processor). If the migration policy is aggressive, these localities can invoke migration. However, when the big picture is considered, it might be the case that it would be better not to act upon these localities as the overall access behavior (big picture) does not favor migration. In most cases, this overall behavior can be better captured using an optimizing compiler.

The overhead due to our migration strategy can be broken into three components. First, there is an overhead due to updating the migration counters (at the end of each update period); we refer to the cost (latency) of an update as $C_u$. Second, there is an overhead in determining the pages to migrate. At the end of each migration period, we determine at most $K$ pages to be migrated. $K$ is a parameter that can be set to different values to implement different migration policies. In our implementation, we keep a pointer the the array of migration counters and after checking $K$ consecutive pages for (potential) migration, we increment this pointer by $K$. So, in successive migration periods, different pages are checked. We call $C_c$ the cost of checking one page for migration. Finally, there is the actual cost of migration a page; we use $C_m$ to denote the migration cost per page. In any realistic evaluation of migration, these overheads should be accounted for. Note that the cost values $C_u$, $C_c$, and $C_m$ are the primary factors for

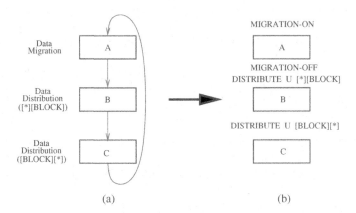

**Fig. 2.** (a) A program fragment that contains three segments. (b) Insertion of compiler directives.

a given implementation that determine the effectiveness of a dynamic data migration strategy. Note that when a data page is migrated the corresponding TLB entry should also be removed. In computing $C_m$, our implementation takes into account this cost as well.

The preceding discussion indicates that it may not be the best strategy to keep migration on all the time and use compiler-directed data distributions for each nest. One problem with such a strategy is that keeping track of migration behavior and updating/checking counters incur runtime overhead. Another problem is the short-lived localities mentioned above. The third potential problem is the fact that (again, as mentioned earlier) trying to use loop/data transformations when non-analyzable references dominate the loop body can lead to misguided optimization which may actually degrade the performance at runtime. Because of these three reasons, it seems to be a better alternative to use compiler-directed transformations and OS-directed migration more judiciously. Our experiments and experience show that most large-scale application codes can be divided into segments, each of which can be optimized using either OS-directed strategy or compiler-directed strategy.

**Switching Between Optimization Strategies.** Since neighboring program segments can be optimized using different optimization strategies, during the course of execution, we need to switch from one optimization strategy to another. To achieve this, we need some support from compiler and architecture. First, to enable/disable dynamic data migration, we assume the existence of two compiler directives: MIGRATION-ON and MIGRATION-OFF. When migration is already on (resp. off), executing MIGRATION -ON (resp. MIGRATION -OFF) directive does not have any effect. Another compiler directive is DISTRIBUTE and has the following format:

DISTRIBUTE <Array-Name> <[D1][D2][D3]...[Dm]>

where Array-Name is the name of the array to be distributed (or redistributed) and [D1][D2][D3]...[Dm] is the type specifier. Note that this directive can be used both to distribute data at the beginning of the program, or to redistribute data (if it is used in the middle of execution). Our optimization strategy can use all these three directives in the same application code. Consider for example the code sketch shown in Figure 2(a), where we have three program segments: A, B, and C. Assume that the compiler detected that the segment A should be optimized using migration and the segments B and C should be optimized using data distribution. Assume further that the data distributions (for a given two-dimensional array U) demanded by segments B and C are [*][BLOCK] and [BLOCK][*], respectively. Figure 2(b) shows the compiler directives inserted by our approach to implement these decisions.

## 3   Experimental Setup and Methodology

To test the effectiveness of our hybrid strategy and compare it with previous approaches to memory locality, we set up a simulation environment and performed experiments with twelve benchmark codes. Figure 3 lists important characteristics of our benchmarks. In this figure, the second column indicates whether the application has regular (denoted R), irregular (denoted I), or mixed (denoted M) access patterns. Experimenting with codes that exhibit different access patterns allows us to measure the robustness of our optimization strategy. Swim, Mgrid, Applu, Compress, Li, and Perl are from Spec'95 benchmark suite. Chromakey is a large digital image processing application. Protocol is a program that implements a wireless application protocol. TPC-D (Q1), TPC-D (Q3), TPC-D (Q6) are C implementations of three different queries from TPC-D which represents a broad range of decision support (DS) applications that require complex, long running queries against large complex data structures. TPC-C is the C version of a database benchmark used for comparing OLTP performance on various hardware and software configurations. The third column in Figure 3 specifies the input used for the corresponding benchmark. The fourth and fifth columns give, respectively, the number of instructions (in UltraSparc) and the number of data references for each benchmark.

| Benchmark | Type | Input | Instructions | Data References |
|-----------|------|-------|-------------|-----------------|
| Applu | R | training | 526.0M | 122.9M |
| Chromakey | M | 44.4MB | 819.2M | 427.7M |
| Compress | I | training | 58.2M | 17.9M |
| Li | I | train.lsp | 186.8M | 79.3M |
| Mgrid | R | mgrid.in | 78.7M | 27.9M |
| Perl | I | primes.in | 11.2M | 4.8M |
| Protocol | M | 16.8MB | 624.1M | 210.1M |
| Swim | R | training | 877.5M | 269.7M |
| TPC-C | M | TPC-generated | 127.0M | 55.3M |
| TPC-D (Q1) | M | TPC-generated | 330.5M | 124.2M |
| TPC-D (Q3) | M | TPC-generated | 582.6M | 270.0M |
| TPC-D (Q6) | M | TPC-generated | 328.6M | 122.8M |

**Fig. 3.** Benchmark codes used in this study

Our optimizations are implemented using the SUIF compiler infrastructure [1] from Stanford University. This infrastructure consists of a small kernel and a toolkit of compiler passes built on top of the kernel. The kernel defines the intermediate representation, provides functions to access and manipulate the intermediate representation, and structures the interface between different compiler passes. The optimization toolkit applies loop-level parallelism and data locality optimizations commonly used in commercial optimizing compilers. Our SUIF implementation takes an input code, analyzes the memory references in loops, and inserts migration and data distribution directives in the code. The compile-time optimizable code segments are also optimized using SUIF.

| Simulation Parameter | Value |
|---|---|
| **Architectural Parameters** | |
| Number of Processors | 8 |
| Processor Speed | 1GHz |
| Memory Capacity Per Processor | 64 MB |
| Local Memory Access Latency | 100 cycles |
| Remote Memory Access Latency | 300 cycles |
| Data L1 Cache Per Processor | 16 KB, 2-way, 32 byte blocks, 1 cycle latency |
| Instruction L1 Cache Per Processor | 16 KB, 2-way, 32 byte blocks, 1 cycle latency |
| Unified TLB | 32 entries, 4-way, 20 cycle miss penalty |
| Page Size | 4KB |
| **Migration-Related Parameters** | |
| Update Period | 5000 cycles |
| Migration Period | 2000000 cycles |
| Freeze Period | 4000000 cycles |
| $K$ (Number of Pages Checked) | 10 |
| $C_u$ (Update Cost) | 1 cycle |
| $C_c$ (Page Checking Cost) | 10 cycles |
| $C_m$ (Page Migration Cost) | 2560 cycles |

**Fig. 4.** Configuration parameters used in our simulations

Our simulation environment takes as input this SUIF-modified code, the number of processors (that will be used to execute the code in parallel), page size, cache and TLB parameters, and memory size and simulates the parallel execution of the application based on the compiler directives MIGRATION-ON, MIGRATION-OFF, and DISTRIBUTE. This simulator only models data accesses and does not assume a specific inter-processor communication network. At each cycle, it executes an instruction from each processor and records whether it is a local or remote memory access, whether it results in a cache hit, and whether it is a read or write reference. If the data reference is write, it invalidates the copies in other caches. When migration is activated, this execution model is interrupted from time to time. As mentioned earlier, our migration algorithm incurs some overhead; all reported performance improvements include this overhead as well. Although our simulation strategy is not extremely sophisticated, it allows us to evaluate and compare different strategies from the memory locality perspective.

Most of our results have been obtained on a *base configuration*. The important parameters of this base configuration are listed in Figure 4. Later in the paper, we modify some of these parameters to study the sensitivity of our strategy to those parameters. Note that with these values, at the end of each migration period, checking for 10 pages (i.e., $K$=10) and migrating them takes 10*(10+2560) = 25700 cycles. 2560 cycles per page copy cost corresponds to a (16 bytes/10 cycle) speed, and is achievable using memory-to-memory copy operations. Page checking cost involves determining which processor uses the page most and whether this processor is the owner, and is implemented using 10 instructions.

For each code in our benchmark suite, we performed experiments with six different versions:

- *OS (First-Touch):* Under this policy, the processor that first touches (that is, writes to, or reads from) a data page of memory causes that page to be allocated from its local memory. Note that this is a static policy; that is, once the pages have been assigned to memories, they are not re-assigned.
- *OS (Round-Robin):* Under this policy, data pages are allocated in a round-robin fashion from all the parallel processors the program runs on.

- *Migration:* This policy starts with Round-Robin but allows pages to migrate between different memories based on the dynamic data access pattern exhibited by the application being executed.
- *Compiler (Static):* In this strategy, the compiler optimizes the entire application code using both loop and data transformations. The details of this strategy is explained elsewhere [5].
- *Compiler (Dynamic):* In this strategy, the compiler optimizes each nest separately using the unified approach in [5]. Since the same array can have different layouts in different nests, explicit layout transformation codes (copy loops) are inserted in suitable places in the code.
- *Hybrid:* This is the optimization strategy discussed in this paper. As explained earlier, it employs both compiler-directed dynamic data distribution and OS-directed dynamic page migration.

## 4   Results

### 4.1   Results for the Base Configuration

Figure 5 shows the percentage reduction in execution time with respect to the First-Touch policy. The average (percentage) improvements due to Round-Robin, Migration, Static, Dynamic, and Hybrid are 1.64, 7.14, 7.68, 7.74, and 15.62, indicating that our approach outperforms all other versions used in this study. In fact, except for one benchmark (Mgrid), our strategy generates the best result. In Mgrid, Hybrid activates migration which is not very effective, thereby incurring some extra overhead at runtime. We also observe that, in purely irregular applications, our approach uses migration and generates the same result as Migration. As far as the regular applications are concerned, in Swim and Applu, Hybrid and the compiler-based dynamic distribution technique generate the same result. In Mgrid, Hybrid outperforms the pure compiler strategy based on static distribution. In the mixed codes, the Hybrid strategy is the clear winner as these codes contain both regular and irregular segments and can be best optimized using both the strategies. The reason that the Round-Robin strategy performs better than the First-Touch strategy is that in most of the cases data initialization loops are not parallelized; in a First-Touch strategy, this causes all data to be allocated from a single processor's memory.

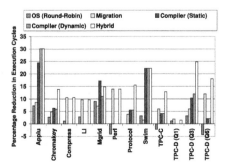

**Fig. 5.** Percentage reduction in execution cycles (with respect to First-Touch)

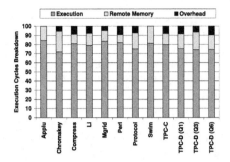

**Fig. 6.** Execution time breakdown of the programs optimized using the hybrid strategy

To illustrate the overheads of dynamic data migration, in Figure 6, we give the execution time breakdown of the programs optimized using our hybrid strategy. In this graph, the execution time of each (optimized) application is divided into three portions: the time spent in execution and cache/local memory accesses (denoted Execution), the time spent in remote memory accesses (denoted Remote Memory), and the time spent during migration (which includes all overheads of updating migration counters, checking pages for migration, and migrating them)—denoted Overhead. We see from these results that the average contributions of Execution, Remote Memory, and Overhead are 78.43%, 15.17%, and 6.40%, respectively. Consequently, we can conclude that in the optimized codes, the migration overheads themselves do not constitute a significant percentage of execution time.

## 4.2 Sensitivity Analysis

Figure 7 shows the impact of migration period (MP) on the effectiveness of our hybrid strategy. Recall that our default migration period was 2000000. We see from Figure 7 that the average reductions when migration period is 1000000, 2000000, 4000000, and 8000000 are 12.26%, 15.61%, 16.19%, and 16.85%, respectively. We also observe that in general working with very small or large migration thresholds does not generate the best results. In fact, for each benchmark, there is an optimum MP, and working with a smaller or larger MP does not bring any additional benefit. This is because a larger MP delays migration and leads to performance loss; similarly, a smaller MP incurs a significant migration overhead. Four applications (Compress, Li, TPC-D(Q3), TPC-D(Q6)) exhibit a different behavior. In these applications, when MP is small, short-lived localities cause unnecessary migrations. Therefore, they benefit from the increased

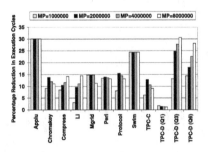

**Fig. 7.** Sensitivity to the migration period (MP)

migration period. In Swim and Applu, on the other hand, the hybrid strategy does not use data migration at all; consequently, their behavior is independent from the migration period used.

## 5    Conclusions and Future Work

Obtaining acceptable speedups on NUMA architecture depends on two major factors: exploiting parallelism and exploiting memory locality. This paper addresses the second factor and proposes a novel memory locality optimization mechanism based on dynamic data migration and automatic data distribution. The idea is to divide a given code into disjoint segments and optimize each segment using either migration or data distribution but not both. Our simulation results indicate that this technique outperforms not only pure migration based or pure data distribution based strategies but also a very aggressive strategy that uses both migration and distribution in each program segment.

## References

1. S. Amarasinghe, J. Anderson, M. Lam, and C.-W. Tseng. The SUIF compiler for scalable parallel machines. In *Proc. the Seventh SIAM Conference on Parallel Processing for Scientific Computing,* February, 1995.
2. J. Anderson, S. Amarasinghe, and M. Lam. Data and computation transformations for multi-processors. In *Proc. the 5th ACM SIGPLAN Symposium on Principles & Practice of Parallel Programming*, pages 166–178, Santa Barbara, CA, July 1995.
3. R. Chandra, D. Chen, R. Cox, D. Maydan, N. Nedeljkovic, and J. Anderson. Data-distribution support on distributed-shared memory multi-processors. In *Proc. the ACM SIGPLAN Conference on Programming Language Design and Implementation*, Las Vegas, NV, 1997.
4. R. Chandra, S. Devine, B. Verghese, A. Gupta, and M. Rosenblum. Scheduling and page migration for multiprocessor compute servers. In *Proc. ASPLOS V,* pages 12–24, October 1994.
5. M. Kandemir, A. Choudhary, J. Ramanujam, and P. Banerjee. Improving locality using loop and data transformations in an integrated framework. In *Proc. the International Symposium on Microarchitecture,* Dallas, TX, December 1998, pp. 285–296.
6. R. LaRowe and C. Ellis. Page placement policies for NUMA multiprocessors. *Journal of Parallel and Distributed Computing,* Vol. 11, No. 2, February 1991,
7. J. Laudon and D. Lenoski. The SGI Origin: A CC-NUMA highly scalable server. In *Proc. the 24th Annual International Symposium on Computer Architecture*, May 1997.
8. W. Li. *Compiling for NUMA parallel machines*. Ph.D. Thesis, Cornell University, Ithaca, New York, 1993.
9. K. McKinley, S. Carr, and C.W. Tseng. Improving data locality with loop transformations. *ACM Transactions on Programming Languages & Systems,* 18(4):424–453, July 1996.
10. B. Verghese, S. Devine, A. Gupta, and M. Rosenblum. Operating system support for improving data locality on CC-NUMA compute servers, In *Proc. ASPLOS VII,* Cambridge, MA, 1996
11. M. Wolf and M. Lam. A data locality optimizing algorithm. In *Proc. the ACM SIGPLAN Conference on Programming Language Design and Implementation*, pages 30–44, June 1991.
12. M. Wolf, D. Maydan, and D. Chen. Combining loop transformations considering caches and scheduling. In *Proc. the International Symposium on Microarchitecture,* pages 274–286, Paris, France, December 1996.
13. M. Wolfe. *High Performance Compilers for Parallel Computing*, Addison-Wesley Publishing Company, 1996.

# Compiler Optimizations Using Data Compression to Decrease Address Reference Entropy

H.G. Dietz and T.I. Mattox

Electrical and Computer Engineering Department,
University of Kentucky,
Lexington, KY 40506-0046
{hankd, tmattox}@engr.uky.edu
http://aggregate.org/

**Abstract.** In modern computers, a single random access to main memory often takes as much time as executing hundreds of instructions. Rather than using traditional compiler approaches to enhance locality by interchanging loops, reordering data structures, etc., this paper proposes the radical concept of using aggressive data compression technology to improve hierarchical memory performance by reducing memory address reference entropy.

In some cases, conventional compression technology can be adapted. However, where variable access patterns must be permitted, other compression techniques must be used. For the special case of random access to elements of sparse matrices, data structures and compiler technology already exist. Our approach is much more general, using compressive hash functions to implement random access lookup tables. Techniques that can be used to improve the effectiveness of any compression method in reducing memory access entropy also are discussed.

## 1 Introduction

Optimization of memory accesses is not a new idea, nor is it new that a compiler should perform the appropriate transformations. However, over the past few years, the natural evolution of computer hardware has yielded a qualitative change in how memory accesses affect processor performance.

### 1.1 Modern Computer Architecture

Logically, processors are more complex than memory, so one would expect them to be slower than memory. In fact, that was the case for much of the history of digital computing. However, through the relatively short history of digital computing, a surprisingly wide variety of different technologies have been used for constructing main memory and processors. Using different technologies, processors and memories have followed different performance curves... both getting faster, but processors increasing in speed at a much greater rate than memories. The result is what we all know: main memory is now much slower than a processor. But the relationship is much more complex than that suggests.

B. Pugh and C.-W. Tseng (Eds.): LCPC 2002, LNCS 2481, pp. 126–141, 2005.

It is true that processor clock rates have been increasing at an impressive rate, but the processors running at these higher clock rates are not the same designs that were used at lower clock rates. Very little of the performance increase in modern processors comes from using the same design with faster gates. For example, the design of an Intel 468DX processor allowed it to run with the then-fast clock frequency of 33MHz and to complete execution of an instruction every few clock cycles. In contrast, the Pentium 4 uses "superscalar" instruction-level parallel execution to complete execution of several instructions every clock cycle — an order of magnitude more work per clock cycle, even ignoring the fact that the Pentium 4's clock ticks at a blazing 2.4GHz. Beyond that, the reason a Pentium 4 can run with a 2.4GHz clock frequency is not simply because it is built using better gates than a 486DX, but also because it carves long logic paths into many pipeline stages. For example, this is why a Pentium III cannot achieve the same clock rate as a Pentium 4 even when they are built with the same technology: a Pentium 4 has much deeper pipelines yielding shorter logic paths for each clock cycle. In summary, processor speed increases are largely enabled by extensive use of superscalar pipelining — all of which comes to a screeching halt when the processor has to wait for a memory read.

Computer architects are very aware of this problem. The solution is to tune the architecture for the kinds of reference patterns that are common and/or those for which performance easily can be improved. Traditionally, the primary hardware mechanism used is a memory hierarchy in which small, fast memories are placed within or near the processor and intended to be used to hold copies of memory blocks that will be referenced with good spatial and/or temporal locality.

The fastest such memory structure is a register file. Compiler writers have long understood register allocation... but there is a twist: the number of registers accessible to the compiler is a function of the instruction set design, so the compiler can only manage as many general-purpose registers on a Pentium 4 as it had on a 486DX. Fortunately, aggressive use of register renaming has allowed computer architects to build hardware that performs on-the-fly reallocation of registers to a much larger pool. For example, the 8 compiler-visible floating point registers of the Intel 486DX turn into 88 within the AMD Athlon. In many processors, special write buffer hardware even attempts to short-circuit-route data being stored from one register into another register which is loading from the address being stored into.

After registers, there are usually two or more levels of cache. Cache line sizes and replacement policies vary, but in general the line size gets bigger and access gets slower as caches get further from the processor. Across processor generations, cache line sizes tend to be increasing in general. Further, most caches now have special provisions for fetching the requested word within a cache line first, rather than fetching the words in sequence.

Even though your program might not use disk-based virtual memory, modern operating systems rely on a page table mechanism to allocate main memory space. Thus, all main memory addresses have to be translated from logical to physical addresses. In most modern machines, this is done by two levels of TLB (translation lookaside buffers) which serve as "caches for address translations." Caches typically are indexed by physical addresses, so that TLBs appear between the processor and L1 cache. The implication is that even if a particular address is in cache, it will be fast to access only if its address is also in the TLB. Although TLBs are often ignored by programmers, they are often very small (typically 32 to 128 entries), so TLB misses can seriously limit performance.

Further complicating all of this, hardware in the latest AMD Athlon and Intel Pentium 4 processors attempts to automatically recognize access patterns and issue prefetch operations. Thus, the old notions of temporal and spatial locality are only part of the story; performance depends on having a memory access pattern that differs only slightly from what the processor was designed to optimize — i.e., that has low entropy.

## 1.2   Memory Access Performance of Modern Architectures

How do all of the above architectural features change how code should be written? The best way to answer such a question is to make some performance measurements on real machines so that the cost of different coding constructs can be accurately estimated. To make the memory access trends more visible, we have restricted our benchmarks to processors that execute the basic IA32 (Intel Architecture, 32-bits) instruction set. This not only eliminates artifacts from use of different instruction sets, but also made it possible to literally use the exact same binary executable on all the machines. Consequently, the memory system effects are not convolved with differences between compilation systems; the one executable was produced using EGS 2.91.66 with the optimizations enabled by the -O1 command line option. An additional benefit in using this instruction set is that all the processors provide the same processor clock cycle timing mechanism.

Most of the architectural features listed above are aimed at improving performance of low-entropy memory access patterns: read sequences that have good spatial and temporal locality or are easily predicted by the hardware. One would hope that repeated references to the exact same word (temporal locality) would be optimized by the compiler to access the word from memory once, and thenceforth from a register. Thus, the lowest entropy memory reference pattern is generally assumed to be a stride-1 access pattern in the increasing address direction. Have these architectural changes achieved speed-up for this read access pattern? As Figure 1 clearly shows, the answer is yes; from the 100MHz Pentium to the most modern Athlon and Pentium 4 an order of magnitude speedup is seen.

It is important to note that, because processors are heavily pipelined, memory access latency can be partly overlapped with loop overhead. It is not possible to separate-out the test loop overhead; any memory access latency that is completely overlapped with loop overhead would appear to be zero and inefficient loop implementations would make memory seem faster. For this reason, all of the graphs in this paper include the loop overhead.

That good speedup is achieved for a low-entropy reference pattern is not surprising. To determine if good speedup is also achieved for high-entropy reference patterns, we selected a simple random number generator — RANQD1 [PrT88] — and used that to

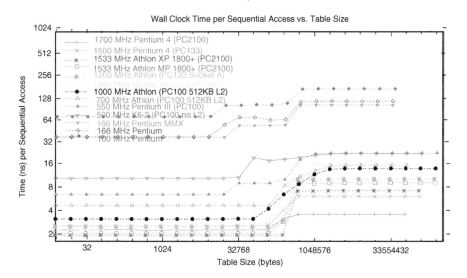

**Fig. 1.** Low-Entropy Memory Read Access Pattern Times

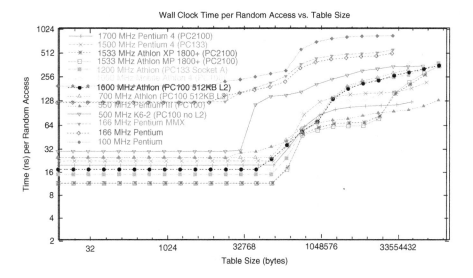

**Fig. 2.** High-Entropy Memory Read Access Pattern Times

generate the address sequence. Ironically, a random number generator does not generate the highest entropy memory access sequence, but is a good model for the type of high-entropy memory reference pattern commonly seen in programs. The good news is that, as Figure 2 shows, good speedup is also achieved for this high-entropy pattern.

However, viewing Figures 1 and 2 together reveals a disturbing fact: newer processors generally have larger differences between the best sequential time and the worst random time. The 100MHz Pentium had only a time factor of 13.3 penalty for a bad reference pattern, whereas an Athlon MP had a time factor of 127.5 penalty .

Of course, some differences are due to differing clock rates; looking at raw counts of clock cycles is an arguably purer measure. These results, respectively for the sequential access pattern and for the random access pattern, are in Figures 3 and 4.

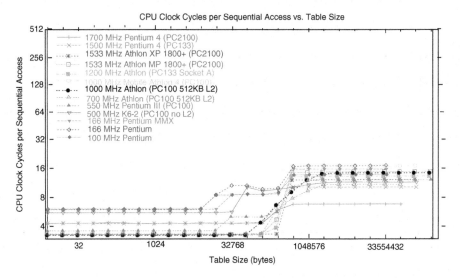

**Fig. 3.** Low-Entropy Memory Read Access Pattern Clock Cycles

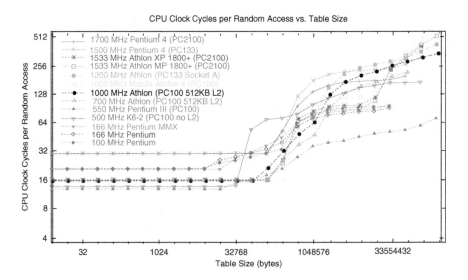

**Fig. 4.** High-Entropy Memory Read Access Pattern Clock Cycles

In summary, the cost of memory references is getting  further from constan t; access times are a complex function of the access pattern with costs currently ranging over  at least two orders of magnitude.  High entropy memory access patterns can take hundreds of clock cycles per read — and  many  operations can be executed per clock cycle. Executing as many as a thousand instructions to avoid a single high-entropy memory reference can yield speedup! This huge payoff makes it practical to consider very complex mechanisms for reducing address reference entropy.  Throughout this paper, our focus is using compression to decrease address reference entropy — in some cases, the total size of the compressed data structures is actually larger than the original data.

## 2   Compression to Reduce Access Entropy

Although we believe the fully general concept of using compiler technology to employ compression for the purpose of reducing address reference entropy to be entirely new, there are a few special cases in which compression has been used to improve memory system performance.

Although our focus is using compiler technology to apply compression to reduce entropy of data references, the work most similar in concept involves hardware technology to operate on compressed code.  Shortly after the invention of VLIW (Very Long Instruction Word) architecture, it was recognized that VLIW instructions often contained redundant or empty fields.  Although the fact was not widely published, the Multiflow Trace architecture took advantage of this fact by having processor hardware fetch compressed blocks of VLIW instructions and decompress them on the fly.  An even more aggressive compression scheme was used for encoding instructions for the complex instruction set of the Intel 432 [ARM81]: instructions were Huffman encoded as bit sequences that were extracted directly from the code stream by the processor hardware.  Although modern processor architecture implementations could benefit from such a hardware-driven approach, the benefit is not as great as one might expect because code stream address reference entropy is relatively low — spatial locality is very good.

Very recent work [ZhG02] attempts to achieve modest compression for dynamically-allocated data structures, but the majority of compiler techniques have been developed to translate code written as "dense" matrix operations to use "sparse" data structures [BiW95]. The sparse representations assume that the majority of data elements have the same value (most often, zero).  Despite this constraint, these compiler code and data transformations, and the associated analyses, are very closely related to our more general notion of using compression as a memory address entropy-reducing transformation.  In particular, the analysis that determines what code would be impacted if the representation of a particular data structure were to be changed is directly applicable.  In fact, the analysis we presented in [JuD92] also would suffice for that purpose.

The generalized problem of using compressed data structures with non-sparse data can be subdivided into four classes based on two simple attributes:

1. **Is the data structure read-only?** Compression algorithms for read-only data structures, especially those with compile-time constant values, can be very computationally expensive provided that the decompression algorithm is inexpensive. If the data can be changed during program execution, the efficiency of the compression algorithm is also critical.

2. **Are elements of the data structure accessed in a fixed pattern — i.e., are they ordered?** Given a fixed access pattern, transmitting the data structure from memory to the processor in that order is nearly the same problem as transmitting the data structure through a communications network — the classical application of compression technology. Note that the access order need not access each element precisely once; a structure containing "a,b,c" accessed with the fixed order "c,a,c,c" is essentially the same as sequential access of the structure "c,a,c,c". If a variable access pattern must be supported, compression methods that make decompression of an element dependent on decompression of previous elements are generally inappropriate.

Techniques for fixed access pattern compression are very well developed; thus, the primary contribution here is the concept of using these techniques as a compiler technology. This is discussed in the following section. Given a variable access pattern and read-only data, new compression techniques are needed. Section 2.2 outlines a very aggressive technique for this type of compile-time compression, which is most useful for increasing the efficiency of lookup tables. To efficiently compress given a variable access pattern and changeable data, the compression scheme must have a relatively efficient method for incremental update of the compressed form. Very few such schemes exist; a very brief discussion is given in section 2.3.

## 2.1 Compression with Ordered Access

Compiler technology for recognizing everything necessary to improve ordered access is very well developed. The required information is essentially accumulated as a side-effect of performing traditional loop parallelization dependence analysis. For example, consider the simple loop nest:

```
          DO 10 J=1,100
            DO 10 I=1,100
   10         A(I,J) = A(I,J) * B(I, J)
```

Within this example loop nest, the elements of B are only read; let us further assume that B is in fact an array of constant values known at compile time. The elements of the array A are both read and written. Thus, the example contains both read-only and read-write data structures with a known access order.

For B, because both the element values and the access order are known at compile time, we can apply a traditional communications-oriented compression scheme at compile time. For example, a variant of Huffman encoding, LZW (Lempel-Ziv Welch), or even fractals and wavelets can be used to compress B. Simple type-dependent compression techniques may be particularly appropriate; for example, although mantissa bits vary, it is very likely that the exponent and sign are the same (or differ little) from one floating point value to the next. Further, because the compression is done at compile time, it is feasible to try several alternative compression techniques and pick the most effective.

The compression of **A** is much more difficult to make effective In part, the complexity comes from the fact that the compression algorithm must be incrementally applied (e.g., wavelets cannot be used because they require examining the complete data structure) and must be computationally cheap enough to be applied at every point where the data are changed. However, the fact that compression is applied at run time also makes it infeasible to try several alternatives and pick the most effective. For many incremental compression techniques, it is quite possible that the result of applying compression would be a data structure larger than the original — with the slowdown aggravated by the higher overhead of processing compressed accesses.

## 2.2   Compression with Variable Access, Read-Only Data

With the exception of some of the sparse compression techniques discussed in section 2, virtually all compression techniques in the literature are incapable of supporting a variable access pattern. However, if the elements of the data structure are read-only and known at compile time, there are a variety of techniques that can be used to compress the lookup table without compromising random access. The basic technology is creation of a **compressive hash function**: a hash function that implements a given mapping using a lookup table that contains fewer entries than there are domain elements.

A **hash function** is a mapping of domain (input or key) values into range (function or return) values. Normally, the ideal is to find a hash function that is minimal and "perfect" — i.e., that implements a domain-to-range mapping by *onto* and *1:1* indexing of a lookup table. However, a perfect hash function only provides rapid indexing: it does not provide compression of the data. In order to provide compression, a compressive hash function maps multiple domain elements, whose range values were equivalent, to the same lookup table entry. A **minimal perfect compressive hash** would have precisely one hash table entry for each unique range value, but any compressive hash function will provide some compression while supporting fully variable random access patterns.

Let $L(k)=v_k$ be the original table lookup function implemented by indexing an array of values, $a[]$, such that $v_k=a[k]$. If there exist two values of $k$, $k_i$ and $k_j$ such that $k_i{\neq}k_j$ and $L(k_i){\equiv}L(k_j)$, then $a[k_i]$ and $a[k_j]$ are essentially copies of the same range value and one might be able to be eliminated from storage as redundant. It is common that lookup functions have many such redundant entries; further, there are techniques that can be used to transform the lookup problem to create such redundancies (see sections 3 and 4). The problem of finding a compressive hash function, $L'(k)=v_k$, is thus the problem of finding an index transformation function, $H(k)=x_k$, which maps into a table with fewer entries than $a[]$, such that for all pairs of values $k_i$ and $k_j$, if $H(k_i){\equiv}H(k_j)$, then $L(k_i){\equiv}L(k_j)$. Notice that $L(k_i){\equiv}L(k_j)$ does not imply $H(k_i){\equiv}H(k_j)$; duplicate entries can also exist in the compressed form, provided that the total array size is still reduced. Similarly, having the compressed array contain entries that are not targeted by any value of $k$ also merely reduces the compression factor achieved. Of course, optimizing the compression factor is not our goal; minimizing average access cost by taking advantage of lower memory access entropy is.

There are many approaches that can be used to search for a good hash function $H(k)$ and the array contents that it requires in order to perform the correct mapping. Fundamentally, the problem of reverse-engineering an efficient hash function from the array contents becomes exponentially more difficult as larger domains and ranges are considered. Achieving higher compression generally has the same impact on complexity of the search, or, equivalently, generates hash functions that are computationally too complex to be useful. Our approach can be summarized as:

(1) Compute the minimum possible size of the hash table, $s$, by counting redundant entries in $L(k)$. If modulus operations are expensive, round $s$ up to the next largest power of two. Also initialize a hash table, $e[s]$ to all "empty" entries.

(2) Generate a potential hash function, $H(k)$, which ensures that, for all values of $k$, $0 \leq H(k) < s$. If $s$ is a power of two, this can be accomplished using bitwise AND $(s-1)$ in $H(k)$.

(3) Evaluate $H(k)$ for all values of $k$. In essence, this is done by evaluating $H(k_i)=x_i$ and then examining $e[x_i]$ for either of two conditions:

- If $e[x_i]$ is empty, set $e[x_i]=L(k_i)$ and mark the entry as full.
  (Serial numbering is often a good way to handle empty/full marking.)

- If $e[x_i]$ is full and $e[x_i] \neq L(k_i)$, record the conflict.
  If the hash function must be perfect, goto step 5;
  otherwise, continue with lossy compression (sections 5 and 6).

(4) Combine evaluations of conflicts and the computational cost for $H(k)$;
    record it as the new "best found so far" if appropriate.

(5) Increase $s$ if the array size seems too small to afford a computationally efficient hash function.

(6) Exit if available search time has elapsed, sufficiently good solution has been found, or $s$ has become too large.
    Otherwise, go to step 2.

Notice that it was not specified how one generates the potential hash function in step 2. There are many viable alternatives. Techniques we have used include:

- Searches of fixed collections of known-effective forms

- Enumerative searches (as per the Superoptimizer [Mas87])

- Genetic programming (GP) [Koz92]

- Adaptive methods that attempt to correct specific conflict(s) from previous hash functions

- Various curve-fitting techniques

Of these, the fixed-collection and GP methods have thus far proven to be most effective. However, further research is needed to find more efficient ways to handle very hard hash compression problems. Currently, overnight or longer runs are often needed to find appropriate hash functions.

### 2.3   Compression with Variable Access, Changeable Data

As discussed above, it is very difficult to find an appropriate compressing hash function for an arbitrary mapping... and the creation process is not incremental. Except when the rate of change of entries is low enough to permit use of a fixed hash compression augmented by a conventional hash table with linear rehash used to identify changed entries, we currently know of no effective approach.

## 3   Accuracy and Range Precision Filtering

Although programmers often take the position that every value computed within their program should be computed with as much precision as possible, what really matters is the accuracy of the results. Precision simply indicates how many bits are used to represent a value; accuracy describes how many of the bits carry correct and useful information. Because various savings are possible in operating on lower precision values, it is generally desirable to make the storage precision of values equal to or slightly greater than the accuracy of those values. The only benefit in maintaining precision much higher than accuracy is that it saves the programmer from having to be aware of what the accuracy of their computations truly is — in other words, it facilitates bad programming practice.

Although integer values are absolutely accurate, the precision required for integer values is determined by the range of values. For example, an integer variable that ranges from 0 to 100 does not require storage with 32-bit precision; 7 bits would suffice. A value that ranges from 10000 to 10100 also can be stored in just 7 bits. In fact, a value that ranges from 10000 to 10200 and is always a multiple of 2 also can be stored in just 7 bits. Range compression also can be applied to floating point values that have a very limited range of exponent values.

Thus, when compression techniques are being applied, the compression techniques should not be constrained to produce values that are identical to the full precision, but only to preserve the accuracy and range of the original values.

For example, consider a typical lookup table. Each entry is usually either the result of a very complex computation or an empirically measured quantity — after all, if entries were determined by a cheap formula, few programmers would bother constructing a lookup table. However, even if complex computations were carried out using very high precision, the accuracy of the results placed in the table is likely to be far lower than the precision of the intermediate calculations used to compute them. Low accuracy also is common for empirical data. Thus, even if subsequent calculations using values from the lookup table require high precision arithmetic, storage of the table entries need not. More generally, a lossy compression scheme that recovers the table entries only approximately is acceptable provided that accuracy is not compromised. Alternatively, accuracy information can be used to filter the table before compression, reducing entropy by changing values to conform with other values in the table when the change does not compromise accuracy.

It is useful to further note that, if the accuracy and range values vary widely over portions of a lookup table, it may be appropriate to subdivide the table on this basis.

Although static accuracy analysis is not particularly difficult for a compiler to implement, an informal survey conducted by Dietz in the early 1990s of scientific Fortran codes then in use at Purdue University revealed that few, if any, results printed by these programs had any significant digits as determined by the standard static analysis. Despite this, the codes seem to produce reasonably accurate answers, apparently with several significant digits. The discrepancy lies in the fact that compensating errors are common and worst-case loss of accuracy is very rare, so static analysis was far too conservative. For this reason, we suggest that the programmer should use a **pragma** to explicitly state the accuracy that should be preserved.

## 4   Synthetic Range Filtering

In some cases, accuracy and range precision filtering are not very helpful. For example, a table of floating point numbers often will have relatively random bit patterns in the mantissas. It may be exceedingly difficult to compress such data. However, an interesting trick can be used to simplify the search.

Let $L(k)=v_k$ be the original table lookup function. If the return value has $b$ bits, then $v_k$ is really the bit vector $v_k[0..b-1]$. Instead of searching for a single compressed lookup function, $L'(k)=v_k$, we can search for a set of compressed lookup functions $L'_0=v_k[0..b_0-1]$,   $L'_1=v_k[b_0..b_1-1]$,   ...,   $L'_m=v_k[b_{m-1}..b-1]$. This effectively synthetically restricts the range for each compressed lookup function, significantly reducing the apparent entropy of the values and consequently making appropriate functions easier to create. Because the bit vectors can be stored as packed fields within a table, there is little or no additional storage overhead associated with the decomposition into bit vectors.

If the compression achieved for the decomposed bit vectors is comparable to the compression achieved without decomposition, having $m$ lookup table references instead of 1 will introduce enough overhead to make decomposition inappropriate. However, the reduced ranges often yield significantly higher compression for some of the $m$ compressed lookup functions. Thus, decomposition into $m$ lookup tables may significantly reduce the total space needed for lookup tables. If this reduction allows the tables to reside in a higher level of memory (e.g., L2 cache rather than main memory), computing $m$ decomposed lookup functions can be significantly faster than performing a single compressed lookup.

Another way to synthetically reduce the range is to convert bit positions that are constant across all lookup values into "don't care" bit positions. The bit positions that are constant ("stuck" at 0 or 1) can be obtained straightforwardly. Let $O$ be the bitwise OR of all the values and $A$ be the bitwise AND of all the values. The *active* bit positions are then those in $O$ AND NOT$A$. The inactive bit positions can thus be treated as "don't care" values within the lookup function(s) and the correct bit position values can be inserted by bitwise ANDing with the *active* set (computed above) followed by bitwise ORing with *A*.

## 5   Individual Exceptions

Suppose that a particular table lookup operation, $L(k)=v_k$, is equivalent to a cheaper lookup operation $L'(k)=v_k$ for all $k{\neq}x$. The single exception can be corrected by code like:

```
if (k≡x) {
      return(v_x);
} else {
      return(L'(k));
}
```

This correction method can be generalized to correct multiple flaws in *L'* by coding either a binary tree or a linear nest of if tests.

Unfortunately, as discussed in the introduction, modern processors are heavily pipelined; thus, performance depends critically on the processor correctly guessing whether to take or not to take each conditional branch. One implication is that the binary tree can be slower than the linear nest because the branch directions are less predictable. In any case, branches often will be mispredicted. We can avoid branch misprediction by converting each if statement into a masking operation like the following C code:

```
t = k^x;
m = ((t | -t) >> (WORDBITS-1));
return((m & (v_x ^ L'(k))) ^ v_x);
```

In this code, assume that *K*, *x*, t, and m are 2's complement signed integers. The value of t will be non-zero *iff* $k{\neq}x$. For any non-zero value of t, the expression (t | -t) will yield a negative integer value. A signed shift right of a negative value by the number of bits in a word minus one essentially replicates the sign bit, making m have the value -1. The same process gives m 0 if t is 0. Thus, m can be used as a bitmask to conditionally enable part of the computation. The returned result is $v_x$ if m is 0 (i.e., $k{\equiv}x$). Otherwise, because $v_x{^\wedge}v_x$ is 0, the result is just *L'(k)*. We can further optimize this code to:

```
t = k^x;
m = ((t | -t) >> (WORDBITS-1));
return((m & L''(k)) ^ v_x);
```

By replacing the table entries of *L'(k)* with $L''(k)=(L'(k) ^\wedge v_x)$;, we can avoid the overhead of one of the exclusive-OR operations.

## 6    "Lossy" Compression

A "lossy" compression scheme is one in which the values recovered from the compressed form are not identical to the original, but have similar properties. In many cases, a lossy compression scheme can yield significantly higher compression than a lossless scheme. For example, JPEG image encoding achieves high compression using a lossy scheme, but the compression technique is carefully engineered so that the lost information is usually visually unimportant. Thus, the question is: how can a lossy compression scheme be engineered to provide similar benefits for reducing memory access entropy?

### 6.1    The Basic Approach

The surprising answer is that a compression scheme that only yields a correct value for *some* inputs can dramatically decrease access entropy. Suppose that a particular table lookup operation, $L(k)=v_k$, is approximated by a lossy compressed lookup operation $L'(k)=v'_k$. It is possible to construct $L'(k)$ such that, for some values of $k$, $v \equiv v'$; i.e., the lossy scheme returns the correct value. Let $p$ be the probability that $k$ is selected such that $L'(k)$ is correct. By using $L'(k)$ rather than $L(k)$ for those values of $k$ that yield correct results, we can reduce the memory access entropy by an amount proportional to $p$.

The only remaining problem is how to select when to use $L'(k)$ and when to use $L(k)$. This can be solved by creating an auxiliary correctness-check function, $C(k)$ that returns *true* only for values of $k$ for which $L'(k)$ yields the correct answer. An implementation of $C(k)$ can be created trivially by using a lookup table with a single bit for each possible value of $k$. However, lossy compression of $C(k)$ also can be applied to create a lookup function $C'(k)$. The only constraint is that for all $k$ such that $C'(k) \equiv true$, $C(k) \equiv true$. If there exists at least one value of $k$ such that $C'(k) \equiv false$ and $C(k) \equiv true$, then the effect is that the probability of using $L'(k)$ is reduced by the sum of the probabilities of those values of $k$ incorrectly classified by $C'(k)$.

One further optimization is possible. Since $L(k)$ will not be evaluated for values where the correctness-check function returns *true*, it is possible to create a residual lookup function, $R(k)$, such that $R(k) \equiv L(k)$ for all $k$ where the correctness-check function returns *false*. There are several different ways to produce $R(k)$.

An obvious approach is to treat $R(k)$ as a new $L(k)$, and to recursively apply the search for a possibly lossy, but cheaper, lookup function $L'(k)$. It should be noted, however, that the recursive application is slightly more complex because $R(k)$ is only defined for certain values of $k$, not for all values between a minimum and maximum. This complication is easily accounted for in the search.

Alternatively, a valid $R(k)$ always can be produced by using an arbitrary (imperfect) hash function with linear rehashing. Each hash bucket in $R$ would contain an input/output value pair; if the input does not match, the sequentially next hash bucket is examined, and so on, until the the value is found. The sequential re-hash is very friendly to both caches and TLBs, so even performing several probes can take only a small fraction of the time required for a random lookup using $L(k)$. Of course, this last optimization applies only when $p$ is sufficiently large; for small values of $p$, directly using $L(k)$ is faster because the lookup table for $L(k)$ is comparably sized or smaller than the one for $R(k)$ — the table for $L(k)$ does not need to hold values of $k$.

## 6.2  A Simple Example

For example, one test case that we have examined is a lookup table taken from a weather prediction code. This table can be viewed as a lookup function $L(k)$, $0 \leq k < 742,600$, which returns a 32-bit floating point value.

It happens that many of the entries are 0, so the table is somewhat sparse — although not sparse enough for the usual sparse data structure methods to be directly useful. It is trivially easy to recognize that a very good choice for a lossy compressed $L'(k)$ is literally the function $L'(k)=0$. There are 297,613 entries computed incorrectly by $L'(k)=0$ (40%). If all values of $k$ are equiprobable, $p=0.6$.

The obvious implementation of $C(k)$ is a lookup table containing 742,600 bits — a mere 92,825 bytes compared to 2,970,400 in the original data structure. This is small enough that both $L'(k)$ and $C(k)$ fit within the L2 cache of most modern processors. However, it is possible to achieve a still smaller cache footprint by lossy compression of $C(k)$. In this case, one of our hash search codes was able to create a 32,768-byte table that can be used to implement $C'(k)$ such that $C'(k)$ is overly conservative in estimating $C(k)$ for less than 0.01% of the values of $K$, essentially leaving $p$ unaffected. However, the hash function for $C'(k)$ is a degree-3 polynomial requiring three multiplies and two adds to be evaluated to index the appropriate byte, which would take significantly longer than the L2-cache access for $C(k)$ — so use of a compressed $C'(k)$ is not worthwhile in this case. If 32,768 bytes fit in L2 cache and 92,825 bytes did not, use of $C'(k)$ may have been justified. In general, the choice is made by plugging-in the cost metrics for the particular target machine's memory access structure; further, it is not necessary to search hash function forms that exceed the cost that the target machine would have for $C(k)$.

Continuing our example, is it appropriate to replace $L(k)$ with $R(k)$? As discussed above, $C(k)$ finds that there are 297,613 values of $k$ that are incorrectly evaluated by $L'(k)$. For simplicity, assume that the recursive approach is ignored and we instead accept an imperfect hash function with linear rehash. For virtually any data, it is easy to find such a hash function that has an average of less than 1 linear rehash per lookup. However, the imperfect hash function must not only store the 297,613 result values, but also the value of $k$ that each result is produced by. Because there are 742,600 possible values of $k$, storing each $k$ value would require a minimum of 23 bits. For alignment reasons, one would certainly round that up to at least 24 bits, and perhaps to 32 bits per $k$ value. At 32+32 bits per table entry, the table for $R(k)$ is 2,380,904 bytes — whereas the original table for $L(k)$ was 2,970,400 bytes. This constitutes a savings of just under 20%, which is probably not sufficient to justify using $R(k)$, because $R(k)$ will be slower for the values of $k$ that require linear rehashes. Of course, if this size difference would allow $R(k)$ to fit in cache where $L(k)$ does not, it would be worthwhile; our example just happens to be too large to fit $R(k)$ in L2 cache on most modern processors.

On a 1GHz Athlon 4 laptop, the use of $L'(k)$, $C(k)$, and $L(k)$ as described above gave a speedup of 1.4x to 2.1x over use of $L(k)$ alone. The variability reflects changes in the reference pattern; clearly, for some reference patterns, the use of compression would yield slowdown due to the extra overhead of evaluating $C(k)$. It is likely that a better compressive hash would yield significantly greater average speedup, but the interesting fact is that our existing software was able to create the above compression scheme quickly enough so that integration of the technique in a compiler could yield acceptably short compilation times.

Generally, read-only data structures that are accessed in fixed patterns are even easier to compress. If the same 742,600-entry table used for the above example is accessed in a fixed order, the lossless compression scheme used in **gzip** reduces the binary data structure to less than 14% of its original size. Optimal use of compression to reduce memory access entropy requires much more research, but obvious cases are worth compressing now.

## 7    Conclusion

In this paper, we have outlined a family of new methods for achieving higher performance from the complex memory access mechanisms used in superscalar pipelined processors. Speedup is obtained by using very aggressive compression technology, especially lossy compressive hash functions, to reduce the entropy of memory access patterns. Decreasing entropy of references is all that matters; adding lossy compressed data structures can simultaneously increase total memory footprint and decrease entropy.

Accepting that some compression problems are unsolvable or would take to long to solve, the new techniques easily could be integrated into a compiler using existing compiler analysis combined with directives or pragmas to help identify appropriate data structures. Our ongoing research centers on more efficient methods for creating compressive hash functions.

This paper represents neither a completed study nor a final answer as to how compression should be used. Rather, it was written because we had long been applying some of these techniques in obscure special cases, but only recently discovered that they have been rendered important and common by modern processor architecture. The evolution of memory systems will no doubt necessitate far more research into exotic methods for improving access pattern entropy.

## References

[ARM81]    *iAPX 432 General Data Processor Architecture Reference Manual*, Intel, January 1981, Appendix A.2, pp. A-13 - A-22.

[BiW95]    A. J. C. Bik, H. A. G. Wijshoff, "Advanced Compiler Optimizations for Sparse Computations," *Journal of Parallel and Distributed Computing*, Vol. 31, No. 1, 1995, pp. 14-24.

[JuD92]    Y-J. Ju and H. G. Dietz, "Reduction of Cache Coherence Overhead by Compiler Data Layout and Loop Transformation," *Languages and Compilers for Parallel Computing*, edited by U. Banerjee, D. Gelernter, A. Nicolau, and D. Padua, Springer-Verlag, New York, New York, 1992, pp. 344-358.

[Koz92]    J. R. Koza, *Genetic Programming: On the Programming of Computers by Means of Natural Selection, MIT Press, 1992.*

[Mas87]    H. Massalin, "Superoptimizer — a look at the smallest program," ASPLOS II, 1987, pp. 122-126.

[PrT88]    W.H. Press, S.A. Teukolsky, W.T. Vetterling, B.P. Flannery, *Numerical Recipes in C*, Cambridge University Press, 2nd edition, 1988, p. 284.

[ZhG02]    Y. Zhang and R. Gupta, "Data Compression Transformations for Dynamically Allocated Data Structures," *International Conference on Compiler Construction*, April 2002, pp. 14-28.

# Towards Compiler Optimization of Codes Based on Arrays of Pointers

F. Corbera, R. Asenjo, and E.L. Zapata

Computer Architecture Dept., University of Malaga
{corbera, asenjo, ezapata}@ac.uma.es

**Abstract.** To successfully exploit all the possibilities of current computer/multi-computer architectures, optimization compiling techniques are a must. However, for codes based on pointers and dynamic data structures these optimization techniques have to be necessarily carried out after identifying the characteristics and properties of the data structure used in the code. In this paper we present one method able to automatically identify complex dynamic data structures used in a code even in the presence of arrays of pointers. This method has been implemented in an analyzer which symbolically executes the input code to generate a set of graphs, called RSRSG (Reduced Set of Reference Shape Graphs), for each statement. Each RSRSG accurately describes the data structure configuration at each program point. In order to deal with arrays of pointers we have introduced two main concepts: the multireference class, and instances. Our analyzer has been validated with several codes based on complex data structures containing arrays of pointers which were successfully identified.

## 1 Introduction

Programming languages such as C, C++, Fortran90, or Java are widely used for non-numerical (symbolic) and numerical applications. All these languages allow the use of complex data structures usually based on pointers and dynamic memory allocation. The use of complex data structures is very helpful in order to speedup code development and, besides this, it also may lead to reducing the program execution time. However, compilers are not able to successfully optimize codes based on these complex data structures for current computers or multicomputers.

More precisely, when dealing with pointer-based data structures usually built at run time, current compilers are not able to capture, from the code text, the necessary information to exploit locality, automatically parallelize the code, or carry out other important optimizations. In other words, if the compiler is not aware of the properties fulfilled by the data structure used in the code, it is impossible to apply certain optimizations. For instance, if the compiler does not know that a certain loop is traversing a doubly linked list, then important techniques such as data prefetching, locality exploiting or parallelism detection, cannot be applied.

With this motivation, the goal of our research line is to propose and implement new techniques that can be included in compilers to allow for the automatic optimization of real codes based on dynamic data structures. As a first step, we have selected the shape analysis subproblem, which aims at estimating at compile time the shape the data

B. Pugh and C.-W. Tseng (Eds.): LCPC 2002, LNCS 2481, pp. 142–156, 2005.

will take at run time. Given this information, subsequent analysis (not implemented yet) would focus on particular optimizations, for example, to exploit the memory hierarchy or to detect whether or not certain sections of the code can be parallelized because they access independent data regions.

There are several ways this shape analysis problem can be approached, some of which are based on explicit programmer annotations [9], and others are based on abstracting the properties of data structures by means of "path expressions" [11], "matrices" [6] or graphs. We have focussed on graph-based methods as they are able to explicitly keep information about dynamic objects not pointed to by any pointer variable. In these graphs the nodes represent the "storage chunks" and edges are used to represent references between them. Some of these graph-based methods use just one graph to approximate all possible memory configurations for each statement in the code [2,12,13], whereas other methods permit the existence of several graphs per statement to represent the information more accurately [10,8,14]. Our own method belongs to the later class, and it is described in [4,5]. Basically, our analyzer generates a reduced set of reference shape graphs (RSRSG) for each statement in the code. Each RSRSG approximates the data structure at each corresponding program point. We have compared our analyzer with other related works in [4,5], but we emphasize here that to the best of our knowledge, our analyzer is the only one able to accurately identify the data structure at each statement of a real C code. The analyzed codes are based on complex data structures such as doubly linked lists, trees, and octrees among others, and combinations of them, such as a doubly linked list of pointers to trees where the leaves point to doubly linked lists, etc.

However, our analyzer was not able to handle arrays of pointers as part of the dynamic data structure. Therefore, in this paper we describe how we extend our method to deal with structures containing arrays of pointers. Please, note that this is the main goal of this paper and that the analyzer details (which are already covered in [4,5]) can not be tackled here due to space constraint. Again, as far as we know, there is no other previous technique able to automatically identify complex data structures comprising arrays of pointers. However, arrays of pointers are frequently included in the definition of complex and dynamic data structures such as sparse matrices and quad/octrees, as we see in Sect. 5, and therefore they deserve to be taken into account in the area of shape analysis research.

The rest of the paper is organized as follows. In Sect. 2 we provide an overview of our shape analysis method, briefly summarizing our previous work for the sake of completeness, as the next sections are based on these ideas. Sect. 3 introduces new contributions to deal with arrays of pointers, such as the multiselector and instance ideas. These new issues lead to new steps in shape analysis which are described in Sect. 4. In Sect. 5 we present the experimental results obtained after feeding our analyzer with several codes based on structures comprising arrays of pointers. Finally, we conclude with the main contributions and future work in Sect. 6.

## 2 Method Overview

Basically, our method presented in [4,5] is based on approximating all possible memory configurations that can appear after the execution of a statement in the code. We call a collection of dynamic structures a *memory configuration*. These structures comprise several memory chunks, that we call *memory locations*, which are linked by references. Inside these memory locations there is room for data and for pointers to other memory locations. These pointers are called *selectors*. Each statement in the code will have a set of *Reference Shape Graphs* (RSG) associated with it, which are called a *Reduced Set of Reference Shape Graphs* (RSRSG). The RSGs are graphs in which nodes represent memory locations which have similar reference patterns. To determine whether or not two memory locations should be represented by a single node, each one is annotated with a set of properties. Now, if several memory locations share the same properties, then all of them will be represented by the same node. These properties are described in [4,5], but to understand the experimental results we have to explain one of them: the share information. This property can tell whether at least one of the locations represented by a node is referenced more than once from other memory locations. In order to hold the shared information we use two kinds of attributes for each node: *SHARED(n)* states if any of the locations represented by the node $n$ can be referenced by other locations by different selectors, and *SHSEL(n, sel)* points out if any of the locations represented by $n$ can be referenced more than once by following the same selector *sel* from other locations.

As we have said, all possible memory configurations which may arise after the execution of a statement are approximated by a set of RSGs we call RSRSG. To move from the "memory domain" to the "graph domain", the calculation of the RSRSGs associated with a statement is carried out by the **symbolic execution** of the program over the graphs. In this way, each program statement transforms the graphs to reflect the changes in memory configurations derived from statement execution. The **abstract semantic** of each statement states how the analysis of this statement must transform the graphs. The whole symbolic execution process can be seen by looking at Fig. 1. For each statement in the code we have an input $RSRSG_i$ and the corresponding output $RSRSG_o$ representing the memory configurations after statement execution. During the symbolic execution of the statement all the $rsg_{ij}$ belonging to $RSRSG_i$ are going to be updated. The first step comprises graph division to better focus on the several memory configurations represented by the RSG. Pruning removes redundant or nonexistent nodes or links that may appear after the division operation. Then the abstract interpretation of the

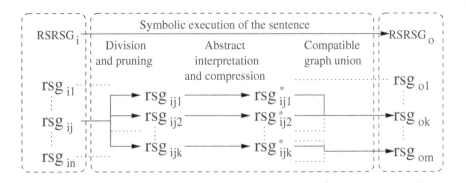

**Fig. 1.** Schematic description of the symbolic execution of a statement

statement takes place and usually the complexity of the RSGs grows. In order to counter this effect, the analysis carries out a compression operation. In this phase each RSG is simplified by the summarization of compatible nodes, to obtain the $rsg^*_{ijk}$ graphs. Furthermore, some of the $rsg^*_{ijk}$ can be fused into a single $rsg_{ok}$ if they represent similar memory configurations. This operation greatly reduces the number of RSGs in the resulting RSRSG.

In the next two sections we present the new extension that allows our analyzer to deal with dynamic data structures comprising arrays of pointers, as these kinds of data structures are widely used in C codes. Due to space constraints we have tried to present a clear idea of our extensions using English and examples, but more technical details are in [3].

## 3   Multiselectors

We can view an array of pointers as a set of $n$ selectors (links), all with the same name. Our original method, briefly described in the previous section, only deals with single selectors (which represent single links). Thus, the problem arising with the arrays of pointers is that a single selector name represents several links, and all of them belong to the same memory location (due to having been allocated by the same *malloc* instruction).

We illustrate all this with the following example. Figure 2 shows an example of a complex data structure definition comprising two arrays of pointers, and it also illustrates the corresponding memory configuration after the execution of the last "malloc()" statement. As we note, *sel* is a single selector which can point to a single memory location and which can be modified by statements like "x→sel=...". These kinds of selectors can be managed by our previous analyzer. However, *sel1* and *sel2* represent arrays of selectors. The difference between *sel1* and *sel2* is that we know the size of the *sel1* array at compile time, but the size of *sel2* is defined at run time. In any case, we now want to deal with both types of arrays of selectors, which now have to be modified by statements like "x→sel1[i]=..." or "x→sel2[i]=...".

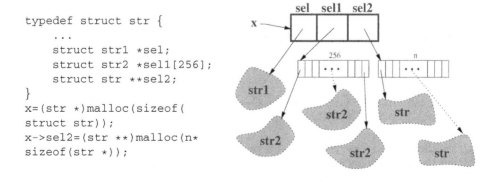

```
typedef struct str {
    ...
    struct str1 *sel;
    struct str2 *sel1[256];
    struct str **sel2;
}
x=(str *)malloc(sizeof(
struct str));
x->sel2=(str **)malloc(n*
sizeof(str *));
```

**Fig. 2.** Example of data structure containing arrays of pointers

Since $sel1$ and $sel2$ are not single selectors, we have called them *multiselectors*. In order to take into account multiselectors in our method we have introduced in our analyzer two new important concepts: **instance** and **multireference class**. The idea is the following: since our method is already able to deal with single selectors our goal is now to include a previous step in the symbolic execution process to focus on one of the selectors included in a particular multiselector. In other words, a statement like "x→sel1[i]=..." is going to update a single selector (a particular selector included in the multiselector $sel1$), but before applying the symbolic execution, first we have to identify the particular sel1[i] which is going to be updated. The instances and multireference classes will help us to develop this preprocessing stage.

### 3.1 Instances

An instance of a multiselector represents a subset of links belonging to this multiselector. In other words, an instance identifies a subregion in the array of pointers. For example, for the statement $x \rightarrow sel[i]$ the analyzer creates an instance in the multiselector $sel$ (the one directly pointed to by $x$), which represents the $i$ position of array $sel$. This way, this instance can be processed and modified by the analyzer as if it were a single selector.

In our method, the set of variables which are used to index the arrays of pointers is called *IVARS*. Now, an instance, $ins$, is identified by two sets, $< ivs, vivs >$ where:

- $ivs = \{iv \in \mathit{IVARS}\}$, is the set of index variables which identifies the array position represented by the instance.
- $vivs = \{iv \in \mathit{IVARS}\}$, is the set of index variables that have previously visited the array position represented by the instance, but which are currently indexing other array positions.

  The reason to keep the $vivs$ set, is to achieve a more accurate description and processing of the link represented by $x \rightarrow sel[i]$ inside a loop body in which the variable $i$ does not take the same value twice. Therefore, the reference $x \rightarrow sel[i]$ always identifies a different position of the array $sel$ and the analyzer will be able to avoid updating regions of the data structures already updated in a previous iteration of the loop.

  The functions $ivs(ins)$ and $vivs(ins)$ provide the $ivs$ and $vivs$ sets respectively. Now, we can say that there are two types of instances:
- *Single instance*. These instances represent exactly one position of the array and they can be handled as a single selector. The instance $ins$ is a *single instance* if $ivs(ins) \neq \emptyset$, which means that there is an index variable in the $ivs$ set for the corresponding $ins$ instance.
- *Multiple instance*. These instances represent more than one array position, i.e. one array region. Now, if $ins$ is a *multiple instance*, then $ivs(ins) = \emptyset$.

We illustrate all these concepts with an example. In Fig. 3 we can see a graph associated with the statement 4 of the code presented in the same figure. Actually, at this program point, the pointer variable (pvar) $tree$ is pointing to the root of the tree represented by node $n1$. This tree root contains an array of pointers to the children, called

```
...     (tree pvar points to a
          previously created tree)
1       for (i=0; i<n; i++) {
2           j = ...
3             if (j == i) {
4                 tree->child[j] = ....
5                 ...
6             }
7             else {
8                 ...
9             }
10      }
11  }
```

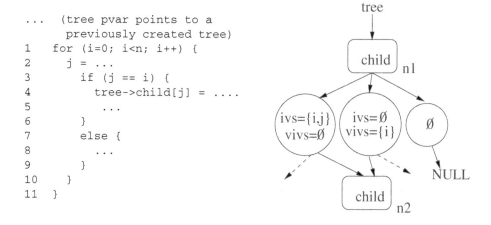

**Fig. 3.** Code example and graph representation of the instances

*child*. Therefore, the node $n1$ contains the *child* multiselector. In this example, for this multiselector, there are three instances represented by three circular nodes.

If statement 4 is reached, clearly index variables $i$ and $j$ share the same value and the corresponding RSRSG will reflect this fact. Actually, the first instance, identified by $< \{i, j\}, \emptyset >$ (which means $ivs = \{i, j\}, vivs = \emptyset$), represents the single array position indexed by variables $i$ or $j$. Clearly, this is a single instance as index variables $i$ or $j$ have a single value at this program point and this way they index a single array position. The $vivs = \emptyset$ for this instance states that this array position was not previously visited by any index variable.

The second instance is identified by $< \emptyset, \{i\} >$. This is a multiple instance representing all the array positions not indexed at the current statement by any index variable but previously visited by the index variable $i$ in previous iterations of the loop at statement 1. Finally, the last instance, identified by $\emptyset$ ($< \emptyset, \emptyset >$), represents all the other array positions: not indexed now or before by index variable $i$.

For example, if $i = 5$, at statement 4, the instance $< \{i, j\}, \emptyset >$ represents the position 5 of the array, the instance $< \emptyset, \{i\} >$ represents positions 0 to 4 and the instance $\emptyset$ identifies positions 6 to the final one.

### 3.2  Multireference Classes

As we saw in Sect. 2, our method symbolically executes each statement of the code, and some of the operations included in the symbolic execution are graph compression and union and graph division. Graph compression and union operations are necessary to avoid an explosion in the number of nodes and graphs associated with each statement to describe the data structure at each program point. On the other hand, the goal of the division operation is to focus on the area of the graph which is going to be modified by the symbolic execution of a statement, leading to a much more accurate updating of the RSRSGs. These operations were defined and work well for single selectors, but

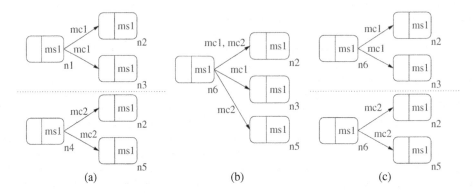

**Fig. 4.** Compression and division with multireference classes

something new has to be introduced to also deal with multiselectors: the multireference classes, $(mc)$.

After the allocation of a new memory location, multiselectors are labeled with a certain multireference class. During the graph compression and union operations, compatible nodes which represent similar memory locations are fused or *summarized* into a single one. When two nodes are summarized the destinations of their *selectors* and *multiselectors* may be joined as well, but multiselector preserves their multireference class. Thus, if for a later statement the analyzer wants to focus on one of the summarized nodes, it is possible to separate them, thanks to the multireference classes.

We can better illustrate this with the example in Fig. 4. First we note in Fig. 4 (a) that nodes $n_1$ and $n_4$ have the same multiselector $ms_1$, but links from node $n_1$ are labeled with $mc_1$ and those from $n_4$ belong to the multireference class $mc_2$. Let's suppose that nodes $n_1$ and $n_4$ are compatible and can be summarized into a new node $n_6$ in Fig. 4 (b). Some of the destination nodes are also joined but the multireference classes allow the analyzer to accurately focus on node $n_1$ or $n_4$ if they have to be modified later (Fig. 4 (c)).

Having introduced these two key concepts associated with multiselectors we can move on to briefly describe how the symbolic execution of the statements has to be modified to take into account this new information.

## 4   Extended Symbolic Execution for Multiselectors

As we said in Sect. 2, the symbolic execution of a statement carries out the generation of the output $RSRSG_o$ which captures the modifications, due to this statement, in the data structures represented by the input $RSRSG_i$. Basically, as we explained in Fig. 1, the symbolic execution process first focusses on the section of the graphs which are going to be updated, to subsequently carry out the abstract interpretation of the statement which conveniently modifies the graphs. Finally, graphs are compressed and some of them joined for the sake of memory wastage minimization.

This scheme is valid for statements in which only single selector are involved. However, if the statement includes multiselectors, $x \rightarrow sel[i] = NULL$, $x \rightarrow sel[i] = y$

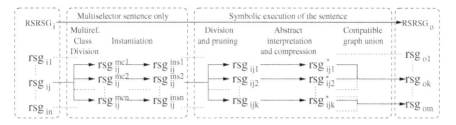

**Fig. 5.** Extension of the symbolic execution to also deal with multiselectors

and $y = x \to sel[i]$, the analyzer must first identify the $i$ position of the array of point-ers to focus on the particular link represented by $sel[i]$. If we are able to do this, then we can later apply the single selector procedure because we have translated a multi-selector into a single selector. Since we are carrying out an analysis at compile time, sometimes the method has to behave conservatively: if we cannot identify the particular $i$ selector we have to update all the links that may be represented by the $sel[i]$ selector. Fortunately, the analyzer normally avoids inaccurate updates since it is able to exclude several links that are definitely not represented by $sel[i]$. Basically, in order to focus on a single selector from a multiselector, the analyzer implements two previous steps as we can see in Fig. 5: multireference class division and instantiation. These two pre-processing stages are executed only for the symbolic execution of statements involving multiselector, and are briefly described next.

### 4.1   Multireference Class Division

For a given statement like $x \to sel[i]$, the multireference class division operation just splits the different configurations of the links represented by multiselector $sel$ into sev-eral graphs. These different configurations are in the same graph after a graph union operation and may coexist in the graph domain for the sake of memory saving. How-ever, in the memory domain those configuration are exclusive and the analyzer has to separate them. In other words, in order to increase the accuracy of the method, before updating a graph, the analyzer looks for the most precise description of the memory configurations which are going to be updated.

More precisely, given an $rsg_i$ to be updated by a statement, the multireference class division will split the $rsg_i$ into as many graphs $rsg_i^{mc_i}$ as there are multireference classes in the multiselector, as we can see in Fig. 5. Note that the number of multiref-erence classes that may appear in a multiselector is limited as a multireference class is just an identifier of a subset of links that may be represented by a multiselector. Since the number of links represented by a multiselector is finite (due to there being a finite number of nodes), the number of subsets of links is also finite.

This operation can be better illustrated by the example in Fig. 6 where we can see a hypothetical $rsg_i$ before the execution of statement of the type "$a \to col[i] = ...$". In this graph, the pointer variable $a$ is pointing to a memory location containing the multiselector $col$. There are two instances associated with this multiselector which are identified by $(< \emptyset, \{i\} >)$, instance $ins_1$, and $\emptyset$, instance $ins_2$. Both instances are pointing to other locations and the links are labeled with two multireference classes, $mc_1$ and $mc_2$.

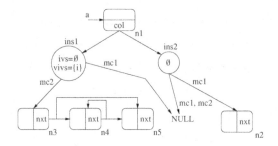

**Fig. 6.** An example of graph that has to be updated

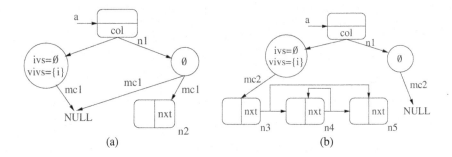

**Fig. 7.** Graphs obtained after the multireference class division

Put simply, this graph represents an array of pointers, $a$, where the already visited positions (instance $ins_1$) are pointing to NULL, $mc_1$, or to single linked lists of two or more elements ($n_3$, $n_4$, and $n_5$), $mc_2$, depending of the followed path reaching the statement in the control flow graph. On the other hand, non-visited positions of array $a$ (instance $ins_2$) may point to a single memory location $n_2$, $mc_1$, or to NULL, $mc_1, mc_2$.

The multireference class division operation generates the two different graphs we can see in Fig. 7. The first graph, Fig. 7 (a), is obtained just by keeping the links belonging to multireference class $mc_1$, whereas the second graph, Fig. 7 (b), keeps those links of the multireference class $mc_2$. Now we have identified two possible memory configurations (two possible data structures) that may reach the statement "$a \rightarrow col[i] = ...$". Note that in this example, these two memory configurations reach the same statement after following two different paths in the control flow graph of the analyzed code. The analyzer has to conservatively update each memory configuration according to the new "$a \rightarrow col[i] = ...$" statement because at compile time the analyzer does not know which path is going to be the one executed at run time.

### 4.2   Instantiation

After the multireference class division, several graphs $rsg_i^{mc_i}$ are going to be modified by the instantiation operation. The goal now is to focus on the particular $i$ position of the array of pointers to successfully translate a multiselector into a single selector. In order to do this, the analyzer has to generate a new single instance to represent the $i$ link of the multiselector $sel$. This particular link will be later processed as a single selector by the subsequent compiler passes as can be seen in Fig. 5.

More precisely, for a statement of the type $x \rightarrow sel[i]$, the new single instance has to fulfill that $ivs = \{i, ...\}$. In the worst case, the new instance would inherit all the links which point to other memory locations from the other already existing instances. This is the most conservative case in which the analyzer is not able to extract more precise information about the particular $i$ position of the array involved in the statement. However, in most cases, the analyzer would be able to identify some relations between index variables. These relations are stored in an *index variable relation table, IVRT*, which is going to help in reducing the number of links that the new single instances have to inherit.

This $IVRT(iv_1, iv_2, st)$ table has to be generated in a preprocessing compiler pass to store the relations between index variables $iv_1$ and $iv_2$ for the statement $st$. The *IVRT* table also holds the relations between an index variable now (in the current iteration of a loop) and before (in a previous iteration) using the expression $IVRT(iv, va(iv), st)$, where $va(iv)$ represents the old values taken by $iv$ in previous iterations of the loop. The possible values for $IVRT(iv_1, iv_2, st)$ are: **eq**, if $iv_1$ and $iv_2$ have the same value at $st$; **neq**, if they are different; or **unk**, if the relation between them is unknown. We are also studying including in the $IVRT$ generation pass more precise array region descriptions such as those presented in [7] which also deals with non-affine access functions.

The *IVRT* holds key information regarding the initialization of the links corresponding to the new single instance. This way, the new single instance $< \{i\}, \emptyset >$ has to inherit all the links of the *compatible* instances, which are those that do not contain $j$ in the $ivs$ set where $IVRT(i, j, st) = neq$. This is due to the fact that if $i \neq j$ in $st$, then the instances with $ivs = \{j, ...\}$ do not represent the $i$ position of the array. Besides, if $IVRT(i, va(i), st) = neq$, then the new single instance $< \{i\}, \emptyset >$ will not inherit the links of instances of the type $< ..., \{i, ...\} >$.

We can better explain these ideas by reference to Fig. 7. Let's suppose that the analyzer has found out in a previous step that $IVRT(i, va(i), st) = neq$, which means that for the code statement $st$ the index variable $i$ has a new value which has never been taken by this variable in this statement $st$ (in a previous iteration). Now, the analyzer has to generate a new single instance $< \{i\}, \emptyset >$ as we see in Fig. 8. Note that this new instance only inherits the links of the $\emptyset$ instance since the $< \emptyset, \{i\} >$ instance identifies already visited positions of the array and we know that $i$ now has a different value.

The number of instances that can appear in any multiselector is limited by the number of index variables and, as we said, an instance is just a pair of sets of index variables. In addition, in these sets they will not appear all possible index variables, but just those involved in the traversing of an array of pointers. These index variables are removed from the instances when the symbolic execution leaves the loop in which the array of pointer is traversed. Subsequently, instances with the same sets are fused and consequently the number of instances decreased.

Due to space constraints we cannot cover additional important issues such as *IVRT* generation and index variable analysis and scope; however, these are described in [3].

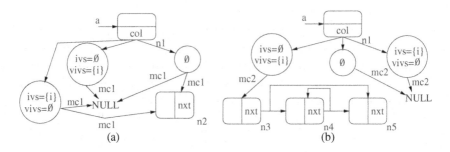

**Fig. 8.** Resulting graphs after instantiation

## 5   Experimental Results

With the previously described ideas we have extended the analyzer presented in [4,5] to allow for the automatic detection of the data structures at each program point for codes based not only on single selectors but also on multiselectors. With this analyzer we have analyzed several codes in which the dominant data structure comprises arrays of pointers.

As we have seen, the set of properties associated with a node allows the analyzer to keep in separate nodes those memory locations with different properties. Obviously, the number of nodes in the RSRSGs depends on the number of properties and also on the range of values these properties can take. The higher the number of properties the better the accuracy in the memory configuration representation, but also the larger the RSRSGs and memory wastage.

Fortunately, not all the properties are needed to achieve a precise description of the data structure in all the codes. That is, simpler codes can be successfully analyzed taking into account fewer properties, and complex programs will need more compilation time and memory due to all the properties that have to be considered to achieve accurate results. Bearing this in mind, we have implemented the analyzer to carry out a progressive analysis which starts with fewer constraints to summarize nodes, but, when necessary, these constraints are increased to reach a better approximation of the data structure used in the code. More precisely, the compiler analysis comprises three levels: $L_1$, $L_2$, and $L_3$, from less to more complexity.

The analyzed codes are the sparse matrix vector multiplication, sparse matrix matrix multiplication, sparse LU factorization, and the kernel of the Barnes-Hut N-body

**Table 1.** Time and space required by the analyzer to process several codes

|  | Time | Space (MB) |
|---|---|---|
| Level | $L_1$ / $L_2$ / $L_3$ | $L_1$ / $L_2$ / $L_3$ |
| S.Mat-Vec | 0'03"/0'04"/0'05" | 0.92/1.03/1.2 |
| S.Mat-Mat | 0'12"/0'14"/0'16 | 1.19/1.31/1.49 |
| S.LU fact. | 2'50"/3'03"/- | 3.96/4.18/- |
| Barnes-Hut | 61'24"/69'55"/0'54" | 40.14/42.86/3.06 |

simulation. In Table 1 we present the time and memory required by the analyzer to process these codes in a Pentium III 500 MHZ with 128 MB main memory. The first three codes were successfully analyzed in the first level of the analyzer, $L_1$. However, for the Barnes-Hut code the highest accuracy of the RSRSGs was obtained in the last level, $L_3$, as we explain in Sect. 5.2. For the Sparse LU factorization, our analyzer runs out of memory in $L_3$. We now briefly describe the results for the analyzed codes.

## 5.1   Sparse Codes

Here we deal with three sparse irregular codes which implement sparse matrix operations: matrix vector multiplication, $r = M \times v$, matrix by matrix multiplication, $A = B \times C$, and sparse LU factorization, $A = LU$.

In the two first codes, sparse matrices $M$, $A$, and $B$ are stored in memory as an array of pointers, $row$, pointing to doubly linked lists which store the matrix rows. Matrix $C$ is similarly stored by columns instead of by rows. The sparse vectors $v$ and $r$ are also doubly linked lists. This can be seen in Fig. 9(a). Note that vector $r$ grows during the matrix vector multiplication process.

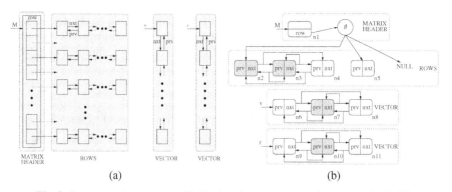

(a)                                                                (b)

**Fig. 9.** Sparse matrix-vector multiplication data structure and compacted RSRSG

On the other hand, the sparse LU factorization solves non-symmetric sparse linear systems by applying the LU factorization of the sparse matrix. Here, the sparse matrix is stored by columns. However, this code is much more complex to analyze due to the matrix filling, partial pivoting, and column permutation which takes place in the factorization in order to provide numerical stability and preserve the sparseness. After the analysis process, carried out by our analyzer at level L1, the resulting RSRSGs accurately represent the data structure at each program point for the three codes.

Regarding the sparse matrix vector multiplication, in Fig. 9(b) we present a compact representation of the resulting RSRSG for the last statement of the code. Nodes where the $SHARED(n)$ property is true are shaded in the figures. In this RSRSG we can clearly see the three main data structures involved in the sparse matrix vector multiplication ($M$, $v$, and $r$). Each vector is represented by three nodes and the central one represents all the middle items of the doubly linked list. The sparse matrix is pointed to by pointer variable $M$ which is actually an array of pointers with the multiselector $row$. This multiselector has, for the last statement of the code, a single instance ($\emptyset$) representing all the positions (pointers) of the array. In the RSRSG we can see that these pointers can point to $NULL$ (there is no element in the row), to a single node (the row has just one entry), or to a doubly linked list of two or more elements. For the matrix matrix multiplication, matrices $A$, $B$, and $C$ are also clearly identified by three graphs like the one just described before. The same happens for the in-place sparse LU factorization where the resulting LU matrix is stored where the original matrix A was.

To properly interpret this graph representation of the sparse matrices we have to say that the analyzer also knows that the $SHSEL(n, sel)$ for all the nodes and all selectors is false. Remember that $SHSEL(n, sel)$ =false means that all the locations represented by $n$ can not be referenced more than once by following the same selector $sel$ from other locations. This leads to several conclusions: (i) the doubly linked lists are acyclic when traversed by following just one kind of selector ($nxt$ or $prv$), since the $SHSEL(n, nxt)$=false points out that a node can not be pointed to twice by other nodes using selector $nxt$ (the same for $prv$); (ii) different pointers of the array $row$ point to different rows, as $SHSEL(n_2, row) =$ false; (iii) besides this, the doubly linked lists do not share elements between them.

Using this information, a subsequent compiler pass would be able to identify the traversals of the rows for prefetching or locality exploiting. Furthermore, the analyzer would state that the sparse matrix rows/columns can be updated in parallel for some loops of the codes, and that it is also possible to update each row/column in parallel.

## 5.2   Barnes-Hut N-Body Simulation

This code is based on the algorithm presented in [1] which is used in astrophysics. In Fig. 10(a) we present a schematic view of the data structure used in this code. The bodies are stored by a single linked list pointed to by the pvar $Lbodies$. The octree represents the several subdivisions of the 3D space. Each leaf of the octree represents a subsquare which contains a single body and therefore points to this body stored in the $Lbodies$ list. Each octree node which is not a leaf has an array $child$ of eight pointers to its children.

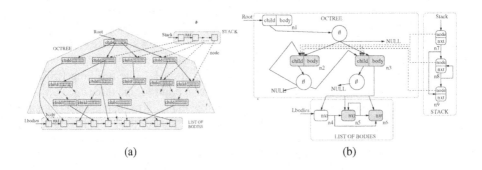

(a)                                        (b)

**Fig. 10.** Barnes-Hut data structure and compacted RSRSG

The three main steps in the algorithm are: (i) The creation of the octree and list (ii) for each subsquare, compute the center of mass and total mass; and (iii) for each particle, traverse the tree, to compute the forces on it.

All the traversals of the octree are carried out in the code by recursive calls. Due to the fact that our analyzer is still not able to perform an interprocedural analysis, we have manually carried out the inlining of the subroutine and the recursivity has been transformed into a loop. This loop uses a stack pointing to the nodes which are referenced during the octree traversal. This stack is also considered in Fig. 10 (a) and obtained in the corresponding RSRSG, Fig. 10 (b). The first step of the code, (i), is successfully analyzed in level $L_1$ but the best accurate description of the data structures used in steps (ii) and (iii) are obtained in level $L_3$.

However, regarding Table 1, there is paradoxical behavior that deserves explanation: $L_3$ expends less time and memory than $L_1$ and $L_2$. In $L_3$ *SHARED* and *SHSEL* remain false for more nodes and links which leads to more nodes and links being pruned during the abstract interpretation and graph compression phase of the symbolic execution of the statements. This leads to significantly reducing the number of nodes and graphs, which reduces memory and time requirements.

## 6    Conclusions and Future Work

In this work we have extended our shape analysis techniques to allow for the automatic detection of dynamic data structures based on arrays of pointers that we have called multiselectors. In order to accurately support multiselectors we propose the use of multireference classes and instances. On the one hand, the multireference classes point out which are the possible configurations of links that may coexist for a given statement. On the other hand, the instances are the key to focussing on the particular position of the array of pointers which is actually involved in a statement including a reference to a multiselector ($sel[i]$).

To validate these techniques we have implemented them in an analyzer which can be fed with C code and returns the data structures at each program point. This analyzer has reported very accurate descriptions of the data structures used in the tested codes, requiring a reasonable amount of memory and time. To the best of our knowledge there is no other implementation able to achieve such successful results for complex C codes like the ones presented here.

Information about data structure is critical in order to carry out further compiler optimizations such as locality exploiting or automatic parallelization. In the near future we will approach the issue of these additional compiler passes, but before this we want to tackle the recursive calls problem.

## References

1. J. Barnes and P. Hut. *A Hierarchical O(n· log n) force calculation algorithm.* Nature v.324, December 1986.
2. D. Chase, M. Wegman and F. Zadeck. *Analysis of Pointers and Structures.* In SIGPLAN Conference on Programming Language Design and Implementation, 296-310. ACM Press, New York, 1990.

3. Francisco Corbera. *Automatic Detection of Data Structures based on Pointers*. Ph.D. Dissertation, Dept. Computer Architecture, Univ. of Málaga, Spain, 2001.
4. F. Corbera, R. Asenjo and E.L. Zapata *Accurate Shape Analysis for Recursive Data Structures*. 13th Int'l. Workshop on Languages and Compilers for Parallel Computing (LCPC'2000), IBM T.J. Watson Res. Ctr., Yorktown Heights, New York, NY, August, 2000.
5. F. Corbera, R. Asenjo and E. Zapata *Progressive Shape Analysis for Real C Codes.*, IEEE Int'l. Conf. on Parallel Processing (ICPP'2001), pp. 373-380. Valencia, Spain, September 3-7, 2001.
6. R. Ghiya and L. Hendren. *Is it a tree, a DAG, or a cyclic graph? A shape analysis for heap-directed pointers in C*. In Conference Record of the 23rd ACM SIGPLAN-SIGACT Symposium on Principles of Programming Languages, pp. 1-15, St. Petersburg, Florida, January, 1-24, 1996.
7. J. Hoeflinger and Y. Paek *The Access Region Test*. In Twelfth International Workshop on Languages and Compilers for Parallel Computing (LCPC'99), The University of California, San Diego, La Jolla, CA USA, August, 1999.
8. S. Horwitz, P. Pfeiffer, and T. Reps. *Dependence Analysis for Pointer Variables*. In Proceedings of the SIGPLAN Conference on Programming Language Design and Implementation, 28-40, June 1989.
9. J. Hummel, L. J. Hendren and A. Nicolau *A General Data Dependence Test for Dynamic, Pointer-Based Data Structures*. In Proceedings of the SIGPLAN Conference on Programming Language Design and Implementation, pages 218-229. ACM Press, 1994.
10. N. Jones and S. Muchnick. *Flow Analysis and Optimization of Lisp-like Structures*. In Program Flow Analysis: Theory and Applications, S. Muchnick and N. Jones, Englewood Cliffs, NJ: Prentice Hall, Chapter 4, 102-131, 1981.
11. A. Matsumoto, D. S. Han and T. Tsuda. *Alias Analysis of Pointers in Pascal and Fortran 90: Dependence Analysis between Pointer References*. Acta Informatica 33, 99-130. Berlin Heidelberg New York: Springer-Verlag, 1996.
12. J. Plevyak, A. Chien and V. Karamcheti. *Analysis of Dynamic Structures for Efficient Parallel Execution*. In Languages and Compilers for Parallel Computing, U. Banerjee, D. Gelernter, A. Nicolau and D. Padua, Eds. Lectures Notes in Computer Science, vol 768, 37-57. Berlin Heidelberg New York: Springer-Verlag 1993.
13. M. Sagiv, T. Reps and R. Wilhelm. *Solving Shape-Analysis problems in Languages with destructive updating*. ACM Transactions on Programming Languages and Systems, 20(1):1-50, January 1998.
14. M. Sagiv, T. Reps, and R. Wilhelm, *Parametric shape analysis via 3-valued logic*. In Conference Record of the Twenty-Sixth ACM Symposium on Principles of Programming Languages, San Antonio, TX, Jan. 20-22, ACM, New York, NY, 1999, pp. 105-118.

# An Empirical Study on the Granularity of Pointer Analysis in C Programs

Tong Chen, Jin Lin, Wei-Chung Hsu, and Pen-Chung Yew

Department of Computer Science, University of Minnesota
{tchen, jin, hsu, yew}@cs.umn.edu

**Abstract.** Pointer analysis plays a critical role in modern C compilers because of the frequent appearances of pointer expressions. It is even more important for data dependence analysis, which is essential in exploiting parallelism, because complex data structures such as arrays are often accessed through pointers in C. One of the important aspects of pointer analysis methods is their granularity, the way in which the memory objects are named for analysis. The naming schemes used in a pointer analysis affect its effectiveness, especially for pointers pointing to heap memory blocks. In this paper, we present a new approach that applies the compiler analysis and profiling techniques together to study the impact of the granularity in pointer analyses. An instrumentation tool, based on the Intel's Open Resource Compiler (ORC), is devised to simulate different naming schemes and collect precise target sets for indirect references at runtime. The collected target sets are then fed back to the ORC compiler to evaluate the effectiveness of different granularity in pointer analyses. The change of the alias queries in the compiler analyses and the change of performance of the output code at different granularity levels are observed. With the experiments on the SPEC CPU2000 integer benchmarks, we found that 1) finer granularity of pointer analysis show great potential in optimizations, and may bring about up to 15% performance improvement, 2) the common naming scheme, which gives heap memory blocks names according to the line number of system memory allocation calls, is not powerful enough for some benchmarks. The wrapper functions for allocation or the user-defined memory management functions have to be recognized to produce better pointer analysis result, 3) pointer analysis of fine granularity requires interprocedural analysis, and 4) it is also quite important that a naming scheme distinguish the fields of a structure in the targets.

## 1 Introduction

The pervasive use of pointer expressions in C programs has created a serious problem for the C compilers. Without proper pointer analyses, compilers would not have accurate knowledge of what memory objects may have been accessed by indirect references. Consequently, many other important analyses, such as data dependence analysis on arrays and complex data structures, may suffer from the conservative assumptions about the targets of pointers. Hence, pointer analysis plays a critical role in C compilers in exploiting parallelism [12]. It provides the analysis base for other analysis and parallelizing techniques.

B. Pugh and C.-W. Tseng (Eds.): LCPC 2002, LNCS 2481, pp. 157–171, 2005.

Many pointer analysis methods have been proposed [1, 2, 3]. Among all the pointer analyses, the points-to analysis [2, 4, 5, 6, 7, 8, 9, 10, 15] is the most widely used. A points-to analysis aims to produce a set of potential targets for each indirect reference so that the alias relationship among pointers can be determined by comparing their target sets. Efforts have been put in searching for a good points-to analysis [11, 12, 13, 21].

The effectiveness of a pointer analysis is generally determined by two factors: the *algorithm* used, and the *granularity* of the points-to targets specified in the compiler. For example, the algorithms used by compilers may have different flow-sensitivity or context sensitivity. The algorithm may also be applied inter-procedurally or only intra-procedurally.

To calculate the target sets, the address space of memory objects in a program should first be assigned *names*. The *granularity* of the names represents the precision of the *naming schemes* used in pointer analysis. Different naming schemes may lead to different granularity in pointer analyses. In general, there are two types of memory objects: the local or global variables defined in the program, and heap memory blocks allocated at runtime. The pointers that point to global or local variables are called stack-oriented pointers; and the pointers that point to memory blocks are called heap-oriented pointers [5]. For heap-oriented pointers, their target objects are anonymous. Compilers have to assign them names internally before the target sets could be calculated. For example, if the compiler assigns the entire heap space with only one name, the entire heap space will be viewed as only one large memory object. All of the pointers point to different memory locations in the heap space will have the same target in their target sets, and they will all be aliases. On the other hand, for stack-oriented pointers, global and local variables usually have explicitly given variable names in the program, and with well-defined types. However, if the compiler treats an entire data structure with many fields as a single memory object, all of the pointers point to the different fields of the data structure will be aliases.

The granularity of the target objects and its related naming schemes not only affect the results of a pointer analysis, but also the efficiency of its algorithm. Finer granularity will allow better distinction among different memory objects, and hence, fewer aliases. However, it may lead to a larger name space and possibly larger target set sizes, and hence, longer time and more storage requirement for a points-to analysis.

Various naming schemes have been proposed in the past [10, 16, 24, 27, 28]. For anonymous heap memory objects, the place where they are allocated is used to name them. For memory objects of structure type, the field names may be used in their names. Some experiments have been done [25, 29] and showed the importance of proper naming methods. However a comprehensive study on the impact of the granularity on pointer analysis has not been done. Most of the previous studies focus primarily on the algorithms. One reason is that it is not trivial to implement different naming schemes in conjunction with various pointer analysis algorithms. Another reason is that the heap memory objects have not received enough attention in the past. In most compilers, only very simple naming schemes are used for heap memory blocks. However, a recent study shows that the number of heap-oriented pointers is quite significant in most SPEC CPU2000 programs [17]. Hence, it is important to look at the impact of naming schemes and the granularity on the pointer analysis and the optimizations that use the results of the pointer analysis.

In this paper, we study this problem using a new approach that combines the profiling techniques and the compiler analysis. We developed an instrumentation and profiling tool set based on the Intel's Open Research Compiler (ORC) [14]. Different naming schemes are simulated and the precise target sets of indirect references (e.g. pointers) are collected at runtime for the points-to analysis. We then feed the results of the points-to analysis back to the ORC compiler. The improvement on the results of alias queries in other compiler analysis and optimizations and the performance of the code thus generated are also measured. Our experiments are conducted on SPEC CPU2000 integer benchmarks and on Intel Itanium computers.

The suggested approach does not have to implement pointer analyses with different granularity in a compiler. It is much easier to simulate these analyses with a runtime tool. The points-to set collected by this tool is an upper bound result and reveals the potential of different granularity. Using the optimizations in the ORC compiler as consumers makes the measurement of effectiveness meaningful. However, we have to admit that some import issues, such as the impact of the algorithm, are not covered in this paper.

The main contributions of this paper include:

- A comprehensive study on the naming schemes and the granularity of the pointer analysis. We found that the widely used simple naming schemes are inadequate. Wrapper functions and self-management functions that contain system memory allocation functions (such as *malloc()*) need to be carefully analyzed. It is also important for a pointer analysis to consider the fields of a data structure.
- A set of instrumentation and profiling tools to study issues related to pointer analysis. We develop a tool that is capable of calculating precise target sets for each pointer reference. This tool set is independent of the pointer analysis used in a compiler. ,
- The impact of the pointer analysis on compiler optimizations. We feed the target sets collected at runtime back into the ORC compiler to help later analyses and optimizations, and measure the performance improvement on Itanium. It provides a very direct way to study the impact of naming schemes and granularity on performance.

The rest of the paper is organized as follows: The background knowledge of points-to analysis is introduced in the next section. Section 3 and section 4 describe, in detail, how the instrumentation and profiling tool works, and how the runtime results are fed back to the ORC compiler to evaluate different naming schemes and granularity levels. The experiment results are presented in section 5. The conclusions are presented in section 6.

## 2  Background

In a points-to analysis, memory objects, such as variables and heap memory blocks, need their *names* so the compiler can identify them as the targets of pointers. A naming scheme sets up a mapping from the memory address space to the symbolic name space. These naming schemes differ in the way memory objects are grouped together, and the names assigned to them. As a result, the naming schemes implicitly determine the granularity of memory objects used within the compiler.

Global variables have explicit and fixed variable names in a program. Therefore, using the variable names sets up a precise one-to-one mapping between their corresponding memory locations and their names. The local variables within a procedure also have explicit variable names. But there may be many instances of a local variable at runtime if the procedure is called recursively. A name for a local variable may represent many instances of the variable in different procedure instances. However, such many-to-one mapping is usually thought as a quite precise.

Heap memory objects have no explicit names assigned to them in the program. The number of memory blocks allocated at runtime by the *malloc()* function is unknown at compile time. The compiler has to group those heap memory blocks and assigns them a name to facilitate points-to analysis.

These anonymous memory objects created by all of the malloc() functions in the program could be assigned the same name[26]. If that is the case, all references accessing to any memory block allocated by the malloc() are aliases. This obviously is not very desirable. Hence, the compiler often assigns names to memory blocks according to the line number of the statement which contains malloc() function in the program. This allows memory blocks allocated at different call sites of the malloc() function to have different names, and hence, be treated as different points-to targets. This is significantly better than the previous naming scheme. However, if the malloc() function is called within the procedure X, and the procedure X is called several times at different call sites. All of the memory blocks allocated at different call sites of procedure X will have the same name.

To avoid such a problem, the compiler can also assign a name according to the calling path at the invocation site of the *malloc()* function in addition to the line number [10]. For example, if procedure X calls procedure Y which in turn calls procedure Z, and a *malloc()* is called within procedure Z. The memory blocks allocated by the *malloc()* can be assigned a name according to its calling path X-Y-Z in addition to its line number. To control the complexity of such a naming scheme, the compiler can use only the last $n$ procedures of a calling path in its naming scheme. In the last example, if n=2, Y-Z will be used. Different n will thus give different levels of granularity to the named memory objects.

When a memory object is a structure type with many fields, the granularity of the memory object can be made even finer by considering each of its field as a different memory object. As a result, two pointers that point to different fields of a memory object of the structure type can be distinguished. However, since C is not a strong-typed language, type casting has to be monitored carefully when fields are considered. Notice that the naming of the dynamically allocated memory blocks and separating the fields of the structure-type memory objects are orthogonal, i.e. they can be used independently in determining the granularity of memory objects.

In the following discussion, the granularity level, G, of a naming scheme will be represented by these two considerations. For example, G=n means that the last n procedures in the calling path are used, but fields are not considered. When n=0, it is the degenerate case of assigning the entire heap space with only one name; when n=1, only the line number is used. G=nf means the fields are also considered in addition to the calling path.

# 3  Target Sets in Different Naming Schemes

## 3.1  Overview

We developed an instrumentation and profiling tool to simulate different naming schemes and collect their target sets of indirect references. Our approach takes advantage of the fact that the addresses of memory objects and references are all available at runtime.

The selected naming scheme is simulated by setting up a mapping at runtime from the addresses of memory objects to their names according to the naming scheme. Targets of a pointer are identified by looking up the mapping with the addresses of the references to their names. The target sets thus obtained represent approximately the best results that these naming schemes and pointer analyses can be expected to achieve.

To facilitate the lookup process, shadows are used to record the address-name mapping. There are three contiguous data segments in a program: the global variable segment, the heap memory segment and the local variables segment. A library routine for system memory allocation is provided to assure that the heap space is allocated in a compact space so as to keep the shadow space for heap compact. A corresponding shadow entry in the shadow segment is assigned to each of the memory blocks allocated. The sizes of the shadow segments can be dynamically adjusted to be large enough to hold the address-name mapping for all of the memory blocks allocated at runtime. The name of a memory object is stored in its shadow entry in the shadow segment with the same offset as that in the data segment (see Fig. 1). As a result, the offset can be used in the lookup process to quickly locate the shadow entry that stores the name. Such a shadow data structure makes its modification very easy - just overwrite the old value and no delete operation is needed. However, this method doubles the size of memory required by a program.

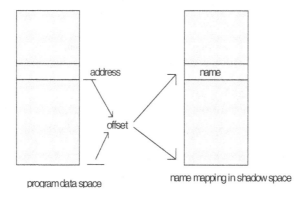

**Fig. 1.** The shadow for naming schemes

There are several advantages using this approach. First, this tool provides a uniform platform to study the granularity of the points-to analysis. The effectiveness of different granularity levels can be compared using this framework. It is much easier to develop such a profiling tool than to implement different naming schemes and pointer analyses in a real compiler. Secondly, the precise target sets for each naming scheme can be collected at runtime. These results are roughly the best any compiler implementation can be expected to achieve. Hence, the obtained results do not depend on the quality of the implementation of these naming schemes and points-to analyses in a real compiler. This is a very significant advantage especially because the results of an inter-procedural points-to analysis are heavily dependent on how it is implemented. The third advantage is that the results of our measurements can be fed back to the ORC compiler, and we can study their actual impact on the other analyses and the optimization phases that are the clients of the points-to analysis. The fourth advantage is that we can study the potential performance improvement on a real machine, i.e. Itanium, not on a simulator.

However, such a profiling method also has its limitations. Since our results are collected during runtime, they could be input dependent and the coverage of the program limits our studies only to the parts that are actually executed at runtime. With the measurements from a suite of benchmarks and the focus of the study is not on a particular program, we believe that the results of our study can reflect the general characteristics of real applications.

Our profiling tool has two major components: an instrumentation tool developed on the Intel's ORC compiler [14], and a set of library routines written in C. Application programs are first instrumented by the modified ORC compiler to insert calls to the library routines. Then at runtime, these library routines simulate different naming schemes and collect the target sets of indirect references.

### 3.2 Instrumentation

The instrumentation tool in the ORC compiler inserts function calls to invoke our library routines to generate and process traces. They simulate different naming schemes for every memory object, and calculate target sets for every indirect reference. We describe some of the details in the followings:

- Procedure calls. At every entrance and exit of a procedure call in the program, a library call is inserted with the call site ID of the procedure passed as one of the parameters. The call site ID is pushed into or popped out of the calling path stack to maintain the current calling path.
- Memory objects. When a memory object becomes alive, a library call is inserted with the starting address, the length, and the name (for variables only) of the memory object passed as its parameters. The name of the variables helps us to identify which variable is actually referenced when the runtime results are fed back to the compiler. The way a name is assigned to a heap memory block is determined by the selected naming scheme. This library call sets up the mapping from the addresses of this memory object to its name by writing the name in the corresponding shadow entry. The number of entries to be written is determined by the size of this memory object. Global variables, local variables and heap memory blocks are instrumented differently:

- Global variables become alive at the beginning of a program. The mapping of global variables is initialized only once when the program starts. Scope may be an issue for global variables. Global variables are visible only in the files in which they are declared. The initialization procedure for global variables is instrumented in each file as a new procedure at the end of the file, and these procedures are invoked at the beginning of the main function. The starting address of a global variable can be accessed by the address-of operation. The length is determined by the type.
  - Local variables become alive each time the procedures in which they reside are called. The address for a local variable may not remain the same for each invocation of the procedure. Therefore, we have to insert library function calls at the beginning of each procedure to set up the address-name mapping for local variables. Variables can be ignored if their addresses are not taken. The starting address of a local variable can be accessed by the address-of operation.
  - Heap memory blocks become alive when they are allocated through calls to system memory allocation functions, such as *malloc()* and *calloc()*. Library function calls are insert after these functions. The starting address is the return value of the memory allocation function, and the size of the memory blocks can be obtained from the parameters of these memory allocation functions.
- Indirect references. Each indirect memory reference is instrumented with its address and the reference ID passed as parameters to the library function call in order to collect its target set at runtime.
- Typecast. The instrumentation of type cast is needed only when we want to identify the type of a memory object. The instrumentation tool also generates a file to describe the layout of each structure type. Therefore, the heap memory blocks for data structures with fields can be sliced into smaller objects according to their fields.

### 3.3  Assign Names

Global and local variables already have their given names. Hence, there is no need to assign names to them. For heap memory blocks, we simulate naming schemes by using different lengths of the calling path. The calling path stack is maintained by instrumented library functions. When a heap memory block is allocated, the top $n$ elements in the calling path stack are checked, if G=n.

When the fields are considered, the field ID associated with the name assigned to the memory object is written into the shadow. The instrumentation tool generates a file to describe the layout of each structure type to help break down memory objects to their fields.

For example, there is a memory object, and its name determined by the calling path is g_*name*. The memory object's starting address is addr_*start* and its size is *object_size*. If this memory object is of structure type or array of structure type, the $k$th field of this memory object will be assigned the name  (g_*name*, k). Assume the offset and the size of this field are *offset* and *field_size*, and the size of the structure is *struct_size*. To set up the mapping, all address, *addr*, in this memory object will be given name (g_*name*, k), when the following two conditions hold.

1. *addr_start* ≤ *addr* < addr_start+object_size
2. *offset* ≤ *(addr-starting) mod struct_size* < *offset+ field_size*.

When references accessing different fields of this memory, the targets can be distinguished because they have different field IDs.

### 3.4 Collect Target Sets

The target of each instance of reference is collected by looking up the shadow with the address value of the reference. The target set of a reference is accumulated according to the reference ID and stored in a hash table.

The target sets computed by the tool are flow sensitive and path sensitive. Only the targets that can reach a reference at runtime are put into its target set. The previous value of a pointer is overwritten after the pointer is re-assigned. The possible targets in not-taken branches are also ignored.

If we want to make the target sets context insensitive, targets coming from different calling contexts are not distinguished and are stored together. We can also make the target sets context sensitive by attaching each target a tag to indicate its call site. However, our evaluation method requires calling context insensitive results, because it is not directly supported in the ORC compiler to generate multiple versions for different calling contexts.

## 4   Evaluate Naming Schemes

The effectiveness of naming schemes is evaluated by feeding the target sets collected at runtime back to the ORC compiler, and observing the changes in the alias queries and in the performance of the generated code. The optimizations in the ORC compiler are used as typical clients of the points-to analysis.

### 4.1  The ORC Compiler

The Open Research Compiler, or the ORC compiler [14], originated from the Pro64 compiler [19] developed by the Silicon Graphic Inc. The ORC compiler is for C, C++ and Fortran90. It has most of the analyses and optimizations available in modern compilers. It performs pointer analyses, scalar optimizations, loop transformations, inter-procedural analyses, and code generation. Profiling and feedback-directed optimizations are also supported by this compiler.

There are three stages of analysis for each procedure: loop-nest optimizations (LNO), scalar global optimizations (WOPT), and code generation optimizations (CG). The LNO stage does loop related optimizations [23], such as parallelization, and unimodular transformations. The WOPT stage contains some general optimizations, such as partial redundancy elimination [22], copy propagation and strength reduction. The CG stage focuses on generating optimized binary code. The inter-procedural analysis is supported by the IPA component.

The pointer analysis in the ORC compiler starts from a flow-free pointer  analysis, which is similar to Steengaard's algorithm [8]. This pointer analysis is done inter-procedurally when the inter-procedural analysis is turned on. A flow-sensitive pointer analysis is then applied intra-procedurally to get more precise results. Some simple rules, such as the address-taken rule, are used to help alias analysis. The alias information stored in the internal representations is maintained across different stages.

When using the ORC compiler as a base for comparison, we try to tune the compiler so that the best results could be brought about by the change of the naming scheme. The optimization level is always set at O3. The inter-procedure analysis is turned off, because the current version of the ORC compiler has unstable inter-procedural analysis which may fail in some benchmarks. Therefore the result of ORC compiler just represents the capability of a practical compiler, not a state-of-art compiler. However, the moderate pointer analysis in the ORC compiler actually makes the changes in granularity clear If the ORC had very powerful pointer analysis, it is unclear where the pointer analysis is overdone.

## 4.2 Feedback

The target sets of indirect references are fed back to the ORC compiler. The target sets may be different when different naming schemes are used, and thus the results of the optimizations in the compiler may be different. Two things are measured: the performance of the generated code on Itanium, and the results of alias queries within the optimization phases.

The changes in the performance on Itanium directly reflect the impact of different naming schemes in the ORC compiler. However, the performance changes are determined by many factors. In this study, we also measure the changes in the result of alias queries in the optimization phases, which somewhat reflect the subtle changes in the pointer analysis.

The major optimizations are done in the WOPT and CG stages. In order to feed back to different stages, the instrumentation is done at different stages so that the feedback information can match. The instrumentation is also done incrementally because the impact of the feedback to WOPT should be considered when the instrumentation at CG is done. The target sets collected at runtime by the profiling tool are fed back to the two stages, replacing the alias analysis result produced by the ORC compiler. In the WOPT stage, the static single assignment (SSA) form [20] is generated based on the target sets fed back from the runtime. Many optimizations in WOPT, such as partial redundant elimination and dead code elimination, are built upon the SSA form. In the CG stage, the results of alias queries are also replaced by the target sets fed back from the runtime. We instrument the ORC compiler to record the changes in alias queries.

The profiling information is limited to the portions in a program that is reached during the execution. There is no alias information for the references that are not reached at runtime. These references are conservatively assumed to be aliased with all other references.

## 5  Experiment Results

Experiments are conducted on the SPEC CPU2000 integer benchmarks. First, the distribution of the results of alias queries in the ORC compiler is reported. Then each benchmark is instrumented, and target information for each indirect references at different granularity levels are collected at runtime. The benchmarks are compiled again with the collected alias information. Due to the improved alias information, some alias queries which used to return may alias now return no alias. The changes of alias queries are reported again to show the impact of pointer analysis with different granularities. Finally, the compiled benchmarks are executed again to measure the impact on execution time.

## 5.1  Alias Queries

As in typical compilers, an alias query in the ORC compiler returns one of the following three results: not alias, same location, and may alias. The first two cases are accurate results, while the third one , may alias, is conservative and could be improved by more precise pointer analyses. Since a pointer expression references either a variable or a heap memory block, the alias pairs that return may alias can be further classified into: three categories: between two  variables (v-v), between a variable and a heap memory object (v-h), and between two heap memory blocks (h-h).   Fig. 2 shows the distribution of the returned values from the original ORC compiler. On average, the queries which return may alias accounts for 54.4% of all queries. This high percentage indicates that there could be great potential for improvements. As shown in Fig. 2, the majority of the may alias queries are related to heap memory blocks. Although there are frequent v-h (variable to heap objects) type queries returning may alias, many of them should be turned into no alias by a stronger inter-procedural pointer analysis.  For the rest of aliases among heap blocks, the following experiments are conducted to study the impact of granularity levels on pointer analyses.

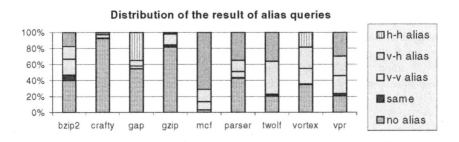

**Fig. 2.** Distribution of the result of alias queries

## 5.2  Query Enhanced by Feedback

After program instrumentation and runtime collection of target sets information, the benchmarks are compiled with the ORC compiler again. This time, the ORC compiler is provided with target information for pointer expressions collected from instrumented runs. Now the ORC compiler is able to give more accurate answers to alias queries. Some queries that used to return *may alias* now may return no alias. The

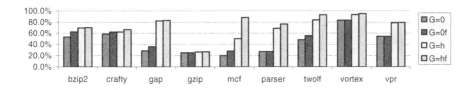

G = 0: all heap memory blocks are given one name.
G=1, 2, 3: the calling path of length 1, 3 or 3 is used to name the heap memory blocks.
G=a: the whole calling path is used to name the heap memory blocks.
G=m: the user memory management function is recognized to name the heap memory blocks.

**Fig. 3.** Percentage of no-alias queries changed with granularity

percentage of the changes is reported in Fig. 3. The queries involving un-reached references are excluded.

There are several observations based on Figure 3.

- There are more than 30% improvements even when G is 0. The reason is that the ORC compiler uses a default symbol to represent all memory objects outside of a procedure to simplify inter-procedural analysis. Such granularity is too coarse. A normal inter-procedural points-to analysis can do much better. .

- For most of the benchmarks, except for bzip2 and mcf, heap memory analysis with line number (G=1) does not improve much. However, for twolf and vpr, G=2 greatly reduces the number of may alias. Further increase of the calling path for heap pointer analysis (G=3) makes little difference.

- G=a does not bring further improvements. Therefore, there are little incentives to consider very long calling path. Some simple analyses, for example, suggested in Intel's compiler group [12], are sufficient.

### 5.3  User Managed Memory

In the benchmark gap and parser, the pointer analysis is insensitive to the naming scheme for heap memory objects. The reason is that the heap memory space is managed by programmers. Therefore, the calling path of system memory allocation does not help. If the functions in which the user manages the heap memory can be recognized, our tool can treat them like malloc(). For example, after we explicitly recognize user managed memory allocation functions, the query improvement improved drastically from 30.8 % to 82.2% in gap, and from 29.9% to 68.4% in parser. See G=m in Figure 3.

Although the user managed memory allocation functions are very difficult, if not impossible, for compiler to recognize them. The major difficulty is to trace the size of memory space accessed through each pointer so that the no overlap can be proved. For programs with user managed memory allocation functions, speculation or dynamic optimization may be needed.

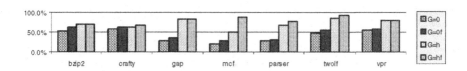

**Fig. 4.** Percentage of no-alias queries changed with field granularity

## 5.4 Fields of Heap Memory Blocks

The fields can affect the pointer analysis in two ways: 1) the pointer analysis can distinguish the points-to sets of different fields that are defined as pointer type; and 2) the pointer analysis can distinguish the targets pointing to different fields of a structure. In our approach, the target sets collected at runtime have the same effects as considering fields in points-to set. Whether to consider fields in target sets is another potential variation.

It is easy to divide a structured variable into finer granularity using their type definition. However, there is no data type defined for heap memory blocks. They can be divided into finer granularity using their fields of structure type only when the memory blocks with the same name are cast to and used as the same type. The type casting of heap memory blocks are traced to identify conditions in which this analysis is applicable. The naming scheme could be based on G=1 or G=2, or G=m such that the heap memory blocks in the same group have the same type. We represented such granularity as G=hf.

The change of queries when fields are considered is reported in Fig. 4. By comparing the result of G=0 and G=0f, and comparing the result of G=h and G=hf, it can be observed that it is important for pointer analysis to consider the fields of both variables and heap memory blocks.

## 5.5 Performance Enhanced by Profiling

Pointer analyses at finer granularity might significantly improve the results of alias queries. It is also interesting to know what would be the impact on the actual optimizations. In this section, the target sets collected at runtime are fed back to the WOPT and the CG phases in the ORC compiler. Optimizations in the two phases are performed with the feedback information, and thus improved results of alias queries. The performance improvement of the benchmark is shown in Fig. 5. After the user memory management functions are recognized in gap and parser, the performance improvement is 20.1% and 12.3%, respectively.

The performance improvement is in proportion to the improvement to alias queries to a lower less a degree. The performance gain of an optimization may depend on many other analyses and the characteristic of the code. Therefore, the improvements of alias queries may not always contribute to overall performance. Half of the benchmarks achieved more than 10% of improvement in performance with finer granularity.

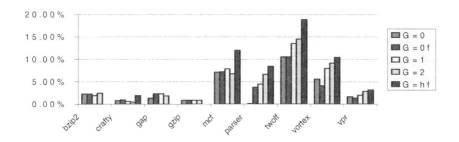

**Fig. 5.** Performance improvement for different granularity levels

## 6  Conclusions

We conduct a comprehensive study on the naming schemes and the granularity of the pointer analysis. We implement a set of instrumentation and profiling tools to study issues related to pointer analysis. Each benchmark is instrumented with our tool to collect target sets information at runtime. Such target sets information is fed back into the ORC compiler automatically to help later analyses and optimizations. This approach provides a direct way to study the impact of naming schemes and granularity on performance

Our experiment results suggest that pointer analysis for heap memory blocks may yield a good return. The commonly used naming scheme that names memory objects with the statement line number of the malloc() function call improves only slightly over the approach that treats heap memory blocks as one entity. However, naming such dynamic allocated memory objects with respective calling path contributes more. Some programs have their own dynamic memory allocation and management routines. It is important for the compiler to recognize such routines to enable more effective naming schemes.

By simulating naming schemes with calling path and field information, the point-to information provided to the ORC compiler greatly improves the results of alias queries. The improved results from alias queries in turn significantly increase the effectiveness of compiler optimizations. Since the point-to information fed back to the compiler is collected at runtime, this approach may not be used directly to generate real code. However, it provides a useful guideline to the potential of pointer analyses at finer granularity.

## References

[1]  David R. Chase, Mark Wegman, and F. Kenneth Zadeck. Analysis of pointers and structures. In Proceedings of SIGPLAN'90 Conference on Programming Language Design and Implementation, page 296-310, June 1990.

[2]  W. Landi and B.G. Ryder. A safe approximate algorithm for interprocedural pointer aliasing. In proceedings of the SIGPLAN'92 Conference on Programming Language Design and Implementation, page 235-248, July 1992.

[3]   X. Tang, R. Ghiya, L. J. Hendren, and G.R. Gao. Heap analysis and optimizations for threaded programs. In Proc. Of the 1997 Conf. On Parallel Architectures and Compilation Techniques, Nov. 1997

[4]   Choi, M. Burke, and P. Carini. Efficient flow-sensitive interprocedural computation of pointer-induced aliases and sife-effects. In Proceedings of the ACM 20th Symposium on Principles of Programming Languages, pages 232-245, January 1993.

[5]   Maryam Emami, Rakesh Ghiya, and Laurie J. Hendren. Context-sensitive interprocedural points-to analysis in the presence of function pointers. In Proceedings of the ACM SIGPLAN '94 Conference on Programming Language Design and Implementation, pages 242-256, June 1994.

[6]   Nevin Heintze and Olivier Tardieu. Demand-Driven Pointer Analysis. ACM SIGPLAN Conference on Programming Language Design and Implementation 2001.

[7]   Robert P. Wilson and Monica S. Lam. Efficient context-sensitive pointer analysis for C programs. In Proceedings of the ACM SIGPLAN'95 Conference on Programming Language Design and Implementation, pages 1-12, June 1995.

[8]   Bjarne Steensgaard. Points-to analysis in almost linear time. In Conference Record of the 23rd ACM SIGPLAN-SIGACT symposium on Principles of Programming Languages, Pages 32-41, January, 1996.

[9]   Bixia Zheng. Integrating scalar analyses and optimizations in a parallelizing and optimizing compiler. PhD thesis, February 2000.

[10]  Ben-Chung Cheng. Compile-time memory disambiguation for C programs. PhD. Thesis, 2000.

[11]  Michael Hind and Anthony Pioli. Evaluating the effectiveness of Pointer Alias Analysis. Science of Computer Programming, 39(1):31-35, January 2001

[12]  Rakesh Ghiya, Daniel Lavery and David Sehr. On the Importance of Points-To Analysis and Other Memory Disambiguation methods For C programs. In Proceedings of the ACM SIGPLAN'01 Conference on Programming Language Design and Implementation, page 47-58, June 2001.

[13]  Markus Mock, Manuvir Das, Craig Chambers, and Susan J. Eggers. Dynamic Points-to Sets: A Comparison with Static Analyses and Potential Applications in Program Understanding and Optimzation. ACM SIGPLAN-SIGSOFT Workshop on Program Analysis 14for Software tools and Engineering, June 2001.

[14]  Roy Ju, Sun Chan, and Chengyong Wu. Open Research Compiler for the Itanium Family. Tutorial at the 34th Annual International Symposium on  Microarchitecture.

[15]  N. D. Jones and S. S. Muchnick,. A Flexible Approach to Interprocedural Flow Analysis and Programs with Recursive Data Structures.  ACM SIGPLAN-SIGACT Symposium on Principles of Programming Languages, 1982.

[16]  S. Zhang, B. G. Ryder, and W. Landi. *Program decomposition for pointer aliasing: A step towards practical analyses.* In Proceedings of the 4th Symposium on the Foundations of Software Engineering, October 1996.

[17]  Tong Chen, Jin Lin, Wei-Chung Hsu and Pen-Chung Yew, On the Impact of Naming Methods for Heap-Oriented Pointers in C Programs, International Symposium on Parallel Architectures, Algorithms, and Networks, 2002.

[18]  Spec CPU2000, http://www.specbench.org/osg/cpu2000/.

[19]  G. R. Gao, J. N. Amaral, J. Dehnert, and R. Towle. The SGI Pro64 compiler infrastructure: A tutorial. Tutorial presented at the International Conference on Parallel Architecture and Compilation Techniques, October 2000.

[20]  Fred Chow, Raymond Lo, Shin-Ming Liu, Sun Chan, and Mark Streich, Effective Representation of Aliases and Indirect Memory Operations in SSA Form, Proc. of 6th Int'l Conf. on Compiler Construction, pp. 253-257, April 1996.

[21]  Shapiro, M., and Horwitz, S., The effects of the precision of pointer analysis. Static Analysis 4th International Symposium, SAS '97, Lecture Notes in Computer Science Vol 1302, September 1997.

[22]  F. Chow, S. Chan, R. Kennedy, S.-M. Liu, R. Lo, and P. Tu. Anew algorithm for partial redundancy elimination based on SSA form. In Proc. of SIGPLAN 97 Conference on Programming Language Design and Implementation, page 273-286, May 1997.

[23]  Michael E. Wolf, Dror E. Maydan, and Ding-Kai Chen, Combining Loop Transformations Considering Caches and Scheduling, Int'l J. of Parallel Programming 26(4), page 479-503, August 1998.

[24]  Amer Diwan, Kathryn S. McKinley, J. Eliot and B. Moss, Type-Based Alias Analysis, SIGPLAN Conference on Programming Language Design and Implementation, pages 106--117, June 1998

[25]  Yong SH, Horwitz S, Reps T. Pointer Analysis for Programs with Structures and Casting. SIGPLAN Conference on Programming Language Design and Implementation, vol 34, pages 91-103, 1999-

[26]  Erik Ruf. Context-Insensitive Alias Analysis Reconsidered. In ACM SIGPLAN '95 Conference on Programming Language Design and Implementation (PLDI'95), La Jolla, California, vol 30, pages 13-22, June 1995.

[27]  D. Choi, M. G. Burke, and P. Carini. Efficient flow-sensitive interprocedural computation of pointer induced aliases and side effects. In Conference Record of the Twentieth Annual ACM Symposium on Principles of Programming Languages, pages 232--245, January 1993.

[28]  Barbara G. Ryder, William A. Landi, Philip A. Stocks, Sean Zhang, and Rita Altucher, A Scheme for Interprocedural Modification Side-Effect Analysis with Pointer Aliasing, ACM Transactions on Programming Languages and Systems (TOPLAS), 23(2), March 2001, pages 105--186.

[29]  Michael Hind and Anthony Pioli, An Empirical Comparison of Interprocedural Pointer Alias Analyses. IBM Report #21058, December 1997.

# Automatic Implementation of Programming Language Consistency Models*

Zehra Sura[1], Chi-Leung Wong[1], Xing Fang[2], Jaejin Lee[3],
Samuel P. Midkiff[2], and David Padua[1]

[1] University of Illinois at Urbana-Champaign, Urbana, IL 61801
{zsura, cwong1, padua}@cs.uiuc.edu
[2] Purdue University, West Lafayette, IN 47907
{xfang, smidkiff}@purdue.edu
[3] Seoul National University, Seoul 151-742, Korea
jlee@cse.snu.ac.kr

**Abstract.** Concurrent threads executing on a shared memory system can access the same memory locations. A consistency model defines constraints on the order of these shared memory accesses. For good run-time performance, these constraints must be as few as possible. Programmers who write explicitly parallel programs must take into account the consistency model when reasoning about the behavior of their programs. Also, the consistency model constrains compiler transformations that reorder code. It is not known what consistency models best suit the needs of the programmer, the compiler, and the hardware simultaneously. We are building a compiler infrastructure to study the effect of consistency models on code optimization and run-time performance. The consistency model presented to the user will be a programmable feature independent of the hardware consistency model. The compiler will be used to mask the hardware consistency model from the user by mapping the software consistency model onto the hardware consistency model. When completed, our compiler will be used to prototype consistency models and to measure the relative performance of different consistency models. We present preliminary experimental data for performance of a software implementation of sequential consistency using manual inter-thread analysis.

## 1 Introduction

A consistency model defines the constraints on the order of accesses to shared memory locations made by concurrently executing threads. For any shared mem-

* This material is based upon work supported by the NSF under Grant No. CCR-0081265, and the IBM Corporation. Any opinions, findings, and conclusions or recommendations expressed in this material are those of the authors and do not necessarily reflect the views of the NSF or the IBM Corporation. Also supported in part by the Korean Ministry of Education under the BK21 program and by the Korean Ministry of Science and Technology under the National Research Laboratory program.

B. Pugh and C.-W. Tseng (Eds.): LCPC 2002, LNCS 2481, pp. 172–187, 2005.

ory system, it is important to specify a consistency model because that determines the set of possible outcomes for an execution, and enables the programmer to reason about a computation performed by the system.

The simplest and most intuitive consistency model for programmers to understand is sequential consistency (SC). SC requires that all threads "appear to" see the same order of shared memory accesses. Between two consecutive writes to a shared memory location, all threads that access the location see exactly the same value, and that value is consistent with the program order.

Most hardware systems implement consistency models that are weaker than SC [1], i.e. they impose fewer constraints on the order of shared memory accesses. This allows more instruction reordering, thus increasing the potential for instruction level parallelism and better performance. Popular hardware consistency models are weak ordering and release consistency, both of which allow reordering of shared memory accesses. These consistency models assume synchronization primitives that the programmer uses to specify points in the application program where shared memory accesses must be made coherent.

Thus, programmers writing explicitly parallel programs must take into account the consistency model when reasoning about the behavior of their programs. If the consistency model allows indiscriminate reorderings, it makes the task of writing well-synchronized programs difficult. Consider the following code:

```
Thread 1              Thread 2
a = ...;
x = 1;                while (x==0) wait;
                      ...= a;
```

This code uses a busy-wait loop and the variable x (initially set to zero) as a flag to ensure that the value of a read by Thread 2 is the value that is assigned to a by Thread 1. There are no data dependences between statements within a thread. So, for the weak or release consistency model, the access to a in Thread 2 may happen *before* the while loop has finished execution, or the assignment to a in Thread 1 may happen *after* the assignment to x. Therefore, there is no guarantee what value of a will be read in Thread 2. For these consistency models, the burden is on the programmer to insert proper synchronization constructs to disallow undesirable reorderings.

The ideal consistency model must be simple for programmers to understand. This is especially important because programmers for a general purpose language form a wide user base with varied skill levels.

We are building a compiler infrastructure that uses software to bridge the gap between the hardware consistency model and the consistency model assumed by the programmer. Our compiler is based on the Jikes Research Virtual Machine (Jikes RVM)[1] [2] which is an open-source Java Virtual Machine from IBM. Today, Java is the only widely-used, general-purpose language that defines a consistency model as a part of the language specification [6], i.e. the Java Memory Model. When completed, our compiler will allow users to experiment with alternative consistency models. It is designed to abstract out the effect of

---

[1] Originally called Jalapeño.

the consistency model on compiler transformations. The compiler will take as inputs a specific consistency model to be assumed by the programmer (henceforth called the software consistency model), and the consistency model provided by the target hardware (i.e. the hardware consistency model). The compiler will perform aggressive inter-thread analysis and optimizations to generate machine code based on the specific hardware and software consistency model(s) chosen.

Many different consistency models have been designed in the past, and new consistency models are still being designed. Since our compiler infrastructure abstracts out the consistency model and parameterizes it, it will allow rapid prototyping of new consistency models. Also, all the analyses and optimizations are to be "truly" portable, i.e. they will be reusable for all hardware and software consistency models we can envision. The availability of a common system platform and compiler algorithms for different consistency models will reduce the number of variables in performance comparison tests. This will allow reliable performance comparisons between different consistency models. Thus, our compiler will serve as a test-bed for developing and evaluating new software consistency models that balance ease of use and performance requirements. Such a test-bed is needed because the programming language community has little experience designing software consistency models. Problems with the Java Memory Model [14] illustrate the difficulty of this task.

We have modified the Jikes RVM to provide a sequentially consistent implementation. SC defines the strongest constraints among popular consistency models that are feasible to implement, i.e. a sequentially consistent implementation has the least flexibility to reorder instructions for optimized execution. Thus, the cost of implementing SC using software gives the maximum performance degradation that can be suffered by any feasible software consistency model implementation on a particular hardware system. We used manual inter-thread analysis to estimate this cost for our compiler using a set of benchmark programs, and found it to be negligible (Section 4). However, a simple implementation using the analyses provided in the Jikes RVM distribution gives slowdowns of 4.6 times on average. Thus, precise inter-thread analysis is important for a software implementation of consistency models that does not sacrifice performance.

The outline of the rest of this paper is as follows. In Section 2, we describe the overall system design for the compiler infrastructure we are developing. In Section 3, we explain the analyses and optimizations that are important from the perspective of implementing different consistency models. In Section 4, we give preliminary experimental data for the performance of a sequentially consistent implementation. Finally, in Section 5, we present our conclusions.

## 2   System Design

For well-synchronized programs that contain no data races, all shared memory access reorderings possible under a relaxed consistency model (e.g. release consistency) that is weaker than SC are also legitimate under SC. So there is no inherent reason for the run-time performance of these programs to be different for *any* two consistency models that are equivalent to, or weaker than SC. Thus, it should be possible to provide the user with a consistency model different from the hardware consistency model without suffering performance degradation. The performance of a software implementation of a consistency model is contingent on the compiler's ability to determine, without needing to be overly conservative, all the reorderings that lead to a legitimate outcome. This depends on the precision with which the compiler can analyse the interaction of multiple threads of execution through shared memory accesses. To provide the software consistency model, the compiler inserts *fences* at required points in the generated code. Fences are special hardware instructions that are used for memory synchronization.

To support multiple consistency models, the following features are used:

1. ability to *specify the consistency model* so that it can be parameterized,
2. rigorous *program analysis* for shared memory accesses,
3. constrained *code reordering transformations*, and
4. *fence insertion* to mask the hardware consistency model.

Constrained code reordering transformations and fence insertion have been implemented. They are discussed in detail in Sections 3.5 and 3.6 respectively. Inter-thread analysis algorithms are currently under development, and we discuss some of the issues involved in their design in Section 3.4.

We do not have a suitable notation for specifying the consistency model as yet. The notation we develop must be:

1. easy to use for the person experimenting with different consistency models.
2. easy to translate to a form that can be used by the compiler.
3. expressive, i.e. the design space of new consistency models must not be limited by the ability to specify them in a certain way.

Java uses dynamic compilation, so the choice of a consistency model can be made during program execution, and run-time values can be used to guide this choice. Also, compiler directives may be used to allow different consistency models for code segments within the same program. This flexibility will make it possible for the developer to freely experiment and perhaps gain a better understanding of the complexities involved in the design of software consistency models.

Figure 1 illustrates the relationship between the different components of the compiler. Given the source program and a software consistency model, the program analysis determines the shared memory access orders to enforce. Code reordering transformations use this information to optimize the program without changing any access orders that need to be enforced. Fence insertion also uses this information along with knowledge of the hardware consistency model, and generates code that enforces the access orders required by the software consistency model. It does this by emitting fences for those access orders that are not enforced by the hardware, but are required by the software consistency model.

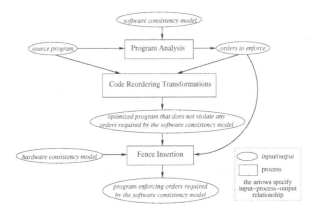

**Fig. 1.** Components in the design of the compiler

## 3   Compiler Techniques

### 3.1   Delay Set Analysis

An execution is invalid when it yields results, visible outside the program, that can only occur if the consistency model is violated. A *delay set* is a set of constraints on program execution order such that if these constraints are enforced, the outcome of the program is always valid according to the consistency model.

In [16], Shasha and Snir show how to find the minimal delay set. They construct a graph where each node represents a program statement. Edges in the graph are of two types: directed program edges (these represent constraints on the order of execution of statements within a thread as determined by the program order), and undirected conflict edges.

A conflict edge exists between two accesses if they are accesses to the same memory location from different threads, they may happen in parallel, and at least one is a write access. Alias analysis and thread-escape analysis (discussed in Section 3.2) help determine if there are accesses to the same memory location from different threads, and MHP and synchronization analysis (discussed in Section 3.3) help determine if they may happen in parallel. The conflict edges can be *oriented* by giving them a direction that represents the order of the two accesses during an execution of the program.

A minimal solution to the delay set analysis problem is the set of program edges in all *minimal mixed* cycles. A mixed cycle is one that contains both program and conflict edges, so a mixed cycle spans at least two threads in the program. Also, since the cycles are minimal, any other cycle in the graph will contain one or more of these minimal cycles within itself. Cycles represent inconsistent executions, because their presence means that there is an orientation of the conflict edges in the graph that is not consistent with the constraints required by the program. The set of program edges in the cycles is the delay set, i.e. the set of constraints that if enforced, prevents an orientation of conflict edges that gives rise to a cycle. If the program edges in this set are honored, then it is impossible at run-time for an orientation of the conflict edges to occur that gives rise to an inconsistent outcome.

In [9], Krishnamurthy and Yelick show that all exact delay set analysis algorithms for multiple-instruction multiple-data (MIMD) programs have a complexity that is exponential in the number of program segments. For single-program multiple-data (SPMD) programs, a large number of threads can be approximately modeled as two threads, resulting in an exponent of two, and therefore a quadratic algorithm [8]. The algorithms of [8,9] have been implemented, and they give good compile time performance on their set of benchmarks.

In general, programs can have arbitrary control flow and multiple threads may execute different code segments. It is difficult to analyse these programs to accurately determine the conflict edges in the program graph. We will use or develop precise alias analysis, synchronization analysis, and dependence analysis to find the set of conflict edges required for delay set analysis.

We are investigating modified path detection algorithms to find mixed cycles in a program graph. These algorithms have the property that they can be parameterized to be conservative and fast running, or precise and executing in worst case exponential time. They can be adjusted dynamically for different program regions, allowing more precise information to be developed "on demand".

In Java, every thread is an object of class `java.lang.Thread` or its subclasses. Therefore, we can use a type-based approach to approximate the runtime instances of threads.

### 3.2   Thread Escape Analysis

Escape analysis is used to identify all memory locations that can be accessed by more than one thread. Our analysis is concerned only with thread escaping accesses, and not the more general lifetime or method escaping properties. We are developing an algorithm for this to be as precise as possible. Because our algorithm is specialized for thread escaping accesses, we expect it to be faster than the more general escape analysis algorithms [3,15].

Figure 2 shows a program fragment from *raytracer*[2]. The method `run` creates an instance of the `Interval` object (referenced by `interval`). This object is used only in the statement `render(interval)`, so it can only escape through the call `render(interval)`. In `render`, the value of `interval` is initially accessible only by the thread that assigns this value, and it is never passed to another thread or assigned to static variables. So, `interval` always references a non-escaping object when `render(interval)` is called by `run`, and the fields `interval.width`, `interval.yto`, and `interval.yfrom` are thread local. This information can be derived by a context-sensitive, flow-sensitive escape analysis [3].

Classical optimizations can be applied to uses of `interval` in `render` even if `run` (and hence `render`) is executed by multiple threads. This will not violate the correctness for any consistency model because the object referenced by `interval`

---

[2] A benchmark program in the Java Grande Forum Multithreaded Benchmarks suite.

```
public void run() {
    Interval interval = new Interval(...);
    ...
    render(interval);
    /* interval is not used hereafter */
    ...
}

public void render(Interval interval) {
    int row[] = new int[interval.width * (interval.yto - interval.yfrom)];
    ...
    for (y = interval.yfrom+interval.threadid; y < interval.yto;
                y += JGFRayTracerBench.nthreads) {
        ylen = (double) (2.0*y) / (double) interval.width - 1.0;
        ...
    }
    ...
}
```

**Fig. 2.** Example program to illustrate thread local objects

```
public void render(Interval interval) {
    int width = interval.width;
    int yto = interval.yto;
    int yfrom = interval.yfrom;
    int row[] = new int[width * (yto - yfrom)];
    ...
    for (y = yfrom+interval.threadid; y < yto;
                y += JGFRayTracerBench.nthreads) {
        ylen = (double) (2.0*y) / (double) width - 1.0;
        ...
    }
    ...
}
```

**Fig. 3.** Optimization using information about thread local objects

does not escape the thread it was created in. Thus, redundant loads can be removed from **render** because no other thread can access the object referred by **interval**. The optimized **render** method is shown in Figure 3.

## 3.3   MHP and Synchronization Analysis

May-happen-in-parallel (MHP) analysis determines which statements may execute in parallel. We are developing an efficient (low order polynomial time) algorithm to perform MHP analysis that builds on previous work [13]. We use a program thread structure graph, similar to a call graph, that allows parallelism between code regions to be easily determined.

Synchronization analysis [4] is used to refine the results of MHP analysis. For two statements $S1$ and $S2$ that are in different threads and may happen in parallel, it attempts to determine if $S1$ must execute before $S2$, or after $S2$. This can reduce the number of possible executions, and improve the precision of other analyses. For example, concurrent global value numbering [12] can become more precise since the values assigned to a variable in one thread that can reach a use of that variable in another thread can be determined more accurately. Also, the precision of delay set analysis improves because synchronization analysis can determine orders on pairs of shared memory accesses from different threads that would otherwise be assumed to conflict.

## 3.4    Issues in the Design of Analysis Algorithms

To gauge the true effect of a consistency model on performance, the compiler must use detailed inter-thread analysis. The analyses and optimizations must be precise, otherwise this may lead to missed opportunities for code reordering optimizations. This will adversely affect software consistency models that are stronger than others being tested. The performance for the strong consistency models will not reflect their true potential, and so fair comparisons between different consistency models will not be possible.

We will be implementing alias analysis, concurrent global value numbering (CGVN), thread-escape analysis, MHP analysis, synchronization analysis, and delay-set analysis. There are several issues that make it challenging to design analysis algorithms for our compiler:

*Run-time compilation*: Faster compilation is always desirable, but for a system where the compile time contributes to the run-time, speed of compilation is imperative. Our system uses dynamic compilation, so it is important that it does not spend too much time performing analyses and optimizations. Thus, the algorithms we use must be *fast*.

*Dynamic class loading*: Due to Java's dynamic class loading feature, it is possible that a method being analyzed contains calls to other unresolved methods. This can result in incomplete information for analysis. Thus, we plan to implement algorithms that are designed to be *incremental*. A set of classes that are interdependent or mostly used together can be packaged into an archive (for example, as a JAR file). For these classes, inter-procedural and inter-class analysis information that is independent of the dynamic context can be determined statically and included in the package. Later, when a class from this package is first used in an application, the archived analysis results will be readily available for the dynamic compiler to incorporate into its current context. This helps to improve both the speed and accuracy of the analysis. Ideas from the design of the Net-Beans [19] and Eclipse [18] platforms can be used to integrate a static package that provides analysis information into a dynamic execution at run-time.

*Incomplete program information*: Dynamic class loading and JIT compilation require that the analyses and optimizations be done with incomplete program information. E.g., when an object is passed to an unresolved method, escape analysis cannot determine if the object is thread-escaping since it does not know whether the method makes the object accessible to another thread. Thus, a lack of information leads to conservative and imprecise analysis, which can degrade performance. There are two ways to handle incomplete program information:

1. The analysis can be *optimistic* and assume the best-case result. Thus, when faced with lack of information, escape analysis would assume an object is non-escaping. The compiler will then perform checks when methods are compiled later to ensure that previous assumptions are not violated. If a violation occurs, it triggers a recompilation to patch up code previously generated.

2. The analysis makes conservative assumptions when faced with lack of information, but always generates safe code. Later, when more information

becomes available, methods can be *recompiled* and more precise results obtained. To avoid expensive re-analysis overhead, only execution hotspots will be recompiled. These hotspots typically include code sections with many fences because fences are expensive. Recompiling the code using more analysis information allows greater freedom to reorder code and may eliminate some fences. The cost model for recompiling must take into account both the number of fences in the hotspot, and the potential benefit in performance of the transformed code after recompilation.

Both approaches require an adaptive recompilation system that allows methods to be recompiled during execution of the program.

## 3.5    Reordering Transformations

Code reordering transformations are sensitive to the consistency model being supported because they can change the order of accesses to shared memory locations. Therefore, optimization algorithms developed for single-threaded sequential programs that use code motion or code elimination cannot be directly applied to shared memory systems with multiple threads of execution.

Consider the following example, where r1, r2, and r3 are registers, and a and b are aliased.

```
1.  Load r1, [a]    // "a" contains the address of a memory location to load from
2.  Load r2, [b]    // "b" contains the same address as "a"
3.  Load r3, [a]
```

If redundant load elimination (RLE) is applied to this code segment, the third instruction can be transformed into Move r3, r1. However, this transformation will violate SC if there is another thread that executes between the first and second Load, and changes the value of the memory location given by a. In this case, r3 gets an older value than r2, even though the assignment to r3 occurs after the assignment to r2. Thus, the RLE transformation appears to reorder code by changing the order of statements 2 and 3.

Transformations must be inhibited if they reorder code in cases where delay set analysis determines that the software consistency model may be violated. For best performance, there must be few instances where a transformation is inhibited.

Our initial implementation targets SC as the software consistency model. We examine all transformations in our compiler to determine if they are valid for a sequentially consistent execution. Our compiler is built using the Jikes RVM, so we focus on optimizations implemented in the Jikes RVM. We modify transformations so that they are not performed for instances that can potentially violate the software consistency model; however, these transformations are performed, even in sequentially consistent programs, where they are shown to be safe by the analyses previously described. Optimizations in the Jikes RVM that are affected are redundant load elimination, redundant store elimination, loop invariant code motion, scalar replacement of loads, and loop unrolling.

In the Jikes RVM, optimization phases are structured such that redundant load/store elimination is done before most other optimizations. Thereafter, the number of accesses to memory variables are fixed in the code. Further optimizations work on the results of these load/store instructions and temporary variables. When tailoring optimization phases to account for a particular memory model, the effects of code motion on the relative ordering of load/store instructions have to be accounted for. However, *elimination* of loads and stores is not a cause for concern at this stage if only temporary variables are being eliminated. For example, common subexpression elimination (CSE) done across basic blocks, as currently implemented in the Jikes RVM, eliminates common subexpressions involving only temporary variables that cannot be changed by another thread. So this CSE does not need to be modified for different consistency models.

In previous work [10,12], we give algorithms to perform optimizations such as constant propagation, copy propagation, redundant load/store elimination, and dead code elimination for explicitly parallel programs. These algorithms are based on concurrent static single assignment (CSSA) graphs. CSSA graphs are constructed from concurrent control flow graphs and they preserve the SSA property for parallel programs, i.e. all uses of a variable are reached by exactly one static assignment to the variable. CSSA graphs and delay set analysis enable us to encapsulate the effects of the consistency model. Thus, the algorithms described can be reused for different consistency models by supplying the consistency model as a parameter to the optimization engine. We will apply these techniques in the compiler we are developing.

**Example.** We illustrate the use of inter-thread analysis to modify transformations in our compiler: we show how delay-set analysis influences RLE using the toy example in Figure 4. This example is based on a code segment extracted from *lufact*[3] and simplified for clarity. We assume that the software memory model is SC, and that the execution uses only two threads.

```
Thread 0                        Thread 1
...                             ...
P1: while (!sync.flag1) ;       S1: ...= col_k[l];
P2: col_k[l] = ...;             S2: sync.flag1 = true;
P3: sync.flag2 = true;          S3: while (!sync.flag2) ;
                                S4: ...= col_k[l];
...                             ...
```

**Fig. 4.** Code segment to illustrate delay-set analysis

For the example, global value analysis and alias analysis are used to determine that all instances of col_k[l] refer to the same element of a single array object. The benchmark program *lufact* performs Gaussian elimination with partial pivoting for a matrix. The rows of the matrix are distributed for processing amongst different threads. However, Thread 0 is responsible for assigning the pivot element (col_k[l] in the example) each time. It uses shared variables sync.flag1 and sync.flag2 for synchronization to avoid conflicts (the benchmark program uses volatile variables to implement barriers for this purpose).

---

[3] A benchmark program in the Java Grande Forum Multithreaded Benchmarks suite.

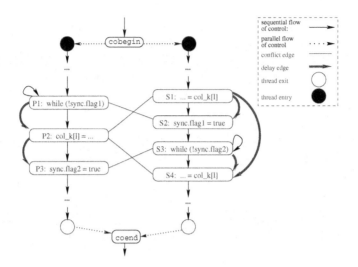

**Fig. 5.** Program graph for the example of Figure 4 showing delay edges

The program graph with delay edges is shown in Figure 5. There are conflict edges between P1 and S2 for the synchronization using `sync.flag1`, between P3 and S3 for the synchronization using `sync.flag2`, between P2 and S1 for the write-read access to `col_k[l]`, and between P2 and S4 for the write-read access to `col_k[l]`. These result in the following three cycles in the program graph:

1. P1,P2,S1,S2: the corresponding delay edges are P1-P2 and S1-S2.
2. P2, P3, S3, S4: the corresponding delay edges are P2-P3 and S3-S4.
3. P2, S1,S4: the corresponding delay edge is S1-S4.

The delay edges are enforced by inserting fences as discussed in Section 3.6.

If we consider each thread in isolation without any consistency model constraints, RLE may be applied to the access `col_k[l]` at S4. Thus, by traditional analysis, the value of `col_k[l]` accessed at S1 may be stored in a register and reused at S4. However, this is invalid for SC because it effectively reorders the access at S3 and the access at S4. Inter-thread delay set analysis can recognize this, and the delay edge from S3 to S4 prevents the reuse of the value accessed at S1.

Note that the synchronization is important to guarantee consistent execution, and it is the effect of the synchronization variable `sync.flag2` that ensures the RLE optimization is not incorrectly applied in this instance. For SC, the presence of an intervening conflicting access is needed to disallow the reordering of two conflicting accesses to the same shared variable. Taking this fact into account helps to perform optimizations in as many instances as possible without being overly conservative.

### 3.6   Fence Insertion

Fence instructions force memory accesses that were issued previously to complete before further processing can occur. They can be used to enforce necessary orders for a consistency model, and thus it is possible to mask the hardware consistency model by another stricter[4] consistency model [11]. Thread-based escape analysis, MHP analysis, synchronization analysis, and delay-set analysis determine the points in the code where fences must be inserted.

We describe two techniques that optimize the number of fences inserted. First, register hazards (i.e. write/write, write/read, and read/write operations to the same register) in conjunction with the store order from the processor enforce an order for all accesses to a particular memory location that occur within the same thread. This is exploited to reduce the number of fences that are inserted. Second, two orders to be enforced can overlap, i.e. in the sequence of operations:

`load A;       load B;       load C;`

it is possible that the orders to be enforced are A before C and B before C. Fences can be inserted in at least two ways: by placing a fence immediately after A and immediately after B, or, more efficiently, by placing a single fence after B that enforces both of the orders.

When developing an algorithm that makes the best use of program control flow to optimize fence insertion, additional complexity is added for programs with loops and branches. We have implemented a fast, flow-insensitive algorithm, and a slower, but more precise, flow sensitive form of the analysis [5]. The experimental data in Section 4 was obtained using the whole-procedure, flow-sensitive algorithm for fence insertion.

## 4   Experiments

We are implementing the compiler infrastructure described using the Jikes RVM on an IBM AIX/PowerPC platform. The IBM PowerPC supports a relaxed consistency model that is similar to weak ordering and provides *sync* instructions that can be used as fences. The Jikes RVM is a Java virtual machine written mostly in Java. It does dynamic compilation for the whole program, i.e. before any method is executed, machine code is generated for the entire method. This allows fences to be inserted to enforce the software consistency model. The Jikes RVM also supports an adaptive recompilation system that can be used to optimize in the presence of dynamic class loading.

We obtained preliminary experimental results for a software implementation of SC using both simple analysis and manual inter-thread analysis. We describe simple analysis in Section 4.1 and manual inter-thread analysis in Section 4.2. The goal of the experiments is to obtain quantitative numbers to estimate the performance of an implementation of the compiler we have described. As a first step, we focus on using SC as the programming language consistency model. This is because SC is a natural and intuitive programming model and is one of the most expensive consistency models to implement.

---

[4] A stricter consistency model specifies stronger constraints on the ordering of shared memory accesses.

For this study, we choose benchmark programs that have a small code size, because that makes them amenable for manual analysis to be applied. We use well-synchronized Java programs because these programs introduce no more constraints for a sequentially consistent programming model than a relaxed consistency model. The synchronization required for these programs is the same for SC as for popular hardware consistency models. We rely on program analyses to detect the set of "required" synchronizations, i.e. the set of shared memory access orders that must be enforced in program threads.

## 4.1  Simple Analysis

The simple analysis is the default analysis that is provided in the Jikes RVM distribution. There is no MHP, synchronization, or delay set analysis. The escape analysis is a simple flow-insensitive analysis. Initially, all variables of reference type are assumed not to be pointing to any thread-shared objects. The analysis then marks a reference variable as pointing to a thread-shared object if:

1. it stores the result of a load from a memory location, or
2. it is the operand of a store to a memory location, or
3. it is the operand of a return statement (and not a method parameter), or
4. it is the operand of a throw statement, or a reference move statement.

The performance using this conservative simple analysis provides a lower bound of the performance using automatic inter-thread analysis. The simple analysis may conservatively mark arguments of method calls as pointing to thread-shared objects, even if the object is never passed to another thread. Therefore, using this analysis can degrade performance even when the program is single-threaded.

## 4.2  Manual Inter-thread Analysis

The analysis results are statically determined and supplied to the compiler by inserting special directives in the program. These directives mark the accesses to thread-shared memory objects that need to be synchronized. Although the directives are inserted manually, we have the compiler implementation in mind when we insert them. Logically, we mark an access if:

- the access involves a thread escaping object, i.e. the object is assigned to or obtained from a class field, or passed to or obtained from another thread.
- MHP and delay set analysis cannot prove the thread escaping object is accessed exclusively.

Therefore, we expect the performance using manual inter-thread analysis to be the upper bound of the performance using automatic inter-thread analysis. Note that it is an upper bound because we did not consider dynamic class loading in manual analysis. In the automatic analysis, we may only have partial program information due to unloaded classes.

## 4.3   Experimental Data

Table 1 gives execution times obtained for the benchmark programs. The first seven programs are from the SPECJVM98 Benchmark suite, the next two are from ETH, Zurich[5], and the remaining are from the Java Grande Forum Benchmark suite v1.0. Except for the first six, all the programs are multithreaded.

Our goal is not to provide higher performance, but comparable performance with an easy-to-understand-and-use consistency model. We compare the slowdown when running the benchmark programs with SC, versus using the default consistency model implemented in the Jikes RVM.

The data presented in Table 1 gives the average times taken over 4 runs of each program on an IBM SP machine with 8 GB of memory and using 4 375MHz processors. The 'Original' column is the execution time for the program using the default Jikes RVM Java memory model. Column 'Simple' is the time taken for an implementation of sequential consistency that uses the simple analysis previously described. Column 'Manual' is the time taken for an implementation of sequential consistency that uses precise, manual, inter-thread analysis. Note that the slowdown numbers are shown in parentheses.

**Table 1.** Performance, in seconds, with (i) simple escape analysis, and (ii) manual escape and delay-set analysis

| Benchmark | Original | Simple | Manual |
|---|---|---|---|
| _201_compress | 16.812 | 224.924 (13.379) | 17.038 (1.013) |
| _202_jess | 9.758 | 29.329 (3.006) | 9.777 (1.002) |
| _209_db | 30.205 | 41.232 (1.365) | 30.560 (1.011) |
| _213_javac | 15.964 | 36.706 (2.299) | 15.606 (0.978) |
| _222_mpegaudio | 13.585 | 174.478 (12.843) | 13.457 (0.991) |
| _228_jack | 19.371 | 41.070 (2.120) | 19.326 (0.998) |
| _227_mtrt | 4.813 | 26.516 (5.509) | 4.822 (1.002) |
| elevator | 22.507 | 22.509 (1.000) | 22.508 (1.000) |
| philo | 15.391 | 15.817 (1.028) | 15.465 (1.004) |
| crypt | 23.579 | 32.688 (1.386) | 23.563 (0.999) |
| lufact | 3.177 | 3.514 (1.106) | 3.182 (1.001) |
| series | 141.859 | 378.768 (2.670) | 141.065 (0.994) |
| sor | 4.137 | 35.776 (8.648) | 4.137 (1.000) |
| sparsematmult | 3.788 | 26.062 (6.880) | 7.499 (1.979) |
| moldyn | 71.756 | 446.406 (6.221) | 71.190 (0.992) |
| montecarlo | 13.973 | 28.852 (2.065) | 13.846 (0.991) |
| raytracer | 145.145 | 1015.980 (7.000) | 145.237 (1.001) |

For simple escape analysis, the average slowdown was 4.6, and 12 of the 17 benchmarks showed slowdowns greater than 2 times. However, for manual analysis, none of the benchmarks showed any significant slowdowns, except *sparsematmult*. *sparsematmult* showed a slowdown of 2 times. It performed poorly because the analysis techniques we have described are not sufficient to eliminate false dependences in the program that occur due to indirect array indexing. However, other techniques can be applied to reduce the slowdown for *sparsematmult*. For example, speculative execution or run-time dependence analysis can be used.

---

[5] Thanks to Christoph von Praun for these.

Our results show that for well-synchronized programs, it is feasible to implement consistency models in software without performance degradation. So, it is worthwhile to develop precise and efficient analysis algorithms for this purpose.

## 5   Conclusion

We have outlined the design of a compiler that allows the consistency model to be a programmable feature. This compiler can be used to prototype and test new consistency models, and to determine the effect of a consistency model on compiler transformations and run-time performance.

We obtained an estimate for performance degradation due to a software implementation of sequential consistency that uses manual analysis. For all benchmark programs except one, there was no slowdown. This demonstrates the usability of software consistency model implementations to provide ease-of-use to programmers, and justifies the development of precise and efficient inter-thread analysis algorithms for this purpose.

## References

1. Sarita V. Adve and Kourosh Gharachorloo.: Shared memory consistency models: A tutorial. IEEE Computer, pages 66-76, Dec 1996
2. B. Alpern, et al: The Jalapeno virtual machine. IBM Systems Journal, Feb 2000
3. J.-D. Choi, M. Gupta, M. Serrano, V.C. Sreedhar, and S. Midkiff: Escape analysis for Java. Proceedings ACM 1999 Conference on Object-Oriented Programming Systems (OOPSLA 99), pages 1-19, Nov 1999
4. P.A. Emrath, S. Ghosh, and D.A. Padua: Event synchronization analysis for debugging parallel programs. Proceedings of Supercomputing, pages 580-588, 1989
5. Xing Fang: Inserting fences to guarantee sequential consistency. Master's thesis, Michigan State University, July 2002
6. J. Gosling, B. Joy, G. Steele, and G. Bracha: The Java Language Specification, Second Edition. The Java Series, Addison-Wesley Publishing Company, Redwood City, CA 94065, USA, 2000
7. Mark D. Hill: Multiprocessors should support simple memory-consistency models. IEEE Computer, pages 28-34, Aug 1998
8. Arvind Krishnamurthy and Katherine Yelick: Optimizing parallel SPMD programs. Seventh Workshop on Languages and Compilers for Parallel Computing, Aug 1994
9. Arvind Krishnamurthy and Katherine Yelick: Analyses and optimizations for shared address space programs. Journal of Parallel and Distributed Computing, 38:139-144, 1996
10. J. Lee, S.P. Midkiff, and D.A. Padua: Concurrent static single assignment form and constant propagation for explicitly parallel programs. Proceedings of The 10th International Workshop on Languages and Compilers for Parallel Computing, pages 114-130, Springer, Aug 1997
11. J. Lee and D.A.Padua: Hiding relaxed memory consistency with compilers. Proceedings of The 2000 International Conference on Parallel Architectures and Compilation Techniques, Oct 2000

12. J. Lee, D.A.Padua, and S.P. Midkiff: Basic compiler algorithms for parallel programs. Proceedings of The 1999 ACM SIGPLAN Symposiun on Principles and Practice of Parallel Programming, pages 1-12, May 1999
13. G. Naumovich, G.S. Avruninand, and L.A. Clarke: An efficient algorithm for computing MHP information for concurrent Java programs. Proceedings of Seventh European Software Engineering Conference and Seventh ACM SIGSOFT Symposium on the Foundations of Software Engineering, Sep 1999
14. William Pugh: Fixing the Java memory model. Proceedings of the ACM 1999 Java Grande Conference, June 1999
15. R. Rugina and M. Rinard: Pointer analysis for multithreaded programs. Proceedings of the ACM SIGPLAN 1999 Conference on Programming Language Design and Implementation, pages 77-90, June 1999
16. Dennis Shasha and Marc Snir: Efficient and correct execution of parallel programs that share memory. ACM Transactions on Programming Languages and Systems, 10(2):282-312, Apr 1988
17. C.-L. Wong, Z. Sura, X. Fang, S.P. Midkiff, J. Lee, and D. Padua: The Pensieve Project: A Compiler Infrastructure for Memory Models. The International Symposium on Parallel Architectures, Algorithms, and Networks, May 2002
18. Eclipse Platform Technical Overview. Object Technology International, Inc., July 2001, Available at www.eclipse.org
19. The NetBeans Platform. Sun Microsystems, Inc., Documentation available at www.netbeans.org

# Parallel Reductions: An Application of Adaptive Algorithm Selection*

Hao Yu, Francis Dang, and Lawrence Rauchwerger

Dept. of Computer Science, Texas A&M University,
College Station, TX 77843-3112
{h0y8494, fhd4244, rwerger}@cs.tamu.edu

**Abstract.** Irregular and dynamic memory reference patterns can cause significant performance variations for low level algorithms in general and especially for parallel algorithms. We have previously shown that parallel reduction algorithms are quite input sensitive and thus can benefit from an adaptive, reference pattern directed selection. In this paper we extend our previous work by detailing a systematic approach to dynamically select the best parallel algorithm. First we model the characteristics of the input, i.e., the memory reference pattern, with a descriptor vector. Then we measure the performance of several reduction algorithms for various values of the pattern descriptor. Finally we establish a (many-to-one) mapping (function) between a finite set of descriptor values and a set of algorithms. We thus obtain a performance ranking of the available algorithms with respect to a limited set of descriptor values. The actual dynamic selection code is generated using statistical regression methods or a decision tree. Finally we present experimental results to validate our modeling and prediction techniques.

## 1 Parallel Performance Is Input Dependent

Improving performance on current parallel processors is a very complex task which, if done 'by hand' by programmers, becomes increasingly difficult and error prone. Moreover, due to the inherent complexity and human limitations, true optimizations are hard to achieve. During the last decade, programmers have obtained increasingly more help from parallelizing (restructuring) compilers. Such compilers address the need of detecting and exploiting parallelism in sequential programs written in conventional languages as well as parallel languages (e.g., HPF). They also optimize data layout and perform other transformations to reduce and hide memory latency, the other crucial optimization in modern, large scale parallel systems. The success in the 'conventional' use of compilers to automatically optimize code is limited to cases when performance is independent of the application's input data. When the access pattern of the code (e.g., loops) is statically insufficiently defined, either because it is read–in from a file or it is actually computed (and re-computed) during execution, then the compiler cannot use classic analysis techniques, e.g., data dependence analysis. Unfortunately, this precludes traditional static compiler parallelization and latency hiding techniques from being used in

* This research supported in part by NSF CAREER Awards CCR-9624315 and CCR-9734471, NSF Grants ACI-9872126, EIA-9975018, EIA-0103742, and by the DOE ASCI ASAP program grant B347886.

B. Pugh and C.-W. Tseng (Eds.): LCPC 2002, LNCS 2481, pp. 188–202, 2005.

the optimization of many important modern applications such as SPICE [12], DYNA–3D [15], GAUSSIAN [10], and CHARMM [1], which have input-dependent and/or computation-dependent memory reference patterns.

A particularly important input dependent optimization is the parallelization of reductions (a.k.a. updates). In fact, with the exception of some simple methods using unordered critical sections (locks) reduction parallelization is performed through a simple form of algorithm substitution. For example, a sequential summation is a reduction which can be replaced by a parallel prefix, or recursive doubling, computation [7,8].

In [17] we have presented a small library of parallel reduction algorithms and shown that the best performance can be obtained only if we dynamically select the most appropriate algorithm for the instantiated input set (reference pattern). Also in [17] we have presented a taxonomy of reduction reference patterns and sketched a decision tree based scheme that allows an application to dynamically select the best algorithm for a pattern.

This paper continues this work and presents in more detail a systematic process of memory reference and algorithm characterization. It establishes a predictive model that takes as input a reduction memory reference pattern and a library of parallel reduction algorithms and outputs the performance ranking of these algorithms. All processes for establishing such a predictive model and its use in a real application are automated. Finally we show how this model can be used in the optimization of irregular applications that instantiate reductions.

We believe that the paper's main contribution is a framework for a systematic process through which input sensitive predictive models can be built off-line and used dynamically to select from a particular list of functionally equivalent algorithms, parallel reductions being just one important example. The same approach could also be used for various other compiler transformations that cannot be easily analytically modeled.

## 2    A Library of Reduction Parallelization Algorithms

To use an adaptive scheme that selects the most appropriate parallel reduction algorithm we first need a library of reduction algorithms. Our library currently contains *direct update methods* and *private accumulation and global update methods*. Direct update methods update shared reduction variables during the original loop execution. Methods in this category include *unordered critical sections* [3,19] (not of interest because they don't scale well for arrays) and *local write* [4]. Private accumulation and global update methods accumulate in private storage during loop execution and update the shared variables with each processor's contribution after the loop has finished. Methods in this category include *replicated buffer* [7,8,13,9], *replicated buffer with links*, and *selective privatization* [17]. For brevity, we provide here only a high level description of the methods. Table 1 provides an overview of their relative strengths and weaknesses. See the previously cited literature and [17] for more details.

**Replicated Buffer** (REPBUFS). A reduction operation is an associative recurrence and can thus be parallelized using a recursive doubling algorithm [7,8]. In a similar manner, the REPBUFS scheme privatizes the reduction variables and accumulates in private storage the partial results and thus allows the original loop to execute as a doall.

Then, after loop execution, the partial results are accumulated across processors and the corresponding shared array is updated.

**Replicated Buffer With Links** (REPLINK). To avoid the overhead encountered at the cross-processor reduction phase by REPBUFS, REPLINK links used private elements to avoid traversing unused private elements. For every shared element, a linked list is maintained based on the processor IDs of used private elements.

**Selective Privatization** (SELPRIV). To avoid the overhead encountered by REPBUFS, SELPRIV only privatizes array elements having cross–processor contentions. By excluding unused privatized elements, SELPRIV maintains a dense private space where almost all elements are used. Since the private space does not align to that in REPBUFS, to avoid introducing another level of indirection, the remote references in the original index array are modified to redirect the access to the reserved elements in the dense private space. The cross–processor reduction phase traverses links among private elements corresponding to the same shared element to update the global reduction element.

**Local Write** (LOCALWRITE). LOCALWRITE uses a variation of the 'owner computes' method and is mostly employed in the parallelization of irregular codes. The reference pattern is first collected in an inspector loop [16] and is followed by a partitioning of the iteration space based on the *owner-computes* rule. Memory locations referenced across processors will have their iterations replicated so that they access addresses local to each processor. The authors of LOCALWRITE have recently improved the implementation of this scheme by using a *low overhead graph partitioning (GPART)* technique to reorder the data and thus minimize the cross-processor communications [5]. The *GPART* algorithm works on reduction loops when the data structure of the loop is equivalent to a graph. Because we are not sure how the algorithm performs when applied to loops with multiple reduction statements we have used a more general but less-optimized implementation of LOCALWRITE: We record the iterations that need to be executed on each processor and then predicate the reduction statements in all the (replicated) iterations.

## 3   Pattern Descriptor

Memory accesses in irregular programs take a variety of patterns and are dependent on the code itself as well as on their input data. Moreover, some codes are of a dynamic nature, i.e., they modify their behavior during execution because they often (not necessarily) simulate position dependent interactions between physical entities. In this context we need to quantify the characteristics of a loop containing reductions that matter most to the performance of parallel reduction algorithms. This characterization is not general but specific to our goal of selecting the best algorithm for the input at hand. In Table 1, we present an experimentally obtained qualitative correlation between the values of some attributes of reduction loops and their memory access patterns and their relative performance. These results indicate that the chosen set of attributes, (called a *pattern descriptor*), can be used for modeling and performance ranking of reduction loops.

**Table 1.** Advantages and Disadvantages of schemes. M is the number of iterations; N is the size of reduction array; P is the number of processors.

| Issues | REPBUFS | REPLINK | SELPRIV | LOCALWRITE |
|---|---|---|---|---|
| Inspector Complexity | NO | $O(N)$ | $O(M)$ | $O(M)$ |
| Inspector Applicability | | always | always | limited |
| Extra Space | $O(N \times P)$ | $O(N \times P)$ | $O(N \times P + M)$ | $O(M \times P)$ |
| Pattern change | not sensitive | sensitive | sensitive | sensitive |
| Locality | poor | poor | good | the best |
| Preferred patterns | dense | sparse | sparse | no preference |
| Extra computation | None | None | access my_index() | replicate iterations |

### 3.1 Pattern Descriptor

The various characteristics of a reduction loop can be described by a small number of parameters, put together in a small vector, called a *pattern descriptor*.

Ideally, these attributes would take no overhead to measure, however this is not possible in most cases because they are input dependent (read from a file or computed during execution before the actual reductions take place). We will now enumerate them in no specific order.

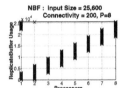 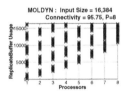 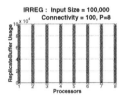

**Fig. 1.** Three classes of memory access patterns whose **CLUS** are defined as *clustered, partially-clustered,* and *scattered,* respectively

**N**, the size of the reduction array is one of the attributes which impacts heavily on the working set of the loop and has to be related to machine model.

**CON**, the Connectivity of a loop is a ratio between the number of iterations of the loop and the number of distinct memory elements referenced by the loop. In [4] it is equivalently defined as the number of edges over the number of nodes of a graph. The higher the connectivity, the higher the ratio of computation to communication will be, i.e., if CON is high, a small number of elements will be referenced by many iterations.

**MOB**, the **Mobility** per iteration of a loop, is directly proportional to the number of distinct subscripts of reductions in an iteration. For the LOCALWRITE scheme, the effect of a high iteration Mobility (actually lack of mobility) is a high degree of iteration replication. MOB is the attribute that can be measured accurately at compile time.

**NRED** is the *number of different reducitons using the same index.* In the cross-processor reduction phase of the REPLINK and SELPRIV schemes, this attribute indicates how many shared reduction elements will be updated while traversing one auxiliary link unit. In the LOCALWRITE scheme, it implies less replication for the same amount of reduction work. Thus, NRED should have larger positive effects on these three schemes comparing to that on REPBUFS scheme.

**OTH**, the **Other work** per iteration of a loop, defines the relative amount of work other than reduction operations. If OTH is high, a penalty will be paid for LOCAL-WRITE to replicate iterations. This attribute is actually dynamic in nature but expensive to measure at run-time. We have thus decided to estimate its value at compile time. Furthermore, we have broken OTH into Memory Read (**OTHR**), Memory Write (**OTHW**) and Scalar Computations (**OTHS**), and then used their relative operation counts for modeling.

**C**, the degree of **Contention** of a reduction element, is the number of iterations referencing it. The C measure is related to the CON measure in the sense that if an element is referenced by many iterations it is quite likely (but not necessarily so) that the loop has many iterations that do reductions on a small number of elements.

**CHR**, the ratio of the total number of references and the space needed for allocating replicated arrays across processors (it is equal to *the number of processors × dimension of the reduction array*). CHR measures the percentage of elements that are referenced if replicated arrays are used. It indicates whether or not to use replicated arrays.

**CLUS**, the **Degree of Clustering**, defines a measurement to classify whether the touched private elements are scattered or clustered on every processor. Fig. 1 shows three classes of memory access patterns whose CLUS values are defined as *clustered*, *partially-clustered*, and *scattered*, respectively. This attribute not only reflects the spatial locality of reductions in private space, but also reflects the structure of the implied graph structure of the reduction loop. For example, in most cases, a fully clustered pattern indicates that data communication occurs mainly between neighbors nodes.

**R**, the **reusability**, measures the frequency and degree of change of the access pattern from one instantiation of the reduction loop to the next. If $R > 1$, then it indicates we can reuse the pattern characterization for $R$ consecutive loop invocations. If $0 < R \leq 1$, then the loop is more or less dynamic. If $R = 0$, then the pattern changes for every invocation. If the pattern is static for the entire execution of a program then it is quite probable that this can be proved at compile time and $R$ does not have to be collected. As previously mentioned, REPLINK, SELPRIV, LOCALWRITE are applicable only when $R > 1$ due to the significant run-time overhead they incur when they are set up (usually part of an inspection). Thus, for a given reduction loop, the **Reusability**, is a crucial factor in the decision whether a more complex reduction algorithm should be considered. The best scheme should have the smallest value of $\frac{R+O}{Speedup}$, where $R$ is the *reusability*, $O$ is the ratio of the set-up phase overhead and the parallel execution time of one invocation of the loop applying a scheme, and $Speedup$ is the speedup of the scheme excluding the set-up phase overhead. We can prove if $R > 0$ at compile time through loop invariant hoisting.

### 3.2   Decoupled Effects of Pattern Descriptor Values on Performances

In this section, we give a qualitative view and discussion of the decoupled effects of the pattern descriptor components on the performance of different reduction parallelization schemes. We should emphasize that while this decoupling is not realistic it is nevertheless useful to uncover qualitative trends.

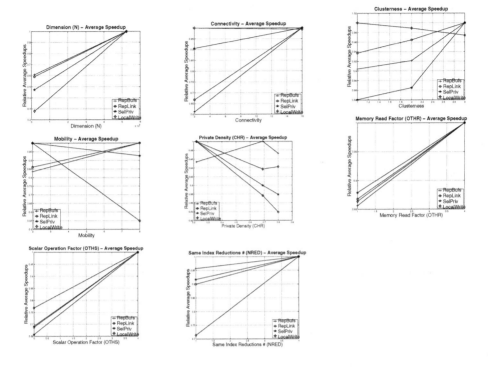

**Fig. 2.** Decoupled Effect of Pattern Descriptor Attributes on performances of different schemes

In Fig. 2, we show the effects of attributes **N, CON, MOB, NRED, OTHR, OTHS, CHR** and **CLUS**. The graphs are based on a factorial experiment to generate a list of attributes that are then used as parameters of a synthetic reduction loop (see Section 4.1). In our experiments, we choose $|A_i|$ values for the $i$th attribute. Each graph in Fig. 2 illustrates the decoupled effect of an attribute, say $A_i$. The vertical axis corresponds to the average speedups normalized by the best average speedup for each scheme.

Table 3 summarizes the trends illustrated in Fig. 2. SELPRIV and LOCALWRITE have better locality and use less space and thus perform better than the REPBUFS scheme. Data replication based schemes (REPBUFS and SELPRIV) consist of two loops: a reduction loop in privatized space and a cross-processor reduction loop. The second loop can be considered as the parallel overhead of these schemes. Thus, when **CON** (previously defined as the ratio between these two loops) increases, the 'privatized' reduction loop dominates and the speedups of REPBUFS and SELPRIV increase. On the other hand, low **CON** values will be helped by LOCALWRITE. High **MOB** values also imply a large number of accesses of the `index` array of the irregular reductions which in turn implies poor performance for the SELPRIV scheme. This is because in this scheme both the original and the `my_index` array redirect references to privatized storage. Higher values for **OTH** increase the relative weight of the privatized reduction loop which implies better performance for the REPBUFS and SELPRIV methods. High **CLUS** values are helped by the SELPRIV scheme because it increases the clustering (gathers references).

| Attributes | RepBufs | SelPriv | LocalWrite |
|------------|---------|---------|------------|
| N    | ↗ | ↑ | ↑ |
| CON  | ↑ | ↗ | – |
| MOB  | ↑ | ↘ | ↓ |
| NRED | – | ↗ | ↑ |
| OTH  | ↑ | ↑ | ↗ |
| CHR  | ↗ | ↓ | ↘ |
| CLUS | ↗ | ↑ | – |

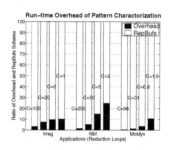

**Fig. 3.** Summary of Effects of attributes in pattern descriptor on the performances of different schemes. (↑: positive effect; ↓: negative effect; ↗: little positive effect; ↘: little negative effect; –: no effect.).

**Fig. 4.** Modeling Overhead. Relative execution times for the parallel reduction loop using the RepBufs scheme (RepBufs) and generating the pattern descriptor (Overhead). **C** denotes the connectivity of the inputs.

## 4    Adaptive Scheme Selection

The *pattern descriptor* can be analyzed by the compiler (rarely) or measured and computed at run-time, either with inspectors or by adopting a simple 'general purpose' technique for the first instantiation of the loop. Some of the attributes of the descriptor are not easy to estimate and/or measure. The characterization of the reduction pattern is achieved by inexpensively computing some scalar values while the references are traversed. Our run-time adaptive reduction parallelization scheme is illustrated in Fig. 5.

The run-time overhead of our technique, represented by the procedures *Compute Pattern Descriptor* and *Select Scheme* in Fig. 5, has been normalized to the RepBufs execution time (because it is assumed without overhead) and shown in Fig. 4.

A realistic prediction scheme cannot rely on the decoupled measurements presented thus far but needs to combine the effect of all attributes as they cover the universe of all possible (realistic) values. Because an exhaustive characterization is impractical we have established a process through which we can sample the $n$-dimensional space of the pattern descriptor, rank the performance of the algorithms in our library and use this mapping to interpolate or reason about any other values of the pattern descriptor. This process is done only once, off-line, as a *setup phase* for each machine installation and it is outlined in Fig. 6.

We will first present the design of the initial map between a set of synthetically generated pattern descriptors and their corresponding performance ranking. This will generate a many-to-one mapping between a limited number of points in the multidimensional space described by the pattern descriptor and the limited number of possible rankings of performance of our library. In fact this number is very limited because we will almost always select the best performing algorithm. Then, we will show how an application can use this mapping to interpolate for its own pattern descriptor and select the best possible algorithm. For this purpose we introduce two methods to generate the prediction code that can then be used by an application at run-time: *Statistical Regression* and *Decision Tree Learning*.

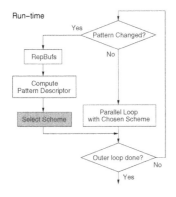

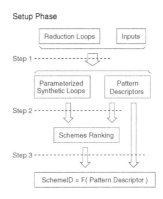

**Fig. 5.** Adaptive Reduction Parallelization at Run-time

**Fig. 6.** Setup phase of Adaptive Scheme Selection

### 4.1  Sample Space Generation, a Factorial Experiment

To measure the performance of different reduction patterns, we have created the synthetic reduction loop in Fig 7 which has been parameterized by most attributes of the pattern descriptor, **N, CON, MOB, NRED, OTHR, OTHS** and **OTHW**. Attributes **CHR** and **CLUS** are used to generate the index array. The various operation types have been grouped in their own loop nests. Because sometimes the native compiler cannot unroll the inner loop nests for different parallel and sequential versions of the loop in the same way we have performed this transformation with our own pre-processing phase. The dynamic pattern depends strictly on the index array. The generation of the index array includes the following steps:

– Assign to each processor the number of touched private elements. The degree of contention of each reduction element and the touched private elements on each processor are normally distributed.
– Decide which elements are touched according to the **CLUS**erness parameter.
– Generate the index array: For any reduction operation in an iteration local to a processor, assign an index value referencing one of the touched elements on the processor. This assignment is random and corresponds to the chosen **CLUS** values.

The synthetic reduction loop is parallelized by all reduction parallelization schemes described in Section 2 using essentially the same *pattern descriptor* as the original synthetic loop. Then, we generate a list of *pattern descriptors* for a factorial experimental design [6]. Specifically, we choose $V_i$ values for the $i$th attribute of the descriptor that

**Table 2.** Values of attributes for the factorial design

| Attributes | N | CON | CLUS | MOB | CHR | NRED | OTHR | OTHS | OTHW |
|---|---|---|---|---|---|---|---|---|---|
| Values | 16384 | 2 | 1 (clustered) | 2 | 0.200 | 1 | 1 | 0 | 0 |
|  | 524288 | 16 | 2 (partial-clustered) | 8 | 0.800 | 4 | 4 | 4 |  |
|  |  |  | 3 (scattered) |  |  |  |  |  |  |

```
DO j = 1, N*CON
  DO i = 1, OTHR
    Read from other arrays
  DO i = 1, OTHS
    Scalar division operation
  DO i = 1, OTHW
    Write to other arrays
  DO i = 1, MOB
    DO l = 1, NRED
      data( l,index(i,j) ) += func
```

```
FOR (each pattern descriptor) DO
  Generate the index array
  FOR (each parallelization scheme) DO
    Instrument the synthetic loop
    Execute the parallel synthetic loop
    Measure speedup
  ENDFOR
  Rank schemes
ENDFOR
```

**Fig. 7.** Synthetic Reduction Loop       **Fig. 8.** Procedure to generate samples

are typical for realistic reduction loops. All the combinations of the chosen values of the different attributes represent a list of pattern descriptors of size $\prod_{i=1}^{A} V_i$, where $A$ is the number of independent attributes of the descriptor. The values of the pattern descriptor for the factorial design are presented in Table 2. The sample space has been generated using the procedure given in Fig. 8. For each measured sample we compare and rank the relative performance of the various reduction algorithms. Finally we obtain the compact map from pattern descriptor to rank.

### 4.2   Model Generation I: Statistical Regression

We have used a set of candidate polynomial models with a reasonable low degree, e.g., up to 3. Then we choose the model which best fits these examples by using a standard statistical package (SAS). The target attribute, the speedup of each scheme, has been fit by a function of the form $speedup = F(patterndescriptor)$.

Corresponding C library routines are generated automatically to evaluate the polynomial $F()$ for each scheme. After computing the *pattern descriptor*, these routines are called to estimate speedups of all schemes, rank them and select the best one. For practical reasons (experimentation time) we limit the maximal degree of models to 3.

### 4.3   Model Generation II: Decision Tree Learning

An alternative process of generating the run-time selection code is building (off-line) a *decision tree* from our limited set of experiments. In general, our problem can be reduced to that of classifying the collected samples into one of a discrete set of possible categories. For each category, only one particular reduction parallelization algorithm is considered best. These kinds of problems are often referred to as *classification problems* for which a well-known technique, "decision tree learning," can be applied.

Decision trees classify instances by organizing the instances in leaf nodes of a tree. Each internal node in the tree specifies a test of an attribute. To classify an instance, we visit the tree by testing the corresponding attributes specified in the root and internal nodes to reach a leaf node. The classification of the leaf node represents the answer. A decision tree is generated in a top-down manner, to choose the best attribute which can be used as a test to partition the training examples. The chosen attribute is used as the test at the root and each possible value of this attribute leads to a descendant. The training examples are partitioned according to the value of the chosen attribute associated to each instance. This process is recursively applied to the descendants and

```
BuildTree
  Input: Samples;    Output: Tree
  Attr = the best attribute to partition samples
  Tree = node to test Attr.
  FOR ( each value(or interval) V of Attr ) DO
    IF ( STOP( Samples(Attr=V) ) THEN
      Tree.child(Attr=V) = BuildLEAF( Samples(Attr=V) )
    ELSE
      Tree.child(Attr=V) = BuildTree( Samples(Attr=V) )
```

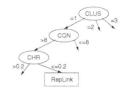

**Fig. 9.** Decision Tree Learning Algorithm. The `Samples` (`Attr=V`) operator returns the subset of Samples in which the `Attr` attributes of the samples is equal to V. The `Tree.child(Attr=V)` operator returns an tree descendent edge whose predicate is `Attr=V`.

**Fig. 10.** A part of a decision tree made by C4.5. By visiting the decision tree along the illustrated path, REPLINK is selected as the best scheme.

the corresponding subset of training examples. A simplified version of the algorithm is described in Fig. 9.

The central choice in this algorithm is the selection of the attribute to test for each node in the tree. The goal is to select the attribute that is most useful for classifying our samples. i.e., that partitions best. For this purpose, a *splitting criterion* is used to measure how well a given attribute separates the training examples according to their target classification. In [11], Quinlan used *gain ratio*, an information-based measure that takes into account different numbers of test outcomes, as the splitting criterion. In the algorithm, it is assumed that each attribute takes discrete values. For continuous attribute A, the $c$ values of A existing in the examples are sorted and the $c - 1$ midway values of every pair of adjacent values partitions the example into $c$ partitions. Notice that the target attribute is a set of classes and it is a discrete variable.

For our experiments we have adopted an available decision tree learning program package: **C4.5** developed by Quinlan [14]. C4.5 can build a decision tree from a set of given examples and classify items using the built tree. Also, C4.5 always tries to produce the minimal tree to avoid over-fitting the training examples.

For adaptive algorithm selection purposes the decision tree learning mechanism is used in two distinct phases. At the installation phase, we build the decision tree which classifies the examples generated by the process described in 4.1 into classes. Each class is associated with one of the parallelization schemes. During program execution a run-time library is used to find the class to which a pattern descriptor belongs and then select the algorithm associated with that class. Since the height of the tree is equal to the number of attributes, the run-time overhead associated with visiting the tree is negligible.

We have built a tree by C4.5 from the all the examples generated in Section 4.1; after simplification, the tree only has 21 leaves. Fig. 10 gives an example to illustrate finding the best scheme by visiting the decision tree.

## 5   Experimental Results

We have collected the performance data (speedups) of reduction loops from several codes which have been parallelized using the reduction schemes described previously and which have been executed with several different input sets. We have then used our prediction model to select the best reduction algorithm and then compared our choice with the actual performance data. Table 3 shows the schemes recommended by both prediction approaches, statistical regression and decision tree learning, with that from experimental results. In most cases, these two prediction processes have recommended the correct solution. We should remark, however, that some times the difference between the first and second algorithm choices did not amount to a significant performance difference. However the trend was almost always predicted correctly.

We have chosen 7 programs from a variety of scientific domains and augmented them with our instrumentation to collect information about the access pattern. This has been done in most cases (for all Fortran codes) automatically using the Polaris compiler [2]. The compiler is capable of extracting the condensed access descriptors of a loop (similar to an inspector loop) and, where it was not possible (SPICE), used our runtime parallelization pass [18] to collect data during actual loop execution. The compiler has inserted calls to a run-time library that compute the various parameters we were interested in. Then we have implemented (by hand) the various reduction algorithms and inserted them one by one for our experiments.

The experimental setup for our speedup measurement consisted of a 16 processor HP-V class system with 4Gb memory and 4Mb cache per processor, running the HPUX11 operating system. It is a directory based cache coherent UMA shared memory machine. Due to the limited size of our input sets and constraints on our single user time allocation for this project we have used only 8 processors.

We have chosen the following well known applications which we will briefly describe here in order to make the paper self-contained. It is important to note that *we have tried, where possible, to use data sets that exercise the entire memory hierarchy of our parallel machine in order to get the performance data of 'real-life' applications.*

**Irreg** is an iterative PDE solver used in CFD applications. It uses an unstructured mesh to model physical structures. The code uses nodes and edges of a graph to represent its mesh. The time is spent computing the forces that are applied to the end points of its edges. After evaluating the forces at each node the program performs an irregular reduction to update them with the new values. The different input sets have almost the same amount of work ($N * CON$). The *Mobility* is 2 because there are two updates to different addresses for each iteration of the reduction loop. **Nbf** is a kernel from the GROMOS molecular dynamics benchmark. It is typical of N-body simulations in that the code maintains a continuously updated list of its neighbors with which it interacts. At every time step forces are evaluated at each node and applied through a reduction operation across the whole data structure of the program. Because the interaction of the molecules changes the Reusability is variable. **Moldyn** is a kernel for the molecular dynamics code CHARMM. It is similar to Nbf in the sense that its nodes interact only with its neighbors. The list of neighbors changes at various times because of the forces applied to them. It is a very dynamic irregular code for which Reusability is low. **Charmm** is the original code for Moldyn. We have used other data sets with sizes of 332,288 and 664,576 in order to produce 'real results'. **Spark98** is a collection of 10 sparse kernels developed by David O'Hallaron at CMU. The sparse matrices are induced from a pair of three-dimensional unstructured finite element simulations of earthquake ground motion in the San Fernando Valley. Each kernel is a program/mesh pair. There are 5

**Table 3.** Modeling Example Result. P = 8; N, CON(nectivity), MOB(ility), NRED, OTHR(other work Memory Read), OTHS(other work Scalar Computation), OTHW(other work Memory Write), CHR, CLUS(terness) are as defined previously. In the last four columns, the schemes are represented by an one digit number. The schemes REPBUFS, REPLINK, SELPRIV and LO-CALWRITE are numbered as 1, 2, 3, 4 respectively.

| APP | Pattern Descriptor | | | | | | | | | Best Scheme(s) | | | |
|---|---|---|---|---|---|---|---|---|---|---|---|---|---|
| | N | CON | MOB | NRED | OTHR | OTHS | OTHW | CHR | CLUS | Real | Syn. | Reg. | Tree |
| Irreg | 100000 | 100 | 2 | 1 | 1 | 0 | 0 | 1 | 1 | 1 | 123 | 132 | 31 |
| | 500000 | 20 | | | | | | 0.99 | 1 | 321 | 132 | 3 | 3 |
| | 1000000 | 5 | | | | | | 0.71 | 3 | 4 | 43 | 43 | 43 |
| | 2000000 | 1 | | | | | | 0.22 | 3 | 3 | 3 | 3 | 34 |
| Nbf | 25600 | 200 | 2 | 1 | 1 | 0 | 0 | 0.25 | 1 | 1 | 213 | 12 | 32 |
| | 128000 | 50 | | | | | | 0.25 | 1 | 12 | 21 | 321 | 3 |
| | 256000 | 5 | | | | | | 0.25 | 1 | 231 | 32 | 3 | 3 |
| | 1280000 | 2 | | | | | | 0.25 | 1 | 23 | 43 | 3 | 3 |
| Moldyn | 16384 | 214 | 2 | 3 | 3 | 3 | 0 | 0.48 | 2 | 21 | 123 | 12 | 312 |
| | 42592 | 70 | | | | | | 0.39 | 2 | 21 | 21 | 213 | 312 |
| | 70304 | 21 | | | | | | 0.34 | 2 | 12 | 213 | 321 | 312 |
| | 87808 | 6 | | | | | | 0.29 | 2 | 1 | 32 | 3 | 312 |
| Spark98 | 21882 | 4.80 | 2 | 3 | 9 | 0 | 0 | 0.20 | 2 | 2 | 231 | 3 | 21 |
| | 90507 | 4.88 | | | | | | 0.18 | 2 | 32 | 321 | 3 | 21 |
| Charmm | 331776 | 17.98 | 2 | 3 | 3 | 0 | 0 | 0.14 | 2 | 123 | 321 | 3 | 21 |
| | 331776 | 8.99 | | | | | | 0.15 | 2 | 3 | 213 | 3 | 21 |
| | 663552 | 4.48 | | | | | | 0.13 | 2 | 2 | 321 | 3 | 21 |
| Spice | 186943 | 0.04 | 28 | 1 | 2 | 0 | 1 | 0.13 | 2 | 3 | 3 | 3 | 3 |
| | 99190 | 0.06 | | | | | | 0.13 | 2 | 3 | 3 | 3 | 3 |
| | 89925 | 0.05 | | | | | | 0.13 | 2 | 3 | 3 | 3 | 3 |
| | 33725 | 0.05 | | | | | | 0.13 | 2 | 3 | 3 | 3 | 3 |
| Fma3d | 174762 | 0.50 | 8 | 3 | 3 | 0 | 0 | 0.13 | 3 | 3 | 3 | 3 | 3 |

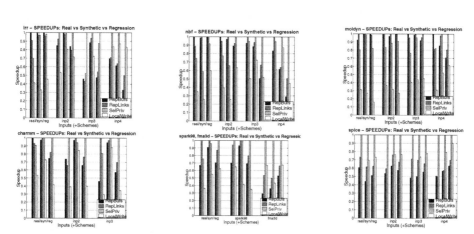

**Fig. 11.** Comparison of Scheme ranks for normalized execution of real applications (*real*), normalized execution of synthetic reduction loop (*syn*) and normalized prediction with a regression model (*reg*)

C programs (smv, lmv, rmv, mmv, hmv) and 2 finite element input data sets (sf10 and sf5). We have chosen the *rmv* kernel which computes irregular reductions. The meshes determine both the size and nonzero structure of the sparse matrices used. We have used the moderate size mesh Sf5 (because the large one was not available to us). It has

30,169 nodes, 410,923 nonzero matrix entries. Reusability is high, there are 3 reduction statements in the loop. Other than reduction statements, there are quite a few other computations and memory references. This code has been transformed by hand because our compiler infrastructure can handle only Fortran code. **SPICE 2G6** is a circuit simulation code written in an older Fortran style. Its main feature is that it does its own memory management inside a statically allocated large array named Value. Therefore all references to arrays are through indirection (subscripted subscripts) which makes almost any compiler analysis impossible. We have transformed the code for parallel execution using the run-time techniques described in [18]. For this paper we have chosen the main loop in subroutine BJT which evaluates the device model and updates the Y matrix of the circuit (this is the reduction loop). The program iterates to a fixed point solving a linear system and then re-evaluating the device model for the newly found values. The model evaluation loop takes between 11% and 45% of total execution time depending on the complexity of the devices and circuits being simulated. The Mobility is 28, which means that there are 28 distinct reduction statements for each iteration. The Connectivity is very low. In order to reuse the information we have used a technique we have named Global Schedule Reuse Control. Instead of proving that addresses do not change from one instance of the loop to the other one, we have checked, at run-time, when a potential address (an integer array) is modified in the global context. Fortunately our conservative method yields only two address changes during the whole program yielding high reusability. **FMA3D** is a finite element method based three-dimensional inelastic, transient dynamic response simulation code from the SPEC CPU2000 suite. We choose one reduction loop in SCATTER_ELEMENT_NODAL_FORCES_PLATQ subroutine. The loop has Mobility 8 and three different reductions sharing the same index (NRED= 3).

## 5.1    Discussion

Table 3 shows the overall results obtained with our modeling approaches. The first ten columns list applications and attributes of pattern descriptor defined in Section 3.1. In the last four columns, we list the best scheme(s) obtained from: execution of real applications (*Real*), execution of synthetic loop with corresponding real pattern descriptors (*Syn.*), recommendation by regression models (*Reg.*) and recommendation by decision tree learning (*Tree*). The schemes REPBUFS, REPLINK, SELPRIV and LOCALWRITE are numbered 1, 2, 3, and 4, respectively. Besides the best scheme we also listed the schemes (whenever applicable) whose speedups are greater than 90% of the best speedup. The last column of Table 3 represents the prediction given by the C4.5 decision tree learning program. We specify all the possible rankings of the best schemes, whose speedups are greater than 90% of the best speedup, as given by C4.5 with the highest probability.

In most cases the estimated rankings are consistent with the experimental rankings. To further investigate the accuracy of the synthetic loop and the regression models, we plotted the relative speedups obtained from the the execution of real applications (*Real*), the execution of synthetic loop with corresponding real pattern descriptor (*Syn.*) and the recommendation by regression models (*Reg.*) in Fig. 11 and also shown in Table 3. In these graphs, each group of bars corresponds to an application-input case

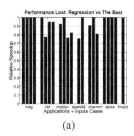 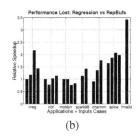 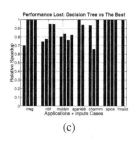

(a)                                    (b)                                    (c)

**Fig. 12.** Performance Comparison. (a) compares the performance of regression prediction and that of the best scheme; (b) compares the performance of regression prediction and that of Rep-Bufs scheme (simplest scheme); (c) compares the performance of decision tree prediction and that of the best scheme To illustrate the effects of the prediction, we assume the reusability of applications is big, thus we do not have to consider the overheads related to schedule reuse.

and each sub-group shows the relative speedups of the four schemes. In most of the cases, although the speedups are not close to each other, the rankings from different sources are consistent. The loss of accuracy occurs because we have not yet been able to accurately model the OTH part of the reduction loops. From a total of 22 application-input cases, the regression approach predicted 14 cases correctly. For the 8 mispredicted cases, only in 5 cases is the mis-prediction more than 10% (lower speedup).

Some of the errors are due to the small number of samples used and imperfect regression models. Table 3 shows that the predictions given by C4.5 are not as accurate as those of the regression approach. From 22 cases, it predicted 10 case precisely, 4 cases with confidence of 90% and 8 cases with confidence less than 90%. Because the decision tree can be represented as a step function and the function in every interval is a constant, it has less extrapolation capability than regression approach. To improve its accuracy the decision tree would need a larger number of samples.

The graphs in Fig. 12 show the effect of our predictions on the performance of real applications. Graph 12(a) indicates that, for most of the patterns, the performance obtained by applying the predicted schemes came close to that of the best schemes. We define an average relative speedup loss (**LOSS**) and use it as a metric of the predictions. In Graph 12(a), for all 22 real application-input cases, the LOSS value of the regression approach is 93.86%. In the four reduction parallelization schemes, REPBUFS is the simplest to implement, thus we compare the performances using recommended schemes with that using REPBUFS. Graph 12(b) compares the relative performance gain between the REPBUFS (the simplest) and the scheme recommended by our model. On the average the LOSS value is 140.20%, a significant performance gain. Graph 12(c), shows that LOSS value for the decision tree method is better than 90%.

## 6    Summary and Future Work

In [17] we have essentially shown that input dependent programs can benefit from adaptively selecting the low level algorithms with which to implement optimizations, e.g., parallel reductions. In this work we have presented a systematic approach of constructing a performance model which, in conjunction with a input data characterization can predict and select the best available algorithm. While the results are good there are several issues which need more work such as to more accurately measure and/or estimate the pattern descriptor of each individual loop instantiation. Also for this purpose a data base (or profile base) of real reduction loops with an experimentally validated pattern descriptor could be useful. Another important conclusion is that Reusability (R) is essential for the ammortization of the overhead of the presented reduction schemes.

# References

1. Charmm: A program for macromolecular energy, minimization, and dynamics calculations. *J. of Computational Chemistry*, 4(6), 1983.
2. W. Blume,et. al  Advanced Program Restructuring for High-Performance Computers with Polaris. *IEEE Computer*, 29(12):78–82, Dec. 1996.
3. R. Eigenmann, J. Hoeflinger, Z. Li, and D. Padua. Experience in the Automatic Parallelization of Four Perfect-Benchmark Programs. *Proc. of the 4-th Workshop on Languages and Compilers for Parallel Computing, Santa Clara, CA, LNCS 589*, pp. 65–83, Aug. 1991.
4. H. Han and C.-W. Tseng. Improving compiler and run-time support for adaptive irregular codes. In *Int. Conf. on Parallel Architectures and Compilation Techniques*, Oct. 1998.
5. H. Han and C.-W. Tseng. A comparison of locality transformations for irregular codes. In *5th Workshop on Languages, Compilers, and Run-time Systems for Scalable Computers*, Rochester, NY, May 2000.
6. R. Jain. *The Art of Computer Systems Performance Analysis*. John Wiley & Sons, Inc., 1991.
7. C. Kruskal. Efficient parallel algorithms for graph problems. In *Proc. of the 1986 Int. Conf. on Parallel Processing*, pp. 869–876, Aug. 1986.
8. F. T. Leighton. *Introduction to Parallel Algorithms and Architectures: Arrays, Trees, Hypercubes*. Morgan Kaufmann, 1992.
9. Y. Lin and D. Padua. On the automatic parallelization of sprase and irregular fortran programs. In *Proc. of the Workshop on Languages, Compilers and Run-time Systems for Scalable Computers*, pp. 41–56, Pittsburgh, PA, May 1998.
10. M. J. Frisch et. al *Gaussian 94, Revision B.1*. Gaussian, Inc., Pittsburgh PA, 1995.
11. T. Mitchell. *Machine Learning*. MIT Press and The McGraw-Hill Companies, Inc., 1997.
12. L. Nagel. *SPICE2: A Computer Program to Simulate Semiconductor Circuits*. PhD thesis, Univ. of California, May 1975.
13. W. M. Pottenger. *Theory, Techniques, and Experiments in Solving Recurrences in Computer Programs*. PhD thesis, CSRD, Univ. of Illinois at Urbana-Champaign, May 1997.
14. Ross Quinlan. *C4.5 Release 8*. http://www.cse.unsw.edu.au/ quinlan/.
15. R. G. Whirley and B. Engelmann. *DYNA3D: A Nonlinear, Explicit, Three-Dimensional Finite Element Code For Solid and Structural Mechanics*. Lawrence Livermore National Lab., Nov., 1993.
16. J. Wu, J. Saltz, S. Hiranandani, and H. Berryman. Runtime compilation methods for multicomputers. In Dr. H.D. Schwetman, editor, *Proc. of the 1991 Int. Conf. on Parallel Processing*, pp. 26–30. CRC Press, Inc., 1991. Vol. II - Software.
17. H. Yu and L. Rauchwerger. Adaptive reduction parallelization. In *Proc. of the 14th ACM Int. Conf. on Supercomputing, Santa Fe, NM*, May 2000.
18. H. Yu and L. Rauchwerger. Run-time parallelization overhead reduction techniques. In *Proc. of the 9th Int. Conf. on Compiler Construction (CC2000), Berlin, Germany*. LNCS 1781, Springer-Verlag, March 2000.
19. H. Zima. *Supercompilers for Parallel and Vector Computers*. ACM Press, New York, New York, 1991.

# Adaptively Increasing Performance and Scalability of Automatically Parallelized Programs*

Jaejin Lee[1,**] and H.D.K. Moonesinghe[2]

[1] Seoul National University, School of Computer Science and Engineering,
Seoul 151-742, Korea
jlee@cse.snu.ac.kr

[2] Michigan State University, Department of Computer Science and Engineering,
East Lansing, MI 48824, USA
moonesin@cse.msu.edu

**Abstract.** This paper presents adaptive execution techniques that determine whether automatically parallelized loops are executed parallelly or sequentially in order to maximize performance and scalability. The adaptation and performance estimation algorithms are implemented in a compiler preprocessor. The preprocessor inserts code that automatically determines at compile-time or at run-time the way the parallelized loops are executed. Using a set of standard numerical applications written in Fortran77 and running them with our techniques on a distributed shared memory multiprocessor machine (SGI Origin2000), we obtain the performance of our techniques, on average, 26%, 20%, 16%, and 10% faster than the original parallel program on 32, 16, 8, and 4 processors, respectively. One of the applications runs even more than twice faster than its original parallel version on 32 processors.

## 1 Introduction

High performance optimizing and parallelizing compilers perform various optimizations to improve the performance of sequential and parallel programs [2]. A problem that most of such compilers currently faced is the lack of information about machine parameters and input data at compile-time. The performance of an algorithm that best solves a problem largely depends on the combination of the input set and the hardware platform executing it. The information about the input and the platform is difficult to obtain or unavailable at compile time. Consequently, it is difficult or sometimes impossible to statically fine-tune the application to the platform. To address this issue, recent

---

* This work was supported in part by National Science Foundation under grant EIA-0130724 and by National Computational Science Alliance under grant ocn, and utilized the Silicon Graphics Origin2000. This work was also supported in part by the Korean Ministry of Education under the BK21 program and by the Korean Ministry of Science and Technology under the National Research Laboratory program.
** The preliminary work of this paper was done when the author was in the Department of Computer Science and Engineering at Michigan State University.

B. Pugh and C.-W. Tseng (Eds.): LCPC 2002, LNCS 2481, pp. 203–217, 2005.

work [1, 7, 14, 20, 21] has been started to explore the feasibility of run-time fine-tuning and optimizations when complete knowledge about the input set and the hardware platform is available.

Automatic parallelizing compilers analyze and transform a sequential program into a parallel program without any intervention of the user. However, in order to achieve maximum performance from the automatically parallelized programs, the user must consider the following factors with regards to the underlying multiprocessor architecture: amount of parallelism contained in the program, cache locality of the program, hardware cache coherence mechanism, workload distribution between processors, data distribution, false sharing, coordination overhead incurred between processors, synchronization overhead, etc. Since these factors manifest synergistically on the performance of parallel loops and the effects differ from one machine to another machine, identifying performance bottlenecks of a parallel program is a tedious and difficult job for the programmer. Consequently, the cost that a programmer pays in order to obtain reasonable performance from an automatically parallelized program adds extra difficulties in developing and maintaining parallel programs.

In this paper, instead of manually identifying the performance bottlenecks from an automatically parallelized program, we avoid executing some parallel loops in parallel if performance degradation of the loops exceeds a predefined threshold value during parallel execution of the program. No knowledge of the parallel program should be assumed from the programmer. Such adaptive execution techniques significantly increase the performance and scalability of automatically parallelized programs. The adaptation and performance estimation algorithms are implemented in a compiler preprocessor. The preprocessor inserts code that automatically determines at run-time the way the parallelized loops must be executed using information obtained by the preprocessor at compile-time and by the code itself at run-time.

Using a set of standard numerical applications written in Fortran77 and running them with our techniques on a distributed shared memory machine (SGI Origin2000), we obtain the performance, on average, 26%, 20%, 16%, and 10% faster than the original parallel programs on 32, 16, 8, and 4 processors respectively.

The rest of the paper is organized as follows: Section 2 describes our parallel programming and execution model assumed; Section 3 presents our algorithm; Section 4 describes the evaluation environment; Section 5 evaluates the algorithm; and Section 6 discusses related work. We conclude in Section 7.

## 2   Our Framework

Figure 1 shows our framework. An automatically or manually parallelized program is fed into the compiler preprocessor. The preprocessor inserts performance estimation and adaptive execution code into the parallel program using target machine specific parameters. The output program from the preprocessor is compiled with a compiler that generates code for the target multiprocessor.

We are particularly interested in adaptive optimization strategies that select code at run-time from a set of statically generated code variants. We generate two different versions of a single parallel loop, one is a sequential version and the other is a parallel version. Since we are interested in running a parallel loop sequentially or in parallel, we focus on the parallel programs that contain large amount of loop level parallelism. A variety of selection algorithms are compared and evaluated with these highly parallel programs: compile-time cost estimation, run-time cost estimation, selection based on

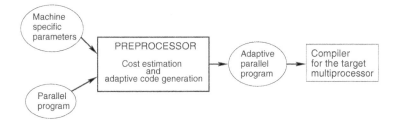

**Fig. 1.** Our framework

execution time, selection based on performance counters, such as the number of grad-uated instructions, and combinations of those strategies. The key observation in this paper is that most of parallel loops are invoked many times so that adaptive execution of the parallel loops is feasible and effective.

The preprocessor inserts instrumentation code in the parallel loop in order to mea-sure, at run-time, the execution time of an invocation or the number of instructions graduated in an invocation. These invocations where execution time, the number of graduated instructions, or both of them are measured are called *decision runs*. Based on the measurements in the decision runs of a parallel loop, the adaptation code de-termines the way of executing the loop, i.e., sequentially or in parallel in the next or remaining invocations.

A drawback of our adaptive execution techniques with decision runs is that we have to run a parallel loop at least once sequentially and at least once in parallel in order to obtain some useful information for adapting the loop to the run-time environment. To compensate this penalty, we combine compile-time cost estimation and adaptive execution techniques. In addition, we introduce the notion of *adaptation window* for run-time cost estimation.

We use the OpenMP parallel programming model as our model of parallel execu-tion. It is a master-slave thread model [13, 5, 17]. Creating slave threads for a parallel loop, distributing the iterations of the loop between threads, cache affinity of each thread executing different iterations, and the synchronization between threads at the end of the loop incur an overhead for running the loop in parallel. We call it *parallel loop overhead*.

## 3   Adaptive Execution Algorithms

We have implemented complier and run-time algorithms that adaptively execute au-tomatically parallelized programs. The same techniques can be applied to the parallel programs generated by hand as long as they use standard parallelization directives used in automatic parallelizing compilers.

Our adaptation scheme has basically three different parts. A compile-time cost estimation model, a run-time cost estimation model, and adaptation strategies using the two models. First, the compile-time cost estimation model (Figure 2) filters parallel loops that contain smaller amount of work than the parallel loop overhead (small loops). Second, the run-time cost estimation model filters highly efficient parallel loops due to large amount of work in the loop. An *efficient parallel loop* is the parallel loop whose speedup is greater than 1. Otherwise, it is an *inefficient parallel loop*. The model counts

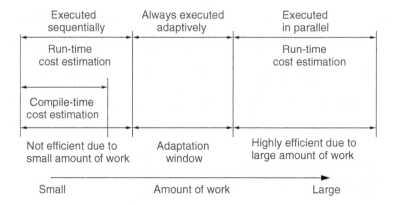

**Fig. 2.** The adaptation scheme

the number of instructions executed in an invocation of the loop at run-time. It also identifies small loops that cannot be handled by the compile-time cost estimation model due to run-time parameters in the loops. Finally, several adaptive execution strategies (including execution time based strategies) determine the way the remaining loops are executed.

## 3.1   Compile-Time Cost Estimation

The compile-time cost estimation model identifies parallel loops that are not efficient due to insufficient amount of work in the loop. It is not beneficial to run this type of loops in parallel because the amount of work in the loop is fairly small compared to the parallel loop overhead. We define a threshold value for the amount of work contained in the loop. If the amount of work is smaller than the threshold value, we run the loop sequentially.

We use a fairly simple cost estimation model. The amount of work ($W$) in a loop can be estimated as a function of the numbers of iterations($n_i$), assignments ($n_a$), floating point addition ($n_{f_{add}}$), floating point multiplication ($n_{f_{mul}}$), floating point subtraction ($n_{f_{sub}}$), floating point division ($n_{f_{div}}$), intrinsic function calls ($n_{fi}$), system function calls ($n_{fs}$), and user defined function calls ($n_{fu}$) Consequently, the estimated amount of work ($W_i$) in an iteration is given by the following formula:

$$W_i = n_a \cdot c_a + n_{f_{add}} \cdot c_{f_{add}} + n_{f_{mul}} \cdot c_{f_{mul}} + n_{f_{sub}} \cdot c_{f_{sub}}$$
$$+ n_{f_{div}} \cdot c_{f_{div}} + n_{fi} \cdot c_{fi} + n_{fs} \cdot c_{fs} + n_{fu} \cdot c_{fu}$$

Where $c_{op}$ is the cost of performing a single operation with type $op$ on the target machine. Thus, the total estimated amount of work in an invocation of the loop is,

$$W(n_i) = n_i \cdot W_i$$

Because we cannot determine at compile-time the actual number of iterations in a loop in general, this formula is parameterized by $n_i$. When we estimate the amount of work in a loop that has branches, we give equal weight to each branch.

We determine the threshold value heuristically. First, we run several representative microbenchmark programs that contain many different type of parallel loops. After

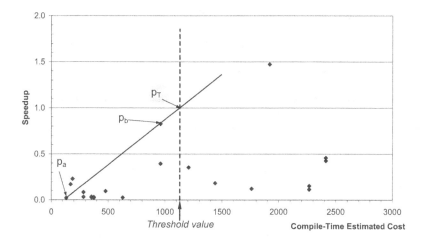

**Fig. 3.** Determining the threshold value with compile-time cost estimation

measuring sequential execution time and parallel execution time of each loop contained in the program on $p$ processors, we plot the speedup of each loop on the Y-axis and the estimated cost (the estimated amount of work) on the X-axis. Then, draw a line from the point that has the lowest estimated cost ($p_a$ in Figure 3) to the point that has the lowest estimated cost among those whose speedup is greater than 0.8 ($p_b$). We choose the cost of the intersecting point with the horizontal line of speedup 1.0 ($p_T$) as our threshold value.

When the loop is multiply nested, it is hard to determine the number of iterations of an inner loop before we run the outer loop. It is because the upper bound, lower bound, and step of the inner loop may change in the outer loop. In other words, it is hard to obtain the cost function parameterized by the numbers of iterations of both the outermost loop and the inner loop. In this case, we simply pass the loop to the run-time cost estimation model.

## 3.2   Run-Time Cost Estimation

While the compile-time cost estimation model estimates the performance of parallel loops that contain small amount of work and that are highly inefficient, the run-time cost estimation model identifies the loops that contain enough amount of computation that can overcome the parallel loop overhead and other overheads incurred during its execution. It also handles the small loops that cannot be handled by the compile-time cost model due to some run-time parameters.

Because the number of instructions executed in a loop is proportional to its amount of work contained in it, we use the number of instructions executed (graduated) in an invocation of a parallel loop as the cost estimation. For the run-time cost estimation model to be effective, the parallel loop must be invoked at least once in the program.

There are two threshold values to be determined in the run-time cost estimation model. One (the lower threshold value) is for the inefficient loops that contain small amount of work and that cannot be handled by the compile-time cost estimation model.

The other (the higher threshold value) is for filtering out highly efficient loops. Heuristically determining the threshold values for the run-time cost estimation model is similar to the compile-time cost estimation model. We run several representative benchmark programs that contain many different type of parallel loops. We measure sequential execution time, parallel execution time, and the number of graduated instructions in the parallel execution of each loop in the benchmark programs on $p$ processors. Then, we plot the speedup of each loop on the Y-axis and the number of graduated instructions (run-time estimated cost) on the X-axis.

For the higher threshold value, we draw a line from the point that has the lowest number of instructions executed ($p_a$ in Figure 4) to the point that has the lowest number of instructions executed among those whose speedup is greater than the *average speedup* of all the loops plotted. ($p_b$ in Figure 4) We choose as our higher threshold value ($T_H$) the cost of the point ($p_H$) whose number of instructions executed is in the middle of the intersecting point with the speedup 1.0 ($p_c$) and the intersecting point with the average speedup ($p_d$).

For the lower threshold value, the method is the same as the compile-time cost estimation model. Draw a line from the point with the lowest cost ($p_a$) to the point with the lowest cost among those whose speedup is greater than 0.8 ($p_e$). We choose the cost of the intersecting point ($p_L$) with the horizontal line of speedup 1.0 as our lower threshold value ($T_L$ in Figure 4).

The region in between the lower threshold value and the higher threshold value is called the *adaptation window*.

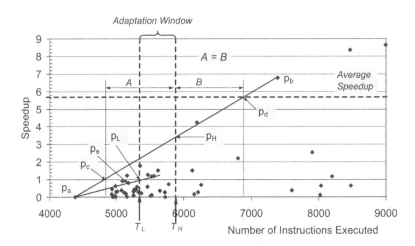

**Fig. 4.** Determining the threshold value with run-time cost estimation. For simplicity, only the essential part of the graph is shown.

### 3.3   Adaptive Execution Algorithms

Depending on the frequency of decision runs and the cost estimation model used, we propose five different adaptive execution schemes: First 2 Invocations with Timing (F2T), Most Recent with Timing (MRT), Static (compile-time) estimation and

**Table 1.** Auto-Parallelizing directives used for SGI MIPSpro Fortran77 compiler

| Directive | Meaning |
|---|---|
| C*$* ASSERT DO (SERIAL) | Instructs the compiler not to parallelize the the loop following the assertion. |
| C*$* ASSERT DO PREFER (CONCURRENT) | Instructs the compiler to parallelize the loop following the assertion, if it is safe to do so. |

**Table 2.** Applications used

| Application | Source | Number of Lines | Data Size and Number of Iterations |
|---|---|---|---|
| Applu | SPECfp2000 | 3980 | Reference input with 20 iterations |
| Hydro2d | SPECfp95 | 4303 | Reference input with 100 iterations |
| Mgrid | SPECfp2000 | 489 | Test input with 40 iterations |
| Su2cor | SPECfp95 | 2271 | Reference input with 100 iterations |
| Swim | SPECfp2000 | 435 | Reference input with 50 iterations |

Most Recent with Timing (SMRT), MRT with Run-time cost estimation (MRTR), and MRT with Static (compile-time) and Run-time cost estimation (SMRTR). Our adaptive schemes are based on the observation that most of scientific applications have one outermost sequential loop and the parallel loops contained in it are invoked multiple times.

**First Two invocations with Timing (F2T).** The parallel loop is executed in parallel and timed when it is first invoked in the program. When it is invoked for the second time, it is executed sequentially and timed. Then we determine whether we run this loop in parallel or sequentially by comparing the two measurements. The loop is executed for the remaining invocations in the program in parallel or sequentially depending on the result of the comparison. The drawback of *First Two Invocations with Timing (F2T)* is that a highly efficient parallel loop has to be executed sequentially once in the decision runs. Also, the measured execution time in the decision runs is not the representive for the remaining invocations of the loop.

**Most Recent with Timing (MRT).** When a parallel loop is invoked for the first time, it is executed in parallel and timed. When it is invoked for the second time, it is executed sequentially and timed again. Then we determine whether we run this loop parallelly or sequentially in the next invocation by comparing the two measurements. However, the way we execute the loop for the remaining invocations is not fixed at this

**Table 3.** Machine specification

| Architecture | Distributed Shared Memory |
|---|---|
| Processor Type (Clock speed) | MIPS R10000 (250MHz) |
| Number of Processors | 128 |
| Total Memory | 128 GB |
| Total Disk | 640 GB |
| Instruction cache size (cache line size) | 32 KB (64 B) |
| Data cache size (cache line size) | 32 KB (32 B) |
| Secondary unified instruction/data cache size (cache line size) | 4 MB (128 B) |

point. Instead, every time the loop is executed, we time it and compare the execution time to its most recent execution time in the other way. If the latter is lower, we change the way it is running. *Most Recent with Timing* can adapt to changes in the workload of the loop across invocations. It uses the recent past of a loop to predict its future behavior. Consequently, if the workload of the loop changes gradually, this strategy works well. However, sudden changes may cause this strategy to work poorly. Similar to F2T, the drawback of MRT is that a highly efficient parallel loop has to be executed sequentially at least once in the first decision runs.

**Static cost estimation and Most Recent with Timing (SMRT).** By combining compile-time performance estimation model with MRT, we can avoid running some loops inefficiently. As shown in Figure 2, the loop that contains smaller amount of work than parallel loop overhead can be filtered out by the compile-time cost estimation model. We run these loops sequentially. Then, the remaining parallel loops are executed by MRT.

**MRT with Run-time cost estimation (MRTR).** MRTR uses the notion of *adaptation window*. The adaptation window consists of the two threshold values of the run-time cost estimation model. In this strategy, a parallel loop is executed in parallel when it is first invoked. We measure the execution time and number of instructions executed (graduated) in the loop. If the number of instructions executed is less than the lower threshold value, the loop is executed sequentially for the remaining invocations. If the number of instructions executed is greater than the higher threshold value, it is executed in parallel for the remaining invocations. Otherwise, its execution in the remaining invocations follows MRT, i.e., the loops with the number of instructions that falls in the adaptation window follow MRT scheme. A parallel loop is niether highly efficient nor highly inefficient if it falls into the adaptation window.

**MRT with Static and Run-time cost estimation (SMRTR).** SMRTR is a combination of Static and MRTR. Before it applies to MRTR, it filters out small inefficient parallel loops with the compile-time cost estimation model (Static) and run them always sequentially. Then, MRTR is used for the remaining parallel loops. For those inefficient parallel loops filtered out by Static, we do not pay the penalty of executing them in parallel at least once in MRTR because their cost is estimated at compile-time. Consequently, we expect that SMRTR gives the best performance.

# 4    Evaluation Environment

## 4.1    Compiler

We have implemented the compiler and adaptive execution algorithms described in Section 3 in our compiler preprocessor. The preprocessor is written in Perl. To identify automatically parallelizable loops in a program, we use SGI MIPSpro Fortran77 compiler [18]. The parallelization information together with the original program is fed into our compiler preprocessor. The preprocessor inserts adaptive execution code and appropriate directives in the original program to direct the compiler of the target multiprocessor machine (SGI Origin2000). The directives inserted are summarized in Table 1. The output program from the preprocessor is compiled by the SGI Fortran77 compiler to generate an executable.

To measure the execution time of an invocation of each loop, we use an SGI system call from *syssgi* to read the processor cycle counter. To count the number of graduated instructions of each loop in an invocation, we use SGI `perfex` library to access processor event counters. The number of graduated instructions from the master thread is counted.

## 4.2   Applications

We evaluate the effectiveness of our algorithms using scientific applications written in Fortran77. We selected applications that are highly parallel. They are Applu, Mgrid, and Swim from SPECfp2000 and Hydro2d and Su2cor from SPECfp95. Table 2 shows the problem sizes and number of iterations used for the applications.

## 4.3   Target Architecture

The code generated by our system is targeted to SGI Origin2000 at the National Center for Supercomputing Applications. All our experiments are done in the dedicated mode of the SGI Origin2000. Table 3 shows the parameters of the architecture.

# 5   Evaluation

Before we evaluate our adaptive execution strategies, we first examine the characteristics of the parallel loops in each application (Section 5.1). We then evaluate the performance of our strategies (Section 5.2).

## 5.1   Characteristics of the Parallel Loops

Table 4 shows the characteristics of the parallel loops in each application. The table gives us the rationale of our adaptive execution strategies. It has one section for all the parallel loops and another for inefficient parallel loops in each application. The first row in the first section shows the total number of parallel loops in each application and their % sequential execution time relative to the sequential execution time of the application. The second row in the first section shows the average number of invocations for each individual parallel loops in the application. The last row in the first section shows the average loop size measured in the number of processor cycles that it takes to execute one invocation of the loop. The first row in the second section shows the total number of inefficient loops in each application for different number of processors. It also shows that their % sequential execution time relative to the sequential execution time of the application and % parallel execution time of inefficient loops relative to the parallel execution time of the application for different number of processors. The second row in the second section shows the average number of invocations for each individual inefficient parallel loops in the application for different number of processors. The last row in the second section shows the average loop size measured in the number of processor cycles that it takes to execute one invocation of the loop in parallel on different number of processors.

We see that the applications are highly parallel and that the parallel loops account for an average of 96.2% of the sequential execution time. Applu, Mgrid, Hydro2d, and Su2cor contains many inefficient parallel loops. More than 30% of their parallel loops

**Table 4.** Characteristics of parallel loops in the applications

| | | | Applu | Hydro2d | Mgrid | Su2cor | Swim | Average |
|---|---|---|---|---|---|---|---|---|
| Parallel | Number of | | 55 | 86 | 11 | 41 | 16 | 41.8 |
| Loops | Parallel Loops | | | | | | | |
| | (% sequential time) | | (95.2%) | (97.3%) | (99.7%) | (88.8%) | (99.8%) | (96.2%) |
| | Average Number | | 8779.7 | 373.0 | 422.7 | 34220.1 | 28.4 | 8764.8 |
| | of Invocations | | | | | | | |
| | Average Loop | | 127.3K | 4.1K | 44.3K | 0.6K | 364.6K | 108.2K |
| | Size (processor cycles) | | | | | | | |
| | | #procs | Applu | Hydro2d | Mgrid | Su2cor | Swim | Average |
| Inefficient | Number of | 2 | 28 | 34 | 1 | 15 | 3 | 16.2 |
| Loops | Inefficient Loops | | (0.9%) | (0.6%) | (0.5%) | (2.8%) | (0.9%) | (1.2%) |
| | (% sequential time) | | (16.5%) | (13.3%) | (0.9%) | (25.2%) | (10.2%) | (13.2%) |
| | (% parallel time) | 4 | 29 | 28 | – | 15 | 3 | 18.8 |
| | | | (0.9%) | (0.2%) | | (2.8%) | (4.2%) | (2.0%) |
| | | | (28.1%) | (20.8%) | | (34.5%) | (21.6%) | (26.3%) |
| | | 8 | 28 | 28 | – | 16 | 3 | 18.8 |
| | | | (0.9%) | (0.2%) | | (2.8%) | (4.2%) | (2.0%) |
| | | | (44.3%) | (28.9%) | | (48.6%) | (33.4%) | (38.8%) |
| | | 16 | 29 | 28 | 1 | 18 | 3 | 15.8 |
| | | | (0.9%) | (0.2%) | (0.2%) | (2.8%) | (4.2%) | (1.7%) |
| | | | (57.2%) | (37.1%) | (1.2%) | (62.5%) | (51.8%) | (42.0%) |
| | | 32 | 32 | 32 | – | 18 | 6 | 22.0 |
| | | | ( 1.4%) | (0.3%) | | (2.8%) | (4.2%) | (2.2%) |
| | | | (79.6%) | (44.8%) | | (70.0%) | (67.1%) | (65.3%) |
| | Average | 2 | 16871.3 | 357.7 | 1042.0 | 80892.9 | 17.3 | 19836.2 |
| | Number | 4 | 16289.6 | 309.4 | – | 80892.9 | 2.3 | 24373.6 |
| | of | 8 | 16871.3 | 337.9 | – | 75837.2 | 2.3 | 23262.2 |
| | Invocations | 16 | 16289.6 | 312.9 | 1.0 | 67458.8 | 2.3 | 16812.9 |
| | | 32 | 15077.8 | 351.9 | – | 67458.8 | 18.0 | 20726.6 |
| | Average | 2 | 1.4K | 0.6K | 0.4K | 0.2K | 368.7K | 74.3K |
| | Loop | 4 | 3.7K | 0.6K | – | 0.2K | 633.4K | 159.5K |
| | Size | 8 | 1.4K | 0.5K | – | 0.5K | 633.4K | 159.0K |
| | (processor cycles) | 16 | 1.4K | 0.5K | 179.2K | 0.4K | 633.4K | 163.0K |
| | | 32 | 1.3K | 0.4K | – | 0.4K | 317.0K | 79.8K |
| Compile-time | Number of | | 18 | 31 | 1 | 32 | 8 | 18 |
| Cost | Parallel Loops | | | | | | | |
| Estimation | (% sequential time) | | (0.51%) | (0.36%) | (0.00%) | (88.50%) | (0.44%) | (17.97%) |
| | Average Number | | 25122.4 | 389.0 | 1.0 | 43801.6 | 37.3 | 13870.3 |
| | of Invocations | | | | | | | |

are inefficient. Inefficient parallel loops do not affect the sequential execution time because they account for at most 2.2% of the sequential execution time on average. However, inefficient parallel loops dominate in parallel execution for all applications but Mgrid. They account for average 13.2% of the parallel execution time of the applications on 2 processors and their execution time covers up to average 65.3% of the parallel execution time on 32 processors. The % parallel execution time of inefficient parallel loops increases as the number of processors increases. This is due to the parallel loop overhead incurred by the inefficient parallel loops. Consequently, we see that inefficient parallel loops are a significant target for optimizations.

Most of the parallel loops are invoked many times (8764.8 times on average). Inefficient parallel loops are invoked much more times than the other parallel loops (for example, 20726.6 times on 32 processors). The size of inefficient parallel loops are much less than the size of other parallel loops except in Mgrid and Swim. Therefore, the overhead involved in executing small parallel loops in parallel is likely to be large compared to their execution time. This means that our serialization technique is an effective optimization technique for parallel programs.

The last section of Table 4 will be explained in Section 5.2.

## 5.2   Results

Figure 5 compares the execution times of the applications under several strategies. For each application, there are 5 groups of bars. Each group corresponds to the number of processors 2, 4, 8, 16, and 32. The leftmost bar (**Base**) in each group corresponds to the execution time of the original parallel program. All parallel loops that are identified by the SGI parallelizing compiler are contained in the original parallel program, and they run in parallel in **Base**. The remaining bars correspond to the our strategies described in Section 3: First Two invocations with Timing (**F2T**), Most Recent with Timing (**MRT**), Static cost estimation (**Static**), Run-time cost estimation (**Runtime**), Static cost estimation and MRT (**SMRT**), MRT with Run-time cost estimation (**MRTR**), and MRT with Static and Run-time cost estimation (**SMRTR**). In each application, all bars are normalized to **Base** (the smaller, the better).

The First Two invocations with Timing (**F2T**) is the worst. This is because it uses only the first two invocations of a parallel loop as decision runs to determine the way it runs for the remaining invocations. Unless the amount of computation of the parallel loop is constant across invocations, the decision is likely to be inaccurate. Also, it runs each parallel loop sub-optimally at least once.

The Most Recent with Timing (**MRT**) is better than **F2T** and often better than **Base**. The reason why it can do better than **F2T** is that it chooses the way to run each

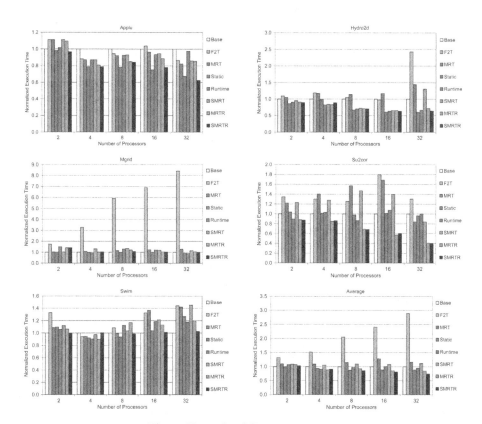

**Fig. 5.** Normalized Execution Time

individual parallel loop in an adaptive manner. However, in the process of doing so, it runs each parallel loop sub-optimally at least once. Under some conditions, changes in the amount of work in a parallel loop across invocations may confuse MRT and make it slow.

Static runs the parallel loops according to the result of static cost estimation model. From the figure, we see that Static is better than Base for most applications (Applu, Hydro2d, and Su2cor). This is because it can estimate the cost of most of the parallel loops in these three applications, and these loops tend to be small (note that it does not estimate the cost of doubly nested parallel loops) and invoked many times in the applications. In addition, it estimates the cost of a parallel loop before it runs. Thus, it does not pay the penalty caused by the decision runs. The last section in Table 4 shows the number of parallel loops whose amount of work is estimated by the static cost model. Note that multiply nested loops are not handled by the static cost model (Section 3.1). It also shows their % sequential time and average number of invocations. Overall, Static is attractive because of its simplicity.

The Run-time cost estimation Runtime is better than F2T, MRT, and Base, but slightly worse than Static. This is because it estimates the cost by counting the number of instructions executed in the loop when the loop is running. Thus, the estimation is accurate. However, in the process of doing so, it runs each parallel loop sub-optimally at least once.

The Static cost estimation with MRT (SMRT) is better than F2T and MRT, but not better than Base. The reason is that the penalty from the decision runs of MRT is much bigger than the benefits obtained from Static. Even though some parallel loops are filtered by Static, running the remaining parallel loops sub-optimally at least once still affects the performance a lot.

The MRT with run-time cost estimation (MRTR) is much better than Base and Static in Applu, Hydro2d, and Su2cor. It is comparable to Static in Mgrid and Swim. Because it estimates the cost of a parallel loop more accurately than Static by using the run-time information, more inefficient loops that tend to be small are filtered by the run-time cost estimation model and are executed sequentially in MRT. Consequently, there is no penalty of running efficient (big) parallel loops sequentially at least once.

As expected, MRT with static and run-time cost estimation (SMRTR) is the fastest. This is because it runs only the parallel loops which fall in the adaptation window at least once sub-optimally. Even though we see a slight performance degradation in Mgrid and Swim due to the penalty caused by decision runs, it significantly reduces the penalty caused by the decision runs of MRT. Moreover, it uses both compile-time and

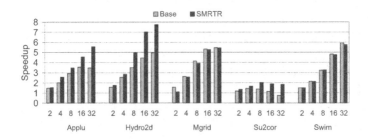

**Fig. 6.** Speedup of Base and SMRTR for each application

run-time cost estimation model. Consequently, it selects inefficient loops more accurately. Overall, SMRTR is the best strategy for adaptively executing the applications. For example, the parallel program with SMRTR runs 26% faster on average than the original parallel program on 32 processors. For Su2cor, SMRTR runs more than twice faster than Base on 32 processors. The speedup obtained with SMRTR for different number of processors is shown in Figure 6.

# 6   Related Work

Recent work has begun to explore the possibilities of optimizations performed at run-time when complete knowledge of the execution environment exists. Many different types of adaptive optimization techniques have been proposed recently in the literature.

Some approaches [8, 16, 6, 15] are based on parameterization of the code at compile-time to restructure it at run-time. Gupta and Bodik [8] dealt with the complexity of loop transformations, such as loop fusion, loop fission, loop interchange, and loop reversal, done at run-time. Saavedra *et al.* [16] proposed adaptive prefetching algorithm that can change the prefetching distance of individual prefetching instructions. Their adaptive algorithm uses simple performance data collected from hardware monitors at run-time. Another adaptive optimization technique, which is based on replication of objects in object oriented programs, is proposed by Rinard *et al.* [14]. To avoid synchronization overhead occurred in updating a shared object, the object is replicated adaptively. Multiple versioning of a loop for run-time optimization was first proposed by Byler *et al.* [3], and modern compilers still use this technique. Diniz et al. [7] used multiple versioning with dynamic feedback to automatically choose the best synchronization optimization policy for object-based parallel programs. Holzle *et al.* [9] proposed a dynamic type feedback technique for improving the performance of object oriented programs. These approaches are similar to our work in that the program dynamically adapts to the environment during its execution using run-time information. However, we neither restructure the code at run-time nor deal with object-oriented programs. We focus on shared memory parallel programs with loop level parallelism, and use different adaptation strategies in order to improve performance and scalability.

Lee [10] proposed a serialization technique of small parallel loops using static performance prediction and some heuristics. A sophisticated static performance estimation model based on the stack distance[12] was proposed by Cascaval *et al.* [4]. A generic compiler-support framework called ADAPT was proposed by Voss and Eigenman [20, 21] for adaptive program optimization. Users can specify types of optimizations and heuristics for applying the optimizations at run-time using ADAPT language. The ADAPT compiler generates a complete run-time system by reading these heuristics and applying them on to the target application. Voss and Eigenman [19] also proposed two run-time test schemes to identify unprofitable parallel loops. Because they used a profiling technique and the execution time of the first invocation of a parallel loop for the tests, their schemes are partially adaptive during the entire execution of an application.

Even though we used a fairly simple static performance estimation model in this paper, our run-time cost estimation models compensate for the inaccuracy caused by the static model. Moreover, our scheme is fully adaptive during the entire execution of an application. Our work is also related to adaptive compilers for heterogeneous Processing In Memory systems [11], where heterogeneity of the system is exploited adaptively.

# 7  Conclusion

This paper presented performance estimation and adaptive execution techniques that determine whether a parallel loop is executed parallelly or sequentially in order to maximize performance and scalability. The adaptation and performance estimation algorithms are in the code that is inserted into the original parallel program by the compiler preprocessor. Applying our adaptation scheme to five highly parallel numerical applications, we obtained 26%, 20%, 16%, and 10% better performance on average than the original parallel programs on 32, 16, 8, and 4 processors, respectively. One of the applications runs even more than twice faster than its original parallel version on 32 processors. The results indicate that our adaptive execution techniques are promising to speed-up the programs that are already parallel.

# References

1. Bowen Alpern et al. The Jalapeño Virtual Machine. *IBM Systems Journal*, 39(1):211–238, February 2000.
2. William Blume, Ramon Doallo, Rudolf Eigenmann, John Grout, Jay Hoeflinger, Thomas Lawrence, Jaejin Lee, David Padua, Yunheung Paek, Bill Pottenger, Lawrence Rauchwerger, and Peng Tu. Parallel programming with Polaris. *IEEE Computer*, 29(12):78–82, December 1996.
3. Mark Byler, James Davies, Christopher Huson, Bruce Leasure, and Michael Wolfe. Multiple Version Loops. In *Proceedings of the International Conference on Parallel Processing (ICPP)*, pages 312–318, August 1987.
4. Calin Cascaval, Luise DeRose, David A. Padua, and Daniel Reed. Compile-Time Based Performance Prediction. In *Proceedings of the 12th Workshop on Languages and Compilers for Parallel Computing (LCPC)*, pages 365–379, August 1999.
5. Rohit Chandra, Leo Dagum, Dave Kohr, Dror Maydan, Jeff McDonald, and Ramesh Manon. *Paralle Programming in OpenMP*. Morgan Kaufmann Publisher, 2001.
6. Alan L. Cox and Robert. J. Fowler. Adaptive Cache Coherency for Detecting Migratory Shared Data. In *Proceedings of the 20th International Symposium on Computer Architectur*, pages 98–108, May 1993.
7. Pedro Diniz and Martin Rinard. Dynamic Feedback: An Effective Technique for Adaptive Computing. In *Proceedings of the ACM SIGPLAN Conference on Program Language Design and Implementation*, pages 71–84, June 1997.
8. Rajiv Gupta and Rastislav Bodik. Adaptive Loop Transformations for Scientific Programs. In *Proceedings of the IEEE Symposium on Parallel and Distributed Processing*, pages 368–375, October 1995.
9. Urs Holzle and David Ungar. Optimizing Dynamically-Dispatched Calls with Run-Time Type Feedback. In *Proceedings of the ACM SIGPLAN Conference on Programming Language Design and Implementation (PLDI)*, pages 326–336, June 1994.
10. Jaejin Lee. *Compilation Techniques for Explicitly Parallel Programs*. PhD thesis, Department of Computer Science, University of Illinois at Urbana-Champaign, October 1999. Department of Computer Science Technical Report UIUCDCS-R-99-2112.

11. Jaejin Lee, Yan Solihin, and Josep Torrellas. Automatically Mapping Code in an Intelligent Memory Architecture. In *Proceedings of the 7th International Symposium on High Performance Computer Architecture (HPCA)*, pages 121–132, January 2001.

12. R. L. Mattson, J. Gecsei, D. Slutz, and I. Traiger. Evaluation Techniques for Storage Hierarchies. *IBM Systems Journal*, 9(2):78–117, December 1970.

13. OpenMP Standard Board. *OpenMP Fortran Interpretations*, April 1999. Version 1.0.

14. Martin Rinard and Pedro Diniz. Eliminating Synchronization Bottlenecks in Object Based Programs Using Adaptive Replication. In *Proceedings of the ACM International Conference on Supercomputing (ICS)*, pages 83–92, June 1999.

15. Theodore H. Romer, Dennis Lee, Brian N. Bershad, and Bradley Chen. Dynamic Page Mapping Policies for Cache Conflict Resolution on Standard Hardware. In *Proceedings of the 1st USENIX Symposium on Operating Systems Design and Implementation*, pages 255–266, November 1994.

16. Rafael H. Saavedra and Daeyeon Park. Improving the Effectiveness of Software Prefetching with Adaptive Execution. In *Proceedings of the Conference on Parallel Algorithms and Compilation Techniques*, October 1996.

17. Silicon Graphics Inc. *MIPSpro Auto-Parallelization Option Programmer's Guide*, 1999.

18. Silicon Graphics Inc. *MIPSpro Fortran 77 programmer's Guide*, 1999.

19. Michael J. Voss and Rudolf Eigenmann. Reducing Parallel Overheads through Dynamic Serialization. In *Proceedings of the International Parallel Processing Symposium*, pages 88–92, April 1999.

20. Michael J. Voss and Rudolf Eigenmann. ADAPT: Automated De-Coupled Adaptive Program Transformation. In *Proceedings of the International Conference on Parallel Processing (ICPP)*, page 163, August 2000.

21. Michael J. Voss and Rudolf Eigenmann. High-level Adaptive Program Optimization with ADAPT. In *Proceedings of the ACM SIGPLAN Symposium on Principles and Practice of Parallel Programming*, pages 93–102, June 2001.

# Selector: A Language Construct for Developing Dynamic Applications

Pedro C. Diniz and Bing Liu

University of Southern California, Information Sciences Institute,
4676 Admiralty Way, Suite 1001,
Marina del Rey, California, 90292
{pedro, bliu}@isi.edu

**Abstract.** Fitting algorithms to meet input data characteristics and/or a changing computing environment is a tedious and error prone task. Programmers need to deal with code instrumentation details and implement the selection of which algorithm best suits a given data set. In this paper we describe a set of simple programming constructs for C that allows programmers to specify and generate applications that can select at run-time the best of several possible implementations based on measured run-time performance and/or algorithmic input values. We describe the application of this approach to a realistic linear solver for an engineering crash analysis code. The preliminary experimental results reveal that this approach provides an effective mechanism for creating sophisticated dynamic application behavior with minimal effort.

## 1  Introduction

The best algorithm for a given computation differs widely depending on the characteristics of its input data and of features of the target architecture. For example there are several sorting algorithms that perform very well when the distribution of the keys is uniform (*e.g., quicksort*) while other algorithms perform much better when the keys either have known boundary properties (*e.g., bucket sort*) or are heavily modal (*e.g., merge sort*). In other scenarios the environment characteristics, rather than the input characteristics impact the choice of algorithm more deeply. For instance, in the context of distributed applications it is possible to trade off computation with communication or simply to offload some of the computation to other nodes if the available bandwidth is adequate. Overall programmers would like to choose a particular implementation among a set of possible alternative implementations of the same functionality depending on input data characteristics, environment conditions or both. While in some cases it is possible to characterize the exact set of conditions for which each alternative implementation should be used (*e.g.,* sorting), in general, programmers must rely on observed behavior to decide which implementation performs best. For scenarios where the choice of which algorithm implementation depends on environment conditions programmers must manually instrument the code with calls to a run-time-system and manually encode the strategies to dynamically

B. Pugh and C.-W. Tseng (Eds.): LCPC 2002, LNCS 2481, pp. 218–232, 2005.

select the appropriate algorithm implementation. Other than being cumbersome and error-prone, the resulting code is complex and hard to port or maintain. The approach proposed in this paper advocates extending an imperative programming language such as C/C++ with a modest set of programming constructs allowing programmers to specify the dynamic behavior of a set of alternative implementations for the same functionality. Programmers use a *selector* construct to associate several code variant implementations of the same function name and to define what the switching policy between the alternative code variants is. Programmers also specify which set of environment variables should be observed for which code variant and associate a *cost* and (optionally) a *probe* function with each code variant. The implementation uses the *probe* and *cost* functions to evaluate, rank and choose the best available variant. Because probing and selecting among a potentially large number of code variants can incur non-negligible overheads the *selector* construct provides a *trigger* function that can disable the probing of code variants for a specific number of invocations or until a relevant environment event occurs. *Trigger* functions provide a powerful mechanism to control the amount of probing overhead and encode the relevant environment conditions under which the alternative variant should be reevaluated. This paper makes the following specific contributions:

- Describes the *selector* construct - a modest set of language extensions for adaptive programming for imperative programming languages.
- Describes a particular implementation of the *selector* to C and outlines a source-to-source code generation scheme for C/C++.
- Presents results of the application of the *selector* construct to a sophisticated linear solver from a real engineering code.

While it is true that programmers can manually implement the functionality of the *selector*, there are several benefits to the approach outlined in this paper. First, it is automated. Programmers are not required to engage in low-level error-prone instrumentation of their codes. Second, the semantic gap between the *selector* semantics and the generated C code is not wide, thereby avoiding programmers second-guessing what the selector code will do.

We see the *selector* as a powerful tool for application and/or library developers whose needs are beyond what optimizing compilers can currently perform. The *selector* provides a set of hooks at the language level that allow programmers to exploit and control run-time behavior of the code without having to master all of the instrumentation details.

The remainder of this paper is organized as follows. The next section presents a concrete example of the application of the *selector* concepts. Section 3 describes the design and implementation of the selector in more detail. Section 4 presents preliminary experimental results of using the *selector* in a large scientific application. We discuss related work in Section 5 and conclude in section 6.

## 2   Example

We now illustrate the application of the *selector* construct in the context of solving large sparse linear systems. In this example we wish to select between three alternative equation reordering algorithms, namely Weighted Nested Dissection (WND), Multiple-Minimum-Degree (MMD) and the Multi-Section (MS). The overall objective of any equation reordering algorithm is to minimize the number of non-zero entries that arise during factorization of the matrix. Minimizing the matrix *fill* results in lower data requirements with the subsequent reduction in number of data memory accesses and arithmetic operations. To address the uncertainty of which method performs the best for a given matrix we define a *selector* as depicted in Figure 1. The *selector* construct defines a set of entries via the **entry** keyword. The *selector* also defines a symbolic name, in this case **Solver** and a list of parameters to be used by all of the entries. In addition to the binding of the entries to a single symbolic name, the *selector* defines for each entry a masking function, a *probe* function, and a *cost* function. Typically the *probe* functions are not considered as doing any useful work in the sense that they create side effects that are non-critical to the overall computation. It is the programmer's responsibility to make sure that probe functions are side-effect-free. These *probe* functions have their arguments either drawn from the *selector* parameter list or environment variables such as **clock**. Environment variables are denoted with the modifier *env* and indicate that the corresponding variable should be sampled before and after the corresponding *probe* function executes. The *cost* functions can be defined elsewhere and need not to be defined in the scope of the *selector*. We have also added, for illustration purposes, a simple *masking* function defined by the **when** keyword. In this case the *masking* function is replaced by the simple predicate (**neq > 1024**) meaning that whenever the predicate does not hold during the evaluation of the various entries, the corresponding entry is not considered.

In this example we have also defined a *policy* function and a *trigger*. A *policy* function defines how to choose the best of the set of evaluated entries. The default *policy* function is to choose the *entry* with the minimum evaluated cost. A *trigger* function defines when should the various entries be evaluated by executing the corresponding *probe* functions. In this example we have defined a parameterized *trigger* function that is active once every **block** invocations of the *selector*. An important point to notice about these functions is that they are defined in the lexical scope of the *selector*. This allows for programmers to access a set of *selector* predefined internal variables generated automatically by the compiler. These variables include for instance the number of entries in the *selector*, (**number_entries**) or the invocation number of the *selector* (**invocation_number**). Other cost related variables are declared implicitly by the *cost* functions on an entry-by-entry basis. The *selector* uses these variables to store the cost metrics associated with each *probe* function to be used for quantitative evaluation of the *cost* functions. Figure 2 illustrates the compiler generated C code for the *selector* in Figure 1. For brevity we have omitted all of the operational code but rather focused on the *selector* syntax.

```
selector Solver(Matrix A, Vector x, Vector b, int neq, int vol) is {
   // The list of alternative code variants.
   entry FactorMMD(A, x, b)
      when (neq > 1024) //this is a simple masking function.
      with probe orderingMMD(A)
      with cost costMetric1(vol, env clock);

   entry FactorWND(A,x,b)
      with probe orderingWND(A)
      with cost costMetric1(vol, env clock);

   entry FactorMS(A,x,b)
      with probe orderingMS(A)
      with cost costMetric2(neq, vol, env clock);

   // One of many possibly policies - typically one although more
   // than one is possible for distinct call sites of the selector.
   // Default policy is to choose the variant with the lowest cost.

   int policy MinCost() {
      int i, idx, min=-1;
      // It is a run-time error if no version is selectable...
      // compiler inserts check. This is also the default policy function.
      for(i = 0; i < number_entries; i++){
         if((selectable[i]) && (cost[i] < min)){
            min = cost[i];
            idx = i;
         }
      }
      for(i=0; i < number_entries; i++)
         selectable[i]=FALSE;
      return idx;
   }

   // The default trigger function is { return TRUE; }
   boolean trigger Every(int block){
      if((invocation_number % block) == 0)
         return TRUE;
      return FALSE;
   }
} // end of the selector construct.

   // Invocation site with specific policy and trigger function.
   // Different call sites could have different policies and
   // trigger functions declared for this selector
   selector Solver(args) with policy MinCost() with trigger Every(10);
```

**Fig. 1.** Example of Linear Solver with Selector Construct

At the *selector* call site the programmer can associate an actual *policy* and *trigger* function and/or provide specific argument values. In the example above the *selector* will reevaluate the set of available entries every 10 invocations. During the successive invocations when no evaluation is required the *selector* uses the code *entry* selected in the previous evaluation. At startup the *selector* forces an evaluation to set up initial conditions. We now describe in detail the behavior of the *selector* generated C code. As outlined in Figure 2, the compiler generates code that evaluates each of the individual probes in the *selector* and chooses the entry as dictated by the user-provided *policy* function. For each *entry* the generated code first determines if that particular *entry* is selectable. It does so by evaluating the predicates (and in general a boolean function) associated with

```
typedef struct Solver_selector_data {
    int number_entries, invocation_number, selected_entry;
    int selectable[3]; // to reflect the masking
    double cost[3];// to store the results of cost functions
    // Cost variables for each entry extracted from cost function args.
    int probe0_var0; // for the vol variable
    double probe0_var1[2]; // env variable with before, after
    int probe1_var0; // for the vol variable
    double probe1_var1[2]; // env variable with before, after
    int probe2_var0; // for the neq variable
    int probe2_var1; // for the vol variable
    double probe2_var2[2]; // env variable with before, after
}
    ...
Solver_selector_data SolverCS0;
// The Selector call site is replaced by the function below.
// Compiler initilizes the Solver_selector_data SolverCS0.
    ...
void SolverCallSite0(Matrix A, Vector x, Vector b,
    int neq, int vol, int trigger_arg0){
    if(Every(trigger_arg0) == TRUE){ // The trigger function invocation
        for(i = 0; i < SolverCS0.number_entries; i++){
            switch(i){
                case 0:
                    if(neq > 1024) SolverCS0.selectable[0] = TRUE;
                    SolverCS0.probe0_var1[0] = clock;// before the probe executes.
                    orderingND(A,x,b);
                    SolverCS0.probe0_var0 = vol;
                    SolverCS0.probe0_var1[1] = clock; // after the probe executes.
                    SolverCS0.cost[0] =
                        (double)costMetric1(SolverCS0.probe0_var0,SolverCS0.probe0_var1);
                    break;
                ... // other cases here.
            }
        }
        SolverCS0.selected_entry = MinCost(SolverCS0);
        if((bounds(SolverCS0.selected_entry,SolverCS0.number_entries)){
            printf(" *** Error: Empty selection (solverCS0) "); exit(1);
        }
    }
    switch(SolverCS0.selected_entry){ // Now selector the variant and execute it.
    case 0:
        FactorND(A,x,b);
        break;
    ... // other cases here.
    }
}
// The original call site would be trasnformed into
SolverCallSite0(A, x, b, volume, number_equations, 10);
```

**Fig. 2.** Selector Code for Selector in Figure 1

each *entry*. Next the generated code invokes the *probe* function and evaluates its run-time performance using the corresponding *cost* function. The next step is for the generated code to invoke the *cost* functions and then its *policy* function. In a typical application the programmer would like to reassess the various alternatives from time to time or in a response to a significant event. For this purpose the *trigger* function is executed before the *selector* assesses the various code variants. If the *trigger* function is inactive, the *selector* chooses the code variant selected in the previous invocation for the same call site or forces the evaluation of the probes if this is the first time the *selector* is invoked. This example illustrates the scenarios the *selector* is designed to handle. First there is a discrete number of alternative implementation for the same functionality. Associated with each *entry* the programmer can define a specific *cost* function and a set of identifiable variables whose run-time values are needed to assess the cost of the *entry*. Last the programmer can define a *policy* and *trigger* functions to control when the choice of code variants should be reevaluated and which variant should be selected. In the next section we describe in more detail the implementation issues of the *selector*. We also describe a set of more advanced features for the *selector*, which include the ability to terminate a sequence of evaluation of *probe* functions as well as the ability to abort the evaluation of a *probe* function based on a time-out specification.

# 3   Selector Design and Implementation

We now describe the basic concepts the *selector* relies on, their syntax and implementation restrictions. Later we describe a series of advanced features that allow for greater flexibility in specifying a richer set of *selector* behaviors for applications that require more sophisticated dynamic behavior.

## 3.1   Basic Concepts

The *selector* relies on four basic concepts illustrated in Figure 3, namely:

- A discrete set of alternative code variants or implementations. These variants must draw their input arguments from a common parameter list to ensure that the arguments passed at the call site to the *selector* can be applied to any of the code variant of the *selector*;
- A set of *cost* functions one per alternative code variant. These *cost* functions provide two pieces of information. First a way to generate a quantitative metric that can be used to rank code variants. Typically *cost* functions will yield floating-point values for comparison purposes. The second piece of information is that the argument list of each cost function implicitly defines the set of metric variables (*e.g.,* wall-clock or number of cache misses) to be used in the evaluation of each code variant. The compiler instruments each code variant based on these variables.
- A *policy* function that defines which of the code variant to choose. The default *policy* function, should it be omitted at the *selector* call site, is to choose the code variant with the minimum cost.
- A *trigger* function that dictates when the *selector* should evaluate the alternative code variants. This function is used to control the amount of time devoted to evaluate alternative code variants mitigating any substantial performance overhead in the search for the best code variant. The default behavior is to evaluate every code variant only once during the first invocation of the *selector*. This situation occurs when the relative performance of the code variants does not change over time but is unknown at compile time.

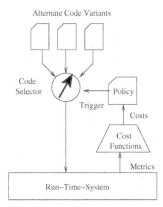

Alternate Code Variants

Code
Selector

Trigger

Policy

Costs

Cost
Functions

Metrics

Run–Time–System

**Fig. 3.** Graphical Illustration of the Selector Concepts

## 3.2   Selector Syntax and Semantics

We have chosen a syntax for the *selector* construct that is closely related to C
as outlined below. Here the parameter list defines the names inside the scope
of the *selector* that can be used for the binding of parameters for each entry
and the lists of arguments `carg0,...,cargC` , `type parg0,...,type pargP`
and `type targ0,...,targT` are simple variable expressions drawn from the *selector* parameters or globally visible variables. At the *selector* call site the programmer must include the keywords `probed selector` or the keywords `sampled
selector` with an argument list that agrees in number and type with the argu-
ment list declared in the *selector*.

```
selector Name (type parm0,...,type parmN) is {
   entry entryName0(arg0,...,argk)
   with cost Cost0(type carg0,...,type cargC);
   ...
   int policy PolicyA(type parg0,...,type pargP) { ... }
   boolean trigger TriggerT(type targ0,...,targT) { ... }
}
```

In the *selector* definition the programmer can specify a series of *policy* and
*trigger* functions. At the call site the programmer indicates which of the defined
*policy* and *trigger* functions that particular site should use as illustrated below.[1]

```
probed selector Name(args) with policy P(args) with trigger T(args);
sampled selector Name(args) with policy P(args) with trigger T(args);
```

We implement two distinct behaviors for the *selector*, namely a *sampled* behavior and a *probed* behavior. The *probed* selector corresponds to the implementation described in section 2. In this behavior, the implementation evaluates all
of the probes of the selectable variants when triggered by an active *trigger* function. The *probe* functions are executed in turn along with their *cost* functions.

---

[1] In many cases the keyword **probed** can be omitted as long as for every entry there
is a probed function. The sampled keyword, however, must be included.

```
// additional selector control variables
int current_entry; // the next code variant to be evaluated
boolean sampling_phase; // controls the sampling across invocations
...
void NameSelector(parm_list){
  if(triggerfunction(arg_list)){
    sampling_phase = TRUE;
    current_entry = 0;
  }
  if(sampling_phase){
    current_entry = nextEntry(current_entry,N,order,selectable);
    switch(current_version){
      ... // invoke the code variant here.
    }
    if(current_entry == number_entries){
    sampling_phase = FALSE;
    selected_entry = policy(arg_list);
    }
  } else {
    switch(selected_entry){
      ... // invoke the selected version in non-sampling phase mode.
    }
  }
}
```

**Fig. 4.** Sampled selector Code Generation Scheme Outline

Next the implementation selects a code variant according to the policy function and executes it. A *sampled selector* does not use any *probe* function for the evaluation of each code variant, but rather the code variant itself. In this situation, and because the actual code variant produces useful work, the implementation cannot simply discard the work. As such a *sampled selector* will work across *selector* invocations and use the actual run of the code variant to determine the code variant cost. At the first invocation the *selector* determines which code variants are enabled. It invokes the first of such code variants and saves the resulting performance metrics as specified by the arguments of the *cost* functions. The implementation then tracks which code variant is to be sampled in the subsequent invocations using internal variables. [2] At each *selector* invocation the compiler generated code first checks if the trigger function holds. If that is the case the selector enters a sampling phase where every subsequent call to the *selector* are used to sample the performance of one of the selectable code variants. Once all of the code variants have been examined during a sampling phase the selector uses the *policy* function to select which code variant to execute. Figure 4 outlines the code generation scheme for the *sampled selector* behavior.

### 3.3    Advanced Selector Features

We now describe a set of advanced *selector* features namely, state and environment variables an early cut-off function.

---

[2] The *sampled selector* implementation evaluates the predicates that dictate which variants are selectable, the predicates when the *trigger* function is first active and during the next N-1 invocations, when the *selector* is sampling the various variants the corresponding *trigger* functions could possibly no longer be active.

**Selector State Variables.** Another aspect of the *selector* is the ability to define `state` variables the programmer can use to define a richer set of policies using *selector* invocation site history. These state variables are declared as ordinary variables in the scope of the *selector* and therefore used by any function defined in the same scope. Eventually this allows the programmer to control aspects such as the evaluation order of the code variants and consequently ameliorating potential run-time overheads of the *selector*.

**Environment Variables.** Typically a *probe* function would require a given environment variable such as wall-clock time or any other raw performance metric to be examined *before* and *after* the actual *probe* function executes. To address this, we define the *env* attribute for variables to be used as arguments in cost functions. and associated two predefined functions `before` and `after` to access the value of the variable before and after the *probe* function executes. The compiler automatically instruments the *probe* function to extract and store at run-time the values of the environment variables before and after the *probe* function executes.

**Early Cut-Off or Break Function.** In some cases the programmer might want to exploit properties of the various code variants in a given selector or simply take advantage of the information gathered in previous evaluations to terminate the evaluation in the current evaluation cycle. At least two scenarios are likely:

- The last evaluated function has yielded good enough expected performance result and no resources should be devoted to exploring alternative variants;
- The last evaluated version exhibits poor performance and subsequent variants are likely to exhibit worse performance due to monotonic properties of the implementations.

To address these concerns the selector includes the possibility of defining an early cut-off, or *break* function for each selector entry as outlined below.

```
entry E
   with cost C() with probe P() with break B(...)
```

After the *selector* has evaluated a given entry's *cost* function it invokes the corresponding *break* function. If this *break* function evaluates to the `boolean` `true` value the *selector* skips the evaluation of the remaining entries and selects the best implementation evaluated so far.

### 3.4   Discussion

One of the guiding principles behind the definition of a *selector* and its syntax was to keep it C-like. The intended target programmers will be a knowledgeable programmer intending to tune a library code or the sophisticated programmer whose need for performance warrants the exploitation of algorithmic trade-offs without engaging in low-level run-time environment programming. The choice of a new script-like language that would include concepts such as "best" and "cost" would present the challenge of teaching yet another scripting language to a programmer whose native programming language will be almost likely C/C++. As such we have define a set of modest extensions to C/C++ to provide hooks so that programmer can explore the notions of dynamically choosing between multiple implementations while retaining a clear, straight-forward vision of that the semantics of the *selector* is. While the approach outlined above can be viewed as fancy C++ template building there are several differences. First the *selector* compiler can perform a substantially more flexible code generation that is currently possible with templates (or at least for currently stable compiler implementations). Furthermore the type checking in the *selector*, while less sophisticated provides for a clearer semantics than in C++ using inheritance rules in templates. Second the *selector* concept is language-independent. Overall our approach has been to offer a simple set of abstractions via a modest set of new keywords and constructs.

## 4    Experimental Results

In this section we describe a preliminary experiment of the application of the *selector* concept described above to a real engineering code.

### 4.1    Example Application and Methodology

For this experiment we have used an existing FORTRAN 77 code for solving a large linear system of equations using a variant of the Cholesky direct factorization method. The segment of the code is structured into three main phases. In the first phase the code reads the input matrix from a file. In the second phase the code factors the input matrix into a lower and upper triangular matrices. In the last phase the code solves the system of equations using two back solve steps. Currently this code can use in isolation one of two competing methods for equation reordering, namely the Multiple-Minimum-Degree (MMD) [9] and the weighted nested dissection (WND) [8] ordering.

Using in this linear solver application we have coded a selector with two entries for the MMD and the WND ordering methods. We also use a cost function that uses the number of non-zero entries in the symbolic-factorization of the matrices as a prediction on how well the corresponding ordering will perform during factorization. At the time of this writing our front-end parser and code generator are not fully operational. As such we have generated the selector code manually using the template that parser will eventually use. This approach allows us to develop a sense for the implementation and performance evaluation details before investing a whole set of resources to a fully automated implementation. The original version of this solver code was written in FORTRAN 77. We have converted the driver component of this application to C to integrate with the selector generated C code. For these experiments we have used 3 input matrices referred to respectively as the **Hood**, the **Knee** and the **I-Beam**. Table 1 summarizes the relevant structural and numeric characteristics of each matrix.

Table 1. Input Data Sets of Linear Solver

| Application | Input Domain | Structure (if any) | Number of Equations | Storage (Mbytes) |
|---|---|---|---|---|
| Hood | Automobile Metallic Structural Analysis | 2D 6-point stencil | 235,962 | 200 |
| Knee | Human Prosthetic Implant | 3D localized neighbors FEM | 69,502 | 553 |
| I-Beam | Civil Engineering | regular linear | 615,600 | 1,311 |

## 4.2   Results

We now describe the performance experimental results obtained with the Solver selector example described above for each of the input matrices. These experiments were carried out on a Sun Blade 100 Workstation with 1Gbyte of internal RAM and running the Solaris 8 operating system. All codes, both FORTRAN and C were compiled with the SunPro compiler using -O optimization level.

We begin this discussion by presenting in Table 2 for each input matrix the time breakdown for solving one linear system with each of the available ordering methods for a single solving run. In reality the applications are structured as multiple solve operations for the same symbolic factorization steps. Table 2 reveals that overall the symbolic factorization has a fairly small weight in the total execution time. However, the choice of which ordering, has a substantial impact on the overall factorization and consequently the overall execution time. Another observation is that although MMD ordering is usually the fastest it produces for these examples the worst execution time. For long runs of solve steps the extra computation power devoted to WND yields substantial gains, even for a single solve step. Next we report on the utilization of a probed selector with the two distinct orderings as referred above.

For each solving variant we have an ordering function as its probe and use the number of non-zeros in the symbolic factorization obtained during the ordering as the prediction of the performance of the factorization step. We use the default policy, as the policy that selects the code variant with the lowest cost metric. For this experiment we enabled all the available code variants and

Table 2. Execution time Breakdown for 3 Input Matrices and 2 Ordering Methods

| Application | Step | MMD | | WND | |
|---|---|---|---|---|---|
| | | Time (secs) | Percent | Time (secs) | Percent |
| Hood | Ordering | 4.49 | 3.26 | 8.04 | 7.81 |
| | Factorization | 130.79 | 94.85 | 92.55 | 89.94 |
| | Solve | 2.59 | 1.73 | 2.31 | 2.24 |
| | Total | 137.87 | 100.0 | 102.90 | 100.0 |
| Knee | Ordering | 2.93 | 0.97 | 7.05 | 5.23 |
| | Factorization | 296.11 | 98.15 | 126.04 | 93.48 |
| | Solve | 2.66 | 0.88 | 1.74 | 1.29 |
| | Total | 301.70 | 100.0 | 134.83 | 100.0 |
| I-Beam | Ordering | 8.96 | 1.03 | 19.25 | 3.40 |
| | Factorization | 731.98 | 84.38 | 418.11 | 73.91 |
| | Solve | 126.49 | 14.49 | 128.33 | 22.69 |
| | Total | 867.87 | 100.0 | 565.69 | 100.0 |

therefore execute all of the associated probes. To evaluate the performance impact of the selector we experience with three selector strategies using trigger and break functions. For this experiment we perform 10 consecutive factorizations of matrices with the same structure followed by a corresponding solve phase. This reflects a computation where the matrix values change slightly but retains the same connectivity.

- *Probe-at-Start*: In this strategy the *selector* probes all of the available variants at the beginning of the execution and then uses the best code variant throughout the remainder of the computation.
- *Check-in-Middle*: In this strategy the *selector* probes all of the code variants at the beginning of the execution. In the middle of the execution the selector reevaluates all of the variants.
- *Reorder-and-Break*: In this strategy the *selector* reevaluates the code variants but starts with the variant that was last selected for execution. In addition it skips the remainder probes if the newly evaluated cost is either better or at most 10% worse than the cost last evaluated for this variant.

Table 3 presents the execution breakdowns for each of the input matrices and for each of the strategies described above. We have separated the amount of time devoted to the probes and compared it with the total execution time.

**Table 3.** Execution Results for Various Selector Strategies

| Application | Strategy | | | | | |
|---|---|---|---|---|---|---|
| | Probe-at-Start | | Check-in-Middle | | Reorder-and-Break | |
| | Total | Selector (%) | Total | Selector (%) | Total | Selector (%) |
| Hood | 1048.71 | 12.46(1.3) | 1059.43 | 25.27(2.5) | 1052.98 | (2.1) |
| Knee | 1339.25 | 9.71(0.8) | 1349.44 | 19.46(1.6) | 1332.70 | 12.60(1.3) |
| I-Beam | 8699.10 | 28.26(0.32) | 8779.83 | 56.35(0.6) | 8864.88 | 36.67(0.41) |

The results in Table 3 reveal that the overhead associated with the probe functions is very small. Even in the case of the naive *Check-in-Middle* strategy the overhead climbs only to a modest 2.5%. This is partly true given the fact that we had only 2 competing variants of code. For larger number of variants the overhead can quickly become significant. As expected the strategy *Reorder-and-Break* reduces the overhead and could be a strategy of choice for selector with large number of code variants. Another noteworthy aspect is that the selector is only as good as the probe functions are. In the case of the **I-Beam** matrix the cost function guides the selector to choose the MMD ordering. This turns out to be the wrong choice for the factorization. A way to combat the inherent unreliability of estimations/predictions of the probes is to use the *sampled selector* version where the real factorization would be used for evaluation.

### 4.3   Discussion

This example illustrate the potential of the selector construct as a way to relieve the programmer of having to deal with explicitly building the instrumentation, control for evaluation and all of the auxiliary data structure associated with a selection scheme. The low programmer effort required to control the overall strategy of the selector is a key aspect of the overall approach In these experiments we had to code only 20 lines of C code to specify both the *trigger*, *cost* and *break* functions. The generated C code was about 200 lines long.

An aspect not focused so far on parallel execution. Clearly parallel execution can exacerbate program execution trade-offs and hence make the application of the selector construct even more appealing (see [6] for an illustrative example). Another important aspect is that parallel execution enables the concurrent evaluation of alternative code variants thereby mitigating the selector overhead even further. We are currently working on extending the code generation scheme to support parallel evaluation as well as testing the abort functionality.

## 5   Related Work

We begin by describing these efforts and then describe the more automated compiler approaches that rely on dynamic profiling to validate or enhance the applicability of traditional compiler analysis or transformations.

### 5.1   Languages for Adaptivity

Voss and Eigenman [10] defined a new language, AL, used to describe compiler optimization strategies. This language uses specific constructs such as constraint and apply-spec to interface with internal compiler transformation passes and focuses on the application of compiler transformation to regions of the code that meet these constraints. The specification also allows the definition of phases of optimization and user-defined strategies. Our approach is very similar to AL in terms of the concept of observing run-time performance and choosing the "best" code variant. A major difference is that AL focuses on tuning the application of compiler transformations whereas we have focused on user-level application tuning. Adve, Lam and Ensink [1] proposed an extension to the class hierarchy of an objected-oriented model of computation with three basic concepts - adaptors, metrics and events. The notion of selector described here is very object-oriented as well. Rather than relying on the syntax and class mechanisms of C++ we have chosen to use a more language-independent approach by requiring the programmer to specify the same set of concepts via functions.

### 5.2   Dynamic Compilation

Dynamic compilation aims at delaying the entry compilation process until run-time. One of the benefits is that run-time data values are accessible and specialized versions of the code can be generated on-the-fly overcoming the inherent limitations of static optimizations. While this approach has been successful in the context of interpreted languages (*e.g.*, in the Hot-Spot compiler from Sun MicroSystems) for C the overheads of implementation seems prohibitively high [4,7], thereby limiting the widespread adoption of this technique.

## 5.3  Feedback-Directed Optimization

In the context of dynamic feedback optimizations researchers have developed fully automated systems that are capable of using run-time profiling information to validate or simply apply transformations. Agesen and Hölzle use run-time information to improve the efficiency of the Polymorphic-In-Line cache (PIC) via the reordering the sequences of the tests to perform faster dynamic dispatching. Bala *et. al* [5] use run-time basic-block statistical data to reoptimize sequences of basic blocks, recompiling non-trivial sequences of basic blocks. The Jalapeño RVM project [3] at IBM uses a simple cost/benefit analysis at run-time to determine which level of optimization to apply when recompiling hot methods. Whereas previous approaches have focused on using run-time data to either validated or enhance the applicability of a given set of transformations, in our own work we have focused on using dynamic feedback to delay the binding of a different set of code variants produced with distinct policies of the same set of transformations [6]. In this approach the compiler, and therefore the compiler writer, must be fully aware of an inherent trade-off for the applications of a given set of programming transformations with distinct policies.

## 6  Conclusion

In this paper we have presented a set of modest extensions to C to allow programmers to easily specify and control the invocation of various code variants for the same functionality. The compiler can generate code automatically using a simple template relieving the programmer from the tedious and error-prone low-level performance evaluation. We have validated this approach for a sophisticated engineering linear solver. For this code the programmer can easily specify a set of cost and run-time strategy functions so that the resulting generated selector code can choose the best available code implementation while exhibiting negligible overheads.

## References

1. V. Adve, V. Lam and B. Ensink, Language and Compiler Support for Adaptive Distributed Applications. In Proc. of the *ACM SIGPLAN Workshop on Optimization of Middleware and Distributed Systems (OM 2001)* Snowbird, Utah, June 2001.
2. O. Agesen and U. Hölzle, Type Feedback vs. Concrete Type Analysis: A Comparison of Optimization Techniques for Object-Oriented Languages. In Proc. of the *ACM Conference on Object-Oriented Programming Systems, Languages and Applications (OOPSLA'95)* 1995.
3. M. Arnold, S. Fink, D. Grove, M. Hind, and P. Sweeney, Adaptive Optimization in the Jalapeño JVM: The Controller's Analytical Model. In Proc. of the *ACM Workshop on Feedback-Directed and Dynamic Optimization (FDDO-3)*, Dec., 2000.
4. J. Auslander, M. Philipose, C. Chambers, S.J. Eggers and B.N. Bershad, Fast, Effective Dynamic Compilation. In Proc. of the *ACM Conference on Programming Language Design and Implementation (PLDI96)*, June 1996.

5. V. Bala, E. Duesterwald, S. Banerjia, Dynamo: A Transparent Dynamic Optimization System. In Proc. of the *ACM Conference on Programming Language and Implementation (PLDI00)*, June 2000.
6. P. Diniz and M. Rinard, Dynamic Feedback: An Effective technique for Adaptive Computing. In Proc. of the *ACM Conference on Programming Language Design and implementation (PLDI97)*, June 1997.
7. D. Engler, Vcode: a retargetable, extensible, very fast dynamic code generation system. In Proc. of the *ACM Conference on Programming Language and Implementation (PLDI96)*, June 1996.
8. G. Karypis and V. Kumar, Multilevel k-way partitioning scheme for irregular graphs. *Journal of Parallel and Distributed Computing*, 48(1):96-129, Jan. 1998.
9. J. Liu, Modification of the minimum degree algorithm by multiple elimination *ACM Transactions on Mathematical Software*, 11(2), pp. 141-153, Jun. 1985.
10. M. Voss and R. Eigenmann, High-Level Adaptive Program Optimization with ADAPT. In Proc. of the *ACM Symp. on Principles and Practice of Parallel Programming (PPOPP'01)*, 2001.

# Optimizing the Java Piped I/O Stream Library for Performance *

Ji Zhang[1], Jaejin Lee[2,**], and Philip K. McKinley[1]

[1] Michigan State University, Department of Computer Science and Engineering,
Software Engineering and Network Systems Laboratory,
East Lansing, MI 48824, USA
{zhangji9, mckinley}@cse.msu.edu
[2] Seoul National University, School of Computer Science and Engineering,
Seoul 151-742, Korea
jlee@cse.snu.ac.kr

**Abstract.** The overall performance of Java programs has been significantly improved since Java emerged as a mainstream programming language. However, these improvements have revealed a second tier of performance bottlenecks. In this paper, we address one of these issues: the performance of Java piped I/O stream library. We analyze commonly used data transfer patterns in which one reader thread and one writer thread communicate via Java piped I/O streams. We consider data buffering and synchronization between these two threads, as well as the thread scheduling policy used in the Java virtual machine. Based on our observations, we propose several optimization techniques that can significantly improve Java piped I/O stream performance. We use these techniques to modify the Java piped I/O stream library. We present performance results for seven example programs from the literature that use the Java piped I/O stream library. Our methods improve the performance of the programs by over a factor of 4 on average, and by a factor of 27 in the best case.

## 1 Introduction

Due to wide acceptance of Java as a mainstream programming language, the performance of Java programs is increasingly important. With the emergence of new Java virtual machine implementations and new compiler optimization techniques, such as just-in-time compilation and hot-spot detection with dynamic

---

* This work was supported in part by the U.S. Department of the Navy, Office of Naval Research under Grant No. N00014-01-1-0744, and in part by National Science Foundation grants CCR-9912407, EIA-0000433, and EIA-0130724. This work was also supported in part by the Korean Ministry of Education under the BK21 program and by the Korean Ministry of Science and Technology under the National Research Laboratory program.
** Corresponding author. The preliminary work of this paper was done when the author was in the Department of Computer Science and Engineering at Michigan State University.

B. Pugh and C.-W. Tseng (Eds.): LCPC 2002, LNCS 2481, pp. 233–248, 2005.

compilation, the overall performance of Java programs has been significantly improved. However, these improvements have revealed a second tier of performance bottlenecks.

Java is inherently a multi-threaded programming language. In some multi-threaded Java programs, data is processed and transferred from one thread to another in a pipeline fashion. A common example is *proxy server*, a middleware component often used to mitigate the limitations of mobile hosts and their wireless connections [1,2,3]. Adopting the terminology of the IETF Task Force on Open Pluggable Edge Services (OPES) [4], proxies are composed of many *proxylets*, which are functional components that can be inserted, added and removed dynamically at run time without disturbing the network state. Example proxylet services include transcoding data streams into lower-bandwidth versions, scanning for viruses, and introducing forward error correction to make data streams more resilient to losses. In an earlier study [5], our group designed a composable proxy framework based on detachable Java I/O streams. Using piped I/O among proxylets produces a flexible framework that can be reconfigured at run time in response to changing environmental conditions or user preferences. However, this investigation also revealed shortcomings of the Java piped I/O classes in terms of performance.

In this paper, we investigate how to improve the performance of Java piped I/O stream library. We found that the Java pipe library is implemented in a very inefficient way. Because Java pipes are widely used, well beyond our own proxy-based systems, their efficiency may significantly impact on the performance of many programs. We analyze data transfer patterns between different threads that are used in Java piped I/O stream library. We consider data buffering, synchronization between different threads, and the thread scheduling policy used in the Java virtual machine. Based on our observations, we propose several optimization techniques that can significantly improve Java piped I/O stream performance. We use these techniques to modify the Java piped I/O stream library. Our experimental results show that these techniques improve the performance of some example programs from the literature using the Java pipe library by over a factor of 4 (by a factor of 27 in the best case) on average. Also, we demonstrate that the most effective technique to use depends on the run-time environment.

The remainder of the paper is organized as follows: Section 2 describes Java piped I/O stream library, and Section 3 presents our proposed methods. Section 4 describes the evaluation environment, and Section 5 presents results of our experiments. Related work is discussed in Section 6, and our conclusions are given in Section 7.

## 2   Java Piped I/O Stream

In this section, we review the use and implementation of Java pipes.

### 2.1   Using Java Piped I/O Stream

The PipedInputStream and PipedOutputStream classes in the Java library provide a mechanism to transfer a stream of bytes between different threads. Before transferring data between threads, a pipe between the two threads is created. Subsequently, one thread can write data to the PipedOutputStream, and the other thread can read data from the PipedInputStream. Figure 1 shows the process of creating a pipe by using `connect` method of PipedInputStream.

```
// create the piped input
PipedInputStream pipeIn = new PipedInputStream();
// create the piped output
PipedOutputStream pipeOut = new PipedOutputStream();
// connect the piped input with the piped output.
pipeIn.connect(pipeOut);
```

**Fig. 1.** Creating a pipe

Two methods are available for reading data from the pipe: `PipedInputStream.read()` and `PipedInputStream.read( byte[] b, int off, int len )`. The `read()` method reads one byte from the pipe; the `read(b, off, len)` method reads a byte-array, `b[]`, from the pipe. The length of the byte-array is specified by `len`. The first byte read is stored at `b[off]` and the kth byte read is stored at `b[off+k-1]`.

Similarly, two methods are available for writing data to the pipe: `PipedOutputStream.write( int b )` and `PipedOutputStream.write( byte[] b, int off, int len )`. The `write(b)` method writes a byte, b, to the pipe; the `write( b, off, len )` method writes a byte-array `b[]` to the pipe. The length of the array written to the pipe is specified by `len`. The first byte written to the pipe is `b[off]` and the kth byte is `b[off+k-1]`. Figure 2 shows how to read and write data using the pipe created in Figure 1.

```
...
byte byteOut;                                    byte byteIn;
byte[] byteArray = new byteArray[MAX];           byte[] byteArray = new byteArray[MAX];
...                                              ...
// preparing output values (byteOut and byteArray)  ...
...                                              ...
pipeOut.write(byteOut);                          byteIn = pipeIn.read()
...                                              ...
pipeOut.write(byteArray,0,MAX);                  pipeIn.read(byteArray,0,MAX);
...                                              ...
         Writer Thread                                   Reader Thread
```

**Fig. 2.** Writing and reading data on a pipe

The writer can invoke a synchronized method `PipedOutputStream.flush()` in order to notify the reader that bytes are available in the pipe. The `flush` method simply invokes `notifyAll()`; it is not related to the flushing mechanisms of the underlying operating system.

## 2.2   Implementation in Sun JDK 1.3.1

The UML class diagram in Figure 3 shows the Java pipe read-write mechanism. When the pipe is connected, a PipedInputStream object reference is assigned to

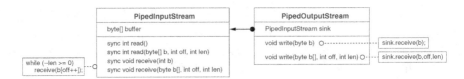

**Fig. 3.** The UML diagram of the Java pipe read/write

the variable `sink` in the `PipedOutputStream` class. When the writer invokes `write` method to write data to the pipe, the `PipedOutputStream` object calls the `receive` method of the `PipedInputStream` object with the parameters of the `write` method.

The `PipedInputStream` encapsulates all the key functions of the pipe including protection of critical sections with synchronization. The `buffer` in `PipedInput-Stream` is shared between the writer and reader. The writer deposits data to `buffer` by calling a `write` method and the reader extracts data from the `buffer` by calling a `read` method. Two methods, `receive(b)` and `receive(b,off,len)`, in `Piped-InputStream` are called by the `write` method in `PipedOutputStream` to write to the buffer one byte and an array of bytes, respectively.

Figure 4 describes the synchronization mechanism of Java pipe in `read()` and `receive(b)` methods. The `read()` and `receive(b)` methods are synchronized. When the reader calls `read()`, it checks if there are any data unread in `buffer`. If not, the reader notifies the writer and blocks itself. The reader wakes up 1000 ms later or is woken up by a `notifyAll` method invoked by the writer. If at least one byte is available in `buffer`, `read()` reads a byte from `buffer`. When the writer calls `receive(b)` through `write`, it checks if there is any free space in `buffer`. If not, the writer notifies the reader and blocks itself. It wakes up 1000 ms later or is woken up by `notifyAll` invoked by the reader. If the shared buffer is not full, then `receive(b)` writes a byte to the shared buffer.

```
while( no data in the buffer ) {          while( no free space buffer ){
  notifyAll();                              notifyAll();
  wait(1000);                               wait(1000);
}                                         }
// read one byte from the buffer          // write one byte to the buffer
ret = byte [out++];                       buffer[in++] = b;
return ret;
```
             (a)                                                   (b)

**Fig. 4.** Synchronization mechanism in Java pipe. (a) Synchronized method `read()` called by the reader. (b) Synchronized method `receive(b)` called by the writer.

Figure 5 shows the implementation of `read(b,off,len)` and `receive(b,off, len)`. The `read(b,off,len)` method first calls `read()` to read one byte from `buffer`, and then copies the remaining bytes byte-by-byte from `buffer` in a loop. The implementation of the `receive(b,off,len)` method is quite simple: it repeatedly calls `receive(b)` `len` times.

However, the implementation and the algorithms used in Java pipe library are inefficient for the following reasons:

```
b[off]=read();                          while (--len >= 0) {
off++; len--;                             receive(b[off++]);
while(len > 0 &&                         }
  there are bytes left in the buffer) {
  Copy one byte from the buffer to b[off];
  off++;
  len--;
}
```

              (a)                                      (b)

**Fig. 5.** Implementation of `read(b,off,len)` and `receive(b,off,len)` in Java pipe. (a) Synchronized method `read(b,off,len)`. (b) Synchronized method `receive(b,off,len)`.

1. The `receive(b, off, len)` method repeatedly calls `receive(b)`. This design incurs at least one method invocation when each byte is transferred.
2. The `read(b, off, len)` method uses byte-by-byte copying, which is very inefficient.
3. Synchronization overhead is high. The methods `read` and `receive` are synchronized methods and use wait/notify synchronization. Monitor operations are involved in both synchronized methods and wait/notify synchronization. When the switching frequency between the reader and writer is high, the synchronization overhead becomes high.
4. The concurrency level is low. The granularity of synchronization is an entire method. Thus, the operations inside the synchronized methods cannot be interleaved.

In this paper, we develop optimization techniques for the Java piped I/O stream library to overcome these inefficiencies.

## 3 Our Approach

In this section, we introduce five different optimization techniques for Java piped I/O stream library.

### 3.1 Array Copying (ArrC)

In the Java piped I/O stream library, the method `read(b,off,len)` uses byte-by-byte assignments to copy bytes from the shared buffer to the byte array b, and the method `receive(b,off,len)` repeatedly calls the method `receive(b)` to copy multiple bytes to the shared buffer from the byte array b. The byte-by-byte copying and repeated method invocations cause unnecessary overhead.

In many cases, it is more efficient to use a native method `System.arraycopy` provided by the Java library to copy data from a byte array to another. The method signature is `System.arraycopy(Object src, int src_position, Object dst, int dst_position, int length)`.

We rewrote `read(b,off,len)` in the library with `System.arraycopy` by replacing repeated byte-by-byte copying, as shown in Figure 6.

```
b[off]=read();                              while( no data in the buffer ){
off++; len--;                                   notifyAll();
while(len>0 &&                                  wait(1000);
    there are bytes left in the buffer) {   } // if no byte left in the buffer, then block
  Copy one byte from the buffer to b[off];  Array-copy the bytes from the buffer to b;
  off++;
  len--;
}
```

                    (a)                                         (b)

**Fig. 6.** Modification of `read(b,off,len)`. (a) Original code (b) Modified code with
`System.arraycopy`.

In addition, we modify `receive(b,off,len)` in the library. Instead of repeatedly calling `receive(b)`, we place the synchronization inside the method and use
array copying to directly copy a certain number of bytes from the shared buffer to
the byte-array `b`, as shown in Figure 7.

```
                                            while (len > 0) {
                                                while( no free space in the buffer ){
                                                    notifyAll();
while (--len >= 0) {                                 wait(1000);
  receive(b[off++]);                              }// if no free space, then block
}
                                                Array copy data from b to
                                                    the space available in the buffer;

                                                len = len - number of bytes copied;
                                            }
```

                    (a)                                         (b)

**Fig. 7.** Modification of `receive(b,off,len)`. (a) Original code. (b) Modified code with
`System.arraycopy`.


## 3.2   Buffering (Buff)

The basic idea of modifying the library with buffering is to add two extra buffers,
input and output, on both ends of the pipe. These buffers are not shared between
the reader and the writer. Read and write operations use these buffers, and do not
directly access the shared buffer. When the output buffer buffer is full, it is written
to the shared buffer. Similarly, when the input buffer is empty, it is filled from the
shared buffer. This concept is illustrated in Figure 8. The size of each buffer is 1024
bytes.

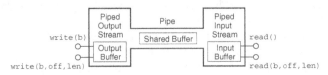

**Fig. 8.** Buffering mechanism

There is one issue that needs to be considered when the buffering technique is used. When the communication between two theads through a pipe depends on the specific pattern of the bytes transferred, the buffering technique may cause deadlock. Calling the flush method is required after writing the data to the pipe in order to prevent deadlock.

### 3.3   Combining Buffering with Array Copying (Buff&ArrC)

Buffering increases the size of data to be transferred through the pipe at one time. As a result, it boosts performance of data transfer. When the data size to be transferred is large, the array copying technique is more effective than the case when the size is small. Thus, it is natural to combine buffering and array copying. We add input and output buffers at both ends of the pipe. When writing (reading) to (from) the pipe, we write (read) to (from) the output (input) buffer. When the output or input buffer is full, we use array copying to transfer data between the output or input buffer to the shared buffer in the pipe.

### 3.4   Synchronization Elimination (SE&ArrC)

Java pipes use a typical producer-consumer model, with wait and notify synchronization between PipedOutputStream (the producer) and PipedInputStream (the consumer). We find that the synchronization mechanism in Java pipe is inefficient and the degree of concurrency can be increased. First, most of the methods in the Java pipe library including the read and receive methods are synchronized methods. To enter a synchronized method, the calling thread must acquire the lock of the synchronized method. This locking mechanism includes monitor-enter and monitor-exit operations and is expensive. Second, when a thread invokes wait, the state of the thread is switched from *runnable* to *not runnable*. When notify is invoked by the other thread, the state of the waiting thread is switched from *not runnable* to *runnable* [6]. This procedure creates thread scheduling overhead [7]. Because receive and read methods are synchronized, the writer and reader cannot execute concurrently.

In order to increase the degree of concurrency and to decrease synchronization and thread scheduling overhead, we completely eliminate synchronization between receive and read using a nondeterministic algorithm. In Java pipes, the PipedInputStream class contains a 1024-byte circular shared buffer accessed by both the reader and writer, and the range of available data in the buffer is specified with the shared variables in and out. Our algorithm, shown in Figure 9, uses a 1025-byte circular shared buffer (Figure 10) instead of the 1024-byte shared buffer. Only 1024 bytes in our shared buffer is avaliable for the writer to fill in. There are two shared pointer variables in and out. The variable in points to the location in the buffer where the next byte is written, and out points to the location where the next byte is read. The variable out is modified only by the reader and the variable in is modified only by the writer. The two variables increase in a circular manner (modulo 1025). To explain our algorithm, we denote the range of the circular buffer in the following way:

$$\mathcal{B}[x, y] = \begin{cases} [x, y] & \text{if } x \leq y \\ [x, 1024] \cup [0, y] & \text{otherwise} \end{cases}$$

$$\mathcal{B}[x, y) = \begin{cases} [x, y) & \text{if } x \leq y \\ [x, 1024] \cup [0, y) & \text{otherwise} \end{cases}$$

where $0 \leq x, y \leq 1024$. Then, the range of data that is valid in the buffer for the reader is $\mathcal{B}[\texttt{out}, \texttt{in})$, and for the writer is $\mathcal{B}[\texttt{in}, \texttt{out-1})$. Thus, the range of the buffer that is operated on by the reader and the writer at one time is $\mathcal{B}[\texttt{out}, \texttt{out-1})$, and it is 1024 bytes long. If $\texttt{in} = \texttt{out}$ then the buffer is empty, and if $(\texttt{in} + 1) \% \texttt{buffer.length} = \texttt{out}$ then the buffer is full.

In $\texttt{read(b, off, len)}$, the reader first takes a snapshot of the shared variables $\texttt{in}$ and $\texttt{out}$ and store their values in new local variables $\texttt{Lin}$ and $\texttt{Lout}$. Then, we use $\texttt{Lin}$ and $\texttt{Lout}$ to determine whether the shared buffer is empty in the $\texttt{while}$ loop. The reader exits the loop only when there are valid data in the buffer. If the shared buffer is empty, we use $\texttt{Thread.yield()}$ in order to let the writer execute by yielding the execution of the current thread (reader). If the shared buffer is not

```
while(true){
  Lin=in;
  Lout=out;
  if (Lin == Lout)
    // buffer is empty
    Thread.yield();
  else
    break;
}
Compute the range of available
  data in the buffer;
Use array copying to copy len bytes
  from the buffer. The data to be
  read begins at buffer[Lout];
Lout = (Lout + number of bytes copied)
    % buffer.length;
out = Lout;
```

read(b, off, len)

```
while(len > 0){
  while(true){
    Lin=in;
    Lout=out;
    if ((Lin + 1) % buffer.length == Lout)
      // buffer is full
      Thread.yield();
    else
      break;
  }
  Compute the range of empty
    elements in the buffer
  Use array copying to copy len bytes
    to the buffer. The location to
    be writen begins at buffer[Lin];
  Lin = (Lin + number of bytes copied)
      % buffer.length;
  in = Lin;
  len = len-number of bytes copied;
}
```

receive(b, off, len)

Fig. 9. Synchronization elimination in the Java pipe implementation

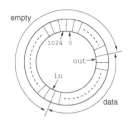

Fig. 10. The circular buffer

empty, the reader exits the loop and copies data from the shared buffer to the destination byte array b by using array copying. When copying data, the portion of the shared buffer that can be accessed by the reader is solely determined by Lin and Lout, and it is $\mathcal{B}[\text{Lout}, \text{Lin})$. The variable in is increased only by the writer in the circular manner after its local copy Lin is made by the reader. Since out is increased only in the circular manner by the reader, out = Lout, and the following conditions are ensured by the writer when in is modified:

$$\text{in}' < \text{Lout} \qquad \text{when in} < \text{out}$$
$$\text{in}' < \text{Lout} + 1025 - 1 \text{ otherwise}$$

Where in' is the modified value of in by the writer. Therefore, in is always in $\mathcal{B}[\text{Lin}, \text{Lout})$. Thus, $\mathcal{B}[\text{Lout}, \text{Lin}) \subseteq \mathcal{B}[\text{out}, \text{in})$, and the reader always operate on the valid data in this range. After copying data, the reader sets Lout to the new location: Lout = (Lout + length of data copied) % buffer.length, and commits Lout to the shared variable out (out = Lout;). The case of receive(b, off, len) is symmetrical to read(b, off, len).

### 3.5   Combining SE with Buffering (SE&ArrC&Buff)

This approach is similar to Buff&ArrC. We add output and input buffers at both ends of the pipe. However, we use the SE&ArrC algorithm to transfer data between the output/input buffers and the shared buffer in the pipe.

## 4   Evaluation Environment

We evaluated our techniques on a synthetic benchmark and seven different example programs taken from the literature. Figure 11 shows the synthetic benchmark used in the experiments. SOURCE_SIZE is the size of the source array in the writer. PACKET_SIZE is the number of bytes to be transferred at a time in the pipe. In the experiments, we set SOURCE_SIZE ($= 128$KB) to be a multiple of PACKET_SIZE, and varied PACKET_SIZE from 1 byte to $2^9$ bytes. By doing so, we see the relationship between the packet size and the performance in addition to the performance of our techniques. In order to focus on the performance of the Java pipe, we try to minimize other factors such as caching, file read, file write, and other computations, in the synthetic benchmark. We assume the total data size (DATA_SIZE) is 1MB. We transfer the same source array 8 times and measure the execution time.

Table 1 describes the seven programs we used in our experiments.

We evaluated the benchmark programs on a dual-processor 800MHZ Pentium III SMP with 32KB L1 and 256KB L2 caches, and 256MB main memory, running Redhat Linux 7.2. Table 2 shows two different JVM configurations used in our experiments. However, we do not compare the performance of Java pipe across different JVM configurations.

Sun JDK supports two threading models, *native threads* and *green threads* [17], depending on the way how Java threads are mapped to the native threads of the underlying OS. *Native threads* in Solaris is many-to-many mapping, i.e., multiple Java

```
byte[] src = new byte[SOURCE_SIZE];          byte dst[] = new byte [SOURCE_SIZE];
off = 0;                                      off = 0;
Prepare src;                                  int dataIn = 1;
remainingData = DATA_SIZE;                    while ( dataIn > 0 )
Start Timer;                                    dataIn= pipeIn.read(dst,off,PACKET_SIZE);
while ( remainingData > 0 ){                  Stop Timer;
  pipeOut.write(src,off,PACKET_SIZE);
  remainingData = remainingData - PACKET_SIZE;
  off = off + PACKET_SIZE;
  if(off >= SOURCE_SIZE)
    off = 0;
}
pipeOut.flush();
PipeOut.close();
```

Thread 1: writer                                      Thread 2: reader

**Fig. 11.** The synthetic benchmark

**Table 1.** Applications used in our experiments

| Name | Description | Size (lines) |
|------|-------------|--------------|
| RhymingWords [8] | Four threads collaborating. The first thread reads data from a file. The second sorts the data. The third reverses the data, and the last thread writes the data to StdOut. | 252 |
| TestThread [9] | One thread generates a random number. The other thread writes the number to StdOut. | 29 |
| SystemStream [10] | One thread reads bytes from StdIn. The other writes the bytes to StdOut. | 69 |
| JavaClassExample [11] | One thread generates random floating point numbers. The other thread writes the average of the numbers to StdOut. | 88 |
| XY [12] | One thread reads data from a file. The other thread changes the letter 'X' into 'Y' in the data and writes the data to StdOut. | 140 |
| Fibonacci [13] | One thread generates Fibonacci numbers and converts them into bytes. The other thread converts the bytes back to integers. | 101 |
| IntByte [14] | One thread converts integers into bytes. The other thread converts the bytes back to integers. | 88 |

threads are mapped to multiple LWPs and the JVM leaves the thread scheduling to the OS (Figure 13(a)). Because there are no LWPs in Linux, each thread is directly mapped to a process (Figure 13(b)) [16]. *Green threads* is many-to-one mapping, i.e., multiple Java threads are mapped to one LWPs (Light Weight Processes) in Solaris or a process in Linux, and the JVM takes care of scheduling Java threads [17]. Thus, performance enhancement from parallelism cannot be realized using green threads.

The effect of `Thread.yield()` in Linux depends on the thread model. While `Thread.yield()` is simply neglected by the JVM in native threads, it yields exe-

**Table 2.** Java Virtual Machines used in our experiments

| | |
|---|---|
| Sun JDK 1.3.1 with native threads [15] | Java 2 Runtime Environment, Standard Edition Java HotSpot Client VM |
| Sun JDK 1.3.1 with green threads [16] | Java 2 Runtime Environment, Standard Edition Classic VM |

cution to the next thread with the highest priority in the waiting queue in green threads.

## 5   Evaluation

### 5.1   Synthetic Benchmark Experiments

The performance results of our techniques with the synthetic benchmark are shown in Figure 12. Base is the benchmark using the original Java piped I/O stream library.

When we use the array copying technique (ArrC), the data transfer rate increases very fast as the packet size increases. When the packet size is 512B, ArrC is

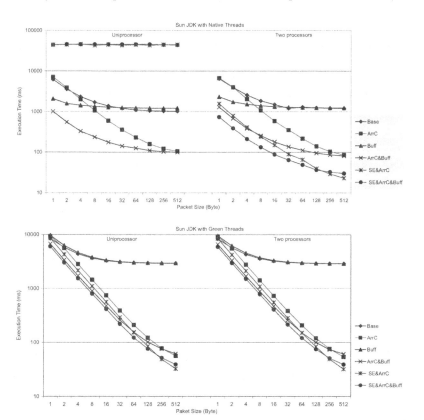

**Fig. 12.** The performance of the synthetic benchmark

**Table 3.** The best technique depends on the environment

|  | One processor | | Two processors | |
|---|---|---|---|---|
|  | Small ($< 256B$) | Large ($\geq 256B$) | Small ($< 256B$) | Large ($\geq 256B$) |
| Native threads | ArrC&Buff | ArrC&Buff | SE&ArrC&Buff | SE&ArrC |
| Green threads | SE&ArrC&Buff | SE&ArrC | SE&ArrC&Buff | SE&ArrC |

33 times faster than Base on average. When the packet size is small, however, we observe slowdown with ArrC when using a single processor. This is because the native method (`System.arraycopy`) invocation overhead is high with the small packet size.

The buffering technique (Buff) is beneficial when the packet size is small because it increases the size of data to be transfered to the shared buffer in the pipe. However, it causes extra overhead of data copying between the input/output buffer and the shared buffer in the pipe. When the packet size is large, the benefit becomes less significant than the copying overhead.

The combination of array copying and buffering (ArrC&Buff) exhibits the best performance on one processor with native threads and is better than each of the others when the packet size is small. When the packet size is large, its performance is close to ArrC. This is because buffering incurs an extra overhead of copying data.

Except for the Sun JDK *native threads* on one processor, SE&ArrC is the fastest when the packet is greater than or equal to 256B. When the packet size is smaller than 256B, the combination of all the techniques (SE&ArrC&Buff) is preferred. The performance difference between SE&ArrC and SE&ArrC&Buff on different packet sizes is likely caused by the extra data copying overhead incurred by buffering.

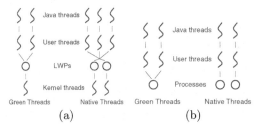

**Fig. 13.** Green threads and native threads. (a) Solaris. (b) Linux.

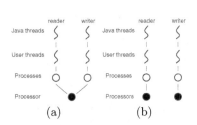

**Fig. 14.** Thread scheduling on physical processors in Linux with native threads. (a) one physical processor. (b) Two physical processors.

In the case of Sun JDK with *native threads* on one processor, both SE&ArrC and SE&ArrC&Buff slow down significantly. They are even slower than Base. We also see that their performance does not vary as the packet size changes (about 44 seconds). This can be explained by a close study of thread scheduling issues of Sun JVM on Linux. In this case, the reader is mapped to one process and the writer to the other [16]. These two processes are running on one processor (Figure 14(a)). When the writer deposits data to the shared buffer and the buffer is full, it calls `Thread.yield`, but this function is ignored in native threads. Thus, the reader will not be scheduled until the current process finishes its time slice assigned by Linux. A similar situation occurs for the reader when the buffer is empty. Thus, it takes approximately two time slices to finish transferring data whose size is the same as the size of the shared buffer between the reader thread and the writer thread.

In Linux, the time slice assigned to each process is about 20 ms. The size of the shared buffer in the Java pipe library is 1KB and the data size to be transferred in our experiment is 1MB. The estimated transfer time is $2 \times 20ms \times (1MB/1KB) = 40,960ms = 41s$, which matches the result of the experiment, 44 seconds, very well.

On the contrary, when two processors are available in the native threads model, the reader and the writer can be mapped to two processes and these two processes run on the two processors in parallel (Figure 14(b)).

From the results, we see that the most effective technique varies depending on the number of physical processors, the threading model, and the packet size. Table 3 summarizes the results in different situations.

## 5.2   Experiments with Real Programs

In real applications, there are many other factors that affect the performance of the Java pipes, such as the existence of threads other than the reader and writer, file I/O, and so on. The execution time of each real example program is shown in Figure 15. The execution time is normalized to the programs with the original Java

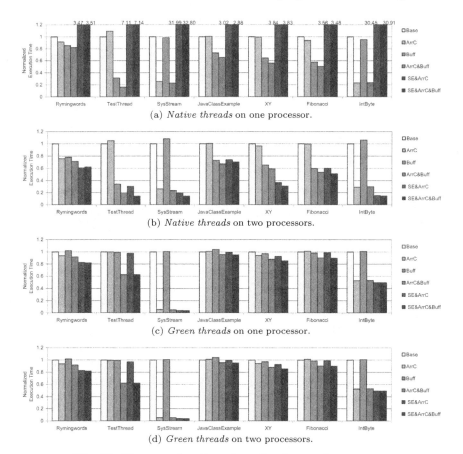

(a) *Native threads* on one processor.

(b) *Native threads* on two processors.

(c) *Green threads* on one processor.

(d) *Green threads* on two processors.

**Fig. 15.** The execution time of our 7 real example programs

pipe library (Base). Table 4 shows the average packet size (the len argument in read and write (or receive)) used in each program. When the packet size is small (RhymingWords, TestThread, JavaClassExample, XY, and Fibonacci), the results conform to our expectation based on Table 3: ArrC&Buff and SE&ArrC&Buff are preferred with native threads on one and two processors, respectively. SE&ArrC&Buff is the fastest using green threads. When the packet size is large (SystemStream and IntByte), the best techniques with green threads (SE&ArrC) and with native threads on one processor (ArrC&Buff) are as expected in Table 3. With native threads on two processors, the best technique (SE&ArrC&Buff) is different from Table 3 (SE&ArrC). However, the performance difference is not significant. In the best case (SystemStream with SE&ArrC using green threads), we obtained a speedup of 27.

Table 5 summarizes the average speedups obtained from our best optimization technique based on Table 3 for each application. The appropriate implementation of Java piped I/O stream library could be chosen at run-time depending on the environmental conditions.

**Table 4.** Average packet size

| Program | Read | Write |
|---|---|---|
| RhymingWords | 7 | 1 |
| TestThread | 1 | 1 |
| SystemStream | 500 | 250 |
| JavaClassExample | 1 | 1 |
| XY | 1 | 1 |
| Fibonacci | 1 | 1 |
| IntByte | 512 | 1024 |

**Table 5.** Average speedup obtained from our best optimization technique for each application

| | One processor | Two processors |
|---|---|---|
| Native threads | 2.58 | 3.87 |
| Green threads | 4.83 | 4.76 |

# 6   Related Work

Guyer and Lin [18] showed the importance of optimizing the software library in high performance computing and scientific computing. They showed that applying an optimization to the library could yield much more performance improvement than an analogous conventional optimization. Optimizing the library needs more effort, but the cost can be amortized by many applications. They proposed an annotation language, which provides the information needed to optimize the library at compile time. Our work is an example of library optimization, and our results show that the library optimization is not trivial, i.e., in many cases, there is no single optimization method that gives the best performance.

Bogda and Holzle [19] pointed out the importance of eliminating overhead caused by unnecessary synchronization in Java. They proposed a technique that creates separate functions for shared variables and local variables to avoid functions accessing both a shared object and a local object. Ruf [20] proposed a technique for statically removing unnecessary synchronization in both the standard library and runtime system of Java. Objects that are synchronized only by a single thread at compile-time are detected and redundant synchronization is removed. Boyapati and Rinard [21] introduced a new static type system, which can ensure that a well-typed program is free of data races. By detecting data races, Some of the unnecessary synchronization that is inserted conservatively in the program can be removed. However, the synchronization mechanism in Java pipe library cannot be removed by that technique. Our implementation of Java pipes does not use any synchronization provided by Java, but still ensures correctness.

Goetz [22] found that the transfer rate of unbuffered data transfer is much lower than that of buffered data in Java I/O. McCluskey [23,24] showed that buffering is effective for Java file I/O, while our work focuses on Java piped I/O stream between different threads.

## 7    Conclusions and Future Work

In this paper, we presented optimization techniques for the Java piped I/O stream library: array copying, buffering, synchronization elimination, and combinations of them. We analyzed commonly used data transfer patterns between threads that use the Java piped I/O stream library to transfer data. Our observation is based on data buffering, data copying mechanism, synchronization between threads, and the thread scheduling policy used in the Java virtual machine. Based on these observations, we modified the Java piped I/O stream library using those optimization techniques.

By using a synthetic benchmark, we found that the optimization techniques exercise different performance in different environments, such as size of data transferred at a time (packet size), number of processors, and threading model. The best optimization technique depends on the run-time environment.

We evaluated our techniques with seven different example programs from the literature. Our experimental results show that these techniques improve the performance of the programs using Java piped I/O stream class library by a factor of 4 on average and by a factor of 27 in the best case.

## Acknowledgments

The authors thank the anonymous reviewers, Hank Deitz, Paul Foutrier, Samuel P. Midkiff, and Bill Pugh for their useful comments.

*Further Information.* A number of related papers and technical reports of the Software Engineering and Network Systems Laboratory can be found at the following URL: http://www.cse.msu.edu/sens.

## References

1. B. R. Badrinath, A. Bakre, R. Marantz, and T. Imielinski, "Handling mobile hosts: A case for indirect interaction," in *Proc. Fourth Workshop on Workstation Operating Systems*, (Rosario, Washington), IEEE, October 1993.
2. Y. Chawathe, S. Fink, S. McCanne, and E. Brewer, "A proxy architecture for reliable multicast in heterogeneous environments," in *Proceedings of ACM Multimedia '98*, (Bristol, UK), September 1998.

3. M. Roussopoulos, P. Maniatis, E. Swierk, K. Lai, G. Appenzeller, and M. Baker, "Person-level routing in the mobile people architecture," in *Proceedings of the 1999 USENIX Symposium on Internet Technologies and Systems*, (Boulder, Colorado), October 1999.

4. L. Yang and M. Hofmann, "OPES architecture for rule processing and service execution." Internet Draft draft-yang-opes-rule-processing-service-execution-00.txt, February 2001.

5. P. K. McKinley, U. I. Padmanabhan, and N. Ancha, "Experiments in composing proxy audio services for mobile users," in *Proceedings of the IFIP/ACM International Conference on Distributed Systems Platforms (Middleware 2001)*, (Heidelberg, Germany), pp. 99–120, November 2001.

6. M. Campione, K. Walrath, and A. Huml, *The Java Tutorial: A Short Course on the Basics, Third Edition*. Addison-Wesley, 2001.

7. Sun Microsystems, "Multithreaded programming guide." 806-5257-1, January 2001.

8. M. Campione and K. Walrath, *The Java Tutorial: Object-Oriented Programming for the Internet, First Edition, Online Version*. Addison-Wesley, 1996.

9. R. Gagnon, "Ral's how to: Java thread."
   $http : //www.rgagnon.com/javadetails/java - 0140.html$.

10. Java Power, "Java power scratch book."
    $http : //www.javapower.ru/faq/sb/java\_io7.htm$.

11. D. Kramer, P. Chan, and R. Lee, *The Java(TM) Class Libraries, Second Edition, Volume 1*. Addison-Wesley, February 1998.

12. J. Weber, *Special Edition Using Java*. Que, November 1996.

13. E. R. Harold, *Java I/O*. O'Reilly & Associates, March 1999.

14. P. Hyde, *Java Thread Programming*. SAMS, August 1999.

15. Sun Microsystems, "Java 2 SDK for solaris developer's guide." 06-1367-10, February 2000.

16. C. Austin, "Java technology on the Linux platform: A guide to getting started," October 2000.    $http : //developer.java.sun.com/developer/technicalArticles/Programming/linux/$.

17. Sun Microsystems, "Java on Solaris 7 developer's guide." 805-4031, 1998.

18. S. Z. Guyer and C. Lin, "Optimizing the use of high performance software libraries," in *The 13th International Workshop on Languages and Compilers for Parallel Computing (LCPC 2000)*, pp. 227–243, August 2000.

19. J. Aldrich, C. Chambers, E. G. Sirer, and S. J. Eggers, "Static analyses for eliminating unnecessary synchronization from Java programs," in *Static Analysis Symposium*, pp. 19–38, 1999.

20. E. Ruf, "Effective synchronization removal for java," in *ACM SIGPLAN Conference on Programming Language Design and Implementation*, June 1999.

21. C. Boyapati and M. Rinard, "A parameterized type system for race-free Javaprograms," in *16th Annual Conference on Object-Oriented Programming, Systems, Languages, and Applications (OOPSLA)*, 2001.

22. B. Goetz, "Tweak your IO performance for faster runtime :increase the speed of Java programs by tuning IO performance," *Java World*, November 2000.

23. G. McCluskey, "Java I/O performance," *;login: - The Magazine of USENIX & SAGE*, December 1998. $http : //www.usenix.org/publications/login/online.html$.

24. G. McCluskey, "Tuning Java I/O performance."
    $http : //developer.java.sun.com/developer/ technicalArticles/Programming/PerfTuning/$, Mar 1999.

# A Comparative Study of Stampede Garbage Collection Algorithms

Hasnain A. Mandviwala[1], Nissim Harel[1],
Kathleen Knobe[2], and Umakishore Ramachandran[1]

[1] College of Computing, Georgia Institute of Technology
{mandvi, nissim, rama}@cc.gatech.edu
[2] HP Labs - Cambridge Research Laboratory
kath.knobe@hp.com

**Abstract.** *Stampede* is a parallel programming system to support interactive multimedia applications. The system maintains temporal causality in such streaming real-time applications via *channels* that contain *timestamped* items. A Stampede application is a coarse-grain dataflow pipeline of timestamped items. Not all timestamps are *relevant* for the application output due to the differential processing rates of the pipeline stages. Therefore, *garbage collection (GC)* is crucial for Stampede runtime performance. Three GC algorithms are currently available in Stampede. In this paper, we ask the question how far off these algorithms are from an *ideal garbage collector*, one in which the memory usage is exactly equal to that which is required for buffering only the relevant timestamped items in the channels? This oracle, while unimplementable, serves as an empirical lower-bound for memory usage. We then propose optimizations that will help us get closer to this lower-bound. Using an elaborate measurement and post-mortem analysis infrastructure in Stampede, we evaluate the performance potential for these optimizations. A color-based people tracking application is used for the performance evaluation. Our results show that these optimizations reduce the memory usage by over 60% for this application over the best GC algorithm available in Stampede.

## 1 Introduction

Emerging applications such as interactive vision, speech, and multimedia collaboration require the acquisition, processing, synthesis, and correlation (often *temporally*) of streaming data such as video and audio. Such applications are good candidates for the scalable parallelism available in clusters of SMPs. In a companion paper [10] we discuss the need for higher level data abstractions to match the unique characteristics of this class of applications. *Stampede* [9] is a parallel programming system for enabling the development of such applications. The programming model of Stampede is simple and intuitive. A Stampede pro-

B. Pugh and C.-W. Tseng (Eds.): LCPC 2002, LNCS 2481, pp. 249–264, 2005.
© Springer-Verlag Berlin Heidelberg 2005

gram consists of a dynamic collection of threads communicating timestamped data items through *channels*[1].

A Stampede computation with threads and channels is akin to a coarse-grain dataflow graph, wherein the nodes are threads and channels and the links are the connections among them. Threads can be created to run anywhere in the cluster. Channels can be created anywhere in the cluster and have cluster-wide unique names. Threads can *connect* to these channels for doing input/output via *get/put* operations. A timestamp value is used as a *name* for a data item that a thread puts into or gets from a channel. Every item on a channel is uniquely indexed by a *timestamp*. Typically in a Stampede computation, a thread will *get* an item with a particular timestamp from an input connection, perform some processing[2] on the data in the item, and then *put* an item with that same timestamp onto one of its output connections. Items with the same timestamp in different channels represent various stages of processing of the same input.

The time to process an item varies from thread to thread. In particular, earlier threads (typically faster threads that perform low level processing) may be producing items *dropped* by later threads doing higher level processing at a slower rate. Only timestamps that are completely processed affect the output of the application, while a timestamp that is dropped by any thread during the application execution is *irrelevant*. The runtime system of Stampede takes care of the synchronization and communication inherent in these operations, as well as managing the storage for items put into or gotten from the channels. The metric for efficiency in these systems is the rate of processing *relevant* timestamps (*i.e.,* timestamps that make it all the way through the entire pipeline). The work done processing irrelevant timestamps represents an inefficient use of processing resources.

In a Stampede computation, the creation of threads, channels, and connections to channels are all dynamic. Since the channels hold timestamped data there is an issue as to when to get rid of data from channels that are no longer needed by any thread (current and future). We refer to this issue as the *garbage collection* problem in Stampede. The traditional GC problem [12,7] concerns reclaiming storage for heap-allocated objects (data structures) when they are no longer "reachable" from the computation. On the other hand, Stampede's GC problem deals with determining when timestamped items in channels can be reclaimed. The runtime system determines that a specific timestamp (which is not a memory pointer but an index or a tag) will not be used anymore. Thus storage associated with all items that are tagged with this timestamp can be reclaimed. Stampede prescribes a simple set of rules for timestamp values that can be associated with an item by a thread (or its children). Further it imposes

---

[1] Stampede also provides another cluster-wide data abstraction called *queues*. Queues also hold timestamped data items and differ in some semantic properties from the channels. From the point of view of the focus of this paper these differences are immaterial and hence we will not mention them in the rest of the paper.

[2] We use "processing a timestamp", "processing an item", and "processing a timestamped item" interchangeably to mean the same thing.

a discipline of programming that requires each thread to mark an item (or a set of items) on a channel as garbage once the thread is finished using that item by issuing a *consume* operation for that item. Using all this information, the runtime system discerns when items can be garbage collected from channels.

In a companion paper [8], we have presented a distributed garbage collection algorithm for Stampede that does not use any application-level knowledge. In a more recent paper [5], we have introduced a new algorithm, called *dead-timestamp based garbage collection (DGC)*, that uses an application-level task graph to make runtime decisions on the interest set for timestamps. We show that using such application-level knowledge can result in a significant space advantage (up to 40%) compared to the earlier algorithm that does not use such knowledge.

In this paper, we ask the question how far off are these GC algorithms from an *ideal?* We define ideal as the case where the memory usage is exactly that which is required for processing relevant timestamps. While implementation of such an oracle is infeasible, it nevertheless serves as an empirical lower-bound for memory usage. We then propose two optimizations to the DGC algorithm that is expected to get us closer to this lower-bound:

1. The first optimization is to globally propagate the information that a particular timestamp value is irrelevant using the task graph.
2. The second optimization is to buffer only the most recent few items in a channel. This optimization gives a producer of items some measure of direct control over garbage collection. The intuition is that downstream computations in interactive applications need only the most recent items and will skip over earlier ones.

The rest of the paper is organized as follows. We discuss related work in Sec. 2. Sec. 3 presents a summary of algorithms that are currently available in Stampede for garbage collection. In Sec. 4, we present the proposed enhancements to the DGC algorithm. The measurement infrastructure in Stampede that allows us to gather the performance data for comparing these algorithms are presented in Sec. 5. We introduce the definition for Ideal GC in Sec. 5.1. In Sec. 6, we discuss the performance of the current algorithms as well as the proposed enhancements with respect to the ideal. We present concluding remarks in Sec. 7.

## 2   Related Work

The traditional GC problem (on which there is a large body of literature [12,7]) concerns reclaiming storage for heap-allocated objects (data structures) when they are no longer "reachable" from the computation. The "name" of an object is a heap address, *i.e.*, a pointer, and GC concerns a transitive computation that locates all objects that are reachable starting with names in certain well-known places such as registers and stacks. In most safe GC languages, there are no computational operations to generate new names (such as pointer arithmetic) other than the allocation of a new object. Stampede's GC problem is an orthogonal problem. The "name" of an object in a channel is its timestamp, *i.e.*, the timestamp is an index or a tag. Timestamps are simply integers, and threads can compute new timestamps.

The problem of determining the interest set for timestamp values in Stampede has similarity to the garbage collection problem in Parallel Discrete Event Simulation (PDES) systems [3]. However, the application model that Stampede run-time system supports is less restrictive. Unlike Stampede, PDES systems require that repeated executions of an application program using the same input data and parameters produce the same results [4]. To ensure this property, *every* timestamp must *appear* to be processed *in order* by the PDES system. A number of synchronization algorithms have been proposed in the PDES literature to preserve this property. Algorithms such as Chandy-Misra-Bryant (CMB) [1,2] process the timestamps strictly in order, exchanging null messages to avoid potential deadlocks. There is no reliance on any global mechanism or control. Optimistic algorithms, such as Time Warp [6], assume that processing a timestamp out of order by a node is safe. However, if this assumption proves false then the node rolls back to the state prior to processing the timestamp. To support such a roll back, the system has to keep around *state*, which is reclaimed based on calculation of a Global Virtual Time (GVT). The tradeoff between the conservative (CMB) and optimistic (Time Warp) algorithms is space versus time. While the former is frugal with space at the expense of time, the latter does the opposite.

On the other hand, the Stampede programming model does not require in-order execution of timestamps, nor does it require that every timestamp be processed. Consequently, Stampede does not have to support roll backs. If nothing is known about the application task graph, then similar to PDES, there is a necessity in Stampede to compute GVT to enable garbage collection. The less restrictive nature of the Stampede programming model allows conception of different types of algorithms for GVT calculation like the one described in [8]. In [5] we have proposed yet another algorithm that uses application-level knowledge enabling garbage collection based entirely on local events with no reliance on any global mechanism.

## 3   Algorithms for Garbage Collection in Stampede

There are three competing mechanisms for GC in Stampede: a *REFerence count based garbage collector (REF)*, a *Transparent Garbage Collector (TGC)* [8], and a *Dead timestamp based Garbage Collector (DGC)* [5]. Each algorithm represents a specific point in the tradeoff between information needed to be provided to the runtime system and the corresponding aggressiveness for eliminating garbage.

- **Reference Count Based Garbage Collector:**
  This is the simplest garbage collector. As the name suggests, a thread associates a reference count with an item when it *puts* it in a channel. The item is garbage collected when the reference count goes to zero. Clearly, this garbage collector can work only if the consumer set for an item is known

*a priori.* Hence this algorithm works only for static graphs where all the connections are fully specified.

- **Transparent Garbage Collector:**

  The TGC algorithm [8] maintains two *state variables* on behalf of each thread. The first is the *thread virtual time*, and the second is the *thread keep time*. The former gives the thread an independent handle on timestamp values it can associate with an item it produces on its output connections. The latter is the minimum timestamp value of items that this thread is still interested in getting on its input connections. Thread keep time advances when an item is consumed, and thread virtual time advances when a thread performs a *set virtual time* operation. The minimum of these two state variables gives a lower bound for timestamp values that this thread is interested in. TGC is a distributed algorithm that computes a *Global Virtual Time (GVT)* that represents the minimum timestamp value that is of interest to any thread in the entire system. So long as threads advance their respective virtual times, and consume items on their respective input connections the GVT will keep advancing. All items with timestamps less than GVT are guaranteed not to be accessed by any thread and can therefore be safely garbage collected. This algorithm is entirely transparent to the specifics of the application, and hence needs no information about the application structure.

- **Dead Timestamps Based Garbage Collector:**

  The DGC algorithm [5] is inspired by the observation that even in dynamic applications, it may be possible to discern all the *potential* channel, thread, and connection creations by analyzing the application code at compile time. Under such circumstances, it is possible for the application programmer to supply the runtime system with a task graph that is a maximal representation of the application dynamism. A task graph (see Figure 1) for a Stampede application is a bipartite directed graph with *nodes* that represent either *threads*, which perform a certain computation, or *channels*, which serve as a medium for buffer management between two or more threads. Directed edges between nodes are called *connections*. A connection describes the direction of the data flow between two nodes. Both types of nodes, threads and channels, have input and output edges called input and output connections. The DGC algorithm determines a *timestamp guarantee* for each node (thread or channel). For a given timestamp T, the guarantee will indicate whether T is *live* or whether it is guaranteed to be *dead*. A timestamp T is live at a node N if (a) T is a relevant timestamp, *and* (b) there is some further processing at N on T (*i.e.*, T is still in use at N). Otherwise T is a dead timestamp at

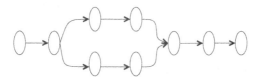

**Fig. 1.** An abstract task graph

node N. If the node is a thread, "in use" signifies that the node is still processing the timestamp; if the node is a channel, "in use" signifies that the timestamp has not been processed by all the threads connected to that channel. DGC use the application supplied task graph to propagate timestamp guarantees among the nodes. The algorithm generates two types of guarantees: *forward* and *backward*. The forward guarantee for a connection identifies timestamps that might cross that connection in the future. Similarly, the backward guarantee for a connection identifies timestamps that are dead on that connection. Using these guarantees, a node can *locally* separate live timestamps from dead ones, and garbage collect items with dead timestamps.

# 4    Enhancements to the DGC Algorithm

The three GC algorithms have been implemented in the Stampede system. In the case of DGC, the forward and backward propagation of timestamp guarantees are instigated by put/get operations on channels. In a companion paper [5], we experimentally compared the performance of these three GC algorithms in the context of a real-time color-based people tracker application that was developed at Compaq CRL [11]. We use *memory footprint* - the amount of memory used for buffering timestamped items in the Stampede channels by the application as a function of real time - as the metric for performance evaluation. This metric is indicative of the instantaneous memory pressure of the application. We showed that the memory footprint of the DGC algorithm for the color-based people tracker application is reduced anywhere from 16% to 40% compared to the other two algorithms.

In this section, we consider optimizations that can further reduce the memory footprint of the application. The first optimization is specific to DGC and concerns the global propagation of the timestamp guarantees. The second optimization is more generally applicable to any GC algorithm, and concerns associating specific attributes with a channel to hasten garbage collection.

## 4.1    Out-of-Band Propagation of Guarantees (OBPG)

Our current implementation of DGC propagates forward and backward guarantees by piggy-backing them with the put/get operations. The limitation to this approach is that a node guarantee cannot be propagated along the graph until either (a) a *put* is performed by the thread node, or (b) a *get* is performed on the channel node. A more aggressive garbage collection would be possible if these guarantees are made available globally. It is conceivable to use *out of band* communication among the nodes to disseminate these guarantees. However, there will be a consequent increase in overhead in the runtime system for this out-of-band communication. To understand this trade-off, the first optimization evaluates the following hypothetical question: *How much reduction in memory footprint can be achieved by instantly disseminating the node guarantees to all other nodes in the graph?* Clearly, instantaneous propagation is not practically feasible but this helps us to understand the potential performance limit for such an optimization.

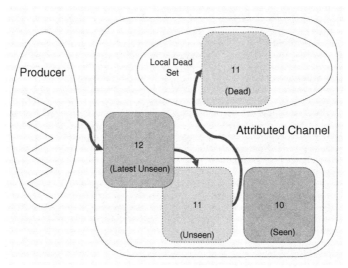

**Fig. 2.** An Attributed Channel. Implementing the KL*n*U optimization where $n = 1$.

## 4.2   Attributed Channels

– **Keep Latest 'n' Unseen.** The second optimization stems from the fact that in real-time applications, downstream computations are mostly interested only in the *latest* item produced by an upstream computation. Coupled with this fact is our earlier observation that upstream computations are lighter than the downstream ones, resulting in a large number of items becoming irrelevant. For example, in [5], we show that in the people tracker application only one in eight items produced by the digitizer thread reaches the end of the pipeline. The proposed optimization is to associate an *attribute* with a channel that allows it to discard all but the *latest* item. The basic idea is that when a producer puts a new item, the channel immediately gets rid of items with earlier timestamps if they have not been gotten on *any* of the connections. We refer to this set of earlier timestamps as the *dead set*. Since a Stampede application depends on timestamp causality, this optimization will not allow an item with an earlier timestamp to be garbage collected even if *one* connection has gotten that item from this channel. We generalize this attribute and call it *keep latest n unseen (KLnU)*, to signify that a channel keeps only the last *n* items. The value of *n* is specified at the time of channel creation and can be different for different channels. Further, it should be clear that this attribute gives local control for a channel to garbage collect items that are deemed irrelevant and is in addition to whatever system-wide mechanism may be in place for garbage collection (such as DGC).

Fig. 4.2 shows how attributed channels work. The producer thread has just produced an item with timestamp 12. Items with timestamps 10 and 11 are already present in the channel. Item with timestamp 10 has been gotten by a consumer, while 11 has not been gotten by any consumers so far. Thus

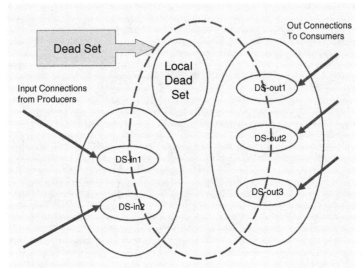

**Fig. 3.** Propagation of Dead Sets. The arrows indicate the direction of flow of dead sets into the given node.

upon put of item with timestamp 12, timestamp 11 can be added to the dead-set of this channel while 10 cannot be.

– **Propagating Dead Sets.**
Similar to the forward and backward guarantee propagation in the basic DGC algorithm, we consider propagating the *local* dead-set information from a node to other nodes in the graph. We call this optimization *Propagating Dead Sets (PDS)*.

Fig. 4.2 shows the state of a node in a given task graph. This node will receive dead-set information from all the out edges due to backward propagation. Similarly, it will receive dead-set information from all the in edges due to forward propagation. The dead-set for a node is computed as the *union* of the local dead-set and the *intersection* of the dead-set information of all the in and out edges incident on that node.

In [5], we introduced the notion of dependency among input connections incident at a node. This information allows timestamp guarantees to be *derived* for dependent connections. For e.g., if connection $A$ to a channel is dependent on connection $B$ to another channel, and if the guarantee on $B$ is $T$ (that is no timestamps *less than* $T$ will be gotten on $B$), then the guarantee on $A$ is $T$ as well. In a similar vein, we propose dependency among output connections. For e.g., let $A$ and $B$ be out connections from a given channel, and let $A$ be dependent on $B$. If the timestamp guarantee on $B$ is $T$ (that is no timestamps *less than* $T$ will be gotten on $B$), then the guarantee on $A$ is $T$ as well.

Figure 4.2 shows the connection dependency for the color-tracker pipeline (Fig. 5). As can be noticed from the table, for the video frame channel the out connections to the histogram and target-detection threads are dependent on the out connection to the change-detection thread. This dependency implies

| Channel Name | Out Connection | Dependent Connections | Channel Name | Out Connection | Dependent Connections |
|---|---|---|---|---|---|
| Video Frame | C1 | C6, C9 | Motion Mask | C3 | C5, C8 |
| Video Frame | C2 | no dep. | Motion Mask | C5 | no dep. |
| Video Frame | C6 | C1 | Motion Mask | C8 | no dep. |
| | | | Hist. Model | C4 | no dep. |
| | | | Hist. Model | C7 | no dep. |

**Fig. 4.** Out Connection Dependency. The depencies stated here are for the real-time color people-tracker pipeline illustrated in figure 5.

that timestamps in the dead-set of the change-detection thread, would never be gotten by either the histogram or the tracker threads. Therefore, the dead-set from the change-detection thread serves as a shorthand for the dead-sets of all three out connections emanating from the video frame channel. Thus the dependent connection information allows faster propagation of dead-set information to neighboring nodes during get/put operations.

- **Out-of-Band Propagation of Dead Sets (OBPDS).**
  The PDS optimization assumes that the dead-set information is propagated only upon get/put operations by neighboring nodes. In Sec. 4.1 we observed the potential for more aggressive garbage collection if local information is disseminated more globally. This optimization investigates the performance potential for out-of-band communication of the the dead-set information to *all* nodes in the graph, and call it OBPDS.

The KL$n$U attribute to a channel has applicability to any GC algorithm. However, the PDS, and OBPDS optimizations are specific enhancements to the DGC algorithm since they require application knowledge.

## 5   Methodology

Stampede is implemented as a runtime library on top of standard platforms (x86-Linux, Alpha-Tru64, x86-Solaris). The three GC algorithms mentioned in Sec. 3 have been implemented in Stampede. The TGC algorithm is implemented in the Stampede runtime by a daemon thread in each address space that periodically wakes up and runs the distributed GVT calculation algorithm. As we mentioned earlier, for the DGC algorithm forward and backward propagations are instigated by the runtime system upon a put/get operation on a channel.

We have developed an elaborate measurement infrastructure that helps us to accumulate the memory usage as a function of time in the Stampede channels. Events of interest are logged at run-time in a pre-allocated memory buffer that is flushed to disk at the successful termination of the application. Some of the interesting events that are logged include, memory allocation times, channel put/get times, and memory free (or GC) times. A post-mortem analysis program then uses these logged events to generate metrics of interest such as the application's mean memory footprint, channel occupancy time for items, latency in processing etc.

## 5.1   Ideal GC

We define an *Ideal Garbage Collector (IGC)* as one in which the memory footprint of the application is exactly equal to that needed to buffer only *relevant* items of the application. Thus the memory footprint recorded by IGC represents a lower bound for an application.

## 5.2   Simulating IGC and the Proposed Optimizations

We use the runtime logs and post-mortem analysis technique to simulate IGC as well as answer the *what if* questions raised in Sec. 4. This strategy is akin to using trace-driven simulation to predict the expected performance of an architectural idea in system studies. Essentially, we use the runtime logs as a trace. The events such as get/put/consume are all recorded in the logs with their respective times of occurrence. The logs contain the GC times for all item on all channels. However, either for simulating IGC or for studying the effect of the optimizations we simply ignore these log entries. Instead, using the logs and the specific optimization being investigated, the post-mortem analysis program *computes* the times when the items will be garbage collected in the presence of that optimization. For IGC we use the logs and postem-mortem analysis to accumulate the memory usage for only the relevant items.

## 6   Performance of GC Algorithms

We use a real-time color-based people tracker application developed at Compaq CRL [11] for this study. Given a color histogram of a model to look for in a scene, this application locates the model if present. The application task graph is shown in figure 5.

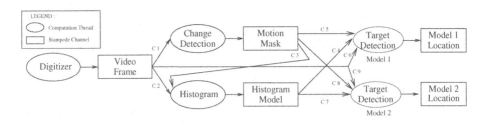

**Fig. 5.**  Color Tracker Task Graph

Any number of models can be tracked simultaneously by cloning the target detection thread shown in the figure and giving each thread a distinct model to look for in the scene. The digitizer produces a new image every 30 milliseconds, giving each image a timestamp equal to the current frame number. The target detection algorithm cannot process at the rate at which the digitizer produces images. Thus not every image produced by the digitizer makes its way through the entire pipeline. Each thread gets the latest available timestamp from its input channel. To enable a fair comparison for all the proposed optimization strategies, the digitizer reads a pre-recorded set of images from a file; two target detection threads are used in each experiment; and the same model file is supplied to both the threads. Under the workload described above, the average message sizes delivered to the digitizer, motion mask, histogram, and target detection channels are 756088, 252080, 1004904, and 67 bytes respectively.

We use *memory footprint* metric to evaluate the proposed optimization strategies. As we mentioned in Sec. 4, memory footprint is the amount of memory used for buffering timestamped items in the channels by the application as a function of real time, and is indicative of the instantaneous memory pressure exerted by the application. To associate real numbers with the memory footprint, we also present the *mean memory usage* of the application.

All experiments are carried out on a cluster of 17, 8-way 550 MHz P-III Xeon SMP machines, each with 4GB of main memory running Redhat Linux 7.1 and interconnected with Gigabit Ethernet. The Stampede runtime uses a reliable messaging layer called CLF implemented on top of UDP. We conduct our experiments using two configurations. In the first configuration all threads and channels shown in figure 5 execute on one node within a single address space. Thus there is no need for inter-node communication in this configuration. In the second configuration, threads and channels are distributed over 5 nodes of the cluster. The channel into which a thread 'puts' items is colocated with that thread in the same address space. Due to the distribution of threads in different address spaces, the messaging layer as well as the network latencies play a part in determining the performance of the application. CPU resources, however, are not shared.

## 6.1    Performance of TGC, REF and DGC

In our earlier work [5], we presented a comparison of the DGC, REF, and TGC algorithms in the context of this same application. Figure 7 and figure 6 summarize the results of this comparison. The primary conclusion from that work is that although the latency for processing a relevant timestamp through the entire pipeline increased for DGC due to the in-line execution of transfer functions on puts and gets, the percentage increase was nominal (2.7% and 0.5% compared to TGC 3.2% and less than 0.1% compared to REF for 1-node and 5-node configurations, respectively [5]). However, the mean memory usage and standard deviation for memory usage for DGC were both much lower that that of either TGC or REF. Figure 7 also shows the simulated results for IGC. The IGC result is really that of an oracle that knows the set of relevant timestamps exactly. It gives a lower bound for memory usage and serves to point out the disparity of realizable implementations (such as DGC) from the ideal. As can be

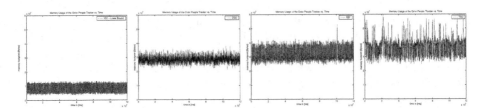

**Fig. 6.** Memory Footprint. The four graphs represent the memory footprint of the application (distributed over 5 nodes) for the three GC algorithms and the additional Ideal: (left to right)(a) Ideal Garbage Collector (IGC), (b) DGC-Dead timestamps GC, (c) REF-Reference Counting, (d) TGC-Transparent. We recorded the amount of memory the application uses on every allocation and deallocation. All three graphs are to the same scale, with the y-axis showing memory use (bytes x $10^7$), and the x-axis representing time (milliseconds). The graphs clearly show that DGC has a lower memory footprint than the other two but still much lower than IGC. In further comparison with REF and TGC, DGC deviates much less from the mean, thereby requiring a smaller amount of memory during peak usage.

|  | *Config* 1 : 1 *node* | | | | *Config* 2 : 5 *nodes* | | | |
|---|---|---|---|---|---|---|---|---|
|  | *Average* *Latency* *(ms)* | *Mean* *Memory* *usage* *(B)* | *Memory* *usage* *STD* | *%* *w.r.t.* *IGC* | *Average* *Latency* *(ms)* | *Mean* *Memory* *usage* *(B)* | *Memory* *usage* *STD* | *%* *w.r.t.* *IGC* |
| *TGC* | 491,946 | 24,696,845 | 6,347,450 | 616 | 554,584 | 36,848,898 | 5,698,552 | 444 |
| *REF* | 489,610 | 23,431,677 | 6,247,977 | 585 | 556,964 | 32,916,702 | 4,745,092 | 397 |
| *DGC* | 505,594 | 17,196,808 | 4,143,659 | 429 | 557,502 | 28,118,615 | 2,247,225 | 339 |
| *IGC* | N/A | 4,006,947 | 1,016,427 | 100 | N/A | 8,292,963 | 2,903,339 | 100 |

**Fig. 7.** Metrics (1 and 5 node configurations). Performance of three GC algorithms and IGC is given for the color people-tracker application. The fifth and the last column also give the percentage of *Mean Memory usage* with respect to IGC.

seen, the mean memory usage of DGC (which is the best performer of the three GC techniques) is still 429% (on 1AS config.) with respect to that of IGC. This is the reason for exploring further optimization strategies.

## 6.2   Performance of the Proposed Optimizations

In this subsection we consider the performance potential of each of the proposed optimizations. As we mentioned in Sec. 4, the KLnU optimization has general applicability. However, in this study we use the DGC algorithm as the base for evaluating all the performance enhancements.

– **Performance of Out-of-Band Propagation of Guarantees (OBPG)**
  Figure 8 (c) shows the results for this optimization. As we mentioned earlier in Sec. 4, to assess the performance limit for this optimization, zero time is assumed for the out-of-band dissemination of the timestamp guarantees. Comparing the results with those for DGC (figure 8 (b)), it can be seen that

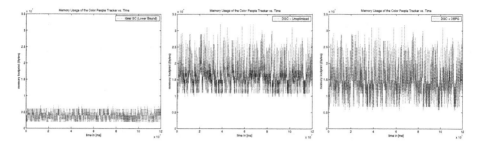

**Fig. 8.** Memory Footprint. The tracker application was run on 1 Address Space (on a single node). The memory footprint graphs above show results for (from left to right) : (a) Ideal GC - Lower Bound (IGC), (b) the unoptimized DGC implementation, (c) DGC optimized with Out-of-Band Propagation of Guarantees (OBPG).

the peak memory usage is lower with this optimization. However, the difference is almost insignificant. The reason is two-fold both of which stem from the nature of this particular application. First, later stages in the pipeline do more processing than earlier stages. Therefore, backward guarantees are more useful in hastening garbage collection than forward guarantees. Second, the task graph is highly *connected* (see figure 5). Later threads (such as the target detection thread) need input directly from earlier channels (such as the video frame channel). Thus GC events from later stages of the pipeline are directly getting fed back to earlier stages reducing the benefits of the OBPG optimization.

– **Performance of Keep Latest $n$ Unseen (KL$n$U)**
  For this optimization, we associate the KL$n$U attribute ($n = 1$, i.e., a channel buffers only the most recent item) with all the channels in the color tracker pipeline. Figure 9 (a) and figure 10 show the effect of the KL$n$U optimization over DGC. Compared to DGC (unoptimized) there is only a modest (16% - 26% reduction in memory usage) improvement due to this optimization. This is surprising since we expected that this optimization will allow each channel to be more aggressive in eliminating garbage locally. Recall that even though the buffering is limited to just the most recent item, a channel still cannot GC earlier items that have been gotten by at least one out connection to

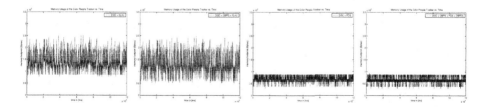

**Fig. 9.** Memory Footprint. The tracker application was run again on 1 Address Space (on a single node). The memory footprint graphs above show results for: (from left to right) (a) DGC with KL$n$U , (b) DGC with OBPG and KL$n$U optimizations, (c) DGC with PDS, and (d) DGC with OBPG and OBPDS.

preserve timestamp causality. The surprisingly small reduction in memory usage is a consequence of this fact.

- **Performance of Propagating Dead Sets (PDS)**

  Figure 9 (c) and (d) show the results of the PDS optimization. Compared to DGC (unoptimized) the reduction in memory usage is large (59% - 55%). The significant improvement due to this optimization is quite surprising at first glance. This optimization combines two effects: first, nodes propagate the dead-set information forwards and backwards using the application task graph; second, a channel aggressively incorporates the incoming dead-set information using the dependency information on its out connections. Analysis of our runtime logs reveal that it is the latter effect that aids the effectiveness of this optimization. For e.g., the video frame channel can use the dead-set information that it receives from the change-detection thread immediately without waiting for similar notification from the histogram and target-detection threads.

- **Performance of Out-of-Band Propagation of Dead Sets (OBPDS)**

  This optimization is similar to OBPG, with the difference that dead-set information is disseminated out-of-band instead of timestamp guarantees. As in OBPG, we assume that this dissemination itself takes zero time to assess the performance limit of this optimization. Figure 10 shows a small reduction (approximately 500KB) in memory usage compared to DGC (unoptimized). As we observed with the OBPG optimization, the relatively little impact of this optimization is due to the connectedness of this particular application task graph.

Overall, the combined effect of the proposed optimizations is a reduction in memory usage of 62% on 1 AS, and 65% on 5AS, respectively, compared to DGC (unoptimized).

| | *Config 1 : node* | | | | *Config 2 : 5 nodes* | | | |
|---|---|---|---|---|---|---|---|---|
| | *Mean Memory usage (B)* | *Memory usage STD* | *% w.r.t. DGC* | *% w.r.t. IGC* | *Mean Memory usage (B)* | *Memory usage STD* | *% w.r.t. DGC* | *% w.r.t. IGC* |
| *DGC − Unoptimized* | 17,196,808 | 4,143,659 | 100 | 429 | 30,359,907 | 2,486,790 | 100 | 366 |
| *DGC + OBPG* | 15,509,662 | 4,774,496 | 85 | 387 | 22,076,617 | 5,609,878 | 73 | 266 |
| *DGC + KLnU* | 14,480,981 | 3,222,947 | 84 | 361 | 22,500,410 | 2,181,028 | 74 | 271 |
| *DGC + OBPG + KLnU* | 13,201,657 | 3,764,269 | 77 | 329 | 16,456,518 | 4,396,111 | 54 | 198 |
| *DGC + PDS* | 7,016,269 | 981,811 | 41 | 175 | 13,770,987 | 2,910,143 | 45 | 166 |
| *DGC + OBPG + OBPDS* | 6,497,603 | 1,235,326 | 38 | 162 | 10,556,471 | 3,226,764 | 35 | 127 |
| *IGC Lower − Bound* | 4,006,947 | 1,016,427 | 23 | 100 | 8,292,963 | 2,903,339 | 27 | 100 |

**Fig. 10.** Metrics (1 and 5 node configurations). Performance of different GC algorithms with combinations of different optimizations is presented for the tracker application. Percentage *Mean Memory usage* of optimizations with respect to that of Unoptimized DGC and IGC are also presented in the figure.

### 6.3   Summary

We considered a number of potential optimizations to enhance the performance of garbage collection. Of the ones considered, the PDS scheme is implementable while OBPG and OBPDS are mainly to understand the limits to performance of implementable strategies. The performance benefits of the PDS optimization is sensitive to several factors that are application-specific: number of attributed channels, the value of $n$ chosen for the KL$n$U attribute, the connectedness of the task graph, and the dependencies among the in/out connections to nodes in the graph. Some counter-intuitive results emerged from the performance study. First, disseminating the timestamp guarantee of DGC or the dead-set information of PDS to all the nodes did not result in substantial savings. In hindsight, this seems reasonable given the connectedness of the color-based people tracker task graph. Second, the KL$n$U optimization in itself was not sufficient to get substantial reduction in memory usage. The propagation of the dead-set information, and use of the dependency information on the out connections of channels was the key to achieving most of the performance benefits.

There is a danger in generalizing the expected performance benefit of these optimizations simply based on the results of one application. Nevertheless, it appears that knowledge of the dependency information on the out connections of channels is a crucial determinant to the performance potential of these optimizations. A question worth investigating is the performance potential for incorporating out connection dependency in the original DGC algorithm. Another question worth investigating is the extent to which the TGC and REF algorithms will benefit in the presence of attributed channels.

## 7   Concluding Remarks

Stampede is a cluster programming system for interactive stream-oriented applications such as vision and speech. A Stampede application is composed of threads that can execute anywhere in the cluster, communicating timestamped items via channels (that can be created anywhere in the cluster as well). An important function performed by the Stampede runtime system is garbage collection of timestamped data items that are no longer needed by any threads in the application. In interactive applications for which Stampede is targeted, it is common for threads to work with the most recent items in a channel and skip over earlier timestamps. Thus the performance of a Stampede computation is crucially dependent on the efficiency of garbage collection.

Our earlier work has proposed *distributed* transparent garbage collection algorithm. In a more recent work, we have proposed a new algorithm that uses an application task graph to *locally* compute guarantees on timestamps that are needed by a given node in the graph and propagate such guarantees to other nodes. In this paper, we have first quantified how far off are the memory usages in these existing algorithms from an *ideal garbage collector*, one that buffers exactly the items that are processed fully in the task graph. Armed with this knowledge, we propose optimizations that help us get closer to the empirical limit suggested by the ideal garbage collector. The first optimization is to make the timestamp guarantees of our previous algorithm available to all the nodes in the graph. The second optimization is to buffer only a few of the most recent items in each channel. This optimization gives local control to the producer of items to declare some timestamps as *dead* in a channel and allows dissemination of this information to other nodes in the graph. The proposed optimizations are evaluated with the measurement and post-mortem analysis infrastructure available in Stampede using a color-based people tracker application. The results show over 60% reduction in the memory usage compared to our most aggressive garbage collection algorithm that is based on timestamp guarantees.

# References

1. R. E. Bryant. Simulation of Packet Communication Architecture Computer Systems. Technical Report MIT-LCS-TR-188, M.I.T, Cambridge, MA, 1977.
2. K. Chandy and J. Misra. Asynchronous distributed simulation via a sequence of parallel computation. *Communications of the ACM*, 24:198–206, 1981.
3. R. M. Fujimoto. Parallel Discrete Event Simulation. *Comm. of the ACM*, 33(10), October 1990.
4. R. M. Fujimoto. Parallel and distributed simulation. In *Winter Simulation Conference*, pages 118–125, December 1995.
5. N. Harel, H. A. Mandviwala, K. Knobe, and U. Ramachandran. Dead timestamp identification in stampede. In *The 2002 International Conference on Parallel Processing (ICPP-02)*, Aug. 2002. To Appear.
6. D. R. Jefferson. Virtual time. *ACM Transactions on Programming Languages and Systems*, 7(3):404–425, July 1985.
7. R. Jones and R. Lins. *Garbage Collection : Algorithms for Automatic Dynamic Memory Management*. John Wiley, August 1996. ISBN: 0471941484.
8. R. S. Nikhil and U. Ramachandran. Garbage Collection of Timestamped Data in Stampede. In *Proc.Nineteenth Annual Symposium on Principles of Distributed Computing (PODC 2000), Portland, Oregon*, July 2000.
9. R. S. Nikhil, U. Ramachandran, J. M. Rehg, R. H. Halstead, Jr., C. F. Joerg, and L. Kontothanassis. Stampede: A programming system for emerging scalable interactive multimedia applications. In *Proc. Eleventh Intl. Wkshp. on Languages and Compilers for Parallel Computing (LCPC 98), Chapel Hill NC*, August 7-9 1998.
10. U. Ramachandran, R. S. Nikhil, N. Harel, J. M. Rehg, and K. Knobe. Space-Time Memory: A Parallel Programming Abstraction for Interactive Multimedia Applications. In *Proc. Principles and Practice of Parallel Programming (PPoPP'99), Atlanta GA*, May 1999.
11. J. M. Rehg, M. Loughlin, and K. Waters. Vision for a Smart Kiosk. In *Computer Vision and Pattern Recognition*, pages 690–696, San Juan, Puerto Rico, June 17–19 1997.
12. P. R. Wilson. Uniprocessor garbage collection techniques, Yves Bekkers and Jacques Cohen (eds.). In *Intl. Wkshp. on Memory Management (IWMM 92), St. Malo, France*, pages 1–42, September 1992.

# Compiler and Runtime Support for Shared Memory Parallelization of Data Mining Algorithms⋆

Xiaogang Li, Ruoming Jin, and Gagan Agrawal

Department of Computer and Information Sciences,
Ohio State University, Columbus OH 43210
{xgli, jinr, agrawal}@cis.ohio-state.edu

**Abstract.** Data mining techniques focus on finding novel and useful patterns or models from large datasets. Because of the volume of the data to be analyzed, the amount of computation involved, and the need for rapid or even interactive analysis, data mining applications require the use of parallel machines. We have been developing compiler and runtime support for developing scalable implementations of data mining algorithms. Our work encompasses shared memory parallelization, distributed memory parallelization, and optimizations for processing disk-resident datasets.

In this paper, we focus on compiler and runtime support for shared memory parallelization of data mining algorithms. We have developed a set of parallelization techniques that apply across algorithms for a variety of mining tasks. We describe the interface of the middleware where these techniques are implemented. Then, we present compiler techniques for translating data parallel code to the middleware specification. Finally, we present a brief evaluation of our compiler using apriori association mining and k-means clustering.

## 1 Introduction

Analysis of large datasets for extracting novel and useful models or patterns, also referred to as *data mining*, has emerged as an important area within the last decade [5]. Because of the volume of data analyzed, the amount of computation involved, and the need for rapid or even interactive response, data mining tasks are becoming an important class of applications for parallel machines.

In recent years, large shared memory machines with high bus bandwidth and very large main memory have been developed by several vendors. Vendors of these machines are targeting data warehousing and data mining as major markets. Thus, we can expect data mining applications to become an important class of applications on large SMP machines.

This paper reports on runtime and compiler support for easing implementations of data mining algorithms on shared memory machines. We have observed that parallel versions of several well-known data mining techniques, including apriori association mining [1], k-means clustering [7], and k-nearest neighbor classifier [5], share a relatively similar structure. The main computation in these algorithms involves updating a

---

⋆ This work was supported by NSF grant ACR-9982087, NSF CAREER award ACR-9733520, and NSF grant ACR-0130437.

B. Pugh and C.-W. Tseng (Eds.): LCPC 2002, LNCS 2481, pp. 265–279, 2005.

*reduction object* using associative and commutative operators. The main issue in maintaining correctness is avoiding race conditions when multiple threads may want to increment the same element.

Based upon this observation, we have developed a set of techniques for parallelizing data mining algorithms. Our set of techniques include full replication, full locking, fixed locking, optimized full locking, and cache-sensitive locking. Unlike previous work on shared memory parallelization of specific data mining algorithms, all of our techniques apply across a large number of common data mining algorithms. The techniques we have developed involve a number of tradeoffs between memory requirements, opportunity for parallelization, and locking overheads. The techniques have been implemented within a runtime framework. This framework offers a high-level interface and hides the details of implementation of the parallelization techniques.

We have also used this framework and its interface as a compiler target. Starting from a data parallel version of a data mining algorithm, our compiler generates code for the interface for our runtime framework. Our experience in implementing the compiler has shown the use of a runtime framework significantly simplifies the compiler implementation. This paper describes our parallelization techniques, runtime framework, compiler implementation, and an evaluation of our compiler using apriori association mining and k-means clustering.

The rest of the paper is organized as follows. We survey the parallel data mining algorithms in Section 2. The interface and functionality of our middleware is described in Section 3. The language dialect we use is presented in Section 4. Our compiler techniques are presented in Section 5. Experimental evaluation of our prototype compiler is the topic of Section 6. We compare our work with related research efforts in Section 7 and conclude in Section 8.

## 2   Parallel Data Mining Algorithms

In this section, we describe how several commonly used data mining techniques can be parallelized on a shared memory machine in a very similar way. Our discussion focuses on three important data mining techniques: apriori associating mining [1], k-means clustering [7], and k-nearest neighbors [5].

### 2.1   Apriori Association Mining

Association rule mining is the process of analyzing a set of transactions to extract *association rules* and is a very commonly used and well-studied data mining problem [1,19]. Given a set of transactions[1] (each of them being a set of items), an association rule is an expression $X \rightarrow Y$, where $X$ and $Y$ are the sets of items. Such a rule implies that transactions in databases that contain the items in $X$ also tend to contain the items in $Y$.

Formally, the goal is to compute the sets $L_k$. For a given value of $k$, the set $L_k$ comprises the frequent itemsets of length $k$. A well accepted algorithm for association mining is the *apriori* mining algorithm [1]. The main observation in the apriori technique is that if an itemset occurs with frequency $f$, all the subsets of this itemset

---

[1] We use the terms *transactions*, *data items*, and *data instances* interchangeably.

also occur with at least frequency $f$. In the first iteration of this algorithm, transactions are analyzed to determine the frequent 1-itemsets. During any subsequent iteration $k$, the frequent itemsets $L_{k-1}$ found in the $(k-1)^{th}$ iteration are used to generate the candidate itemsets $C_k$. Then, each transaction in the dataset is processed to compute the frequency of each member of the set $C_k$. k-itemsets from $C_k$ that have a certain pre-specified minimal frequency (called the *support level*) are added to the set $L_k$.

A simple shared memory parallelization scheme for this algorithm is as follows. One processor generates the complete $C_k$ using the frequent itemset $L_{k-1}$ created at the end of the iteration $k-1$. The transactions are scanned, and each transaction (or a set of transactions) is assigned to one processor. This processor evaluates the transaction(s) and updates the counts of candidates itemsets that are found in this transaction. Thus, by assigning different sets of transactions to processors, parallelism can be achieved. The only challenge in maintaining correctness is avoiding the possible race conditions when multiple processors may want to update the count of the same candidate.

## 2.2   k-Means Clustering

The second data mining algorithm we describe is the k-means clustering technique [7], which is also very commonly used. This method considers transactions or data instances as representing points in a high-dimensional space. Proximity within this space is used as the criterion for classifying the points into clusters.

Three steps in the sequential version of this algorithm are as follows: 1) start with $k$ given centers for clusters; 2) scan the data instances, for each data instance (point), find the center closest to it, assign this point to the corresponding cluster, and then move the center of the cluster closer to this point; and 3) repeat this process until the assignment of points to cluster does not change.

This method can also be parallelized in a fashion very similar to the method we described for apriori association mining. The data instances are read, and each data instance (or a set of instances) are assigned to one processor. This processor performs the computations associated with the data instance, and then updates the center of the cluster this data instance is closest to. Again, the only challenge in maintaining correctness is avoiding the race conditions when multiple processors may want to update center of the same cluster.

## 2.3   k-Nearest Neighbors

k-nearest neighbor classifier is based on learning by analogy [5]. The training samples are described by an n-dimensional numeric space. Given an unknown sample, the k-nearest neighbor classifier searches the pattern space for k training samples that are closest, using the euclidean distance, to the unknown sample.

Again, this technique can be parallelized as follows. Each training sample is processed by one processor. After processing the sample, the processor determines if the list of k current nearest neighbors should be updated to include this sample. Again, the correctness issue is the race conditions if multiple processors try to update the list of nearest neighbors at the same time.

## 3     Parallelization Techniques and Middleware Support

In this section, we initially focus on the parallelization techniques we have developed for the data mining algorithms we described in the last section. Then, we give a brief overview of the middleware within which these techniques are implemented. We also describe the middleware interface.

### 3.1     Parallelization Techniques

In the previous section, we have argued how several data mining algorithms can be parallelized in a very similar fashion. The common structure behind these algorithms is summarized in Figure 1. The function *op* is an associative and commutative function. Thus, the iterations of the foreach loop can be performed in any order. The data-structure *Reduc* is referred to as the *reduction object*. Every element of this object is referred to as a *reduction element*.

The main correctness challenge in parallelizing a loop like this on a shared memory machine arises because of possible race conditions when multiple processors update the same element of the reduction object. The element of the reduction object that is updated in a loop iteration ($i$) is determined only as a result of the processing. For example, in the apriori association mining algorithm, the data item read needs to matched against all candidates to determine the set of candidates whose counts will be incremented. In the k-means clustering algorithm, first the cluster to which a data item belongs is determined. Then, the center of this cluster is updated using a reduction operation.

The major factors that make these loops challenging to execute efficiently and correctly are as follows:

- It is not possible to statically partition the reduction object so that different processors update disjoint portions of the collection. Thus, race conditions must be avoided at runtime.
- The execution time of the function *process* can be a significant part of the execution time of an iteration of the loop. Thus, runtime preprocessing or scheduling techniques cannot be applied.
- In many of algorithms, the size of the reduction object can be quite large. This means that the reduction object cannot be replicated or privatized without significant memory overheads.

```
{ * Outer Sequential Loop *}
While() {
    { * Reduction Loop *}
    Foreach(element e) {
        (i, val)   =   process(e) ;
        Reduc(i)   =   Reduc(i) op  val ;
    }
}
```

**Fig. 1.** Structure of Common Data Mining Algorithms

– The updates to the reduction object are *fine-grained*. The reduction object comprises a large number of elements that take only a few bytes, and the foreach loop comprises a large number of iterations, each of which may take only a small number of cycles. Thus, if a locking scheme is used, the overhead of locking and synchronization can be significant.

We have developed a number of techniques for parallelizing this class of loops. The comparison of our work with existing work on shared memory parallelization is presented in the related work section. Our work has shown that three techniques are the most competitive and can all out-perform each other under certain conditions. These techniques are, *full replication*, *optimized full locking*, and *cache-sensitive locking*. For motivating the optimized full locking and cache-sensitive locking schemes, we also describe a simple scheme that we refer to as *full locking*.

**Full Replication:** One simple way of avoiding race conditions is to replicate the reduction object and create one copy for every thread. The copy for each thread needs to be initialized in the beginning. Each thread simply updates its own copy, thus avoiding any race conditions. After the local reduction has been performed using all the data items on a particular node, the updates made in all the copies are *merged*.

We next describe the locking schemes. The memory layout of the three locking schemes, *full locking*, *optimized full locking*, and *cache-sensitive locking*, is shown in Figure 2.

**Full Locking:** One obvious solution to avoiding race conditions is to associate one lock with every element in the reduction object. After processing a data item, a thread needs to acquire the lock associated with the element in the reduction object it needs to update.

In our experiment with apriori, with 2000 distinct items and support level of 0.1%, up to 3 million candidates were generated. In full locking, this means supporting 3 million locks. Supporting such a large numbers of locks results in overheads of three

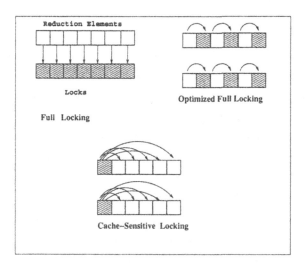

**Fig. 2.** Memory Layout for Various Locking Schemes

types. The first is the high memory requirement associated with a large number of locks. The second overhead comes from cache misses. Consider an update operation. If the total number of elements is large and there is no locality in accessing these elements, then the update operation is likely to result in two cache misses, one for the element and second for the lock. This cost can slow down the update operation significantly.

The third overhead is of false sharing. In a cache-coherent shared memory multi-processor, false sharing happens when two processors want to access different elements from the same cache block. In full locking scheme, false sharing can result in cache misses for both reduction elements and locks.

**Optimized Full Locking:** Optimized full locking scheme overcomes the the large number of cache misses associated with full locking scheme by allocating a reduction element and the corresponding lock in consecutive memory locations, as shown in Figure 2. By appropriate alignment and padding, it can be ensured that the element and the lock are in the same cache block. Each update operation now results in at most one cold or capacity cache miss. The possibility of false sharing is also reduced. This is because there are fewer elements (or locks) in each cache block. This scheme does not reduce the total memory requirements.

**Cache-Sensitive Locking:** The final technique we describe is *cache-sensitive locking*. Consider a 64 byte cache block and a 4 byte reduction element. We use a single lock for all reduction elements in the same cache block. Moreover, this lock is allocated in the same cache block as the elements. So, each cache block will have 1 lock and 15 reduction elements.

Cache-sensitive locking reduces each of three types of overhead associated with full locking. This scheme results in lower memory requirements than the full locking and optimized full locking schemes. Each update operation results in at most one cache miss, as long as there is no contention between the threads. The problem of false sharing is also reduced because there is only one lock per cache block.

### 3.2  Middleware Functionality and Interface

We have developed a middleware in which the various parallelization techniques we described earlier have been implemented. The middleware serves two goals. First, it offers a high-level interface for the programmers to rapidly implement parallel data mining algorithms. Second, it can serve as a compiler target. By generating code for the middleware interface, the compiler need not generate separate code for each of the parallelization approaches we support. This work is part of our work on developing a middleware for rapid development of data mining implementations on large SMPs and clusters of SMPs [8]. Our middleware targets both distributed memory and shared memory parallelization, and also includes optimizations for efficient processing of disk-resident datasets.

For shared memory parallelization, the programmer is responsible for creating and initializing a reduction object. Further, the programmer needs to write a local reduction function that specifies the processing associated with each transaction. The initialization and local reduction functions for k-means are shown in Figure 3. As we discussed earlier, a common aspect of data mining algorithms is the *reduction object*. Declaration

```
void Kmeans::initialize() {
    for (int i = 0; i < k; i++) {
        clusterID[i]=reducobject->alloc(ndim + 2);
    }
    {* Initialize Centers *}
}
void Kmeans::reduction(void *point) {
    for (int i=0; i < k; i++) {
        dis=distance(point, i);
        if (dis < min) {
            min=dis;
            min_index=i;
        }
    }
    objectID=clusterID[min_index];
    for (int j=0; j< ndim; j++)
        reducobject->Add(objectID, j, point[j]);
    reducobject->Add(objectID, ndim, 1);
    reducobject->Add(objectID, ndim + 1, dis);
}
```

**Fig. 3.** Initialization and Local Reduction Functions for k-means

and allocation of a reduction object is a significant aspect of our middleware interface. There are two important reasons why reduction elements need to be separated from other data-structures. First, by separating them from read-only data-structures, false sharing can be reduced. Second, the middleware needs to know about the reduction object and its elements to optimize memory layout, allocate locks, and potentially replicate the object.

Two granularity levels are supported for reduction objects, the *group* level and the *element* level. One group is allocated at a time and comprises a number of elements. The goal is to provide programming convenience, as well as high performance. In apriori, all $k$ itemsets that share the same parent $k - 1$ itemsets are typically declared to be in the same group. In k-means, a group represents a center, which has $ndim + 2$ elements, where $ndim$ is the number of dimensions in the coordinate space.

After the reduction object is created and initialized, the runtime system may *clone* it and create several copies of it. However, this is transparent to the programmer, who views a single copy of it.

The reduction function shown in Figure 3 illustrates how updates to elements within a reduction object are performed. The programmer writes sequential code for processing, except the updates to elements within a reduction object are performed through member functions of the reduction object. A particular element in the reduction object is referenced by a group identifier and an offset within the group. In this example, *add* function is invoked for all elements. Besides supporting the commonly used reduction functions, like addition, multiplication, maximum, and minimum, we also allow user defined functions. A function pointer can be passed a parameter to a generic reduction function. The reduction functions are implemented as part of our runtime support. Several parallelization strategies are supported, but their implementation is kept transparent from application programmers.

After the reduction operation has been applied on all transactions, a *merge* phase may required, depending upon the parallelization strategy used. If several copies of the reduction object have been created, the merge phase is responsible for creating a single correct copy. We allow the application programmer to choose between one of the standard merge functions, (like add corresponding elements from all copies), or to supply their own function.

## 4    Data Parallel Language Support

We now describe a data parallel dialect of Java that can be used for expressing parallel algorithms for common data mining tasks. Though we propose to use a dialect of Java as the source language for the compiler, the techniques we will be developing will be largely independent of Java and will also be applicable to suitable extensions of other languages, such as C or C++.

We use three main directives in our data parallel dialect. These are for specifying a multi-dimensional collections of objects, a parallel for loop, and a reduction interface.

**Rectdomain:** A rectdomain is a collection of objects of the same type such that each object in the collection has a *coordinate* associated with it, and this coordinate belongs to a pre-specified rectilinear section.

**Foreach Loop:** A foreach loop iterates over objects in a rectdomain, and has the property that the order of iterations does not influence the result of the associated computations.

```
Interface Reducinterface {
    { * Any object of any class implementing *}
    { * this interface is a reduction variable *}
}
public class KmPoint implements Disk-resident {
    double x1, x2, x3;
    KmPoint (String buffer) {
        { * constructor for copying to/from a buffer *}
    }
}
public class Kcenter implements Reducface {
    static double [] x1,x2,x3;
    static double[] meanx1, meanx2, meanx3;
    static long[] count;
    Kcenter (String buffer) {
        { * constructor for copying to/from a buffer *}
    }
    void Postproc() {
        for(i=0; i < k; i++) {
            x1[i]=meanx1[i]/count[i];
            x2[i]=meanx2[i]/count[i];
            x3[i]=meanx3[i]/count[i];
        }
    }
    void Assign(KmPoint point,int i,double dis) {
        meanx1[i]+=point.x1;
        meanx2[i]+=point.x2;
        meanx3[i]+=point.x3;
        count[i]+=1;
    }
}

public class Kmeans {

    public static void main(String[] args) {
        Point< 1 > lowend = .. ;
        Point< 1 > hiend = .. ;
        RectDomain< 1 > InputDomain=[lowend:hiend];
        KmPoint[1d] Input=new KmPoint[InputDomain];

        while(not_converged) {

            foreach (p in InputDomain) {
                min=9.999E+20;
                for (i=0; i < k; i++) {
                    int dis = Kcenter.distance(Input[p],i);
                    if( dis < min) {
                        min=temp;
                        minindex=i;
                    }
                }
                Kcenter.Assign(Input[p],minindex,min);
            }
            Kcenter.Finalize();
        }
    }
}
```

**Fig. 4.** k-means Clustering Expressed in Data Parallel Java

**Reduction Interface:** Any object of any class implementing the reduction interface acts as a *reduction variable* [6]. The semantics of a reduction variable are analogous to those used in version 2.0 of High Performance Fortran (HPF-2) [6]. A reduction variable has the property that it can only be updated inside a *foreach* loop by a series of operations that are associative and commutative. Furthermore, the intermediate value of the reduction variable may not be used within the loop, except for self-updates.

Another interface we use is *Disk-resident*. Any class whose objects are either read or written from disks must implement this interface. For any class which implements the reduction interface, or represents objects that are disk-resident, we expect a constructor function that can read the object from a string. In the case of a class that implements the reduction interface, such constructor function is used for facilitating interprocessor communication. Specifically, the code for the constructor function is used for generating code for copying an object to a message buffer and copying a message buffer to an object. Similarly, for any dataset which is either read or written to disks, the constructor function is used to generate code that reads or writes the object.

The data parallel Java code for k-means clustering is shown in Figure 4. $k$ is the number of clusters that need to be computed. An object of the class KmPoint represents a three-dimensional point. The variable Input represents a one-dimensional array of points, which is the input to the algorithm. In each iteration of the foreach loop, one point is processed and the cluster whose center is closest to the point is determined. The function Assign accumulates coordinates of all points that are found to be closest to the center of a given cluster. It also increments the count of the number of points that have been found to be closest to the center of a given cluster. The function Postproc is called after the foreach loop. It determines the new coordinates of the center of a cluster, based upon the points that have been assigned to the cluster. The details of the test for termination condition are not shown here.

## 5   Compiler Implementation

In this section, we describe how our compiler translates a data mining application written in the data parallel dialect to a middleware specification.

The use of middleware considerably simplifies the task of compiler, because task planning, asynchronous I/O operation and synchronization are all transparent to the compiler. Moreover, the compiler does not need to generate significantly different code to use different parallelization techniques.

As illustrated in previous sections, a typical application in our target class comprises an initialization of an array of reduction elements, an iterator which specifies the input data and local reduction function that operates on the instance, and a finalization function to handle output. Accordingly, our compiler needs to: 1) Generate function to initialize reduction elements, 2) For each data parallel loop that updates an object of reduction interface, generate local and global reduction functions, and 3) Generate the finalization function.

A special template called a reduction element is implemented in our middleware to make synchronizations transparent to users. Each reduction element corresponds to one

```
void Kmeans::initialize()  {
    ReplicationDM ( double )::preinitialize();
    int reduct_buffer=reducobject->alloc(k*4+1);
    for (int i = 0; i < k; i++) {
        (*reductionElement)(reduct_buffer, i)=0 ;
        (*reductionElement)(reduct_buffer, i+1)=0 ;
        (*reductionElement)(reduct_buffer, i+2)=0 ;
        (*reductionElement)(reduct_buffer, i+3)=0 ;
    }
    Replication_DM< double > ::post_initialize();
}
```

**Fig. 5.** Compiler Generated Initialization Function for k-means

```
void Kmeans::local_reduction(void* block) {
    int *datablock=(int *) block;
    int instance_number = *datablock;
    double *instance=(double*)(datablock)+1;
    double min;
    double temp;
    int min_index;
    KmPoint Input ;
    for (;instance_number>0;instance_number-) {
        scandata(instance, &Input) ;
        min=max_number;
        for(int i=0;i<;i++) {
            temp = distance( Input, i);
            if( temp < min) {
                min=temp;
                minindex=i;
            }
        }
        assign( Input, minindex, min);
    }
}

void Kmeans::scandata(int*instance, KmPoint* Input )
{
    memcpy(&Input.x1,instance,sizeof(double));
    instance+=sizeof(double);
    memcpy(&Input.x2,instance,sizeof(double));
    instance+=sizeof(double);
    memcpy(&Input.x3,instance,sizeof(double));
    instance+=sizeof(double);
}

void Kmeans::assign(KmPoint& Input, int index, double dis )
{
    reducObject->Add(reduct_buffer,index, Input.x1);
    reducObject->Add(reduct_buffer,index+1, Input.x2);
    reducObject->Add(reduct_buffer,index+2, Input.x3);
    reducObject->Add(reduct_buffer,index+3, 1);
    reducObject->Add(reduct_buffer,K*4+1, dis);
}
```

**Fig. 6.** Compiler Generated Local Reduction function for k-means

block in the memory, and all reduction elements are shared by all consumer processes at runtime.

The responsibilities of initialization function typically include allocation of reduction elements and setting the initial values. In generating the initialization function, we gather static information from the class declaration of reduction interface to decide the number of reduction elements to be allocated. For applications where this cannot be known until runtime, such as apriori associate mining, we use symbolic analysis. Figure 5 shows the initialization function of kmeans. After allocating reduction elements, the statements that set the initial value of each element are translated directly from the constructor of the object of reduction interface.

Generating local reduction function is quite straight-forward. The operations within the foreach loop can be extracted and put into a separate function, which simply becomes the local reduction function. However, as high level representation of the reduction interface in our dialect of Java is translated to reduction elements, reference and updates of the reduction interface must also be translated to reference and updates of the corresponding reduction elements. The compiler generated local reduction function is shown in Figure 6.

Currently for the data mining applications we have studied, the global reduction function is just a call to a method of the middleware that performs reductions on all reduction elements. The detailed operations are transparent to our compiler.

The last task of our compiler is generating a finalization function to specify the output. The finalization function typically also includes the termination condition for the sequential loop surrounding the foreach loop. This is done by simply translating the functions called after the foreach loop in the source code.

# 6   Experimental Results

In this section, we focus on evaluating our compiler and runtime framework. We use two common data mining algorithms, apriori association mining and k-means clustering.

Our first experiment demonstrates that each of the three parallelization techniques we have developed can out-perform others depending upon the problem characteristics. Our second set of experiments compare the performance of compiler generated codes with hand-coded versions.

Through-out this section, the versions corresponding to the full replication, optimized full locking and cache-sensitive locking are denoted by `fr`, `ofl`, and `csl`, respectively.

## 6.1   Evaluating Different Parallelization Techniques

This experiment was performed using a Sun Microsystem Ultra Enterprise 450, with 4 250MHz Ultra-II processors and 1 GB of 4-way interleaved main memory.

We used apriori association mining for this experiment. The size of the reduction object in k-means clustering is usually quite small, and as a result, almost identical performance is seen from all three techniques.

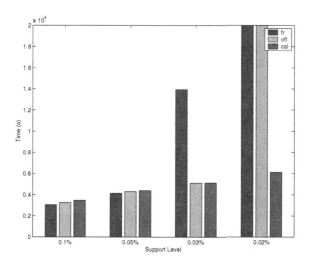

**Fig. 7.** Relative Performance of Full Replication, Optimized Full Locking, and Cache-Sensitive Locking: 4 Threads, Different Support Levels

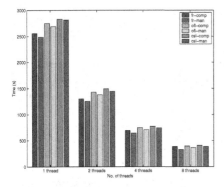

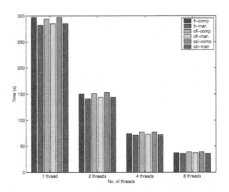

**Fig. 8.** Comparison of Compiler Generated and Manual Versions - Apriori Association Mining

**Fig. 9.** Comparison of Compiler Generated and Manual Versions - k-means clustering

We use a dataset with 2000 distinct items, where the average number of items per transaction is 20. The total size of the dataset is 500 MB and a confidence level of 90% is used. We consider four support levels, 0.1%, 0.05%, 0.03%, and 0.02%.

The results are shown in Figure 7. These results were obtained using a In apriori association mining, the total number of candidate item-sets increases as the support level is decreased. Therefore, the total memory requirement for the reduction objects also increases. When support level is 0.1% or 0.05%, sufficient memory is available for reduction object even after replicating 4 times. Therefore, `fr` gives the best performance. At the support level of 0.1%, `ofl` is slower by 7% and `csl` is slower by 14%. At the support level of 0.05%, they are slower by 4% and 6%, respectively. When the support level is 0.03%, the performance of `fr` degrades dramatically. This is because replicated reduction object does not fit in main memory and memory thrashing occurs. Since the memory requirements of locking schemes are lower, they do not see the same effect. `ofl` is the best scheme in this case, though `csl` is slower by less than 1%. When the support level is 0.02%, the available main memory is not even sufficient for `ofl`. Therefore, `csl` has the best performance. The execution time for `csl` was 6,117 seconds, whereas the execution time for `ofl` and `fr` was more than 80,000 seconds.

## 6.2   Evaluating Compiler Generated Codes

We next focus on comparing the performance of compiler generated codes with manually coded versions. We use apriori association mining and k-means clustering for this purpose.

These experiments were conducted on a SunFire 6800. Each processor in this machine is a 64 bit, 900 MHz Sun UltraSparc III. Each processor has a 96 KB L1 cache and a 8 MB L2 cache. The total main memory available is 24 GB. The Sun Fireplane interconnect provides a bandwidth of 9.6 GB per second.

The results obtained from apriori are shown in Figure 8. We used a 1 GB dataset for our experiments. We compared the compiler generated and manual versions corresponding to the three parallelization techniques we have developed. These six versions are denoted as `fr-comp`, `fr-man`, `ofl-comp`, `ofl-man`, `csl-comp`, and `csl-man`, respectively.

On this dataset, the reduction object fits into main memory even after being replicated for 8 threads. As a result, full replication based versions give the best performance. All versions achieve a relative speedup greater than 6.5 on 8 threads.

In comparing the performance of compiler and manual versions, the compiler versions are consistently slower by between 5% and 10% than the corresponding manual versions. An exception to this is the `fr-comp` version on 8 threads, which is almost 20% slower than `fr-man`.

In comparing the compiler generated and manual versions, the main difference arises because the compiler generated version performed extra copying of the input data, whereas the manual version analyzed data directly from the read buffer. As the code becomes more memory bound, the impact of extra copying gets larger. This, we believe, is the reason for a more significant slow-down of the compiler version using full replication on 8 threads.

The results obtained from k-means are presented in Figure 9. We used a 1 GB dataset, comprising 3 dimensional points. The value of $k$ we used was 100. We again experimented with six versions.

Because of the small size of reduction object and a higher amount of computation in each iteration, the performance of the three parallelization techniques is almost identical. The relative speedups are greater than 7.5 in all cases. The performance of compiler generated versions is nearly 5% slower than the performance of the corresponding manual versions in all cases.

# 7    Related Work

Shared memory parallelization has been widely studied by a number of compilation projects. We believe that our approach is distinct in two specific ways. First, we are not aware of compilation efforts focusing on the cache implications of locking. Second, our compiler generates code for a runtime framework that implements a number of parallelization techniques.

Rinard and Diniz have developed the technique of adaptive replication [15] which has some similarities with our approach. They perform replication at runtime for reduction elements that are accessed frequently and therefore, the associated locks can incur large synchronization costs. Our experiences with data mining codes has shown that synchronization costs are not significant. Instead, the cache misses in accessing locks are the significant cost, and are addressed by our optimized full locking and cache-sensitive locking techniques.

A number of research projects in recent years have focused on parallelization of indirection array based reductions [2,4,10,11,3,16]. In such reductions, the reduction array is typically accessed using an indirection array. The indirection array can be analyzed as part of a runtime preprocessing or *inspector* phase to determine the element(s) accessed during a particular iteration. Such analysis can be done in a small fraction of the cost of execution of the entire loop. However, this is not an applicable solution for data mining algorithms.

Many researchers have focused on shared memory parallelization of data mining algorithms, including association mining [18,13,14] and decision tree construction [17]. Our work is significantly different, because we focus on on a common framework for parallelization of a number of data mining algorithms and involve compiler support.

# 8    Conclusions

In this paper, we have focused on providing runtime and compiler support for shared memory parallelization of data mining applications. With the availability of large datasets in many scientific and commercial domains, we expect that data mining will be important class of applications for parallel computers. We have presented a set of parallelization techniques, a runtime framework implementing these techniques, and a compiler that translates data parallel code to the runtime interface.

Our work has resulted in the following observations. First, we have shown that the three parallelization techniques we have focused on, involving replication or locking with different granularities, can all outperform each other based upon the problem characteristics. Second, our compiler implementation experience has shown that a runtime framework can significantly ease the code generation task. Experimental results from our compiler have shown that the performance of compiler generated code is competitive with the performance of hand-written code.

# References

1. R. Agrawal and J. Shafer. Parallel mining of association rules. *IEEE Transactions on Knowledge and Data Engineering*, 8(6):962 – 969, June 1996.
2. W. Blume, R. Doallo, R. Eigenman, J. Grout, J. Hoelflinger, T. Lawrence, J. Lee, D. Padua, Y. Paek, B. Pottenger, L. Rauchwerger, and P. Tu. Parallel programming with Polaris. *IEEE Computer*, 29(12):78–82, December 1996.
3. E. Gutierrez, O. Plata, and E. L. Zapata. A compiler method for the parallel execution of irregular reductions in scalable shared memory multiprocessors. In *ICS00*, pages 78–87. ACM Press, May 2000.
4. M. Hall, S. Amarsinghe, B. Murphy, S. Liao, and M. Lam. Maximizing multiprocessor performance with the SUIF compiler. *IEEE Computer*, (12), December 1996.
5. Jiawei Han and Micheline Kamber. *Data Mining: Concepts and Techniques*. Morgan Kaufmann Publishers, 2000.
6. High Performance Fortran Forum. Hpf language specification, version 2.0. Available from http://www.crpc.rice.edu/HPFF/versions/hpf2/files/hpf-v20.ps.gz, January 1997.
7. A. K. Jain and R. C. Dubes. *Algorithms for Clustering Data*. Prentice Hall, 1988.
8. Ruoming Jin and Gagan Agrawal. A middleware for developing parallel data mining implementations. In *Proceedings of the first SIAM conference on Data Mining*, April 2001.
9. Ruoming Jin and Gagan Agrawal. Shared Memory Parallelization of Data Mining Algorithms: Techniques, Programming Interface, and Performance. In *Proceedings of the second SIAM conference on Data Mining*, April 2002.
10. Yuan Lin and David Padua. On the automatic parallelization of sparse and irregular Fortran programs. In *Proceedings of the Workshop on Languages, Compilers, and Runtime Systems for Scalable Computers (LCR - 98)*, May 1998.

11. Honghui Lu, Alan L. Cox, Snadhya Dwarkadas, Ramakrishnan Rajamony, and Willy Zwaenepoel. Compiler and software distributed shared memory support for irregular applications. In *Proceedings of the Sixth ACM SIGPLAN Symposium on Principles & Practice of Parallel Programming (PPOPP)*, pages 48–56. ACM Press, June 1997. ACM SIGPLAN Notices, Vol. 32, No. 7.

12. S. K. Murthy. Automatic construction of decision trees from data: A multi-disciplinary survey. *Data Mining and Knowledge Discovery*, 2(4):345–389, 1998.

13. Srinivasan Parthasarathy, Mohammed Zaki, and Wei Li. Memory placement techniques for parallel association mining. In *Proceedings of the 4th International Conference on Knowledge Discovery and Data Mining (KDD)*, August 1998.

14. Srinivasan Parthasarathy, Mohammed Zaki, Mitsunori Ogihara, and Wei Li. Parallel data mining for association rules on shared-memory systems. *Knowledge and Information Systems*, 2000. To appear.

15. Martin C. Rinard and Pedro C. Diniz. Eliminating Synchronization Bottlenecks in Object-Oriented Programs Using Adaptive Replication. In *Proceedings of International Conference on Supercomputing (ICS)*. ACM Press, July 1999.

16. Joel H. Saltz, Ravi Mirchandaney, and Kay Crowley. Run-time parallelization and scheduling of loops. *IEEE Transactions on Computers*, 40(5):603–612, May 1991.

17. M. J. Zaki, C.-T. Ho, and R. Agrawal. Parallel classification for data mining on shared-memory multiprocessors. *IEEE International Conference on Data Engineering*, pages 198–205, May 1999.

18. M. J. Zaki, M. Ogihara, S. Parthasarathy, and W. Li. Parallel data mining for association rules on shared memory multiprocessors. In *Proceedings of Supercomputing'96*, November 1996.

19. Mohammed J. Zaki. Parallel and distributed association mining: A survey. *IEEE Concurrency*, 7(4):14 – 25, 1999.

# Performance Analysis of Symbolic Analysis Techniques for Parallelizing Compilers[*]

Hansang Bae and Rudolf Eigenmann

School of Electrical and Computer Engineering,
Purdue University, West Lafayette, IN
{baeh, eigenman}@purdue.edu

**Abstract.** Understanding symbolic expressions is an important capability of advanced program analysis techniques. Many current compiler techniques assume that coefficients of program expressions, such as array subscripts and loop bounds, are integer constants. Advanced symbolic handling capabilities could make these techniques amenable to real application programs. Symbolic analysis is also likely to play an important role in supporting higher–level programming languages and optimizations. For example, entire algorithms may be recognized and replaced by better variants. In pursuit of this goal, we have measured the degree to which symbolic analysis techniques affect the behavior of current parallelizing compilers. We have chosen the Polaris parallelizing compiler and studied the techniques such as range analysis – which is the core symbolic analysis in the compiler – expression propagation, and symbolic expression manipulation. To measure the effect of a technique, we disabled it individually, and compared the performance of the resulting program with the original, fully-optimized program. We found that symbolic expression manipulation is important for most programs. Expression propagation and range analysis is important in few programs only, however they can affect these programs significantly. We also found that in all but one programs, a simpler form of range analysis – control range analysis – is sufficient.

## 1  Introduction

Automatic program parallelization has been studied and developed intensely in the last two decades, especially in an effort to automatically detect parallelism present in numerical applications. As a result, advanced analysis and transformation techniques exist today, which can optimize many programs to a degree close to that of manual parallelization. The ability of a compiler to manipulate and understand symbolic expressions is an important quality of this technology [1]. For instance, the accuracy of data dependence tests, array privatization, dead

---

[*] This material is based upon work supported by the National Science Foundation under Grant, No. 9974976-EIA, 9975275-EIA, and 0103582-EIA. Any opinions, findings, and conclusions or recommendations expressed in this material are those of the authors and do not necessarily reflect the views of the National Science Foundation.

B. Pugh and C.-W. Tseng (Eds.): LCPC 2002, LNCS 2481, pp. 280–294, 2005.

code elimination, and the detection of zero-trip loops increases if the techniques have knowledge of the value ranges assumed by certain variables.

Several research groups have developed symbolic analysis capabilities to make the most of program analysis techniques implemented in their compilers [1,3,4,5,6,7,8]. The Polaris parallelizing compiler [2] has incorporated advanced symbolic analysis techniques in order to effectively detect privatizable arrays, to determine whether a certain loop is a zero-trip loop for induction variable substitution, and to solve data dependence problems that involve symbolic loop bounds and array subscripts. Range Propagation [3] is the basis for this functionality. It can determine the value ranges that symbolic expressions in the program can assume. Polaris' symbolic nonlinear data dependence test – the Range Test [4] – makes use of Range Propagation. The Range Test is the main advanced data dependence test in the Polaris compiler. Expression propagation is another important technique, which can eliminate symbolic terms by substituting them with known values. Furthermore, symbolic expression simplification is essential in several passes in the Polaris compiler.

The major impediment in adopting certain symbolic analysis techniques is their relatively high cost [5,9]. For example, in one of our experiments, the Polaris compiler exhausted the available memory space that kept the range information of that program. Whether or not this cost is worth expending is not known, as the techniques' effectiveness in the context of an advanced optimizing compiler and with contemporary application programs has not been studied. These facts motivated our effort to quantify the gains of symbolic analysis techniques. We present the results as follows. Section 2 outlines the analysis techniques we measured. Section 3 describes our experimental methods and metrics. Section 4 discusses the results in detail. Section 5 reviews related work, and Section 6 presents our conclusion.

## 2  Symbolic Analysis Techniques in Polaris

We categorize the studied techniques into three groups. First, Range Propagation and the Range Test are the most important techniques that deal with symbolic terms in array subscripts. Second, Expression Propagation is a conventional technique to transform symbolic expressions into more analyzable form. Third, Symbolic Expression Simplification was included, because it provides essential functionality that several Polaris passes make use of.

### 2.1  Range Propagation and Range Test

The Range Analysis technique determines the value ranges assumed by variables at each point of a program. It does this by performing *abstract interpretation* [10] along the control and data flow paths. The results are kept in a *range dictionary* [3], which maps from variables to their ranges. Polaris supports two levels of range dictionaries. The *control range dictionary* collects information by inspecting control statements, such as IF statements and DO statements. The *abstract interpretation (AI) range dictionary* subsumes the control range dictionary and

```
IF (m.GT.5) THEN                              IF (j.GT.0.AND.j.LT.3) THEN
  n = m + 4      {m>=6}                          DO i = 1, imax
  DO i = 1, m    {m>=6, n=m+4}          S1:        a(3*i+j) = a(3*i) + 3.14*i
    a(i) = 3.14*n {m>=6, n=m+4, 1<=i<=m}         ENDDO
  ENDDO                                         ENDIF
ENDIF
           (a)                                              (b)

                k = 0
           L1:  DO i = 1, 10                L1:  DO i = 1, 10
           L2:    DO j = 1, m               L2:    DO j = 1, m
                    k = k + 2                        ...
                    ...              ->             ENDDO
                  ENDDO                             a(2*i*m) = ...
                  a(k) = ...                      ENDDO
                ENDDO
                                  (c)


                                          DIMENSION a(10000), a0(2:30)
                                     !$OMP PARALLEL
                                     !$OMP+PRIVATE(A0,K,TPINIT,I)
                                          DO tpinit = 2, 30, 1
                                            a0(tpinit) = 0.0
     DIMENSION a(10000)                   ENDDO
     ...                             !$OMP DO
     DO k = 1, 10                         DO k = 1, 10, 1
       DO i = 1, imax                       DO i = 1, imax, 1
         a(3*k) = a(3*k) + 3.14*i             a0(3*k) = a0(3*k)+3.14*i
       ENDDO                                ENDDO
       DO i = 1, 1000           ->          DO i = 1, 1000, 1
         a(2*k) = a(2*k) + 3.14*i             a0(2*k) = a0(2*k)+3.14*i
       ENDDO                                ENDDO
     ENDDO                                ENDDO
                                     !$OMP END DO NOWAIT
                                     !$OMP CRITICAL
                                          DO tpinit = 2, 30, 1
                                            a(tpinit) = a(tpinit)+a0(tpinit)
                                          ENDDO
                                     !$OMP END CRITICAL
                                     !$OMP END PARALLEL
                                  (d)
```

**Fig. 1.** The Range Propagation technique and its applications. (a) Contents of the range dictionary. (b) Loop that can be parallelized with the Range Test. (c) Induction variable substitution. (d) Reduction transformation.

collects additional information from all assignment statements. Figure 1(a) shows an example code and the contents of the range dictionary.

One objective of this study is to determine the effectiveness of the range dictionary. The Polaris compiler currently uses range dictionary information to detect zero-trip loops in the induction variable substitution pass, to determine array sections referenced by array accesses in the reduction parallelization pass, and to compare symbolic expressions in the Range Test. Figure 1(c) illustrates the case of induction variable substitution. Suppose the range dictionary for the shown code section keeps the range for the variable m, which is also the upper bound of the loop L2. If it is possible to prove that m is greater than or equal to one, based on range dictionary information, the loop L2 is not a zero-trip loop, and induction variable substitution can be applied safely in the array a, as shown in the right-hand side code. Otherwise, the compiler keeps the original code or generates multi-version loops.

The Polaris compiler is able to recognize array reductions and translate them into parallel form [11]. *Privatized Reductions* is one possible translation variant, shown in Figure 1(d). The range information for k was used to determine the accessed region of array a. This information is then used as the dimension of the private copy a0, and for the bounds of the preamble and postamble loop of the parallel reduction operation. If the range information were not available,

Polaris would use the declared dimension of the array a instead, which may be too large, causing overhead in the preamble and the postamble.

The most important application of range analysis is the Range Test. The test performs many comparisons between symbolic expressions in order to analyze array subscripts. The comparison procedure determines the arithmetic relationship of two expressions by examining the difference of the two expressions. If the difference contains a symbolic expression, the range information of that expression is searched in the range dictionary. Figure 1(b) shows a simple example. Since the possible value of j is either one or two, the Range Test can determine that there is no loop-carried dependence in the statement S1.

## 2.2 Expression Propagation

By propagating the expression assigned to a variable to the variable's use sites, symbolic expressions can deliver more accurate information. Polaris can propagate constant integer, constant logical, and symbolic expressions within a procedure and across procedures. Real-valued expressions can also be propagated, but this option is switched off by default.

Before analyzing individual subroutines, Polaris performs interprocedural expression propagation, during which assignments to propagated expressions are inserted at the top of each procedure. Then, these expressions are propagated to possible call sites. This process iterates until no new expressions are discovered. Subroutine cloning is performed during this process, if the same subroutine is called with two different expressions.

Intraprocedural expression propagation is performed on each subroutine after the induction variable substitution pass. This Polaris pass introduces variables for which propagation can be important, as our measurements will show. However, other than this effect, intraprocedural expression propagation is essentially subsumed by intraprocedural and range propagation. As mentioned earlier, this technique can also propagate real-valued expressions and array expressions. We will include this option in our measurements as well.

## 2.3 Symbolic Expression Simplification

The simplification of symbolic expressions is important, as compiler–manipulated expressions tend to increase in complexity, making them difficult to analyze. Nearly all Polaris passes make use of expression simplifier functions. For instance, the procedure performing symbolic expression comparison assumes that the two expressions are reduced to their simplest form. Polaris provides the following three simplifying techniques for symbolic expressions:

- Combine: A+4*A -> 5*A
- Distribute: A*(3+B) -> 3*A+A*B
- Divide: 3*A/A -> 3

# 3    Experimental Methodology

The fully-optimized programs serve as the baseline of our measurements. Starting from these programs, we disabled each compiler technique individually. For techniques that contain several levels of optimization, we took measurements with increasing levels. We compared the resulting, transformed code with the base code to examine the difference in the number of parallelized loops, and we measured the overall program performance of the parallel programs. In order to understand the performance impact of the techniques on the programs before parallel code generation, we also measured the performance of the transformed programs executed sequentially (i.e., without OpenMP translation).

## 3.1    Benchmark Suite

Table 1 shows our benchmark suite. We selected scientific/engineering programs written in Fortran77 from the floating point benchmarks in SPEC CPU95, from the Perfect Benchmarks and from the serial version of NAS Parallel Benchmarks. We chose the SPEC CPU95 over CPU2000 codes because Polaris requires Fortran77 input. All SPEC CPU2000 Fortran77 programs are present in the SPEC CPU95 suite. Since they are essentially the same codes, we expect that the results in terms of the number of parallelized loops would be the same for the SPEC CPU2000 codes. However, the speedup of the parallel programs is expected to be higher for the SPEC CPU2000 compared to the CPU95 codes, due to the larger input data sizes. Several Perfect Benchmarks with their original input data sets execute in only a few seconds on today's machines. Therefore we have increased the problem sizes of ARC2D and TRFD. Among the four NAS benchmarks written in Fortran77, we found that symbolic analysis makes a difference only in MD. We included this code in our figures.

## 3.2    Set-Up and Metrics

The Polaris compiler outputs parallel programs written in OpenMP, which we compiled using the Forte compiler to generate code for Sun workstations. We used a four-processor shared-memory Sun E-450 system for our experiments. The following shows all settings for this experiment. The compiler flag "-stackvar" allocates all local variables on the stack, and "-mt" is needed for multithreaded code.

**Table 1.** Benchmark suite

| Code | # Lines | Serial time | Code | # Lines | Serial time |
|---|---|---|---|---|---|
| APSI | 7361 | 57.8 | TURB3D | 2100 | 183.6 |
| HYDRO2D | 4292 | 80.3 | WAVE5 | 7764 | 96.3 |
| MGRID | 484 | 54.5 | ARC2D | 4650 | 55.1 |
| SU2COR | 2332 | 55.0 | MDG | 1430 | 27.1 |
| SWIM | 429 | 84.7 | TRFD | 580 | 126.0 |
| TOMCATV | 190 | 96.1 | MG | 1460 | 57.4 |

| | |
|---|---|
| - CPU: 480 MHz UltraSPARC II | - Number of processors: 4 |
| - Memory: 4GB | - Operating System: SunOS 5.8 |
| - Compiler: Forte 6.1 | - Compiler flags: -fast -stackvar -mt -openmp |

We use the overall program speedup – serial execution time of the original code divided by parallel execution time of the transformed code – as a metric for presenting the performance of the programs, and also briefly describe the features of the transformed codes, such as the number of parallelized loops to explain the quality of the transformed codes.

## 4   Results and Analysis

### 4.1   Impact on Sequential Execution of Transformed Programs

In a first experiment, we ran all transformed benchmarks without compiling OpenMP directives and compared them with the original programs. In this way, we could observe the effect of each technique on the performance before parallel code generation. Such effects are due to (1) direct changes of the source code by the techniques and (2) affected restructuring transformations. Our expression propagation techniques are implemented such that they perform direct substitutions of the source code. Also, the expression simplification techniques affect the programs directly. Among the restructuring transformations that are affected by symbolic analysis are induction variable substitution and reduction transformations. Understanding these performance effects is important because they represent degradation that is not a result of the parallel execution or lack thereof.

We found that expression propagation can introduce overhead. For example, expression propagation made a statement longer than a hundred lines in APSI, disabling code generation by the backend compiler. TURB3D ran 144% longer because of the overhead from expression propagation. SU2COR increased by 9%. All other programs showed no more than 5% overhead after program transformation.

We found that the expression simplification technique is necessary for many benchmarks. For instance, TRFD ran 240% longer after disabling the combining functionality for simplification. That means that, without this technique, the restructured program would run so inefficiently that it would offset much of the gain from parallel execution.

Another interesting situation is the reduction transformation. Sometimes, this transformation is expensive because of inefficient preamble and postamble, as shown in Figure 1(d). This happened after certain compiler techniques were disabled in our experiments, resulting in insufficient information for data dependence analysis. We deal with that situation further in the following subsection.

In order to observe the effect of each compiler technique on the parallel program performance, we ran all benchmarks on four processors. We describe the result of the experiments category by category in the following subsections.

### 4.2   Range Analysis

Table 2 shows the characteristics of the transformed codes, with enabled/disabled techniques that relate to range analysis. The figures in each column represent

**Table 2.** Number of parallel loops with and without range analysis. RT stands for Range Test. The figures in each colum describe: "total (lost outer-level)" parallel loops. "=" means the code is identical with the base code, The "No AIRD" row shows the results with no AI range dictionary used; in "No RD" both the AI and the control range dictionary are switched off; The last row "No RT" serves as a reference showing the effect of disabling the Range Test.

| Code | APSI | HYDRO2D | MGRID | SU2COR | SWIM | TOMCATV | TURB3D | WAVE5 | ARC2D | MDG | TRFD | MG |
|------|------|---------|-------|--------|------|---------|--------|-------|-------|-----|------|-----|
| Base | 141 | 92 | 10 | 54 | 16 | 6 | 24 | 185 | 126 | 20 | 5 | 35 |
| No AIRD | 141(2) | = | = | = | = | = | = | 185(2) | = | 20 | 5 | = |
| No RD | 139(10) | 92(3) | = | = | = | = | 24 | 181 | = | 19(2) | 11(2) | 35(7) |
| No RT | 122(7) | 89 | 8 | 44 | 7 | = | 22 | 160(7) | 125 | 13(1) | 8(2) | 24(2) |

the total number of parallel loops in the program. The numbers in parentheses explain how many outer level parallel loops were lost. For example, without the range dictionary, Polaris found 92 parallel loops in HYDRO2D. Although the base code and the code with disabled range dictionary have the same number of parallel loops, three outer–level loops could no longer be found parallel.

As expected, many programs benefit from the Range Test, since it is the only advanced data-dependence test used in Polaris. (Polaris also includes an optional Omega test. The performance when using this test instead of the Range Test is essentially the same as the "No RD" version.) More importantly, the table shows that the computation of full range information using the AI range dictionary is necessary only for APSI and WAVE5. This means that the relatively inexpensive control range dictionary is sufficient for Polaris to analyze the other codes. The table further shows that half of the benchmark codes do not need any range information – they can still be analyzed as accurately as the fully-optimized code. Although many subscripts contain symbolic terms, these terms cancel out in comparison operations. For example, the two expressions i+m-3 and i+m+5 can be compared by the test without the need for range information.

Figure 2 shows the program performance on four processors. Three programs APSI, WAVE5, and TURB3D achieved speedup less than one. This is due to the fact that we have used the "eager parallelization scheme" in Polaris. That is, the compiler is conservative in its profitability analysis – it avoids the parallelization of small parallel loops only if there is a provable disadvantage. This is appropriate for our study, where we are interested in the compiler's ability or inability to detect parallelism. In addition, TURB3D is included without advanced interprocedural analysis, which could improve the performance of the code significantly, but was not yet available in our version of Polaris.

In terms of program performance, four benchmarks, HYDRO2D, WAVE5, MDG and TRFD, benefit from the range dictionary. The code section in Figure 3 shows the case that needs range analysis in HYDRO2D. This loop accounts for 5% of the serial execution time, and is the main factor of the performance difference. After induction variable substitution, the array tst contains symbolic subscripts i-mq+j*mq. The range information for the variable mq (mq>=1) enables the Range Test to compare expressions such as j*mq and 1-mq+(j-1)*mq, allowing the compiler to

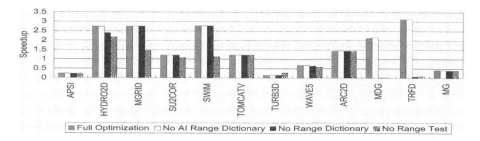

**Fig. 2.** Program performance with and without Range Analysis

```
   k = 0
   DO j = 1,nq                              DO j = 1,nq
      DO i = 1,mq                              DO i = 1,mq
         ...                         ->            ...
         k = k + 1                               tst(i-mq+j*mq) = DMIN1(tcz, tcr)
         tst(k) = DMIN1(tcz, tcr)            ENDDO
      ENDDO                                ENDDO
   ENDDO
```

**Fig. 3.** Need for range dictionary in HYDRO2D

disprove the output dependence on `tst`. The performance gain after disabling the Range Test in `TURB3D` comes from not parallelizing small loops.

The phenomenal performance loss in `MDG` comes from an inefficient reduction transformation. Remarkably, `INTERF_do1000` and `POTENG_do2000`, the most time-consuming loops in `MDG`, were parallelized even without the Range Test. However, a small other loop was transformed very inefficiently without Range Analysis. The loop looks like a reduction operation, but is a fully parallel loop. This fact can be detected by the Range Test with range dictionary information. However, without range information, the loop ends up being transformed as an array reduction, which is highly inefficient due to large pre/postambles in this case. The graph indicates the control range dictionary is sufficient to detect the explicit parallelism in the loop. In `TRFD`, Polaris was unable to parallelize the two most time-consuming loops without any range dictionary. Instead, many small inner loops were parallelized, causing significant performance degradation.

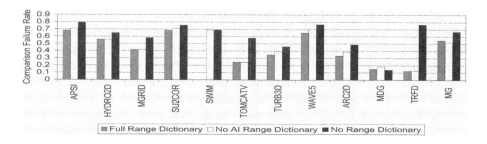

**Fig. 4.** Expression comparison failure rate

**Table 3.** Cost of range anlaysis. (a) Percent compilation time of range analysis. The analysis time spans from 0.63 seconds to 153 seconds with full range dictionary, and from 0.38 seconds to 21 seconds only with control range dictionary. (b) Normalized memory requirement (1=No range analysis). The memory requirement spans from 33 Megabytes to 266 Megabytes with full range dictionary, and from 33 Megabytes to 125 Megabytes only with control range dictionary.

(a)

| Code | APSI | HYDRO2D | MGRID | SU2COR | SWIM | TOMCATV | TURB3D | WAVE5 | ARC2D | MDG | TRFD | MG |
|---|---|---|---|---|---|---|---|---|---|---|---|---|
| Full | 27.0 | 16.8 | 6.8 | 5.9 | 14.9 | 9.9 | 7.0 | 9.4 | 15.6 | 13.4 | 17.8 | 8.4 |
| Control | 3.1 | 9.5 | 1.6 | 2.0 | 6.6 | 8.6 | 2.7 | 3.6 | 4.7 | 4.3 | 7.1 | 2.4 |

(b)

| | | | | | | | | | | | | |
|---|---|---|---|---|---|---|---|---|---|---|---|---|
| Full | 2.13 | 1 | 1 | 1.06 | 1 | 1 | 1 | 1.05 | 1.07 | 1.12 | 1 | 1.15 |
| Control | 1 | 1 | 1 | 1.01 | 1 | 1 | 1 | 1 | 1 | 1.02 | 1 | 1.02 |

The results in this section indicate that Range Analysis is performance-critical for a small set of benchmarks only. Figure 4 shows that the range information affects the compiler, nevertheless. It presents the failure rate of expression comparison during the Range Test. It clearly shows that Polaris is able to make better decisions, thanks to range information, in all but one program. In MDG, the number of comparisons is less without the Range Dictionary. The lack of range information made several monotonicity tests fail during the Range Test, making further comparisons useless. MG has more comparison failures with full range analysis because it creates more complex expressions in the range dictionary. While there could be a simple fix in this case, it points out a generic issue. Advanced program analysis tends to generate more complex compiler-internal representations, necessitating more powerful manipulation algorithms.

Table 3 shows the cost of range analysis. In many programs the analysis takes a significant fraction of the overall execution time of the compiler. Full range analysis is significantly more expensive than the analysis based on the control range dictionary. Given the limited benefit from full range analysis, this simpler form of analysis may be preferable for practical compiler implementations. On the other hand, the additional memory requirement for full range analysis is small, except for a 213% increase in APSI.

### 4.3   Expression Propagation

The effects of expression propagation on the benchmark codes are presented in Table 4. Interprocedural propagation helped Polaris find more parallel loops in MDG and TRFD. Moreover, additional intraprocedural expression propagation was essential in finding outer-level parallelism in TRFD. The reason is that the potential dependence caused by a variable introduced by induction variable substitution was disproved by propagating information to the use site of that variable. For the benchmark APSI, interprocedural expression propagation provided information that helped the compiler recognize that an outermost loop had only one iteration and serialize this loop. This explains why Table 4 shows more outer-level parallelism *without* that technique.

**Table 4.** Number of parallel loops with and without expression propagation. "*" means outer-level parallelism. Expression propagation was not applied to the base code for WAVE5.

| Code | APSI | HYDRO2D | MGRID | SU2COR | SWIM | TOMCATV | TURB3D | ARC2D | MDG | TRFD | MG |
|------|------|---------|-------|--------|------|---------|--------|-------|-----|------|-----|
| Base | 141 | 92 | 10 | 54 | 16 | 6 | 24 | 126 | 20 | 5 | 35 |
| No IntraEP | 141 | = | = | 54 | = | = | 24 | = | 20 | 6(1) | = |
| No InterEP | 141(*1) | 92 | 10 | 54 | 16 | = | 25 | 126 | 17 | 8(2) | 35(2) |
| No EP | 141(5,*1) | 92 | 10 | 54 | 16 | = | 25 | 126 | 17 | 8(2) | 35(2) |

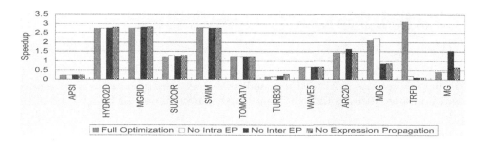

**Fig. 5.** Program performance with and without expression propagation

In MDG and TRFD, expression propagation improved performance, as presented in Figure 5. The most time-consuming loops POTENG_do2000 in MDG and OLDA_do100 and OLDA_do300 in TRFD were not parallelized without interprocedural expression propagation and even without additional intraprocedural expression propagation for the case of TRFD. However, expression propagation does not make much difference in terms of execution time for the SPEC benchmarks. For some benchmarks, the actual substitution of the propagated expression incurred a slight overhead because of the increased strength of the operation. Using 1+i1+2**(6+(-2)*1)+k1*2**(7+(-2)*1) instead of i1+i120 a huge number of times in TURB3D is an example of the potential disadvantage of expression propagation.

The OpenMP translation of Polaris is responsible for the odd behavior of ARC2D when interprocedural expression propagation was disabled. The code section in Figure 6(a) accounts for the performance difference. The left-hand-side code was generated with interprocedural expression propagation, whereas the right-hand-side code was generated without this technique. Both outermost loops are parallel. Polaris detected the original array work as private. Expression propagation helps Polaris determine that only an array subrange of size jmax, where jmax is definied in the subroutine, is actually needed as private. Since OpenMP does not support partial arrays to be declared private, Polaris chooses to allocate from the heap a smaller array and use array expansion rather than privatization. Unfortunately, this turns out to perform less than privatizing the full array in this case.

```
       SUBROUTINE filery(jdim, ...)                    SUBROUTINE filery(jdim, ...)
       ...                                             ...
       jdim = jmax                             !$OMP+PRIVATE(..., work)
       ...                                             ...
       ALLOCATE (work0(1:jdim, ...))                 DO n = 1, 4
       DO n = 1, 4                                     DO k = kbegin, kup
         DO k = 1, kmax-1                                DO j = jlow, jup
           DO j = jlow, jup                                work(j,k,i) = ...
             work0(j,k,1,my_cpu_id) = ...                 ...
       ...
                                          (a)
       !$OMP PARALLEL                                  DO j = 2, ju-jl, 1
             DO j = 2, ju-jl, 1                          jx = ju+(-jl)
       !$OMP DO                                  !$OMP PARALLEL
             DO k = 2, ku, 1                     !$OMP DO
               f(ju+(-j), k) = ...                      DO k = kl, ku, 1
               ... = f(2+ju+(-j), k)                      f(jx, k) = ...
             ENDDO                                        ... = f(2+jx, k)
       !$OMP END DO NOWAIT                              ENDDO
             ENDDO                              !$OMP END DO NOWAIT
       !$OMP END PARALLEL                       !$OMP END PARALLEL
                                                      ENDDO
                                          (b)
```

**Fig. 6.** Code sections of ARC2D with and without expression propagation. (a) Privatization in subroutine FILERY (b) Loop blocking in subroutine XPENTA.

**Table 5.** Number of parallel loops with and without expression simplifier. SU2COR could not be parallelized without combining functionality.

| Code | APSI | HYDRO2D | MGRID | SU2COR | SWIM | TOMCATV | TURB3D | WAVE5 | ARC2D | MDG | TRFD | MG |
|------|------|---------|-------|--------|------|---------|--------|-------|-------|-----|------|-----|
| Base | 141 | 92 | 10 | 54 | 16 | 6 | 24 | 185 | 126 | 20 | 5 | 35 |
| No Divide | = | 92 | = | 54 | = | = | 24 | 185 | = | = | 6(1) | = |
| No Distribute | 130(15) | 92(3) | 8 | 48 | = | 6 | 23 | 177(7) | 125 | 15(2) | 11(2) | 31(8) |
| No Combine | 121(11) | 89 | 8 | N/A | 7 | 6 | 22 | 156(11) | 129(1) | 13(2) | 9(2) | 24(4) |

However, without expression propagation, there were four loop nests where the outer loop was no longer parallel, setting off the performance gain in Figure 6(a). Those four loops have similar shapes. Figure 6(b) shows one of them. With expression propagation, the compiler could substitute jx with ju-j and remove the assignment to jx, making it possible to do loop-blocking utilizing OpenMP directives. The subroutine containing this loop is called 400 times, and the value of ju-jl is 288, making the number of fork-joins in the right-hand side loop 114799 more than that of the left-hand side loop. MG speeds up only with intraprocedural expression propagation. In other configurations, the parallelizer performs reduction transformation that introduces huge overhead in preambles/postambles.

We have also measured the effectiveness of more specific options of expression propagation. These are the propagation of array expressions and propagation of real expressions. The base code was generated with array expression propagation and without real expression propagation. In general, the effects of these techniques are negligible compared to other techniques examined in this section. However, we have seen code examples where propagation generated very long expressions, which is undesirable.

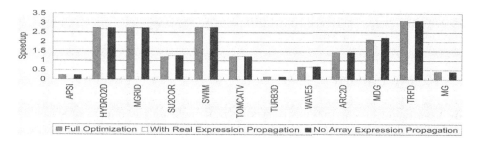

**Fig. 7.** Program performance with and without expression propagation

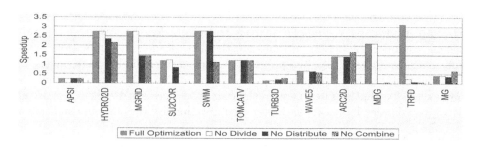

**Fig. 8.** Program performance with and without expression simplifier

## 4.4 Expression Simplifier

In general, the symbolic expression simplifier turned out to be important. This
is because nearly all passes implemented in Polaris use that functionality. For instance, the Range Test assumes the two expressions to be compared are in their
simplest form before the comparison. Table 5 shows the effects of this technique
on the benchmark codes. The combining capability plays a more important role
in helping the Range Test than the other two capabilities, because it performs
the actual simplification in the expression manipulation. On the other hand, can-
celing common factors in the denominator and the numerator does not happen
frequently, so the effect was negligible, except for TRFD.

Figure 8 shows the overall performance of each program without the expression simplifier. As we have seen in this section, TRFD again shows an extreme
performance loss. For TURB3D, disabling the simplifier resulted in serializing small
loops with a performance gain.

An important additional consideration is the expression simplifier's impact on
memory usage during program analysis. Polaris could not fully analyze SU2COR
with expression simplification turned off because it exhausted its swap space
(2 GB).

As in the case without expression propagation, ARC2D shows odd behavior
without the combining capability. It turned out that the code section responsible
for this behavior runs faster with inner-level parallelism, which is not true in general. Without the combining capability, the compiler could only find inner-level

parallelism, which happened to perform better because of insufficient number of iterations at the outer level.

## 5   Related Work

We have found no comprehensive studies that measure the impact of symbolic analysis techniques, as presented in this study. However, a number of projects have developed compile-time symbolic analysis techniques similar to those considered in this paper. Haghighat and Polychronopoulos proposed a methodology for the discovery of certain program properties that are essential in the effective detection and efficient exploitation of parallelism [6]. The authors' methodology was implemented as a symbolic analysis framework for the Parafrase-2 parallelizing compiler. Induction variable substitution, dead-code elimination, symbolic data dependence test, and program performance prediction were suggested as possible analysis techniques that could benefit from the symbolic analysis framework. The authors also showed their analyzer performed well, especially in detecting complex induction variables such as induction variables in conditional statements.

Fahringer proposed symbolic analysis techniques to be used as part of a parallelizing compiler and a performance estimator for optimization of parallel programs [7]. He suggested an algorithm for computing lower and upper bounds of symbolic expressions based on a set of constraints, to be used in comparing symbolic expressions, simplifying systems of constraints, examining non-linear array subscript expressions for data dependences, and optimizing communications. Another functionality he suggested is the capability of estimating the number of integer solutions to a system of constraints, which can be used to support detection of zero-trip loops, elimination of dead code, and performance prediction of parallel programs. His techniques were implemented for the Vienna Fortran Compilation System (VFCS), a High-Performance-Fortran-style parallelizing compiler. His technique for comparing symbolic expressions enabled hoisting communication out of loop nests in FTRVMT, a dominant loop in OCEAN.

There were also efforts to analyze symbolic expressions across procedure boundaries. Havlak constructed interprocedural symbolic analysis mechanisms as an infrastructure for the Parascope compilation system [8]. His analysis is based on the program representation in Thinned-gated single-assignment (TGSA) form – an extended form of Static single-assignment (SSA), and operates interprocedurally by relating a call graph to each value graph for a procedure. During the analysis, information such as passed values, returned values, array subscripts and bounds, loop bounds, and predicates are considered. The effectiveness of his technique was measured only by comparing dependence graphs.

Recent research deals with symbolic analysis by formulating it as a system of constraints. Pugh and Wonnacott's research on nonlinear array dependence analysis [12,14] suggested a method of obtaining certain conditions under which a dependence exists. Value-based dependence analysis, which delivers more accurate information, was also described by a set of constraints, and the author suggested uninterpreted function symbols as a way of representing non-affine terms that could exist during dependence analysis. Rugina and Rinard's work on symbolic bound analysis [15] proposed a scheme to compute symbolic bounds for each pointer and array index variable at each program point, and to compute a set of symbolic regions that a procedure accesses. They reduced the systems of constraints to linear programs to obtain symbolic bounds.

## 6 Conclusion

We have measured the impact of symbolic analysis techniques, specifically range propagation, expression propagation, and symbolic expression simplification. Using several SPEC CPU95, Perfect, and NAS benchmarks we have analyzed the techniques' ability to help recognize parallelism and improve program performance.

We have found that all techniques make a significant difference in at least one of the programs. Expression simplification is important for most programs, while full range propagation does not affect the program performance substantially. Somewhat unexpected, interprocedural expression propagation was only relevant for two of the programs. More complex programs are affected more significantly. Symbolic analysis effects performance the most in the Perfect Benchmarks and the least in the NAS benchmarks. This suggests that the techniques will impact full-scale applications more significantly than measured in our experiments.

In our analysis we found that secondary effects of symbolic analysis techniques can make a performance difference. For example, in several program sections, the techniques helped recognize parallel loops that were too small to improve performance and introduced overhead instead. Improved performance estimation capabilities could help remedy these situations and would thus be important complements of advanced program analysis techniques.

We found that the simpler form of range propagation, which derives information from control statements only, had the same effect as full range analysis in all but one programs. In terms of the resulting program performance, the two forms of range analysis were equivalent. Furthermore, full range analysis consumed significantly more compile time. These findings are significant, as they will allow compiler developers to implement advanced optimization techniques that rely on symbolic analysis without high compile-time expenses. It holds in particular for the Range Test, which is able to analyze data dependences in the presence of nonlinear and symbolic subscripts.

## References

1. W. Blume and R. Eigenmann. An overview of symbolic analysis techniques needed for the effective parallelization of the perfect benchmarks. In *Proceedings of the 1994 International Conference on Parallel Processing*, pages 233–238, August 1994.
2. W. Blume, R. Doallo, R. Eigenmann, J. G. J. Hoeflinger, T. Lawrence, J. Lee, D. Padua, Y. Paek, B. Pottenger, L. Rauchwerger, and P. Tu. Parallel programming with polaris. *IEEE Computer*, pages 78–82, December 1996.

3. W. Blume and R. Eigenmann. Symbolic range propagation. In *Proceedings of the 9th International Parallel Processing Symposium*, pages 357–363, Santa Barbara, CA, April 1995.

4. W. Blume and R. Eigenmann. Nonlinear and symbolic data dependence testing. *IEEE Transactions on Parallel and Distributed Systems*, 9(12):1180–1194, December 1998.

5. P. Tu and D. A. Padua. Gated SSA-based demand-driven symbolic analysis for parallelizing compilers. In *Proceedings of the 1995 International Conference on Supercomputing*, pages 414–423, 1995.

6. M. R. Haghighat and C. D. Polychronopoulos. Symbolic analysis for parallelizing compilers. *ACM Transactions on Programming Languages and Systems*, 18(4):477–518, July 1996.

7. T. Fahringer. Efficient symbolic analysis for parallelizing compilers and performance estimators. *The Journal of Supercomputing*, 12(3):227–252, May 1998.

8. P. Havlak. *Interprocedural Symbolic Analysis*. PhD thesis, Dept. of Computer Science, Rice University, May 1994.

9. W. Blume and R. Eigenmann. Demand-driven symbolic range propagation. In *Proceedings of the 8th Workshop on Languages and Compilers for Parallel Computing*, pages 141–160, Columbus, OH, 1995.

10. P. Cousot and R. Cousot. Abstract interpretation: A unified lattice model for static analysis of programs by construction or approximation of fixpoints. In *Proceedings of 4th ACM Symposium*, pages 238–252, 1977.

11. W. M. Pottenger and R. Eigenmann. Idiom recognition in the polaris parallelizing compiler. In *Proceedings of the 9th International Conference on Supercomputing*, pages 444–448, 1995.

12. W. Pugh and D. Wonnacott. Nonlinear Array Dependence Analysis. In *Proceedings of 3rd Workshop on Languages, Compilers and Run-Time Systems for Scalable Computers*, November 1994.

13. V. Aslot and R. Eigenmann. Performance characteristics of the spec omp2001 benchmarks. In *Proceedings of the 3rd European Workshop on OpenMP (EWOMP'2001)*, Barcelona, Spain, September 2001.

14. W. Pugh and D. Wonnacott. Constraint-based array dependence analysis. *ACM Transactions on Programming Languages and Systems*, 20(3):635–678, May 1998.

15. R. Rugina and M. C. Rinard. Symbolic bounds analysis of pointers, array indices, and accessed memory regions. In *Proceedings of the SIGPLAN Conference on Programming Language Design and Implementation*, pages 182–195, Vancouver, Canada, June 2000.

# Efficient Manipulation of Disequalities During Dependence Analysis

Robert Seater and David Wonnacott

Haverford College, Haverford, PA 19041
davew@cs.haverford.edu
http://www.cs.haverford.edu/people/davew/index.html

**Abstract.** Constraint-based frameworks can provide a foundation for efficient algorithms for analysis and transformation of regular scientific programs. For example, we recently demonstrated that constraint-based analysis of both memory- and value-based array dependences can often be performed in polynomial time. Many of the cases that could not be processed with our polynomial-time algorithm involved negated equality constraints (also known as *disequalities*).

In this report, we review the sources of disequality constraints in array dependence analysis and give an efficient algorithm for manipulating certain disequality constraints. Our approach differs from previous work in that it performs efficient satisfiability tests in the presence of disequalities, rather than deferring satisfiability tests until more constraints are available, performing a potentially exponential transformation, or approximating. We do not (yet) have an implementation of our algorithms, or empirical verification that our test is either fast or useful, but we do provide a polynomial time bound and give our reasons for optimism regarding its applicability.

## 1 Introduction

Constraint-based frameworks can provide a foundation for efficient algorithms for analysis and transformation of "regular scientific programs" (programs in which the most significant calculations are performed on arrays with simple subscript patterns, enclosed in nested loops). For example, the detection of memory-based array data dependences is equivalent to testing the satisfiability of a conjunction of constraints on integer variables. The individual constraints may be equalities (such as $i = j + 1$), inequalities (such as $1 \leq i \leq N$), and occasionally disequalities (such as $i \neq j$). (For a discussion of the Omega Test's constraint-based approach to both memory-based (aliasing) and value-based (dataflow) dependence analysis, see [1,2].)

Satisfiability testing of a conjunction of inequality constraints on integer variables ("integer linear programming") is NP-complete [3], and value-based dependence analysis introduces the further complexity of negative constraints. One might not expect that the constraint-based approach to dependence analysis could yield an efficient algorithm, but empirical tests (such as [1]) have found

B. Pugh and C.-W. Tseng (Eds.): LCPC 2002, LNCS 2481, pp. 295–308, 2005.

these techniques to be efficient in practice. We recently investigated the reasons for this efficiency [2], and found that most constraints come from a simpler domain for which polynomial-time satisfiability testing is possible.

While it is possible to construct an arbitrarily complicated integer linear programming problem via memory-based dependence analysis [4], almost all of the problems that arise are conjunctions of equality and inequality constraints from the *LI(2)-unit* subdomain. An inequality constraint is said to be in the *LI(2)* subdomain if it can be expressed in the form $ai + bj + c \geq 0$. It is said to be in *LI(2)-unit* if $a, b \in \{-1, 0, 1\}$. The existing Omega Library algorithms [5] perform satisfiability testing of conjunctions of LI(2)-unit inequality and equality constraints in polynomial time.

Negative constraints, even within the LI(2)-unit subdomain, can also cause exponential behavior of the Omega Library. However, almost all of the conjunctions of constraints that are negated during value-based dependence analysis are so redundant (with respect to other constraints) that the Omega Test can replace them with a single inequality (for example, $1 \leq i \leq N \wedge \neg(i = 1 \wedge 1 \leq N)$ will be converted to $1 \leq i \leq N \wedge \neg(i \leq 1)$, and then to $2 \leq i \leq N$ ). As long as each negated conjunction can be replaced with a single inequality (and the individual constraints are still LI(2)-unit), the Omega Test performs value-based dependence testing in polynomial time.

Many of the cases that could not be processed with our polynomial-time algorithm involved conjunctions of *disequalities* (negated equality constraints). Disequalities can be produced by disequalities in `if` statements, by equality tests in `if-else` statements, during the negation step of value-based analysis, or when an uninterpreted function symbol is used to represent a non-linear term.

Disequalities can be converted into disjunctions of inequalities ($\alpha \neq \beta \Leftrightarrow (\alpha < \beta \vee \alpha > \beta)$). However, when this is followed by conversion to disjunctive normal form, the size of the problem increases exponentially. Lassez and McAloon [6] observed that, for constraints on real variables, disequalities are *independent*. That is, if no one disequality eliminates all solutions, there is no way for a finite number of disequalities to *add up* and together make the system unsatisfiable. Unfortunately, it is in general possible for disequalities to add up for constraint systems with integer variables. We have developed an algorithm to identify disequalities that cannot add up despite our use of integer variables. We call such disequalities *inert*, and use the term *ert* for disequalities that can add up. Satisfiability testing of $r$ inert disequalities can be handled with $2r$ satisfiability tests of conjunctions of inequalities, rather than the $2^r$ needed for ert disequalities.

This paper is organized as follows: Section 2 provides formal definitions of inert and ert disequalities, and gives the (very simple) algorithm for satisfiability testing. Section 3 gives our inertness test, and Section 4 discusses the impact it would have on the data structures used in the Omega Library. Section 5 gives the reasons why we believe the test would be useful during dependence analysis. Section 6 discusses related work, and Section 7 presents our conclusions.

## 2   Inert (and Ert) Disequality Constraints

From this point on, we consider satisfiability testing of a conjunction of $m$ inequalities and $k$ disequalities on $n$ integer variables. In practice, we may manipulate a mixture of equality, inequality, and disequality constraints, but we ignore equalities here in the interest of simplicity (we could, in principle, convert each equality into a conjunction of inequalities).

Any disequality constraint $\alpha \neq \beta$ can be treated as a disjunction of inequalities $(\alpha < \beta \lor \alpha > \beta)$. However, a satisfiability test of a conjunction of $m$ inequalities and $k$ disequalities using this approach involves $2^k$ satisfiability tests of conjunctions of $m + k$ inequality constraints (after conversion to disjunctive normal form).

Lassez and McAloon [6] observed that, for constraints on real variables, disequalities are *independent*. That is, if no one disequality eliminates all solutions, there is no way for a finite number of disequalities to add up and together make the system unsatisfiable. Thus, satisfiability testing of a conjunction of $m$ inequalities and $k$ disequalities on real variables can be treated as $2k$ satisfiability tests of $m + 1$ inequalities.

Unfortunately, disequality constraints on integer variables can add up. For example, the three disequalities shown (as dashed lines) in Figure 1a together eliminate all integer solutions in the grey region bounded by the three inequalities (solid lines). In Figure 1b, a collection of four disequalities parallel to the bounding inequalities could eliminate all integer solutions. However, no finite set of disequalities can add up to eliminate all integer solutions in Figure 1c, and disequalities that are not parallel to the bounding inequalities cannot be important in eliminating all integer solutions in Figure 1b. Thus, the opportunity for disequalities to add up depends on the nature of the inequalities and disequalities.

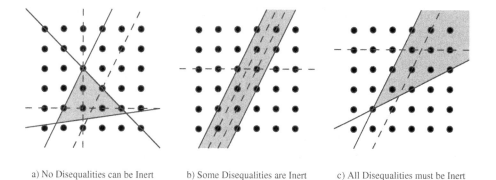

a) No Disequalities can be Inert         b) Some Disequalities are Inert         c) All Disequalities must be Inert

**Fig. 1.** Inertness of Disequalities on Integer Variables

We therefore give the following definitions:

Given a feasible conjunction of inequalities $C$ and relevant disequality $d$,

We say $d$ is **inert in C** if, for any finite conjunction of disequalities $D$, $C \wedge d \wedge D$ is satisfiable $\Leftrightarrow$ both $C \wedge d$ and $C \wedge D$ are satisfiable.

Otherwise, we say that $d$ is **ert in C**.

Note that inertness is not defined when $C$ is infeasible or $d$ is not relevant (in the sense used by Lassez and McAloon [6], i.e. $d$ is relevant if $C \wedge \neg d$ is satisfiable). Our algorithm for satisfiability testing of a conjunction of inequality and disequality constraints follows immediately from this definition:

1. Let $C$ be the inequality constraints and $D$ the disequalities.
2. Test $C$ for satisfiability. If $C$ is unsatisfiable, $C \wedge D$ must be unsatisfiable, so return *false*.
3. Optionally, test each $d \in D$ for relevance (by testing satisfiability of $C \wedge \neg d$), and discard irrelevant disequalities. Note that irrelevant disequalities may be treated as either inert or ert without affecting the result.
4. Test each $d \in D$ for inertness.
5. For each inert disequality $i \in D$, test the satisfiability of $C \wedge i$. If $C \wedge i$ is unsatisfiable, $C \wedge D$ must be unsatisfiable, so return *false*.
6. Let $E$ be the conjunction of all ert disequalities in $D$. Test $C \wedge E$ for satisfiability by treating each $e \in E$ as a disjunction of inequalities. Return the result of this test (if $D$ contains no ert disequalities, return *true*).

Thus, if we can perform polynomial-time tests for (a) the inertness of a disequality (in Step 4), and (b) the satisfiability of a conjunction of inequalities (in Steps 2, 3, and 5), the overall algorithm is polynomial in the number of inequalities and inert disequalities. The test is still exponential in the presence of ert disequalities (due to Step 6), but we will have reduced the exponent: for $i$ inert disequalities and $e$ ert disequalities, the number of satisfiability tests of conjunctions of inequalities is $2i + 2^e$ rather than $2^{i+e}$. Since our existing polynomial-time test requires constraints from LI(2)-unit subdomain, we seek a quick test for inertness within this domain.

Our algorithm for testing inertness is made of two tests that formalize, and generalize for higher dimensions, two insights that are evident from Figure 1. The "closure test" is based on the observation that all disequalities are inert if the set of inequalities is "closed", as in Figure 1a. The "parallel test" finds cases in which parallel inequalities bound an open prism, as in Figure 1b; in this case disequalities that are parallel to the boundaries are ert.

Note that there may be other approaches to polynomial-time satisfiability testing for systems of constraints in the LI(2)-unit subdomain, but our approach follows the philosophy of the Omega Test: produce an algorithm that is efficient in the common cases, but general enough to handle the full logic. This lets us apply a single algorithm to fully LI(2)-unit systems, systems with a few constraints that are slightly more complex, or arbitrarily complex systems of constraints (the last of which may, of course, require unacceptable amounts of memory or time).

# 3   A Complete Inertness Test for LI(2) Constraints

In this Section we describe a general algorithm for determining inertness of an LI(2) disequality $d$ in a conjunction of $m$ LI(2) inequalities $C$ on $n$ variables. We assume that $C$ is known to have at least on integer solution.

We begin, in Subsection 3.1, by stating a theorem about inertness and outlining an informal proof (so far, our attempts at a full proof have clearly been beyond the scope of this paper). In Subsection 3.2, we give a motivation for the *Closure Test* and an intuitive understanding of how and why it works. In Subsection 3.3 we give detailed pseudocode for the algorithm. In Subsection 3.4, we give and prove upper bounds for the time complexity and space complexity of the algorithm. In Subsection 3.5, we prove the accuracy of the closure test algorithm. In Subsection 3.6, we describe the *Parallel Test* which covers some additional cases which are not accounted for by the closure test. These two tests are the key components to the algorithm to determine inertness. In fact, the proof of correctness (given in 3.7) is just a proof that those tests are sufficient to completely determine inertness.

## 3.1   Inertness and Non-parallel Rays

Inertness testing can be viewed as the search for rays contained in $C$ that are not parallel to the hyperplane defined by $\neg d$.

**Theorem 1.** Given $C$, a feasible conjunction of inequalities with integer (or rational) coefficients, and $d$, a disequality relevant to $C$, $d$ is inert in $C$ iff $\forall$ rays $r \subseteq sol(C), r \parallel d$.

If all rays contained in $C$ are parallel to $d$, $C$ must be either closed or open in a direction parallel to $d$, and $d$ is ert in $C$ (recall Figure 1a and the slanted disequalities in Figure 1b).

If $C$ contains a ray $r$ that is not parallel to $d$, $d$ must be inert in $C$: Since $C$ is convex, any ray parallel to $r$ with an origin within $C$ contains only points in $C$. Consider the set of rays $R$ that are parallel to $r$ and originate from the integer solutions to $C \wedge \neg d$. Each ray in $R$ must contain an infinite number of integer points in $C$ (assuming that $r$ is defined, like all our constraints, with integer coefficients). For $d$ to be ert when $C \wedge d$ is satisfiable (which must be the case if $C$ contains a ray not parallel to $d$), there must be some set of disequalities $D$ for which $C \wedge d \wedge D$ is unsatisfiable and $C \wedge D$ is satisfiable. $C \wedge d \wedge D$ can only be unsatisfiable if every integer solution in $C$, including those on $R$, is eliminated by some disequality. Since each ray $R_i$ in $R$ contains an infinite number of integer points, there must be at least one disequality in $(D \wedge d)$ that eliminates all the points in $R_i$. Since $d \not\parallel r$, $d$ cannot eliminate any $R_i$, and $D$ eliminates all points in $R$, including all integer solutions to $C \wedge \neg d$. Thus, $C \wedge D$ must be unsatisfiable, and $d$ cannot be ert in $C$.

## 3.2    Closure Test: Overview and Motivation

The *Closure Test* determines whether or not each of the variables in $d$ is bounded both above and below. To determine whether or not a variable $v$ is bounded above, we could compute the transitive closure of the "upper bound" relation among the variables (and a single node representing constants). That is, $y$ is an upper bound of $x$ if there exists a constraint $ax \leq by + c)$. $x$ is bounded above iff it has a path to the constant node or to both $y$ and $-y$ for some variable $y$. Recall that in LI(2), there are no bounds of the form $ax \leq by + dz + c$. We actually use a "sloppy" variation on transitive closure that only guarantees accurate bound on the variables in $d$, to gain a slight reduction in complexity.

It may be tempting to think of determining the boundedness of each variable as equivalent to determining boundedness of $C$, but that is not the case, and the distinction is important. Any closed region can be trivially made to be open by adding an *irrelevant variable* which is not mentioned in any of the constraints. For instance, adding $z \geq 0$ to $C$, where $z$ is not mentioned anywhere else in $C$, will make $C$ open even if it was closed beforehand. However, as far as inertness is concerned, we don't care about the irrelevant variables. This is because $d$ will be extruded infinitely far (without being bounded by $C$) along each of those variables. Therefore, any ray which "escapes" only along irrelevant variables is necessarily parallel to $d$. Recall that rays parallel to $d$ do not give us any information about the inertness of $d$, and that we are only concerned with the existence of non-parallel escaping rays. For these reasons, it is very important that our test treat regions which are only open along irrelevant variables as being closed. In summary, we really want to determine the boundedness of the variables of $C$ which are relevant to $d$.

## 3.3    Closure Test: The Algorithm

In this section, we describe the actual algorithm for performing a closure test on a set of variables (namely those in $d$).

For each variable $x$ in $d$, we will determine if $x$ is bounded above and if $-x$ is bounded above. Since the lower bound of $x \in d$ is the same as the upper bound of $-x$, we will determine both upper and lower bounds of each variable. However, framing the question entirely as upper bounds will make the algorithm more readable and will make storing and retrieving the information easier.

We will need the following additional storage space to run the algorithm:

a boolean array of length $n$, recording if a variable has been reached or not.
a boolean table of indirect upper bounds
    one row per variable and per negative of each variable
    one column per variable and per negative of each variable
    one "constant bound" column
    one "modified" column

Pseudocode for the algorithm is as follows:

```
Indirect_Bound(integer x)
    mark x as ''reached''     // prevent infinite recursion
    look at all upper bounds on x and set the appropriate
                        column in the row for x to true
    set the ''modified'' column for x iff any columns were set
    if no constant bound and no +y/-y pair is checked for x
        foreach single variable bound on x which is not ''reached''
            call this Indirect_Bound recursively on it
            set (to true) the column for each variable returned
        // note that there are no multi-variable bounds in LI(2)
    return the list of bounds on x (the true entries in x's row)
```

We run this algorithm on each variable in d, and on the negative of each variable in d. After doing so, we need to do some post-processing:

(1) If any variables in $d$ are entirely unbounded (0 entries in the "modified" column), the the region is unbounded. Otherwise, run the next test.
(2) For each variable in $d$, check to see if it is either bounded by a constant or bounded by $y$ and $-y$ for some variable $y$. If each variable is bounded in this manner, then the region is bounded. Otherwise, the region is bounded.

Interpret the results of the algorithm as follows:

If the region is bounded, the $d$ is ert.
If the region is unbounded, then $d$ might still be ert, so we run the Parallel test.

If we were not working over the LI(2) (or LI(2)-unit) domain, then there would also be the possibility of a multiple variable bound.

## 3.4  Closure Test: Time Complexity

Pre-processing and initializing the table will take $O(n^2)$ time.

Post-processing takes $O(m)$ in order to scan the relevant entries in the table, since the density of the constraints is bounded to 2.

Naively examined, the recursive function will take $O(m^2n)$ time, however amortized analysis reveals that the test actually takes $O(mn)$ time. That is, by recording our progress in the table, we save a linear amount of time by consulting the table instead of re-deriving some of the information.

The functions is called at most once on each of the $n$ variables. At each call, each of the (up to $m$) upper bounds has to be examined. Each of those might return as many as $m$ upper bounds which have to be merged with the existing upper bounds. However, the total number of upper bounds is at most $m$, since each equation only provides one bound on $x$. The algorithm takes advantage of this fact by not returning previously visited bounds, and thus the total amount of work spent on returning upper bounds in $O(m)$. Thus, the total amount of work done over all $n$ recursive calls is $O(nm)$. Consequently, the overall time complexity is $O(n^2 + mn)$.

## 3.5   Closure Test: Accuracy

Recall that the quadratic time complexity is achieved because we don't return upper bounds which have already been encountered. However, this means that the bound in question has already been returned to the original variable we are testing, so it is already accounted for. Of course, the upper bounds recorded in the table may be incomplete for the variables which don't appear in $d$, but we still get accurate information on the variables in $d$.

Intuition If is $x$ is eventually bounded by $y$ and $-y$, then we can use back substitution to create two constraints of the form

$$x + y + c_1 \geq 0$$
$$x - y + c_1 \leq 0$$

Solving for the intersection of those two lines gives us a (constant) bound on $x$ (although not necessarily a tight one).

## 3.6   The Parallel Test

The *Parallel Test* is based on the fact that if there are two parallel inequalities, one on each side of $d$, then $d$ will not be inert. For some disequality of the form

$$a_1 x_1 + ... + a_n x_n \neq c_0$$

we look for a pair of inequalities of the form

$$a_1 x_1 + ... + a_n x_n \leq c_1,$$
$$a_1 x_1 + ... + a_n x_n \geq c_2$$

with $c_2 \leq c_0 \leq c_1$. If such constraints are present in $C$, then $d$ is ert in $C$.

The Omega Library uses a hash table to facilitate identification of parallel constraints, so this test should take constant time. Even without this hash table, it would only take $O(m)$ time to scan the $m$ constraints.

Note that outside of the LI(2) subdomain, it is possible to have a case in which $d$ is contained in a "prism" with sides that are not parallel to $d$. Thus our parallel test is not sufficient to identify all ert disequalities if $C$ includes constraints outside of this subdomain.

## 3.7   Combining the Two Tests

In this section, we bring together the closure and parallel tests to create a single tests which will completely determine inertness.

**Conjecture:** Let $d$ and $C$ be LI(2) (or LI(2)-unit). If $d$ is ert in $C$, then either the closure test or the parallel test will identify it as such. If $d$ is inert, then neither the Closure Test nor the Parallel test will identify it as ert.

That is, the Closure and Parallel tests completely determine inertness. We will validate this conjecture by proving the following theorem.

**Definition:** Consider a hyperplane (in our case $d$) and a conjunction of linear constraints $C$. Let $r$ be a ray which originates on $d$. If $r$ is completely contained within $C$ but does not intersect the boundary of $C$, then $r$ is said to **escape C from d**.

For the following theorem and proof, we will use "$\overline{d}$" to denote the hyperplane defined by the negation of the disequality $d$.

**Theorem 2.** If there are not two non-redundant constraints parallel to $d$ and there exists some ray $r$ such that

(a) $r$ is not bounded by $C$,
(b) the initial point of $r$ satisfies $C$ and lies on $d$, and
(c) $r \parallel d$,

then there must exist a ray $r'$ such that

(a) $r$ is not bounded by $C$,
(b) the initial point of $r$ satisfies $C$ but not $d$, and
(c) $r \nparallel d$.

**Remark:** The theorem exactly says that $d$ is inert in $C$ only if both tests fail to return "ert". Proving this theorem will also validate the completeness conjecture.

**Proof:** Since there are not two constraints parallel to $d$, at least one of the two half spaces defined by $d$ doesn't contain a constraint parallel to $d$. Consider that half space (or one of them if both fit the criteria). By "down" we will mean directly towards $d$ and by "up" we will mean directly (perpendicularly) away from $d$. Angles will be implicitly measured from the plane $d$ "upwards".

We will prove that, if all non-parallel rays are blocked by $C$, then all rays are blocked by $C$. Thus we will have proven the converse of the theorem and the theorem will follow.

By assumption, there must be some ray, $r'$, which is

(1) parallel to $d$, and
(2) has initial point on $d$ and within the bounds of $C$
(3) which is not bounded by $C$.

If not, then we will construct a valid $r'$ with the following algorithm, beginning it with $n = 0$.

**Algorithm:** We are given a ray $r_n$. If it is not bounded by $C$, then stop. We have found a valid $r'$. If so, then there are three ways for $r_n$ to be bounded by (intersect with) a constraint in $C$.

(a) A constraint that is parallel to $d$.
(b) A constraint $c$ such that $r_n$ points into $d$. That is, the angle of $r_n$ up from the projection of $r_n$ onto $d$ is positive.

(c) A constraint $c$ such that $r_n$ does not point into $d$. That is, the angle of $r_n$ up from the projection of $r_n$ onto $d$ is negative.

The Theorem gives us that $(a)$ is not the case.

If $(c)$ is the case then that constraint must also block $r_p$. This result is a contradiction with our assumption that $r_p$ is not blocked by $C$ and thus cannot occur.

If $(b)$ is the case, then consider a new ray, $r_{n+1}$, of smaller angle, which is not blocked by the same constraint. Run the algorithm on this new ray. Since there are only a finite number of constraints in $C$, then eventually a ray will be produced which is blocked by one of the other two cases. Since we are given that $case(a)$ does not occur, we know that eventually we will produce a ray which is not bounded by $C$.

Consequently, if both the Parallel Test and the Closure Test do not return "ert", then a non-parallel ray must escape – making $d$ inert in $C$.

### 3.8 Generalizations

The algorithms above work when all inequalities and disequalities are in the LI(2) subdomain. If a formula contains a small number of disequalities outside of this subdomain, we can safely (if expensively) treat them as ert. However, if a formula contains one non-LI(2) inequality, we must (in the absence of an inertness test) treat *all* disequalities as ert.

We are currently investigating extensions of our inertness test, focusing on the use of linear programming techniques to perform a direct test for the existence of a ray $r$ that is not parallel to $d$: we simply determine if an objective function that is perpendicular to $d$ is unbounded. However, it is not clear that the overall complexity of this approach can be made low enough to make it helpful in dependence testing.

We could also try to identify the extreme rays of $C$, and then determine whether or not any of them are not parallel to $d$. However, if a system has many extreme rays and few disequalities, this might prove to be much slower than our approach.

It is also worth noting that any disequality that contains a variable that does not appear in any inequality (or equality) constraint can trivially be satisfied (essentially by treating the disequality as an equality, solving for the new variable, and then setting it to some other value).

## 4     The Representation of "Simplified" Relations

As the Omega Test and Omega Library [5] served as the foundation for our prior work on polynomial time array dependence analysis, it is the obvious framework for implementation of the algorithms presented here. Such an implementation would involve major modifications to the Omega Library's core data structures. The library is designed to transform relations defined by arbitrary Presburger

Formulas [7], possibly with certain uses of uninterpreted function symbols [8], into a "simplified form". This transformation happens automatically during satisfiability testing and at other times; it prevents redundant analysis, and thus presumably provides a great speed advantage over a system that evaluates every query based on an unsimplified relation.

The simplified form is a variant of disjunctive normal form in which individual "conjuncts" (conjunctions of equality and inequality constraints, possibly with local existentially quantified variables) are connected by disjunction ($\vee$). Depending on the query performed, this simplified form may or may not include redundant conjuncts, equalities, or inequalities.

Note that simplification may not always be beneficial, and deferring it to the proper point is an important strategy for getting good performance from the Omega Library. For example, consider queries for value-based dependence analysis, which have the form $C_0 \wedge \neg C_1 \wedge \neg C_2 \wedge \ldots \wedge \neg C_N$, where the $C_i$'s are conjuncts. The Omega Library uses information in $C_0$ to reduce the cost of negating the other conjuncts. If we were to simplify each negated conjunct and then combine the results with $\wedge$, the cost would be dramatically higher for many cases (see [1] for details).

Even if our polynomial-time disequality algorithm has proven that a system of constraints is satisfiable, converting it into simplified form can increase its size exponentially, since each non-redundant disequality will be converted into a disjunction. We could solve this problem by allowing disequality constraints within the individual conjunct data structures. This approach would have benefits even if all disequalities where ert: except in cases where redundancy is to be removed, the Omega Library could stop testing for satisfiability as soon as it has proven a relation is satisfiable. The current algorithms produce the entire disjunction and then test each conjunct for satisfiability. This could provide some part of the speedup shown under "privatization analysis" in [9, Table 13.2], but in a more generally applicable context.

An equivalent approach would be to simply allow negated equality constraints in simplified relations. This approach could be taken even further, to allow more general negated constraints, or other formulas that cannot be handled efficiently (or at all). The current Omega Library can (in principle) handle arbitrary Presburger Formulas when it is not restricted to our provably polynomial subdomain. However, when faced with certain uses of uninterpreted function symbols, or when restricted to provably polynomial cases, the Omega Library replaces any set of constraints that it cannot handle with a special constraint identified simply as *unknown*.

It might be possible to modify this algorithm to annotate each *unknown* with the unsimplified formula that produced it, in case later manipulation of the relation provides information that lets the library handle the offending constraint. However, without extensive empirical testing, it is hard to know whether the overhead involved in this approach would be worthwhile.

The above changes have the potential to improve the accuracy, speed, and ease of use of the Omega Library, since polynomial-time simplifications could be performed early without causing a decrease in later accuracy (this approach would also make the efficiency less sensitive to the timing of simplifications).

# 5    Implementation Status and Future Work

We do not currently have an implementation of our algorithms, and thus we do not have empirical verification that they are either fast or effective in practice. Given the nature of the changes discussed in the previous section, we do not expect to have an implementation any time soon.

However, we do have reason to hope that our algorithms will be applicable during dependence analysis. Our studies of the constraints that arise in practice [1,2] suggest that disequalities often involve loop index variables used in `if` statements or in subscripts. For programs with scalable parallelism, some or all loops are bounded by symbolic constants (typically program parameters), which are not themselves bounded above. In this case, we expect the disequalities to be inert. When all disequalities are inert and the constraints obey the other conditions given in [2], memory- and value-based dependence testing can be done in polynomial time.

Before undertaking any implementation effort, we plan to investigate algorithms for projection and gist in the presence of disequalities. It may be the case that some of the insights of Imbert [10] can be combined with our definition of inertness in some useful way.

# 6    Related Work

Most other work on handling negated constraints during dependence analysis focuses on producing approximate results or deferring satisfiability tests until more constraints are available. The Omega Library's negation algorithms [11,9] and the algorithms for manipulating "Guarded Array Regions With Disjunction" (GARWD's) in the Panorama compiler [12] are examples of the deferral approach (the proposals at the end of Section 4 were directly inspired by the GARWD algorithms). The drawback with deferring negation is, of course, that we will be forced to choose some other approach if we do not get any helpful constraints before we must answer a satisfiability query.

Our work with identifying inert disequalities complements this approach, and there should be no problem with combining the two. When disequalities are inert, they can be tested directly; when they are not, satisfiability testing should be delayed as long as possible.

We do not know of any other work on polynomial-time satisfiability testing of disequalities on integer variables. Our work on identifying inert disequalities on integer variables was driven by a frustrated desire to apply the work of Lassez and McAloon [6], which is relevant only to real (or rational) variables.

# 7   Conclusions

Disequality constraints can cause exponential behavior during dependence analysis, even when all constraints are in the otherwise polynomial LI(2)-unit domain. We have developed a polynomial-time algorithm to identify certain inert disequalities within this domain, in which case satisfiability testing is polynomial in the number of inequalities and inert disequalities, but exponential in the number of ert disequalities.

The integration of our algorithms into the Omega Library would require a redefinition of the central data structure representing a "simplified" problem, and would thus be a major undertaking. However, it might provide opportunities for improving the speed and accuracy with which the Omega Test handles other queries.

## Acknowledgments

This work is supported by NSF grant CCR-9808694.

## References

1. William Pugh and David Wonnacott. Constraint-based array dependence analysis. *ACM Trans. on Programming Languages and Systems*, 20(3):635–678, May 1998.
2. Robert Seater and David Wonnacott. Polynomial time array dataflow analysis. In *Proceedings of the 14th International Workshop on Languages and Compilers for Parallel Computing*, August 2001.
3. Michael R. Garey and David S. Johnson. *Computers and Intractability: A Guide to the Theory of NP-Completeness*. W.H. Freeman and Company, 1979.
4. D. E. Maydan, J. L. Hennessy, and M. S. Lam. Efficient and exact data dependence analysis. In *ACM SIGPLAN '91 Conference on Programming Language Design and Implementation*, pages 1–14, June 1991.
5. Wayne Kelly, Vadim Maslov, William Pugh, Evan Rosser, Tatiana Shpeisman, and David Wonnacott. The Omega Library interface guide. Technical Report CS-TR-3445, Dept. of Computer Science, University of Maryland, College Park, March 1995. The Omega library is available from http://www.cs.umd.edu/projects/omega.
6. Jean-Louis Lassez and Ken McAloon. Independence of negative constraints. In *TAPSOFT 89: Proceedings of the International Joint Conference on Theory and Practice of Software*, 1989.
7. G. Kreisel and J. L. Krevine. *Elements of Mathematical Logic*. North-Holland Pub. Co., 1967.
8. Robert E. Shostak. A practical decision procedure for arithmetic with function symbols. *Journal of the ACM*, 26(2):351–360, April 1979.
9. David G. Wonnacott. *Constraint-Based Array Dependence Analysis*. PhD thesis, Dept. of Computer Science, The University of Maryland, August 1995. Available as ftp://ftp.cs.umd.edu/pub/omega/davewThesis/davewThesis.ps.
10. Jean-Louis Imbert. Variable elimination for disequations in generalized linear constraint systems. *The Computer Journal*, 36(5):473–484, 1993. Special Issue on Variable Elimination.

11. William Pugh and David Wonnacott. An exact method for analysis of value-based array data dependences. In *Proceedings of the 6th International Workshop on Languages and Compilers for Parallel Computing*, volume 768 of *Lecture Notes in Computer Science*. Springer-Verlag, Berlin, August 1993.

12. Junjie Gu, Zhiyuan Li, and Gyungho Lee. Experience with efficient array data flow analysis for array privatization. In *Proceedings of the 6th ACM SIGPLAN Symposium on Principles and Practice of Parallel Programming*, pages 157–167, Las Vegas, Nevada, June 1997.

# Removing Impediments to Loop Fusion Through Code Transformations

Bob Blainey[1], Christopher Barton[2], and José Nelson Amaral[2]

[1] IBM Toronto Software Laboratory, Toronto, Canada
blainey@ca.ibm.com
[2] Department of Computing Science, University of Alberta, Edmonton, Canada
{cbarton, amaral}@cs.ualberta.ca

**Abstract.** Loop fusion is a common optimization technique that takes several loops and combines them into a single large loop. Most of the existing work on loop fusion concentrates on the heuristics required to optimize an objective function, such as data reuse or creation of instruction level parallelism opportunities. Often, however, the code provided to a compiler has only small sets of loops that are control flow equivalent, normalized, have the same iteration count, are adjacent, and have no fusion-preventing dependences. This paper focuses on code transformations that create more opportunities for loop fusion in the IBM®XL compiler suite that generates code for the IBM family of PowerPC®processors. In this compiler an objective function is used at the loop distributor to decide which portions of a loop should remain in the same loop nest and which portions should be redistributed. Our algorithm focuses on eliminating conditions that prevent loop fusion. By generating maximal fusion our algorithm increases the scope of later transformations. We tested our improved code generator in an IBM pSeries™ 690 machine equipped with a POWER4™ processor using the SPEC CPU2000 benchmark suite. Our improvements to loop fusion resulted in three times as many loops fused in a subset of CFP2000 benchmarks, and four times as many for a subset of CINT2000 benchmarks.

## 1   Introduction

Modern microprocessors such as the POWER4 have a high degree of available instruction level parallelism and are typically nested within a relatively slow memory subsystem with non-uniform access times. Both of these machine characteristics make the distribution of memory references within a program critical to achieving high performance. In many scientific applications, the structure of loop nests operating on dense data arrays is a primary determinant of overall performance. Compilers with advanced automatic loop restructuring capabilities have emerged to address this performance opportunity [1].

Two important and complementary transformations typically performed in a loop restructuring compiler are loop fusion and loop distribution. Important design decisions when implementing loop optimization include (a) the order in

B. Pugh and C.-W. Tseng (Eds.): LCPC 2002, LNCS 2481, pp. 309–328, 2005.

which these phases should be executed, and (b) whether the *smartness* of the loop optimization algorithm should be placed (i) in loop fusion, (ii) in loop distribution, or (iii) in both.

In this paper we introduce the algorithms used for loop fusion in the IBM XL Fortran and VisualAge® for C++ for AIX compilers. In these compilers maximal loop fusion is performed first and then selective loop distribution takes place, *i.e.,* the smartness is placed in the distribution phase of the loop optimization process. These compilers target the PowerPC architecture and have been in continuous production use since the introduction of the POWER architecture in 1990. In this paper we report performance results for the new IBM processor, the POWER4. The POWER4 processor features two microprocessors running in excess of 1 GHz on a single chip along with a large shared L2 cache and control logic for an even larger off-chip L3 cache and high bandwidth chip-to-chip communication. Each microprocessor features 8 parallel functional units executing instructions in an out-of-order fashion along with dedicated L1 data and instruction caches. As in the POWER3™ processor, the POWER4 data caches include support for automatic prefetching of linear reference streams.

The fusion of small loops to generate larger loops decreases the number of loop branches executed, creates opportunities for data reuse, and offers more instructions for the scheduler to balance the use of functional units. Possible negative effects of loop fusion are increased code size, increased register pressure within a loop, potential overcommiting of hardware resources and the formation of loops with more complex control flow. Increased code size can affect the instruction cache performance. Higher register pressure has the potential of resulting in code with undesirable spilling instructions. Architectures such as the POWER4 achitecture contain hardware support for prefetching linear reference streams. If a loop contains more reference streams than can be prefetched by the hardware, one or more of the reference streams will be plagued by cache misses, causing performance degradations. Loops with complex control flow have a longer instruction path length and can have negative side effects on later optimizations such as software pipelining.

The loop fusion algorithm used in this compiler scans the code to find pairs of normalized loops that can be fused and greedily fuses them. Two loops can be fused if they are control equivalent, have no dependences, and their bounds conform (see Section 4). In order to be fused, there must be no intervening code between the loops. In some situations the code that is between the loops has no data dependences with one of the loops. In this case the code can be moved either before the first loop or after the second loop. In this paper we describe our implementation of this data movement operation. We also implement loop peeling to allow the fusion of loops that originally had non-conforming bounds. Our algorithm processes loops in the same nesting level in a given control flow, moving intervening code, peeling iterations, and fusing loops until no more loops can be fused. We present experimental results comparing the loop fusion algorithm with and without these improvements.

In previous work published on loop fusion, the decision to fuse a set of loops was based on the evaluation of an objective function — usually a measurement of data reuse and/or estimates of resource usage [4, 6, 10]. In our implementation the decision of how the code should be aggregated into a set of loop nests is delayed until loop distribution. Therefore, we can apply maximal loop fusion without regard to resource usage or to the benefits of fusion. For compile time and implementation efficiency we use a greedy algorithm and do not consider cases in which an early fusion might prevent a later, potentially more profitable, fusion.

The main contributions of this paper are:

- A new algorithm that eliminates conditions that prevent loop fusion and increase the scope of later loop restructuring transformations.
- An implementation of the new fusion algorithm in the IBM production compilers for the eServer pSeries, and measured performance on the eServer pSeries 690 that is built around the new POWER4 processor.
- Experimental results that show that the algorithm increases the number of loops fused when compared with the algorithm in the original compiler.

The rest of the paper is organized as follows: Section 2 briefly introduces the POWER4 Architecture, which was used for the performance measurements. Section 3 describes the general loop optimizer that is used in this compiler. Section 4 describes the loop fusion algorithm and Section 5 presents some preliminary experimental results. Section 6 reviews related work.

## 2   The POWER4 Architecture

The POWER4 is a new microprocessor implementation of the 64-bit PowerPC architecture designed and manufactured by IBM for the UNIX®server market. It features two processor cores running at speeds up to 1.3 GHz placed onto a single die. Four of these dies are placed together to form one multi-chip module (MCM), containing eight processor cores. Each of the two processors on the die has a dedicated 64 KB direct mapped L1 instruction cache, a dedicated 32 KB 2-way set associative L1 data cache and a unified 1 KB 4-way set associative TLB supporting 4 KB and 16 MB page sizes. The two processors share a single 8-way set associative 1.44 MB on-chip combined L2 cache. Each 4 chip (8 processor) MCM has an attached 128 MB L3 cache and dedicated memory controller. For the experiments presented in this paper we used a dual MCM pSeries model 690 server. This machine runs at 1.1 GHz and has 64 GB of main memory[3].

Each L1 instruction cache can support up to 3 outstanding misses and each L1 data cache can support up to 8 outstanding misses. The L1 data cache and the L2 and L3 shared caches include support for automatic prefetching of linear reference streams. Each processor maintains a 12-entry prefetch address filter queue and up to 8 concurrent active prefetch streams. The L2 cache is organized into 3 slices, each 480 KB in size and can offer more than 100 GB/s in bandwidth [12].

## 3     Overview of Loop Optimizations

In the XL compilers, most optimizing transformations are applied to each loop
nest in functions by the iterative application of several specialized passes. Loop
fusion enlarges the scope in which later optimizations are applied. Fusion creates opportunities to improve data reuse, to generate coarser grain parallelism,
to exploit the use of hardware prefetch streams, to improve the allocation of architected register files, and to improve the scheduling for load/store or floating-
point dominated code, or for code that combines both types of operations. The
larger scope available for these later optimizations is due to the aggregation of
more code into a smaller number of loop nests. In order to reap these benefits
we implement maximal fusion first, and later redistribute the code into separate
loop nests. The distributor reaggregates code according to a set of constraints
and the optimization of an objective function. If the original loop structure is
already optimal, the distributor will usually re-create it. Thus the loop fusion
phase performs maximal fusion without concern for potential negative effects in
the code.

Figure 1 presents the sequence of transformations applied to the code, including loop fusion and loop distribution. Starting on the left of the figure, the early
optimizations, aggressive copy propagation and dead store elimination, create
opportunities for loop interchanging and loop unroll and jam. Conventional copy
propagation algorithms do not move computations into a loop to prevent the en-
largement of the dynamic path length of the loop. Our aggressive propagation,
however, does move statements into a loop to enable the creation of perfectly
nested loops. Figure 2 illustrates the aggressive copy propagation performed in
this compiler. The original code is in Figure 2(a). After copy (and expression)
propagation the code in Figure 2(b) is obtained, and after the dead store elimination, the code in Figure 2(c) results. Although the multiplication x*y now needs
to be computed in every iteration of the inner loop, the combination of these two
optimizations generates a perfectly nested loop that can be advantageous both
for loop permutation and unroll-and-jam. Furthermore, the computation of x*y
can be moved back out of the loop after the loop optimizer has completed.

Next, maximal loop fusion is performed. The goal is to enhance the scope
for optimization in the loop distributor and not necessarily to improve performance on its own. Working with larger portions of the code, the distributor will

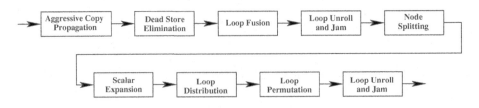

**Fig. 1.** Loop Optimizations

```
for(i=0 ; i<k ; i++)          for(i=0 ; i<k ; i++)          for(i=0 ; i<k ; i++)
{                             {                             {
  s = x*y;                      s = x*y;                      for(j=0 ; j<n ; j++)
  for(j=0 ; j<n ; j++)          for(j=0 ; j<n ; j++)            V[i][j] = V[i][j] + x*y;
    V[i][j] = V[i][j] + s;        V[i][j] = V[i][j] + x*y;    }
}                             }
         (a)                           (b)                           (c)
```

**Fig. 2.** Example of aggressive copy propagation followed by dead store elimination

encounter more opportunities to explore data reuse, generate coarser grained parallelism, exploit prefetch, improve the use of architected registers, and schedule operations to the fix point, floating point, and load/store units.

After loop fusion, the compiler applies common-subexpression elimination, and *node splitting*. In order to keep the size of the data dependence graphs (DDGs) under control, complex statements are allowed in the code representation at this level. Each one of these statements is a *node* in the DDG. Because these nodes represent complex statements, a node may participate in multiple dependence relations. Node splitting separates a complex statement into two or more simpler statements, each participating in a disjoint dependence relation. In some cases node splitting allows the loop distributor to distribute two portions of a statement into separate loop nests. For instance, such a split is profitable when one part of the statement has self-dependences that prevent parallelization and the other part parallelizable.

The scalar expansion transformation identifies the use of scalars that induce anti or output dependences across loop iterations. In a traditional scalar expansion algorithm, each one of these scalar variables would be expanded into arrays with as many dimensions as required to eliminate the dependences. In this compiler, the expansion is limited to one dimension, and the variables are marked as *expandable* but the actual generation of the arrays is postponed until the code generation phase. At that point the expansion might not be necessary because of code aggregation done by the loop distributor or, if expansion is necessary, the required storage could be overlaid with existing temporary storage.

It is important to strike the right balance between the multiple conflicting goals of the loop distributor. In this compiler suite the loop distributor first identifies the minimal segments of code that must be distributed as a unit. For instance, if an *if* statement is encountered, the test along with the code that appears in both branches, up to but not including the join node, form a unit of code. These code units are called *aggregate* nodes. Aggregate and statement nodes, which form maximal strongly connected components of the DDG are grouped together to form π-nodes, named after the definition by Kuck [13]. Degenerate π-nodes are also formed from the remaining statement and aggregate nodes that are not part of any strongly connected component. A π-node may contain from a single statement to an arbitrarily complex portion of code. π-nodes are the units that the distributor works with.

Some of the characteristics of a $\pi$-node that are relevant for the loop distribution algorithm include: register requirements,[1] load/store usage, number of floating point and fixed point operations executed, and the number of prefetchable linear streams.[2] Another important attribute taken into consideration by the distributor is whether the code in a $\pi$-node is self-dependent or not. A $\pi$-node that is not dependent on itself is parallelizable and should be aggregated only with other non-self-dependent nodes.

Once the $\pi$-nodes are formed, the distributor creates an affinity graph that is an undirected weighted graph whose nodes correspond to $\pi$-nodes and whose weighted edges represent the affinity between the nodes. Currently the only measure of affinity used in the compiler is the potential for data reuse between the code in the nodes. The compiler uses a greedy algorithm in the distributor: it attempts to aggregate nodes in decreasing order of affinity. The decision about aggregating two $\pi$-nodes is based not only on the affinity in the graph, but also on whether aggregation would satisfy data dependences and whether aggregation is desirable based on node attributes. For instance, if the aggregation of two $\pi$-nodes would exceed the use of the existing prefetching streams, the nodes are usually not aggregated. Likewise self-dependent (non-parallelizable) nodes are usually not aggregated with non-self-dependent (parallelizable) nodes. Decisions about aggregating nodes are conditioned to the potential increase in data reuse.

After loop distribution, loop permutation and unroll and jam are performed. These transformations are limited in their application to perfectly nested loops and benefit from the loop distributor's efforts to isolate perfect nests.

## 4   Loop Fusion Algorithm

In the XL compiler suite, loop normalization takes place prior to loop fusion. In other words, whenever possible, the loop starting count, its increment, and its direction (always increasing the index) are normalized. We divide loops into two classes: loops that are *eligible* for fusion and loops that are not eligible for fusion. Examples of loops that are *non-eligible* for fusion include loops that were specified to be parallel loops by the programmer (in OpenMP for instance), loops for which normalization fails, non-counted loops, and loops with side entrances and side exits. In order to be fused, two loops that are *eligible* for fusion must satisfy the following conditions:

- they must be conforming,
- they must be control equivalent,
- they must be adjacent, and
- there can be only forward dependences between the loop bodies.

---

[1] Loop body size is used as an estimator for register pressure.

[2] The number of prefetchable linear streams is an important characteristic for the optimization of code for the Power4 because this architecture has a hardware stream prefetching mechanism that is triggered by regular data accesses.

```
                                          do i1 = 1, n
                                            a(i1) = a(i1) * k1
                                          end do
   subroutine f(a,b,c,d,n,m,ds)           do i2 = 1, n-1
   real a(n),b(n),c(n),d(m)                 d(i2) = a(i2) - b(i2+1) * k2
   real k1, k2, k3                         end do
   a = a * k1                              ds  = 0.0
   d(1:n-1) = a(1:n-1) - b(2:n) * k2       do i3 = 1, m
   ds = sum(d)                               ds = ds + d(i3)
   if(n<m)                                 end do
     c(n-2) = n                            if(n<m)
   else                                      c(n-2) = n
     c(n-2) = m                            else
   b(2:n-1) = a(1:n-2) + b(1:n-2) / c(1:n-2)  c(n-2) = m
   end                                     do i4 = 1, n-2
                                            b(i4) = a(i4) + b(i4) / c(i4)
                                          end do
```

(a) Fortran 90 Code                    (b) Fortran 77 Code

**Fig. 3.** Fortran 90 and Fortran 77 versions of the code for running example

Two normalized loops are *conforming* if they have the same iteration count. A set of loops is *control equivalent* if, whenever one of the loops of the set is executed, all of the other loops must be executed. We say that a loop is executed if its exit test is executed at least once. Two loops are determined to be control equivalent using the dominator and post-dominator properties of the loops. If loop $L_j$ dominates loop $L_k$ and $L_k$ post-dominates $L_j$ then the two loops are control equivalent. Two loops $L_j$ and $L_k$ are *adjacent* if there is no intervening code between them, *i.e.*, in the Control Flow Graph, $L_k$ is the immediate successor of $L_j$.

We use the contrived running example presented in Fortran 90 and Fortran 77 in Figure 3 to illustrate our loop fusion algorithm. This code example has four loops accessing four different arrays, a, b, c, d. We assume that there is no overlap between the memory locations of these arrays, *i.e.*, there is no i and j such that the address of x(i) overlaps with the address of y(j), where x and y represent the arrays a, b, c, and d.

Figure 4 presents the LoopFusion algorithm. The algorithm operates one nest level at a time processing the outermost nesting level first and then moving toward the innermost level (step 1). First the algorithm partitions all the loops that are at the same nest level into sets of loops that are control equivalent. In step 4 all loops that are not eligible for fusion are removed from the set. Since all the loops in a set are control flow equivalent, dominance defines a total order over the set. Therefore, we can use the notion of moving *forward* and moving in *reverse* order through the set. The loop fusion algorithm iterates, alternating forward and reverse passes over the set, until it finds no more loops to be fused. Fusions and code movements that take place during a pass through a set of loops change the control flow graph and the dominance order between the loops. Therefore, before each pass the control flow graphk and the dominance relations are recomputed. The iterations processed in the while loop starting at step 7

```
LoopFusion
1.    foreach NestLevel N_i from outermost to innermost
2.            Gather identically control dependent loops in N_i
              into LoopSets
3.            foreach LoopSet S_i
4.                    Remove loops non-eligible for fusion from
                      S_i
5.                    FusedLoops ← True
6.                    Direction ← Forward
7.                    while FusedLoops = True
8.                        if |S_i| < 2
9.                            break
10.                       endif
11.                       Build Control Flow Graph
12.                       Compute Dominance Relation
13.                       FusedLoops =
                              LoopFusionPass(S_i,Direction)
14.                       if Direction = Forward
15.                           Direction = Reverse
16.                       else
17.                           Direction = Forward
18.                       endif
19.                   endfor
20.           end while
21.   endfor
```

**Fig. 4.** Loop Fusion Algorithm

alternate between forward and reverse passes through the loop set until no loops
are fused during a pass. In the code example of Figure 3, all loops are eligible for
fusion and control equivalent, thus all four loops are in the same set, and have
the following dominance order: $i1 \rightarrow i2 \rightarrow i3 \rightarrow i4$ (we will identify the loops
in the example by their index variables).

In a forward pass the LoopFusionPass algorithm presented in Figure 5 traverses a set of control flow equivalent loops in dominance order, while during a
reverse pass the traversal is in post-dominance order. The function Intervening
Code$(L_j, L_k)$ checks whether the two loops are adjacent, *i.e.*, if there is intervening code between them. We use the dominance relation to determine the
existence of intervening code. An aggregate node $a_x$ *intervenes* between loops
$L_j$ and $L_k$ if and only if $L_j$ properly dominates $a_x$, $L_j \prec_d a_x$, and $L_k$ properly post-dominates $a_x$, $L_k \prec_{pd} a_x$. Because the loops $L_j$ and $L_k$ are control
equivalent, there cannot be a side entrance or a side exit to the intervening code
between the two loops. If we find intervening code between $L_j$ and $L_k$, we check
if the intervening code can be moved either before the first loop or after the
second one (step 3). Our algorithm allows for a portion of the intervening code
to be moved above the first loop while the remainder of that code is moved

```
LoopFusionPass(S_i, Direction)
1.    FusedLoops = False
2.    foreach pair of loops L_j and L_k in S_i, such that L_j
              dominates L_k, in Direction
3.          if IntervENINGCODE(L_j, L_k) = True and
              IsIntervENINGCODEMovABLE(L_j, L_k) = False
4.              continue
5.          endif
6.          σ ← |κ(L_j) − κ(L_k)|
7.          if L_j and L_k are non-conforming and
              σ cannot be determined at compile time
8.              continue
9.          endif
10.         if DependenceDistance(L_j, L_k) < 0
11.             continue
12.         endif
13.         MoveIntervENINGCODE(L_j, L_k, Direction)
14.         if IntervENINGCODE(L_j, L_k) = False
15.             if L_j and L_k are non-conforming
16.                 L_m ← FuseWithGuard(L_j, L_k)
17.             else
18.                 L_m ← Fuse(L_j, L_k)
19.             endif
20.             S_i ← S_i ∪ L_m − {L_j, L_k}
21.             FusedLoops = True
22.         else
23.             continue
24.         endif
25.    endfor
26.    return FusedLoops
```

**Fig. 5.** Loop Fusion Algorithm

after the second loop. This is necessary when a portion of the intervening code cannot be moved down because of dependences with $L_k$ and the remainder of the code cannot be moved up because of dependences with $L_j$. The algorithm IsIntervENINGCODEMovABLE checks for this condition.

If the two loops do not conform, *i.e.*, if they have different iteration counts, they could be made to conform by guarding iterations of one of the loops. We are only considering loops that were normalized (loops for which normalization failed were eliminated in step 4 of the LoopFusion algorithm). In step 6 we compute the difference between the upper bound of the two loops, $κ(L_j)$ and $κ(L_k)$ and store the result in $σ$. Observe that this is a symbolic subtraction as the value of $σ$ may not be known at compile time. In step 7 we abandon our attempt to fuse the loops $L_j$ and $L_k$ if $σ$ cannot be determined at compile time.

On the other hand, if $\sigma$ is a known constant, a guard is placed in the fused loop to inhibit the extra execution of one of the loop bodies (see step 16).

Figure 9 presents the algorithm FUSEWITHGUARD used to fuse two non-conforming loops $L_j$ and $L_k$. A new loop, $L_m$ is created with the larger upper bound of the two loops (step 1). A guard branch is then created at the beginning of the loop (step 2) and the bodies of $L_j$ and $L_k$ are included within the guard (steps 3 and 4). The guard branch checks to see if the current iteration count is less than the lower upper bound of the two loops. The bodies of the original loops are then copied into the new loop, preserving the dominance relation between them. An else statement is then inserted to guard the second loop body (step 5). The longer loop is inserted in the else statement (step 6). This guarded fusion creates more code growth than an alternative technique that would simply guard the shorter loop. However, it is preferable in this compiler because it favors a later index set splitting transformation because it will allow the common portions of the fused loop to remain together.

In step 10 we check if the dependence relations between the bodies of loops $L_j$ and $L_k$ prevent fusion. This test is performed last because checking for dependences between loop bodies is the most expensive loop fusion condition that needs to be tested. If there is a negative dependence distance from $L_j$ to $L_k$, the loops cannot be fused. In the IBM XL compiler suite, data dependences are computed on demand. For our algorithm, this computation is based on the SSA data flow representation within the context of a loop. The information about references to arrays is summarized in matrices of subscripts. These matrices are used along with vectors representing the bounds of surrounding loops to determine the dependence relation between two loop bodies, or between a loop body and intervening code. If there are dependences, the dependence analysis produces a dependence vector consisting of a distance or direction for each loop surrounding the reference pair.

The intervening code between loops $L_j$ and $L_k$ may itself contain loops. These loops are treated as regular code and are moved if dependences allow. During a forward pass, the intervening code is only moved up (step 13). This restriction on the direction of code movement during a pass is a result of an engineering design. A collection of data structures is used to store the control flow graph, the dominator and post-dominator trees, and the SSA data flow graph. We allow these data structures to become inconsistent after the fusion of loops and the movement of intervening code within a pass of the algorithm. These structures are rebuilt at the end of each pass. It would have been possible to modify the interface to these structures to allow them to be updated as fusion progressed, however we do not believe our approach has a noticeable effect on running times and it maintains the original interface. Because code is not moved down (or up) during a forward (or reverse) pass, even if all the intervening code is movable, the part of the code that must move down (or up), because of dependences, is not moved in this step. In this case the two loops do not become adjacent and cannot be fused in the same pass. Therefore, in step 14 we check once more if the loops are adjacent before fusing the two loops in step 18 and updating the

```
do i5 = 1, n                          ds  = 0.0
    if (i5 < n-1)                     if(n<m)
        a(i5) = a(i5) * k1                c(n-2) = n
        d(i5) = a(i5) - b(i5+1) * k2  else
    else                                  c(n-2) = m
        a(i5) = a(i5) * k1            do i5 = 1, n
    end do                                if (i5 < n-1)
    ds  = 0.0                                 a(i5) = a(i5) * k1
    do i3 = 1, m                              d(i5) = a(i5) - b(i5+1) * k2
      ds = ds + d(i3)                     else
    end do                                    a(i5) = a(i5) * k1
    if(n<m)                               end do
      c(n-2) = n                          do i3 = 1, m
    else                                    ds = ds + d(i3)
      c(n-2) = m                           end do
    do i4 = 1, n-2                         do i4 = 1, n-2
      b(i4) = a(i4) + b(i4) / c(i4)          b(i4) = a(i4) + b(i4) / c(i4)
    end do                                end do
```

(a) After Fusing i1 and i2 into i5                 (b) After moving intervening code up

**Fig. 6.** Completing first forward pass in running example

loop set in step 20. When all the intervening code is movable, the movement of the portion of the intervening code that can move up in step 13 prepares the loop set for a potential fusion in the next pass of the algorithm.

In the example of Figure 3(b) the first two loops to be compared are i1 and i2. There are no dependences that prevent their fusion, they are adjacent, but they are non-conforming. The test in step 15 in Figure 5 is true and the two loops are fused using the algorithm in Figure 9. This fusion results in the loop i5 shown in Figure 6(a).

The next comparison is between loops i5 and i3. There are no dependences preventing fusion, and the loops are non-adjacent but the intervening code (initialization of ds) is movable to the point before i5. However, the difference between the iteration count of the two loops cannot be determined at compile time (we assume that n and m are not known until run time), and fusion of i5 and i3 fails.

Next i5 and i4 are compared, the two loops can be made to conform, there are no dependences preventing fusion, and all the intervening code (which includes loop i3 and the if-then-else before i4) can be moved. Because of the dependence on d between i5 and i3, i3 only can be moved down to the point after i4. The dependence on c(n-2) requires the aggregate node that contains the if-then-else to be moved up to the point before i5. The MOVEINTERVEN-INGCODE algorithm moves the intervening code that can be moved up to the point before i5 resulting in the code shown in Figure 6(b). However, the test on step 14 fails, and the loops cannot be fused in this pass.

The control flow graph is rebuilt and the dominance and post-dominance relations recomputed before a reverse pass starts. In the reverse pass the loops i4 and i3 are compared, but they cannot be fused because we cannot determine the difference in their iteration count at compile time. Next, i4 and i5 are compared.

```
ds   = 0.0                          ds   = 0.0
if(n<m)                             if(n<m)
   c(n-2) = n                          c(n-2) = n
else                                else
   c(n-2) = m                          c(n-2) = m
do i5 = 1, n                        do i6 = 1, n
   if (i5 < n-1)                       if (i6 < n-2)
       a(i5) = a(i5) * k1                 if (i6 < n-1)
       d(i5) = a(i5) - b(i5+1) * k2           a(i6) = a(i6) * k1
   else                                       d(i6) = a(i6) - b(i6+1) * k2
       a(i5) = a(i5) * k1                 else
   do i4 = 1, n-2                             a(i6) = a(i6) * k1
       b(i4) = a(i4) + b(i4) / c(i4)      b(i6) = a(i6) + b(i6) / c(i6)
   end do                             else
   do i3 = 1, m                          if (i6 < n-1)
       ds = ds + d(i3)                       a(i6) = a(i6) * k1
   end do                                    d(i6) = a(i6) - b(i6+1) * k2
                                         else
                                             a(i6) = a(i6) * k1
                                      end do
                                      do i3 = 1, m
                                         ds = ds + d(i3)
                                      end do
```

(a) After moving intervening code          (b) After fusing i5 and i4 into i6

**Fig. 7.** Final reverse pass on running example

The only intervening code (loop i3) can be moved down below i4. The difference in iteration count between i4 and i5 is 2 and there are no dependencies that prevent fusion. The intervening code between i4 and i5 is moved down (in step 13) resulting in the code shown in Figure 7(a). The two loops are then fused resulting in the code in Figure 7(b) and the reverse pass terminates. The next forward pass will result in no additional fusions and the algorithm will terminate.

As discussed in Section 3, the code is organized into aggregate nodes. An aggregate node is a minimum code segment that must be moved as a unit. Examples of aggregate nodes include a single statement, a nest of loops, or an if-then-else statement with arbitrarily complex code in each branch. The algorithm in Figure 8 checks if all the aggregate nodes in the intervening code found between two loops $L_j$ and $L_k$ can be moved to other places in the program. In step 1 we build the set InterveningCodeSet containing all the aggregated nodes that are *intervening code* between the two loops. An aggregate node $a_x$ is intervening code between two loops $L_j$ and $L_k$ if $L_j$ properly dominates $a_x$, $L_j \prec_d a_x$ and $L_k$ properly post-dominates $a_x$, $L_k \prec_{pd} a_x$.

We cannot move aggregate nodes that might have side effects. Instances of code that have side effects include volatile load/store, statements that perform I/O, and unknown functions that might contain such statements. If any of the aggregate nodes in the intervening code between two loops have or may have side effects, the intervening code is *non-movable* (step 2).

When determining the direction in which an aggregate node $a_x$ can move, we need to take into consideration the data dependences between $a_x$ and the remaining aggregate nodes in the intervening code, as well as the data dependence relations with the loops $L_j$ and $L_k$. Thus we build a Data Dependence Graph $G$ for the nodes in the aggregate node set (step 4). Then we traverse $G$ in topological order to build the CanMoveUpSet, the set of nodes that can be moved to the point before the loop $L_j$ (steps 5 to 10). A node $a_y$ can move up if

```
ISINTERVENINGCODEMOVABLE(L_j, L_k)
1.    InterveningCodeSet ← {a_x|L_j ≺_d a_x and L_k ≺_pd a_x}
2.    if any node in InterveningCodeSet is non-movable
3.        return False
4.    Build a DDG G of InterveningCodeSet
5.    CanMoveUpSet ← ∅
6.    foreach a_y ∈ G in topological order
7.            if CanMoveUp(Predecessors(a_y)) and L_j δ̸ a_y
8.                CanMoveUpSet ← CanMoveUpSet ∪{a_y}
9.            endif
10.   endfor
11.   CanMoveDownSet ← ∅
12    foreach a_z ∈ G in reverse topological order
13.           if CanMoveDown(Successors(a_z)) and a_z δ̸ L_k
14.                CanMoveDownSet ← CanMoveDownSet ∪{a_z}
15.           endif
16.   endfor
17.   if InterveningCodeSet −
          (CanMoveUpSet ∪ CanMoveUpSet) = ∅
18.       return True
19.   return False
```

**Fig. 8.** Algorithm to check if all intervening code can be moved

```
FUSEWITHGUARD(L_j, L_k)
1.    Create L_m with upper bound max(κ(L_j), κ(L_k))
2.    Insert Guard Bound for min(κ(L_j), κ(L_k)) at beginning
      of L_m
3.    Copy body of L_j to L_m, within guard
4.    Copy body of L_k to L_m, after L_j body, within guard
5.    Insert else statement
6.    if (κ(L_j) > κ(L_k))
7.        Copy body of L_j to L_m, after else statement
8.    else
9.        Copy body of L_k to L_m, after else statement
10.   endif
```

**Fig. 9.** Algorithm to fuse loops using a guard statement

there are no data dependences between the preceding loop $L_j$ and $a_y$, $L_j \not\delta a_y$, and all the predecessors of $a_y$ in $G$ can also move up.

Similarly, in steps 11 to 16 we traverse $G$ in reverse topological order to build the set of nodes that can move down, the CanMoveDownSet. In order to move a node $a_z$ down, there must be no dependences between $a_z$ and the second loop $L_k$, and all of $a_z$'s successors must be able to move down. The test in step 17 tests if every aggregate node in the InterveningCodeSet can be moved either up or down.

The MoveInterveningCode called in step 13 of the LoopFusionPass uses the sets created by the IsInterveningCodeMovable to move code. If called during a forward pass, it simply traverses the DDG and moves any aggregate node that can move up to the point before the first loop $L_j$. Likewise, when called during a reverse pass, it moves all nodes that can move down to the point after the second loop $L_k$.

## 5   Results

We implemented the algorithms presented in Section 4 in the development version of the IBM XL compiler suite and ran benchmarks compiled with this modified compiler on an IBM eServer pSeries 690 machine built with the POWER4 processor. Figure 10 presents preliminary results for the SPEC2000 and SPEC95

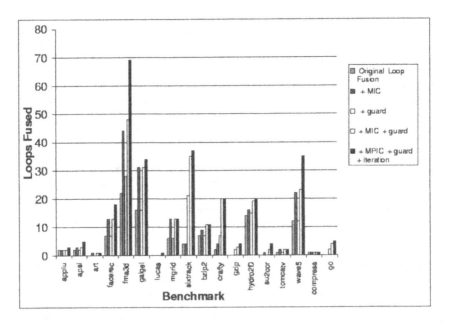

**Fig. 10.** Number of loops fused with each version of the compiler[3]

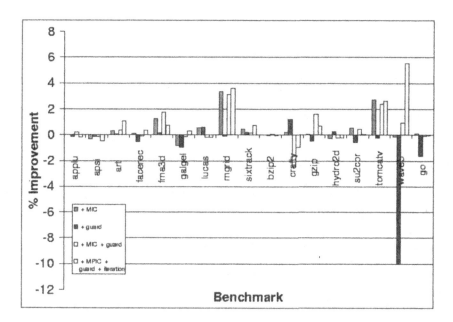

**Fig. 11.** Execution times for selected SPEC benchmarks with multiple versions of the compiler suite

benchmark suites. We only include in the figures of results the benchmarks in which our loop fusion algorithm affects code transformations, *i.e.*, benchmarks in which more loops are fused as a result of our algorithm. Also, benchmarks from SPEC95 which also occur in the SPEC2000 suite were not repeated.

We compare five versions of our algorithm with an implementation of basic loop fusion. Figure 10 presents the number of loop fusions that occurs in each version of the compiler. The versions of the compiler are:

**Original:** It is a basic loop fusion algorithm in which no code transformations are performed to try and make loops fusible.

**+MIC:** Does a single forward pass of the algorithm and moves any intervening code that can be moved up. If all of the intervening code cannot be moved up, fusion fails.

**+MPIC:** Part of the intervening code is moved up. In order for fusion to benefit from this, the iteration step must be included.

**+guard:** Non-conforming loops are fused using the guard branch. It does not, however, allow intervening code between two loops to be moved.

**+MIC +guard:** Combines guarding and simple code motion.

**+MIC +guard +iteration:** Complete implementation of the iterative algorithm executing as many passes as required for maximal fusion.

The results in Figure 10 indicate that each of the transformations affect different benchmarks. The movement of intervening code (columns *MIC* and *MPIC*) results approximately doubles the number of loops fused in fma3d, galgel, facerec, and mgrid. The number of loops fused with *MPIC* or without *MIC* partial movement of intervening code is the same. This is to be expected because moving partial intervening code (move some statements up in current pass and the remainder down in the reverse pass) only benefits when the iteration step is added. The more complex *MPIC* pass, however, does not result in performance degredations when compared to the simpler *MIC* pass.

When loops are made to conform through the use of guard branches (*guard*), five times as many loops are fused in sixtrack, three times as many loops are fused in crafty and 27% more loops are fused for fma3d. Both gzip and go had 2 loops fused where none were fused in the original algorithm. However, for all other benchmarks, no extra loops are fused.

Combining the movement of intervening code with the guard branches for loop conformation (*MIC* and *guard*) produces a dramatic increase in the number of fused loops for many benchmarks.

Finally, the addition of the iteration step, in combination with the *MPIC* and *guard* options resulted in even more loops fused in several benchmarks (apsi, facerec, fma3d, galgel and sixtrack). This demonstrates that there are cases in which moving intervening code below the second loop (reverse pass) and splitting intervening code to move part of the intervening code above the first loop and the rest below the second loop can be very beneficial.

The technique to generate more fusion that we report in this paper is an enabling technology for optimizations that take place later in this compiler framework. We are now addressing some of those optimizations and finding ways in which they will benefit from the larger scope provided by our improved fusion. Nonetheless, a paper reporting advancement of compiler technology would not be complete without run times for SPEC benchmarks. Therefore, we present the running times for the different versions of the compiler in Figure 11. In the current version of the compiler, the impact of the increased fusion in the running times is modest. The most significant performance change is in wave5, where tripling the number of loops fused resulted in an improvement of 5.1% in the running time. The other significant performance change is in mgrid, where doubling the number of loops fused resulted in an improvement of 3.6% in the running time. We are in the process of obtaining run-time measurements using hardware counters in the POWER4 (performance of caches, load/stores completed, *etc.,*) to offer better explanations for the performance changes.

When non-conforming loops are fused as a result of adding guard statements, control flow is introduced into the loop body. The insertion of control flow into a loop might inhibit software pipelining. Thus, we would expect to see a degradation in performance in this case. We are currently investigating several of the benchmarks (crafty, fma3d and sixtrack) to determine if there were benefits to loop fusion (*i.e.*, data reuse) which offset the negative effects of introducing control flow. We are also working on a variation of index set splitting that will be able to identify branches within a loop and peel or split the loop to remove control flow splits.

# 6    Related Work

In this paper we presented improvements to the maximal loop fusion algorithms in the IBM XL Fortran and VisualAge for C compilers. Scant work has been published on maximal loop fusion followed by a loop distributor. In contrast, there has been extensive studies and experimentation with weighted loop fusion. Weighted loop fusion associates non-negative weights with each pair of loop nests. These weights are a measurement of the gains that are expected if the two loops were fused. Examples of gains represented in weighted loop graphs include potential for array contraction, improved data reuse, and improved local register allocation. Given such a weighted graph representing potential fusions, the goal of weighted loop fusion is to group the loop nests into clusters in a way that minimizes the total weight of edges that cross cluster boundaries [14].

In Gao *et al.*, a Loop Dependence Graph (LDG) provides a measure for the number of arrays that can be contracted when two loops are fused. Contracted arrays can be represented by a small number of scalar variables, thus removing memory instructions through the elimination of multiple load/stores of the same array. Their solution for this modified weighted loop fusion problem is based on the max-flow/min-cut algorithm [6]. The LDG based solution for loop fusion focuses on solving the problem of moving data between the cache and the registers, while our approach also takes into consideration the data cache performance.

Kennedy and McKinley used a polynomial reduction of the Multiway Cut problem to prove that solving the weighted loop fusion problem to maximize data reuse is NP-Hard. They also provide a greedy algorithm and a variation of the max-flow/min-cut algorithm to find approximated solutions for loop fusion [10]. Megiddo and Sarkar propose an integer linear programming solution for weighted loop fusion based on the Loop Dependence Graph (LDG) [14].

In [11] Kennedy and McKinley introduce the concept of *loop type*. In their experiments they used two types of loops: *parallel loops* are loops that have no loop-carried dependences, and *sequential loops* are loops that have at least one loop-carried dependence. In order to be fused, two loops must be of the same type, and must be conformable at level $k$, *i.e.* they are at the same level of perfect nests and all their outer loops are conformable. Two loops are conformable if they have the same iteration count. When performing *Unordered Typed Fusion* they try to produce the fewest loops without giving priority to any loop type. Through a reduction of the Vertex Cover problem they show that the Unordered Typed Fusion problem is NP-Hard. On the other hand, the Ordered Typed Fusion exercises a preference for fusing loops of a given type. For instance, parallel loops should be fused first — and thus potentially prevent some later fusion of sequential loops — when data reuse is not a concern. They propose a greedy algorithm to solve the Ordered Typed Fusion problem.

Loop distribution was introduced in Muraoka's Ph.D. thesis to improve parallelism [15]. Kuck introduced the idea of using a portion of the dependence graphs in the loop distribution algorithm, and defined of a $\pi$-block as a strong

---

[3] Measurements were not done using the official SPEC tools.

connected component of the data dependence graph [13]. Kennedy and McKinley designed a loop distribution algorithm for loops with complex control flow that does not replicate statements or conditions [9]. Hsieh, Hind, and Cytron extend the algorithm to allow the distribution of loops with multiple exits [8]. A comprehensive discussion of loop transformations is found in Bacon *et al.* [2].

In addition to improving data locality and reducing loop overhead, loop fusion can increase the granularity of parallelism and minimize loop synchronization. Some research on loop fusion focuses on multi-processor architectures and programs that can run in parallel. Singhai and McKinley developed a heuristic to fuse loops, taking into account both data locality and parallelism subject to register pressure [16].

Gupta and Bodik introduce a technique for loop transformations, including loop fusion, to be decided at run time instead of compile time [7]. Kennedy and McKinley provided an algorithm for fusing a collection of parallel and sequential loops that minimizes parallel loop synchronizations while maximizing parallelism [10].

## 7     Final Remarks

Many papers address the problem of optimizing the set of loops that should be fused to increase data reuse through graph partition and related techniques. However, there has been scant documentation of the actual process of combining code motion with fusion to enable maximal loop fusion and allow the redistribution of these loops at a later phase. Thus the description of the maximal loop fusion algorithms in this paper is an important contribution. Our algorithm is fast — there are no noticeable changes in the compile time when the fusion algorithm is implemented — and easy to implement and debug.

Our next line of study will include removing the restriction that all the loops that are fused must be control equivalent. We will investigate techniques similar to the ones described by Chen and Kennedy [5] that allow the critical path of a loop to be increased when there is a potential for benefits due to increased data reuse.

The loop distributor is also being enhanced in light of the new loop fusion implementation. Larger loop nests are being created, which are providing new scenarios for the loop distributor to to evaluate and deal with.

Loop alignment is another well known loop transformation which we are also working on. Performing loop alignment on loops that have a known distance negative dependence will allow even more loops to be fused.

A form of Index Set-Splitting is currently being developed that will analyze the guard branches generated by the FuseWithGuard algorithm and create new loops (through loop peeling or loop splitting) that do not contain the guards. This optimization will eliminate the control flow splits introduced during fusion, which should increase opportunities for later optimizations, such as software pipelining.

We believe this work provides an excellent framework to enhance the number of loops which are fused in a program. This loop fusion enables other optimizations, such as loop distribution, to make better decisions on how to organize loops to increase performance. While the runtime results presented do not indicate this work had any improvement on overall performance, we are confident that it does create more opportunities for other optimizations and work is currently underway to enhance these optimizations to benefit from these fusion results.

## Acknowledgements

The work reported in this paper uses the infrastructure built by many hands. We thank the Toronto Portable Optimizer (TPO) and Toronto Optimizing Backend (TOBEY) teams for building this infrastructure. Special thanks to Jim McInnes, Ryan Weedon, and Roch Archambault for extensive and fruitful discussions. This research is supported by an IBM Centre for Advanced Studies (CAS) fellowship and by grants from the National Sciences and Engineering Council of Canada (NSERC), including a grant from the Collaborative Research Development (CRD) Grants program.

## Trademarks

The following terms are trademarks or registered trademarks of International Business Machines Corporation in the United States, other countries, or both: IBM, PowerPC, POWER3, POWER4, pSeries, VisualAge.

UNIX is a registered trademark of The Open Group in the United States and other countries.

## References

1. A. W. Lim an S.-W. Liao and M. S. Lam. Blocking and array contraction across arbitrarily nested loops using affine partitioning. In *Proceedings of the ACM SIGPLAN Symposium on Principles and Practice of Parallel Programming*, pages 103–112, June 2001.
2. D. F. Bacon, S. L. Graham, and O. J. Sharp. Compiler transformations for high-performance computing. *ACM Computing Surveys*, 26(4):345–420, 1994.
3. Steve Behling, Ron Bell, Peter Farrell, Holger Holthoff, Frank O'Connell, and Will Weir. The power4 processor introduction and tuning guide. Technical Report SG24-7041-00, IBM, November 2001.
4. C. Ding and K. Kennedy. The memory bandwidth bottleneck and its amelioration by a compiler. In *2000 International Parallel and Distributed Processing Symposium*, pages 181–189, Cancun, Mexico, May 2000.
5. C. Ding and K. Kennedy. Improving effective bandwidth through compiler enhancement of global cache reuse. In *International Parallel and Distribute Processing Symposium*, San Francisco, CA, April 2001. ´

6. Guang R. Gao, Russ Olsen, Vivek Sarkar, and Radhika Thekkath. Collective loop fusion for array contraction. In *1992 Workshop on Languages and Compilers for Parallel Computing*, pages 281–295, New Haven, Conn., 1992. Berlin: Springer Verlag.

7. R. Gupta and R. Bodik. Adaptive loop transformations for scientific programs. In *IEEE Symposium on Parallel and Distributed Processing*, pages 368–375, San Antonio, Texas, October 1995.

8. B.-M. Hsieh, M. Hind, and R. Cytron. Loop distribution with multiple exits. In *Proceedings of Supercomputing*, pages 204–213, November 1992.

9. K. Kennedy and K. S. McKinley. Loop distribution with arbitrary control flow. In *Proceedings of Supercomputing*, pages 407–417. IEEE Computer Society Press, November 1990.

10. K. Kennedy and K. S. McKinley. Typed fusion with applications to parallel and sequential code generation. Technical Report CRPC-TR94646, Rice University, Center for Research on Parallel Computation, 1994.

11. Ken Kennedy and Kathryn S. McKinley. Maximizing loop parallelism and improving data locality via loop fusion and distribution. In *1993 Workshop on Languages and Compilers for Parallel Computing*, pages 301–320, Portland, Ore., 1993. Berlin: Springer Verlag.

12. Kevin Krewell. Ibm's power4 unveiling continues: New details revealed at microprocessor forum 2000. In *Microprocessor Report: The Insider's Guide to Microprocessor Hardware*, November 2000.

13. D. J. Kuck. A survey of parallel machine organization and programming. *ACM Computing Surveys*, 9(1):29–59, March 1977.

14. Nimrod Megiddo and Vivek Sarkar. Optimal weighted loop fusion for parallel programs. In *ACM Symposium on Parallel Algorithms and Architectures*, pages 282–291, 1997.

15. Y. Muraoka. *Parallelism Exposure and Exploitation in Programs*. PhD thesis, University of Illinois at Urbana Champaign, Dept. of Computer Science, February 1971. Report No. 71-424.

16. S. Singhai and K. McKinley. A parameterized loop fusion algorithm for improving parallelism and cache locality. *The Computer Journal*, 40(6):340–355, 1997.

# Near-Optimal Padding for Removing Conflict Misses

Xavier Vera[1], Josep Llosa[2], and Antonio González[2]

[1] Institutionen för Datateknik, Mälardalens Högskola
P.O. BOX 883, Västerås, 721 23, Sweden
xavier.vera@mdh.se
[2] Computer Architecture Department, Universitat Politècnica de
Catalunya-Barcelona
Jordi Girona 1-3, Barcelona, 08034, Spain
{josepll, antonio}@ac.upc.es

**Abstract.** The effectiveness of the memory hierarchy is critical for the performance of current processors. The performance of the memory hierarchy can be improved by means of program transformations such as padding, which is a code transformation targeted to reduce conflict misses. This paper presents a novel approach to perform near-optimal padding for multi-level caches. It analyzes programs, detecting conflict misses by means of the Cache Miss Equations. A genetic algorithm is used to compute the parameter values that enhance the program. Our results show that it can remove practically all conflicts among variables in the SPECfp95, targeting all the different cache levels simultaneously.

## 1 Introduction

Memory performance is critical for the performance of current computers. Memory is organized hierarchically in such a way that the upper levels are smaller and faster. The uppermost level typically has a very short latency (e.g. 1-2 cycles) but the latency of the lower levels may be a few orders of magnitude longer (e.g. main memory latency may be around 100 cycles). Thus, techniques to keep as much data as possible in the uppermost levels are key to performance.

In addition to the hardware organization, it is well known that the performance of the memory hierarchy is very sensitive to the particular memory reference patterns of each program. The reference patterns of a given program can be changed by means of transformations that do not alter the semantics of the program. These program transformations can modify the order in which some computations are performed or can simply change the data layout. *Padding* is an example of the latter family of techniques. Padding is based on adding some dummy elements between variables (inter-variable padding) or between elements of the same variable (intra-variable padding).

Padding has a significant potential to remove cache misses. In fact, it can remove most conflict misses by changing the addresses of conflicting data, and some compulsory misses by aligning data with cache lines. However, finding the

B. Pugh and C.-W. Tseng (Eds.): LCPC 2002, LNCS 2481, pp. 329–343, 2005.
© Springer-Verlag Berlin Heidelberg 2005

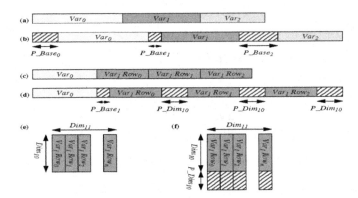

**Fig. 1.** Data layout: (a) before inter-variable padding, (b) after inter-variable padding (c) before padding, (d) after padding, (e) 2-D array, (f) 2-D array after intra-variable padding

optimal padding for a given program is a very complex task, since the options are almost unlimited and exploring all of them is infeasible. For very simple programs, the programmer intuition may help but in general, a systematic approach that can be integrated into a compiler and can deal with any type of program and cache architecture is desirable. This systematic approach requires the support of a locality analysis method in order to assess the performance of different alternatives.

In this paper, we propose an automatic approach to perform both inter- and intra-variable padding in numeric codes, targeting any kind of multi-level caches. It is based on a very accurate technique to analyze the locality of a program that is known as Cache Miss Equations (CMEs) [6] and a genetic algorithm in order to search the solution space. Earlier, we have proposed techniques to estimate the locality of a possible solution in a very few seconds [2, 21], in spite of the fact that a direct solution to the CMEs is an NP problem. The proposed genetic algorithm converges very fast and although it does not guarantee that the optimal solution is found, we show that after padding, the conflict miss ratio of the evaluated benchmarks is almost negligible. Besides, comparing our method with previous frameworks that address padding [17, 19], it turns out that in 91% of the cases our approach yields better results.

The rest of this paper is organized as follows. Section 2 presents the padding technique and its performance is evaluated in Section 3. Section 4 outlines some related work and compares our method with previous approaches. Finally, Section 5 summarizes the main conclusions of this work.

## 2   Padding

This section presents our method for guiding both inter- and intra-variable padding. In this paper we refer to the cache size of L1 (primary) cache as $C_s$.

$mem_i$ is the original base address of variable number $i$ ($Var_i$) and $P\_Base_i$ stands for the inter-variable padding between $Var_i$ and $Var_{i-1}$. $dim_{ij}$ stands for the size of the dimension $j$ of $Var_i$ ($D_i$ is the number of dimensions) and $S_i$ is its size. $P\_Dim_{ij}$ is the intra-variable padding applied to $dim_{ij}$, and $P\_S_i$ is the size of $Var_i$ after padding (see Figure 1). We define $\Delta_i$ as $P\_S_i - S_i$.

## 2.1 Inter-variable Padding

When inter-variable padding is applied only the base addresses of the variables are changed. Thus, padding is performed in a simple way. Memory variable base addresses are initially defined using the values given by the compiler. Then, we define for each memory variable $Var_i$, a variable $P\_Base_i$, $i = 0 \ldots k$:

$$0 \le P\_Base_i \le C_s - 1$$

Note that padding a variable is equivalent to modifying the initial addresses of the other variables (see Figure 1). Thus, after padding, the memory variable base addresses are computed as follows:

$$BaseAddr(Var_i) = mem_i + \sum_{k=0}^{k \le i} P\_Base_k$$

## 2.2 Adding Intra-variable Padding

The result of applying both inter- and intra-variable padding is that all base addresses and sizes of every dimension of each memory variable may change. They are initially set according to the values given by the compiler. For each memory variable $Var_i$, $i = 0 \ldots k$ we define a set of variables $\{P\_Base_i, P\_Dim_{ij}\}$, $j = 0 \ldots D_i$

$$0 \le P\_Base_i, P\_Dim_{ij} \le C_s - 1$$

After padding, memory variable base addresses are computed in the following way (see Figure 1):

$$BaseAddr(Var_i) = mem_i +$$
$$+ \sum_{k=0}^{k < i}(P\_Base_k + \Delta_k) + P\_Base_i$$

and the size of the dimensions are:

$$Dim_i(Var_j) = dim_{ji} + P\_Dim_{ji}$$

## 2.3 Model

For the sake of uniformity in the analysis presented here, we assume that both inter- and intra-variable padding are applied[1] In presence of a multi-level cache,

---

[1] To apply only inter-variable padding, set all $P\_Dim_{ij}$ to 0.

the cost function to minimize is the miss penalty, which can be estimated as follows:

$$miss\_penalty = \sum_l \mu_l * number\_misses_l$$

where $\mu_l$ is the latency of the cache level $l$. Our work focuses in obtaining the values of the variables

$$\{P\_Base_i, P\_Dim_{ij}\}$$

that minimizes the miss penalty. When having only a single level cache, minimizing the miss penalty is the same as minimizing the number of misses.

Let $f$ be the function that represents the miss penalty for each possible value of the padding variables:

$$f \longmapsto miss\_penalty \tag{1}$$

$$f(\underbrace{[0, C_s - 1]}_{P\_Base_0} \times \underbrace{[0, C_s - 1]^{D_0}}_{P\_Dim_{0j}} \times \ldots \times \underbrace{[0, C_s - 1]}_{P\_Base_k} \times \underbrace{[0, C_s - 1]^{D_k}}_{P\_Dim_{kj}}) =$$
$$= f(P\_Base_0, \underbrace{P\_Dim_{0j}}_{D_0}, \ldots, P\_Base_k, \underbrace{P\_Dim_{kj}}_{D_k})$$

Note that $[0, C_s - 1]^{D_i}$ represents the domain of the different $P\_Dim_{ij}$ of the variable $Var_i$. There is no need to consider larger domains: if two references do not conflict on a cache of size $S$, they will not conflict on a cache of size $nS$ (larger by a factor of $n$). Therefore, we use the cache size of the smallest cache in the hierarchy (which in practice is L1).

Our problem can be expressed as follows:

$$MIN \quad f(P\_Base_0, \underbrace{P\_Dim_{0j}}_{D_0} \ldots, P\_Base_k, \underbrace{P\_Dim_{kj}}_{D_k})$$

$$0 \leq P\_Base_i, P\_Dim_{ij} \leq C_s - 1$$

$$i = 0 \ldots k$$

where $f$ is called the *objective function*.

Since $f$ is a pseudo-polynomial function [4], the relationship between padding and the number of misses is nonlinear. $P\_Base_i$ and $P\_Dim_{ij}$ can take only integer values, thus, our problem can be seen as a nonlinear integer optimization (NLP) one.

One of the challenges in NLP is that some problems exhibit local minima. Algorithms that propose to overcome this problem are named *Global Optimization*. Real functions have been studied deeply [20, 12, 7]. Unfortunately, integer functions are hard to optimize. There are some studies based on {0,1} valued integer functions [10], but in general, this is a hard and time-consuming problem. Hence, the use of heuristics is necessary. Tabu search [8] obtains promising theoretical results, but only partial implementations have been reported so far. On the other hand, simulated annealing [13] and genetic algorithms [9, 11] have been used for years with very good results.

```
ALGORITHM:
Supply a population P₀
i=1
while (not finish)
    Pᵢ=Selection(Pᵢ₋₁)
    Pᵢ=Reproduce(Pᵢ)
    i=i+1
end
```

**Fig. 2.** Simple Genetic Algorithm

Our proposal is based on the use of a genetic algorithm to optimize function $f$. We implemented a direct-search that makes the same number of evaluations as our approach for the sake of comparison. In none of the cases did it yield better results than the genetic algorithm and the miss penalty was 26.9% larger on average.

## 2.4  Genetic Algorithm

Algorithms for function optimization are generally limited to convex regular functions. However, there are lots of functions that are not continuous, non differentiable or multi-modal. It is common to solve this problem by means of stochastic sampling.

Genetic Algorithms (GAs) [9] are a particular type of stochastic methods, that simulate the evolution of a population. Figure 2 shows the simplest GA. It starts from a random generated population, and it makes the population evolve by means of basic genetic operators (selection, mutation and crossover) [9] applied to individuals of the current population, to produce an improved next generation. The probabilities for crossover and mutation, as well as the size of the initial population, are set experimentally.

**Genetic Algorithm Parameters.** The use of GAs requires the determination of the following issues: chromosome representation, selection function, genetic operators and the termination criteria.

Each individual is made up of a set of chromosomes, which represents the variables. In our work, each individual is one configuration of padding (identified by all the inter- and intra-variable padding factors), and the chromosomes represent one single padding factor. The fitness of those individuals is computed using the objective function (eq. 1). The fittest individual is the one that has a set of padding factors that results in a smallest miss penalty.

Genetic algorithms require the natural parameter set of the optimization problem to be coded as a finite-length string over some finite alphabet such as alphabet {0,1}. Therefore, each chromosome is made up of a sequence of genes from a certain alphabet.

It has been shown that using large alphabets gives better results [15]. Thus, we have used the alphabet $\{0, \ldots, 2^k - 1\}$, where $k$ is the greatest divisor of the

$log_2 C_s$ that is lower than $log_2 C_s$. This is the largest value of $k$ that guarantees that a single padding factor consists of at least two genes for every cache size. This is not a restriction because the compilers know the cache size. Thus, this computation can be done automatically.

**Example.** Let us assume a cache of 32KB. Thus, $log_2(32 \times 2^{10}) = 15$. The set of divisors is $divisors = \{1, 3, 5, 15\}$. Hence, the greatest divisor less than 15 is 5, and we will use the alphabet $\{0, \ldots, 31\}$, representing each single padding with 3 genes. For instance, a padding factor of 10017 is represented by the following three genes:

$$\underbrace{01001}_{gene_0=9} \underbrace{11001}_{gene_1=25} \underbrace{00001}_{gene_2=1}$$

$$\underbrace{\qquad\qquad\qquad\qquad\qquad}_{chromosome}$$

Genetic operators provide the basic search mechanism of the GAs, creating new solutions based on the solutions that exist. The *selection* of individuals to produce successive generations plays an extremely important role. We have adopted one of the selection schemes that gives better results, which is known as *remainder stochastic selection without replacement* [9].

### 2.5  Implementation of Padding

Given a loop nest, our objective function ($f$ in eq. 1) consists of the CMEs generated in a parameterized way, weighted with the latencies of each cache level. We generate a set of parameterized equations for each cache level, where the parameters are the padding factors. We have developed some techniques that exploit the special characteristics of the CMEs [2] in order to speed-up the process of counting solutions in them. To further reduce the computation cost, we propose to study a subset of the iteration space instead of the whole iteration space [21]. This subset is used to study the L1 cache, and the resulting misses are passed to the following cache levels.

Our experiments have shown that an initial population of size equal to 30 is enough to achieve a good solution. We find that if we set crossover probability to 0.9 and we choose a mutation probability of 0.001, the genetic algorithm gives near-optimal results after 15 generations.

## 3  Performance Evaluation

### 3.1  Experimental Framework

We have implemented our padding technique for Fortran codes through the Polaris Compiler [16] and the Ictineo library [1].

We evaluate the CMEs using our own polyhedra representation [2]. The size of the sample is set according to a confidence interval of width 0.05 and a 95% confidence [21]. We use the central point of this interval as an estimation of the actual miss ratio.

We have optimized several applications taken from the SPECfp95 that give an insight into how our tool can remove conflict misses. For each application, we have chosen the most time-consuming loop nests that in total represent between the 60-70% of the whole execution time, using the reference input data. Results for different cache architectures, including multi-level caches, are reported. A fully-associative cache has been evaluated as a reference point to estimate the amount of conflict misses that are not removed by the padding technique.

## 3.2   Experimental Evaluation

Figure 3 shows, for the 6 SPECfp95 programs analyzed, the miss ratio of a direct-mapped cache before and after applying inter-variable padding. Note that the figures for the different cache sizes (32KB, 16KB, 8KB, and 4KB) have different scales. Note also that the SPECfp95 applications have a relatively small working set with respect to current applications. Thus, the results for the smaller cache sizes may be more representative of what we can expect today for larger caches and bigger applications. Two sets of programs can be distinguished:

- **Set1** is composed of programs Tomcatv and Swim. The miss ratio of this set of programs is highly affected by cache size. In addition many of the misses are due to conflicts [5].
- **Set2** is composed of programs Su2cor, Hydro, Mgrid, and Applu. The miss ratio of this set of programs is quite insensitive to the cache size. In addition all the programs of this set have practically no conflict misses [5].

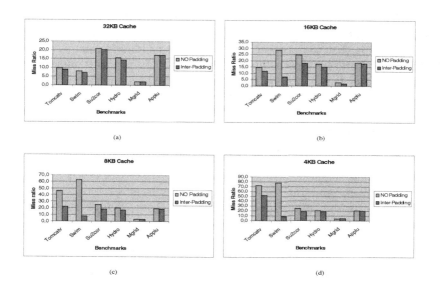

**Fig. 3.** Miss ratio before and after inter-variable padding for different cache sizes

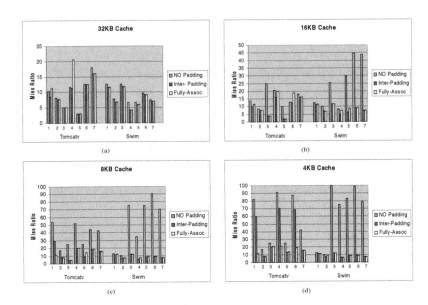

**Fig. 4.** Miss ratio for the Tomcatv and Swim loop nests before and after inter-variable padding for different cache sizes

**Inter-Variable Padding.** Since the objective of padding is to eliminate conflict misses, for **Set2** we obtain a small improvement when applying inter-variable padding due to the low number of conflicts. Su2cor, which is the program with the highest conflict miss ratio in this set, experiences the highest improvement (e.g 27% miss rate reduction for a 16KB cache). In addition, another source of improvement is that the proposed inter-variable padding technique also aligns the data structures with cache lines, which reduces compulsory misses.

On the other hand, inter-variable padding provides a huge improvement in miss ratio for **Set1**. Note that for both programs, a small improvement is obtained for a 32KB cache (Figure 3.a). This is caused by the fact that almost no conflicts arise for 32KB caches or bigger for these programs due to the relatively small working set of the SPECfp95 applications. However, the smaller the cache the bigger the miss ratio and the bigger the improvement that inter-variable padding obtains.

For the Swim program, the miss ratio grows from 8.1% to 24.8%, 62.9%, and 77.9% when the cache is reduced from 32KB to 16KB (Figure 3.b), 8KB (Figure 3.c), and 4KB (Figure 3.d) respectively. However, when we apply inter-variable padding, the miss ratio is kept almost constant (7.1%, 7.2%, 7.8% and 8.2% respectively). This is because most of the misses of this program are caused by conflicts between different data structures (inter-variable conflict misses) and the algorithm practically obtains the optimal padding among them.

For the Tomcatv program, the miss ratio also grows significantly when the cache size is reduced (9.5%, 14.8%, 46.0%, and 72.1% respectively for the dif-

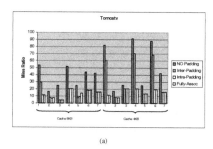
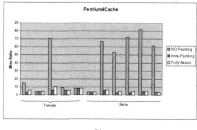

(a)                                          (b)

**Fig. 5.** (a) Miss ratio for different Tomcatv loop nests before and after inter- and intra-variable padding (b) Miss ratio for the Tomcatv and Swim loop nests for the Pentium 4 L1 cache

ferent cache sizes). In this program, we also obtain a considerable improvement when applying inter-variable padding for caches smaller than 32KB. However, the miss ratio after inter-variable padding varies significantly with the cache size (8.8%, 11.8%, 21.6%, and 52%). This variation is caused by capacity misses that grow when the cache is reduced, and by intra-variable conflict misses (e.g. conflicts among distinct rows and columns of the same array) whose frequency also grows when the cache is reduced. Inter-variable padding does not remove the latter type of conflicts, which are the target of intra-variable padding.

Figure 4 details the miss ratio for the main loop nests of the programs in **Set1** (note again the different scales for the different cache sizes). The figure shows the miss ratio for each loop before and after applying inter-variable padding. It also shows the miss ratio for a fully-associative cache after inter-variable padding.

For the Swim program loop nests 1 and 2 have practically no improvement due to inter-variable padding (excepting a slight improvement due to alignment) because they have no conflict misses. Note also that these two loop nests have almost the same miss rate regardless of the cache size. On the other hand, loop nests 3 to 7 have an extremely large miss ratio. As an extreme case, loop nest 3 has a miss ratio close to 100% for a 4KB cache, which after inter-variable padding is reduced to 11.8%. Note that inter-variable padding removes all the conflict misses for all Swim loops since the miss rate after inter-variable padding and the fully-associative miss rate are practically identical.

The Tomcatv program has several loop nests that deserve special comments. For the 32KB and 16KB, the proposed inter-variable padding technique practically removes all conflict misses. For the 8KB cache, inter-variable padding removes all conflict misses from all loop nests except for loop 1. In this case, inter-variable padding reduces the miss ratio from 53.6% to 29.2% but not all conflict misses are removed since the fully-associative miss ratio is 11.4%. An analysis of this loop shows that there are also intra-conflict misses.

In the case of a 4KB cache, inter-variable padding achieves about the same miss rate as a fully-associative cache for loop nests 2, 3, 5, and 7. As a noticeable case, the miss ratio of loop 7 has been reduced from 42.3% to 15.8%. For the other loop nests there is a significant improvement but the miss ratio is still far

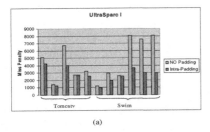 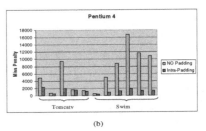

(a)                                        (b)

**Fig. 6.** Miss penalty before and after intra-padding for (a) UltraSparc I (b) Pentium 4 cache architectures

from that of the fully-associative cache. An analysis of these three loop nests revealed that most of the remaining misses are intra-variable conflict misses.

**Intra-Variable Padding.** Inter-variable padding cannot remove intra-variable conflict misses. The objective of intra-variable padding is to eliminate them.

We have shown in the previous section that Tomcatv is the only program of our benchmarks that has a significant intra-variable conflict miss ratio, in particular for caches of 4KB and 8KB. Figure 5.a shows the miss ratio for the different loop nests of the Tomcatv program. The figure shows the miss ratio for each loop after applying inter- and intra-variable padding. It also shows the miss ratio before padding and that of a fully-associative. As we observed before, inter-variable padding does not remove all conflict misses because there are intra-conflict misses. Intra-variable padding achieves about the same miss rate as the fully-associative cache, which means that the proposed padding algorithm removes practically all conflict misses.

Figure 5.b details the miss ratio for the main loop nests of the programs in **Set1** for a 8KB 4-way set associative cache with 64B lines, which is the L1 cache architecture of the new Pentium 4 processor [3]. Intra-variable padding achieves about the same miss ratio as the fully associative cache, reducing the average miss ratio from 62.5% to 4.18% for the Swim program, and from 23.6% to 4.6% for the Tomcatv.

### 3.3    Multi-level Caches

We experimentally evaluated multi-level padding for uniprocessors. Cache analyses were made for two different configurations:

– UltraSparc I:
  - 16KB, 32B line direct-mapped L1 cache
  - 512KB, 64B line direct-mapped L2 cache
– Pentium 4
  - 8KB, 64B line 4-way set-associative L1 cache
  - 256KB, 128B line 8-way set-associative L2 cache

For both processors, the L2 latency is approximately 3 times the latency of L1, so for computing the cost function, we define the miss penalty in multiples of L1 latency (e.g. a hit has no penalty, a L1 miss adds a penalty of 1, and a L2 miss adds a penalty of 3). We analyzed the most significant loop nests from Tomcatv and Swim, applying intra-variable padding. Figure 6.a shows the miss penalty for the different loop nests assuming a cache architecture such as UltraSparc I. Intra-variable padding reduces 21.7% the average miss penalty for the Tomcatv program, and it reduces the average miss penalty by 50.7% for the Swim program. Figure 6.b details the same information for the Pentium 4 architecture. Again, intra-padding reduces drastically the miss penalty for both programs. In the case of Tomcatv, average miss penalty is reduced by 57.2%, whereas it drops 86.6% in the case of Swim.

**Optimization Time.** Finally, padding has to be performed in a reasonable amount of time in order to be included as an optimization step of a compiler. In our case, it took about 3 minutes to optimize each program[2] This amount of time can be significantly reduced if the technique is guided by a locality analysis in order to apply padding only to those loop nests that can benefit from it. The locality analysis developed in this work could easily be extended to provide such information.

## 4   Related Work

Caches improve the speed of programs by reducing the number of accesses to the slow upper levels of the memory hierarchy. Conflict misses may represent the majority of intra-nest misses and about half of all cache misses for typical programs and cache architectures [14].

Some padding techniques have been previously proposed by other authors.

Rivera and Tseng [17, 18] propose several simple heuristics that are addressed to eliminate conflicts in some particular cases. They mainly focus on conflicts that occur on every loop iteration, addressing only inter-padding for uniformly generated references (so they can not remove conflict misses for references such as B(i,j) and C(k,j)). On the other hand, they do not use intra-padding to remove cross-interferences. In the case they can not remove all the conflicts, no changes are done to the data layout. Besides, they use the padding algorithm devised to avoid conflict misses for direct-mapped caches to remove conflict misses for set-associative caches, without taking in account that interferences arise in different situations for different cache architectures. A set contention in a set-associative cache does not mean there is an interference. They presented an extension of this work targeting multi-level caches [19].

Figure 7 and Figure 8 compare their method with ours. We have studied all the main loop nests of the programs in **Set1** (see Section 3.2), which are the ones that suffer heavily from conflict misses.

---

[2] In a Pentium III at 600 MHZ.

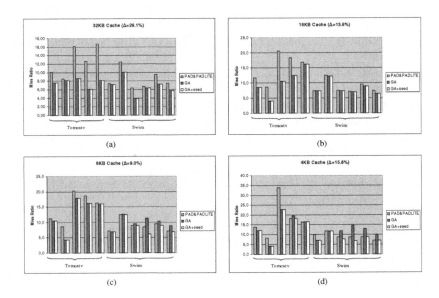

**Fig. 7.** Comparison with Rivera et al's method for direct-mapped caches. $\Delta$ stands for the relative decrease in miss ratios our method achieves compared to theirs.

Figure 7 compares both methods for 32KB, 16KB, 8KB and 4KB direct-mapped caches. Notice different scales for each chart. First column presents the miss ratios obtained running Rivera et al's method. We use the best result yielded by their two approaches PAD and PADLITE. The second column shows the miss ratios obtained by our approach. GA performs better in all the cases for 32KB and 16KB caches. However, we observe that in some cases Rivera et al's heuristics obtain better results when studying 8KB and 4KB caches.

In order to improve the population in successive iterations, the presence of good individuals in the first population may help. Thereby, we include in the initial solution two individuals (seeds) that represent the original solution provided by the compiler and the one obtained by running PADLITE [17]. The third column presents the results for this variant (called GA+seed). It gives better results for all cache configurations, yielding 29.1%, 13.6%, 9% and 15.6% smaller miss ratios for the 32KB, 16KB, 8KB and 4KB caches respectively.

Finally, we compare the different padding techniques for multi-level caches. Figure 8 shows the miss penalty for UltraSparc I and Pentium 4 cache architectures. Our method improves the miss penalty, compared to Rivera et al's method, by 8.1% and 8.9% for UltraSparc I and Pentium 4 architectures respectively.

Ghosh, Martonosi and Malik [6] propose a padding technique for direct-mapped caches based on using the CMEs for conflicting arrays that have the same column size. Their technique finds the optimal padding if there is a padding such that the total number of replacement misses after padding is zero. However, if such a padding does not exist, their technique does not provide any solution. Note that replacement misses include both conflict and capacity misses and one

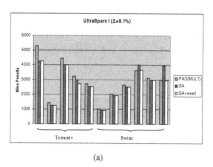 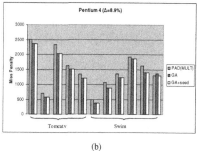

|  |  |
|---|---|
| (a) | (b) |

**Fig. 8.** Comparison with Rivera et al's method for multi-level caches. $\Delta$ stands for the relative decrease in miss penalty our method achieves compared to theirs.

may expect the case where replacement misses cannot be decreased up to zero to be common. In their experiments, this only happens for one out of the seven loops examined but most of their benchmarks are small kernels.

Our technique differs and improves these two previous approaches in the fact that it is a technique to search the solution space for the optimal padding, for any type of reference pattern that corresponds to affine references. It always produces a padding scheme that reduces conflict misses and usually is very close to the optimal. It is not targeted to avoid conflicts in some particular cases but it considers any type of conflicts, using both inter- and intra-padding to remove self- and cross-conflicts. Besides, our algorithm works fine for both direct-mapped and set-associative caches, generating the best padding scheme for each kind of architecture.

Recently, Vera and Xue [22] have presented a method that extends the CMEs to further analyze whole programs. We believe that our padding approach can be easily adapted to this new analysis technique. In that way, the padding factors could be optimized at a global program level considering the interactions of the different loop nests.

## 5   Conclusions

Cache memory performance is critical for the efficient execution of numerical applications. Padding is a program transformation that reduces conflict misses. In this work, we have proposed the use of genetic algorithms in order to perform near-optimal padding.

The evaluations show that, for the programs that have conflict misses, we achieve a significant improvement. For instance, for a 8KB 4-way associative cache, which is the L1 cache of the new Pentium 4 processor [3], we can reduce the miss ratio of the Swim program from 62.5% to 4.18% and the miss ratio of the Tomcatv program from 23.6% to 4.6%. Furthermore, the miss penalty for Pentium 4 is reduced by 79.27%. Besides, for the programs without conflict misses padding slightly reduces the compulsory misses due to a better alignment of arrays with cache lines.

Finally, an exhaustive evaluation of the programs with a high number of conflict misses reveals that the proposed technique practically removes all the conflict misses for all the loops analyzed, both inter- and intra-variable conflicts.

## Acknowledgments

This work has been supported by the ESPRIT project MHAOTEU (EP 24942) and the CICYT project 511/98. We would like to thank the anonymous referees for providing helpful comments in earlier drafts of this paper.

## References

1. E. Ayguadé et al. *A uniform internal representation for high-level and instruction-level transformations.* UPC, 1995.
2. N. Bermudo, X. Vera, A. González, and J. Llosa. An efficient solver for cache miss equations. In *IEEE International Symposium on Performance Analysis of Systems and Software (ISPASS'00)*, 2000.
3. D. Carmean. *Inside the Pentium 4 Processor Micro-Architecture (www.intel.com/pentium4)*, 2000.
4. P. Clauss. Counting solutions to linear and non-linear constraints through Ehrhart polynomials. In *ACM International Conference on Supercomputing (ICS'96)*, pages 278–285, Philadelphia, 1996.
5. A. Fernández. A quantitative analysis of the SPECfp95. Technical Report UPC-DAC-1999-12, Universitat Politècnica de Catalunya, March 1999.
6. S. Ghosh, M. Martonosi, and S. Malik. Cache miss equations: a compiler framework for analyzing and tuning memory behavior. *ACM Transactions on Programming Languages and Systems*, 21(4):703–746, 1999.
7. Gill, Murray, and Wright. *Practical optimization.* Academic Press, 1981.
8. Glover and Laguna. *Tabu search.* Kluwer, 1997.
9. D. Goldberg. *Genetic algorithms in search, optimizations and machine learning.* Addison-Wesley, 1989.
10. Hansen, Jaumard, and Mathon. Constrained nonlinear 0-1 programming. *ORSA Journal on Computing*, 1995.
11. J. Holland. *Adaptation in natural and artificial systems.* The University of Michigan Press, Ann Arbor, 1975.
12. Host, Pardalos, and Thoai. *Introduction to global optimization.* Kluwer, 1995.
13. Kirkpatrick, Gelatt, and Vecchi. Optimization by simulated annealing. *Science 220*, 1983.
14. K. S. McKinley and O. Temam. A quantitative analysis of loop nest locality. In *Proc. of VII Int. Conf. on Architectural Support for Programming Languages and Operating Systems (ASPLOS'96)*, 1996.
15. Z. Michalewicz. *Genetic algorithms+Data structures=Evolution Programs.* Springer-Verlag, 1994.
16. D. Padua et al. *Polaris developer's document*, 1994.
17. G. Rivera and C.-W. Tseng. Data transformations for eliminating conflict misses. In *ACM SIGPLAN '98 Conference on Programming Language Design and Implementation (PLDI'98)*, pages 38–49, 1998.

18. G. Rivera and C.-W. Tseng. Eliminating conflict misses for high performance architectures. In *ACM Internacional Conference on Supercomputing (ICS'98)*, 1998.
19. G. Rivera and C.-W. Tseng. Locality optimizations for multi-level caches. In *Supercomputing (SC'99)*, 1999.
20. Torn and Zilinskas. *Global optimization.* Springer-Verlag, 1989.
21. X. Vera, J. Llosa, A. González, and C. Ciuraneta. A fast implementation of cache miss equations. In *8th International Workshop on Compilers for Parallel Computers (CPC'00)*, 2000.
22. X. Vera and J. Xue. Let's study whole program cache behaviour analitically. In *International Symposium on High-Performance Computer Architecture (HPCA 8)*, Cambridge, Feb. 2002.

# Fine-Grain Stacked Register Allocation for the Itanium Architecture

Alban Douillet[1], José Nelson Amaral[2], and Guang R. Gao[3]

[1] Dept. of Computer Science, University of Delaware,
Newark, DE 19716, USA
`douillet@capsl.udel.edu`
[2] Dept. of Computing Sciences, University of Alberta,
Edmonton, Alberta, T6G 2E8, Canada
`amaral@cs.ualberta.ca`
[3] Dept. of Electrical Engineering, University of Delaware,
Newark, DE 19716, USA
`ggao@capsl.udel.edu`

**Abstract.** The introduction of a hardware managed register stack in the Itanium Architecture creates an opportunity to optimize both the frequency in which a compiler requests allocation of registers from this stack and the number of registers requested. The Itanium Architecture specifies the implementation of a Register Stack Engine (RSE) that automatically performs register spills and fills. However, if the compiler requests too many registers, through the *alloc* instruction, the RSE will be forced to execute unnecessary spill and fill operations. In this paper we introduce the formulation of the fine-grain register stack frame sizing problem. The *normal* interaction between the compiler and the RSE suggested by the Itanium Architecture designers is for the compiler to request the maximum number of registers required by a procedure at the procedure invocation. Our new problem formulation allows for more conservative stack register allocation because it acknowledges that the number of registers required in different control flow paths varies significantly. We introduce a basic algorithm to solve the stack register allocation problem, and present our preliminary performance results from the implementation of our algorithm in the Open64 compiler.

## 1 Introduction

The problem of minimizing data traffic between the memory and the registers of a processor — known as the register allocation problem — has occupied researchers for many years. Whether selecting a set of values to be *promoted* to registers [5], or minimizing the number of values spilled from registers to memory [4,3], the goal is to minimize the number of loads and stores actually executed at runtime to reduce memory traffic and thus reduce the execution time of the program.

Register allocation algorithms work with the constraint that a processor has a fixed — and often small — register set. Besides the increased traffic with

B. Pugh and C.-W. Tseng (Eds.): LCPC 2002, LNCS 2481, pp. 344–361, 2005.
© Springer-Verlag Berlin Heidelberg 2005

memory caused by the unavoidable spill operations, reusing the same register to store multiple temporary values introduces write after read (WAR), and write after write (WAW) dependencies in the instruction stream. Such dependences are not intrinsic to the program being executed, but are a consequence of register reuse.

Another unintended consequence of the small fixed-size register file is that the load and store instructions required for register spilling must be fetched from memory and issued, thus these instructions compete with other instructions for space in the instruction and the data cache and further increase the memory traffic.

In order to eliminate these avoidable dependences, out-of-order issue processors often have extra *non-architected* registers — or *reservation stations* — that are not visible to the compiler. This extra storage can be used at runtime to rename the registers selected by the compiler, eliminating the extra dependences and allowing more instruction level parallelism. Unfortunately loads and stores inserted by the compiler to spill values to memory cannot be eliminated from the instruction stream at runtime. Therefore these spill instructions increase the memory traffic even when some of the non-architected storage could be used to save the value been spilled[9,10].

An alternative design that eliminates many of these problems is adopted in the Intel Itanium Architecture [6,7,8]. In the Itanium a portion of the register file is implemented as a very deep stack. In the first processor in the Itanium family, the top 96 positions of this register stack are implemented as physical registers, while the remainder of the stack is mapped to memory. An instruction, called *alloc* , is provided to enable the compiler to specify how many registers will be used by each procedure. This instruction allows for up to 96 registers to be allocated at once. The architecture also provides a *register stack engine* (RSE), a hardware mechanism that automatically copies to and from memory the bottom portion of the stack that does not fit in the 96 physical registers. To the best of our knowledge, the Itanium architecture is the only architecture that uses such a mechanism.

Whenever the accumulated allocations in a program exceed 96 registers, the RSE transfers values between the memory and the registers to make room for the new allocation. Therefore the compiler still has to solve the register allocation problem in a similar fashion as it does for architectures without a register stack. However it is now possible to make new tradeoffs between serialization caused by the creation of WAR and WAW dependences and the allocation of more registers. Moreover the allocation instruction itself has a cost that needs to be taken into consideration when multiple allocation instructions are used in a procedure to reduce the accumulated register allocation.

The *alloc* instruction was designed to be called once at the beginning of every function. In this paper, we propose the *fine-grain allocation of stacked registers*, *i.e.,*we propose to use more than one *alloc* instruction in each procedure in order to reduce the number of unnecessary register spills and fills. In Section 2, we describe the register stack and the *alloc* instruction. In Section 3, we introduce a motivating example and clearly formulate the multi-*alloc* problem. In Section 4, we describe an algorithm to solve the multi-*alloc* problem. The experimental results are presented in Section 5 and show that a finer-grain use of the *alloc* instruction can lead to improvements at run-time.

## 2    Register Stack and Allocation Instruction

The Itanium architecture has 128 integer general purpose registers. Of those, 32 are static registers accessed and allocated by the compiler using conventional mechanisms. A *register stack* is implemented in the remaining 96 registers. Because the architecture maintains a backing storage where portions of the stack can be spilled, from the point of view of the application, this stack can grow unbounded. Stacked registers are organized into *frames*, one per function invocation. The size of the frames are set using the *alloc* instructions[1]. Each individual alloc instruction can resize the current register stack frame to up to 96 registers.

Whenever the total number of stacked registers allocated surpasses 96, a hardware mechanism, called the *Register Stack Engine* (RSE) automatically spills enough values to the backing storage to make room for a new allocation request. When physical registers become available (e.g. due to the completion of a function invocation, the RSE fills these registers with values that had been previously spilled. The spill/fill operations are asynchronous with the execution of the instructions of the running application.

### 2.1    The Allocation Instruction

The alloc instruction has four parameters: the number of inputs, $i$, the number of locals, $l$, the number of outputs, $o$, and the number of rotating registers, $r$. The size of the frame allocated is given by $l + o$. The input registers are a subset of the local registers. The output registers of a caller procedure overlap with the input registers of the callee to allow the passage of parameters via registers. The rotating registers are a subset of the stacked registers allocated in the current frame with the restriction that $0 \leq r \leq l + o$. Rotating registers are used to enable the implementation of dynamic single assignment in software pipelined loops. The execution of an alloc instruction may either grow or shrink the register frame of the current procedure. The parameters of the alloc instruction specify the size of the current frame, and that this new size is effective immediately upon completion of the instruction.

For simplicity, in the remaining of this paper we consider the *alloc* instruction to have a single parameter that is the size of the frame. Unless otherwise stated, henceforth, all references to number of registers, refer to stacked registers. We say that a function requires $n$ registers for its execution if in at least one of its execution paths $n$ stacked registers are accessed. Notice that not all the

---

[1] The *alloc* instruction should actually be named *resize* instruction. Indeed it does not only allocate registers but also deallocate them if needed. The effect of the instruction is only a change of size of the register stack frame.

executions of the function will need the allocation of $n$ registers, as the function might not execute the path that requires the maximum number of registers. Consider, for instance, a function $foo$ that requires 60 registers and that calls a function $bar$ that also requires 60 registers. Figure 1(a) shows the register stack after the allocation of registers for the function $foo$. Figure 1(b) illustrates that when $bar$ executes there is not enough registers to allocate its 60 registers (see the shaded area). Therefore some of the registers previously allocated to $foo$ must be saved to memory (spilled) to make room for the registers required by $bar$ (Figure 1(c)). The register frame of $bar$ wraps around to use the space emptied by spilling the lower part of $foo$'s frame. Now consider that we have used our technique in $bar$ and have provided multiple $alloc$ instructions for different paths of $bar$. If the current invocation of $bar$ only requires 10 registers, the pattern of allocation will be the one shown in Figure 1(d), and no register spilling by the RSE would be required.

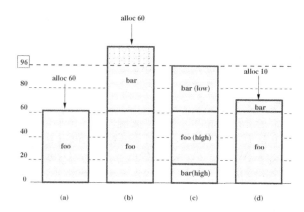

**Fig. 1.** Example of the Effects of the $alloc$ Instruction

In this paper we explore the use of multiple alloc instructions in a procedure in order to reduce the number of unnecessary spills/fills performed by the RSE. Our intuition is that if the compiler is forced to use a single alloc instruction per procedure, this instruction must inserted early in the procedure and must request the allocation of the maximum number of registers used in any control path through the procedure. If the total number of allocated registers over all the active functions exceeds 96, then the RSE must spilled values in all called procedures. Meanwhile the actual register requirement in some control paths may be considerably smaller than the maximum among all control paths.

## 2.2   RSE Modes of Operation

An important factor in the optimization of the placement of $alloc$ instructions by the compiler is the policy used to perform the spill and fill operations by the RSE. The Itanium architecture proposes four spill/fill policies for the RSE implemented as modes of operation. The four modes of operations offer combinations of *eager* and *just-in-time* loads and stores. A load/store is said to be just-in-time when it is executed when an *alloc* instruction triggers it or by the return of a procedure. A load/store is said to be eager when the RSE speculatively loads/stores registers from/to memory before an *alloc* instruction asks for it or the procedure returns. Through the eager execution of load/stores, the RSE will hopefully make enough space for the next *alloc* instruction and will not stall the execution of the program waiting for the spills to be executed.

Although the algorithm discussed in this paper is independent of the mode of operation of the RSE. the "eager loads/eager stores" mode of operation would be the most efficient one for applications with many function calls. However, the Itanium processor only implements the "just-in-time loads/just-in-time stores".

## 3   Problem Statement and Motivating Example

In this section we introduce a simple example that we will used throughout the paper to motivate and describe the execution of our multi-*alloc* algorithm.

### 3.1   Motivating Example

We consider the problem of efficiently inserting *alloc* instructions in the code of a function $f$ in a program $P$. We explain what we mean by "efficient" through the following example. We are given the Control-Flow Graph (CFG) $G$ of $f$ and the *local register requirement* ($lrr$) of every basic block of $G$, *i.e.*,the number of *stacked* registers that must be allocated for each basic block of $G$. For instance, $lrr(A) = 10$ means that basic block $A$ requires that at least 10 registers be allocated from the register stack to execute properly. We assume that the CFG is acyclic — we will deal with loops later. Also, the $lrr$ values are known and our problem formulation takes place after the register assignment phase[2].

Figure 2 shows the CFG $G$ that we will use throughout the paper. The big boxes represents the basic blocks of $G$ while the number in the little boxes attached to the basic blocks are the $lrr$ value of the corresponding basic block. For instance, $lrr(C) = 20$ and $lrr(F) = 96$.

The *alloc* instructions have not been inserted in the code of $f$ yet. For instance, the basic block $A$ can only be executed if there are at least $lrr(A) = 10$ registers allocated on the stack. Thus, we must make sure that,

> **Criterion 1:** For every control-flow path $C$ of $G$, there will be enough registers allocated to allow the execution of every basic block of $C$ .

Figure 3 presents an allocation instruction insertion scheme that satisfies *Criterion 1*.

---

[2] Usually named *register allocation phase*, but we want to avoid any confusion with the traditional register allocation problem.

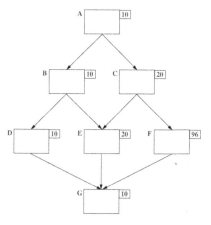

**Fig. 2.** The CFG $G$ of a routine $f$ where every basic block is associated with its $lrr$ value

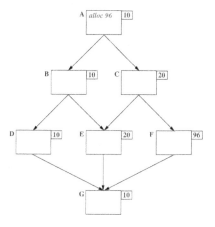

**Fig. 3.** The *alloc* instruction allocates enough registers so that every basic block in $G$ can execute properly

Now, thanks to the *alloc* instruction in A, 96 registers are allocated for every basic block in $G$, the program is correct and $f$ can be executed. The allocation value of the *alloc* instruction was chosen as equal to the maximum $lrr$ value of all the basic blocks in $G$. This is the *normal* usage of the *alloc* instruction described in the Intel Itanium Architecture manuals[6,7,8]. Note that the *alloc* instruction must be executed before any other instruction that uses a stacked register is executed.

Unfortunately, depending on the control-flow path to be executed, we may allocate more registers than actually required and therefore trigger unnecessary memory traffic. For instance, if the control-flow path $[A, B, D, G]$ is executed at run-time, 96 registers are allocated but only 10 are used. It would be more efficient if,

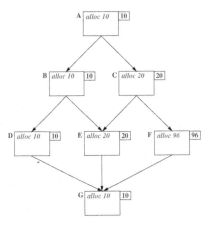

**Fig. 4.** An *alloc* instruction is inserted in every basic block of $G$ to allocate the exact number of registers required by any basic block

**Criterion 2:** For every control-flow path of $G$, we do not allocate more registers than actually required.

Using this criterion, we could have the other extreme for the insertion of the allocation instructions shown in Figure 4.

Now, we have satisfied *Criteria 1* and *2* but we, obviously, used unnecessary *alloc* instructions that create a non-negligible increase on the code size and will slow down the program. For instance, the *alloc* instruction in $D$ is redundant and could be removed because basic block $B$, the only parent of $D$, already allocated enough registers for $D$ to execute. Thus, we need another criterion to generate an efficient alloc insertion,

**Criterion 3:** In any control-flow path in $G$, only "necessary" *alloc* instructions are inserted.

To apply criterion 3, we try to use a simple algorithm that eliminates the *alloc* instruction from a basic block $v_i$ if all the paths that lead to $v_i$ have allocated enough registers to satisfy the *lrr* of $v_i$. Unfortunately, as shown in Figure 5, this algorithm fails to satisfy *Criterion 3*: for the control-flow path $[A, C, E, G]$, the *alloc* instruction in basic block $E$ is not necessary. However our algorithm failed to eliminate that instruction because the control-flow path $[A, B, E, G]$ does not allocate enough registers before reaching $E$.

We want to move the *alloc* instruction that is in $E$ in Figure 5 to another place, so that it is not executed in the path $[A, C, E, G]$. On the other hand, we do not want to move the *alloc* from $E$ to $B$, because in that case we would allocate too many registers (20 instead of 10) for the path $[A, B, D, G]$ and violate *criterion 2*. Thus, we would like the *alloc* instruction to appear between $B$ and $E$. We insert an artificial basic block in the CFG when we have no

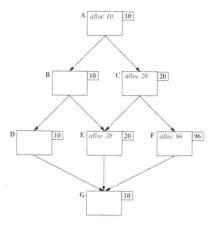

**Fig. 5.** The *alloc* instruction are all necessary except the one in $E$ for the control path $[A, B, E, G]$

place for the *alloc* instruction that would satisfy all three criteria. Because the allocation instruction insertion phase occurs late in the code generation phase, the insertion of an artificial basic block in the CFG can be costly in term of updating hyperblocks, scheduling, and live ranges. Therefore we need another criterion for our definition of efficient allocation insertion in order to ensure that this method is only used as a last resort,

**Criterion 4:** The number of artificial basic blocks inserted in $G$ is minimum.

### 3.2  Problem Formulation

In practice we are concerned with the number of *alloc* instructions executed at runtime, therefore when applying *Criterion 3* we want to take into consideration the frequency of execution of each control path. Thus we now assume that we are also given a function $w(C)$ that specifies the frequency of execution of the control path $C$ when the function $f$ is executed. To implement the third condition we define $N(G, w)$, the number of alloc instructions executed for the control flow graph $G$ under the frequency of execution $w$ as:

$$N(G, w) = \sum_{C \in P(G)} \sum_{v_i \in C} w(C).has_{alloc}(v_i)$$

where $P(G)$ is the set of all control-flow paths of $G$, $v_i \in C$ indicates that the basic block $v_i$ is in part the control path $C$, and the function $has_{alloc}(v_i)$ returns 1 if the basic block $v_i$ contains an *alloc* instruction and 0 otherwise. Because the *alloc* instruction can have a long latency (RSE spills/restores) and because the *alloc* instruction introduces new false dependencies with the instructions using the registers being allocated, the less *alloc* instructions executed at run-time, the better (*Criterion 3*). We can now present our problem statement.

---

**Multiple Alloc Problem Statement:** Given an acyclic control-flow graph $G = (V, E)$ for a procedure $f$, a register assignment for the variables of $f$, and a frequency of execution $w(C)$ for each control-flow path of $f$, find an allocation instruction insertion scheme $A$ of $G$ such that all the following conditions are satisfied:

(i) **Correctness Criterion:** for every control-flow path $C$ of $G$, enough registers are allocated to allow the correct execution of each basic block in $C$.

(ii) **Fitness Criterion:** for every control-flow path $C$ of $G$, the number of registers allocated does not exceed the maximum local register requirement of any basic block in $C$.

(iii) **Efficiency Criterion:** the average number of *alloc* instructions executed at run-time, $N(G, w)$, is minimized.

(iv) **Sparseness Criterion:** the number of artificial basic blocks inserted in the CFG is minimized

---

The criteria of the problem statement are sorted in decreasing priority order. For instance, the efficiency criterion must be satisfied before trying to satisfy the sparseness criterion.

In Figure 6 we provide a solution that satisfies all the requirements of our problem statement. A control-flow path may include more than one *alloc* instruction, because a given basic block may belong to multiple control paths. The artificial basic block $H$ has been inserted between $B$ and $E$ to allocate 20 registers for

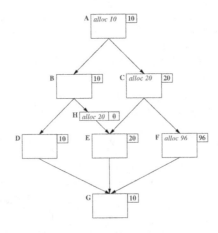

**Fig. 6.** A solution to our example

the execution of $E$ without the instruction interfering with the control-flow path $[A, C, E, G]$. *Criteria 1-3* are satisfied while the number of artificial basic blocks inserted is minimized. In any control path, when the flow of execution reaches a basic block, either enough registers have already been allocated or the basic block contains the appropriate *alloc* instruction. Also, after any *alloc* instruction that allocates $r$ registers, at least $r$ registers are actually used later in the CFG. Finally, $N(G, w)$ is minimized and equal to $4 + 2 + 1 + 1 = 8$ when considering the control-flow paths in the following order: $[A, B, D, G]$, $[A, B, H, E, G]$, $[A, C, E, G]$ and $[A, C, F, G]$.

## 4   Solution Method

In this section we introduce an heuristic algorithm that generates a multiple *alloc* instruction placement. Given a CFG annotated with the *lrr* for each basic block, this algorithms finds a set of *alloc* instructions that satisfies criterion 1. Although this algorithm does not minimize the number of artificial basic blocks inserted, our observation indicates that few such blocks are actually inserted in the code. In its current formulation, the algorithm assumes that all control-flow paths have the same frequency of execution.

### 4.1   The Algorithm

Before inserting the *alloc* instructions, the following intermediate values need to be computed.

$lrr(A)$: Local Register Requirement of basic block $A$. As defined earlier, it is the maximum number of live registers at any point in basic block $A$. To be executed, $A$ requires that $lrr(A)$ registers be allocated on the stack.

$orr(A)$: Outgoing Register Requirement of basic block $A$. It is the minimum number of stacked registers required by any control-flow path in the CFG that originates in $A$, $A$ included, and ends at the exit node. The $orr(A)$ can be defined recursively by: $orr(A) = max(lrr(A), min(orr(S_1), \ldots, orr(S_n)))$ where the $S_1, \ldots, S_n$ are the direct successors of $A$ in the CFG.

Given a register assignment, the $lrr(A)$ and the $orr(A)$ are intrinsic properties of $A$. The following two values are determined by the placement of *alloc* instructions:

$alloc(A)$: Number of registers allocated by the *alloc* instruction in $A$. If there is no *alloc* instruction in $A$, then $alloc(A) = 0$.

$maa(A)$: Minimum Actually Allocated. The value represents the minimum number of registers actually allocated in any control-flow path that originates in the start node of the CFG and ends in $A$, $A$ included. The $maa(A)$ can be defined recursively by: $maa(A) = max(alloc(A), min(maa(P_1), \ldots, maa(P_n)))$ where $P_1, \ldots, P_n$ are the direct predecessors of $A$ in the CFG.

```
        // Computation of the orr values
1:      for every BB $v_i$ in the CFG in reverse topological order {
2:          $orr(v_i) \leftarrow max(lrr(v_i), min(orr(S_{i_1}, \ldots, S_{i_{n_i}})))$ }

        // The main algorithm
3:      for every BB $v_i$ in the CFG in topological order {

            // if $V_i$ has no predecessor, we automatically insert an
            // alloc instruction.
4:          if $v_i$ has no predecessor in the CFG {
5:              insert $alloc(orr(v_i))$ in $v_i$;
6:              $maa(v_i) \leftarrow alloc(v_i)$;
7:              next BB; }

            // We analyze the $v_i$ and its predecessors.
8:          all_paths_need_alloc $\leftarrow$ TRUE;
9:          no-path_need_alloc $\leftarrow$ TRUE;
10:         must_insert_locally $\leftarrow$ FALSE;
11:         for all the predecessors $P_j$ of $v_i$ {
12:             if $maa(P_j) < lrr(v_i)$ {
13:                 candidate$(P_j) \leftarrow$ TRUE;
14:                 no_path_needs_alloc $\leftarrow$ FALSE; }
15:             else {
16:                 candidate$(P_j) \leftarrow$ FALSE;
17:                 all_paths_need_alloc $\leftarrow$ FALSE; }
18:             if candidate$(P_j)$ AND $P_j$ has at least 2 successors
19:             AND $orr(P_j) < orr(v_i)$ {
20:                 must_insert_locally $\leftarrow$ TRUE; }
21:         }

            // When enough registers are allocated in all incoming path
            // we do not need to insert any alloc instruction.
22:         if no_path_needs_alloc {
23:             $maa(v_i) \leftarrow min_{\{j\,candidate(P_j)\}}(maa(P_j))$;
24:             next BB; }

            // When none of the predecessors has enough registers allocated,
            // or when there exists one predecessor $P$ with not enough register
            // allocated where $orr(P) > orr(v_i)$, then we must insert an alloc
            // instruction in $v_i$.
25:         if all_paths_need_alloc OR must_insert_locally {
26:             insert $alloc(orr(v_i))$ in $v_i$;
27:             $maa(v_i) \leftarrow alloc(v_i)$;
28:             next BB; }

            // Otherwise we insert an alloc instruction in every predecessor
            // that requires it.
29:         for all the predecessors $P_j$ of $v_i$ such that candidate$(P_j)$=TRUE {
30:             insert $alloc(orr(v_i))$ in $P_j$;
31:             $maa(P_j) \leftarrow alloc(P_j)$; }
32:         $maa(v_i) \leftarrow min_j(maa(P_j))$;
33:     }
```

**Fig. 7.** The multi-*alloc* placement algorithm

For performance, multiple *alloc* instructions should not be placed inside loop nests. Therefore, for the multi-*alloc* algorithm, each loop nest is represented as an aggregate node in the CFG, *i.e.*, a single virtual basic block with a single set of values (*lrr*, *orr*,...). The *lrr* of a loop nest is the maximum register requirement of all the basic blocks in the loop nest. This is a conservative approach to loop nests, but effective in practice.

Before applying our algorithm, we inserted empty basic blocks on the entrance edges of loops to make sure the algorithm is able to insert *alloc* instructions in the predecessors of loop entry basic blocks if necessary. The inserted basic blocks have only one successor and therefore the insertion of an *alloc* instruction is compatible with the fitness criterion.

Our multi-*alloc* placement algorithm is shown in Figure 7. First (lines 1-2), a bottom-up topological traversal is performed to compute the *orr* values using the *lrr* values.

Then each basic block is considered in topological order (line 3). If the basic block has no predecessor in the CFG, we insert an *alloc* instruction in the block (lines 4-6). If the basic block requires zero stacked registers, insert $alloc(orr(v_i))$ is converted into a no-operation.

Given a node $v_i$, we check all the immediate predecessors of $v_i$ to identify which ones are candidates for the placement of an *alloc* instruction (lines 11-16). A predecessor $P_j$ of $v_i$ is a candidate for an *alloc* placement if its $maa(P_j)$ is smaller than $lrr(v_i)$.

If all the incoming paths of $v_i$ need an *alloc* instruction, then the *alloc* instruction is placed in $v_i$ itself (lines 19 and 25). The number of registers allocated is equal the maximum number of registers that will be required in any path leaving $v_i$, $orr(v_i)$. By allocating $orr(v_i)$ instead of $lrr(v_i)$, we prevent the need for the insertion of another *alloc* instruction in at least one path leaving $v_i$.

If there exists at least one incoming path that does not need the *alloc* instruction, the algorithm inserts one *alloc* instruction in each of the incoming paths that need it (lines 27-29). Finally we update the $maa(v_i)$ value (line 30).

## 4.2   Application to Our Motivating Example

The application of the algorithm to our motivating example is shown on Figure 8. In this figure each basic block is annotated with its *lrr*, *orr*, and *maa* values. Figure 8(a) shows the CFG after the computation of the *orr* values(lines 1-2). Then the CFG is traversed in topological order (line 3). The first basic block, $A$, has no predecessor therefore we insert an *alloc* instruction (line 4-6) with $alloc(A) = orr(A)$ (Figure 8(b)). Next basic block $B$ is visited. Because $lrr(B)$ is equal to $maa(A)$ (an immediate predecessor of $B$) no *alloc* instruction is needed in $B$ (lines 11,14-15). Assume that the algorithm visits $C$ next. $A$ is the only predecessors of $C$, and $maa(A)$ is smaller than the $lrr(C)$. Therefore an *alloc* instruction must be inserted in $C$. Because $A$, the only predecessor of $C$, has a lower *orr* value, the insertion must be in $C$ (lines 17-19, Figure 8(c)). When the algorithm visits $D$, its only predecessor $B$ has enough registers allocated

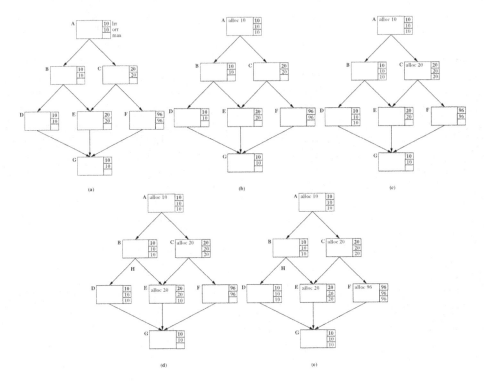

**Fig. 8.** Application of the algorithm on our motivating example

$(lrr(D) \leq maa(B))$ (lines 11,15-16), thus $D$ does not need an *alloc* . As for $B$ we do not insert an *alloc* instruction in $D$. $E$ has two predecessors and only one incoming path, from $B$, requires the insertion of an *alloc* instruction. Because $orr(B) < orr(E)$, the insertion must be local (lines 17-19, Figure 8(d)). Then the algorithm continues and an *alloc* instruction is inserted in $F$ but not in $G$ (Figure 8(e)).

### 4.3   Algorithm Analysis

**Time Complexity**

**Theorem 1.** *The algorithm is linear in the number of basic blocks in the CFG.*

*Proof.* The algorithm traverses the CFG in topological order and only visits the predecessors of every basic block. Visiting a predecessor is equivalent to following an edge backwards. In a CFG each node can have at most 2 immediate successors. Thus the number of edges in a CFG is proportional to the number of nodes. Therefore the entire loop can be executed in linear time in the number of nodes.

For the same reason, the insertion of artificial basic blocks does not change anything to the time complexity.                                                                     □

**Criteria Satisfaction.** First we prove that the two first criteria of our problem statement are satisfied.

**Theorem 2.** *The algorithm proposed returns an allocation instruction insertion scheme that satisfies the correctness criterion.*

*Proof.* The algorithm traverses the graph in top-down topological order. For each basic block, the algorithm tests if enough registers have been allocated for every incoming path to the basic block (line 11). If an *alloc* instruction is required to satisfy the local register requirement of the basic block, the algorithm inserts one either directly in the basic block (lines 4-6 or 24-26), either earlier in the faulty paths (lines 27-30). Therefore the correctness criterion is satisfied.     □

The fitness criterion is not satisfied as our example shows for the basic block $E$ in Figure 8(e). If the control-flow paths comes from $C$, then we repeat the *alloc* instruction.

Because the algorithm does not take into account the frequency of execution of any given control-flow paths of $G$, the algorithm cannot return an allocation instruction insertion scheme that satisfies efficiency criterion. However, if each control-flow path has the same frequency of execution, then we believe that the algorithm satisfies the criterion in most of the cases.

Since we do not insert new basic blocks in the CFG at all, the number of inserted basic blocks is obviously optimal.

## 5     Experiments and Results

### 5.1     Experimental Framework

We implemented the multi-*alloc* algorithm with the two optimizations in the industry-strong Open64 compiler ([1,2]. The *alloc* instructions are inserted right after the register allocation phase but before the last instruction scheduling phase of the compiler. Our experiments were performed in an HP workstation i2000 equipped with a single 733MHz Itanium processor and 1GB of memory and running Debian Linux 2.4.7.

Currently we have tested the implementation on 6 SPEC CPU2000 benchmarks programs. We measured the number of *alloc* instructions inserted and

| Benchmark | Average number of *alloc* inserted | Largest number of *alloc* inserted | Absolute number of registers saved | Relative number of registers saved | Best number of registers saved | Execution time |
|---|---|---|---|---|---|---|
| 164.gzip | 1.92 | 11 | 1.31 | 14.50% | 5.16 | +28.58% |
| 175.vpr | 1.74 | 32 | 1.46 | 13.06% | 15.78 | +18.26% |
| 181.mcf | 1.26 | 4 | 1.50 | 14.93% | 6.44 | +8.09% |
| 186.crafty | 2.77 | 25 | 1.66 | 20.10% | 19.95 | +56.61% |
| 254.gap | 2.50 | 23 | 1.20 | 16.98% | 3.61 | +30.01% |
| 256.bzip2 | 1.63 | 12 | 1.20 | 14.81% | 3.01 | +22.50% |
| average | 1.97 | * | 1.38 | 15.73% | * | +27.34% |

**Fig. 9.** Number of registers saved and *alloc* instructions inserted for each of the seven benchmarks tested

the number of registers saved due to our algorithm. We compare our results to the standard algorithm for the *alloc* instruction, *i.e.,*an algorithm that inserts a single *alloc* in each procedure entrance. On average, we allocate 1.38 less registers per procedure with a maximum of 19.95 registers saved. We use 1.97 *alloc* instructions on average with a maximum of 32 instructions in a procedure. This average is weighted by the frequency of execution of each basic block.

## 5.2   Implementation Considerations

For simplicity, the algorithm presented in this paper assumes that the *alloc* instruction has a single parameter, *i.e.,* the size of the current register stack frame. However, in the *alloc* instruction in the Itanium architecture specifies the number of input, output, local, and rotating registers. Thus an implementation of the algorithm has to include different strategies for each type of register.

The rotating registers overlap with the local and output registers. In our current implementation, the *alloc* instructions requests rotating registers only when the number of rotating registers required is less than the sum of local and output registers. If this is not the case, then obviously there can be no downstream loop that uses rotating registers. A downstream loop that requires rotating registers would have been taken into account in the *orr* values.

The input registers are easily handled because they are part of the local section of the register stack frame. Input registers are used to specify how many registers in the new stack frame overlap with the previous stack frame.

The local registers and the output registers were the only types of registers that require modifications to the simplified algorithm. Each basic block needs the full set of values (*lrr*, *orr*, *maa* and *alloc*) for each of the two types of registers. Thus, an *alloc* instruction is inserted in a basic block if either local or output registers are required (OR statement).

In some cases the introduction of a second parameter forces us to insert more *alloc* instructions to preserve the correctness of the program. This situation happens when two different control flows reach a function call and the number of local registers allocated in each incoming path is distinct. Consider, for instance, the example shown in Figure 10. Each *alloc* instruction is annotated with two numbers: the number of local registers to the left, and the number of output registers to the right. Because of automatic register renaming, r32 is always the first register in a stack frame. If we consider only the number of registers required in each basic block, the *alloc* instruction in basic block $C$ is not necessary because there are enough registers allocated in either incoming path. However, if block $\dot{C}$ has a function call that expects three output registers, there is a problem: the boundary between local and output register depends on the incoming path: if we reach block $C$ from block $A$, then $r42$ is the first output register. Whereas, if the flow comes from $B$, the first output register is $r52$. Therefore, at the function call site, there is no way to tell at compile time which register is the first output register. We must insert an *alloc* instruction before the function call to ensure that the output registers start at $r42$ regardless of the incoming path as shown in our example.

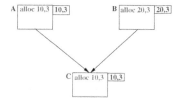

**Fig. 10.** Necessary extra *alloc* instruction for function calls

## 5.3   Results

Table 9 shows our results for the six benchmarks tested. These numbers are weighted by the frequency of execution of each basic block in the routine. Thus the basic blocks and *alloc* instructions in a control-flow path that is executed 1 out of 10 times that the routine is executed is weighted by 0.1. Then we take the average for all the routines in the benchmark.

The number of registers saved can be significant with a maximum of 19.95 registers for one routine of *186.crafty*. The number of registers not allocated thanks to our optimization is low: 1.38 on average. Nonetheless, the algorithm reduces the register stack frame size of a routine by 15.73%, on average. These results are explained by the relatively low register pressure in the SPEC2000 benchmarks.

Although the algorithm does not try to limit the number of *alloc* instructions inserted in a given routine, the average number of instructions inserted is 1.97. By adding one more *alloc* instruction per routine, we can manage to reduce the number of registers allocated by 15.73%. However, in some rare cases the number of *alloc* instructions inserted is high. For instance in one routine of *175.vpr* the algorithm inserted 32 *alloc* instructions. We are investigating such cases to identify opportunities for improvement. We are to notice the direct relation between the average number of *alloc* instructions inserted and the execution time.

Despite the savings in register allocated, the execution time of the programs has been increased by up to 56.61% for *186.crafty*. The main reason is the cost of the *alloc* instruction itself that was not taken into account by the algorithm. This instruction is expensive and introduces false dependences that can break a good instruction schedule. Moreover the insertion of basic blocks to host *alloc* instructions at the entrance of loops results in the insertion of branch instructions as well. Finally, most of the time, the difference between the number of registers allocated between two *alloc* instructions is small and inserting a second *alloc* instruction does not pay off.

## 6   Future Work

Future generations of processors of the Itanium family are expected to have a much more efficient Register Stack Engine. We anticipate that the implementation of eager spill and eager fill modes in the RSE will lead to a more effective application of the idea of using multiple *alloc* instructions introduced in this paper. Moreover we plan to study the following modifications to the original algorithm:

- The algorithm could use an *alloc* instruction immediately before a loop entry to reduce the number of registers allocated to the number of variables live at that point in the program, and another *alloc* instruction at the loop exit to restore the number of registers required by the paths that leave the loop.
- A similar solution could be used around function calls. In the Itanium architecture, there are 96 registers available in the register stack. As long as all the cumulative number of registers requested by active functions is less then 96, there will be no spills and fills. Using this observation, we could delay the time when the 96 register threshold value is reached by shrinking the current register stack frame as much as possible right before every function call.
- When feedback profiling information is available, the multiple *alloc* placement algorithm can favor placing the least number of *alloc* instructions in the control paths that have the highest frequency of execution. The placement of *alloc* instructions in other paths would be secondary to this constraints.
- the insertion of *alloc* instructions could be triggered by a profitability analysis, and be restricted to the places where the gain is significant enough. The registers could be allocated in chunks, or *quanta*, of 5 or 10 up to the maximum needed by the function. It would reduce the number of *alloc* instructions in the program (efficiency criterion) with a limited cost for the fitness criterion. This idea follows from the implementation of efficient dynamic memory allocation algorithms.

## 7   Conclusion

In this paper, we tried to solve the problem of inserting *alloc* instructions in Itanium code in order to achieve a finer-grain allocation scheme and reduces the number of blocking spills and restores with the register stack engine. We defined four subgoals: correctness, fitness, efficiency and stability and proved that the problem was NP-complete.

Then we propose a heuristic that solves the first two criteria: correctness and fitness. The algorithm is linear and achieves ...

However the algorithm did not consider the frequency of execution of the control-flow paths in the CFG and the resulting code could be further improved. Also, the eager allocation modes were not available in the Itanium processor used for the the experiments, although it would a efficient source of improvement.

The next step is now to consider the frequency of execution of control-flow paths and try different levels of optimizations by releasing the fitness constraint for instance.

# Acknowledgments

We would like to acknowledge Gerolf Hoflehner and Jim Pierce for their contributions and for insightful comments about our approach to the problem. This research is supported by the National Science Foundation (NSF), by the National Security Agency (NSA), by the Defense Advanced Research Projects Agency (DARPA), and by the Natural Sciences and Engineering Research Council (NSERC) of Canada. We would also like to thank Intel Corporation for their generous donations.

# References

1. Open research compiler for itanium processors. http://ipf-orc.sourceforge.net/, January 2002.
2. Open64 compiler and tools. http://open64.sourceforge.net/, January 2002.
3. D. Callahan and B. Koblenz. Register allocation via hierarchical graph coloring. In *SIGPLAN 91 Conference on Programming Language Design and Implementation*, pages 192–203, Toronto,ON, June 1991.
4. G. J. Chaitin. Register allocation & spilling via graph coloring. In *SIGPLAN 82 Symposium on Compiler Construction*, pages 98–105, June 1982.
5. F. C. Chow and J. L. Hennessy. The priority-based coloring approach to register allocation. *ACM Transactions on Programming Language and Systems*, 12(4):501–536, October 1990.
6. Intel Corporation. *Intel Itanium Architecture Software Manual vol1-4*, December 2001. revision 2.0.
7. Intel Corporation. *Intel Itanium Processor Reference Manual for Software Development*, December 2001. revision 2.0.
8. Intel Corporation. *Intel Itanium Processor Reference Manual for Software Optimization*, November 2001. http://developer.intel.com/design/itanium/.
9. R. Govindarajan, H. Yang, J. N. Amaral, C. Zhang, and G. R. Gao. Minimum register instruction sequence problem: Revisiting optimal code generation for dags. In *15th International Parallel and Distributed Processing Symposium*, San Francisco, CA, April 2001.
10. R. Govindarajan, H. Yang, J. N. Amaral, C. Zhang, and G. R. Gao. Minimum register instruction sequencing to reduce register spills in out-of-order issue superscalar architectures. *IEEE Transactions on Computers*, 2002.

# Evaluating Iterative Compilation

G.G. Fursin[1], M.F.P. O'Boyle[1], and P.M.W. Knijnenburg[2]

[1] ICSA, School of Informatics, University of Edinburgh, UK
[2] LIACS, Leiden University, The Netherlands

**Abstract.** This paper describes a platform independent optimisation approach based on feedback-directed program restructuring. We have developed two strategies that search the optimisation space by means of profiling to find the best possible program variant. These strategies have no *a priori* knowledge of the target machine and can be run on any platform. In this paper our approach is evaluated on three full SPEC benchmarks, rather than the kernels evaluated in earlier studies where the optimisation space is relatively small. This approach was evaluated on six different platforms, where it is shown that we obtain on average a 20.5% reduction in execution time compared to the native compiler with full optimisation. By using training data instead of reference data for the search procedure, we can reduce compilation time and still give on average a 16.5% reduction in time when running on reference data. We show that our approach is able to give similar significant reductions in execution time over a state of the art high level restructurer based on static analysis and a platform specific profile feedback directed compiler that employs the same transformations as our iterative system.

## 1    Introduction

Traditional approaches to compiler optimisations are based on static analysis and a hardwired compiler strategy which can no longer be used in a computing environment where the platform is rapidly changing. Modern architectures have very complex internal organisations: high issue widths, out-of-order execution, deep memory hierarchies, etc. However, compiler machine models are necessarily simplified to be tractable and only take into account a small part of the actual system. Such models provide very rough performance estimates which, in practice, are too simplistic to statically select the best optimisations. What is required is an approach which evolves and adapts to architectural change without sacrificing performance.

This paper examines a feedback assisted approach based on traversing an optimisation space. Early results suggest that such an approach can give significant reductions in execution time over purely static approaches with, on average, a 20.5% improvement over the highest optimisation levels provided by the native compiler. Although such an approach is usually ruled out in terms of excessive compilation time, it is precisely the approach used by expert programmers when the application is to be executed many times. Embedded systems are an extreme example of this, allowing the cost of compilation to be amortised over many shipped products.

B. Pugh and C.-W. Tseng (Eds.): LCPC 2002, LNCS 2481, pp. 362–376, 2005.

In previously published work [2,7], we have shown the use of *iterative compilation* in optimising program performance. Different transformations are applied, corresponding to points in the transformation space, and their worth evaluated by executing the program. Several evaluations, based on a compiler search strategy, are performed to a certain pre-defined maximum number, with the compiler selecting the best one. Related work in the area of linear algebraic libraries has also shown good performance [13].

However, the main drawback of previous work is that it has focused solely on tuning compute-intensive kernels where the optimisation spaces being searched are relatively trivial. Clearly, for iterative compilation to be considered a realistic optimisation approach, it must be shown to be able to find good results on the large spaces that arise for realistic applications with a relatively few number of evaluations.

Although iterative approaches can find good results, they may be inappropriate if the data size, for instance, is different from that actually encountered at runtime. In order to investigate this phenomenom, we applied our approach to training data before applying the selected transformation to distinct reference data. In all cases our approach outperforms the native optimising compiler.

Finally, we compared our approach to a state-of-the-art profile driven optimiser that is present in the Compaq compiler for the Alpha processors. There are many optimisations used in this optimiser, including all of the high level source to source transformations that are used by our system, plus many others. This optimiser collects runtime data to steer its optimisation process, like our approach. However, unlike our approach, it uses this data, by certain fixed heuristics, in a fixed strategy. We show that our searching techniques outperform this static approach significantly, even though the static profile driven optimiser has access to additional transformations not considered by our scheme that can dramatically improve execution time, such as software pipelining.

The paper makes the following contributions:

- For the first, time it demonstrates that iterative compilation outperforms static approaches on realistic non-kernel benchmarks.
- It demonstrates that good optimisations can be found with variable runtime data.
- It demonstrates significant reductions in execution time compared to a state-of-the art native high level restructurer that employs statically (among others) the same transformations as our system with few evaluations.
- It demonstrates significant reductions in execution time over an existing platform specific feedback directed optimiser that employs (among others) the same optimisations as our system.

This paper is organised as follows. Section 2 describes the benchmarks and platforms investigated. Section 3 shows comparatively how performance is affected by different transformations. Section 4 describes the overall compiler infrastructure and the iterative compilation strategies implemented. This is followed in Section 5 by an evaluation of this approach. Section 6 provides a brief review of related work and Section 7 provides some concluding remarks.

## 2    Benchmarks and Platforms

We consider the following SPEC95 FP benchmarks: Tomcatv, Swim and Mgrid
with the reference data input sets. The following platforms are used:

**Alpha 21164** 500MHz. In-order. Digital UNIX V4.0D. F77 V5.0. 8K L1.
**Alpha 21264** 500MHz. Out-of-order. Digital UNIX V4.0E. F77 V5.2. 64K L1.
**Pentium II** 350 MHz. Windows 2000 Professional. Compaq F77 V6.1 16K L1.
**Pentium III** 600MHz. Red Hat Linux 6.1. g77 2.95.1. 16 k L1.
**HP-PA 9000/712** 80 MHz. OS A.09.07 F77.9.0. 128K L1.
**Ultrasparc** 300 MHz. SunOS 5.7, g77 2.95.1. 16K L1.

All comparative experimental data is with respect to the native compilers at
their highest optimisation level. We later compare our approach against the
Compaq high level restructurer which is only available on the Pentium and
the 2 Alphas. The Compaq compiler with the optimisation level set to -O5
becomes a high level restructurer which applies all of the transformations of
our system. This compiler, moreover, applies other loop transformations as
well, including software pipelining that is well known to boost program
performance.

Furthermore, on the Alpha platforms this compiler allows profile driven optimisation where it uses runtime data to drive these loop transformations. We
compare our approach against this option also.

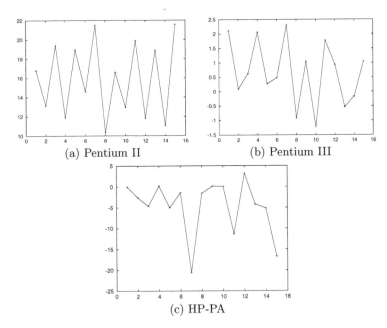

(a) Pentium II                    (b) Pentium III

(c) HP-PA

**Fig. 1.** Percentage reduction in execution time for varying pad sizes: Swim

## 3    Impact of Program Transformations

It is well-known that program transformations have a variable impact on program performance and that finding the best transformation sequence is a difficult task. In this section we wish to empirically demonstrate not only the non-linear impact of program transformations, but how this varies across machines, demonstrating the challenge in developing generic compilers that can adapt to different platforms.

### 3.1    Transformations

Here we examine the impact of 3 well known transformations, array padding, loop unrolling and tiling on selected benchmarks and platforms.

*Padding.* Array padding is used to reduce conflict misses in cache based architectures [10]. Figure 1 shows the reduction in execution time due to padding

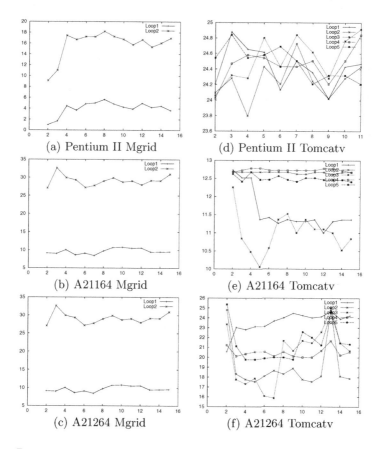

**Fig. 2.** Percentage reduction in time for varying unroll factors: Mgrid + Tomcatv

with respect to the original code on Swim across three of the platforms. This oscillatory behaviour is not particularly surprising and is well studied [8], however, it does highlight the difficulty for an optimising compiler in determining whether array padding should be considered and finding the best factor, particularly when moving from one platform to another. For instance, on the Pentium II, array padding gives, on average, a clear improvement, even if small changes in parameter values give wide variation in behaviour. In the case of the Pentium III, however, it has little impact on performance while for the HP-PA it should generally be avoided.

*Loop Unrolling.* Loop unrolling is a well known optimisation used to expose more instruction level parallelism (ILP) to the back end scheduler and reduce the relative overhead of memory access. Figure 2 show the impact of loop unrolling on 21162, 21264 and the Pentium II when applied to Mgrid and Tomcatv. We have highlighted the impact on the most time consuming loops: two in the case of Mgrid and five in the case of Tomcatv. In absolute terms there is much less variability than in the case of padding, though clearly in the case of Mgrid, unrolling loop 1 gives a much greater reduction in execution time than loop 2. Similarly the best unroll factor varies from platform to platform. In the case of Tomcatv, all 5 loops benefit from unrolling and there is generally no large absolute difference between different unroll factors. However, unrolling by a factor of 5 on loop 3 on the A21164 gives particularly poor performance, and an unroll factor of 13 on the A21264 seems surprisingly beneficial to all loops.

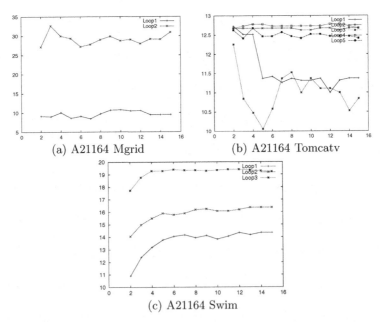

(a) A21164 Mgrid

(b) A21164 Tomcatv

(c) A21164 Swim

**Fig. 3.** Percentage reduction in execution time for varying tile sizes: A21164

*Loop Tiling.* Loop tiling [8] is used to improve cache utilisation by exploiting temporal and spatial locality. Figure 3 show the impact of loop tiling on the three benchmarks on the A21164. Here we again highlight two of the main loops in Mgrid, this time we just focus on two loops for Tomcatv and three for Swim. In the case of Mgrid, tiling is beneficial for tile sizes greater than 4 for loop 1 but should be avoided for loop 2. It is beneficial for all tile sizes in the case of Swim, with those greater than 14 giving the greatest reduction in execution time. However, tiling always gives poor performance on Tomcatv, due to the lack of intra-loop locality within this program [8].

Although the impact of program transformations has been well studied, this section has shown that high-level transformations can have a significant impact on performance even when compared to modern high performance native compilers. It is not the intention of this paper to *explain* processor behaviour in the presence of transformations, rather that, as the figures shown in this section suggest, such behaviour will be difficult to accurately predict. Thus, designing an optimising strategy that works well across such platforms is highly non-trivial. In the next section we develop two compiler strategies that are intended to be suitably generic.

# 4   Compiler Strategies

The main objective of a compiler strategy is to decide which transformations to apply, guided by information in the form of static analysis, execution time, or heuristics which are meant to reduce the transformation space to consider. While the majority of research in optimisation via high level restructuring has relied on static information, here we are primarily concerned with developing techniques that have no architectural knowledge and are solely based on dynamic information.

## 4.1   Strategy 1

This strategy uses data and loop transformations in a cost-conscious manner. Rather than search through a large space of all possible loop and data transformations, it targets those sections of the program that dominate program execution and considers restricted loop and data transformations in separate phases reducing the number of combinatorial options by imposing a phase order.

Initially, the program is profiled and those subroutines that dominate execution time are marked. Within each marked routine, those loop nests that dominate execution are also marked as are the arrays referenced within them. After this initially marking phase, we consider data transformations on those arrays marked as significant. As data transformations are global in effect, they are considered first on the assumption that local loop transformations can later compensate for some adverse effects that can be caused locally by the global data transformations. In this strategy, the only data transformation considered is array padding and this is applied to the first dimension of the marked arrays inter-procedurally. If there are $p$ padding factors to consider and $a$ arrays, then the number of different padding combinations is $p^a$. To reduce this complexity, we pad each array the same amount, reducing the complexity to $p$. For this new padded program, we now consider loop transformations.

Loop tiling (with tile sizes ranging from 2 to the range of the loop bounds) is considered for all those loop nests marked initially as significant. Each loop nest is considered in turn and tiled. When the best tile size is determined, it is recorded before moving on to the next loop nest. To avoid combinatorial explosion, each loop is optimised in isolation, ignoring the effect of transforming one loop on the rest of the program. Once the tile factors for each significant loop have been determined, they are all applied to give a new program. Finally loop unrolling is applied in a similar manner.

## 4.2   Strategy 2

This strategy again focuses on the three transformations considered before: array padding, loop tiling, and loop unrolling. Once again, profiling is used to determine those arrays and loop nests of interest. This time, however, rather than combine the best padding, tiling and unroll factors, we randomly search for the best combination. One or more loops and arrays are randomly selected and random tile, pad and unroll factors applied. This avoids the coupled behaviour of transformations (where the best form of one transformation plus the best form of another gives a sub-optimal value when combined), without having to exhaustively search a large space.

Both strategies retain the best version found so far at each evaluation, so that after evaluating a fixed number of transformed programs, the best transformed program is returned as the final selected program. As is immediately apparent, neither of these strategies contain any platform or program specific information. The next section evaluates to what extent they may improve performance.

## 5   Experimental Results

In this section we evaluate the two iterative search strategies. This is followed by an evaluation of the use of smaller training data as a mechanism to reduce overall compilation time.

Finally, we evaluate our iterative approach against an existing high level restructurer and a feedback directed optimiser that employ (among others) the same transformations as our iterative system.

### 5.1   Evaluating Iterative Search Strategies

The first search strategy was allowed to run for 200 evaluations[1] and Table 1 shows the reduction in execution time found across the platforms and benchmarks. In all cases we improve on the best obtainable performance of the native

---

[1] An evaluation consists of 3 parts: ($i$) transform the program, ($ii$) compile it with the native compiler, and ($iii$) execute the program.

compiler and give on average a 20.5% reduction in execution time. Tomcatv is most improved by program optimisations considered in this paper and Swim the least, though on the 21264 a 40% improvement is found. Comparing different platforms, the 21264 is most improved by the program optimisations considered in this paper and the PIII the least.

**Table 1.** Strategy 1: Percentage reduction in execution time

|        | PII  | PIII | HP-PA | US    | 21164 | 21264 | Avg. |
|--------|------|------|-------|-------|-------|-------|------|
| Tomcatv| 31.4 | 25.3 | 38.6  | 22.6  | 13.5  | 25.4  | 26.1 |
| Swim   | 21.7 | 2.31 | 8.35  | 17.73 | 22.6  | 40.0  | 18.8 |
| Mgrid  | 18.1 | 1.29 | 17.38 | 15.1  | 32.6  | 15.4  | 16.6 |
| Avg.   | 23.7 | 9.63 | 21.4  | 18.5  | 22.9  | 26.9  | 20.5 |

In Figure 4 we show how the first search strategy performs with respect to the number of evaluations. The reduction in execution time of the current best program version is shown for three of the six different platforms across the three benchmarks. At each evaluation a new program version is selected by the strategy. If the new program selected is an improvement on the best version so far, we see an improvement in execution time reduction and the new program becomes the current best version. Otherwise the current best version is retained and we see no change in execution time reduction. In the case of Tomcatv, the most significant performance gains are made within 40 evaluations. In the case of Swim, higher performance gains are made for these three platforms, taking approximately 40 evaluations to find the majority of the available performance gains. Finally, in the case of Mgrid, after just 18 iterations the search strategy finds good program optimisations across the three platforms.

Despite the complex behaviour of transformations across platforms and their interaction with each other, our first iterative strategy has shown that it can perform well across all platforms. Interestingly, the rate at which it finds good candidate optimisations is broadly similar for each target machine.

Although the first strategy finds good performance with relatively few evaluations, this may still be too time consuming in practice. Therefore, we now evaluate Strategy 2 with a maximum of 15 evaluations and compare its performance against the native compiler, restricting our attention to 3 of the 6 platforms. What is immediately apparent from the results in Table 2, is that the second strategy is able to find considerable reductions in execution time despite the small number of evaluations. On the Pentium, it achieves 75% of the performance found using Strategy 1 and over 85% on the two Alphas.

If we examine in detail how fast the strategy finds good results as shown in Figure 5, we find that within just 5 evaluations, significant reductions in execution time are found. Considering the size of the optimisation search space considered, this is a significant result.

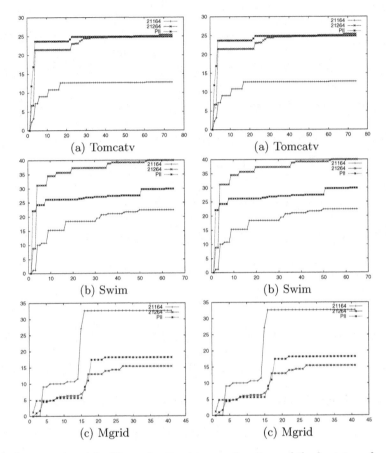

**Fig. 4.** Strategy 1 and 2 : The reduction in execution time of the best transformation found so far by strategy 1 wrt the number of evaluations. Performed on 3 platforms.

**Table 2.** Strategy 2: Percentage reduction in execution time

|          | PII  | 21164 | 21264 | Avg. |
|----------|------|-------|-------|------|
| Tomcatv  | 24.6 | 9.9   | 22.0  | 18.8 |
| Swim     | 14.5 | 19.0  | 33.0  | 22.6 |
| Mgrid    | 14.5 | 30.5  | 14.8  | 19.9 |
| Avg.     | 17.8 | 19.8  | 23.2  | 20.2 |

## 5.2   Evaluating the Use of Training Data to Determine Transformation

Although we have shown that our approach outperforms native compilers in every case with relatively few evaluations, this still may be too expensive. In this experiment we therefore use the smaller training data (and hence shorten evalua-

**Table 3.** Strategy 1: Training Data: Percentage reduction in execution time

|          | PII  | PIII | HP   | US    | A21164 | A21264 | Avg.  |
|----------|------|------|------|-------|--------|--------|-------|
| Tomcatv  | 32.5 | 25.3 | 38.6 | 22.6  | 11.9   | 19.4   | 25.05 |
| Swim     | 21.5 | 0.09 | 3.2  | 14.0  | 23.1   | 38.6   | 16.7  |
| Mgrid    | 12.1 | 0    | 0    | 0     | 31.8   | 5.1    | 8.16  |
| Avg.     | 22   | 8.5  | 13.9 | 12.21 | 22.3   | 21     | 16.63 |

**Table 4.** Strategy 2: Training Data: Percentage reduction in execution time

|          | PII  | A21164 | A21264 | Avg.  |
|----------|------|--------|--------|-------|
| Tomcatv  | 25.4 | 11.2   | 22.3   | 19.6  |
| Swim     | 28.4 | 23.9   | 35.7   | 29.3  |
| Mgrid    | 11.5 | 32.7   | 4.3    | 16.16 |
| Avg.     | 21.7 | 22.6   | 20.76  | 21.68 |

**Table 5.** Strategy 1 and 2: Percentage reduction in execution time wrt a high level restructurer -O5

|          | A21164 | A21264 | PII  | Avg.  |
|----------|--------|--------|------|-------|
| Tomcatv  | 12.3   | 25.4   | 22.3 | 20    |
| Swim     | 27.9   | 38.2   | 20.3 | 28.8  |
| Mgrid    | 4.3    | 10.5   | 18.0 | 10.9  |
| Avg.     | 14.8   | 24.7   | 20.2 | 19.6  |

|          | A21164 | A21264 | PII   | Avg.  |
|----------|--------|--------|-------|-------|
| Tomcatv  | 8.3    | 23.7   | 14.6  | 15.5  |
| Swim     | 20.1   | 31.8   | 11.9  | 21.2  |
| Mgrid    | 0      | 8.3    | 16.1  | 8.13  |
| Mgrid    | 12.23  | 21.26  | 14.16 | 14.9  |

tion time) from the SPEC benchmark suite in order to find a good optimisation and then apply the resulting best optimisation to the actual reference data. Use of the training data will also give an insight into how iterative compilation performs in the presence of different data sets and sizes.

As can be seen in Table 4, the first iterative strategy using training data never performs worse than the native optimiser and in the majority of case gives significant reduction in execution time. On average there is a 16.63% improvement which compares favourably with the 20.5% average found using solely the reference data (Table 1). Using training data we reduce the evaluation time and obtain over 80% of the execution time reduction when using the actual reference data. In the case of Mgrid, performance gain was found on only 3 of the 6 platforms, showing that its performance is more closely related to the actual runtime data.

If we apply the second strategy with just 15 evaluations to three of the six platform, we find the results shown in Table 5, where we have on average a 21.68% improvement. If we compare the execution time reduction of Strategy 2 against Strategy 1 on each machine, we see that their performance is almost identical when using training data. Furthermore, if we compare the execution time reduction of Strategy 2 using training data with the performance obtained using reference data (Table 2), the training data actually gives slightly better results due to the random nature of the search strategy.

## 5.3   Comparison Against an Existing Static High Level Restructurer

The previous sections have shown that iterative compilation can give good performance improvements over the native compiler in relatively few iterations and in the presence of smaller training data.

In order to further evaluate the use of iterative compilation in high level restructuring, this section compares our approach to an industrial high level restructurer. The Compaq compiler has an option (-O5) which enables high level restructuring and is integrated within the entire compiler chain. This restructurer uses an elaborate phase ordered strategy based on sophisticated static analysis and considerable architectural knowledge. Loop transformation optimisations that are used by the Compaq compiler include loop blocking, loop distribution, loop fusion, loop interchange, loop scalar replacement, and outer loop unrolling. It moreover employs array padding and software pipelining. Hence this compiler uses the same transformations as our iterative system, and several that are not implemented by us.

We applied Strategies 1 and 2 to the three platforms (where the Compaq compiler is available) with high level restructuring enabled. Thus, we are applying high level transformations which are then fed into a native compiler which may, in turn, apply further high level transformations. The results are given in Tables 6 and 7. Overall Strategy 1 is able to reduce execution time by 19.6% and Strategy 2 by 14.9%. Thus a techniques that evaluates just 15 program transformations is able to give significant execution time reduction when compared to a state of the art optimiser.

In only one case does Strategy 2 fail to make an improvement and in this case simply achieves the same performance as the native high level restructurer as we are using the native high level restructuring as our backend compiler. This ability to make use of the best available vendor supplied compiler technology is a useful feature of our approach. However, for a strictly fair comparison, we should compare our approach using the native low level optimiser (-O4) as our backend compiler, to Compaq's high level restructurer (-O5) which also makes use of the native low level compiler as its backend compiler. In such a case, strategies 1 and 2 give 9.92% and 8.6%, respectively, reduction in execution time when compared to the Compaq high level restructurer, using the same native low level optimiser.

Thus we are able outperform an existing high level restructurer, and furthermore can use that same restructurer as a backend to further improve performance. The ability to adapt to improvements in vendor supplied system software is a useful feature of our approach.

## 5.4    Comparison Against an Existing Profile-Directed Compiler

We have shown that our technique outperforms native compilers, with full optimisation enabled, and an existing static high level restructurer. Here we show our generic approach also outperforms an existing profile-directed compiler. The Compaq compiler on the two Alphas has accesses to low level profile tools that allows it to gather information during one execution in order to improve code generated for the next run [5]. This can be done under two modes: with full low level optimisation on (-profile -O4) and with full low level optimisation on *plus* high level restructuring (-profile -O5). Hence on the Alphas the Compaq compiler can drive the same loop transformations as our system using profile data. The difference between the Compaq compiler and our system lies in the fact that the Compaq compiler uses predefined heuristics in a predefined order to select transformations whereas our system performs a search procedure. In this section we show that searching outperforms highly tuned static heuristics significantly.

We plotted the speedups of these two different modes against the native compiler in Figures 6, 7, and 8 (-profile -O4, -profile -O5). We also plotted the speedups of all other approaches described in this paper. Namely, the original native (-O4) execution time, the native high level restructurer time (-O5). For further comparison, we also plotted the results of both strategies using the native compiler as the backend compiler (-it st 1/2 -O4), and the native compiler with high level restructuring enabled as the backend (-it st 1/2 -O5).

As can be immediately seen, the iterative approaches outperform the Alpha's profile directed approach in all cases. Furthermore, iterative compilation with a simple native compiler (-it st 1/2 -O4) even outperforms the profile directed approach using high level restructuring (-profile -O5) in most cases. In the majority of cases the A21264 benefits more from optimisation than the A21164, except in the case of mgrid where (-O5) optimisation dramatically improves performance for both the profile directed and iterative approaches on the A21164. Interestingly, the Alpha's profile directed compilation actually performs better without the use of high level restructuring on the A21164. It is not immediately apparent why this is the case, possibly high level restructuring may interfere with the profiler.

Overall, Strategy 1 reduces the execution time on average by 16.52% when compared to the profile directed compiler, while Strategy 2 reduces the execution time by 12.48%.

Once again these performance gains are made with the Compaq high level restructurer (-O5) as our backend compiler. However, for a strictly fair comparison, we should compare our approach using the native low level optimiser (it st 1/2 -O4) as our backend compiler against Compaq's profile directed approach using a high level restructurer (-profile -O5) which also makes use of the native low level compiler as its backend compiler. In such a case, strategies 1 and 2 give 9.8% and 8.5%, respectively, reduction in execution time when compared to the Compaq's profile directed, high level restructurer; both using the same native low level optimiser.

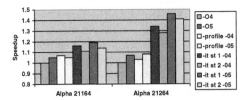

**Fig. 5.** Tomcatv: Speedup

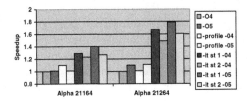

**Fig. 6.** Swim: Speedup

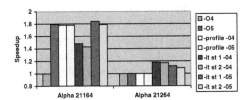

**Fig. 7.** Mgrid: Speedup

Thus, our generic approach outperforms even highly optimised platform specific, feedback directed approaches.

## 6    Related Work and Discussion

Feedback directed optimisation [11] is a basic technique used in computer architecture where hardware resources are dedicated to tracing and predicting program behaviour. Similarly, in low-level compilers profile guided compilation is widely used to determine execution path, allowing improved program optimisation.

Due to the limits of static analysis, systems for generation highly optimised versions of BLAS routines are proposed which probe the underlying hardware for platform specific parameters [13,1]. In the SPIRAL project a feedback directed search approach is applied to DSP algorithms that can be expressed as tensor products Within this domain, excellent versions of DSP algorithms can be found in a relatively short number of executions [9].

Wolf, Maydan and Chen [14] have described a compiler that also searches for the optimal optimisation based on a fixed order of the transformations. However, they solely use a static cost model to evaluate the different optimisations which inevitably approximates system behaviour and does not adapt to architectural change. A similar approach has been taken by Han, Rivera and Tseng [6] which uses a model to search for tile and pad sizes; again such an approach is restricted by the use of static models. Finally, Chow and Wu [4] apply "fractional factorial design" to decide on the number of experiments to run for selecting a collection of compiler switches, rather than trying to explore a program optimisation space in a platform independent manner.

Feedback directed high level transformations have also recently become more popular. In [12] a framework is described which allows remote on-line optimisation of a program while it is running, gaining the benefits of actual knowledge of runtime parameters without the overhead of compilation on the critical path. Our approach is similar in spirit in that different optimisations are tried and the best selected, theirs on-line ours off-line. However, the main distinction is that we have developed generic search strategies based on investing a systematic transformation optimisation space. Dynamic online optimisations found in Java just-in-time compilers [3] also make use of runtime behaviour in determining program optimisation. However, such approaches only consider a fixed predetermined number of optimisations.

## 7 Conclusion

This paper has described an aggressive compiler framework that outperforms static optimisation approaches and that allows optimisers to adapt to new platforms by way of feedback directed iterative compilation. By decoupling strategy from implementation, we have implemented two architecture blind generic optimisation approaches. These rely on our framing the problem of optimisation as that of traversing a transformation space in order to minimise the object function of execution time. We have shown that for three SPEC FP benchmarks, across six platforms, we reduce the execution time by 20.5% on average. When restricting the number of evaluations to just 15, we achieve a reduction of 20.2% across 3 of the platforms. We have also shown that good performance can be achieve when smaller training data is used giving over 80% of the performance achieved using reference data.

For a fair comparison, we compared our approach to that of a native high level restructurer. Using the same native backend compiler we obtain a reduction in execution time of almost 10% on average. Moreover, if we compare our approach to a platform specific profile directed high level optimiser that employs the same transformations as our system plus several more, we also obtain a reduction in execution time of almost 10% on average. Furthermore, we are able to adapt and use the high level restructurer as our backend compiler, where we are able to further improve performance, reducing execution time by 12% on average when compared to the platform specific profile directed high level optimiser.

We have shown, for the first time, that iterative compilation is viable for large optimisation spaces found in general programs and that good performance may be achieved regardless of platform. Future work will investigate both the use of models to further reduce the number of evaluations required and evaluate other search strategies.

# References

1. J. Bilmes, K. Asanović, C.W. Chin, and J. Demmel. **Optimizing matrix multiply using PHiPAC: A portable, high-performance, C coding methodology**, ICS'97,1997.
2. F. Bodin, T. Kisuki, P.M.W. Knijnenburg, M.F.P. O'Boyle, and E. Rohou **Iterative Compilation in a Non-Linear Optimisation Space** , Profile and Feedback Directed Compilation, PACT, 1998.
3. M.Burke et.al, **The Jalapeno Dynamic Optimizing Compiler for Java**, Proc. of ACM'99 Java Grande Conference, June 1999.
4. K. Chow and Y. Wu, **Feedback-Directed Selection and Characterization of Compiler Optimizations**, FDO, 1999.
5. R.Cohn and P.G. Lowney, **Feedback Directed Optimization in Compaq's Compilation Tools for Alpha**, FDO, 1999.
6. H. Han, G. Rivera and C.-W. Tseng, **Software Support for Improving Locality in Scientific Codes**, CPC, 2000.
7. T. Kisuki, P.M.W. Knijnenburg and M.F.P. O'Boyle, **Combined Selection of Tile Sizes and Unroll Factors Using Iterative Compilation**, PACT, 2000.
8. K. S. McKinley and O. Temam., **A Quantative Analysis of Loop Nest Locality**, ASPLOS, 1996.
9. J. Moura, J. Johnson, R. Johnson, D. Padua, V. Prasanna, M. Puschel, B. Singer, M. Veloso, and J. Xiong. **Generating Platform-Adapted DSP Libraries using SPIRAL**, Proc. HPEC 2001, MIT Lincoln Laboratories.
10. G. Rivera and C.-W. Tseng, **Data Transformations for Eliminating Conflict Misses**, PLDI, 1998.
11. M. Smith, **Overcoming the Challenges to Feedback-Directed Optimizations**, Dynamo'00, 2000.
12. Voss M.J. and Eigenmann R., **A framework for remote dynamic Program Optimization**, Dynamo, 2000.
13. R.C. Whaley and J.J. Dongarra. **Automatically tuned linear algebra software**. Proc. Alliance, 1998.
14. M.E. Wolf, D.E. Maydan, and D.-K. Chen. **Combining loop transformations considering caches and scheduling**. *Int'l. J. of Parallel Programming*, 26(4):479–503, 1998.

# Author Index

# Lecture Notes in Computer Science

For information about Vols. 1–3739

please contact your bookseller or Springer

Vol. 3789: A. Gelbukh, Á. de Albornoz, H. Terashima-Marín (Eds.), MICAI 2005: Advances in Artificial Intelligence. XXVI, 1198 pages. 2005. (Subseries LNAI).

Vol. 3788: B. Roy (Ed.), Advances in Cryptology - ASI-ACRYPT 2005. XIV, 703 pages. 2005.

Vol. 3785: K.-K. Lau, R. Banach (Eds.), Formal Methods and Software Engineering. XIV, 496 pages. 2005.

Vol. 3784: J. Tao, T. Tan, R.W. Picard (Eds.), Affective Computing and Intelligent Interaction. XIX, 1008 pages. 2005.

Vol. 3783: S. Qing, W. Mao, J. Lopez, G. Wang (Eds.), Information and Communications Security. XIV, 492 pages. 2005.

Vol. 3781: S.Z. Li, Z. Sun, T. Tan, S. Pankanti, G. Chollet, D. Zhang (Eds.), Advances in Biometric Person Authentication. XI, 250 pages. 2005.

Vol. 3780: K. Yi (Ed.), Programming Languages and Systems. XI, 435 pages. 2005.

Vol. 3779: H. Jin, D. Reed, W. Jiang (Eds.), Network and Parallel Computing. XV, 513 pages. 2005.

Vol. 3778: C. Atkinson, C. Bunse, H.-G. Gross, C. Peper (Eds.), Component-Based Software Development for Embedded Systems. VIII, 345 pages. 2005.

Vol. 3777: O.B. Lupanov, O.M. Kasim-Zade, A.V. Chaskin, K. Steinhöfel (Eds.), Stochastic Algorithms: Foundations and Applications. VIII, 239 pages. 2005.

Vol. 3776: S.K. Pal, S. Bandyopadhyay, S. Biswas (Eds.), Pattern Recognition and Machine Intelligence. XXIV, 808 pages. 2005.

Vol. 3775: J. Schönwälder, J. Serrat (Eds.), Ambient Networks. XIII, 281 pages. 2005.

Vol. 3774: G. Bierman, C. Koch (Eds.), Database Programming Languages. X, 295 pages. 2005.

Vol. 3773: A. Sanfeliu, M.L. Cortés (Eds.), Progress in Pattern Recognition, Image Analysis and Applications. XX, 1094 pages. 2005.

Vol. 3772: M. Consens, G. Navarro (Eds.), String Processing and Information Retrieval. XIV, 406 pages. 2005.

Vol. 3771: J.M.T. Romijn, G.P. Smith, J. van de Pol (Eds.), Integrated Formal Methods. XI, 407 pages. 2005.

Vol. 3770: J. Akoka, S.W. Liddle, I.-Y. Song, M. Bertolotto, I. Comyn-Wattiau, W.-J. van den Heuvel, M. Kolp, J. Trujillo, C. Kop, H.C. Mayr (Eds.), Perspectives in Conceptual Modeling. XXII, 476 pages. 2005.

Vol. 3769: D.A. Bader, M. Parashar, V. Sridhar, V.K. Prasanna (Eds.), High Performance Computing - HiPC 2005. XXVIII, 550 pages. 2005.

Vol. 3768: Y.-S. Ho, H.J. Kim (Eds.), Advances in Multimedia Information Processing - PCM 2005, Part II. XXVIII, 1088 pages. 2005.

Vol. 3767: Y.-S. Ho, H.J. Kim (Eds.), Advances in Multimedia Information Processing - PCM 2005, Part I. XXVIII, 1022 pages. 2005.

Vol. 3766: N. Sebe, M.S. Lew, T.S. Huang (Eds.), Computer Vision in Human-Computer Interaction. X, 231 pages. 2005.

Vol. 3765: Y. Liu, T. Jiang, C. Zhang (Eds.), Computer Vision for Biomedical Image Applications. X, 563 pages. 2005.

Vol. 3764: S. Tixeuil, T. Herman (Eds.), Self-Stabilizing Systems. VIII, 229 pages. 2005.

Vol. 3762: R. Meersman, Z. Tari, P. Herrero (Eds.), On the Move to Meaningful Internet Systems 2005: OTM 2005 Workshops. XXXI, 1228 pages. 2005.

Vol. 3761: R. Meersman, Z. Tari (Eds.), On the Move to Meaningful Internet Systems 2005: CoopIS, DOA, and ODBASE, Part II. XXVII, 653 pages. 2005.

Vol. 3760: R. Meersman, Z. Tari (Eds.), On the Move to Meaningful Internet Systems 2005: CoopIS, DOA, and ODBASE, Part I. XXVII, 921 pages. 2005.

Vol. 3759: G. Chen, Y. Pan, M. Guo, J. Lu (Eds.), Parallel and Distributed Processing and Applications - ISPA 2005 Workshops. XIII, 669 pages. 2005.

Vol. 3758: Y. Pan, D.-x. Chen, M. Guo, J. Cao, J.J. Dongarra (Eds.), Parallel and Distributed Processing and Applications. XXIII, 1162 pages. 2005.

Vol. 3757: A. Rangarajan, B. Vemuri, A.L. Yuille (Eds.), Energy Minimization Methods in Computer Vision and Pattern Recognition. XII, 666 pages. 2005.

Vol. 3756: J. Cao, W. Nejdl, M. Xu (Eds.), Advanced Parallel Processing Technologies. XIV, 526 pages. 2005.

Vol. 3754: J. Dalmau Royo, G. Hasegawa (Eds.), Management of Multimedia Networks and Services. XII, 384 pages. 2005.

Vol. 3753: O.F. Olsen, L.M.J. Florack, A. Kuijper (Eds.), Deep Structure, Singularities, and Computer Vision. X, 259 pages. 2005.

Vol. 3752: N. Paragios, O. Faugeras, T. Chan, C. Schnörr (Eds.), Variational, Geometric, and Level Set Methods in Computer Vision. XI, 369 pages. 2005.

Vol. 3751: T. Magedanz, E.R. M. Madeira, P. Dini (Eds.), Operations and Management in IP-Based Networks. X, 213 pages. 2005.

Vol. 3750: J.S. Duncan, G. Gerig (Eds.), Medical Image Computing and Computer-Assisted Intervention – MICCAI 2005, Part II. XL, 1018 pages. 2005.

Vol. 3749: J.S. Duncan, G. Gerig (Eds.), Medical Image Computing and Computer-Assisted Intervention – MICCAI 2005, Part I. XXXIX, 942 pages. 2005.

Vol. 3748: A. Hartman, D. Kreische (Eds.), Model Driven Architecture – Foundations and Applications. IX, 349 pages. 2005.

Vol. 3747: C.A. Maziero, J.G. Silva, A.M.S. Andrade, F.M.d. Assis Silva (Eds.), Dependable Computing. XV, 267 pages. 2005.

Vol. 3746: P. Bozanis, E.N. Houstis (Eds.), Advances in Informatics. XIX, 879 pages. 2005.

Vol. 3745: J.L. Oliveira, V. Maojo, F. Martín-Sánchez, A.S. Pereira (Eds.), Biological and Medical Data Analysis. XII, 422 pages. 2005. (Subseries LNBI).

Vol. 3744: T. Magedanz, A. Karmouch, S. Pierre, I. Venieris (Eds.), Mobility Aware Technologies and Applications. XIV, 418 pages. 2005.

Vol. 3742: J. Akiyama, M. Kano, X. Tan (Eds.), Discrete and Computational Geometry. VIII, 213 pages. 2005.

Vol. 3740: T. Srikanthan, J. Xue, C.-H. Chang (Eds.), Advances in Computer Systems Architecture. XVII, 833 pages. 2005.